Coolidge, Austin Jacobs; Mainsfield, John Brainard

History and Description of New England

Maine

Coolidge, Austin Jacobs; Mainsfield, John Brainard

History and Description of New England

Maine

Inktank publishing, 2018

www.inktank-publishing.com

ISBN/EAN: 9783747703786

HISTORY AND DESCRIPTION

OF

NEW ENGLAND.

MAINE.

BY

A. J. COOLIDGE AND J. B. MANSFIELD.

BOSTON:
AUSTIN J. COOLIDGE,
39 COURT STREET.
1860.

PREFACE.

This volume, which is intended to furnish a good historical and descriptive account of every town and important plantation in Maine, from the earliest settlement to the present time, forms one of a series upon all the New England States. The matter has been prepared from State documents, town records, actual observation, conversation with citizens, and a wide range of correspondence. The information respecting the plantations was gathered from entirely reliable sources, and will be of particular interest, not only to the people of Maine who desire to see a knowledge of the rich settling lands in this State published more widely, but to all who wish to find a good opening for themselves or their friends, in the pursuits of agriculture or the mechanic arts, in a territory which God has adorned with beauty and luxuriance, with the prospect of a sure reward.

A list of the post-offices not contained in the body of the work is added, which, with the villages in each town, can be readily found in the copious index. The names of all the Senators and Representatives in Congress, from the organization of the State to the present time, as well as the Electors of President, the Governors and candidates for the gubernatorial office, together with the respective dates of election and terms of service, and the popular vote for each, are set forth in conveniently arranged tables. These are the result of much labor, and will be of service not to the politician alone, but to every one who wishes to have at hand so important an accompaniment of the civil history of the Commonwealth.

The "Dirigo" State having now attained the fortieth year of her age, although, with a single exception, the youngest of the Atlantic sisters, is sufficiently advanced to be more widely introduced to the world. In fact, through her hardy and enterprising sons, in every clime, the mother's fame is increasing. With a view to contribute to a better acquaintance with her moral, intellectual, and pecuniary worth, this work is respectfully submitted.

CONTENTS.

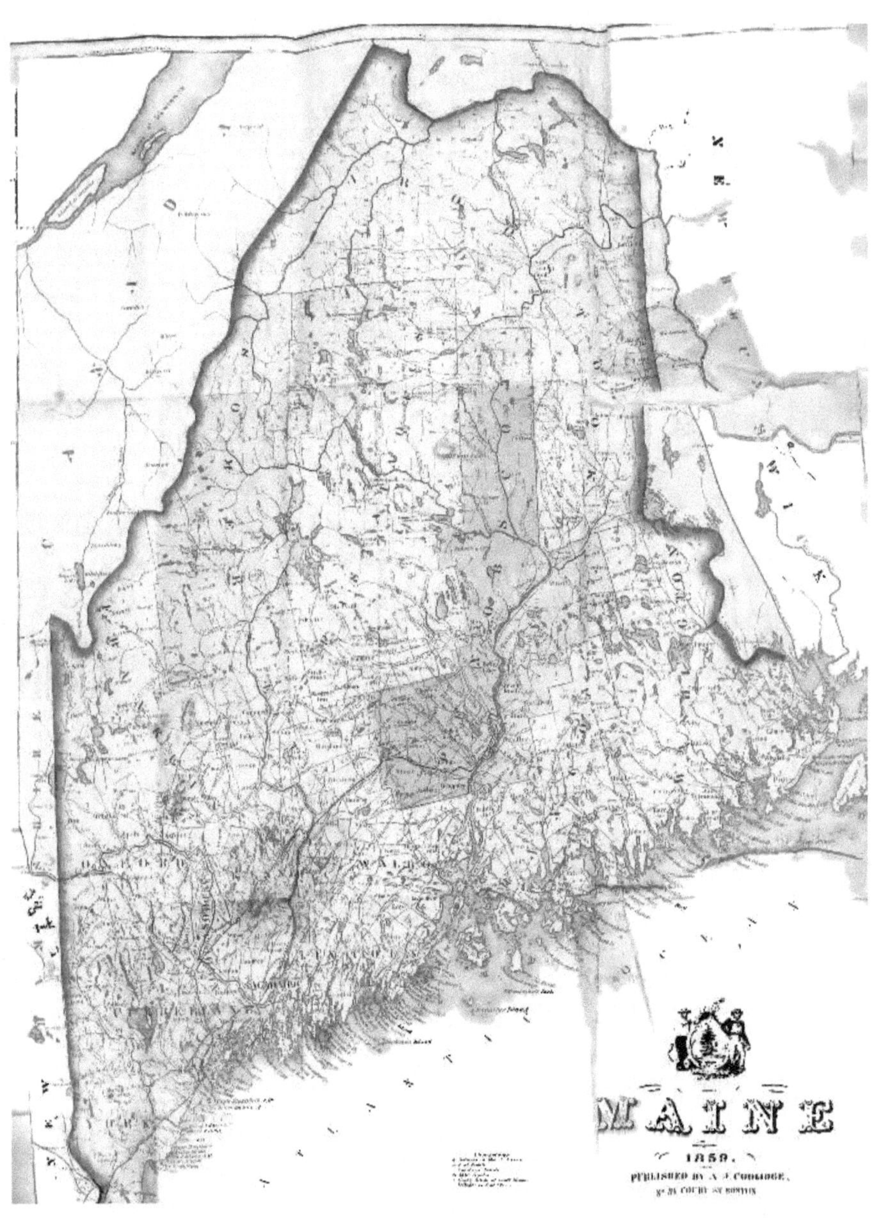
MAINE
1859.

HISTORY

AND

DESCRIPTION OF NEW ENGLAND.

CHAPTER I.

DISCOVERY AND SETTLEMENT.

New England occupies a geographical position between the parallels of 41° and 48° of north latitude, and the meridians of 67° and 74° of longitude west from Greenwich, or between 3° and 10° east from Washington. It comprises the six northeastern States of the American confederacy; namely, Maine, New Hampshire, Vermont, Massachusetts, Rhode Island, and Connecticut, — the whole covering an area of 65,038 square miles.

The discovery of New England — the honor of which, according to the testimony of the most reliable authors, belongs to John Cabot and his son Sebastian — occurred in 1497, five years after Columbus had made his first voyage of discovery, and had raised the veil that concealed the continent from the eyes of Europe.

Inspired by the success of Columbus, envious of his fame, and jealous of the acquisitions that might be made by the Spanish crown, the Cabots fitted out an expedition, under the patronage and authority of Henry VII., of England, consisting of two caravels, with one hundred and fifty men each. This expedition, encouraged by the merchants of London and Bristol, sailed from the latter port in the early part of May; and, on the 24th of June, the most sanguine expectations of the voyagers were realized by the sight of land. As the morning breeze and the rising sun cleared up the fog, the rock-bound coast of Labrador[1] reëchoed the roar of the beating surge, and the summits of its icy

[1] It has generally been supposed that the part of this continent first seen by the Cabots was Newfoundland, but Biddle in his Memoir of Sebastian Cabot, p. 52, has

peaks came fully into view. The discoverers pushed further to the north, but were compelled by their sailors, who were frightened at the idea of perpetual day, to turn back; and, accordingly, they bore southward as far as 35° north latitude.

Fully aware of the importance of this voyage to the British crown, and familiar with the maxims and prevalent notions of those days, which made new countries, not inhabited by civilized nations, the absolute property of the discoverers, there is no doubt that it was the intention of the Cabots to make the most of their voyage. But historians do not agree as to the extent of their explorations; and, as no records were left by them sufficiently in detail to set the matter at rest, we must fall back upon the statements of others which are deemed most reliable. Holmes, in his Annals, quoting a passage from Peter Martyr's Decades, "De rebus Oceanicis et novo orbe," concludes that they ranged the coast as far south as Florida.[1] There is some obscurity in Martyr's statement, but it is quite evident that a large portion of the Atlantic coast passed before their eyes.[2] Here a mutiny broke out among the crews, and the expedition was obliged to return to England, without attempting any further explorations, or settlements on any part of the coast.

The English, by virtue of the discoveries made on this voyage, which were confirmed by subsequent expeditions, set up their original claim to the principal part of North America. But, because the Cabots made no settlement, some writers dispute the validity of the claim. This, however, is rather a question for statesmen and jurists to discuss.

The gold that Columbus had obtained from the natives of Hispaniola on his first voyage, and which he presented to his patrons and friends, stimulated the spirit of adventure; and private expeditions, for the purpose of searching for the golden treasures which the New World was

rendered it quite certain that it was Labrador, adducing, among other proofs, a description of the land (thought to be Cabot's) as "full of white bears," which has never been applicable to Newfoundland.

[1] Holmes's Annals, p. 13, and note vi. at end, (ed. 1829).

[2] Martyr, B. 6, p. 267. This writer represents the Cabots to have met with obstructions from ice, and turned southward, following the line of the coast, till in about the latitude of Gibraltar and the longitude of Cuba, which would only bring them off Cape Hatteras. But, from his mention of Cuba bearing upon their left, it would seem that he meant that they took a southerly course to about 35° north latitude, thence a southwesterly course till nearly off Cuba. It is but fair in this case to allow the reader the benefit of the original, which is as follows: "Quare coactus fuit, uti ait, vela vertere et Occidentem sequi: tetenditque tamen ad meridiem, littore sese incurvante, ut Herculei freti latitudinis fere gradus equârit: ad Occidentemque profectus tantum est, ut Cubam insulam a læva, longitudine graduum pene parem, habuerit."

supposed to possess, were fitted out in Spain and Portugal, by those who had been the companions of Columbus. Alonso de Ojeda, an officer in the Spanish naval service, was one of the earliest of these adventurers. Having obtained the royal license for his enterprise, the merchants of Seville equipped him with four ships for the voyage; and, on the 20th of May, 1499, he sailed from the port of St. Mary's, in Spain. He took with him, as companion for the voyage, a Florentine gentleman, by the name of Amerigo Vespucci, whose services, on account of his superior attainments in all that pertained to the science of navigation, were of the utmost importance to Ojeda, in navigating the uncertain and dangerous seas of an unknown and distant clime. While in this subordinate position, however, Vespucci coveted the fame which the success of the voyage would create for its projector; and, as early certainly as 1510, he published an account of the voyage, claiming to have been himself the principal discoverer, and demanding that the new world should be called by his name. This claim was soon after unjustly conceded to him; and, by general consent, this new quarter of the globe has ever since been called AMERICA.[1] But neither to Vespucci nor to Columbus belongs the honor of making the first discovery of this continent, but to John Cabot alone, of all the voyagers of the fifteenth century; and to Italy belongs, without dispute, the imperishable honor of giving birth to the three contestants for this fame.

Europe, at this period, had but too recently emerged from barbarism to take immediate advantage of so great a discovery. Spain and Portugal, however, sent out expeditions to the New World; but while they were making the most of their discoveries in Central and South America, England, France, and the other European powers, remained inactive, — an apology for which must be sought in the unpropitious circumstances in which those governments were then placed.

On the accession of Queen Elizabeth to the throne of England, a more liberal policy was inaugurated, and greater encouragement given to explore, colonize, and settle the new country. Various expeditions were sent to New England during her reign; but all, or nearly all, terminated disastrously to those engaged; and nothing was accomplished in establishing colonies and opening settlements until the commencement of the seventeenth century.

[1] Robertson's America, vol. I. note 22; Holmes's Annals, vol. I. p. 16, note vii. at end, (ed. 1829). Herrera says, that, "to make good his false and assumed claim to the discovery of the continent, he suppressed the name of 'Dragon's Mouth,' which Columbus had given to the entrance into a bay near Trinidad;" and that "he confounded the passages of the two voyages," — that made before, with Columbus, and this made with Ojeda, — in order to make it appear, in fact, that he (Vespucci) was the original discoverer.

England and France, the two rival nations of Western Europe, who for centuries had vied with each other for supremacy, now commenced the race of empire together on the virgin soil of America. Had these two nations — the fiery, impetuous Gaul, and the cool, calculating, and determined Anglo-Saxon — inaugurated the work of colonization together, leaving their national jealousies and animosities at home, and been rivals only in their efforts to promote the welfare and improvement of their colonies, and in developing the resources of the country, the labors of the eighteenth century would not have been thrown over upon the nineteenth. Instead of erecting, as they did, respectively, lines of fortifications along the Mississippi, the Ohio, and the Kennebec, extending from New Orleans to the St. Lawrence, to contest inch by inch each other's progress, they would have been opening wide, for immigration from the liberty-seeking nations of Europe, the eastern and western portals of the country. Instead of maintaining a protracted siege at Louisburg, they would have been constructing the great highways of commerce between the Atlantic and Pacific Oceans even now only in contemplation. In short, had they been employed in these vast enterprises, the moral and the material power of each would have been vastly augmented from year to year, both at home and abroad; and, to-day, America, in her onward progress, would have been more than a century in advance of her present position, — not only in those beautiful arts which embellish life and appeal to the higher parts of a nation's character, but also in those useful ones by which the happiness and comfort of its citizens are secured.

But, unfortunately, the interests of France and England, from the first, were conflicting. Their aims were dominion; the success of the one was regarded as involving the extinction of the claims of the other. The opposing interests of each continued to increase in magnitude, until they were brought together, face to face, and grappled in deadly conflict. Victory oscillated for a time, — now inclining to the standard of France, anon to that of England; but on the Plains of Abraham the die was cast, and victory settled down upon the banner of England. France, unable to recover from so great a defeat, or to prolong the contest with dignity, ceded her American possessions, and retired from the field.

The country, which had been found a wilderness, dense and unbroken, and ancient as the powers of nature, inhabited by roving tribes of savages, living in rude wigwams on the coast and along the banks of the great rivers, was scarcely less than a wilderness on the extinction of the claims of the French. It was so, in fact, for aught that had been done by the great proprietors and corporations. They had expended large sums, it is true, but with the purpose of aggregating treasure, and transferring it to other lands, instead of making the soil and the sea avenues of wealth and happiness to the landless sons of the Old World, who should seek a homestead on these shores.

Failing to establish a system of landed tenantry here, as well as all other schemes of private avarice and lordly aggrandizement, and seeing no prospect of ever recovering their ruined fortunes by further efforts, the great proprietors withdrew from the scene, and relinquished all, in despair and disgust, into the hands of the poor but hardy laboring classes, whom they had been mainly instrumental in removing here.

In 1620, the English Puritans, who had been driven to Holland on account of their non-conformity to the usages of the established church, landed on the shores of Plymouth. Their arrival here was a great epoch in our history. It may with truth be said, that the history of New England, and the continent itself, had its commencement with the landing of the Pilgrims on our shores. Their migration hither, unlike that of those who had preceded them, was not for purposes of gain. Royal patents of extensive territories, or the prospect of an abounding commerce, had no attractions for them. They were poor, persecuted exiles, who had been hunted out of their native land by the bigotry and fanaticism of a powerful and unrelenting Episcopal hierarchy, whose intolerant spirit towards dissenters was only equalled by that of the Church of Rome itself. Self-exile was the only refuge for the dissenter; and religious freedom being the highest and holiest of all earthly considerations, to enjoy it, untrammelled by the surveillance and proscription of the civil power, the Plymouth Pilgrims severed the tenderest earthly ties, and sought on the wild shores of America a refuge from their persecutors, and opportunity to establish a *pure church*, which might be nourished with their prayers and tears through the period of its infantile being, and which, when as strong in the maturity of its years as in the soundness of its principles, might transmit its blessings to their posterity. That single idea led the first Plymouth colonists to these shores; and that single idea supported them under all difficulties, and enabled them to maintain their position in spite of obstacles enough to have utterly prostrated common men. They were rigid in their notions and practices, it is true, and sometimes exceeded what the liberality of the nineteenth century would approve; but, for all their excesses, the circumstances of the times offer a sufficient apology. None can deny the honesty and sincerity of their purposes. They were not the safe men, the conservative men, the timid men, that are now occasionally to be found, who are so very fearful of doing a bad act, that they never do a good one in the course of their whole lives; but they

1*

were men of stern will and indomitable energy, — God-appointed, it might almost seem, to settle ice-and-granite-bound New England. They braved every danger, and resolutely encountered every difficulty, — even such as had before appalled the stoutest hearts and made bankrupt the wealthiest proprietors of England. They had no money to back them; no royal prerogatives to lean upon; nothing but the mere connivance of King James at their movements, and the faith which can only live in a Christian's bosom, to which they clung as the shipwrecked mariner clings to the last plank of his stranded vessel.

Such was the germ of our colonial system, which, after a painful struggle of two centuries, and the trying events of a revolution, ripened into a full-grown republic, the most powerful that the world ever knew. By it and through it a vast system of internal colonization has been prosecuted, the entire continent overrun, and the Anglo-American flag carried to the regions of the setting sun.

From the few, feeble, and unprotected settlements along the rugged coast of New England have sprung thirty-two sovereign and independent states, — possessing territory sufficient for as many more, — which, while being severally towers of beauty and strength, covering their separate peoples and having their distinctive purposes wrought within, are also the colossal supports of the great temple of the Republic which spans the continent from ocean to ocean, and within the walls of which the arts of war and peace are being perfected, without confusion of tongues, among people of various origin.

The colonial epoch may be, for convenience' sake, divided into four periods. The first extends from the establishment of the Popham Colony at Sagadahoc in 1607, to 1660, when the troubles with the natives were beyond pacification, and an exterminating Indian war was opening upon the colonists. During this period, the colonial governments were established, and the troubles with the natives, incident to their establishment, had originated the war with the Pequots in 1637, and that between the Dutch and Algonquins in 1643. These were both short in duration, and a few years sufficed to repair whatever loss they had occasioned to the colonists. This period is also distinguished for the emigration to New England of such men as Brewster, Wilson, Cotton, Shepard, Phillips, Higginson, Shelton, Hooker, Davenport, Winthrop, Bradford, Winslow, Eaton, and the persecuted Roger Williams; and is styled by Dr. Baird the golden age of the colonial cycle.

The second period extends from 1660 to 1720. The colonies had now taken permanent root, when the blast of every misfortune seemed to be let loose upon them. The resistance to the union of church and state, the violent disputes with the home government on the rights of the colonies, and the serious Indian wars, shook the colonies to their very foundations; but they were too firmly grounded to be overturned.

The third period extends from 1720 to 1750. Notwithstanding the troubles which the colonies experienced during this time, on account of the part they had taken in the controversies between France and England, the "Great Awakening," or the great religious revivals, that pervaded all the colonies, occurred. This was the period during which the key-note of the gospel was sounded in the wilderness by such men as Edwards and Prince, Dickinson, Davies, and Finlay, the Tennents, the Wesleys, and that "Prince of preachers," George Whitefield, who, like the angel symbolized in the Apocalyptic vision, traversed colony after colony, preaching the everlasting gospel.

The fourth period extends from 1750 to 1776, and was one of great agitation. The colonies had aided England in another war with France, which terminated with the conquest of the Canadas, which were made over to England by the treaty of Paris, in 1763. Colonial rights were again discussed with the mother country, and with a bitterness that foreclosed all prospect of an amicable adjustment, and the colonies were compelled to make an appeal to the arbitrament of the sword.

Another period embraces the eighty years of our national existence. The initiative for independence was taken by the colonists, July 4, 1776; and, after a severe contest of seven years' duration, they were victorious. Their independence was acknowledged; a republic was organized; and the United States were enrolled among the nations of the earth. Not a century has elapsed since this great event, yet the progress of this Republic has been without a parallel in the world's history. Besides the increase of its territory, its commerce, at that time just beginning to spread its sails to the breeze, now extends over the whole world, compassing oceans, and sweeping along the great stream of traffic from hemisphere to hemisphere; while its internal improvements, — its cities and towns, which have sprung up in every direction, — its highways of travel, — its improvements in the arts and manufactures, — and, above all, the magnetic telegraph, as an instrument of intercommunication, — have made these states the wonder of the world.

Learning has become the preceptor of industry, and labor the body of thought; art the handmaid of religion, and science the elevator of humanity. With such aims as these, there is no destiny too glorious for our country or our people, who, in following the instructions of the Pilgrim Fathers, interpreted by the voice of experience, look above the stars of science and the differing glories of their devotees, to Him who walketh in the midst of the seven candlesticks, and holdeth the stars in his right hand.

CHAPTER II.

MAINE—OUTLINES OF ITS HISTORY.

MAINE is the largest of the New England States, and the most easterly of the United States. It is bounded on the south by the Atlantic Ocean; on the east by the St. Croix river, and by a line running due north from the monument[1] at its source, to St. John river; on the north by St. John and St. Francis rivers, to the head of Lake Pohenagamook, in latitude 47° 31′ 39″, longitude 69° 17′ 31″, thence by a line following the highlands, in a southwesterly direction, to the northeast corner of New Hampshire; and on the west by the state of New Hampshire. Maine is estimated to contain an area of 31,766 square miles, or 20,330,240 acres. The greatest width of the state, from Quoddy Head due west to New Hampshire, is 200 miles; and its greatest length, from Kittery Point to the northeastern angle, is 350 miles.

Whenever the first name on the great roll of American States is pronounced, the imagination is borne in an instant to the remotest east and the most wintry north of a vast national domain, where, in front, the ocean rolls with all its storms, and from behind wave the boundless forests. Colonial enterprise was earlier here than in any other northern state; and yet, of all the Atlantic States, this is the youngest.

For the period of one hundred and ten years after America had become known to Europe, the coast of Maine remained unexplored. No bark had ascended any of its majestic rivers, nor found its way into any

[1] The first surveys of the eastern boundary line were made by Samuel Titcomb and John Harris, in 1797. They established a monument at the head of St. Croix river, in latitude 45° 48′, which was a yellow birch tree, hooped with iron, and on it they inscribed the initials of their names. Joseph Bouchette and John Johnson, surveyors under the treaty of Ghent, erected a new monument, a few feet north of the old one, consisting of a large cedar post, supported by large rocks, and marked "July 31, 1817." This is the monument recognized in the treaty of 1842 by Webster and Ashburton, establishing the eastern and northern boundaries of the state.

of its capacious bays. All that had been done during that time was to engross the lucrative trade of the fisheries along the coast of Newfoundland, and erect temporary residences thereon, for the accommodation of fishermen while prosecuting their business.

Bartholomew Gosnold was the earliest navigator, of whom we have any authentic account, who made the discovery of, and to some extent explored, the coast; but the records of his voyage are so imperfect, that but little is known of its results. He sailed from Falmouth, England, on the 26th of March, 1602, and made land on the 4th of May, in about the 43° north latitude. At what particular place he landed, is not now known, as he erected no monument to mark the spot. The uncertainty of the place of his landing is occasioned by the error in the chart that he sailed by, which, says Weymouth, was more than half a degree out of the true latitude. Williamson thinks he landed at Mount Desert, or Mount Agamenticus, because the central Isle of Shoals, which is in latitude 42° 29′, is south of the land he first saw. He sailed around the southerly side of Cape Cod, discovered the Elizabeth Isles; and, on the 18th of June, in the same year, reëmbarked for England. Gosnold had by this voyage awakened a spirit of adventure; and, from this time, the coast of New England was visited, from year to year, by French, English, and other European navigators, until it was fully explored.

Martin Pring sailed the next year from Milford Haven, and on the 7th of June entered Penobscot Bay. He and his companions were highly pleased with the view they had of a "high country, full of great woods;" and they spoke in enthusiastic terms of the good fishing-grounds and good moorings which they found among the islands. Pring returned to England in August, with a valuable cargo of fish, fur, and sassafras. He pronounced the cod and haddock taken in Penobscot Bay much superior to those taken on the coast of Newfoundland. Among the many curiosities that Pring carried home was a birch-bark canoe, a specimen of aboriginal ingenuity. Gorges says, in his history, that Pring made a perfect discovery of all these eastern rivers and harbors, and brought the most exact account of the coast that had ever yet come to hand.[1]

The success of this voyage of Pring excited the adventurous spirit of the French, and encouraged the English in repeating their visits to these northern shores. France and England were both highly elated with ideas of extensive foreign dominion, and the prospect of an abounding commerce. Yet the means and the measures best fitted for their attain-

[1] "A Brief Narration of the Original Undertakings for the Advancement of Plantations in America." By Sir Ferdinando Gorges, Kt., ch. v. p. 19. London: printed in 1658.

ment were altogether unknown, as well to the statesman as to the speculator. They did not understand that a well-devised plan, a thorough organization, and a vigorous prosecution of that plan, in settling the new country, under the auspices of their respective governments, could give to the enterprise success and permanency. They based their rights on the priority of discovery, nominal possession, or royal commission, not thinking that rights on such a basis were too slender to be seriously defended.

It was a great misfortune to France and England, as well as to this country, that they both coveted the same territory, and were using all possible means to establish their claims to it, either by discovery, nominal possession, or royal patent. The people of both nations were resolved in their purposes; and, with such an object in view, and with the rival feelings and jealousies with which each regarded the other, it might have been foreseen that these counter claims would ultimately produce the most violent controversies, quarrels, and perhaps wars.

On the 8th of November, 1603, Pierre De Monts, one of the court favorites of Henry IV. of France, received from his sovereign a royal patent to all the territory between 40° and 46° north latitude. This extensive region embraced all the present New England States, besides New Brunswick, Nova Scotia, and the Canadas, and was named in the patent "Acadia." De Monts sailed for his new possessions in the ensuing spring, March 7, 1604, and arrived on the southern side of the Acadian peninsula (Nova Scotia), on the 6th of May. He spent the summer in exploring the coast; sailed up the St. John, gave it the name it now bears; and passed the winter of 1604–5 on St. Croix Island, in Passamaquoddy Bay. The winter was severe, and many of his men died. On the opening of the spring, he ranged the coast westerly to the Kennebec, where he erected a cross, and took possession of the country in the name of the king of France. Thence he proceeded to Cape Cod. Some of the places he passed appeared suitable for settlement, but his company was small, and the savages numerous, unfriendly, and thievish; so he returned to St. Croix, and, in September, embarked for France, leaving Dupont, Champlain, and Chauvin to explore the country and perfect a settlement.

During this year, several English gentlemen, to avoid if possible the jealousy of the French, and, at the same time, secure to themselves the advantages of prior possession, despatched George Weymouth across the Atlantic, on a pretended search for the *northwest passage*, the grand idea of the English navigators.

Weymouth sailed from Ratcliffe on the 31st of March, and on the 11th of May hove in sight of Cape Cod. He explored the coast, and erected crosses in several places, by way of establishing his claim to the country;[1] and in June sailed up the Kennebec river, came to anchor off Bath, and proceeded in a boat some distance up the Androscoggin.[2]

On the 10th of April, 1606, James I. of England incorporated two companies, agreeably to their own choice, one called the London company, and the other the Plymouth company; and granted, by royal patent, to both of the companies, all the territory between the 37° and the 45° of north latitude. This, it will be noticed, covered the whole territory that had been granted to De Monts three years previous, — except one degree upon the north, — with the addition of three degrees on the south. On the 20th of December, of the same year, the London company despatched three vessels, with one hundred colonists, for the coast of South Virginia; and in April, 1607, a permanent settlement was established on James river; and there the earliest administration of government was commenced on the continent of America, north of Mexico.

Weymouth anchored off Bath, June, 1605.

A similar enterprise, by the Plymouth company, was matured about the same time, for settling another colony in North Virginia, as the region east of the Hudson was then termed. One hundred emigrants, besides mariners, were engaged in the enterprise; all necessary supplies were procured, and, on the 31st of May, they took their departure in two ships from Plymouth. They had a favorable passage, and, on the 8th of August, landed on the Phipsburg peninsula,[3] at the mouth of the Kennebec river, called by the natives Sagadahoc river. They soon erected several cottages, sunk two or three wells, and commenced an intercourse with the natives. On the 11th, they organized their government by

[1] Purchas, 1659–76; 2 Belknap's Biog., p. 40.

[2] See Address by John McKeen, Maine Hist. Coll., vol. v.

[3] Some modern writers insist that it was upon Parker's Island, others at Arrowsic, and still others at Georgetown; but the recent discovery of the manuscript of "William Strachey Gent.," in the Sloane Collection of the British Museum, published by the "Hakluyt Society," London, 1849, and republished by the Mass. Hist. Soc., Fourth Series, vol. 1, pp. 221–246, has thrown new light upon the point, and hardly leaves room for a doubt that they landed on the peninsula. See also Bartlet's Frontier Missionary, Note B. p. 236.

formally reading their patent. They named the settlement the Sagadahoc colony, and elected their officers — George Popham as president, Captain Rawleigh Gilbert, James Davies, Richard Seymour (the first Episcopal clergyman north of Virginia), Captain Richard Davies, and Captain Harlow, as assistants. Here they built their cabins, and erected a fortification, the remains of which are even now to be seen.

The winter months were fraught with various trials. They suffered much from cold and hunger; and, by the impolitic course they had pursued with the natives, had forfeited their trade and hospitality. Their storehouse took fire in midwinter, and was reduced to ashes, and most of their provisions were destroyed. Three of the principal patrons of the colony died during the winter, one of whom was the President (George Popham).[1] The hostility of the natives, and the various misfortunes that befell the colonists, rendered their situation truly deplorable; and they resolved to quit the country and return to England. As soon as the affairs of the colony could be settled, and arrangements made for leaving, they embarked for home, reporting to their friends and patrons in England, as the cause of their return, that the country was "intolerably cold and sterile, unhealthy, and not habitable by our English nation."[2]

By the untimely end of this colony, some further deaths, and additional discouragements, a fatal blow was given to the spirit of colonization for some years. De Monts, the French patentee, had also met with many reverses and disappointments; and, on learning the disastrous termination of the Sagadahoc colony, abandoned the idea of prosecuting his enterprise any further, and surrendered his patent to Madame De Guercheville, a Catholic French lady, who was desirous of making the experiment of converting the natives to the Catholic faith.

[1] There is a tradition that the colonists, for their amusement in the tedious winter months, among other things, set a company of the natives to hauling a loaded cannon with drag ropes, with the muzzle pointing forward, which, at a favorable opportunity, was discharged, consigning to instant death many of the unsuspecting victims. The Indians, justly incensed at this act of wanton barbarity, assembled in a large body, resolved on the massacre of the whole colony, and made a descent on the storehouse, containing the merchandise and provisions, which were its sole dependence. In the overhauling, they broke open some barrels of powder, which being accidentally ignited, produced a terrific explosion, killing many of their number. The survivors, in their simplicity, understood this as the reproving voice of the Great Spirit for their attempt to exterminate the settlers; and forthwith brought provisions enough to sustain them through the winter, without which every man must have perished from starvation. It is thought by some, upon insufficient evidence however, that Popham fell a victim to the merited revenge of his savage neighbors.

[2] Prince's Annals, p. 35.

She obtained a charter from the king, in confirmation of the patent she had received from De Monts, and immediately sent over her agent (Suassaye), with twenty-five colonists, to take possession of Acadia in her name. He landed on the 16th of May, 1613, at Mount Desert, built a small fort on the south side of the river, and a few cabins around it, erected a cross, celebrated mass, and called the place St. Saviour.

The English, being greatly chagrined at their late defeat in establishing a settlement at Sagadahoc, watched the settlement of the French at St. Saviour with a jealous eye. On learning the important advantages the French were obtaining at this place, in their fur and peltry trade with the natives, Sir Ferdinando Gorges, one of the patrons of the Sagadahoc colony, a man not to be overcome by failure where he saw another successful, determined upon a second expedition. He purchased a ship with his own money, and obtained a master and crew to make a voyage hither; but so strangely had the passion for adventure abated in England, that it was with the greatest difficulty he could find any one willing to engage with him in the enterprise of attempting another settlement, or even in exploring the country. During this time, Captain Samuel Argal, of Virginia, who was in the habit of making occasional visits to these northern shores, for the purpose of taking fish, was cast ashore on one of the islands in Penobscot Bay; and, by closely questioning the natives in regard to the French, learned all the particulars of their recent settlement on Mount Desert, under the auspices of Madame De Guercheville. This intelligence he immediately communicated to the magistrates in Virginia, and they determined at once to expel these Roman Catholic Frenchmen, as intruders on the territory granted by his sovereign majesty James I. to his loyal subjects.

A naval armament was immediately fitted out for the purpose of reducing Mount Desert, consisting of eleven fishing vessels, containing sixty soldiers, and carrying fourteen pieces of cannon. Argal took the place, with scarcely any show of resistance. The inhabitants surrendered themselves as prisoners, to whom Argal offered the alternative of returning to France, or going with him to Virginia, — the latter of which most of them accepted. He broke in pieces the cross the Jesuits had erected; and, by way of taking formal possession of the place, erected another, and inscribed on it the name of King James I. He then proceeded to the island of St. Croix, and destroyed what remained of De Mont's settlement there. From thence he went to Port Royal; and, after setting fire to that place, returned to Jamestown.

These counter claims of the two governments were the principal cause of all the troubles in the colonies. They frequently involved the two nations in war; and it was not until Wolfe led the cohorts of England on to the Plains of Abraham, and British banners waved in triumph over Quebec, that the question of sovereignty was finally settled, and France abandoned her claims.

Gorges succeeded in securing the services of Captain Richard Vines, to take the command of his vessel, than whom no better man could have been obtained to carry out his design, which was ostensibly to engage in fishing and trade, though in reality it was to keep possession of the country against the French. Vines landed at the mouth of Saco river during the fall of 1617, and spent the winter there; at which place, in 1623, Gorges succeeded in establishing a permanent settlement.

After some years of variable fortune and uncertain prospects, he obtained a charter from Charles I. of all the territory between the Kennebec and the Piscataqua, as far north as the source of the latter river. By this charter, dated April 8, 1639, this territory, with its inhabitants, was incorporated into a body politic, and named the province or county of Maine,—a compliment to the queen of Charles I., who, it is commonly supposed, inherited the province in France of that name.[1] By this charter, Gorges, his heirs and assigns, were made absolute lords proprietors of the province, excepting the supreme dominion, faith, and allegiance due to the crown, and the right to exact, yearly, a quarter of wheat, and a fifth of the profits arising from the pearl fishings, and from gold and silver mines.

The territory over which Gorges was made dictator was but little less than one sixth of the area of the present State of Maine, and his proprietorship, thus chartered, was little less than an absolute sovereignty. Sir Ferdinando, whose mind was ever fruitful in expedients, used every possible means to raise his province into distinction, by encouraging settlements, and making grants of the land to gentlemen of rank and influence. He was fully convinced that the growth of his province was surpassed by all its colonial neighbors, not excepting New Hampshire, whilst the seizure of it by the French, who occupied the country east of the Penobscot, was, not without reason, apprehended.

After the death of Gorges, the province fell to his heirs; and, on the 6th of May, 1677, Massachusetts purchased it from them for the sum

[1] Hon. George Folsom, in his Discourse before the Maine Historical Society, in 1846 (vol. II.), denies the generally received notion that the queen owned the "Province of Meyne." He says, "Such is the prevailing impression as to the origin of the name finally given by Gorges to his province; but, unfortunately for its accuracy, the province of Maine, in France, did not appertain to Queen Henrietta Maria, but to the crown; nor is it discoverable that she possessed any interest in that province."

of £1,250 sterling. This event closed the first period in the provincial history of the State.

There are other matters connected with this period, such as the occupation of Bigaduce, now Castine, by D'Aulney, and subsequently by Baron de Castin; the revival of the settlement of Sagadahoc by the celebrated John Smith and Thomas Dermer; the Muscongus or Waldo patent; the Pemaquid patent, and other grants outside of what was then the province of Maine, — a detailed account of all which is given in another part of the work.

The second period extends from this colonial union to the close of the Indian wars, embracing over eighty-three years, and bringing down the history to 1760.[1]

It was but two years before the purchase of the title of Gorges from his heirs in 1677, that the war of King Philip broke out; and the territory of Maine was, for the first time, alarmed by the hostile aspect of the savages. Thenceforth, till 1760, the Indians made the land a wilderness, and as such held it as their own. It is appalling, even now, to read the narratives of the deeds of slaughter which were then perpetrated, and which allowed to three successive generations no secure rest upon their pillows. Every twentieth person in the colony was either slain, or carried into captivity to return no more. Eighty were murdered within three months, between the Piscataqua and the Kennebec. The people lived in garrisons, reaping their fields amidst the hazards of ambush and massacre; and not a few of them withdrew to the more protected towns of Massachusetts. Casco was deserted, Arrowsic was burned, amidst terrible slaughter, and the shores further east entirely devastated. Berwick was defended only at the sacrifice of a gallant family; Wells and York were again and again attacked, with bloodshed; and, at the fight of Black Point, sixty out of ninety combatants were left on the field.

Ten years of peace followed the close of King Philip's war, when the war of King William broke out, and the wild weapons of the Indian, supported by the muskets of the French, were again bathed in blood. This war lasted ten years, and was terminated by the peace of Ryswick. Six years of peace here intervened, when Queen Anne's war began, renewing for ten years more the former misery, before the waste places had been repaired. This war was terminated by the peace of Utrecht: and was soon followed by Lovewell's war, of three years'

[1] The grateful acknowledgments of the authors are due to the Rt. Rev. George Burgess, D. D., for permission to use matter contained in his address before the Maine Historical Society in 1854, published in the fourth volume of their Collections.

duration, memorable for the slaughter of the Roman Catholic missionary, Rasles, at Norridgewock, and the bloody fight at Fryeburg.

The ravages of these Indian wars checked, for a whole century, the advance of the civilizing power of commerce, tillage, and education. It is hardly possible to paint too strongly the disastrous fruits of this harassing strife. Scarcely a foot was won from the forests. On every spot where settlements had been attempted, nothing but the smouldering ruins of habitations and the bleaching bones of their recent occupants met the eye.

The third great period in the history of Maine extends from the close of the Indian wars, in 1760, to the organization of the State, and its admission into the Federal Union in 1820, during which a steady advance was made in the productive industry of the province, — the war of the Revolution scarcely impeding its progress.

There were, in 1760, but thirteen incorporated townships, which formed little more than a streak along the coast from Kittery to Pemaquid. In this year, the two counties of Cumberland and Lincoln were added to the original shire of York. Old claims are revived, new grants obtained; the course of the great rivers is explored, and the coast between the Penobscot and the St. Croix is taken into possession. In 1789, twenty new towns were incorporated, and two new eastern counties were honored with the names of Hancock and Washington. The wrecks of questioned claims and confiscated rights were recovered, and large allotments were granted for the encouragement of education; the advances of the axe upon the forests were steady; mighty woods were floated down every stream; and the whispers of the wind through the pines, hitherto heard only by the wild Indian or the wandering hunter, now mingled with the lowing of the herds, the hum of industry, and the songs of the settler.

The population of Maine, during the first half of these sixty years, increased to eight times its previous number; and, in the last half, it had a threefold increase. In the last war with England, a cloud was cast over the smiling prosperity of the province, and the Penobscot was again made a frontier river; but when that cloud had passed, the three hundred thousand inhabitants of Maine demanded and obtained a separate constitution, as also admission as a State into the Federal Union.

The fourth and last period extends from 1820 to the present time. Of this period, little is as yet historical, in that sense in which history is the record of facts completed. It contains, indeed, the beginning and the end of those ambitious speculations which a stirring people are always but too ready to undertake. Unlimited credit, vast enterprises, fictitious fortunes, and final calamity, followed each other in quick succession; when a new era — that of the lumber business — seemed to dawn upon the country. Immense sums were embarked in this enterprise; but this too failed, bringing upon its projectors, and on capitalists generally, wreck and ruin. That crisis has passed; but it has left a bolder spirit of enterprise, and perhaps even a preference for hazardous undertakings, which are sometimes seen in singular contrast, if not in singular union, with the former cautious habits of the people. Shipwrecks of every kind are the punishment of such adventures; but while the individual sinks, the calamity may sometimes open more speedily the general pathway to success. This period embraces the final settlement of the northeastern boundary. The small diminution of territory was but the loss of so much land; but the decision, while it removed a possible occasion for strife, gave a more distinct view of the wilderness behind. It is still a peculiar feature of Maine, that it contains, and must long contain, such a wilderness.

> " Stern famine guards the solitary coast,
> And winter barricades the realms of frost."

It is at least a background, which somewhat appalls the timid and the easy, so long as, under a genial sky, vast prairies repose untilled along the Mississippi, or the setting sun is reflected from golden hills without an owner. Maine may have a woody desert of her own, larger perhaps than any of the sisterhood of original states; but, inch by inch, the trees will probably fall, and fences, gravelled roads, pleasant cottages, and fields of waving grain, will extend to the Chaudière and to Madawaska.

If we take a step backward in the view of the population of Maine, we shall find that the whole number of its inhabitants, one century ago, did not probably exceed ten thousand; and they were scattered along the coast, occupying only a few salient points, and engaged in lumbering and fishing, — not extending at all into the interior, through fear of savages, who held empire over the forests, and for want of roads. This ten thousand, notwithstanding the outsetting current, under the genial influence of free institutions, has become six hundred thousand. To predict that Maine must be, in some sense, a northern hive, sending forth its young to win wealth in warmer fields, is but to say that it must be what the north always was in Asia, in Europe, and America, either through conquests, through commerce, or through constant emigration. But neither Scandinavia nor Tartary is depopulated by these swarmings of men; nor will Maine be, who can spare her thousands to California, and still keep her hundreds of thousands, quite as worthy and vigorous, at home.

2*

This state, participating in nearly all the great improvements of the age, has gone on steadily developing her resources, and increasing her wealth and power. Her railroad interest, which did not fully open until since 1840, has become one of vast magnitude. There are upwards of four hundred miles of track in operation, at a cost of from $15,000,000 to $20,000,000, penetrating all parts of the state west of the Penobscot, and affording facilities for transportation which greatly augment the value of property, and contribute to the general prosperity. In the year 1856, the several railroads carried upwards of 2,600,000 passengers, for which they received $1,248,404.69, besides $1,073,244.66 for freight and $78,993.46 for mail and other services. These advantages are increased by 555 miles of telegraph; and by the steamboat navigation, which was forced into notice under great discouragements,—requiring some exclusive privileges from the state,—and which is now an important interest, engrossing a large capital.

The slow advance of agriculture into the interior of the State indicates that the energy of the people has turned into other channels than the enlargement and cultivation of their fields at home. Notwithstanding this diversion, the census of 1850 shows seventy-seven thousand persons engaged in agricultural pursuits, who had more than 2,000,000 acres of improved land in their home farms, and 2,500,000 acres unimproved,—the land being valued at $55,000,000, and the implements of cultivation at $2,284,000. The aggregate value of stock, agricultural produce, and articles of home manufacture, exceeds annually $30,000,000, showing that here is a substantial interest not to be overlooked. Agriculture forms the permanent basis of a country's greatness. It is the nursing mother of a wise and virtuous people; and it is fortunate indeed that the recent decline in the lumber trade seems to be creating a deeper interest in the products of the soil. Maine, in 1857, held her third annual agricultural exhibition, thus getting the start of her maternal state, which that year held her first.

But Maine is essentially a *commercial* state, with an extended seacoast of 278 miles, (or 2,486 miles, including bays and islands,) having numerous safe and convenient harbors, with facilities for building, manning, and equipping vessels of every size and class. She has always ranked among the foremost in maritime operations. In ship-building she took the lead at the very start, and has never lost supremacy, but has left her competitors still further behind. In 1820, 27,705 tons of shipping were built; and, in 1855, it amounted to 215,904 tons, divided among 213 barques, 107 brigs, sixty-eight schooners, two sloops, and six steamers. In the fisheries, Maine holds the second rank; in the general aggregate of tonnage, the third; in imports, the seventh; and in exports, the tenth. She has thirteen districts for collection of the revenue.

Her comparative wealth is large. The aggregate valuation of real and personal property in the state in 1850 was $122,777,561, making an average of $210 to every man, woman, and child. Her capital is not idle. Besides the means of its employment before mentioned, upwards of $15,000,000 are embarked in manufacturing operations, with an annual product of more than $25,000,000. There is also a banking capital of $8,107,485, distributed among seventy-nine banks.

In her civil organization, she has fifteen counties, 388 incorporated towns, of which ten have received a city charter; about 350 plantations and settlements, embracing territory and natural capacities sufficient to support a very large population. Touching her moral and social condition, the last census returns exhibited 945 churches, valued at $1,794,209, giving accommodations to 325,997 persons, or 56 per cent. of the entire population, each church having an average value of $1,899, and seating 345 persons; two colleges, one theological and one medical school, with an annual income of $14,000; 131 academies and private schools, with an annual income of $51,187. The report of the Superintendent of Schools for 1857 gave 4,102 school-districts, 3,889 school-houses, 240,764 pupils, and an expenditure of $666,797.58, or $2.59 to each pupil. There are about fifty newspapers (eight of which are daily), circulating among 63,887 subscribers, and having an annual issue of more than 4,000,000 copies. The united libraries of Maine, other than private, embracing the public, the school, the Sunday school, the college, and the church libraries, contain 121,969 volumes.

The pulpit, the school, the press, and the library, then, co-working with the natural and acquired resources of Maine, are an irresistible power, which must give her a distinguished position among the orbs of our political constellation. Her extent of territory, rich soil, long line of sea-coast, excellent harbors and navigable rivers, the enterprise and ingenuity of her people, their regard for education and a faithful administration of duties in the government of the state, are sure precursors of an exalted destiny.

CHAPTER III.

MAINE — ABORIGINAL INHABITANTS.[1]

The Indians of Maine are supposed to be of what is termed by Mr. Pickering, the Lenni Lenápe, or Delaware Stock, and by Mr. Gallatin, in his "Synopsis," the Algonkin Lenape. Says the former of these eminent philologists, "When the Europeans arrived in America, these Indians were in possession of the *eastern* coast of this continent, from Virginia to Nova Scotia; and hence, as we are informed, they were called Wapanachki, or Abenakis, that is, *Men of the east*, or Eastlanders." By La Hontan and other writers, they were called *Algonkins*, or, as more usually written by the French travellers and historians, *Algonquins*. The generic name *Abenaqui*, or Abnaki, has not been used by Europeans in the extended sense above mentioned, but has been restricted to the principal tribes or nations which inhabited a part of Canada, Nova Scotia, and the adjoining north-eastern territory of the United States, now called the State of Maine. This explanation may serve to reconcile, in some manner, the classifications made by different writers. Some of the old writers, as Charlevoix, Abbe Raynal, and La Hontan, as indeed some of the later ones, call all the natives east of the Piscataqua (except the Micmacs or Nova Scotia Indians) Abenaquies. Gallatin, Williamson, and some others, make two great divisions — Abnakis, and Etchemins or Etetchemins, i. e. "canoe-men." Under the Abnakis are usually included the *Sokokis*, or Saco Indians; the *Anasagunticooks*, or Androscoggin tribe; the *Wawenocs*, who dwelt along the coast from Merry-meeting bay to the St. George's; and the *Canibas*, or Kenabes, who occupied the valley of the Kennebec, and who were again divided into the *Norridgewocks*, the *Taconnets*, about Waterville, and the *Cushnocs*, about Augusta. Under the Etchemins are generally reckoned the *Tarratines*,

[1] The following are among the works that have been consulted. Champlain's Voyages; La Hontan's New Voyages; Charlevoix's Histoire de la Nouvelle France; Gookin's Historical Collections of the Indians in New England — *Mass. Hist. Coll. Vol. I.* 146–227; Pickering's Introduction to Rasles' Abnaki Dictionary — *Memoirs Amer. Acad., New Series, Vol. I.* 370; Gallatin's Synopsis of the Indian Tribes — *Transactions of Amer. Antiq. Soc. Vol. II.*; Williamson's Hist. Maine; Language of the Abnaquies, or Eastern Indians, by Wm. Willis — *Maine Hist. Coll. Vol. IV. Art.* 6; Indian Tribes of New England, by Lorenzo Sabine — *Christian Examiner* for January, 1852, and January and March, 1857; Shea's Hist. of Catholic Missions among the Indian Tribes of the United States, 123–162; The Abnaki Indians, by Frederic Kidder — *Maine Hist. Coll. Vol. VI.*

or *Penobscots* (which some writers are at a loss whether to class with the Abnakis or Etchemins), the *Passamaquoddys*, and the *Marachites* or *St. John's* tribe, the last on the east side of the St. Croix, and, consequently, not to be noticed here. Of all the tribes of Maine, the Penobscots and Passamaquoddys, who probably constitute half of the whole Indian population of New England, alone remain. Williamson gives estimates of the numbers of the several tribes about 1615, which far exceed the usual computations, making them in the aggregate about 8,800 warriors, or 30,000 inhabitants, reckoning the Sokokis at 900 warriors; the Anasagunticooks, 1,500; the Wawenoes, 1,100; the Canibas, 1,500; the Tarratines, 2,400; and the Passamaquoddys, 1,400. The great plague of 1617, and subsequent intestine wars in most of the tribes, left but a small fraction of the original number.

To glance briefly at the Abnakis:— Historians tell us that the Sokokis had two branches, one within the great bend of the Saco, at Pequawket or Fryeburg, the other, fifteen or twenty miles below, upon the Great Ossipee — that they were men of valor, but were ruined in Lovewell's fight, in 1725 — that some of them aided the English at Louisburg in 1744, and before the capture of Quebec the tribe was extinct — that Fluellen, Capt. Sunday, and Squando were renowned chiefs:— that the Anasagunticooks claimed dominion along the Androscoggin, from its sources to Merry-meeting bay — that they took part in the ravages during Philip's war at Pemaquid and along Casco bay — that, in 1744, 160 warriors remained, in 1750, most of the tribe joined the St. Francis Indians, and, at the time of the Revolution, about forty might be found scattered among the islands and along the course of the river:— that the Wawenoes or Sheepscot Indians were the immediate subjects of the Great Bashaba, whose residence was near Pemaquid, and who was slain in the war with the Tarratines, the power of the tribe being then broken — that, in 1747, but two or three families were left here, the remnant having gone to Canada:— that the Canibas, more usually called the Norridgewocks, because most of them resided here, were a brave, and yet docile people. They tell us of the great success of the Jesuit missionaries among them, and especially of Gabriel Druillettes, who first came in 1646, of James Bigot in 1688, and of Sebastian Rasles from 1695 to 1724, the biography of whom opens anew the story of jealousies and retaliatory conflicts, that were appeasable only in the death of this indefatigable man — and that the greater portion of the tribe thereupon joined the St. Francis Indians, leaving, in 1760, but thirty warriors, and in 1795 only six or seven families.

But to proceed with the Tarratines or Penobscots, and the Passamaquoddys:— The former were known to the early French and English voyagers, who tell us of the natives about Pentagoet. They were then warlike and powerful. From the time of "King William's war" (1688), their decline was rapid, and many were dispersed among the tribes on the St. Lawrence. In 1754, they were reduced to about 800, and in 1760, war, rum, and famine had left but seventy-three warriors and 400 others. Since the beginning of the present century, however, they have increased. In 1803, they were 347; in 1820, 400; in 1855, 443. Their territory, without doubt, originally extending from the sea-coast at Camden up both sides of the Penobscot and its tributaries to their sources, must have been to a large extent "spirited" away from them; for the Indian cannot be made to comprehend that he has in form of law parted with these lands forever.

The early success of the Penobscots over the Wawenocs has been mentioned. About 1669, it is believed that they were defeated in a battle with the Mohawks. In 1667, or about the time of the treaty of Breda, Baron de St. Castin, who, as an officer in the French service had come to Canada about 1665, upon the disbanding of the troops came and settled down among the natives upon the peninsula Bigaduce (now known by his name), and dwelt in the country about thirty years. He learned to speak their language with fluency — engaged in trade with them, and amassed a large property. He taught them the use of fire-arms, and led their forces in the wars with the English. These ties of friendship were made still stronger by his marriage with the daughter of Madockawando, by whom he had a son, called Castin the younger. The English courted his favor, but were jealous of his influence. In 1688, a party under the lead of Governor Andros pillaged his establishment, under the pretence that he would not recognize English jurisdiction east of the Penobscot. The same act was repeated upon the son in 1703, who was very friendly to the English, and one of his sisters was taken captive. In 1721, he was improperly seized and carried to Boston, where he was kept a prisoner for several months. These outrages were the main causes of enlisting the Penobscots in the *second* and *third* wars against the English. Their participation in the *first* (King Philip's) war had been mainly provoked by the wanton upsetting of a canoe with the wife and child of the far-famed Squando, in the Saco river, and the consequent death of the child, merely to test the idle saying "that a pappoose would swim as naturally as a puppy." Madockawando counselled peace, but the war spirit could not be stayed. The *fourth* war grew partly out of the dispute about lands east of the Kennebec, and partly from the onslaught upon Norridgewock, and the imprisonment of the younger Castin. In the *fifth* war (1744), notwithstanding the strong articles of alliance with the English contained in the Dummer treaty of

1726, the young warriors were in the ascendency, and involved the tribe. The *sixth* and last war (1754), although it incited the other Indians in Maine to various depredations, did not embroil the Penobscots, until after the reckless shooting and scalping of twelve of their number by James Cargill, of Newcastle, and the barbarous murder of Margaret Moxa, a noble and humane Indian woman, who was, at the very time, on an errand of peace and good-will to the garrison at St. George's; added to which was the inhuman butchery of her infant before her eyes, despite her dying entreaties that it might be taken to the fort. This infamous man was tried and acquitted, when he claimed and received a sum from the public treasury, equal to $2,000, for the scalps of his victims. The warriors could be restrained no longer. They plunged into the strife, and, deserted by their French allies, crushed by superior strength, and wasted by the smallpox, intemperance, and famine, they were ready, in 1760, to give in their final submission. From 1675 to this time — eighty-five years — thirty-six years had been spent in war.

The chiefs of the Penobscots have been Madockawando, who had no compeer in all New England but Philip; Mogg, his prime minister, and negotiator of the treaty of 1676; Wenemovet, a cousin of Madockawando, and negotiator of the Dummer treaty; Laron, and Egeremet; — within the last hundred years, Tomer; Osson "the Squire;" Orono, with a European complexion, — thought by some to have been a grandson of the elder Castin, and who flourished during the Revolution, and died in 1801, at the age of 113 years; John Aitteon, grandfather of the present chief or "governor;" Joseph Lolar, father of Capt. Francis; John Aitteon, father of the present governor, who served from 1816 to his death in May, 1858; and Joseph Aitteon, chosen, September 9, 1858, to hold the office for two years. John Neptune, lieutenant-governor, should also be mentioned, as he was contemporary with the last John Aitteon, and, in spite of his frailties, has long virtually shared the honors and influence of the chieftaincy. In religious matters, being Roman Catholics, their leaders have been Fathers Vincent Bigot, and Thury, in the eighteenth century; Gaulin, Rageot, Le Masse, De la Chasse, Lauvergat, Barthuaine, Matignon, Ciquard, and John Cheverus, afterwards a bishop and cardinal, in the last century; — Edmund Demillier from 1833 to 1843, and John Bapst from 1848 to 1850.

After repeated negotiations, the State got possession of all the lands of this tribe except four townships, and the islands in the Penobscot. The townships were sold, and the funds invested for their benefit. Their present home is at Oldtown, upon Indian Island, containing about 300 acres. They are variously engaged in driving logs, in agriculture, and making baskets and ornamental work, living in comparatively comfortable houses, but many of them loving too well the white man's rum to make a rapid advance towards civilized life.

The Passamaquoddys, or Sibayks, are thought by some to have descended from the natives seen by De Monts in 1604; others think, from the Penobscots, as these two tribes well understand each other, the Passamaquoddys, however, being far inferior in energy and intelligence. They do not appear in history until after the conquest of Canada. In 1801, Massachusetts, in consideration of their release of all other lands in Maine, confirmed to them forever fifteen islands in the St. Croix, township No. 2, R. 1, Lire's and Pine Islands in Big lake (one of the Schoodic), and lands at Nemcass Point, which projects into the lake, and at Pleasant Point, in the town of Perry, six miles from Eastport, those at the last place having been increased to 300 acres. Here they have a village and a church. Pleasant Point, in modern times, has been their chief place of abode, but for some years about half of them have dwelt on their township north of Big lake, where also they have a village and church. Here, probably, they dwelt when nothing was known of them upon the coast, as ancient Indian utensils have been exhumed. The township was formerly heavily timbered, but was many years since ravaged by fire. Some $15,000 worth of lumber, however, has lately been sold for their benefit. This tribe, too, is upon the increase. Governor Bernard was informed, in 1764, that their warriors numbered but thirty. It is known, however, that forty or fifty in the Revolution bore arms on the Whig side, and once assisted the people of Machias in repelling an attack by a British flotilla. In 1804, Sullivan estimated them at 130. In 1820, they were 379; in 1848, 405. They are not so well off as the Penobscots, but have been aided by direct grants from the State.

We have given the briefest possible view of this ill-fated race. Ethical and political writers will continue, as heretofore, to find in the weakness and indolence, in the cold and vindictive character of the aborigines, a justification of Anglo-Saxon treatment. The Indians were stolen and enslaved — rum was forced upon them — their lands were taken without any adequate compensation, and they were told to move along. They were heathen, and retaliated. Christianity might, perhaps, have taught them better, if it did not so teach the conquering race, but its effects were not tried. It is admitted that civilization and barbarism cannot dwell together; but let them not, in parting company, deny the existence of gratitude, generosity, and good faith in the feebler race. When treated as foes they were hostile; but they did not first break a peace which had been kept for fifty years. England and France made their domain a battle-ground, bid for their alliance, taught them lessons in atrocity, and accomplished their ruin.

CHAPTER IV.

COUNTIES, CITIES, AND TOWNS OF MAINE.

ABBOTT, situated in the southwestern part of Piscataquis county, embraces an area of 23,040 acres, and is one of the five towns that were granted to Bowdoin College in 1794. Its settlement is of recent date, and hence the town possesses but little material for history. It was incorporated in 1827, and possesses all the elements of a thriving agricultural town. The Piscataquis river flows through the southwest part, on the banks of which are many good farms. There are here two small villages, one post-office, two religious societies (Congregational and Free-will Baptist), and nine school districts, with sixteen schools. Population, 747; valuation, $65,351.

ACTON is situated in the western part of York county, one hundred and five miles from Augusta, and lies on the boundary line between Maine and New Hampshire. The history of the town belongs to that of Shapleigh, from which it was taken, and incorporated in 1830. Hills and valleys diversify its surface, except in the east and northeasterly parts. The soil is stubborn, but with proper attention good crops are obtainable. The town is well watered by several ponds, known by the names of Long, Square, Great East, Garvin's, and Loon. Little Ossipee river lies on the north, Salmon river on the west, and Mousam river towards the northeast of the town. Acton has three villages, — Acton, North Acton, and South Acton, — at each of which there is a post-office and a church; and fourteen school districts, having twelve schools. Population, 1,359; valuation, $213,825.

ADDISON is situated on the sea-coast, on the west side of Indian river, in Washington county. It was settled soon after the close of the Revolutionary war, and organized into a plantation, known as Number Six west of Machias. It became an incorporated town February 14,

1796. It has two villages — Addison Point and Indian River, with a post-office at each; one church edifice (Baptist); fourteen school districts, having twenty-six schools. Population, 1,152; valuation, $206,931.

Albany, Oxford county, lies south of the Androscoggin river, and fifteen miles west of Paris. It was settled soon after the close of the Revolutionary war, and in 1800 contained a population of between sixty and seventy. It was incorporated March 20, 1804. It is drained by Pequawket river, which has its source in a small pond in the northern part of the town. A series of basins, formed by the wear of the river in the solid talcose rock, are objects of great curiosity, one of which is seventy feet deep and forty feet in diameter. The surface of the town is mountainous, and much of it remains uncleared. There is one village in the town, and one post-office. It is divided into eight school districts, with an aggregate of 234 pupils. Population, 747; valuation, $71,843.

Albion, in the northeast corner of Kennebec county, twenty-four miles from Augusta and forty-four miles southwest from Bangor, was first organized in 1802 into a plantation, and called Freetown. In 1804, it was incorporated into a town and called Fairfax, next Lygonia, and lastly Albion.

The town is about six miles square. The soil, in the westerly part, is free from stones, and easily cultivated; the eastern portion is somewhat rocky, but productive. The southern portion is hilly; and well adapted to the cultivation of wheat. The Lovejoy pond, in the western part of the town, is famous for pickerel and perch, and is skirted on all sides with beautiful farms.

Albion has five shingle machines; four saw-mills; one grist-mill, having three sets of stones; fourteen school districts, with twenty-six schools; two post-offices, Albion and South Albion; and five meeting-houses. Population in 1850, 1,604 — which has been increased, by the annexing of Albion Gore, to about 1,650; valuation, $228,597.

Alexander, in the easterly part of Washington county, about midway between its northern and southern extremity, was first settled in 1810. Solomon Perkins, Caleb Pike, George Hill, A. Bohanan, William D. Crockett, Paul Morse, Cyrus Young, and Samuel Cottel were among the first who made Alexander their home, and came principally from Massachusetts and New Hampshire. The settlers obtained the titles to their lands from John Black, agent for the Bingham Purchase.

The town was incorporated in 1835, being prior to that time designated as Plantation No. 16.

The surface is uneven, but there is a variety of good farming land, and the inhabitants depend principally on their agricultural labors for a livelihood. The principal stream is the Wapskanegan, which runs through the centre of the town. Pleasant lake lies in the western part of the town, as also does Burrows lake. Medybemps and Pokey lakes lie partly in this town.

A Congregational and a Methodist society have been organized here, neither of which has a church edifice, holding their meetings in the school-houses. The town contains four school districts; Stephenson's mills, situated on Pleasant lake; and two post-offices — Alexander and Lane's Brook. Population, 544; valuation for 1858, $42,000.

ALFRED, the shire and central town of York county, eighty-eight miles from Boston and twenty-six from Portland, contains about eight thousand acres. The early history of Alfred is involved in that of Sandford, of which it was formerly a part, bearing at that time the name of "North Parish of Sandford," or "Massabesick." The people of Alfred, at the time of its incorporation in 1794, called Sandford "Phillipstown," this being the name of the township before Sandford was incorporated in 1768. The origin of these names may be traced to the owners of the territory, namely, Major William Phillips and Peleg Sandford. Alfred took its name from that early monarch of England, Alfred the Great.

The first settler[1] in Alfred was Simeon Coffin, who moved hither in 1764, and settled on what is now called the Hall Farm, on the west side of the pond. Daniel Gile settled north of Mr. Coffin, and afterward Stephen Coffin and his brother Daniel settled south of him. Many others followed at different periods.

The tragedy connected with the "picture-tree," which stood a little west of Parson Sweet's meeting-house, on which was carved the image of a child's head, is explained thus: the daughter of Peter Morrill, while gathering hemlock near Doughty's Falls, was surprised and captured by Indians, who, to prevent her giving alarm by screams, killed her on the spot, and on their retreat to Canada, carved her likeness on the tree above mentioned. In Alfred, a female captive was murdered at the crossing of Pequawket road, within a mile of the court-house. She was weak, and the Indians killed her to rid themselves of the incumbrance.

The northern part of the town is very hilly, and abounds in granite

[1] The authors are indebted to Mr. Peter Coffin, who has preached among the Shakers here for more than forty years, for much valuable information respecting the early pioneers.

rocks and hard-wood forests. The southern part is comparatively level. Near the centre of the town, on the northeast side of the plain, stands the beautiful village of Alfred. There are two small rivers intersecting this town, which unite to form Mousam river, at a place called Swett's Mill. Each of these streams affords water-power for mills during the greater part of the year; and below their junction the power is sufficient to run factories the whole year. One of these streams rises from Pomegranate pond, and passes through Massabesick pond; the other takes its rise in a dense forest and marsh, called Jebung Woods.

The chief occupation of the first settlers seems to have been lumbering. Several saw and grist mills were early erected; and mechanics of almost every kind began to locate themselves in the neighborhood of the mills.

The court-house, located in the village of Alfred, was erected in 1806, on land given by William Parsons and Dr. Hall. The jail was not built until about two years after. In 1821, a newspaper was started, called the "Eastern Star," but had a short existence. The first framed building erected in town was a school-house, on the site of the present brick hotel, and was designed for, and occupied by, the whole town. In 1803, the brick school-house was put up and opened, and districts were formed. The academy was built in 1823 or 1824.

The first emigrants were from Massachusetts and New Hampshire, where religious instruction was particularly regarded. They soon felt the privation here, and were early in supplying the best means of public worship their situation allowed. A church was formed, comprising the first settlers around Massabesick and Pomegranate ponds, and the contiguous part of Waterboro', under the direction and care of Mr. Merriam and Mr. Little. A second one was soon after formed around Conant's mills, by Mr. Little. In 1780 the two were united under Mr. Prince, and meetings were held regularly in John Knight's barn, a part of which was also occupied by Mr. Knight as a dwelling-house. At this time there were only about twenty members in the church.

About 1782, the order of Shakers had its origin, and a small village of them was soon after formed at Mastcamp, four miles northeast of the principal settlement. In 1793, the society was organized as a body, in the present order and discipline of church-government.

In 1802, the supreme court, which had been held at Kennebunk for the two preceding years, was removed to Alfred, although not without a severe contest; and the bench was occupied by Judges Dana, Cushing, and Thacher. In 1806, the court of common pleas and the York courts were removed to this, the shire town.

There are now five church edifices in the town, — one Congregational, two Baptist, one Methodist, and one Shaker; eleven school districts with ten schools; one bank with a capital of $75,000; and one post-office. Population, 1,319; valuation, $271,600.

ALNA, Lincoln county, on the west side of Sheepscot river, is bounded south by Wiscasset. It was originally a part of Old Pownalborough, — now Dresden, — and its history is included in that town's. It was incorporated in 1794, under the name of New Milford, afterwards changed to Alna.

The town extends about six miles north and south, and four miles east and west. The surface is uneven, — the western part, back from the river, being quite broken, — while other portions abound in ledges and bogs. On the banks of the river, however, good soil is found. Its abundance of berries makes it a place of resort in the fall.

At the head of the tide, near the north line of the town, there is a small village, with two saw-mills and one grist-mill. One mile east, on the river, is another small village, named Puddle Dock, with a ship-yard, where shipbuilding is carried on to a moderate extent. At the south part of the town is another small village, called Sheepscot Bridge, where are one saw and one grist mill, and a ship-yard, doing a moderate business. Agriculture is the general employment.

Alna has two church edifices, — one Congregational, the other Free-will Baptist; also six school districts, with twelve schools; and one post-office. Population, 916; valuation, $182,679.

ALTON, Penobscot county, on the west side of Penobscot river, north of Oldtown, and formerly a part of Argyle, was incorporated a town in 1845. Its surface is generally level, but the soil poor.

There is a small village in the northwest part of the town, on the west side of Dead stream, with a tannery, doing a large and lucrative business; also a saw-mill and a shingle machine, recently put in operation, promising a profitable business. Alton has two post-offices, Alton and Alton Village; and has six school districts, with nine schools. Population, 252; valuation, $13,346.

AMHERST, in the northern part of Hancock county, constitutes a part of Bingham's Purchase. Its settlement was commenced between 1805 and 1808 by Captain Goodell Silsbee, Moses Kimball, Asahel Foster, Jesse Gils, Joseph Day, Judah West, and Elisha Chick. Its progress since has been slow. In 1822, Amherst was set off from the plantation of Mariaville, and, in 1831, was incorporated a town.

3*

Its surface is considerably broken and uneven, and in some parts very rocky. It is watered by some small ponds having their outlet in Union river. Its heavy growth of pine has been mostly cleared off. It has one saw-mill, two clapboard and shingle machines; a large tannery, doing considerable business; one small village; one post-office; one church edifice (Congregational); and four school districts, with three schools. The inhabitants are engaged in agriculture and lumbering. Population, 323; valuation, $43,962.

AMITY, Aroostook county, was incorporated March 19, 1836. The first settlement was commenced in 1826 by Jonathan T. Clifford, Jonathan Greenleaf, and Columbus Dunn. This township was formerly known as "No. 10, first range." The first settlers bought their lands for twenty cents per acre, payable one half in cash, and one half in work on the public highways. Since the incorporation of the town, the lands have been sold to speculators by the state. This has retarded its growth to a very great extent, since settlers can buy of the state, at the Aroostook settlement, much cheaper than of the proprietors of land here, most of whom are non-residents.

The surface is rolling, and well timbered with hard wood. It is watered by branches of the Penobscot, St. John, and St. Croix rivers, which take their rise in this town, and which are large enough for floating lumber, supplied by the surrounding region. It has three school districts, with the same number of schools. Population, 256; valuation for 1858, $23,300.

ANDOVER, Oxford county, was incorporated in 1804, under the name of East Andover, and was then in York county. The first settler was Ezekiel Merrill, — with his wife and six children, — who came from Fryeburg. He drew his effects on hand-sleds — aided by his three sons — through the woods, the only guide being the spotted trail of the Indians. Mrs. Merrill was here two years without seeing the face of any white female, save her own three daughters. The next settlers were mostly from Andover, Mass., and were Jonathan Abbott, Samuel Poor, Sylvanus Poor, Theodore Brickett, Francis Swan, Josiah Wright, John Abbott, Jeremiah Burnham, and others. The title to the land was first obtained by grant from Massachusetts.

The surface is mostly smooth, consisting of large intervals on the river, with a little higher elevation of pine plains. The town is surrounded by mountains, lying mostly without and on the borders, Lone mountain being the only one lying wholly within its limits. The town is well watered by Ellis river, which runs through it, Black brook, Saw-

Lewiston Falls.

yer brook, Frye's brook, — on which is the cataract, — Stony brook, Gardner's brook, and Lone brook. These streams frequently rise so high as to overflow the intervals, and cause great damage to crops; and the soil being sandy, it is difficult to build bridges so strong as to withstand the freshets. The streams abound in trout.

The chief occupation of the settlers is agriculture and lumbering. This town has but one village, which is called Andover Corners. It has seven school districts, with sixteen schools; two churches, both occupied by Congregational societies, with one minister; two post-offices, Andover and South Andover; one grist-mill and one tannery. Population, 710; valuation, $75,390.

ANDROSCOGGIN COUNTY, situated towards the southwest part of the state, has the smallest territory, excepting Sagadahoc, of all the counties, containing an area of about four hundred square miles. The act establishing it was passed March 18, 1854. It was made up from four counties, and comprises fourteen towns, as follows: — Lewiston, Lisbon, and Webster, from the county of Lincoln; Auburn, Danville, Durham, Minot, and Poland, from the county of Cumberland; Livermore and Turner from the county of Oxford; East Livermore, Greene, Leeds, and Wales, from the county of Kennebec. The inhabitants were left at liberty to select for the shire town, either Auburn, Lewiston, or Danville, but were restricted to a location within the limits of the Lewiston Falls Village corporation; and they chose Auburn.

The county is watered by the river whose name it bears, and its tributaries; and possesses, for the most part, a fertile soil, and excellent advantages for manufacturing, which are being largely improved. The leading pursuit of the inhabitants is agriculture, although the manufacturing interest bids fair to be of no secondary importance. The county has also the best facilities for communication, being traversed by the Grand Trunk railway, and the Androscoggin and Kennebec railroad.

The substantial and commodious county buildings are situated a short distance westerly from Lewiston falls. A view of these falls, which so beautifully combine the wildness of nature with the elements and achievements of industrial life, and which seem to belong to the whole county rather than to any part of it, is given in connection with this article.

The inhabitants have full county privileges, except in the matter of choosing senators, for whom they vote with their original counties.

There are three terms of the supreme judicial court, for both civil and criminal business, in this county, commencing on the first Tuesdays of January, July, and August.

The aggregate population of the towns composing the county, was, by the last census returns, 25,748; valuation, $4,152,502.

Anson, Somerset county, situated on the west bank of the Kennebec river, is a large and thriving town. Settlements were made here about the same time as at Norridgewock, by adventurers who pushed up the river, in order to be the first to take possession of the rich alluvial lands on the banks of the Kennebec. When surveyed it was found to be without the limits of the Plymouth Patent, and was accordingly called township Number One west of the Kennebec river, north of the Plymouth Patent. It was incorporated March 1, 1798, by its present name. It was divided, and North Anson was incorporated out of it March 20, 1845; but a reunion took place March 13, 1855. Anson has two villages, North and South Anson, both on the Kennebec river, with a post-office at each; two tanneries, doing a good business; an academy, well patronized; twenty-four school districts, with thirty-six schools; four churches, Congregational, Free-will Baptist, Methodist, and Universalist. Population, 2,016; valuation $310,391.

Appleton is situated in the southwest part of Waldo county, twenty-five miles easterly from Augusta. Settlements were made in this town about 1775. It is watered by the Medomac and the St. George's rivers, and is a very good agricultural town. There are two villages, McLain's Mills and North Appleton, at the latter of which, lime is manufactured to a considerable extent. Lumber, lime, dairy and farm produce form the staples of trade. Appleton has five saw-mills; nine shingle and stave mills; three grist-mills; one tannery; one carriage manufactory; three shoe and boot manufactories; two social libraries; four church edifices, — one Baptist, one Free-will Baptist, one Friends' and one Union, occupied by Methodists and Universalists; two post-offices, — McLain's Mills and North Appleton; and twelve school districts, with twenty-four schools. Population, 1,727; valuation, $206,691.

Argyle, Penobscot county, on the west bank of Penobscot river, twenty miles north from Bangor, was incorporated in 1839. The surface of the town is generally level, — some of it swampy; and the soil poor. There are two saw-mills and two grist-mills; two churches, Methodist and Free-will Baptist; four school districts, with five schools; and one post-office. Population, 338; valuation, $22,573.

Aroostook County, forming the whole northern and northeasterly part of the state, is the largest county, embracing an area of 6,800 square miles, most of which is wild land. It was taken from the counties of Penobscot and Washington. The act establishing it was passed March 16, 1839, at which time its name became identified, far and near, with the controversy with Great Britain respecting the boundary. The act defines it to be "all that part of the state lying north of the north line of the fourth range of townships, north of the Lottery townships, and east of the dividing line between ranges five and six west of the east line of the state, and of a line from the north termination of the said dividing line, and running the same course, to the north line of the state."

This territory was enlarged by act of March 21, 1843, by annexing to the county all of Penobscot county north of the three townships numbered eight, in the sixth, seventh, and eighth ranges of townships west from the east line of the state; and again, by act of March 12, 1844, defining the boundaries between several counties, in which Aroostook acquired from Piscataquis and Somerset counties, all the territory north of the townships numbered ten, and west of the seventh range of townships west of the east line of the state.

It is divided by the state surveys into one hundred and eighty-one townships, and into three districts of registration, known as the first, second, and third districts.

The whole county is well watered by a great number of lakes, ponds, rivers, and brooks, and on many of the streams there is a sufficient fall for propelling machinery. The principal rivers are the St. John, Allagash, Aroostook, Masgunicook, and the Mattawamkeag, which are fed by a great number of tributaries. The principal lakes are Long lake, in the western part; and Portage, Eagle, Square, Cross, and Madawaska, in the northeastern part. Here and there a few bogs may be seen, though the country cannot be called swampy.

Pine Forests of Northern Maine.

The settlements are mostly in the southerly and easterly portions of the county. As yet, only thirteen towns have been incorporated, though many others, called plantations, are being rapidly settled, and will soon become incorporated municipalities.

Houlton was made the shire town. There are two terms of the supreme judicial court, for both civil and criminal business, commencing on the second Tuesday of March, and the third Tuesday of September.

Aroostook has, until lately, been valued only for its timber. It is now gradually recovering from the unwise policy which the state has pursued, in making grants of its land to public institutions and to scheming speculators, instead of encouraging actual settlers. The forests are receding before the sinewy arms of the woodsmen, who are turning their attention from river-driving to clearing up the lands, and to the development of the abundant agricultural resources of the county.

The soil is generally excellent, and of three kinds, — diluvial, alluvial, and soil resulting from the disintegration of the rocks beneath. Limestone is found along the banks of the Aroostook and the St. John, and in some parts of the county is quite abundant. Houlton is remarkable for its limestone soil, which makes it extremely productive, and admirably suited for the growth of grain and grasses. The rich alluvial soils of this county will, when cleared up, yield to no other districts in the luxuriance of their productions. Pop., 12,529 ; Val., $537,438.

ARROWSIC, Sagadahoc county, is an island town in the Kennebec river, near its mouth, and contains about twenty thousand acres, including a large quantity of salt marsh. This island was purchased of the natives by Major Clark and Captain Lake, in 1661, at which time a fort was standing on the west side of the island, at a place now known as Stinson's point, and was occupied by one Hammond, an old trader, who probably erected it to prevent a surprise from the natives. It is not, however, known that Hammond purchased or claimed any land at that place. The Indians destroyed this fort, so tradition says, in resentment for the loss of furs and arms stolen by the English from some of their friends, who lived further up the river. Clark and Lake's fort, which was distant about two miles from Hammond's, was destroyed about the same time by the natives who surprised the former; and Captain Lake, in attempting to flee from it, was mortally wounded. His bones, which were afterwards found, were, it is said, interred in Boston.

The early settlers met with many reverses; and, at times, suffered great privations. During the Indian wars, massacres and conflagrations were of frequent occurrence. A short time before the erection of Fort Halifax, the Norridgewock Indians descended the river, and landing at Arrowsic, killed a Mr. Preble, while he was working in his field; after which they proceeded to his house, murdered his wife, and took his children (a son and two daughters) captives, whom they carried to Canada. Captain Hamden, a relative of theirs, after the peace of Paris, in 1763, proceeded to Canada and obtained their release. Remains of dwellings, and other evidences of Indian depredations, are still to be seen on the island.

Arrowsic was set off from Georgetown and incorporated in 1841. At present, there is little that would be attractive to the traveller. As a summer resort it is, however, much visited by persons in search of health and recreation, — its invigorating breezes, and opportunities for bathing and fishing being unequalled. It has a church edifice; two school districts, with three schools; and one post-office. Population, 311; valuation, $72,875.

Ashland is near the centre of Aroostook county. William Dalton began its settlement about 1835, at the junction of the Great Machias with the Aroostook. Dalton was followed a year or two afterwards by Benjamin Howe, who settled on the Aroostook river, a short distance above him, and still resides there. The township was lotted by Noah Barker, during the years of 1839–40. At that time there were but five families here. The Fairbanks road, leading to Presque Isle, was opened the same year. The Aroostook road, extending from the military road seven miles above Mattawamkeag point to the north line of this township, having been cut through a year or two previous, was not made passable till about 1843. From the termination of this, the Fish river road, which was surveyed and opened in 1839, runs northerly to the mouth of Fish river. A large portion of the township, bordering upon the river and the roads just mentioned, is cleared up and settled. The surface is generally even, and the occupation of the inhabitants about equally divided between lumbering and farming. There is one village on the east side of the river, near the mouth of the Great Machias, which has a public-house, two stores, and a post-office, but no church edifice. This township was once incorporated as a town, but the charter was subsequently revoked, and it has relapsed into its plantation state. There are four school districts. Population, 354.

Athens, Somerset county, on the eastern side of the Kennebec river, about forty miles north from Augusta, was settled about 1782, and incorporated March 7, 1804. It is an excellent farming town, watered by a tributary of the Kennebec. Athens has one village, one post-office, thirteen school districts, and three religious societies, — two Baptist and one Methodist. Population, 1,460; valuation, $245,687.

ATKINSON is in the southern part of Piscataquis county. Its settlement was commenced in 1802, by Byley Lyford, from Canterbury, N. H., who, for two years, was the only inhabitant. In 1807, a saw-mill and grist-mill were built near the centre of the town, by Jonathan and Josiah Colcord, from Nottingham, N. H. Since then three saw-mills and several shingle machines have been erected.

In 1819, the town was incorporated, and named in honor of Judge Atkinson, of the supreme court of New Hampshire, — one of the three original proprietors of the town,—upon which he gave the town a library of about one hundred volumes.

The surface is rolling. The lowlands between the swells are not generally suitable for cultivation. The highlands or swells have a rich, deep soil, free from stone, and easily cultivated.

Atkinson has four church organizations, — Baptist, Congregational, Methodist, and Free-will Baptist; also nine school districts, with the same number of schools. Population, 895; valuation, $111,181.

AUBURN, Androscoggin county, is situated on the west bank of the Androscoggin river, opposite Lewiston. The settlement of the town was commenced in 1786. Samuel Starbird, Thomas Bailey, Samuel Emerson, David Libbey, and one Small, were among the first settlers, although the exact date of their arrival is unknown. In June, 1789, Benjamin True, Jabez, Levi, and Daniel Merrill, from Salisbury, Mass., and Jacob Stevens, from New Gloucester, settled in the eastern part of the town. Subsequently, the tract comprising this town, Poland, and Minot, was granted by Massachusetts to one Baker, and was thence called Bakerstown.[1] In 1795, the whole tract was incorporated in one town, named Poland. In 1802, Poland was divided, and the easterly portion incorporated under the name of Minot. In 1842, Minot was divided, and the easterly part incorporated under the name of Auburn, the territory comprising which was originally granted by Massachusetts to John Bridgham and others, who had a struggle with the Pejepscot proprietors, the latter claiming that their Indian grant included a large portion of this town. The matter was finally settled by Massachusetts paying the Pejepscot claimants for the land. Thus the settlers seem to have obtained the titles to their lands from John Bridgham and others.

Auburn, like many other towns, has its Indian legends. A story is told of a white man, who, at an early period, settled upon an island in the river, above the falls, towards whom the Indians entertained a deadly hatred; and they determined to kill him. For this purpose a

[1] See Poland.

party of about fifty Indians started in their canoes from a point some distance up the river, in the dead of night, guided, as they supposed, by the light that the lonely white man kept continually burning upon the island. But by some means, the white man's suspicions had been awakened, and fearing a night attack by them, he had taken the precaution to build a fire on a hill below the falls, directly in range of his island, and to put out his own fire upon the island. The Indians, lured on by this light, were drawn into the fatal current before they discovered their mistake, — dashed over the falls, and all of them perished.[1]

Auburn.

Many implements of Indian manufacture have been found here, such as axes, war-clubs, and ornaments. Two years since, while the streets were being graded, some ten or twelve Indian skeletons were exhumed, evidently having been buried according to their usual custom, in a sitting posture, with their wampum and war-clubs around them.

The surface of the town is generally uneven, but without mountains. The soil is fertile, especially along the valleys and the banks of the Androscoggin. The town is watered by two very pleasant ponds, in the easterly and central parts, and the Little Androscoggin, a stream of considerable size, which forms a portion of the southerly and easterly

[1] Another version of this story represents that the Indians were about to make a descent upon the settlement at Brunswick, and were intercepted by this island hermit, who by some means had gained a knowledge of their intentions.

boundary, and is a tributary of the larger river of that name. The Androscoggin and Kennebec railroad passes through the town. There are four villages, the most important of which is situated on the banks of the Androscoggin, at what is commonly termed Lewiston Falls. Here are the county buildings, constructed in 1856–57, of brick, with a granite basement, at a cost of $100,000. There are four post-offices, one at each of the villages; sixteen school districts, with the same number of schools; and four churches, — two Universalist, one Baptist, and one Congregationalist.

Auburn is not so much an agricultural as a manufacturing town. Considerable business is done here in the manufacture of house furniture, but the boot and shoe manufacture constitutes the principal business. There are five saw-mills, three flour mills, one peg manufactory, two tanneries, one sash and blind factory, and one iron foundery. The town has one bank, with a capital of $75,000. Population in 1850, 2,840; but since that time there has been a large increase of business and of population, so that at the present time there cannot be less than 4,500 inhabitants. Assessors' valuation for 1858, $652,847.

Augusta, the capital of the state, and the shire town of Kennebec county, is situated on both sides of the Kennebec, and was originally a

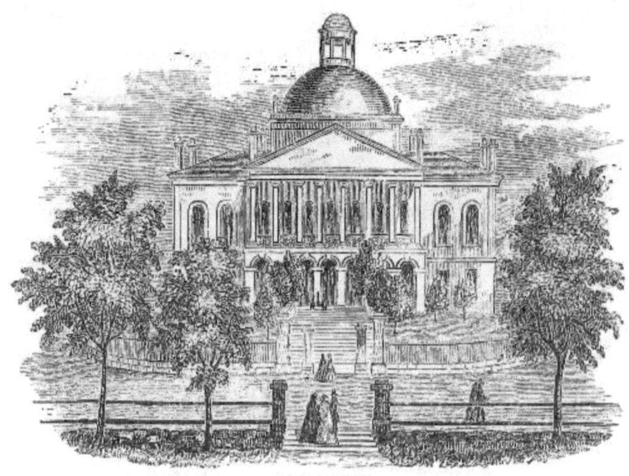

The State House.

part of the Kennebec Patent granted to the Plymouth colony in 1629. It was then occupied by the Cushnoc clan of Indians, a branch of the Canibas tribe, and the Abnaki nation, and from them derived its early name of Cushnoc. It was here that the patentees made the first settlement within the limits of their grant; and it seems to have become a prosperous one as early as 1654, but was depopulated upon the breaking out of King Philip's war, and remained desolate many years. In 1716, a stone fort was built here, and garrisoned at the public expense; but the place was again abandoned on the commencement of Lovewell's war, in 1724, and but little effort toward resettlement was made until after the fall of Quebec in 1760. There is certainly no evidence of such effort previous to the year 1754, during which Fort Western was built by the Kennebec proprietors, under the auspices of Governor Shirley. In connection with this fort a palisade enclosure was made, fifty feet distant from the walls upon all sides, in each of the four corners of which a block-house was erected; but all traces of the fort

Arsenal.

and these outposts had disappeared many years since. The "great house," as it was usually called, still standing on the easterly side of the river about a mile above the bridge, which was built by James Howard, the first and only commandant at Fort Western, has been erroneously supposed by some to have been that fort. This house was for a short time, in the autumn of 1775, the head-quarters of Benedict Arnold when on his expedition to Quebec.

Since the close of the Revolutionary war, the history of the place has been progressive.

Augusta became the shire town of the county of Kennebec in 1799, and the seat of government in 1831. The first bridge across the river was built in 1797, at a cost of $28,000. It decayed, and was rebuilt in

1818. The second bridge was destroyed by fire in 1827, bu was rebuilt the same year, at a cost of $13,000. The post-office was established here in 1794, and the first meeting of the legislature was held in January, 1832. Augusta was incorporated as a town in 1797, and became a city in 1849.

The principal business portion of the town is on the west side of the river. The scenery on the east side is romantic and pleasing. The streets are shaded by trees, and the numerous beautiful public buildings, of white granite, give it a charming appearance. The State House, of which an engraving will be found on a preceding page, is an elegant and spacious structure, built of white granite, and situated on an eminence at the west part of the city. It contains excellent accommodations for all state purposes. The grounds about the building are finely laid out, and decorated with trees, presenting quite a tasty appearance. Immediately in front of this building is the common, a beautiful and extensive plat of land, lying between the State House and the Kenne-

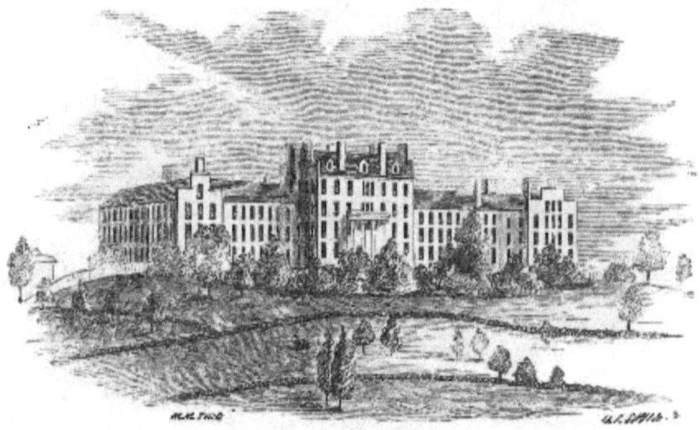

Insane Hospital.

bec river. Directly opposite the common, on the east bank of the river, is the United States Arsenal, erected at a cost of $100.000, consisting of several fine buildings, on beautiful grounds, a view of which is given on the preceding page. The buildings are constructed principally of stone, and present a very fine appearance. The grounds are extensive and well arranged, and surrounded by a costly iron fence. There are at present about two thousand stand of arms deposited here, besides cannon, and various munitions of war. Immediately below the arsenal, on the same side of the river, is the State Insane Hospital, a spacious granite building, occupying a plat of elevated ground of seventy acres, a view of which is here presented. It is an honor to the state and to humanity. Its situation is unrivalled for the beauty of its scenery. It is much admired for its external architecture, and also for its internal arrangements. The centre building and wings are 262 feet long; the centre building being eighty-two feet in length, forty-six feet wide, four stories high, besides the basement and attic, having a chapel in the attic eighty by forty. The wings are ninety feet long in front, and one hundred in the rear, thirty-eight feet wide, and three stories high, divided into 126 rooms, 120 of which are designed for patients, with halls between the rooms twelve feet wide, running the entire length of each wing, and communicating with the dining-rooms in the centre building. The buildings which formerly occupied the site of the edifice just described were destroyed by fire on the 3d of December, 1850, when twenty-seven of the inmates and one of the keepers fell victims to the devouring element. The fire originated about four o'clock in the morning, in the hot-air chamber in one south wing, and spread with great rapidity, destroying every thing in the two south wings, and part of the main building. The books and papers belonging to the hospital were safely removed, and a part of the furniture in a damaged state. The reërection of the buildings was immediately commenced, and the work was completed in the course of two years. This institution is under the superintendence of Dr. Henry M. Harlow, who fills his arduous situation with much ability.

There are excellent public-houses in Augusta, the chief of which are the Augusta House, near the State house, and the Stanley House. About half a mile above the village, a massive dam, with locks, has been erected across the Kennebec, for the purpose of improving the navigation of the river above, and of creating a water-power of great capacity. The length of this dam, exclusive of the stone abutments and lock, is 584 feet, and the height fifteen feet above ordinary high-water mark, forming a pond of the average depth of sixteen feet, and sixteen and a half miles in extent. The immense body of water, and the great and unfailing supply thus brought into use for manufacturing purposes, are almost unsurpassed. The first cost of this great work was about $300,000. This water-power is already used to a very considerable extent in propelling various kinds of machinery. Several saw-mills, a large flouring establishment, sash, door, and blind manufactories, machine shops, and a cotton factory with ten thousand spindles, are in successful operation. Augusta presents advantages for manufacturing establishments equal, if not superior, to any in New England. The chief manufacture is lumber, there being about thirty saws, and one gang of saws, running day and night. The lumber is principally shipped, though large quantities are used in some of the manufacturing operations above enumerated. There are an extensive iron foundery,

4*

two shovel factories, one manufactory of melians, and other smaller manufactories. Shipbuilding has recently averaged about two vessels a year. The town is located in the heart of a large and important state, rapidly increasing in population and wealth, surrounded by a fertile country, rich in every necessary agricultural product, and stored with granite, clay, lumber, lime, iron-ore, and every sort of building material. The facilities here afforded for transportation are of inestimable value to a large manufacturing place. Augusta is traversed by the Kennebec and Portland railroad, which connects with the Penobscot and Kennebec, and thus has easy communication with Bangor, as well as all cities to the westward, while equal facilities are presented by water, — Boston being but eleven hours distant by steamer, and many other places being quite as accessible.

Augusta contains four banks, having an aggregate capital of $363,000; one savings institution; eight church edifices, namely, one Congregational, one Baptist, one Free-will Baptist, one Methodist, one Unitarian, one Universalist, one Episcopal, and one Roman Catholic; a female seminary; twenty-two school districts, with thirty-four schools; and one post-office. Population, 8,225; valuation, $2,492,575.

AURORA, Hancock county, about twenty miles east of Bangor, was settled between 1805 and 1810, by John Gils, and Samuel, Benjamin, and David Silsbee, Samuel Bonsey, Richard Beadle, Moses Ingals, and John Temple. The progress of its settlement has been slow. The chief inducement to settlers has been the lumber business, for the prosecution of which Aurora presents an extensive field. Pine, suitable for lumber, large quantities of which have already been cut off, is still abundant.

It was incorporated a plantation in 1822, and a town in 1831. The surface is rocky and broken, and is watered by four ponds, three of which are called Middle Branch ponds of Union river, the other Gils's pond, all of which have their outlet in Union river.

Aurora has one post-office; three school districts, with four schools. Population, 217; valuation, $33,672.

AVON is situated in the central part of Franklin county. Settlements were commenced here very shortly after the close of the Revolutionary war, by Captain Joshua Soule and Captain Perkins Allen. They were followed soon after by Moses Dudley, Ebenezer Thompson, Mark Whitten, Thomas Humphrey, Charles Dwelley, and Samuel and Jesse Ingraham.

The town was incorporated in 1802. The south and west parts are somewhat uneven, and not wholly settled. The southwestern corner is near the summit of Mount Blue. There is one village in the easterly part of the town, a place of some trade, having a post-office. Sandy river passes through the town in nearly a southeast direction. There are twelve school districts, with eighteen schools. Population, 778; valuation, $80,677.

BAILEYVILLE, Washington county, is situated on the west bank of the St. Croix river, and is some fifteen miles in length, by four miles in width. It became an incorporated town in 1828. It has four school districts, four schools, and one post-office. Population, 431; valuation, $24,700.

BALDWIN, Cumberland county, situated on the western shore of Lake Sebago, was granted, together with the town of Sebago that joins it, in 1774, to the survivors of Captain Flint and company, of Concord, Mass., to whom the government of Massachusetts had granted, about the year 1735, the township No. 3 east of the Connecticut river, (now Walpole); but which, on running the boundary line between Massachusetts and New Hampshire, was found to be in the latter state; consequently Captain Flint and his company lost their grant, and all the labor and money they had expended in settling it. They had occupied it from 1735 to 1751; and from that time until 1774, the proprietors kept no records, or, at least, there are none to be found. It is presumed that many of them had died, and others had become disheartened; but, on the petition of Samuel Whittemore and Amos Lawrence, the grant of these two townships was made to the survivors, and they were required to lay out and settle them on the usual conditions, namely, to locate thirty families here within six years. In 1780, the conditions remaining unfulfilled, it became necessary for them to obtain an extension, to avoid the loss of their second grant; and the state gave them six years more. They were barely able to comply with the terms of the grant within this time, for in 1790 they had only thirty families, and counted close at that. They complained of a great amount of suffering, and their necessities sometimes produced curious, and often amusing, contrivances to meet the exigencies of the times.

Nothing had been done in this town previously to 1800 for religious or educational purposes. Religious meetings were occasionally held here, but were not frequent nor permanent until some twenty-four years later.

On the 23d of June, 1802, the town was incorporated, and named in memory of Loammi Baldwin, one of the early settlers. It had previously been called Flintstown, in honor of Captain Flint, the original grantee. The first meeting for organization of the town was held on the 30th of August following the act of incorporation.

In the year 1824, Rev. Noah Emerson was settled as pastor of the Congregational church, when the Methodists formed themselves into a society, and claimed a share of the ministerial fund. A suit was brought in the supreme court, but resulted adversely to the claimants. The pastoral relation of Mr. Emerson continued until 1850, but his happiness and success were somewhat affected by this unpleasant controversy. Each denomination built a house of public worship, and has sustained preaching most of the time. The Methodists have recently built a new and tasteful edifice on the site of the old one.

The surface of the town is considerably broken, although the soil is well adapted to the growth of grass and grain. Considerable attention has been paid to the cultivation of fruit. Baldwin has an extensive water-power for manufacturing purposes. On the Saco river near the north line of the town are the Great falls, on which a water-power company have commenced extensive operations, the value of which will be much enhanced on the building of the railroad which has been already chartered up the valley of the Saco river. There are ten school districts, with seventeen schools, and one post-office, in town. Population, 1,100; valuation, $156,238.

BANGOR, Penobscot county, a city and port of entry, is situated on the west bank of the Penobscot river, about thirty miles above its mouth. The town extends on the river six miles, and contains an area of about twenty thousand acres. Bangor was originally known as Kenduskeag plantation. The first attempt at settlement was made by Stephen Buzzell, who, with his family, spent the winter of 1769–70 here. During the ensuing spring and summer he was joined by a few others; and, in 1772, the settlement contained twelve families.

The earliest records of any public proceedings are of a meeting of the inhabitants in 1789, at which a vote was passed to build a place of public worship. The act of incorporation was obtained February 25, 1791, at which time the settlement contained a population of 576 inhabitants. Rev. Seth Noble was the representative of the town, who was intrusted with the duty of obtaining its incorporation. He was directed by the inhabitants to have the town called *Sunbury*, — a name which was deemed appropriate on account of its pleasant situation, — and to see that that name was inserted in the act. Mr. Noble, however, had a great partiality for that old psalm-tune, Bangor; and, when the speaker called for the name of the town, recollecting, probably, his tune better than the instructions of his townsmen, Noble answered, Bangor, and so it was named.

In 1814, Bangor was taken possession of by a British fleet, immediately after the destruction of Hampden, to which place it had gone in pursuit of the American corvette, the *Adams*.[1] Considerable property was destroyed by this fleet; and the shipping in the harbor was only saved by the inhabitants binding themselves in the penal sum of $30,000 to deliver the same at Castine at a specified time; but peace being declared before the expiration of the time, no enforcement of the bond ever took place.

In the fall of 1833, a petition for a city charter was forwarded to the legislature. An act of incorporation was obtained the following winter, and carried into effect the next spring. At this time, and for a few years subsequent, the growth of the city was very rapid. Shipbuilding was carried on to a considerable extent; the lumber business was large and lucrative; and many other branches of business were active and prosperous. The rise in the value of real estate, during the period of speculation, hastened the growth of Bangor in a remarkable degree; but the revulsion which followed was disastrous in the extreme. All business activity was, for a season, checked and blasted; while the business community was cramped in its energies to such a degree, that it did not for years recover from the shock. The act of Congress, passed for the relief of those who had become so sadly involved by that sudden reaction in business, relieved many of the citizens of Bangor from vast liabilities, which they never could have liquidated, and from which, otherwise, it would have been impossible for them to escape.

The theological seminary received its charter from the legislature of Massachusetts in 1814. It was originally established in Hampden; but was removed thence to Bangor in 1819, where it is now permanently located. Though under the particular charge of the orthodox Congregationalists, it is equally open to other sects; and students of almost every denomination are found within its walls. The course and term of study are similar to those established at Andover and Princeton. There are three professorships fully endowed; and it is expected a fourth will soon be added. It already has a library of ten thousand volumes. The number of students for the past twenty years has been very uniform, rarely rising above fifty or falling below forty.

The railroad from Bangor to Oldtown was opened in 1836, and being at that time connected directly with the wharf on Exchange street, was the medium of transportation for large quantities of lumber. The completion of the railroad between Bangor and Lincoln will be highly advantageous to Bangor, and the country through which the

[1] See Hampden.

road is to pass. The Penobscot and Kennebec railroad, from Bangor to Waterville, was completed in the fall of 1855.

In 1840, the population of Bangor was little short of nine thousand. Since then, it has nearly, or quite, doubled. The principal calamities which have been of quite serious consequence to the city, were first, the great flood, which occurred in March, 1846, submerging the whole lower part of the city, and rising in the stores on West Market square to the height of over seven feet, sweeping away the Penobscot bridge, which connects the city with Brewer, as well as occasioning damage at various points on the river. The second calamity was the direful visitation of the cholera in 1849.

The location of Bangor is unusually good for the growth of a city, and its business advantages are immense. Its site is pleasant, commanding fine views of the rivers and the adjoining country. The buildings, both public and private, are constructed with neatness and taste, and some in a style of superior elegance. There are several handsome church edifices and other public buildings; and within a few years several new and elegant blocks of stores have been erected, and many splendid and convenient private residences. The new market building, completed in 1856, at a cost of $35,000, is built on piles in the Kenduskeag river, directly opposite the custom-house and post-office. It evinces in its construction much architectural taste. The hall above will seat two thousand people, and it is one of the finest buildings in the state. The public houses are excellent.

Bangor has an extensive coasting trade, which has greatly increased within the last few years. It has also a large southern and West India trade. In 1848, it became a port of entry. The river at Bangor is sufficiently deep to float the largest vessels, the tide rising, on an average, thirteen feet. Frankfort, about twelve miles below, is the head of winter navigation.

In 1849, steamers commenced running on the Upper Penobscot. The beautiful and picturesque river and forest scenery in that region, the pleasures of a summer trip to the woods and mountains of the interior, and the fresh air of the country, draw many visitors from abroad to the vicinity of Bangor during the warm season. A voyage up the Penobscot, and a tramp to Katahdin, make a most healthful and pleasing summer excursion. Travellers visiting Moosehead lake, and the ponds and forests in its vicinity, on hunting or fishing excursions, pass through Bangor. The number of travellers who bend their steps thitherward increases each year.

Bangor is on one of the noblest rivers in the Northern states — the product of an almost countless number of tributary streams. The city

is seated upon both sides of the Kenduskeag river, and is the mart of one of the most extensive and one of the richest alluvial basins east of the Ohio valley. It is true, that this section of the country is in a high degree of latitude, and that the icy chains of winter are felt with greater force and for a longer period than in more southern climes; but this seeming disadvantage is more than compensated by the unrivalled purity of the air and water — two of the indispensable requisites of health and longevity. There is probably no portion of the country where the great staples of wheat, beef, and wool can be produced with greater facility, where surplus produce can find a market at less expense, or where the industrious agriculturist can reap a surer reward. On a comparison of the present population of this immense territory of which Bangor is the great centre, extending from tide water to Madawaska, with that of older settlements of a less fertile soil, of less navigable facilities, and in nearly as high a degree of latitude, the mind is favorably impressed with the flattering prospects of the valley of the Penobscot, and of Bangor, which must ever possess superior advantages as a mart of trade, and the depot for the agricultural productions of a rich and thriving country extending many miles inland.

Lumbering forms a very large and important branch of business. The amount of lumber surveyed here, up to the close of the year 1855, according to the books of the surveyor-general, amounts to 2,999,847,201 feet. The agricultural and mineral resources of the surrounding country, though extensive, are as yet, in a great degree, undeveloped.

There are in Bangor fifty-nine public schools, fourteen churches divided as follows — one Unitarian, three Congregational, two Baptist, one Free-will Baptist, two Methodist, one Universalist, one Episcopal, two Roman Catholic, and one Swedenborgian; thirteen banks, with an aggregate capital of $1,200,000; two institutions for savings; two library associations, one possessing 1,640 volumes, and the other nearly five thousand; eight benevolent societies; four newspaper establishments, two of which issue a daily paper; one express company, besides others conducted by individual enterprise. Two lines of steamboats navigate the Penobscot, one between Bangor and Portland, and the other between Bangor and Boston. Population, 14,432; valuation, $6,013,709.

Baring, Washington county, is bounded north by the St. Croix river, and east by Calais. Baring was incorporated in 1825, and does a large and extensive business in lumbering. The railroad from Calais to Baring has been completed some years, and yields a fair revenue to the stockholders. All the lumber from the Baring mills is taken by the cars to tide water at Calais — there being four or five trains employed in the service each day, each train carrying some fifty thousand feet of lumber. The conveniences for manufacturing and conveying the lumber to the wharves are very complete — it being run directly from the mills on to the cars, where it is not disturbed till piled on the wharves ready for shipment.

Baring has one post-office, and one school district, with nine schools. The inhabitants are industrious and prosperous, and are principally engaged in the lumber business. Population, 380; valuation, $63,632.

BARNARD, Piscataquis county, is the western half of a township six miles square, of which Williamsburg is the eastern half. It lies about ten miles northeast from Dover. The town was incorporated in 1834; and has a number of slate quarries, which furnish excellent roofing material; four school districts, having an aggregate summer attendance of sixty-two pupils. Population, 181; valuation, $14,844.

BATH, a city and port of entry, is the capital of Sagadahoc county, situated on the west bank of the Kennebec, twelve miles from its mouth. The first European who is known to have landed in Bath, was Captain George Weymouth, who explored this part of the coast of Maine in the summer of 1605.[1] He sailed up the Kennebec river; and wishing to know the quality of the soil and its adaptation to husbandry, took his boat and a part of the crew, and landed. He says: "We passed over very good ground, pleasant and fertile, and fit for pasture, having but little wood, and that oak, like that standing in our pastures in England, good and great, fit timber for any use. There were also some small birch, hazel, and brake, which could easily be cleared away, and made good arable land."

Such was his expressed opinion of this place when on his voyage here, preparatory to the founding of the colony, which was attempted by Popham a short time after, at the mouth of the river. No attempt, however, was made to settle here by any Europeans, until as late as 1660, when a clergyman by the name of Robert Gutch, came here, and purchased of Robin Hood, an Indian sachem, the territory of the present city and town of Bath, and that which constitutes West Bath. Robin Hood was the original and acknowledged proprietor, and his deed to Gutch bears date May 29, 1660. Gutch came from Salem, Mass., and resided here until 1679, when in crossing a river to fulfil an appointment to preach on the Sabbath, he was drowned.

The settlement progressed so exceedingly slow, that, for upwards of

[1] See Address by John McKeen, Esq., Maine Hist. Coll., vol. v.

three quarters of a century, only a sufficient number of persons had collected here to form a parish. A petition was presented about this time to the General Court of Massachusetts, signed by John Philbrook and forty-six others, "inhabitants of the lands on Kennebec river, bounded southerly by Winnegance river, easterly by Kennebec river, westerly by Stevens's river, and northerly by Merry Meeting bay, in length about nine miles, and in breadth about three,—which, about fourteen years ago, were granted by the Honorable Court to Georgetown,—praying that the said land be set off from Georgetown as a separate parish." The petition was granted September 7, 1753, after which the territory set off was known as the second parish in that town; but such was the poverty of the inhabitants of this parish, that they were called, in derision, by their fellow townsmen, "the twenty-cow parish;" probably from that number of cows on their valuation list. From the rate-bill of 1759, we learn that there were sixty ratable polls here.

Captain William Swanton, who had been a soldier in the French war, and had served in the reduction of Louisburg in 1758, took up his residence here in 1762. He was a shipbuilder, industrious and skilful in his trade, and was the pioneer in that branch of productive industry for which Bath is now so justly noted. From this time the population and business of the place steadily increased. On the 17th of February, 1781, it became an incorporated town, taking its name from Bath, England. The town was favorably situated for commercial enterprise, being located on the bank of a river, extending far into the interior of a country abounding with valuable ship-timber, much sought after by the maritime powers of Europe. On the conclusion of peace with Great Britain, when the restrictive measures, that had been imposed upon American trade were removed, and the channels of commercial enterprise were opened, the inhabitants became actively and profitably engaged in lumbering and shipbuilding. The carrying trade from the Southern states to Europe began to increase, and gave to the shipping of Bath constant employment, which yielded a sure and liberal profit; while the coastwise transportation gave full employment to vessels of a smaller class, many of which were built here. Its commercial prosperity was checked by the last war with England, but on the close of the war it again revived.

In 1847, Bath received a city charter, and, on the establishment of Sagadahoc county in 1854, it became the county seat. The compactly-built portion of the city extends about three miles along the river, and, on an average, half a mile back. It is not laid out with any great regard to regularity; but has some very beautiful streets and many tasteful private residences. The surface of the town is broken, and the streets are made to correspond to its irregularities. The leading business of the town is shipbuilding, and the avocations connected with that pursuit. In this branch of industry it is surpassed only by the cities of Boston, New York, and Philadelphia. During the year ending June 30, 1852, there were forty ships, five brigs, and three schooners built here, having an aggregate of 24,339 tons; in 1853 the amount of tonnage built was 49,400; in 1854 there were fifty-six ships built, besides thirteen other vessels, amounting in all to 58,454 tons. Since that time, however, there has been a great falling off in shipbuilding. During the year 1856, there were only four large ships of one thousand tons each built here.

There are but few places that have advantages for navigation superior to Bath. It has a good harbor, with a sufficient depth of water for the largest ships, and is usually entirely free from ice during the whole year. There is steamboat communication between this place and the towns up the river as far as Waterville, and westerly to Portland and Boston. There is also a branch railroad, that connects with the Kennebec and Portland railroad at Brunswick.

There are twelve church-edifices here, belonging to the several religious denominations; five banks, with an aggregate capital of $750,000; one savings institution; three school districts, and eighteen schools. The schools in the city proper are on the graded system. They are well conducted, and are an honor, not only to the city, but to the state. There are also two or three newspaper establishments in the city. The population in 1850 was 8,020, since which there has probably been some diminution from extensive emigration westward. Valuation for 1858, $6,543,875.

BEDDINGTON is situated in the western part of Washington county, and has an area of 23,040 acres. It is a new town, and but little has yet been done in clearing up and settling it. It was incorporated in 1833. The town is watered by the Narraguagus and Pleasant rivers, on which are some good mill-sites. It has one school district, with forty pupils. Population, 147; valuation, $21,028.

BELFAST, a city, and the shire town of Waldo county, lies on both sides of the river Passagassawaukeag, at the head of Penobscot bay, twelve miles westerly from the mouth of Penobscot river, and thirty miles below Bangor. The territory comprising Belfast formed a part of the Muscongus or Waldo patent, and was purchased by the first settlers in 1769, at the price of twenty cents per acre. It was permanently inhabited the following year by a company from Londonderry, New

Hampshire, who were the immediate descendants of Scotch-Irish colonists, who emigrated from the city of the same name in Ireland, in 1718. Other accessions to the settlement soon took place, and in 1773 the population numbered two hundred. A successful application to be incorporated as a town was made that year, — the name of Belfast being selected at the request of one of the inhabitants who was a native of Belfast, Ireland. In their religious tenets, the first settlers of Belfast were strict Presbyterians. When the Revolution commenced, they took an early and decided stand in favor of independence, and refusing to take the oath of allegiance to Great Britain after the occupation of Castine by an English force in 1779, they were driven from their new homes and did not return to them until peace was declared. The municipal organization of the town was resumed in 1786. Belfast was again invested by the British during the war of 1812.

The first settlement of Belfast was made on the eastern side of the river, but the more favorable position of the opposite shore for communication with the interior country, diverted business to the location now occupied by the compact part of the city. The first church was erected in 1792, and Rev. Ebenezer Price, the first minister, was settled four years after. A post-office was established in 1797, and the town was made a port of entry in 1818. The first newspaper, called the Hancock Gazette, was commenced in 1820, and the first bank was incorporated in 1832. Belfast was made the shire town of Waldo county in 1828. In 1845, a portion of the town, containing about five hundred inhabitants, was set off, and with the western part of Prospect, formed into the present flourishing town of Searsport. A city charter was granted to Belfast in 1850, and accepted in 1853. The first mayor was Hon. Ralph C. Johnson.

The compact part of Belfast is built on an acclivity, which ascends gradually from the water, and is for the most part regularly laid out. The streets are wide, and many of them are ornamented with shade trees. The business portion of the place is mostly built of brick. Among the public buildings are the court-house, erected in 1853, the United States custom-house and post-office, an academy, a stone jail, and six churches, two of which are Congregational, and the others Baptist, Methodist, Unitarian, and Universalist. There are sixteen school districts with twenty-one schools. A well-perfected system of schools is maintained, at an annual expense of $7,000. Shipbuilding and fishing constiture the principal business. There were twenty-six vessels built in 1857, with a combined tonnage of 9,897. The whole amount of the shipping owned in the district in 1857 was 73,475 tons, being exceeded by that of only eleven other ports in the Union. Manufacturing is carried on to some extent, and there are various manufactories of paper, edge-tools, and iron-work. There are two banks, with an aggregate capital of $175,000, and also an insurance company. Three weekly newspapers are published at Belfast. Steamboats, during the summer, daily connect Belfast with Portland, Boston, and Bangor, and seven stage lines afford constant communication with the neighboring cities and towns. The city contains a population of over six thousand; valuation, $1,186,907.

BELGRADE, towards the northwest part of Kennebec county, was originally owned by the Plymouth company, from whom the settlers obtained their titles. The settlement of the town was commenced in 1774, by Philip Snow, from New Hampshire. In 1796, so great had been the increase in the number of inhabitants, that Belgrade was incorporated as a town.

The surface is uneven, and much of it covered by water. There is a connected chain of seven lakes, — five of which are in this town, — reaching over into Sidney and Waterville, the largest of which covers an area of twenty-five square miles. These lakes are interspersed with several islands, one of which is a farm of two hundred acres, and is only accessible from the main land by boat. All of these lakes fall into the Kennebec river, about two miles below the centre of Waterville.

Agriculture is the principal pursuit of the inhabitants, though there are a few manufactories; among which are one shovel factory, one spool factory, and several saw-mills and grist-mills.

There are two villages in this town, — at each of which considerable business is transacted, — bearing the names of the Mills village, and the Depot village. There are three church edifices, namely, Baptist, Unitarian, and Friends'; three post-offices — Belgrade, Belgrade Mills, and North Belgrade; eighteen school districts, with nineteen schools; and an academy, which is in a flourishing condition. Population, 1,722; valuation, $414,843.

BELMONT, Waldo county, is situated six miles west from Belfast, and originally formed a part of the Waldo patent. It subsequently fell into the possession of General Knox, who sold the township to Benjamin Joy and Samuel Parkman. The first settlement was commenced by Daniel Doloff, in 1790, and the town was incorporated February 5, 1814. In 1817, a post-office was established here; and in 1855 the town was divided, the northern half being incorporated under the name of Morrill. At that time it had one church, — Free-will Baptist; one grist-mill, six saw-mills, two stores, and five school districts, with the same number of schools. Population, 750; valuation, about $80,000.

Belfast

BENTON, Kennebec county, is situated on the east side of the Kennebec river, in the northeastern part of the county, and is about twenty-five miles distant from Augusta. It was called Sebasticook until June 19, 1850, when it received its present name. The settlement of this town, which originally belonged to the town of Clinton, was commenced about 1775, and it was incorporated in 1792. Benton is watered by the Sebasticook and the Kennebec rivers, along the banks of which there are some very fine farms. The town has one village, called Sebasticook Corner; one post-office; and ten school districts, with ten schools. Population, 1,189; valuation, $155,992.

BERWICK, York county, situated on the eastern bank of the Piscataqua river, is one of the frontier towns of western Maine, and originally formed a part of the possessions of Sir Ferdinando Gorges. It was called by the Indians Newichawannock, signifying "Come to my house, or place," probably derived from the salutation of some friendly Indian. Settlements were commenced in this town as early as 1624; but to what extent, we have no means of ascertaining. Two men were living here in 1631, whose names were Chadbourne and Gibbins; and Williamson informs us that there were others here about the same time, the names of whom he gives as Frost, Heard, Shapleigh, Spencer, Broughton, Leader, Plaisted, and Wincoll. The earliest title from the Indians on record is a deed, which was obtained by Chadbourne, in 1643, from the chief of the Piscataquas. From this time, for the period of upwards of thirty years, there seems to have been a slow but steady progress in the settlement of the town. The rigors of winter produced here the same privations and sufferings as were experienced in many other of the New England settlements, and not unfrequently in summer was there a great scarcity of provisions. But these sufferings were of small moment compared with the Indian troubles that followed.

In 1675, Berwick was pillaged and partially destroyed by the savages, while on their march for the destruction of the more populous settlements on the coast. It was, however, soon rebuilt, and had more than recovered its losses, when, in 1689, it was attacked by a party of French and Indians from Canada, and entirely destroyed. The inhabitants defended themselves bravely; but, the assailants having every advantage, they were forced to surrender at discretion, — thirty-four having been killed, while the remainder — fifty-four — for the most part women and children, were carried into captivity.[1] In 1703, the settlement had

[1] The commander of this expedition was M. Artel, the same leader who afterwards added to his infamous notoriety by the destruction of Deerfield, Mass., in 1704, when he made captives of Rev. Mr. Williams and others.

5*

scarcely been recommenced, when it was again attacked by the French and their savage allies, and several persons were killed. Even yet, the cup of bitterness was not full; for, four years afterward, two of the settlers were killed while returning from public worship.

The repetition from year to year of these desperate adventures of the savages, aided and abetted by their French allies, was sufficient to blight every hope that might be entertained of the permanent settlement of the place; but the hardihood and determination of the settlers eventually overcame these discouraging obstacles. In 1713, application having been made to the General Court, the settlement was, on the 9th of June of that year, incorporated into a town by the name of Berwick. The area of the town at that time was quite large, embracing, besides its present territory, that of North and South Berwick. The surface of Berwick is generally level, and the soil of a productive character. It is watered by Little river, which runs through the town in a westerly direction, falling into the Salmon Falls river. The principal occupation of the inhabitants is farming.

There are three churches in the town, — a Methodist, a Baptist, and a union house; four tanneries; one pottery; eighteen school districts, with thirty schools; and one post-office. Population, 2,121; valuation, $219,101.

BETHEL, Oxford county, is situated on both sides of the Androscoggin river, and contains an area of 25,920 acres. It was originally granted to Josiah Richardson, of Sudbury, Massachusetts, and others, for services in the French war. It was settled in 1773, under the name of "Sudbury Canada," and became an incorporated town, under its present name, June 10, 1796.

The surface of the town is undulating. There are some highly productive farms along the course of the river. The Grand Trunk railway passes through the town, and affords the most ample facilities to the inhabitants for the transportation of their produce and merchandise to a ready market.

The academy located at this place is in a flourishing condition, and ranks high as an institution of learning. Besides this there are twenty-four school districts; three churches, two of which are Methodist, and one Congregational; and one post-office. Population, 2,253; valuation, $266,498.

BIDDEFORD, York county, situated on the sea-coast, on the western bank of the Saco river, was originally granted by the Plymouth Council to John Oldham and Richard Vines, by patent, bearing date February

12, 1629, (o. s.), and described as "that tract of land lying on the south side of the River Swanckadocke (Saco), containing in breadth, by the sea, four miles, and extending eight miles up into the main land."

On the 25th of June, 1630, Vines, for, or in conjunction with, Oldham,[1] took legal possession of the land. The emigrants who came over with Vines to settle on his land, and those who arrived here in previous expeditions, located chiefly near the sea, on the spot where Vines passed the winter, when here on an exploring expedition in 1616–17.[2] Vines never reaped any benefit from this grant of land, though he made the most commendable exertions to settle it — expending large sums upon it, all which proved unavailing. These frequent outlays soon became a source of pecuniary embarrassment to Vines; and, in consequence, he was compelled to sell his patent to Dr. Robert Child, of Nashaway (now Lancaster, Mass.), after which he removed to Barbadoes, West Indies, about the close of 1645. Dr. Child, not being particularly pleased with his investment, sold to William Phillips, of Boston. Phillips paid the doctor £90 for the town of Biddeford, and took his deed of it, bearing date March 11, 1658–9. Phillips, notwithstanding he had the title of Vines's grant from the Plymouth Council, as well as the deed of the doctor, had apprehensions lest his title, in some unexpected way, might be questioned; and soon after acquired another title from the Indian sachem, Mogg Megone, whose character is so graphically portrayed in one of Whittier's poems. From Phillips all the land titles in Biddeford are derived.

This town has had to contend with all the vicissitudes incident to a frontier settlement, and was twice destroyed by the Indians. The sufferings of the settlers were great in each of these Indian wars. During their continuance, a garrison was erected at Winter Harbor, and maintained at public cost, which, after the conclusion of the war, was dismantled, and the troops were removed.

Biddeford was united to Saco about 1660, and remained a part of that town, until 1718, when it became a distinct, incorporated town, receiving its name from a town in England, from which some of the settlers emigrated.

In the war of the Revolution, Biddeford zealously contributed men

[1] It seems that Oldham never took any interest in the patent; and no record can be found of his having been at any time within its limits. He resided principally at Salem, then called Naumkeag.

[2] Several cellars, now filled up and overgrown with antiquated shrubbery, mark out the locality of this ancient settlement. Apple-trees, rotten with age, and the English cherry, survive here in the midst of oaks and sumachs. It is now a deserted spot, and buried in the most perfect solitude.

and money for its prosecution; since which, its record has been one of constant growth. In 1855, the town became a city.

The surface is rather broken; much of it is rocky and unproductive, though here and there are some good farms. The territory is some ten miles in length, and four in width; and is drained by Little river on the southeast, and by the Saco river on the east. There are quite a number of granite quarries here, which furnish excellent building material, and are worked advantageously and profitably.

Manufacturing operations are large in Biddeford. There are two cotton mills, known by the names of the Pepperell and the Laconia having a capital of one million dollars each. The Pepperell corporation went into operation in 1850, have three mills, and run seventy thousand spindles. They manufacture the various kinds of cotton goods, varying from thirty up to one hundred inches in width, turning out, on an average, 1,200,000 yards each four weeks, and employing from 1,500 to 1,600 operatives, — about 450 males and 1,200 females. The pay-roll averages twenty thousand dollars per month. The Laconia company went into operation in 1845, and has three mills, runs eleven hundred looms, fifty thousand spindles, and employs one thousand operatives. The monthly pay-roll averages about eighteen thousand dollars. There is also a large machine-shop, for the manufacture of cotton machinery. There are five saw-mills, one of which is propelled by steam, in which considerable business is done in the manufacture of the smaller kinds of lumber. In the coarser kinds of lumber for shipping, there is not so much done as formerly. In the way of shipbuilding, Biddeford does but little. There are ten or twelve vessels owned here, which carry on a profitable trade between Biddeford and other Atlantic ports. A portion of the female population is profitably employed in the manufacture of clothing for the Boston market. There are three brick-yards, which have been and still are doing a profitable business, — all the brick edifices in the city being built from the production of these yards.

There are in Biddeford eight church edifices, — two Congregational, two Methodist, one Baptist, two Free-will Baptist, and one Roman Catholic. The town is divided into eleven school districts, having sixteen school-houses and twenty-one schools. The schools are conducted on the graded system. There are two banks, — the Biddeford bank, with a capital of two hundred thousand dollars, and the City bank, with a capital of fifty thousand dollars; one savings institution; and one post-office. Population, 6,095; valuation, $4,821,908.

BINGHAM, Somerset county, is situated on the east side of the Kennebec river, and contains an area of 23,040 acres. The first settlement

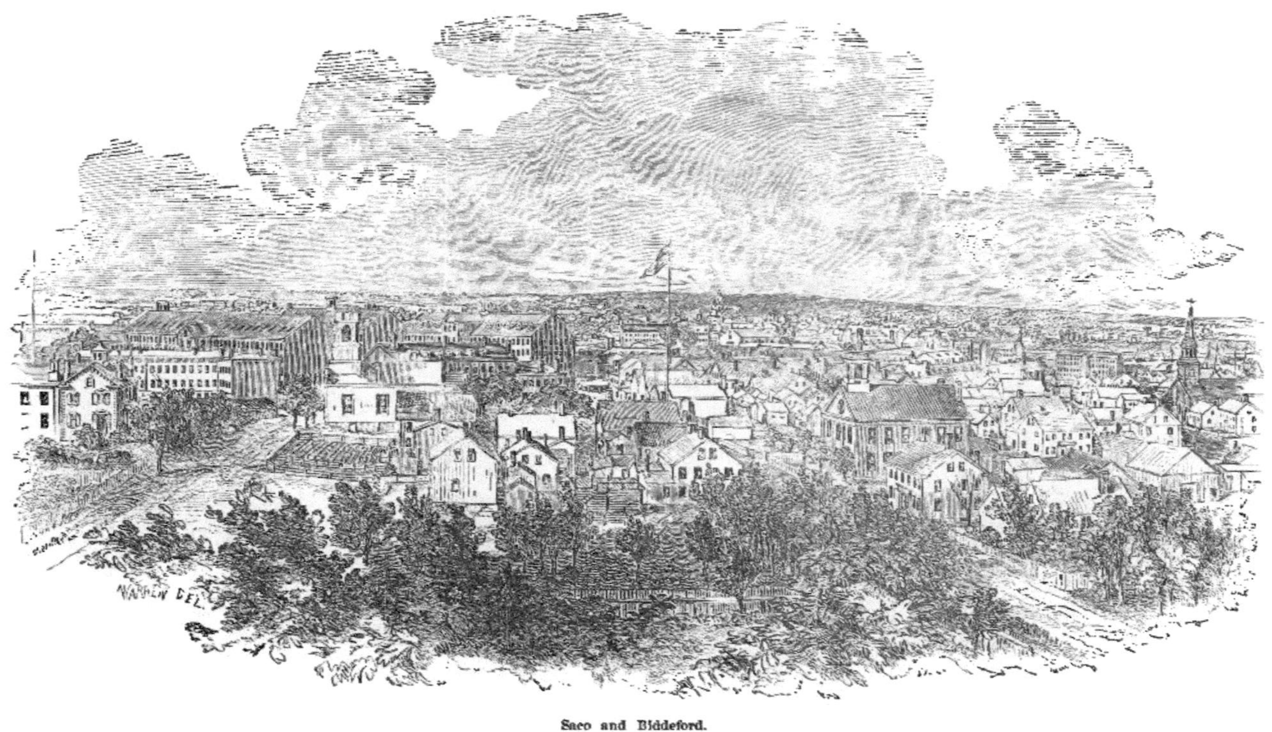

Saco and Biddeford.

was made in this town as early as 1784; and, in 1801, it was surveyed by Philip Bullen. It was incorporated on the 6th of February, 1812, under its present name, which was given in honor of William Bingham, the great landed proprietor in this state. There are two saw-mills and two grist-mills here; three churches, — one Congregational, one Methodist, and one Free-will Baptist; thirteen school districts, with seventeen schools; and one post-office. Population, 752; valuation, $86,322.

BLANCHARD, in the westerly part of Piscataquis county, is distant from Dover twenty-two miles. It embraces an area of six miles square; has one considerable elevation, called Russell's mountain, in the southeastern part; and is drained by the head-waters of the Piscataquis river. Blanchard has one Congregational church, one school district, and one post-office. Population, 192; valuation, $17,130.

BLOOMFIELD, Somerset county, lies on the west side of Kennebec river, thirty-three miles north from Augusta. It contains an area of 11,910 acres, only three hundred acres of which are waste land, and two hundred and nineteen acres are appropriated to highways. This town originally belonged to Canaan, and its early history is blended with the history of that town. It was erected into a separate township and incorporated February 6, 1814. It has a fertile soil, and produces good crops. Its name will be significant so long as recurring seasons shall adorn its hills and vales with the livery of luxuriant growth.

Bloomfield has two church edifices a Congregational, and a Baptist; with twelve schools; one academy, with forty students; one tannery; three grist-mills; two saw-mills; one bank (the Skowhegan), with a capital of $75,000; and one post-office. Population, 1,301; valuation, $256,690.

BLUEHILL is situated in the southwest part of Hancock county, on Bluehill bay. The settlement of the town was commenced April 7, 1762, by Joseph Wood and John Roundy, both from Beverly, Mass. They landed near Fire Falls, so called, where Bluehill bay communicates with a salt-water pond. Here they went to work getting out staves, and making preparation for the settlement of their families, which they moved hither the following spring. Four or five years after, Mr. Wood said to Mr. Roundy, "I hope I may live to see plowing in this town yet." To which Mr. Roundy replied, "I shall not wish to live any longer than *till* that time." This reply shows how discouraging the prospect before them then appeared. The third family in town was formed by the marriage of Colonel Nathan Parker, from Andover, Mass., with Mary, eldest daughter of Captain Wood. Colonel Parker was an officer of the provincial troops at the siege and fall of Louisburg. On his return he was driven with many others to the West Indies, where a number died with the fever, about the close of the year 1761. The family of Samuel Foster, from Andover, was the fourth. They made but a short stay. The fifth was that of Colonel Nicholas Holt, from the same town, who arrived May 27, 1765.

The plantation name of the township was Newport. In 1769, it appears, by the town records, that the settlers had some place which they used for public worship, since, during the previous year, they voted to raise money, "for to hire a person for to preach the gospel to us, and for to pay his board." And at the same meeting a vote was passed to lay out a road to the Penobscot. On the commencement of hostilities with Great Britain, the town chose a committee of correspondence, a committee of inspection, and a committee of safety. From 1779 to 1784, the town meetings were suspended. In 1772, October 7, the Congregational church was formed, numbering eight male and eight female members. The town was incorporated January 30, 1789.

On the 18th of June, 1803, an academy was incorporated, and was endowed by a grant of the western half of township No. 23, Washington county. This tract the trustees of the corporation sold July 28, 1806, for the consideration of $6,252. A part of this sum has been lost to the academy, by the failure of parties to whom it had been intrusted. A principal now remains of $5,064.58; the interest of which is applied to defray the expenses of the institution. This, with the tuition fees, supports the school one half the year. The average number of students in attendance is fifty.

The surface is varied. The only elevation of note is Bluehill, from which the town takes its name. This is a majestic hill near the centre of the town, rising to an altitude of 950 feet above high-water mark. From the bay there is a gradual ascent for about a mile, thence it is quite abrupt to the top, which consists of a huge mass of curl-grained rocks. In the early settlement of the town, it was covered with trees, principally evergreens, which, at a distance, gave it a very dark blue tint; hence its name. It is now entirely bald. The summit affords a delightful view of the village, the bay — interpersed with numerous islands — and the surrounding country.

In the eastern part of the town, there is a valuable granite quarry, from which, in 1855, the sum of $20,000 was realized. There are also about five thousand cords of wood annually shipped from this port. Ship building is carried on to some extent: three or four vessels are built every year, averaging two hundred tons each. The Revolutionary soldiers that went from this town are all deceased. Christopher Osgood, son of Ezekiel Osgood, one of the first settlers, was at the battle of Bunker Hill. Nehemiah Hinckley served through the war, was honorably discharged at West Point, when he returned to Bluehill, where he died at the age of seventy-five. Edith Hinckley, his widow, the daughter of Joseph Wood, the first settler, was born August 3, 1766. She is still living, at the advanced age of ninety-two years, and in the full possession and enjoyment of her physical and mental energies. Rev. Jonathan Fisher was the settled minister here from 1796 to 1837, and died in 1847.

The town has one village; two religious societies, — Baptist and Congregational, each having a place of worship; three post-offices, — Bluehill, Bluehill Falls, and North Bluehill; and eighteen school districts. Population, 1,939; valuation, $350,221.

Boothbay, Lincoln county, is a peninsula, situated between the mouths of the Sheepscot and Damariscotta rivers, and is what was formerly known as Cape Newagen. It is supposed to have been settled as early as 1630; but what progress was made at that time is now unknown. Captain Weymouth — when on his voyage here in 1605 — entered the harbor previously to ascending the Kennebec river. Permission to settle here was purchased in 1666 by Henry Curtis, of the famous sagamore, Robin Hood; but the Indians, taking offence either at the terms of the purchase or some probable encroachment, destroyed the settlement in 1688. It lay a desolate waste for forty years afterwards, and was revived in 1730, by Colonel Dunbar, who gave it the name of Townshend, which it bore for many years.

The town was incorporated on the 3d of November, 1764, retaining its original name until 1842, when it received the name it now bears, in memory of Old Boothbay, in Lincoln county, England. The commercial advantages of this town are equal to any on the coast of Maine; and there is a wide scope for their improvement. The harbor has four entrances; and such is its capacity and superior location, that the English, prior to the Revolutionary war, had projected the establishment of a naval depot here, — all the arrangements for which were made, — but it was abandoned solely on account of the uncertain chances of war. The inhabitants are principally engaged in the foreign and coasting trade, and in the cod and mackerel fisheries. Shipbuilding is also an important branch of business, and employs a large amount of capital: about one hundred vessels, of various sizes, are owned in town. Boothbay has one village, one church edifice (Congregational), seventeen school districts, and one post-office. Population, 2,504; valuation, $239,067.

Bowdoin is situated in the northwest corner of Sagadahoc county, and is supposed to have been settled some years previous to the Revolutionary war. It was incorporated March 21, 1788, and, according to Williamson, contained about 120 families. Bowdoin took its name from the family of Governor Bowdoin. It stands well in an agricultural point of view; has one village, with a capital of some five or six thousand dollars in manufactures; three church edifices, — two of which are Baptist, and one Free-will Baptist; eighteen school districts, and one post-office. Population, 1,857; valuation, $247,813.

Bowdoinham, Sagadahoc county, is situated on the west bank of Kennebec river. This township was claimed by the Plymouth proprietors, who conveyed it, with other lands adjoining, to William Bowdoin, of Boston. But this title was involved in a dispute; for on the 3d of July, 1637, Sir Ferdinando Gorges granted to Sir Richard Edgecomb, of Mount Edgecomb, England, a tract of eight thousand acres, situated near Merry Meeting bay, then called the "Lake of New Somerset." The bounds were so indefinite as to make the place of location extremely uncertain, and neither the grantee nor his heirs paid any regard to the patent till after Queen Anne's war. In 1718, John Edgecomb, of New London, appeared for the heirs, and entered a minute of the grant in the book of claims. This minute seemed to be a description of a tract equal to four miles square on the western bank of the Kennebec river, where it meets Merry Meeting bay.[1] In 1756, the claim was revived by Lord Edgecomb, one of the heirs, who intrusted his business to Sir William Pepperrell, of Kittery. The latter having died without settling the claim, his lordship empowered Nathaniel Sparhawk (Sir William's son-in-law) to pursue it. Mr. Bowdoin brought an action to establish his claim, and showed title from the Plymouth proprietors, and a quitclaim from Abbagadusset, an Indian chief. The court ruled that this should prevail against the obsolete and indefinite grant made by Gorges, and Mr. Bowdoin won the case; but some years afterwards the superior court ruled that this town did not belong to the Plymouth proprietors, and the north line of the town was fixed as the southern boundary of their patent.

The settlement of the town was commenced soon after the building of Fort Richmond; but its progress was so much retarded by the wars with the Indians, and the disputes about the title to the land, that it did not become an incorporated town until 1762. It is now a place of importance. The surface is level and the soil productive. It has an

[1] Book of Claims, p. 82.

invested capital, in trade and manufactures, of upwards of $100,000, and one bank, with a capital of $50,000. The Kennebec and Portland railroad passes through it. Bowdoinham has one village; five churches (two Methodist, a Baptist, Free-will Baptist, and Universalist); two post-offices, — Bowdoinham and East Bowdoinham; and seventeen school districts, with nineteen schools. Population, 2,382; valuation, $529,794.

BOWERBANK, Piscataquis county, is situated north from Dover, the town of Foxcroft intervening. It covers an area of six miles square, and was incorporated in 1839. It has three school districts, one post-office, and one church (Free-will Baptist). Sebec lake, a large body of water, lies mostly in this town. Population, 173; valuation, $17,376.

BRADFORD, Penobscot county, is a pleasant agricultural town, situated about twenty miles north from Bangor. The first clearing preparatory to settling was made in the summer of 1803, by James White and Robert Marshall, who came from Thomaston. White moved his family hither the following year, and Marshall moved his in the spring of 1805. In 1804, two men, by the names of Jennison and Rogers, from Union, settled in the south part of the town; and, in 1806, Wilson and Hildreth moved hither from Thomaston. This was the commencement of the now flourishing town of Bradford. It was organized into a plantation in 1820, — at which time it contained eleven voters, — and was incorporated March 12, 1831. Robert Marshall, the pioneer settler of the town, is still living, and resides on the same farm, and near the same spot, which he first occupied, fifty-three years ago. He is now eighty years of age. A number of the descendants of Joseph Wilson reside in town, and some in other parts of the county. White, Rogers, and Hildreth moved away many years since.

The surface of Bradford is mostly smooth and unbroken, gently undulating, and tolerably free from stones. There are no lakes or ponds in town, and but very little waste land. Dead stream flows through here from northwest to southeast, and falls into the Pushaw stream in Alton. There are a number of good mill-sites on this stream, some of which are already occupied by mills of different kinds. There are three villages with three post-offices in town. At Bradford Corner, there are two neat church edifices, one owned and occupied by the Congregationalists, and the other jointly by the Baptists and Free-will Baptists. The neat town-house stands one mile east of the Corner, and is occupied half the time as a place of worship by the Universalist society. The Methodists hold their meetings at East Bradford school-house.

There is one high school, which is kept one or two quarters in the year, according to the state of finances, and eleven school districts, with twenty-one schools. The population of the town in 1856 was estimated at 1,500, and the valuation, $155,000.

Bradley, Penobscot county, lies on the east bank of the Penobscot river. The first settlers of this town came from different parts of this state, and some from Massachusetts.

The town was incorporated in 1834. Its surface is uneven; but there are few hills of any great height. But little is done in cultivating the soil; and this will not seem strange, when it is known that the only land suitable for cultivation is on the banks of the Penobscot, and that even this is of indifferent quality. Pine lumber once grew here in large quantities; but the lumberman's axe and the fire-king have swept most of it away.

The lumber manufacture is the only branch of productive industry carried on here. At the village, there are fourteen single board saw-mills, three gangs of saws, four clapboard mills, four lath mills, and three shingle mills, nearly all of which are in constant operation during the summer season. Part of the large pond on Nichols stream is in this town. The Greatworks and the Nichols are considerable streams, and both supply good water-power, which is improved to a moderate extent. The Penobscot river, however, furnishes the principal water-power.

There is no place of public worship in town; — the inhabitants attend church, however, at Oldtown and Orono. The only village here is called Greatworks, situated at the falls of the same name, on the Penobscot river, two miles from Oldtown village. A post-office is located at this village. The town is divided into four school districts, with five schools, which are kept from five to six months of the year. Besides these there are some private schools in town. Population, 796; valuation for 1858, $93,525.

Bremen, Lincoln county, is situated in the southern part of the county, and originally belonged to the Pemaquid patent. William Hilton, of Plymouth, Mass., was the first settler, having moved hither with his family, consisting of four sons and three daughters, in the year 1735. He was soon, however, driven back again to Plymouth by the Indians; but on the pacification of the Indian troubles, in 1745, he returned to Bremen; and being an heir, by marriage, to the Brown claim,[1] took

[1] This claim originated from one John Brown, who settled at New Harbor, in the town of Bristol, in 1621, and who, in 1625, bought of the Indian sagamore, Robin Hood.

possession of a lot on said claim for a farm, on which he resided until 1754, the period of the breaking out of the Indian war, when he moved his family to the block-house at Muscongus harbor, a distance of five miles from his farm. This he made his home, continuing, in the mean time, his labors upon his claim. In May, 1755, while he and his three sons, William, Richard, and John, were landing from a boat, they were fired upon by the Indians, who were in ambush, which resulted in the death of William, and the severe wounding of the father and Richard; but John, the youngest son (only seventeen years of age), being unharmed, returned the fire and killed one of the Indians. He then assisted his father and elder brother into the boat, and returned to the block-house, leaving William dead upon the beach. The wound the father received in this encounter proved mortal, he having survived but eight days.

At the incorporation of the town of Bristol, this territory was included as a part of it, and remained as such till 1828, when it became an incorporated town under its present name.

The town has an uneven surface. It is watered by Muscongus and McCurdy's ponds, and is bounded on the west by Pemaquid and Biscay ponds. The occupations of the inhabitants are farming and fishing. Commodore Samuel Tucker, of Revolutionary memory, was a native of this town, and lived and died here.

Bremen has one village; one church edifice, which is owned by the Congregationalists; one post-office, seven school districts, with the same number of schools. Population, 891; valuation, from assessors' books in 1858, $106,411.

BREWER, Penobscot county, is situated on the east side of Penobscot river, extending six miles on the river, and being about three miles wide. Its early history is included in that of Orrington, of which it formed the northern part until February, 1812, when it was set off from that town and incorporated under its present name, in honor of John Brewer, one of its first settlers, and the first postmaster of the town.

The surface is quite even, and the soil a clayey loam, which is considered good for farming purposes, especially along the banks of the river. Brick-making is a prominent business here, there being some twelve or

for fifty skins, a tract of land between Broad bay and Damariscotta river, extending twenty-five miles into the country. This tract of land he and his descendants inhabited till driven away by the Indians; but, though not allowed to occupy it, his descendants claimed the land until 1812, when the matter was adjusted. — *Commissioners' Report*, 1811; *Annals of Warren*, p. 17.

fifteen yards in operation, which manufacture about twelve millions annually. These bricks sell for five dollars per thousand, delivered at the wharf: most of them are shipped to Boston and its vicinity. There is also considerable business done here in shipbuilding; the average for the past five years being about two thousand tons annually. The vessels are mostly of the smaller class, consisting of brigs and schooners, varying from one hundred and fifty to three hundred tons burden. A number of saw-mills are also established here, some of which are propelled by steam; and connected with them are several shingle and lath machines.

There are two villages, both located on the river, about two miles apart. The upper village is directly opposite the city of Bangor, with which it is connected by a toll-bridge. There is a post-office at each village. There are three church edifices, — two Congregational, and one Methodist; and three school districts, with twenty-six schools. Population, 2,628; valuation, $383,261.

Bridgton, is situated in the northwest part of Cumberland county. The grant of this town was made, in 1761, by Massachusetts, to Benjamin Mullikin, Moody Bridges, and Thomas Perley, agents for the proprietors. It was divided into eighty-six shares. Sixty-one of these rights were held by individual proprietors; one was set apart for the support of the ministry; one for the first settled minister; one for Harvard College; one for the support of schools; one for the first settler in the township; and the remaining twenty were held by all the proprietors as a community. These lots were numbered from one to eighty-six; and each claimant received his number by lot. As an encouragement to settlers, the proprietors proposed to give one hundred acres of the common land, lying east of Long pond, to each settler who should have twelve acres of land cleared, a house built, and a family settled in the township, by the year 1771.

In 1767, the proprietors named their township Bridgton, in honor of Moody Bridges, one of their number. Prior to this time, it had been known by the name of Pondicherry.[1]

The first tract of land was granted in 1768, to Captain Benjamin Kimball, from Ipswich, Mass., who bound himself "to settle in the township by the 10th of June of that year; to build a convenient house for the entertainment of the proprietors and others, by the 10th day of September; to keep a store of goods, to be retailed out at a reasonable advance;

[1] This name was humorously given to a tract of country, lying between Long pond and Pleasant mountain, on account of its numerous ponds and abundance of wild cherries.

and also to hold himself in readiness, with a convenient boat of two tons burden, rigged with a convenient sail, to carry passengers and freight from Pierson Town to the head of Long pond and back, whenever called upon by the proprietors, for the term of seven years. For this service, he was to receive six shillings per day for himself, five shillings per day for an assistant, and two shillings and sixpence for his boat."[1] Kimball kept this store for several years, and carried on a considerable trade with the Indians.

The same year the proprietors, for a somewhat similar consideration, contracted with Jacob Stevens to build and keep in repair a saw-mill and a corn-mill. These mills were the first erected in Bridgton, and were built on the stream now known as Stevens's brook.

Owing to unforeseen obstacles, the settlement did not advance as rapidly as anticipated; and additional inducements were held out to settlers. On the night of the 2d of October, 1780, the dwelling-house of Enoch Perley was consumed by fire, together with all the records of the proprietors. Fortunately, however, the field-notes of the surveyor who laid out the township, and the tickets by which the lots were drawn, were preserved. From these, and from memory, a committee, appointed for the purpose, made up a new record, and procured a confirmation thereof by the legislature of Massachusetts in 1783.

In June, 1782, a committee of the proprietors, appointed for the purpose of inquiring into the progress made by the settlers in clearing land and erecting buildings, reported the names of certain persons as having merited each one or more lots, which amounted in the aggregate to fourteen, and were located next to Long pond. These lots have since been designated as "merited" lots. At the same time, arrangements were made for building a public saw-mill on the stream leading from Woods pond to Long pond. The site selected was the same that is now occupied by Mr. Chaplin's mill, in the village known by the name of Pinhook.

For several years the progress of the settlement was much retarded by the Revolutionary war. The inhabitants, though not actually molested during that war, were in constant apprehension of a hostile attack from the Indians. Several of the families broke up and removed to Standish, where they remained till the danger was past. At one time, in consequence of information received that the Indians had attacked the settlement at Bethel (then called Sudbury Canada), and killed one man, and were advancing towards Bridgton, the alarm became so

[1] These conditions are embodied in the deed conveying to Captain Kimball the sixty-first right of land. It bears date April 6, 1768.

6*

great that nearly all the inhabitants determined on evacuating the place, but were spared the necessity by the withdrawal of the enemy. From the close of the war, the settlement advanced more rapidly, and in 1787, the population numbered two hundred and eighty-seven persons.

Bridgton was incorporated as a town February 7, 1794. From that time, the town steadily increased in wealth and population, till 1805, when the part of its territory lying on the easterly side of Long pond, containing about 8,500 acres, was set off to form, in part, the new town of Harrison. Again, in 1834, a portion of the southeast corner of the town, containing about 2,500 acres, was set off to form a part of the new town of Naples. In 1847, the inhabitants, seeking to restore Bridgton as far as possible to its former dimensions, acquired by annexation upon the west, from the towns of Fryeburg and Denmark, a tract of territory containing about 3,700 acres, now known by the name of Texas. The present area of the town is about thirty thousand acres. The land in this region is very productive. There are some excellent and well-cultivated farms in the town and vicinity.

There are twenty-two school districts, and twenty-one public schools, kept, upon an average, about one half the time, and an academy, established in 1818. There are seven religious societies, all having places of public worship, — three Congregational, one Baptist, one Free-will Baptist, one Universalist and one Methodist: also, one Newspaper — the Bridgton Reporter.

Bridgton contains nine saw-mills, six grist-mills, three extensive tanneries, two large carriage manufactories, and several other manufacturing establishments of importance; also, three post-offices. Population, 2,710; valuation, $472,161.

Brighton, Somerset county, was originally a part of Bingham's Kennebec Purchase, and joins the town of Bingham on the east. It is watered by a branch of the Kennebec river, and was incorporated in 1816. The town has one small village, two saw-mills, two grist-mills, one tannery, one church edifice (Free-will Baptist), one post-office, and eight school districts. Population, 748; valuation, $46,919.

Bristol, Lincoln county, is situated at the southern extremity of the peninsula, between the Damariscotta and Muscongus rivers, and embraces the ancient Pemaquid, a place justly celebrated in the early history of New England, as one of the most important settlements on the coast. It is at present particularly interesting from the fact that the monuments of its early history are still remaining, — these being almost the only records that have been left us. Even these, the destroying hand of time has so changed that a wide field is open to speculative inquiry, as scarcely any thing can be determined with certainty. Bristol formed a large part of the Pemaquid patent, granted by the Plymouth Council, February 20, 1631, to Robert Aldsworth and Gyles Elbridge, two merchants, belonging to Bristol, England. The patent covered the entire peninsula, from the sources of the rivers to the sea, including the Damariscove islands, and all others within twenty-seven miles of the main land. The grant was made in consideration of past public services, as well as the promise, on the part of the patentees, to build a town on the grant as soon as practicable.

They commenced the settlement on a point of land, made by the Pemaquid river, as it enters the harbor, covering an area of twenty-seven acres, and which, at that time, was studded with heavy forest trees.[1] In a few years, residences, shops, and trading-houses were numerous enough to indicate that the settlement was in a most prosperous condition.

In 1664, Bristol was claimed by the Duke of York, as being within the patent he held from the crown, of New York and Sagadahoc, of which Sir Edmund Andros was commissioned governor. This gentleman assumed the reins of government in October, 1674,[2] and continued governor over this part of Maine till 1682.[3] He transported many Dutch families here; and Gyles says,[4] that he built a city at the mouth of the Pemaquid river, on the spot represented in the accompanying engraving, and named it Jamestown, in honor of the duke. The great number of old cellars here, in a tolerably good state of preservation, and the paved streets, now covered with soil, seem to corroborate this statement. Gyles also says, that Andros built a fort here, which he named Fort Charles, and garrisoned with a "considerable number of soldiers." This, Andros was of opinion, would fully secure the duke's supremacy.[5] Notwithstanding the arbitrary policy of Andros, and the imperious manner in which he administered the government, — by which he incurred the hatred of every settler in Maine, — the settlements seem to have been generally prosperous. In 1674, Josselyn says, that Pemaquid, Matinicus, Monhegan, Cape Newagen, [now Boothbay,] "where Captain Smith fished for whales," and Muscongus, "now all filled with

[1] Large stumps are now to be seen at low tide, which show what this ancient forest was. The sea, having worn away the shore so as to cover their stumps at flood-tide, has thus preserved them from decay.

[2] Williamson, vol. I., p. 444–5.

[3] Douglas, vol. I., p. 430.

[4] Tragedies of the Wilderness.

[5] Belknap, p. 158.

dwelling-houses, and stages for fishermen, had plenty of cattle, arable land, and marshes."[1]

In 1675, the war of King Philip broke out in Massachusetts, and the eastern Indians, having received repeated injuries at the hands of the English, joined the Massachusetts braves for their extermination. By the untiring exertions, however, of Abraham Shurt, a very influential citizen of Pemaquid, who well understood the Indian character, the impending doom, that, like a storm-cloud in the heavens, had overhung with its sable drapery the settlements along the coast, and Pemaquid in particular, was for a time averted. He called together the chiefs; and, by his great fairness in promising them a just remuneration for the furs that had been stolen from them, and assurances against any future aggression, their hostile feelings were allayed, and pledges of friendship exchanged. But the good faith of the savages was suspected. The traders at some of the neighboring stations were accused of selling them arms and ammunition, and rumors were forthwith put in circulation, that an extensive conspiracy was forming among all the tribes of the province, to completely wipe out, at one decisive blow, all the settlements upon the coast. The government was alarmed at these rumors, and warrants were issued, to "seize every Indian known to be a man-slayer, traitor, or conspirator."[2] These warrants fell into the hands of the basest of men; the same ones, in fact, who had originated and put in circulation the rumors concerning the designs of the Indians. A vessel was fitted out off Pemaquid, and a crew organized, for the purpose of kidnapping the Indians. The intention was, by specious pretexts, to inveigle them on board the vessel, and then to transport them to foreign ports, to be sold as slaves. Shurt, having informed himself of this outrageous proceeding, remonstrated with those who were the prime movers in it; but to no purpose. He next informed the Indians of the plot, and warned them of their danger; but it was so deeply laid, and so adroitly managed, that he was unable wholly to thwart the enterprise. Several Indians were decoyed on board, and dealt with as their betrayers had intended. This fact becoming fully known, the pent-up rage that had long heaved the savage bosom, and which had only been smouldering under the pacific policy of Shurt, now knew no bounds, and burst forth like the fiery torrent of the volcano. A murderous attack was at once made upon all the settlements and trading stations along the coast, and they were destroyed with a vengeance that knew no limit. Pemaquid, the centre of civilization in the wilderness, — one of the first-born cities in the New World, — was

[1] Josselyn's Voyages, p. 200–205. (Harv. Coll. Lib.) [2] Williamson, p. 531, vol. I.

Site of Phips Fort,—Ancient Pemaquid.

now to meet its doom. The torch was applied, and the infant city soon enveloped in one devouring sheet of flame. Tenants ran frantic from their burning dwellings to seek a refuge in the wilderness; but only, in many cases, to have their heads cleft by the tomahawk. Those who escaped did so only because their fleetness of foot carried them beyond the reach of the shower of balls that followed them. Some plunged into the water to escape the vigilant eye of the savage; whilst others made their way to the adjacent islands, and from thence to Boston and other places, where they might find security.

On the termination of this war, in 1678, the settlers again returned, and began to clear away the ruins of the late conflagration, to repair the fort, and to put the place in a state of defence. This had scarcely been attained, and the settlement placed again on a favorable footing, when a revolution broke out in England. William and Mary ascended the throne. War was declared against France; and, as a natural result, the colonies were again called to participate in the struggle. Pemaquid was again destroyed, the French battering down the fort, and taking it by assault. Most of the inhabitants were either killed or taken prisoners, and the fields and habitations that adorned both sides of the river were again reduced to a melancholy waste.

In 1692, three years after, this place fell into the hands of the English; and Sir William Phips, the first governor of Massachusetts under the second charter, commenced its reconstruction, by erecting a new stone fortification on the point of land between the house of Mr. Partridge, as seen in the engraving, and the large rock at the extremity of the point. This fort commanded the river above and below, and its strength was supposed to be amply sufficient for the defence of the place. This supposition, however, proved to be unfounded; for the French recaptured it in 1717–18, though they occupied it but a short time. In 1724, the fort became a rendezvous for the inhabitants of Pemaquid and the surrounding settlements, and continued as such during Lovewell's war. In 1729–30, it had gone considerably to decay, and was repaired by Colonel Dunbar.[1] During the war of the Revolution, fearing it might become a place of defence for the enemy, it was destroyed.

[1] In 1729–30, Colonel David Dunbar, a reduced and indigent colonel in the army, received an appointment as surveyor of the king's woods in America. He also, by the aid of persons who were enemies of the proprietors, obtained a royal order, by which the entire province of Sagadahoc was given into his hands, with directions to settle, superintend, and govern it. He accordingly took up his residence at Pemaquid, and erected a commodious dwelling-house, which he surrounded with a farm, and beautified with a well-cultivated and tasteful garden. — (*Commissioners' Report*, 1811, p. 156.) He repaired the fort that Phips had built, and gave it the name of Fort Frederick; again laid out the

The inhabitants of this town did not take any part in distant operations in the last war with England, preferring to remain at home and defend their own settlement. The following incidents are evidences of the manner in which they carried out their intentions: —

A Spanish brig lay in the harbor of Bristol, having smuggled goods on board destined for that port; and on the afternoon of September 4, 1813, the British brig *Boxer* entered the mouth of the Pemaquid river, for the purpose, it is supposed, of collecting the stipulated salvage, which the Spaniard had not heretofore paid. Before she had accomplished her object, however, the American brig *Enterprise*, which had been cruising off the coast, hove in sight; and the *Boxer* determined on her capture. Nailing her colors to her mast, she bore down upon the *Enterprise*, and engaged her between Pemaquid point and Monhegan island. The conflict lasted forty-eight minutes, during which the *Boxer* was terribly cut up. The shot from the *Enterprise* continued to riddle her, until a gun was fired to leeward by the *Boxer*, — an acknowledgment of her submission and capture. The *Enterprise* then came along side, and took the *Boxer* as her prize to Portland.

The next year, on the 29th of June, the British determined on being revenged on Bristol, for the many chastisements they had received at the hands of her inhabitants; and despatched the frigate *Maidstone* to execute what had long been threatened, namely, the utter demolition of the town. The Bristol boys, however, were prepared to receive them, and treat them to a collation of grape-shot. The *Maidstone* anchored in Fisherman's Island harbor, and sent eight barges into Pemaquid harbor, containing two hundred and seventy-five men. They were met by Captain Sproul, with a force of about one hundred men. The engagement took place during the night, — a dense fog enveloping the rival forces, so that neither the barges nor men could be seen, save by the flashes of the musketry. Not one of Captain Sproul's men was injured during the engagement, which was about an hour in duration; nor is it known that the British suffered any loss. They did not attempt to land, but pushed for New Harbor, about seven miles further east by sea,

city, which had been burnt in 1676, and added to the conflicting titles that already existed in this neighborhood, by regranting the lands, with but little regard to the rights of former occupants. Those that refused to repurchase their lands, and take deeds from him, were violently ejected; and in some cases their houses were burnt, and they themselves threatened with imprisonment. A mammoth petition was gotten up by the proprietors of various grants in the province, and others interested, and laid before the king; and, through the persevering efforts of Levi Waldo, who was largely interested in the Muscongus patent, and the colony agent, Dunbar was removed from authority. — *Sullivan's Hist. of Maine.*

though only one mile by land. Here two boys were stationed on guard, who, as soon as they saw the barges, fired the concerted signal gun, when Captain Sproul, with his command, made all haste to the rescue. William Rodgers, who lived near this spot, seeing the enemy, advised them to make a hasty retreat, or one hundred of the Bristol boys would soon be upon them. They ridiculed his counsel; and, in return for it, an officer, with a profane oath, ordered the bow gun to be discharged at him, which, however, did no injury. Soon after, the Yankees, old and young, assembled in large numbers, eager for the fight. Lodging themselves behind the rocks, they made sad havoc among the English forces, while they were comparatively secure from harm. Soon the foremost barge became disabled, and was replaced by another; but the English, finding that they were suffering considerably, while their enemies were secure, gave up the contest and returned to the ship. Not one of the Bristol boys was hurt during the engagement; while the British lost many in killed and wounded, though the exact number is not known. The *Maidstone* hovered about the coast a few weeks subsequent to this engagement, when she returned to England, where the captain was court-martialed and discharged from the service "for making an attack upon Bristol without orders."

There are some interesting relics of an ancient settlement in this town, about three quarters of a mile above the site of Phips's fort. One

Antiquities in Bristol.

of them is an earthwork, situated on a high bluff, as seen in the engraving, having every appearance of the remains of a fortification. Mr. Williamson, the historian of Maine, and some others, pronounce it the remains of a fort; but offer no conjecture as to when it was erected, or by whom, or for what purpose. Some antiquaries, who think they have sufficient proof of the settlement of New England by a Scandinavian colony prior to the time of Columbus, attribute the work to them. There are also in close proximity to the earthwork, the remains of a tannery, — now a bog of about half an acre, grown up with rushes. The vats are filled up, though the linings are still preserved. With the aid of a pole, these vats can be felt in their length and breadth. The more reasonable solution of the matter is, that this earthwork was constructed by the early settlers as a place for the storage of provisions, and such other property as they might possess; and that the old tannery was built at or about the same time.

The inhabitants of Bristol are mainly of Scotch descent, with a mixture of the Scotch-Irish, a part of whom settled Londonderry, N. H. There are also some of the descendants of the Dutch, who were garrisoned here under the authority of Andros; besides a sprinkling of the German stock, who emigrated under the patronage of Waldo, and settled the town of Waldoboro'.

The territory of the town is very large, and the surface very uneven. Granite is found here; but, as a general thing, of a coarse quality. There are several ponds, three of which have an outlet, called Pemaquid river, which falls into the harbor of that name, at the south part of the town.

The leading pursuit of the inhabitants is seafaring. Something has been done in shipbuilding, though not on a very extensive scale. In the year 1854–55, four ships, one brig, and one schooner were constructed here, making an aggregate of 3,425 tons. At the present writing, the business has fallen off, only one schooner of forty-five tons having been built in 1856. In the way of manufacturing, little or nothing is done.

There are four so-called villages, namely, Bristol Mills, Pemaquid Falls, Round Pond, and Walpole. Post-offices have been established at Bristol, Pemaquid, and Round Pond. There are seven churches in Bristol, three of which are Methodist, two Congregational, and two union meeting-houses; and nineteen school districts, with twenty schools. Population, 2,931; valuation, $251,075.

Brooklin makes one of the extreme southern points of Hancock county, and was formerly a part of the town of Sedgwick, from which it was incorporated in 1849. The inhabitants are engaged principally in fishing and seafaring. During the summer season, a considerable business is carried on in the manufacture of porgy oil. From five hundred to one thousand barrels have been made annually, worth from

$15 to $20 per barrel. The flesh of the fish, after the oil is thus pressed out, is found to be very serviceable upon the soil of this place, which, like many of the sea-board localities, cannot boast of its productiveness. The farms on which it has been used are rapidly improving.

Brooklin has good harbors. A light-house was erected in 1856, on Fly's ledges. There are two small villages, one at the river, near Sedgwick, the other at the corner, near Centre Harbor; five boot and shoe manufactories, two barrel manufactories, six grocery stores, one church edifice, occupied by the Baptists and Congregationalists; one post-office; and ten school districts, with nineteen schools. Population, 1,002; valuation, $77,832.

Brooks is situated near the centre of Waldo county, and was first settled in 1801, by three brothers, — Joseph, John, and Jonathan Roberts. Soon after, Benjamin Cilley, accompanied by his sons, Benjamin, Peter, and Simon, from Buckfield, in the county of Oxford, took up their residence in the town. The settlement was originally called Washington, which it retained till its incorporation in 1818, when it received the name of Brooks, in honor of Governor Brooks of Massachusetts.

Brooks is a small, hilly town, having generally a good soil, with some fine farms. Some attention is paid to agriculture, with good improvement. The town is well watered. Marsh river, which takes its rise here, and empties into the Penobscot at Frankfort, has water-power suitable for mills. The first mills were built by Joseph Roberts, and called Roberts's mills. In the south part of the town is Passagassawaukeag pond, giving rise to Passagassawaukeag river, which runs through Waldo and the upper part of Belfast, and empties into Penobscot bay, affording in its course several excellent water privileges. At the outlet of the pond, in Brooks, are Ellis's mills; and in the southerly part of the town are several small streams, supplying water-power part of the year.

Brooks village is the principal place of business, having mills, stores, and a post-office. Some business is done at Lane's, two miles south of the village. The religious societies are Congregational, Free-will Baptist, Methodist, and Friends'. The first lawyer was Phineas Ashmun, who came in the early settlement as agent for Thorndike, Sears, and Prescott, the proprietors of land in Brooks, Jackson, and Thorndike. He was the first postmaster, holding the office many years, and died at an advanced age. The first physician was Jacob Roberts. The settlers purchased their lands of the proprietors, Thorndike, Sears, and Prescott.

The inhabitants, in general, are temperate, industrious, well-informed, and independent in word and action. Brooks was the native place of Hon. Woodbury Davis, one of the judges of the supreme court of Maine. No town of its size in the county has done more for the cause of freedom and of temperance. It has seven school districts; and two post-offices, — Brooks and South Brooks. Population, 1,021; valuation, $102,343.

BROOKSVILLE, Hancock county, is situated on the eastern shore of Penobscot bay, opposite Islesborough; and, with the exception of the southeast corner, is entirely surrounded by water. It adjoins Sedgwick, and was formed from parts of Castine, Penobscot, and Sedgwick. Its history is almost entirely embodied in the articles on those towns, to which the reader is referred.

The town was incorporated June 13, 1817. The surface is generally uneven, abounding in granite, of which there are several valuable quarries. The principal harbor is Buck's, a deep and safe cove, protected by a small island at its mouth. There are in town, one fulling-mill, three grist-mills, and four saw-mills; also four churches, — Methodist, Baptist, and two Congregational; thirteen school districts; and one post-office. Population, 1,333; valuation, $105,901.

BROWNFIELD, Oxford county, adjoins Fryeburg on the north, and has Conway and Eaton, in New Hampshire, on the west. It was first organized as a plantation in 1787, and incorporated in 1802. It was originally granted by Massachusetts, in three several grants, to Henry Young Brown, who had been a captain in the French war, in consideration, it is supposed, of services rendered in that momentous struggle. He was to settle thirty-eight families therein by June 10, 1770; and, in three years from that time, to have a Protestant minister upon the territory, — as a consideration in part, at least, for his grants. The first clearing of land was made by him, in May, 1765. In the war of 1812, when the population of the town was less than nine hundred, twenty-two persons entered the army, including one captain and three lieutenants. Of these, four died in the service by sickness, and eighteen returned, — two of them having been wounded. The first settled minister of Brownfield was the Rev. Jacob Rice, a graduate of Harvard College in 1765, who was ordained in 1805. The first schoolmaster was "Master Simeon Colby," canonized by seven years' successive rule and service in a single school district here.

The town lies seventy miles southwesterly from Augusta, and forty miles northwesterly from Portland, and on the mail-stage route from Portland, through Fryeburg and Conway, to the notch of the White mountains. It is situated on Saco river, and is intersected by the Little Saco, Shepherd's river, Burnt-meadow and Ten-mile brooks. Much of the soil is of medium quality. Burnt-meadow and Frost mountains, the former rising about two thousand, and the latter about fifteen hundred feet, are within the town, and are resorted to by lovers of extensive and charming views of wild and rural scenery.

The centre village, on Shepherd's river, is the principal place of trade and business in the town. There are two church edifices, one belonging to the Congregationalists, the other to the Free-will Baptists and Methodists; seventeen school districts, three grist-mills, three saw-mills, a large tannery, various small mechanical establishments, and one post-office. Population, 1,320; valuation, $159,636.

Brownville, Piscataquis county, originally No. 5, range 8, north of the Waldo patent, was bargained, by the committee appointed by the Commonwealth of Massachusetts for the sale of eastern lands, to Samuel Fowler, March 2, 1795, for the sum of £2,963 14*s*. 7*d*., of which sum he paid £261. In the month of June, 1803, he, in company with Benjamin Marshall and four others, made a survey of the town, laying it out in lots one mile long from north to south, and half a mile wide. In 1806, the town, falling again into the possession of the Commonwealth, was deeded by Read and Smith, agents for the state, to Moses Brown and Josiah Hills, of Newburyport, Mass. During the summer of that year, Hills moved his family hither, and built a mill on Ebeme river. A part of the wooden dam then built is still in existence. Dr. Isaac Wilkins moved hither from Solon in 1808, and died about 1820. His son George kept the farm after his death, and still resides upon it. In 1810, according to the statement of James Rankin, there were but fifteen families here. The settlement was organized into a plantation in 1819, and incorporated as a town in 1824.

There is one village belonging to Brownville, which is situated in the southwest part of the town; and one post-office; there are two church edifices, belonging to the Congregationalists and Methodists; and nine school districts, with sixteen schools. The slate quarries in this town are of immense value. Two of them are now worked, and give employment to about seventy men, most of whom are of Welsh origin. Population, 787; valuation, $78,987.

Brunswick is situated in the extreme eastern part of Cumberland county. The first settlement within the limits of the town was made by Thomas Purchas in 1628, under a supposed patent from the Plymouth council; but, finding his situation so exposed to the ravages of the

Indians, that he was constantly liable to their depredations, he sought the protection of Massachusetts, by assigning to the then governor, John Winthrop, "all the tract at Pejepscot;[1] lying on both sides of the river Androscoggin, four miles towards the sea." He succeeded, under the protecting arm of Massachusetts, in making a prosperous settlement here, but on the breaking out of King Philip's war it was destroyed by the Indians. Scarcely had it arisen from its ashes, when the colony charter of Massachusetts was annulled by the crown, and the ties which connected the inhabitants of Maine with Massachusetts were greatly weakened, if not entirely sundered. Some of the inhabitants, taking advantage of this state of things, conceived the idea of purchasing this large tract of land of the natives; and, on the 7th of July, 1684, the whole tract that had been taken up by Purchas, and other large tracts, having no very definite limits, were sold by several Indian sagamores to Richard Wharton. The widow and heirs of Purchas made some reservations, and then signed a quitclaim of the whole to Wharton. This is a brief account of the Pejepscot Purchase; the disputed land claims and the vexatious lawsuits that grew out of it, were the most protracted and harassing to be found on the judicial records of the state.

In 1690, the Indians made another incursion, and again burned the town; but it was rebuilt in 1713–14; and, to secure the place against further pillage and destruction, a fort was erected in 1715, near where the village now stands, called Fort George, which, however, proved to be of little service to the inhabitants, as in Lovewell's war, which occurred in 1722, the town was again laid in ashes. It was resettled a third time in 1727, and on the 24th of June, 1737, was incorporated, taking its name from one of the twelve states of the German Confederation. It is now one of the most important towns in the state. The village is very pleasantly situated on a plain near the mouth of the Androscoggin. The Kennebec and Portland Railroad passes through the town, a branch of which has recently been extended from Brunswick to Bath.

Bowdoin College, a view of which is here given, is situated on an elevated plain in the southeast part of the village. It was chartered by the general court of Massachusetts on the 24th of June, 1794, and, at the same time, was endowed with five townships of land;[2] and went

[1] The Indian name, signifying where "angry waters come gushing," referring, probably, to the falls in the Androscoggin. Others, however, give as its meaning, "crooked, like a running snake."

[2] These townships were the present towns of Sebec, Foxcroft, Guilford, Abbott, and Dixmont.

Bowdoin College.

into operation in 1802, receiving the name it now bears in honor of a wealthy and distinguished family of Massachusetts. The medical department was established in 1820. The college has a library of thirty thousand four hundred volumes, and an anatomical cabinet, both which are annually receiving accessions.

Brunswick has eight church edifices, — one Congregational, three Baptist, one Universalist, one Episcopal, one Methodist, and one Free-will Baptist; twenty-four school districts, with twenty-nine schools; three banks, with an aggregate capital of $150,000; and two post-offices, — Brunswick and Oak Hill. It has also one cotton factory — the Cabot Manufacturing Company's — which was built in 1838, and manufactures sheeting; two box factories, one sash and blind factory, six shingle machines, seven saw-mills, two grist-mills, one carding-mill, three machinists, one marble-worker, one soap and candle factory, four carriage builders, nine stores, and two public houses. Population, 4,977; valuation, $1,107,822.

BUCKFIELD is situated in the eastern part of Oxford county. The first effort at settlement within the limits of this town was made by Benjamin Spaulding, in the summer of 1776. The ensuing spring, Thomas Allen and Abijah Buck moved here with their families; and the locality continuing to receive accessions, it was soon pretty thickly settled. In 1788, a survey of the tract was made, which was found to comprise an area of 22,323 acres. Soon after, it was purchased of the Commonwealth of Massachusetts, at the rate of two shillings per acre. The deed of this land bears date November 13, 1788.

7 *

Buckfield was incorporated March 16, 1793, receiving its corporate name in honor of Abijah Buck. The surface of the town, in the south-western part, bordering on Paris, is quite uneven; on the margin of the streams there is some fine alluvial land, which is capable of a high degree of cultivation. There are several rich beds of magnetic iron ore here, from which the very best wrought iron and steel can be made: limestone is also found, which yields lime nearly equal to that of the Rockland quarries: a bed of yellow ochre has also been opened. The town is watered by Twenty-mile river, which is spanned by five bridges. This river is made otherwise useful by sufficient water-power for several mills, and other machinery. The village is located near the centre of the town, in which there are three churches, eight stores, one post-office, an academy, and thirteen school districts. Population, 1,657; valuation, $259,924.

Bucksport, Hancock county, lies on the eastern shore of Penobscot river, eighteen miles below Bangor. It was one of the six townships originally granted by William and Mary to David Marsh, of Haverhill, Mass., and three hundred and fifty others, citizens of Massachusetts and New Hampshire, whose title thereto was confirmed in 1764, by the general court of Massachusetts.

On the 8th of August, 1762, Jonathan Buck, James Duncan, Richard Emerson, William Duncan, and William Chamberlain, the surveyor, came here from Haverhill, Mass., and began the survey of the town, upon the confirmation of the grant. Colonel Buck built a saw-mill on Mill river, a small stream passing through the present village; also a dwelling-house, and a store. The next year Laughlin McDonald[1] and his son Roderick, came here from Fort Pownal, and took up two lots as settlers.

In 1766–67, Asahel Harriman, Jonathan Frye, Benjamin Page, Phineas Ames, Jonathan Buck, Jr., and Ebenezer Buck, came here and settled on lots agreeably to the provisions of the grant, which gave to each actual settler one hundred acres of land. According to the records there were but twenty-one families here in 1775.

The town was incorporated in 1792, and called Buckstown. It was first represented in the general court in 1804, by Jonathan Buck. In 1817 the name was changed from Buckstown to Bucksport, because the latter syllable was significant of its locality, while the former syllable was retained in honor of its founder.

The surface is uneven, but not mountainous, and beautifully diversi-

[1] McDonald was originally from Greenock, in Scotland.

fied with ponds and streams. The majestic Penobscot, as it moves on to the ocean, washes its western and southern sides. It is quite thickly settled for miles along the river, yet there is but one village proper, in which most of the trade is centred.

The principal occupation of the inhabitants is, and ever has been, shipbuilding, in which the most of their capital is invested. About three thousand tons are annually set afloat here. Some thirty sail, each of one hundred tons and upwards, are employed in the fisheries on the Grand Banks. These give employment to more than three hundred men and boys. Besides these there are a large number of vessels engaged in the coasting and foreign trade.

There are four meeting-houses, — one Congregationalist, and three Methodist; eighteen school districts, with twenty-two schools; two seminaries, one Congregational, and one Methodist; one bank, with a capital of $75,000; and four post-offices, — Bucksport, North Bucksport, Bucksport Centre, and East Bucksport. Population, 3,381; valuation, $626,338.

BURLINGTON, Penobscot county, is situated fifty-four miles northeast from Bangor, and about fifteen miles east from the Penobscot, and embraces an area of forty-eight square miles. It is watered by several ponds, which form the principal head waters of the Passadumkeag river, which flows into the Penobscot. It was incorporated in 1832, and has one church (Congregationalist), one post-office, and six school districts, with ten schools. Population, 481; valuation, $28,500.

BURNHAM is situated in the northwest corner of Waldo county, and was settled soon after the close of the war with England. The surface of the town is generally level, but somewhat swampy. It was incorporated in 1824, and is, as yet, but sparsely settled. There is one small village, but no church edifice or public institution of any kind, excepting the district schools, of which there are eight, in the same number of districts: one tannery, two saw-mills, and two shingle machines are in operation here. Burnham has the usual trade of country towns. Population, 784; valuation, $100,000.

BUXTON, York county, was "Number One" of the seven townships granted by the general court of Massachusetts in 1732, to individuals who had served in the war against the Narragansett Indians. In 1735, a surveying commission was appointed, who laid out 123 lots near Salmon falls, on the Saco river. In 1740, the first effort was made in settling the township, by five families who moved here from Massachusetts; but owing to the troubles with the Indians they were soon obliged to leave. Nothing further was done towards settling the township, until the fall of 1750, when seven persons moved in with their families; they were William Hancock from Londonderry, Ireland, John Elden and Job Roberts from Saco, Samuel Merrill, Timothy Haseltine, Joshua Woodman, and John Wilson from Massachusetts. In 1760, the proprietors built a meeting-house, and three years after, Rev. Paul Coffin, a Congregational clergyman from Newbury, was ordained, and remained here as pastor for sixty years, until his death on the 6th of June, 1821. In July, 1772, the township was incorporated, and named by Mr. Coffin from Buxton, England, the home of his ancestors. From that time, the town steadily advanced, without any serious interruption.

The surface is generally level, and the soil good for farming. It is watered by Saco river, and Bonnie Eagle, Duck, and Lilly ponds, and one or two others of smaller size. There are four villages. Salmon falls village, taking its name from the falls in Saco river, on which it is situated, is a place of some business. The fall in the river is about eighty feet to a half mile. The first saw-mill erected in this town was built here in 1770. At the present time, three saws cut about two million feet of boards annually, the most of which are made into boxes and headings, for the West India trade. In the early settlement of the town, salmon were caught in large quantities about the falls. About one mile up the river from this place is the village of Bar Mills, so called from a bar of rock, which extends entirely across the river. The first mills at this place were erected in 1795. There are now on the Buxton side of the river, five saws cutting out about three million feet of boards annually; also a grist and plaster mill, a planing-machine, and shingle and lath machines. The York and Cumberland Railroad passes near this village, and affords good facilities for the transportation of lumber from the mills. Four and a half miles above this is the village of West Buxton, or Moderation Mills, — as it is sometimes called, — which has a woollen factory, and a sash, blind, and door factory. About the same amount of lumber is manufactured here as at Bar Mills. Buxton Centre Village is a place of some business.

There are eight church edifices, — two Congregational, two Methodist, two Free-will Baptist, one Baptist, and one Union house; three post-offices, — Buxton, Buxton Centre, and West Buxton; and seventeen school districts, with the same number of schools. Population, 2,995; valuation, $424,397.

BYRON, Oxford county, is situated at the northern extremity of the county, on Swift river. The town was incorporated in 1833. The first settlers were Samuel Knapp from Massachusetts, Jonas Green from Wilton, James Bawn from Sydney, John Thomas from Norway, J. Stockbridge from Turner, Richard Morrill, and Abraham Reed. The land was purchased of a Mr. Brown, of Newburyport, Mass. The Indian name of this town was Skillertown.

The surface of Byron is very uneven. There are two mountains known by the names of "Turk" and "Broad." Swift river runs through its entire length, and there is also a pond called Garland pond; so that the place is well watered, and is already the site of three mills, for which there is ample power. The principal occupation of the inhabitants is agriculture. Wheat and corn are grown to a large extent. Lumbering, in winter, is extensively carried on. There is but one village in the town, and that is known by the euphonious name of "Hop City," at which the only post-office is located. There are six school districts. Population, 296; valuation, $31,000.

Calais, a port of entry, and embraced in the Passamaquoddy district, is situated at the eastern extremity of Washington county, at the head of the tide waters of the St. Croix. It contains an area of 19,392 acres, and was granted by the state of Massachusetts June 27, 1789, to Waterman Thomas. Having an advantageous location for navigation, and being surrounded by dense forests of valuable pine timber, it soon became the mart for the lumber business, a great many persons being attracted here under the supposition that fortunes could be made. Ship timber was manufactured among the other varieties; and, when Napoleon excluded the English from the Baltic, they resorted to Calais to obtain the supplies necessary for their ship-yards: hence, a large and lucrative trade, which lasted for some years, was carried on between the inhabitants of this town and the British timber-dealers. In 1809, Calais became an incorporated town; and, being the centre of trade for a large inland district, its population and business went on increasing from year to year, and in 1850 it received a city charter.

The St. Croix river at this point is crossed by several bridges, exclusive of the railroad bridge, which connects the city with the town of St. Andrews. A railroad has been completed to the mills in Baring, by which the large amount of lumber cut there is transported to Calais, and shipped to the various markets. Another company has extended this road as far as Lewey's Island, in Princeton, making the entire length about nineteen miles. The telegraph wires between Halifax and Boston pass through this town. A large amount of shipping, employed principally in the coasting trade, is owned here; and, at one time, considerable was done in shipbuilding; but latterly the business has suffered a great decline. Lumbering has ever been and still is the leading pursuit, and as a consequence, a great amount of capital is invested in the trade. There are eight single saw-mills, ten gang saw-mills, eighteen lath-mills, besides clapboard and shingle machines, in active operation.

Several handsome houses of public worship have been erected in Calais, as also an academy, and a few private and select schools. The town is divided into eight school districts; has one bank, with a capital of $100,000; two newspapers; and three post-offices — Calais, Milltown, and Red Beach. Population, 5,500; valuation, $1,172,053.

CAMBRIDGE is situated in the eastern part of Somerset county, seventy miles from Augusta, and is the half of a six-mile-square township, Ripley being the other half. These two towns are divided diagonally, from northeast to southwest, by the Maine stream, which forms one of the tributaries of the Sebasticook river. Cambridge was incorporated in 1834, and hence has very little history but what is common to almost every New England town. The surface is gently undulating, and the soil tolerably good. The town contains one village, one church edifice, five school districts with five schools, one or two stores, a public-house, two grist-mills, two saw-mills, and one post-office. Population, 487; valuation, $30,526.

CAMDEN is situated in the south part of Waldo county, on the west side of Penobscot bay. It was surveyed in the year 1768, by David Fales, at which time not a tree had been felled, nor a building erected in the whole township. The surface is quite broken and mountainous, from the general appearance of which, the Indians called it Megunticook, signifying, "great swells of the sea." Within three or four years after Fales had made the survey, James Richards commenced a settlement at the mouth of the stream, where the principal village now stands; and Peter Ott, a German, commenced one at what is now Rockport village. Others soon followed. Some attempts at farming were made by these settlers, though on a small scale. In 1779, when Castine was in the hands of the British, Camden became the only place of rendezvous for the Americans, a small force of whom were encamped here, under command of Major George Ulmer. The town was incorporated in 1791, and contains an area of 26,880 acres.

During the last war with England, a battery was erected on the top of the mountain, back of the village, consisting of one twelve and one eighteen pounder. This appearance of the ability of the town to defend itself, held the British in check, and they dared not attack it, though they might have taken it at any time had they made the attempt, there being but a handful of soldiers, and no gunners that could manage the battery. The command at the time devolved upon Colonel Foot, whose courage, (although no opportunity was ever afforded the Colonel to set his valor beyond a doubt,) some wicked sceptics have even dared to question. It is reported that when he was expecting an attack by the British, he drew up his force to meet them, and with all the majesty of Napoleon at the Pyramids, delivered them a speech. Drawing his sword from its scabbard, he pointed back to Meguntieook mountain, on which the battery was erected, and exclaimed, "'Soldiers! forty ages behold you.' You are now going into battle, but if you find yourselves under the necessity of retreating, you will find me up in Simon Barrett's barn."[1] Since the close of the war, there have been no incidents in the history of the town worthy of note.

The several mountain peaks here, especially the two Meguntieooks, bald and rugged, one rising to a height of 1,335 and the other 1,457 feet, present, at a distance, a very imposing appearance. There are several ponds, partly or wholly within the limits of the town; namely, Canaan pond, Oyster river pond, Tolman's pond, and Chichawaukie pond.

The manufactories here are principally of the character required by an agricultural community; such as saw-mills, grist-mills, carriage, sash and blind manufactories, and blacksmiths' shops. There are excellent water privileges, which will at some time be valuable; six ship-yards, launching from ten to twelve vessels annually; and extensive and valuable lime quarries, the annual revenue of which is large. It is only surpassed, in this branch of business, by the adjoining city of Rockland.

There are five villages, — Camden Harbor, Rockport, Simonton Corner, Ingraham Corner, and Rockville; four post-offices, — Camden, West Camden, Rockport, and Rockville; eleven religious societies, ten of which have houses of public worship; twenty school districts, with forty-nine schools, besides a high school, supported most of the time. Population, 4,005; valuation, $602,804.

CANAAN, Somerset county, is situated on the east side of the Kennebec river, forty miles north from Augusta, and contains an area of 15,891 acres, of which five hundred are covered with water, and 266 with highways. The plantation name was "Wesserunset." The survey of the town was made by John Jones, in 1779, and it was incorporated under its present name, June 18, 1788. The first settlement

[1] The barn in question was in the town of Hope.

was made here as early as the year 1770. Bloomfield and Skowhegan were formerly included within the limits of this town.

The surface is somewhat rough, though there are many fertile sections. The soil is mainly a clayey loam.

There are six churches in Canaan, — Congregational, Methodist. Baptist, Free-will Baptist, Christian Baptist, and Universalist. The town is divided into twelve school districts, with twenty-six schools. It has one post-office. Population, 1,696; valuation, $216,623.

CANTON is situated in the eastern part of Oxford county, on the Androscoggin river, and was originally a part of the town of Jay. The first efforts at settlement were made in 1790 or 1792, — William Livermore, William French, Joseph Coolidge, and Alexander Shepherd, being among the earliest settlers. They were soon followed by others, who, with those already mentioned, came principally from Massachusetts. This town, prior to its occupation by the white man, was inhabited by the Rockomeca Indians, probably a clan of the Pequawket tribe, who had their residence at Fryeburg. This clan was entirely exterminated by the ravages of the smallpox, during the French war, in 1757. Implements, supposed to have been used by the natives, have been found in this town, several of which are now in possession of some of the inhabitants: an Indian burying-ground, containing many of the bones of the deceased warriors, has also come to light.

Canton was incorporated in 1821. The surface of the outskirts of the town is uneven, while the centre is smooth and level. It is not surpassed by any locality in the state for agricultural purposes. At Canton point, called by the Indians who resided there, Rockomeca point, is a large and beautiful tract of interval, which was, in Indian times, planted with corn, hills of which were seen by the first settlers. The Androscoggin river runs through the town circuitously, its banks being lined with the best of interval. The mountain situated north of the point was also named by the Indians Rockomeca. Whitney pond, in the southerly part of the town, received its name from Whitney, a hunter, who was wounded by the savages and left for dead, but revived. and crawled to a camp, where he took refuge. His companions, being in pursuit of him, discovered what they supposed to be an Indian in the camp, when they fired upon him; and, on coming up, found they had killed their comrade.

There is one village in town, containing a machine shop, for the manufacture of agricultural implements, a tin-ware factory, and an iron foundery. Two church edifices have been erected here, one of which is occupied by the Universalists, and the other by the Baptists and Free-will Baptists. The town is divided into ten school districts, with nine schools, and has two post-offices — Canton and Canton Mills. Population, 1,233; valuation for the year 1857, $165,000.

Cape Elizabeth, Cumberland county, is almost a peninsula, and is separated from Portland by Fore river, which is spanned by a toll-bridge. It contains an area of 12,881 acres, and together with Portland and Richmond Island originally formed a part of the old town of Falmouth.

Richmond Island, the southerly part of the town, is situated about a mile from the mainland, and contains about two hundred acres of land. The first European settler on the island was Walter Bagnall, who came here in 1628, and occupied the island without any title. His sole object seems to have been to drive a profitable trade with the Indians, by every means within his reach. He lived alone upon the island undisturbed, until, by his cupidity, he drew down upon him the vengeance of the natives, who put an end to his life on the 3d of October, 1631. He left a large amount of property, which was soon scattered after his death. Two months afterwards (December 1, 1631), the island was granted, by the council of Plymouth, to Robert Trelawny and Moses Goodyear, merchants of Plymouth, England. In 1637, Richard Gibson, an Episcopal minister, was settled here; and, if tradition be correct, a church was erected about the same time. Gibson left the island in 1640, and went to Portsmouth; from thence, in 1642, he returned to England.

This island, from its local situation on the highway of coasting business, — having the sea, with its ample stores of fish, on the one side, and the forest, with its woods, its furs, and its savage tenants, on the other, — obtained great advantages, and met with a rapid growth. It became a resort for fishermen, and considerable foreign commerce was prosecuted. Before 1648, we have accounts of large ships arriving at the island and taking out cargoes for Europe. In 1638, a ship of three hundred tons was sent here, laden with wine, and, the same year, Mr. Trelawny, one of the proprietors, employed sixty men in the fisheries. In 1639, John Winter, the agent of Trelawny, sent to England, in the bark Richmond, six thousand pipe-staves. The subsequent history of this island has not sustained the promise of its early days. After the death of Winter, — who had been a prime mover in its active operations, — about the year 1648, its commerce declined, its population diminished, and, after the first Indian war, it ceased to be a place of any business or importance. The island is now a single farm, devoted to the production of potatoes, and there is but one solitary house in a place formerly teeming with life and business.

Cape Elizabeth was incorporated 1764, but with only district privileges. The State Reform School, established in 1853, for juvenile offenders, is located here. The building is capable of accommodating 240 boys, and there are nearly the full number in attendance. They are employed in farming, in making clothing, and various mechanical operations. They have religious instruction in the Sabbath school, conducted by volunteers from various religious societies in Portland, and by preaching in the chapel every morning. There is also a good library. Much improvement has been made by the boys, and most of them manifest a gratifying desire to aid in the duties of the institution, and a lively interest in its prosperity and usefulness.

There are three churches — Congregational, Methodist, and Free-will Baptist; eleven school districts, and one post-office called Cape Elizabeth Depot. Population, 2,082; valuation, $256,287.

CARMEL, Penobscot county, is situated twelve miles west from Bangor, and comprises an area of 23,040 acres. It was purchased of the state of Massachusetts, March 2, 1795, by Martin Kinsley, of Hampden, and settled under the auspices of the proprietor. The town was incorporated in 1811. The surface is level, and was originally covered with a heavy growth of pine, a large portion of which is still remaining. Carmel is watered by the Soadabscook and the Kenduskeag streams, which flow in opposite directions, and come so near together, that, during heavy rains, their waters commingle, each taking a portion of the surplus of the other. Along the margin of each of these streams, there are some tracts of fine alluvial land; and a small portion of the town is somewhat swampy. The Penobscot and Kennebec Railroad passes through Carmel. The village is situated near the centre, and is a very active and thriving place of business. The town contains three churches (Methodist, Universalist, and Free-will Baptist), ten school districts, with the same number of schools; and two post-offices, Carmel and North Carmel. Population, 1,225; valuation, $107,228.

CARROLL, situated at the easterly extremity of Penobscot county, is a very good farming town. The surface is somewhat hilly, but most of the soil is capable of cultivation. The first settlements were made here about the year 1831 or 1832. It is watered by the Mattagoodus stream, which flows north into the Mattawamkeag, and by other small streams, that flow south into the Schoodic lakes. Near the centre of the town is a valuable lime quarry.

As yet there is no church edifice, but there are six school districts, each of which supports a school during the summer and winter term. There is also one post-office. Population, 401; valuation, $21,229.

CARTHAGE, Franklin county, formerly No. 4, Abbot's Purchase, lies south of Weld, and west of Wilton and Temple. William Bowley and one by the name of Winter were the first settlers, the former of whom built what are called Bowley's mills, on Webb's river. The town was lotted by Solomon Adams, in 1803.

Carthage was incorporated in 1829. It is drained by Webb's river, which runs southerly. The eastern part is broken by quite a range of mountains, variously denominated the Bear, Saddleback, or Blueberry. Formerly it had extensive forests of pine. A considerable quantity of the land is fit for cultivation. Dr. Perkins, of Farmington, is now the proprietor of the unsold lands. Valuable formations of limestone are found here.

There are two saw-mills and a grist-mill here, which are doing a profitable business. Five schools have been established, having an aggregate winter attendance of 117. The town has one post-office. Population, 420; valuation, $42,142.

CASCO is situated in the northerly part of Cumberland county, having Otisfield upon the northwest and Raymond upon the southeast, from the latter of which it was taken, and incorporated in 1841. It previously comprised nearly one half the territory of Raymond, which was seven and a half miles square.

The surface is uneven, and the soil hard and rocky, but tolerably productive. It is watered by Pequawket river, and the outlet of Great and Little Parker ponds. These ponds are partly in Casco and partly in Otisfield. On the outlet are some good mill sites. Thompson pond is in the northern part of the town, the outlet of which, falling into lake Sebago, furnishes some good mill privileges.

There are three villages, with a post-office at each, bearing the names of Casco, South Casco, and Webb's Mills; four saw-mills, four grist-mills, four shingle machines, one tannery, one carriage factory, three church edifices, — one Free-will Baptist, one Friends' and one Union house; and eleven school districts, with ten schools. Population, 1,046; valuation, $152,314.

CASTINE, Hancock county, one of the earliest settled places in Maine, and one of the most varied and interesting in its historical associations, extending, as they do, through a period of nearly two centuries, is sitnated on the peninsula of Marche-biguatus, commonly called Bigaduce, on the eastern side of Penobscot bay, seven miles from the mouth of Penobscot river. Under the name of Pentagoet, this peninsula became well known to the first settlers of New England; and, as early as 1630, was selected by the Plymouth company for a trading station. The French, and afterwards the Dutch, held possession of the place. D'Aulney, the French governor of Acadie, erected a fort and resided here for seven years. Subsequently, it fell into the hands of the English; but, by the treaty of Breda, it was ceded to the French, in whose control it remained for nearly a century.

Castine perpetuates the name of the Baron de St. Castin, a French nobleman, of an eccentric disposition, who established his residence here in 1667. Forming a close alliance with the Indians and marrying the daughter of Madockawando, their chief, he remained among them for over thirty years. His influence over the natives was so powerful, that, according to La Hontan, they regarded him as their tutelar god. To his exertions may be traced the establishment of Catholicism among them. Castin proved a dangerous enemy to the people of Massachusetts, who made several ineffectual attempts to capture him. He taught the eastern Indians the use of fire-arms, and he coöperated with them in their frequent attacks upon the frontier settlements. After living thirty years a life of seclusion, Castin returned to France, leaving the possession of his dominions to his half-breed son, "Castin the younger," who was a man of some education and intelligence. The Castin family did not finally abandon the peninsula until the termination of the French war of 1744.

Castine became permanently settled by the English in 1760. At an early period of the Revolution, the first settlers evinced their patriotism by taking the crew of a British vessel prisoners, and sending them to General Washington's head-quarters at Cambridge. Four years after this event, in the summer of 1779, the plantation was invested by a British force of 650 men, with three sloops of war. The English government had long been sensible that the establishment of a military post here would be of essential service in checking the ravages of privateers, as well as in securing a supply of timber for the royal navy. Preparations were at once made for fortifying the place, and an extensive fortress was commenced on the summit of the peninsula. Massachusetts determined to dislodge the invaders from her territory, and in a few weeks, the largest American force ever fitted out, consisting of forty-three vessels, carrying two thousand men, and mounting 340 guns, sailed from Boston for Penobscot. At the time of their arrival, the fort was not more than half completed; but, by assiduous labor, the British commander was enabled to put it in a tolerable condition of defence. He had taken the precaution to erect batteries at every point of the peninsula regarded accessible. After being twice repulsed, our forces at last effected a landing on the northwestern bank, by climbing a precipice, with a loss of over one hundred of their number. The British sustained a loss of thirty in the conflict. A battery was erected in front of the enemy's fort, and both parties maintained a cannonading for several days, while the commanders of the American land and naval forces were wasting the time in discussing the expediency of carrying the works by storm. In the mean time, a fleet of seven British ships arrived, and the Americans made an inglorious retreat up the Penobscot river. All their vessels and military stores were either captured or destroyed, the officers and men escaping with difficulty into the woods. This expedition, called in history the "Penobscot Expedition," stands upon record as the most disastrous issue our arms have ever experienced. The commander of the naval forces — Saltonstall — was cashiered, for the incapacity or pusillanimity to which so disgraceful a defeat was justly attributed.

Castine remained in the possession of the enemy until peace was declared. During the war of 1812 it was again occupied by the British, who repaired and strengthened the works erected in the Revolution. Four thousand troops were stationed here at one time. No attempt was made to dislodge them; and the town continued to be the seat of important military operations, as well as of an extensive trade, for nearly a year.

No place in Maine has passed through so many changes as this ancient town. It has been successively possessed by the Indians, French, Dutch, and English. During nearly the whole of the seventeenth century, the flag of France floated over its fort, in defiance of the English, whose attempts to gain a foothold here were unavailing. No less than five naval engagements have taken place on the bosom of its harbor, the English having twice attacked it, and the Americans once. In the language of Judge Sullivan, in his History of Maine, "It has never been without a garrison from 1630 to 1783, and has always been dealt with, by the nations in whose possession it has been, as a place of great importance."

Castine was incorporated in 1796, and then became the shire town of Hancock county, the county buildings being situated in that part of Penobscot which was taken to form Castine. It continued to be the county seat until 1838, when the courts were removed to Ellsworth. After the Revolution terminated, Castine became rapidly settled, and the number of its inhabitants sixty years ago exceeded that at the present day.

For a long time it was the most important mart of business in the eastern part of Maine, and the residence of many distinguished men. Bangor, Belfast, and other places more favorably located, afterwards diverted the trade which centred here.

The most prominent points of historical interest which the old peninsula of Bigaduce affords, are the ruins of Castin's fort, now nearly obliterated; Fort George, erected in the Revolution; a fort at the entrance of the harbor, built by the Americans previous to the last war; and the remains of various batteries, which are of Revolutionary origin. The whole soil of the peninsula abounds in ancient relics. The spade frequently brings to light articles of Indian manufacture; and cannon balls, shells, and other evidences of war, have been found in great numbers. In 1840, a deposit of about six hundred silver coins, mostly French and Spanish, all bearing a date previous to 1680, was exhumed near the bank of the river, a few miles above the town. Castine is becoming a favorite resort during the heat of the summer months; and with its beautiful and expansive scenery, its salubrious breezes, its seclusion and tranquillity, and its historical associations, it must always be attractive to the antiquary and the lover of nature.

The village of Castine occupies a commanding position on the eastern side of the peninsula, which gradually ascends from the shore, and on its summit are to be seen the ruins of the old English fort. The streets are wide and neat, and the private residences are indicative of comfort and good taste. The public buildings are, three churches,—Congregational, Methodist, and Universalist; a custom-house; and a town-hall, formerly the court-house. There is a light-house below the town, on "Dice's Head." Castine is the wealthiest town in Maine in proportion to its size, and is the seat of customs for the Penobscot district. A large number of vessels are owned here, and several ships are built annually. The tonnage of the district, for the year ending June, 1855, was 53,965 tons. The manufacture of cordage and of iron chains is prosecuted to some extent. The principal business of the inhabitants is that of the fisheries, and a large amount of capital is employed in it. An insurance company, with a capital of $70,000, is established here. A steamboat connects Castine, during the summer, with the neighboring towns.

Castine has four school districts, with eight schools; and two post-offices — Castine, and North Castine. Population, 1,260; valuation, $597,360.

Centreville, Washington county, adjoins the town of Machias on the northeast corner, and is watered by Machias river. The history of this town lies somewhere in the future. It was incorporated in 1842, and was formerly known as plantation No. 23, east division. It has two school districts. Population, 178; valuation, $22,801.

CHARLESTON, which is one of the northern tier of towns in Penobscot county, adjoins Piscataquis county, and is twenty-five miles northwest from Bangor. The town was granted July 14, 1802, by the Commonwealth of Massachusetts, to John Lowell, and is six miles square. The settlement was commenced as early as 1795, by Charles Vaughan, and the town was incorporated February 16, 1811. A busy little village has sprung up within its limits. There are ten school districts, with the same number of schools, and one academy; one church edifice, and two post-offices — Charleston and West Charleston. Population, 1,283; valuation, $142,977.

CHARLOTTE is located in the eastern part of Washington county, forty-one miles from Machias, and was incorporated in 1825. The surface is undulating, — the town is fair for farming purposes. It is watered by a large pond in the central part, having its outlet through the town of Pembroke, — called Pennamaquon stream. There are here six school districts, with nine schools; and one post-office. Population, 718; valuation, $45,405.

CHELSEA, Kennebec county, is a small town, situated on the east bank of the Kennebec river, and joins Augusta on the south. Prior to its incorporation in 1850, it composed a part of the town of Hallowell. There are several very good farms in the town; and some which cannot be commended so highly. Yeaton Corner, situated on the river, is the only village in Chelsea. The town is watered by Worromontogus river, which falls into the Kennebec. It has nine school districts, with the same number of schools; and one post-office, called Togus Spring. Population, 1,096; valuation, $146,869.

CHERRYFIELD, Washington county, is situated on both sides of the Narraguagus river, and is thirty miles from Machias. This town was originally No. 11 of what were known as the "Lottery townships," and was incorporated February 9, 1816. Cherryfield is a thriving town, lumbering being the principal business. There are three churches, — a Baptist, Congregationalist, and Methodist; twenty-two saw-mills, three grist-mills, eight school districts, and one post-office, called Narraguagus. Population, 1,648; valuation, $199,992.

CHESTER, Penobscot county, is situated on the west bank of the Penobscot river, opposite the town of Lincoln. It has but recently been settled; but the soil is reported to be of a fertile character, and rewards amply the labors of the husbandman. It was incorporated in 1834, and has a post-office and six school districts, with eight schools. Population, 340; valuation, $12,793.

CHESTERVILLE, Franklin county, is one of the southerly towns of the county, and is about eight miles long, and six in width at the north end. The first white settler entered the township in 1782, and commenced the settlement in the south part, known formerly as Wyman's plantation, so called in honor of its pioneer, Abraham Wyman. In March, 1783, two families moved in, and settled near the central part, designated soon after as the Chester plantation. Some of the early settlers came from Bath, others from York, and a few from New Hampshire and Massachusetts. Rev. Jotham Sewell, born in York, who travelled much in Maine as a preacher, was one of the early settlers; and William Bradbury, who was treasurer of the town for twenty-six years, commenced his fortunes here. Among the hardships and trials which these two pioneers had to endure was that of going to Winthrop, twenty miles, to mill, drawing their grain on a hand sled. Daniel Wyman was also an early settler. The first road was opened through the place in 1780, and the first saw-mill and grist-mill put in motion in 1785.

Chesterville was incorporated February 20, 1802. Much of the land in the centre of the town is flat and low. The hills, which are mostly stony, lie at each end, where the best farms are located. There is considerable meadow, and a large portion of swamp and bog land here. Moose hill lies in the southwest corner of the town, but the highest point of this eminence is believed to be in East Livermore. A spur of the Blabon hill is supposed to be the highest land within the town. It is composed of granite, large quantities of which are annually quarried and wrought into building material. Another place, called the "Bluff," lies northwest of Sand point, and is a ledge almost perpendicular, being about a hundred feet high and thirty rods long.

Chesterville is watered by the Little Norridgewock and McGurdy's rivers, and by another stream, which enters the town near the southeastern extremity. On these streams are some good mill sites, which have been improved. There are also a few ponds, the principal of which is called Parker's, lying in the southeast part of the town, which has several islands.

Chesterville has three villages,—one at the Centre mills, another at Keith's mills, and another just springing up near Sandy river, opposite to Farmington Falls village. At the villages and a few other places, boards, shingles, clapboards, laths, matches, pails, leather, starch, and ship-plank are manufactured. Carding, cloth-dressing, and axe-making are carried on to some extent. The town contains two union meeting-houses, occupied alternately by the different religious denominations; eleven school districts, with twenty-one schools; and three post-offices — Chesterville, North Chesterville, and South Chesterville. Two well-conducted libraries exist here, one of which is in the south part of the town, and the other at North Chesterville — the latter possessing more than two hundred volumes. Population, 1,142; valuation, $140,612.

CHINA is situated in the eastern part of Kennebec county, on the Sheepscot river, about ten miles from Augusta. Its first settlement was made by a family of Clarks, originally from Nantucket, who, while on one of their coasting and fishing expeditions, in the autumn of 1773, ran their vessel up the Kennebec as far as Cobbossee (now Gardiner), where they fell in with one John Jones, who was employed by the Plymouth company to survey this township, in the disposition of which every alternate lot was awarded to actual settlers. The next year (1774) they took up their abode, — Jonathan and Edmund Clark on the west side of China lake, Ephraim and Andrew Clark, and George Fish, a brother-in-law, upon the east side. Soon after James, Judah, and Ichabod Chadwick, and Abner Weeks, from Cape Cod, settled in the south part of the township. In 1775, Abram Burrill settled three miles easterly from the head of the lake, and Michael Norton at Norton's Corner. The titles were obtained from the Plymouth company.

The township was called Jones's plantation until its incorporation, February 8, 1796, when it received the name of Harlem. On the 5th February, 1818, the northern part of Harlem, together with a part of the towns of Fairfax (now Albion) and Winslow, were incorporated into a separate town, called China, and about the year 1822 the remaining part of Harlem was annexed to China.

The land adjacent to the lake rises from its gravel beach in gradual slopes, of no great elevation. In some places, it is wooded to the water's edge; but, for the most part, has been converted into pasturage and tillage. The soil is excellent, and but few towns surpass this in an agricultural aspect. In 1837, when the state government paid a bounty on wheat, China headed the list for the quantity produced.

China lake, a beautiful body of water, intersects the town diagonally and is nearly divided by a promontory into two ponds. The waters are connected by a small passage called "the Narrows." The eastern body of the lake is about six miles long by one mile wide; the western extends into Vassalboro', a distance of three and a half miles from the narrows, and thence is connected by the Sebasticook with the Kennebec. The lake abounds in fish.

The western branch of the Sheepscot river passes through the eastern part of the town, furnishing several good mill privileges. There are many smaller streams, on which are saw-mills and grist-mills. The larger portion of Three Mile pond is in the southwest corner of the town.

There are four villages. China village, at the north end of the lake, is much the largest, and contains two meeting-houses, an academy, several stores and mechanics' shops. South China, beautifully situated at the south end of the lake, contains a meeting-house, three stores, several mechanics' shops, a manufactory for boots and shoes, — incorporated in 1855, under the name of Mechanics' Association, — a hotel, and an excellent public library. Two other meeting-houses are within a short distance. Weeks's Mills, in the southeast part of the town, on the west branch of the Sheepscot, contains a meeting-house, two stores, several mechanics' shops, saw-mills and grist-mills, and a tannery. Branch Mills, at the east part of the town, in the valley of the west branch of the Sheepscot, has a high school, a saw-mill and grist-mill, several manufactories, and two stores.

There are seven churches: the Friends have three, the Baptists two, and the Methodists two. There are three post-offices, — China, South China, and Weeks's Mills; and twenty school districts, with the same number of schools. Population in 1850, 2,769, supposed to be at present about 3,000; assessors' valuation for 1856, $473,401.

CLIFTON is situated in the southwestern part of Penobscot county, and its settlement was commenced about the year 1815, — Benjamin Penney, Eben Davis, and a man by the name of Parks, being among the first settlers. The town was incorporated in 1848, under the name of Maine; but, the inhabitants not feeling pleased with it, at their request it was soon after changed by the legislature to Clifton. The town is of very little importance, either as regards agriculture or manufactures. Its surface is irregular, and the soil is poor, and hard to cultivate. It has four school districts, with seven schools. Population, 306; valuation, $19,305.

CLINTON is situated in the northeast corner of Kennebec county, and was settled about the year 1775. It was soon after organized into a plantation by the name of Hancock, and was incorporated as a town, February 28, 1795, under its present name. The surface is quite level, and the soil is of a productive character. The Sebasticook river passes through the town, and affords water-power for some manufactories. It is also traversed by the Penobscot and Kennebec Railroad. Two villages have grown up within the limits of Clinton, — known as Morrison Corner and Clinton Village. There is a gore of land containing about three thousand acres adjoining the town upon the northeast, which has plantation privileges. It is called Clinton Gore, — is traversed by the Penobscot and Kennebec Railroad, and, it is thought, will soon be annexed to this or one of the adjoining towns. There are two church edifices in Clinton — Congregational and Free-will Baptist; twelve school districts, and two post-offices, — Clinton and Pishon's Ferry. Population, 1,743; valuation, $188,606.

COLUMBIA, situated towards the southwestern part of Washington county, is a very large town, comprising between forty and fifty thousand acres, and was settled soon after the Revolutionary war. It was incorporated February 8, 1796; and is watered by Pleasant river. upon which there are two grist-mills, several saw-mills, and two tanneries. Lumbering has been the leading business; but now the inhabitants are beginning to devote a portion of their attention to the cultivation of the soil. The town has one village, three churches, (Methodist, Congregational, and Baptist,) nine school districts, with fourteen schools; and one post-office. Population, 1,140; valuation, $169,931.

CONCORD, Somerset county, is situated on the west side of Kennebec river, opposite the town of Bingham, and is twenty-five miles from Norridgewock. The history of this town is as yet undeveloped. Its boundaries are extensive, but the soil is not of the best kind, and in fact few advantages are offered for the encouragement of the settler. It was incorporated in 1821; has one church edifice (Free-will Baptist), twelve school districts, with fourteen schools; and one post-office. Population, 550; valuation, $30,376.

COOPER is an unimportant town in the eastern part of Washington county, and is but partially cleared of its original forests. Settlements were commenced here during the war of 1812, and in 1822 it became incorporated. There are two or three swells of land that by proper cultivation would make tolerably good farms. It has no elements of thrift, nor any apparent guaranty for any thing beyond its present condition. A small church was organized by the Congregationalists in 1826, and one by the Baptists in 1828. There are six school districts, with eleven schools; and one post-office. Population, 562; valuation, $36,332.

Corinna is situated in the western part of Penobscot county, twenty-five miles from the city of Bangor. The original proprietor was Dr. John Warren of Boston, to whom the land was sold, by the Commonwealth of Massachusetts, June 30, 1804. In December, 1816, it became an incorporated town. The surface is generally level, the soil yielding good average crops. Corinna is watered by a stream, which flows through the central part of the town, falling into Newport pond. On this stream there are four saw-mills and one grist-mill, a carding machine, and clothing mill. The town contains three churches (Methodist, Congregationalist, and Free-will Baptist), fourteen school districts, an academy, and three post-offices — Corinna, Corinna Centre, and West Corinna. Population, 1,550; valuation, $165,292.

Corinth, situated in the central part of the southern division of Penobscot county, contains an area of 23,040 acres. The town was granted by the State of Massachusetts, to a man by the name of John Peck, December 9, 1794, and its settlement was commenced a few years after. When it had received a sufficient number of inhabitants it was organized into a plantation, with the name of Ohio; and, on the 21st of June, 1811, became an incorporated town, with its present name. The surface is quite level. The inhabitants are nearly all farmers, and their fields, buildings, and surroundings generally, indicate that they are in prosperous circumstances. East Corinth is the principal village, and stretches along for some two miles upon a level street. The principal mechanical operations here are carriage and sleigh making. There are five shops devoted to these pursuits, which manufacture from $15,000 to $20,000 worth annually, — thus proving that there are other sources of wealth in Maine besides the lumber business and mill privileges.

There are three handsome church edifices, which are generally well filled; likewise an academy, which is in a flourishing condition, having had, in the winter of 1856–7, seventy students. During the fall and spring terms, however, there is a much larger attendance. There are fifteen school districts, with thirty-one schools, and three post-offices — Corinth, East Corinth, and South Corinth. Population, 1,600; valuation, $199,964.

Cornish is a small town in the northern part of York county, and is a part of the original tract of land, purchased in 1660, of Captain Sunday, an Indian sagamore, by Francis Small. Settlements were not commenced here till 1776, when a few families moved into the southern part of the town, and called it Francisburgh or Francistown, from the Christian name of the proprietor. It was incorporated February 27, 1794, and contains twelve thousand acres. It received its name, it is said, on account of the large crops of corn produced in the town. This may or may not be the case; but one thing is certain, the soil is very productive, not only in corn, but in other kinds of grain. It is watered by the Saco river, which forms the northern boundary of the town. There are two church edifices (Methodist and Congregational), twelve school districts, with the same number of schools; and one post-office. Population, 1,144; valuation, $198,622.

CORNVILLE, Somerset county, is situated on what was originally the north line of the Plymouth patent; and, being without the jurisdiction of that company, was sold by the Commonwealth of Massachusetts to Moses Bernard and others, receiving the name of Bernardstown. The first efforts at clearing up the forests were made about the year 1790; but no families settled here until 1794. The town was incorporated February 24, 1798, when the name was changed to the one it now bears. At this time, a strip of land, one mile and a half in width, was taken from the Plymouth patent and annexed to this town, increasing its area to 29,440 acres. Cornville has a good soil for tillage, and, like Cornish, although quite remote from it, is said to have received its name on account of the large crops of Indian corn produced within its limits. The town is watered by the Wesserunset stream, a branch of the Kennebec. There are two churches in town — Congregational and Free-will Baptist; twelve school districts, and one post-office. Population, 1,260; valuation, $219,526.

CRANBERRY ISLES, Hancock county, including the islands called Great Cranberry, Little Cranberry, Sutton's, and Baker's islands, are situated from three to six miles off the main land at Mount Desert, of which they originally formed a part; and thirty-five miles from Ellsworth. They were incorporated as a separate town March 16, 1830, and their history must be chiefly sought in connection with that of the parent town.

The agricultural features of these islands need not form any subject for remark, as the character of the soil certainly constitutes no exception to that covering most of the outer islands on the coast. The occupations of the inhabitants, as well as the substantial arrangements of their tables, are furnished from the mute briny world.

There are six school districts, and one post-office. Population, 203; valuation, $38,659.

CRAWFORD, Washington county, is distant thirty-five miles from Machias, and, until its incorporation in 1828, was known by the name of Adams. It is watered by two large ponds, which cover nearly one fourth of the entire area of the town. Crawford has little to recommend it to the agriculturist, and may be ranked among the poor towns of the state.

It has two school districts, with the same number of schools; and one post-office. Population, 324; valuation, $20,994.

CUMBERLAND, Cumberland county, is situated on Casco bay, six miles from Portland. Gray lies partly upon its north and west; Windham touches it upon the west; Falmouth makes its southern boundary, and upon the east and north lie the bay, Yarmouth, and North Yarmouth. Its history belongs to the town of North Yarmouth, of which it formed a part, until 1821, when it was incorporated as a separate town. The surface is level, and back from the sea-shore there is some very good farming land. The Grand Trunk Railway and the Kennebec and Portland Railroad pass through the eastern part. Cumberland contains two church edifices (Congregational and Methodist); eleven school districts, with eighteen schools; and three post-offices — Cumberland, Cumberland Centre, and West Cumberland. Population, 1,656; valuation, $326,815.

CUMBERLAND COUNTY, situated on Casco bay, was organized in 1760, by the same act that defined the boundaries of York county (which had previously been coextensive with the province of Maine), and established Lincoln county upon the east. The line running between Cumberland and York was the same as at present, — on the easterly sides of Saco, Buxton, Limington, and Cornish, as far as to Oxford county. It then turned and ran north two degrees west to the north limits of the province. The northeasterly line of this county was then, as now, the Androscoggin river, up as far as the county of that name. Thence it ran in the same course with the westerly line, north two degrees west to Canada; — so that the territory of Cumberland then covered, besides its present limits, the counties of Androscoggin and Franklin, and parts of Oxford, Kennebec, and Somerset, as now organized; also all the islands in Casco bay. Falmouth was made and continued the shire town, until the incorporation of Portland from it in 1786, since which the latter has been the county seat. Cumberland has now twenty-five towns.

The United States circuit court for the district of Maine holds its terms at Portland, commencing on the 23d days of April and September; and the United States district court holds two of its terms here, commencing on the first Tuesdays of February and December.

The law term of the supreme judicial court for the western district commences on the second Tuesday in July. The jury terms of this court, for *civil* business, commence on the third Tuesdays of January and April, and the second Tuesday of October: — for *criminal* business, on the first Tuesday of March, and the last Tuesdays of July and November. Population of the county, 68,842; valuation, $16,777,054.

CUSHING, Lincoln county, is a seaboard town, situated on the west bank of St. George's river, opposite to the town of St. George, which composed a part of its territory until 1803: St. George was the plantation name of the two towns, and they both formed a part of the Waldo patent. They were settled by emigrants from Ireland, brought here in 1733 under the auspices of General Waldo. In the year 1753, a very strong stone fortress was built in this town, which was garrisoned by a company of provincial troops under the command of Major Burton. Cushing was incorporated January 28, 1789, and now contains 8,600 acres. The surface is very rocky, and presents but a poor field for the operations of the farmer. The town contains two religious societies, each having a house of worship (Baptist and Union); six school districts, with the same number of schools; and one post-office. Population, 807; valuation, $90,688.

CUTLER, Washington county, is situated on the sea-coast, thirty-five miles east of Machias. The original settlers of the town were Ephraim Andrews, John Davis, Robert Cates, and John Maker, who came from the town of Machias and settled here about the year 1785, depending, at that time, for a subsistence, on farming and fishing. In 1812, the plantation contained thirty families. In the war with Great Britain (1813), an American cutter lying in the harbor was captured by the crew of a British armed vessel, and some of the inhabitants were plundered; not, however, without some resistance on their part. The settlers obtained the titles to their lands from John C. Jones, and after his death, from Joseph Cutler, of Newburyport, in honor of whom the town was named.

Cutler was incorporated in 1817. The surface is broken by hills and ledges of rock, between which are some valuable meadows, producing grass of a good quality. The scenery is very delightful, and from an elevation of land called the "Look-out," a fine view is gained of the Bay of Fundy, with its countless sails moving to and fro. The town is watered by Little river. Cutler harbor is one of the best in the state, being protected from storms by high land on each side, and by an island at the mouth, on which the government has erected a light-house:

it is also of sufficient depth for vessels of the largest size to ride at anchor, and, being always free from ice, is accessible at every season of the year. The facilities for ship-building are great, though but few vessels have been built here, — two ships and eight or ten schooners being the extent of the business in this line. The *California*, a packet-ship of seven hundred tons, and a small schooner of thirty tons, launched in the spring of 1857, are among the number.

The lumber business is carried on to some extent, there being an incorporated company, known by the name of the Cutler Mill-dam Company, and several private individuals, engaged in the trade. This company have erected a new mill at Schooner brook, comprising one saw for long lumber, two shingle machines, one lath machine, and a box machine. There is another mill at the head of Little Machias bay. In 1835, a wealthy company from England purchased a piece of land in this town, called the Eastern Head, and commenced opening a mine, out of which they succeeded in extracting some valuable ore, including some copper and gold; but the enterprise has since been abandoned.

There is but one meeting-house in town, which is occupied alternately by the Methodists and Baptists. Cutler is divided into seven school districts, with ten schools, and has two post-offices — Cutler and North Cutler. Population, 820; valuation for 1857, $71,000.

DAMARISCOTTA, Lincoln county, is situated on the eastern bank of Damariscotta river, opposite the town of Newcastle, and its ship-building interests have ever been large. It originally formed a part of the Pemaquid Patent, and was settled about 1640, by men who left Pemaquid in search of new and easier fields of enterprise. The land titles were involved in all those controversies and vexatious lawsuits, with which the Pemaquid Patent was harassed. During the Indian wars, the settlers tasted the bitterness of warfare with the savages, having been frequently driven off or massacred by them. Damariscotta was more properly an outpost of Pemaquid, rather than a central point, exercising a controlling influence on the surrounding settlements.

On the incorporation of Nobleboro', the territory of Damariscotta was included in, and formed a part of, that town; but, in 1849, in compliance with the wish of its inhabitants, it was created a distinct municipality. The surface is uneven, and the land moderately productive. A village has sprung up on the banks of the river, and frequently, in the seasons of lumbering and ship-building, which are the principal occupations, presents quite a lively aspect.

Damariscotta has two public-houses, seven ship-builders, two caulkers and gravers, three sail-makers, five pail factories, three carriage-builders, one grist-mill, and two tanneries; it has also three churches — Baptist, Methodist, and Universalist; six school districts, with seven schools; one bank, with a capital of $50,000; and one post-office — called Newcastle. Population, 1,328; valuation, $377,242.

DANVILLE, Androscoggin county, is situated on the south side of Androscoggin river, opposite Lewiston, and was originally a part of the Pejepscot Purchase. The settlement of the town was commenced in 1764, and it was incorporated March 6, 1802, under the name of Pejepscot, which was retained until February 1, 1819, when it was changed by act of the legislature.

The surface of Danville is generally even and tolerably productive, and it is watered by the Androscoggin river. The Grand Trunk Railway passes through one corner of Danville, and forms a junction with the Androscoggin and Kennebec Railroad. The town contains two public-houses, three saw-mills, two shingle machines, one grist-mill, one tannery, one pail factory, one carriage factory, and one marble-worker: also three church edifices (Free-will Baptist, Methodist, and Universalist), eleven school districts, with eight schools, and two post-offices — Danville and West Danville. Population, 1,636; valuation, $392,715.

DAYTON, York county, on the west side of Saco river, which divides it from Saco and Buxton, was set off from Hollis in 1854. It was first settled about 1753, by John and Andrew Gordon, of Biddeford, who were driven off by the Indians, but afterward returned. Some articles of pewter ware have been ploughed up within a few years, supposed to have been buried by them before being driven off. Andrew was killed, by the fall of a tree, in 1804. *The Landing*, originally called Russell lot, was settled about 1760, by John and Edward Smith. John Smith of Biddeford settled near the block-house about 1762, was lieutenant under General Pepperrell in the expedition against Louisburg, and served also in the Revolutionary war. Zebulon Gordon, the first plantation clerk, settled in 1772. Quite a number settled about 1787; others about 1800. Rev. Simon Lock came from Barrington, N. H., in 1792, settled in the south part of the town, and was soon installed pastor of the Baptist church in Lyman, continuing such till his death, September 6, 1831. His widow died November 2, 1851, aged 102 years, ten months, and nineteen days. Jesse Lock, a son, still lives in this town. He represented Hollis in the Massachusetts legislature from 1812 to 1816.

A block-house for holding goods and trading with the Indians, built

9 *

in 1729, about eighty rods below the falls, was garrisoned with ten or fifteen men until 1759, when the cannon were transferred to Castle William, in Boston harbor.[1] The early settlers of this and adjoining towns used this as a place of refuge from the Indians in times of alarm and danger. Dayton furnished seven men for the struggles of the Revolution, one of whom (Jacob Rhoades) is still living here, and draws a pension.

The surface of the town is undulating, without any high hills. It is interspersed with small streams, and abounds in springs of pure water. The Boiling Spring, so called, is quite a curiosity. It is two or three rods in diameter and seven or eight feet deep, bottomed on quicksand. The water is very clear, and boils up sometimes in one part, sometimes in another, changing fantastically from place to place every few minutes. The soil is well adapted to grazing, to the growth of English grasses, Indian corn, and other grains, and to fruit-trees. English hay, oats, potatoes, apples, as well as neat-stock and the products of the dairy, are sent to market. Before the Revolution, the inhabitants depended mostly on lumber, which they bartered for corn.

There was considerable activity in business here until within twenty years. The valley of the Saco furnished valuable timber, much of which was manufactured into lumber and rafted to Saco market, or hauled to Portland. Previous to the war of 1812, some four or five stores were supported at Little Falls landing, about a mile above the Biddeford line. At Union Falls is a valuable water-power. In 1807 or 1808, a dam and four or five saw-mills were built on the Dayton side, and were operated until 1837, when they were swept away by a freshet, and have never been rebuilt, — since which the village has gone backward. The privilege is apparently to become valuable again, having been purchased by the Saco and Biddeford Water-Power Company, which in 1856 commenced the erection of a stone dam, that will cost from $15,000 to $20,000.

There are, however, in the town two saw-mills, two grist-mills, one shingle machine, one carding machine, and one edge-tool manufactory.

There is not a church within the present limits of the place, the Hollis meeting-house being just over the line. Dayton has seven school districts, with five schools. Population in 1854, 819; valuation, $119,000.

DEBLOIS, in the western part of Washington county, originally comprised a portion of Bingham's "South Million-acre Purchase," and for many years was held in trust under Bingham's will, — Colonel

[1] Folsom's Hist. Biddeford, p. 222, 248.

Black, of Ellsworth, acting as agent for the trustees. Colonel Black sold this deed to William W. Woodbury and Daniel C. Emery, the stipulations of the sale being that the deed should be delivered on the payment of the purchase-money. While it was held in this form, Woodbury and Emery conveyed their interest to the City Bank of Portland, which corporation was already a tenant in common of thirty-three sixty-fourths of said tract, as also of other townships adjoining Beddington, being the ungranted lands of Cherryfield, and half of township No. 22, in Hancock county. The City Bank paid the balance of the purchase-money due by Woodbury and Emery, and therefore became proprietors of the land, which they subsequently disposed of to William Freeman, Jr., of Cherryfield. The town was incorporated in 1850, and received its name in honor of Thomas Amory Deblois, late president of the City Bank of Portland. It has one school district, with one school; and one post-office. Population, 126; valuation — no return.

Dedham is situated in the northwesterly part of Hancock county. The first settlement was made by Nathan Phillips, about the year 1810. It was incorporated as a town, in 1837, under its present name, at the suggestion of Reuben Gregg, who had formerly lived in Dedham, Mass.

The surface of Dedham presents nothing but rocks piled on rocks immensely high, with yawning gulfs between. There are ten mountain peaks in the town, and about the same number of ponds. The waters, with the exception of those of Fitz pond, all find their outlet in Union river. Fitz pond has two outlets, one in Union river, the other in Eastern river. How the inhabitants can obtain a living in Dedham, it is difficult to conceive. They are at least entitled to great credit for the roads they have built over this sterile country.

There is but one village in Dedham, located in the western part of the town, which contains the only post-office. The tanning business and lumbering are carried on to some extent; and a flour and grist mill has just been completed. There is one church edifice, occupied by the Baptists. The town is divided into six school districts, with ten schools. Population, 516; valuation, \$55,094.

Deer Isle, Hancock county, comprises in its municipality three islands on the eastern side of Penobscot bay, called Great Deer Isle, Little Deer Isle, and Isle Au Haut. Little Deer Isle, the most northerly of the group, has an area of one thousand acres, which is well suited for agriculture, and supports a considerable number of inhabitants. Great

Deer Isle is about ten miles in length from north to south, and near five miles in width, the northern part being tolerably level, while the south is rough. Isle Au Haut is estimated to contain about 3,500 acres; has generally a bold shore, and possesses one or two good harbors. The combined territory of these three islands amounts to 14,320 acres.

This town receives about one twelfth part of all the fishing bounty paid by the United States. The inhabitants in the south part are almost exclusively engaged in fishing, while those in the northern part are employed in the coasting trade. Deer Isle contains four churches, Methodist, Baptist, and two Congregational; an academy; thirty school districts, with an aggregate of 1,480 pupils; one fulling-mill, three grist-mills, two saw-mills, one brickmaker, one sash and blind factory, one shingle machine, one tannery, three ship-builders, and four post-offices — Deer Isle, South Deer Isle, Green's Landing, and Oceanville. Population, 3,037; valuation, $227,042.

DENMARK is situated in the southern part of Oxford county, and joins Fryeburg on the southeast. It was formed from a grant made by Massachusetts to the Fryeburg Academy, and two other grants made by that state to private individuals, together with a strip from the town of Brownfield. Denmark was settled in 1788–89. Among the original settlers were Ezra Stiles, David Porter, Nathaniel Symonds, Thomas Bragdon, Nathaniel McIntire, Ephraim Jewett, William Davis, Parson and Thomas Pingree, Elias Berry, and Cyrus Ingalls, several of whom came from Andover, Mass. The territory comprising this town was included in the tract formerly known under the Indian name of Pequawket.

Denmark was incorporated February 20, 1807. Its surface is hilly and very stony. The principal mountain is known by the name of Pleasant mountain, and is rather peculiar in appearance, being about eight or ten miles in circumference at its base, and two thousand feet above the level of the sea, while it is entirely unconnected with any other elevation of land. A dwelling-house has been erected on its summit, which is very much frequented by pleasure-seekers during the warm summer months, and the view from its towering height is said to be not inferior to that from the summit of Mount Washington. The Saco river bounds Denmark partly on the west. There are in town Beaver, Granger, and Moose brooks, and some streams of less note. Moose brook issues from the pond of the same name, and is the largest stream here, having at its head a most excellent water-power, made serviceable in propelling the machinery contained in a grist-mill, two saw-mills, a cloth-dressing mill, a carriage factory, a shingle and planing machine, and a cabinet shop. At this spot is centred the principal part of the population of Denmark.

The lumber business was formerly considerable; but now agricultural pursuits occupy the attention of the inhabitants. Fruit is raised to some extent, and stock-raising is moderately carried on. There are two church edifices here — Congregational and Universalist; fourteen school districts, with the same number of schools; and one post-office. Population, 1,203; valuation for 1857, $184,749.

DENNYSVILLE is situated in the eastern part of Washington county, about seventeen miles west from Eastport. The original settlers were mostly from Hingham, Mass.; and among them were Theodore Lincoln, Theophilus Wilder, William Kilby, and Solomon Cushing. The first settlement was made in 1786. The proprietors of this township (which for many years included the territory of Pembroke, and also that of Perry, adjoining), were Thomas Russell, Benjamin Lincoln, and John Lowell, who purchased it from the state of Massachusetts; and from them the settlers obtained the titles to their lands. Dennysville was incorporated in 1818, taking its name from the river which bordered it, called, at the time of its settlement, Denny's river, from an Indian called "Denny," who had his hunting-ground in this neighborhood.

The surface, like that in most of the towns on the seaboard in Maine, is broken and hilly. There are no lakes, ponds, or considerable streams. The manufacture of lumber — boards, shingles, and laths — is the principal occupation of the inhabitants. There is also a factory for the making of pails, tubs, and churns, and a tannery. In agriculture, little is done beyond raising hay and stock. Dennysville has one church, occupied by the Congregationalists; two school districts, with four schools; and one post-office. Population, 458; valuation, $99,853.

DETROIT, situated in the southeast corner of Somerset county, thirty-nine miles from Augusta, was incorporated in 1838, under the name of Chandlerville, which it retained till it received its present name, in 1841. It is watered by the two branches of the Sebasticook, which unite here. The Penobscot and Kennebec Railroad passes centrally through the town. Detroit has one saw-mill, one shingle machine, and two tanneries; five school districts, with eight schools; and one post-office. Population, 517; valuation, $50,685.

DEXTER, Penobscot county, is the most northwesterly town in the county. It is built on the height of land between the Kennebec and Penobscot rivers, fifty-eight miles northeast from Augusta, and thirty miles northwest from Bangor. The township was surveyed in 1792; but no settlement was attempted until 1801, when David Smith commenced the enterprise.

The first family which moved to the town was that of Ebenezer Small, of Gilmanton, N. H. A large delegation from other parts of New Hampshire followed, among whom were Joseph Tucker, Seba French, William Mitchell, Simeon and John Safford, the Shepleys, the Smiths, and the Maxwells. Besides these, several families from the western part of the state emigrated here. In 1803, the boundaries of the town were established (a plan of which was drawn by Simeon Safford), and it was partitioned into lots, and disposed of to settlers. The town was incorporated in 1816, and received its present name, in honor of Hon. Samuel Dexter. The post-office was established in 1818, the

Dexter.

mail from Bangor to Skowhegan being carried once a week, on horseback, by Daniel Hayden. The first meeting-house (Universalist) was erected in 1829.

Dexter is a fine specimen of a New England town, abounding in hills, vales, and ponds, and is regarded as among the best farming towns in the county, though it is more generally known for its excellent water-power, and the general thrift and enterprise of its inhabitants. The village lies at the outlet of a beautiful pond of about one thousand acres, fed entirely by springs, furnishing a safe and unfailing water-power, never affected by freshets or drought. The fall in this pond is 150 feet in three quarters of a mile,—there being nine improved privileges within this distance, turning sixteen large wheels, which propel a great variety of machinery.

There are twenty stores in town; also, five factories, employing 225 hands, by the aid of which there are annually thrown into the market 820,000 yards of flannel, 15,000 pairs of blankets, and 30,000 yards of cassimeres and tweeds, consuming in their manufacture 420,000 pounds of wool. The cost for labor is $50,000 per annum; and for stock, $250,000. Besides the above, there are also in active operation a tannery, which cures annually ten thousand hides; a machine shop; and an establishment largely engaged in the manufacture of orange and lemon boxes, which are made by a new and peculiar process, capable of turning out thirty thousand per annum. The manufacture of cabinet furniture, sashes, blinds, and doors, is also carried on extensively. A grist-mill was erected in 1854, with five sets of stones, to which, during the drought of that year, grain was brought a distance of forty miles; a fact which attests both the value of the privilege and the excellence of the mill. Besides the mechanical establishments already enumerated, there are five shingle machines, one brick-yard, one carding machine, two pail factories, and six saw-mills.

The already large and still increasing business of this inland town demands better facilities for transportation, and a railroad is contemplated to Newport, a distance of thirteen miles, to intersect with the railroad from Bangor to Augusta and Portland. A charter has been granted, surveys made, and the road will doubtless be completed at an early day.

A violent tornado passed over this town in 1848, by which the largest trees were torn up by the roots, and the strongest buildings completely crushed.

There are two printing-offices in Dexter; and ten school districts, each having excellent school-houses; and here the remark may be made, that, in any state, the character of the school-houses furnishes a very correct rule by which to judge of the character of the inhabitants of a town. Where comfortable, well-arranged school-houses are found, there also dwell industrious, thrifty, intelligent, and virtuous communities. There are eighteen schools, with nine hundred pupils, and a school fund yielding $2,000 annually: and four churches — Universalist, Baptist, Methodist, and Congregational. Population, 1,948; valuation, $267,561.

DIXFIELD, Oxford county, is situated on the north side of the Androscoggin river, opposite the town of Peru, and was granted by Massachusetts to Jonathan Holman and others. Ezra Newton, with his wife and her sister, spent the winter of 1793 in this town, and left upon return of spring. They are supposed to have been the first persons who made any habitation here. John Marble came with a yoke of oxen in the spring of 1793; but no permanent settlement was made until 1795, when John Marble, Gardner Brown, Amos Trask, Levi Newton, David Torrey, and John Gould came, accompanied by their families. The settlers obtained the titles to their lands from Dr. Elijah Dix.

The town was incorporated June 21, 1803. The surface is broken: the principal elevations being Large and Small Sugar-loaf, and Aunt Hipsy's mountains. It is drained by the Androscoggin river; and contains no lakes or ponds of note. Agriculture is carried on quite extensively, and the principal articles of manufacture are woollen goods. There are two shingle machines, one saw-mill, one grist-mill, and one carding machine; also, three church edifices — one of which is occupied by the Universalists, the other by the Congregationalists and Methodists, and the third by different denominations; eleven school districts, and two villages, — Dixfield and East Dixfield, — each of which has a post-office. Population, 1,180; valuation, $153,729.

DIXMONT is the southwest corner town of Penobscot county, and was known in the original survey as No. 3, range one, north of the Waldo patent. It was first granted by the state of Massachusetts to Bowdoin College, from the trustees of which, John J. Blaisdell of Parsonsfield purchased three thousand acres, at one dollar per acre; but, failing to make the payment at the stipulated time, the purchase reverted to the trustees of the college, from whom the settlers on this tract obtained the titles to their lands. The remainder of the township, 20,040 acres, was purchased by Dr. Elijah Dix,[1] of Boston, July 12, 1801, for the consideration of $21,431, and from him, and the mountain in the southerly part, the town takes its name.

The first permanent settlers were Friend Drake, Elihu Alden, John Bassford, Benjamin Brown, and nine others. The town was incorporated in 1807, during which year a malignant fever broke out, of which many of the settlers died, — retarding for a time the progress of the settlement. During the last war with England, some of the inhabitants were drafted into the army, and others volunteered. None were killed, however; but several received severe wounds, among whom was Charles Peabody, now living, who was struck in the ankle by a cannon ball, making amputation of the leg necessary.

The surface is uneven and broken; but most of the soil is fit for cul-

[1] Dr. Dix never had a permanent residence in town, but made occasional visits for the purpose of business. He died here, while on a visit, May, 1809, and was interred in the burial-ground near Dixmont Corner.

tivation. The two highest elevations are known as Peaked and Harris mountains, the former lying in the easterly part of the town, and the latter in the southerly part. The altitude of Harris mountain is 1,160 feet above the level of the sea, and on its summit is an observatory, erected by the superintendent of the United States coast survey (Professor Bache) in 1854. Butman's pond is the only natural one in Dixmont, and covers an area of about forty acres. Butman's stream, the outlet of this pond, falls into a pond in Plymouth. Martin's stream flows through the northwest part of the town.

Dixmont contains four small villages — Dixmont Corner, North Dixmont, East Dixmont, and Dixmont Centre; three houses for public worship, occupied by the several religious denominations; twelve school districts, with twenty-one schools; three saw-mills, three shingle machines, two flour and grist-mills, one brickmaker, one edge-tool maker, one pail-maker, and one tannery; as also four post-offices — one at each of the villages. Population, 1,605; valuation, $209,621.

Dover is situated at the extreme southern part of Piscataquis county. The settlement was commenced in 1801, by Eli Towne from Pepperell, Mass., who moved his family here in June, 1802. During the following eight years, Abel Blood and Nathaniel Chamberlain from Charlton, Mass., Eleazer, Seth, and John Spaulding, and Job Parsons from Norridgewock, William Huston from Anson, William Mitchell and Joel Doore from Athens, James Rowe from Waterville, and Paul Lambert from Winthrop, all in this state, came here and settled with their families. The titles to the land were derived from the Vaughan family, who came over from England, and purchased the township of the state of Massachusetts. It was organized into a plantation in 1816, and incorporated as a town in 1822.

The surface is generally uneven, but not hilly. There are no mountains, lakes, or ponds. The Piscataquis river forms the northern boundary, upon which the only village is situated, which is connected by a bridge with the neighboring village and town of Foxcroft; thus presenting to the eye of a stranger but one village, both of which, for beauty and neatness, are surpassed by very few in the state.

There are five church edifices in town, (two Baptist, one Free-will Baptist, one Universalist, and one Methodist). The pulpits of all these are usually supplied, and the congregations respectable in numbers. It may be remarked in this connection, that the Congregational church stands in the village of Foxcroft; but a large portion of the members of the church and parish reside in Dover. There are five post-offices — Dover, East Dover, South Dover, West Dover, and Dover South Mills.

Most of the people are engaged in agriculture. There are four saw-mills, and machines for making shingles and clapboards; one flour-mill, two tanneries, two carriage manufactories, one woollen factory, in successful operation; and the usual number of mechanical trades. The Piscataquis Observer is printed here. There are seventeen school districts, with eighteen public schools. Dover is the shire town of the county, and contains at the present time a population of about 2,500; valuation, $405,000.

Dresden, situated in the western part of Lincoln county, on the eastern bank of Kennebec river, formerly embraced the present towns of Alna, Wiscasset, and Perkins. The territory comprised in Dresden, Alna, and Wiscasset, was sold by the Indians to Christopher Lawson, on the 10th of October, 1649, and Lawson sold the same to Messrs. Lake and Clark. Lake resided on his purchase till he was killed by the Indians. It was afterwards owned by Sir Biby Lake, Edward Hutchinson, and others. A fort was erected in this town in 1754, about a mile above the northern end of Swan island, now the town of Perkins, and called Fort Shirley, in compliment to Governor Shirley, the then governor of the province of Massachusetts. Major Samuel Goodwin commanded Fort Shirley till it was dismantled. Pownalborough was incorporated February 13, 1760, receiving its name from Governor Pownal, who succeeded Governor Shirley. It was the shire town of the county of Lincoln for thirty-four years.

Dresden was settled about 1750. Three brothers, William, Charles, and Rowland Cushing, took up their residence here in 1760, and were distinguished men in the service of the county. The town was incorporated June 25, 1794, from what was termed the west precinct of Pownalborough, and took the name of Dresden, from a town of that name in Germany, whence some of the inhabitants had emigrated under the auspices of General Waldo. Major John Polereczky, a Frenchman, and a distinguished soldier in the American army under General Rochambeau, took up his residence in this town after the close of the war, and was for fifteen years town clerk.

The surface is mostly even, and is watered by Eastern river and the Kennebec. Dresden has two villages; three church edifices — Congregational, Episcopal, and Methodist; nine school districts; three post-offices — Dresden, Dresden Mills, and South Dresden: also two saw-mills, two grist-mills, three tanneries, and one brickyard. Population, 1,419; valuation, $270,613.

Durham is situated in the southern part of Androscoggin county, on the south side of the Androscoggin river, and contains an area of about seventeen thousand acres. This town originally formed a part of the Pejepscot Purchase, of which Colonel Royall of Medford, Mass., was a large proprietor, and from him it was called Royallston, until its incorporation February 17, 1789. William Gerrish was the first settler. This town is connected with that of Lisbon by a bridge crossing the Androscoggin. The land is suitable for agriculture, in which the inhabitants are principally engaged.

Durham contains three villages, known as Southwest Bend, West Durham, and South Durham, at each of which there is a post-office; six church edifices — Methodist, Congregationalist, Free-will Baptist, Universalist, Quaker, and Union; seventeen school districts, with thirty-three schools; three grist-mills, two saw-mills, three shingle mills, three clapboard mills, six blacksmith's shops, thirty shoe shops, and five stores. Population, 1,886; valuation, $376,358.

EASTBROOK, Hancock county, is situated about twenty miles north-east from Ellsworth, and not quite so far from the head of tide-water in Taunton bay. It is a six-mile-square township; was incorporated in 1836; has two ponds of considerable size, and is also watered by a branch of Union river. It has two saw-mills, and three school districts, with eighty-two children between the ages of four and twenty-one years, thirty-seven of whom are said to attend school. Population, 212; valuation, $32,811.

EAST LIVERMORE, Androscoggin county, is situated on the east side of the Androscoggin river. The first settlement, in what is now called East Livermore, was made in the year 1786, by Abram Weston, formerly of Lincoln, Mass. Other settlers came in soon after, among whom were Elisha Smith, Thomas Dascom, and Elijah Mills. Elijah Livermore, from whom the town took its name, and Colonel Fuller, were the proprietors of the soil, and from them the first settlers obtained their titles. The Indian name of the township was "Rockomeca," signifying "great corn land."

East Livermore was incorporated in 1843, having been set off from Livermore, of which it was formerly the part lying east of the Androscoggin river. The southwesterly part of the town is generally level, and the soil sandy; but the northeasterly part is more uneven, with quite prominent hills, and many southern slopes, which render it excellent for farming purposes. East Livermore has become somewhat celebrated for the raising of fine breeds of cattle; in fact, the town for several years has received the first premiums at the fairs for its splendid teams, which are of the Durham breed. Moose hill is situated in the extreme northeast corner, and overlooks the whole town: southerly, and at its foot, is a small pond, bearing the same name. An interval, some half a mile in width, situated on the western side of the town, on the river, extends nearly its whole length.

East Livermore has but one village, situated in the extreme northwest corner, at the falls of the Androscoggin river, and known by the name of Rockomeca Falls. This village has some six or eight stores and shops, a public-house (known by the name of the Rockomeca house), a shingle mill, a saw-mill, a grist-mill, a carriage factory, and a shoe manufactory, employing some fifty hands. The fall of water on the Androscoggin river at this village, is some fifty feet to the half mile. The water-power is surpassed at very few places in New England; and from the location of the village, being the terminus, at present, of the Androscoggin Railroad, it bids fair some day to be a large manufacturing place. The inhabitants are mostly engaged in agricultural pursuits, the chief products being wheat, corn, potatoes, and apples in abundance.

There are four church edifices in town — Baptist, Free-will Baptist, Methodist, and Universalist; eight school districts, with eight schools; and three post-offices — Livermore Falls, East Livermore, and Strickland's Ferry. Population, 891; valuation, $200,000.

East Machias, Washington county, situated on both sides of East Machias river, was set off from Machias and incorporated in 1836. It is watered by the above-mentioned river, which receives the waters of a large pond from the east, and then falls into Machias river and bay at the southern extremity of the town. These afford water-power sufficient to drive sixteen saw-mills, six shingle mills, and several lath mills. East Machias is a flourishing little town, and does annually considerable business in lumbering and ship-building. There are three churches — Baptist, Congregational and Methodist; two school districts, and fifteen schools; one of the best academies in the state; and one post-office. There are also three grist-mills, one tannery, six ship-builders, three pail-makers, three edge-tool makers, and one carriage maker. Population, 1,905; valuation, $313,894.

Eastport, Washington county, is an island situated in Passamaquoddy bay, and is about five miles long, and nearly two miles in its greatest width. It originally included within its limits a few islands lying contiguous to it, as also the present town of Lubec. Settlements were commenced here in 1780; but in consequence of the dispute between

England and the United States regarding the boundary line, it had but a slow growth; after the settlement of the disputed question, however, it increased much more rapidly. Until its incorporation, February 24, 1798, it was known as Moose Island, which was then changed to the name it now bears, in consequence of its being the most eastern port in the United States.

During the last war with England, to prevent the town from being captured by the English, two companies of militia were detached from the brigade of General Blake, then stationed upon the Penobscot river, and quartered here, under the command of Major Philip Ulmer. These troops were relieved within a year, by companies belonging to the regular army, under command of Colonel George Ulmer, who, in his efforts to prevent smuggling and illicit intercourse with the enemy, having given offence to some of the inhabitants, was dismissed from the command, and Major Perley Putnam, of Salem, appointed in his place. On the 5th of July, 1814, a small British expedition was secretly despatched from Halifax, which was joined by a fleet from Bermuda, the whole consisting of the *Ramillies,* a seventy-four gun ship, having on board Commodore Sir Thomas Hardy; the *Martin*, sloop of war; the brig *Boxer;* the *Bream;* the *Terror*, a bomb ship; and several transports, carrying a large body of troops, commanded by Colonel Thomas Pilkington. This expedition arrived in front of Eastport on the 11th of July, when the commodore demanded a surrender of Fort Sullivan, allowing only five minutes for an answer. Major Putnam, at first, refused; but, through the importunate persuasions of the inhabitants, he at length reluctantly struck his flag,— the terms of capitulation being that all the public property should become the prize of the British; but the private rights and interests of the inhabitants were to be respected. Forthwith upwards of one thousand men, and a battalion of artillery, with women and children, were set on shore from the shipping by means of barges; fifty or sixty pieces of cannon were landed; possession was taken of the fort, and the British flag immediately hoisted. The captors then seized upon the custom-house property, and took $9,000 in unfinished treasury notes, which they by the boldest threats and artifices endeavored to make the collector sign; but he absolutely refused, declaring that "death would be no compulsion." Prizes were made of several vessels; large quantities of goods were seized for breach of blockade; and all property belonging to other persons than the inhabitants of Eastport was declared forfeited.

After a while a trade was opened by the British, which was too strong a temptation for the citizens of Maine to resist; and, though the general government used every effort to prevent smuggling, they were

10*

unable wholly to suppress it. The British officers having declared that they had no design to carry on offensive operations, this expedition being only for the purpose of obtaining possession of the islands in Passamaquoddy bay, about two thirds of the islanders reluctantly submitted to the requirement of taking the oath of allegiance, while the other third left the place to seek some spot where the "powers that be" were more in accordance with their opinions. The enemy then declared that they had possession of what was their due by the treaty of 1783, and immediately proceeded to erect batteries, upon which they mounted the cannon they had landed. Having appointed a deputy collector of customs, the commodore with his squadron departed, leaving upon the island eight hundred troops, who remained here for three years after the conclusion of peace, under the plea that the island was included in the original limits of New Brunswick.

In 1839, the principal part of the business portion of the place was destroyed by fire, but was soon rebuilt. The village is situated on the south end of the island, and contains about one hundred warehouses and stores, a telegraph station, and a custom-house, built at an expense of thirty-five thousand dollars. Upon a hill in the centre of the town is Fort Sullivan, usually garrisoned by a company of United States artillery. The village is compactly built; and a covered bridge connects it with the town of Perry, while a ferry communicates with Lubec. The people are chiefly engaged in commercial pursuits, — many vessels being built and owned here, and the fisheries carried on to a considerable extent. The harbor is one of the finest and most spacious on the New England coast, and is never closed by ice. Communication is had daily by steamers with the Upper St. Croix, St. Andrew, and Calais, and tri-weekly with Portland and Boston. Some trade is carried on here by land, but the greater part is by water. The town has one district and eight schools, conducted on an excellent system, and a library. There are seven meeting-houses — Unitarian, Congregational, Baptist, Methodist, Episcopalian, Christian, and Roman Catholic; one planing mill, one shingle mill, one tannery, one grist-mill, one lath manufactory, six pail-makers, one carriage builder, one door, sash, and blind factory, and four ship-builders; also, a post-office. Population, 4,125; valuation, $660,519.

EDDINGTON, Penobscot county, is situated on the east side of Penobscot river, and has an area of nine thousand acres. It was granted on the recommendation of Congress, by the Commonwealth of Massachusetts, June 14, 1785, to Jonathan Eddy and nineteen others, for services rendered during the Revolutionary war. The settlement of the town was commenced immediately after the grant was made, and it was incorporated February 22, 1811, taking its corporate name from the original grantee, Jonathan Eddy.

The surface of Eddington is uneven, and in some parts broken; but the soil is good. There are two villages, one situated on the Penobscot river, and the other at the eastern extremity of the town; two churches — Methodist and Universalist; seven school districts, with fourteen schools; and two post-offices — Eddington and East Eddington; it has also one saw-mill, one grist-mill, three shingle mills, two pail-makers, one carding machine, and one carriage builder. Population, 696; valuation, $101,283.

Eden, Hancock county, is situated on the northern part of Mount Desert island, and embraces an area of twenty-two thousand acres, about one thousand of which are covered by water. Its early history belongs to the town of Mount Desert, of which it formed a part until its incorporation. The surface and soil are similar to those of Mount Desert. The leading pursuits of the inhabitants are navigation and agriculture. Eden has one village, four religious societies (Baptist, Free-will Baptist, Methodist, and Congregational), three of which have meeting-houses; fourteen school districts, with twenty-one schools; and four post-offices — Eden, West Eden, Bar Harbor, and Salisbury Cove. It has also two saw-mills, two shingle mills, and five ship-builders. Population, 1,127; valuation, $103,809, although the present actual value is estimated as high as $400,000.

Edgecomb, Lincoln county, is situated on the peninsula formed by the Sheepscot and Damariscotta rivers, and joins Boothbay on the north. It was originally settled in 1744, by Samuel Trask and others, who took up their lands and established their claims by possession, in which they remained undisturbed for the period of ten years, when their title was challenged by a party of adventurers from Boston, who pretended to have a deed of the tract from the Indian sagamores. They failed to establish the genuineness of their deed, and were obliged to abandon their pretensions. The settlers suffered very much from the attacks of the Indians, and such other privations as were incident to life in a new country. The town was incorporated in 1774. Jeremisquam island, and another lying directly east of it, belonged to Edgecomb until they were incorporated by the name of Westport, in 1828. The town has considerable trade, and has been favorably known for its ship-building. There are two churches — Congregational and Free-will Baptist; eight school districts, with fifteen schools, and two post-offices; also one saw-mill, three grist-mills, one shingle mill, two ship-builders, four brickmakers, and one carding machine. Population, 1,231; valuation, $167,730.

EDINBURGH, Penobscot county, is situated on the west bank of the Penobscot river, twenty-five miles north of Bangor. It was incorporated in 1835, and is drained by several small streams. The town is entirely agricultural, and but sparsely settled. It has one church edifice (Free-will Baptist), two school districts, with two schools; and one post-office. Population, 93; valuation, $11,307.

EDMUNDS, Washington county, formerly plantation No. 10, was selected in preference to No. 5, now the city of Calais, by Colonel Aaron Hobart of Abington, Mass., who purchased the territory, containing 17,696 acres, for the sum of £2,200, from the state of Massachusetts, August 3, 1786; and Rufus Putnam of Boston, and three others, were appointed to survey the same.

The first settler was James Neil, an Irish deserter from the British army, who, on his way hither, shot and killed his two pursuers. He built a log house in 1775, where he continued till 1793, when he moved to New Brunswick. The next settlement was in 1785, by John Oliver and his mother, (who also moved to New Brunswick in 1793,) and by Captain Elijah Ayers, Jr., Samuel Scott, and William Hurley, who moved to Nova Scotia about the time the others did to New Brunswick. Richard Harper and family lived here a few years, and then moved to No. 2. Harper went to sea, was taken by the French, and died in prison. In 1787, Nathaniel Hobart, son of Aaron, arrived, engaged in the mill and lumber business, tarried ten years, became discontented, sold to Phineas Bruce, an eminent lawyer of Machias, and moved to New York. He was a graduate of Harvard College of 1784. In 1788, Benjamin Shaw and Daniel Smith settled. In 1791, Shaw's house and barn were burned down, and he moved with his family to New Brunswick. Smith lived here twenty-five years. In 1792, Isaac Hobart, son of the first proprietor, settled, living in a camp while his house and mill were being built. After the death of his father, he purchased the wild lands belonging to the heirs, and became owner of three fourths of the township, now in possession of his three sons, Aaron, Isaac, and Benjamin. The father moved in 1826 to Eastport, where he died in 1847, aged seventy-five. From 1788 to 1800, others settled, some of whom moved away. Among others, Samuel Runnels and family came in 1796. He had been a soldier of the Revolution, and deserves special notice. When he heard of the "Lexington fight," he started immediately from Prospect, where he then lived, and arriving at head-quarters, enlisted in Colonel Knowlton's regiment, and served through the whole war, was in many battles, was wounded at Long Island, was with Washington in New Jersey at the crossing of the Delaware; and in the battle of Trenton killed a Hessian captain and took his sword. He received a pension of ten dollars per month for a few years before his death, which occurred in this town, September 4, 1833, at the age of eighty-two. Aaron Hobart, first proprietor, died in 1808, previous to which the settlers obtained their titles from him, but have since acquired title from Isaac Hobart.

The town of Edmunds was incorporated in 1828. The surface is uneven, but without high hills or deep valleys. The place was selected for its valuable wood and timber, rather than its agricultural qualities; yet the cultivation of the soil is not neglected. The raising of cattle, especially cows for the dairy, receives good attention. There is an abundance of water, furnished by several ponds and small streams. Edmunds has one church edifice, occupied by the Methodists, and six school districts, with the same number of schools. The manufactures consist chiefly of all kinds of lumber. There are four saw-mills, four lath machines, and four shingle machines. The average annual manufacture of lumber is estimated at 1,200,000 feet of long lumber, 1,500,000 each of shingles and laths. There is a mill for carding wool, which has been in operation many years. In 1856, a factory for making pails and churns was erected. There is a ship yard, at which a moderate business is done. Population, 416; valuation for 1857, $63,127.

Elliot, situated in the western part of York county, on the eastern bank of the Piscataqua river, belonged to Kittery until March 1, 1810, when it was erected into a distinct municipality. While an adjunct of Kittery, it bore the name of Sturgeon Creek, and was called the north parish. Walter Neal, the agent of Mason and Gorges, made grants of land here in 1632; but a settlement was made a few years previous to that date.

Elliot is small in territory, but is very thickly settled. The surface is level, and the soil well adapted to agriculture, in which pursuit the inhabitants are principally engaged. It is watered by the Piscataqua river. The western part of Elliot, near the banks of the river, and vicinity, are adorned with handsome cottages, attached to which are gardens, blooming with flowers. In summer, the well-cultivated farms teeming with luxuriant vegetation; the fine orchards, their trees laden with fruit; and the beautiful and placid Piscataqua, its waters shaded by the foliage of the trees which line its margin, — form a *coup d'œil* not often seen. Viewed by a denizen of the hot and close atmosphere of a city, it makes him yearn to have a habitation in a spot like this, where he might behold Nature in all her loveliness, and quaff the invigorating country air.

A small pond, lying on the northeastern part, is the only body of water in town. Additional activity is given to the place by the Portsmouth and Portland Railroad, which traverses the town from north to south.

Elliot has three religious societies — Congregational, Methodist, and Wesleyan Methodist; an academy, eight school districts, with the same number of schools; and two post-offices — Elliot and Elliot Depôt. It has also two saw-mills, two grist-mills, two shingle machines, two tanneries, and one brickmaker. Population, 1,803; valuation, $320,658.

Elliotsville is situated in the southern part of Piscataquis county, not many miles from Moosehead lake. The first settler was Samuel G. Bodfish, who came here from Kennebec county in 1826. Two years after, Daniel Briggs and John Drake from Buckfield, Joseph Sawyer and Ebenezer Sawyer from Buxton, William Burnell and G. F. Burnell from Portland, settled here, and began to make their "clearings." These were the only settlers in town until about 1830. The north half was a grant to the heirs of William Vaughan; and four thousand acres in the southern half was a grant to Saco free bridge corporation. Some of the settlers obtained their titles from E. G. Vaughan, and others from Mr. Bridge of Augusta. The town was incorporated in 1835.

The surface is uneven and rather broken. There are two elevations, called Peaked and Barren mountains. It is watered by Wilson's stream, which runs through the entire length, and by Ship-pond stream, which takes its name from Ship pond, of which it is the outlet. There are also several smaller ponds.

While there are some of almost all denominations in Elliotsville, yet they have no settled minister and no church edifice. There are three school districts, with three schools, and one post-office; also one shingle machine and one clapboard machine. Population, 200; valuation, $10,884.

Ellsworth, the shire town of Hancock county, is situated on both sides of Union river, at the head of ship navigation, about four miles from the entrance of the river into the sea. Its plantation name was New Bowdoin, and the first settlements were made in 1763. Colonel Meletiah Jordan, Benjamin Joy, Colonel Jones, George Lord, and

Nathaniel and Major John Jellison, who came from the western part of the state and from Massachusetts, were among the first who took up their abode within the limits of Ellsworth. Notwithstanding its favorable location for ship-building and navigation, its progress was slow, and it was not incorporated till February 26, 1800.

Ellsworth has acquired considerable notoriety on account of the troubles with the Roman Catholic inhabitants, which took place in the year 1854. The difficulties commenced in consequence of a Catholic boy in one of the public schools declining to read in the New Testament, which was followed by a refusal on the part of the Catholic

Ellsworth.

children generally to go through that exercise. Many of them also, though not compelled to read the book themselves, were very disorderly while others were doing so; to prevent a recurrence of which, the most unruly ones were expelled. This was followed by the prosecution of the school committee, instigated by the Catholic priest (Mr. Bapst), and a withdrawal of all the children from the public schools. The case went to the supreme court, and the action of the committee was sustained, while the town defrayed the expenses of the defence. The citizens, in consequence of the determined efforts of the Romanists to obtain the control of their common school system, were soon embroiled in a religious controversy of a most violent character, which was magnified into an undeserved importance by being mixed up with the issues of party politics. Several persons were attacked, knocked down, and stoned by the Papists; and the citizens, in retaliation, took summary vengeance upon them. Subsequently, Mr. Bapst the priest was seized by some of the Protestants, tarred and feathered, ridden upon a rail, forced to leave town, and threatened with the penalty of death if he ever returned. These stringent proceedings with the priest awed the Romanists into good behavior, and thus ended the difficulty. In May, 1856, however, their chapel was burned down by an incendiary; but from the fact of its being insured for much more than its real cost, and that every thing valuable which it contained had been previously removed, a strong suspicion was entertained that its destruction was planned to obtain the insurance. It may be as well to state, that those who were instrumental in the ill advised proceedings towards the priest were arrested and brought before the grand jury, but no bill was found. Since these proceedings, the disaffected class have emigrated from the town largely, till scarce half their original number now remain.

Ellsworth is an uncommonly large town, containing an area of between sixty and seventy thousand acres. The surface is considerably broken, particularly on the west bank of the river. It is well watered by two large ponds, and by Union river and its tributaries. The leading pursuits of the inhabitants are lumbering, ship-building, coasting, and agriculture. The mechanical or manufacturing establishments consist of nine saw-mills, two grist-mills, nine lath machines, one shingle machine, one machine shop, one tannery, one carding machine, one pottery, eight brick-yards; and thirteen ship-building, five pail, two edge-tool, one carriage, and eight box making establishments, in all of which there is an invested capital of upwards of $2,000,000. There were two banks, which, in 1858, closed up their affairs. Ellsworth supports one weekly newspaper, as well as five religious societies — Baptist, Methodist, Congregational, Spiritualist, and Catholic; the Baptist and Congregational having houses of public worship. A high school has been established; besides which there are nineteen school districts, with twenty-three schools. The inhabitants are accommodated by four post-offices — Ellsworth, Ellsworth Falls, North Ellsworth, and West Ellsworth. Population, 4,009; valuation, $675,945.

Emden, Somerset county, is situated on the west side of Kennebec river, about forty miles north from Augusta. The first settlements in this town were commenced on the river in 1779 by Amos Patridge, George Mitchell, and William Hamblin. Samuel Hutchins and a Mr. Young located on Seven Mile brook in 1782. They were followed, in 1788, by Captain John Gray from Wiscasset, and in 1790 by Thomas

McFaden from Georgetown, Joseph Cleaveland, with his sons Jonathan and Luther, and Edward Savage. John Chamberlain, and his sons Jeremiah and Stephen, settled here about the same time. Chamberlain the elder was the son of the John Chamberlain, that shot Paugus, the Indian chief.[1]

The town was incorporated June 22, 1804, and organized on the 16th of August following; Thomas McFaden, one of the first settlers, being chosen clerk. He died in 1846, at the advanced age of one hundred years and twenty days. The surface of the town is hilly, and is well watered by a number of ponds and streams; among which are the Great Hancock pond, covering 1,538 acres; the Small Hancock pond, 325 acres; and Tahi pond, 133 acres, besides several smaller ones. The Kennebec river, which forms the eastern boundary of the town, is here dotted with about twenty islands, some of which are large enough for cultivation. Colby's Island contains about sixty acres; McFaden's, thirty-five acres; Ayer's Island, settled by Moses Ayer in 1790, contains ninety-seven acres, and lies nearly opposite the centre of the town. It belongs to the town of Solon. Seven Mile brook crosses the southwest corner of the town, and is skirted on both sides by rich intervals. The Hancock, Tahi, and Martin streams afford some valuable mill sites; which are occupied, however, by only two saw-mills. The religious denominations are Baptist, Methodist, Free-will Baptist, and Universalist, which are nearly equal in numbers. There are thirteen school districts, with the same number of schools; and three post-offices — called Embden, West Embden, and Embden Centre. Population, 971; valuation, $130,073.

Enfield, Penobscot county, is a small town situated on the eastern bank of the Penobscot, opposite the mouth of the Piscataquis. It was incorporated in 1835, and contains an area of fifteen thousand acres. The original settlers came partly from Buckfield, and partly from Bangor.

Cold Stream pond, five miles long and two miles wide, forms most of the eastern boundary of the town. It is a fine sheet of water, fed mostly by springs, and well supplied with the finny tribe. On the completion of the Milford and Lincoln Railroad, the vicinity of this pond will doubtless become a fashionable place of resort for people from the city during the summer months, there being ample facilities for boating, fishing, and gunning. Cold stream is the outlet, and falls into

[1] See Fryeburg.

the Passadumkeag, about two miles above its junction with the Penobscot.

The surface of the western half of the town is quite level. The soil is a clayey loam, and requires considerable dressing to make it productive. The eastern part is rather broken, but the soil is strong and produces good crops. In the northeast part there are some fine granite ledges, which will ultimately be valuable for building material. Enfield has excellent water privileges; and two saw-mills, one carding machine, and one shingle machine, are already in operation. This would be a safe location for large manufacturing establishments, freshets and drought being unknown.

There are five school districts, with seven schools, in each of which one or two terms of school are taught during the year. There is no church edifice, but religious meetings are held by Baptists and Methodists, and sometimes by other denominations, in private dwellings. There are two villages, namely, Enfield and West Enfield, the former of which is the principal, situated at the outlet of Cold Stream pond, in the southeast part of the town. A post-office has been established at each of these villages. Population, 396; valuation, $27,163.

ETNA is situated in the southwest part of Penobscot county, and was settled in the year 1807,— Dr. Benjamin Friend, Phineas Friend, James Harding, Dennis and Reuben Dennett, and Bela, Asa, and Calvin Sylvester being among the early settlers. General John Crosby of Hampden owned the township at this time, and it was known by the name of Crosbytown. It was incorporated in 1820. The surface is rather broken, but the soil is good, and well adapted to the growth of grass and grain. It is watered by the Kinsley and Soadabscook streams. The inhabitants are, for the most part, engaged in agricultural pursuits. Etna contains one church edifice (Baptist), and has two villages,— one at the railroad station, in the north part of the town, and the other in the centre of the town. There are eight school districts, with eight schools; one saw-mill, one shingle mill, and two post-offices — Etna. and Etna Centre. Population, 802; valuation for 1857, about $100,000.

EXETER, Penobscot county, was granted to Marblehead academy, by Massachusetts, in 1793, the exterior lines of the township having been run in 1792 by Ephraim Ballard and Samuel Weston. The township was lotted in 1800 by Moses Hodsdon, of Kenduskeag. The first "chopping" was done June 6, 1800, by Lemuel Tozier and John Durgin, at Hill's Corner; and the first settlement was made in 1801 by Lemuel Tozier, who was immediately followed by Reuben Seavey, Joseph

Pease, and Josiah Barker. The town was incorporated in 1811, and J. Pease Jr. was upon the first board of selectmen. He died July 2, 1857, aged seventy-two. Mr. Barker yet survives. Among the early proprietors were Benjamin Joy and William Turner, of Boston; for whom Dr. John Blaisdell acted as agent. Hence, prior to its incorporation, the place was called "Blaisdell Town." The first school was taught in 1804 by Ann Stevens, who is still living. The first representative was Winthrop Chapman, who is still a prominent citizen.

The surface is uneven. The land is excellent for farming purposes, and the inhabitants, as a consequence, devote much of their attention to this branch of industry. The principal stream is the Kenduskeag, on which are five saw-mills, two shingle-mills, two grist-mills, and a carding and clothing mill. The first mills were built by Levi Stevens, in 1813, where now stand the Cutler mills.

There are five villages in Exeter — Exeter Corner, Canney's Corner, Hill's Corner, Exeter Mills, and Cutler's Mills. There are four post-offices, — called Exeter, Exeter Mills, East Exeter, and South Exeter; thirteen public schools, one high school, and four church edifices — Congregational, Baptist, Methodist, and Free-will Baptist. Population, 1,853; valuation, $242,197.

Fairfield, Somerset county, situated on the west side of Kennebec river, twenty-six miles north from Augusta, was first settled as early as 1774. Fairfield is a large town, embracing forty-two square miles, and was incorporated June 18, 1788. Its scenery is very beautiful, which fact, in all probability, gave rise to its name. It possesses a very productive soil, and is watered by Marston stream, which falls into the Kennebec in the north part of the town.

The principal village is called Kendall's mills, situated on the Kennebec, in the southeast part of the town, three miles distant from Waterville. There is an excellent water-power here, on which are located several saw-mills, and machines for cutting clapboards, laths, and shingles. The town contains five church edifices — three Methodist, one Universalist, and one Friends'; twenty school districts, with sixteen schools; twenty-eight saw-mills, two grist-mills, two tanneries, four shingle mills, two carriage builders, one door, sash, and blind maker, and six post-offices — Kendall's Mills, Fairfield, Fairfield Corner, North Fairfield, Somerset Mills, and Larone. Population, 2,452; valuation, $418,074.

Falmouth, Cumberland county, is a seaport town on Casco bay, and originally embraced the present towns of Cape Elizabeth and Westbrook, and the city of Portland, having an area of eighty square miles, including all the islands upon its coast. Its history is given in the article on Portland. It was incorporated in 1718, taking its name from a seaport town in England. It is watered by the Presumpscot river, and traversed by the Grand Trunk Railway and the Kennebec and Portland Railroad. Considerable is done in the fisheries in Casco bay, and sometimes a few ships are built. Brick-making also forms a branch of industry. Falmouth contains one village, called Piscataqua; three church edifices — two Congregational, and one Baptist; thirteen school districts, with the same number of schools; an academy, known as the Oak Grove Seminary; and two post-offices — Falmouth and West Falmouth. It has one saw-mill, one grist-mill, one tannery, three brick-makers, and three ship-builders. Population, 2,147; valuation, $401,273.

FARMINGDALE, Kennebec county, was formed from parts of the towns of Gardiner, Hallowell, and West Gardiner, and incorporated in 1852. The land was cleared with the intention of settlement in 1787, by James and Henry McCausland, from Cape Elizabeth, who obtained their titles from Sylvester Gardiner. Farmingdale has an uneven surface, and is watered by Jenning's pond, Cold stream, and the Kennebec, — the latter forming its eastern boundary. There are six ship-builders in town, who are engaged to some extent in the business, having an invested capital of about half a million of dollars. Farmingdale has three school districts, and one post-office. Population, about 800; valuation for 1858, $373,545.

FARMINGTON, the shire town of Franklin county, is situated in that part of Maine known as the Sandy river valley, thirty miles from Augusta, and about seventy miles from Portland. The first exploration of this town, with a view to settlement, was made by Stephen Titcomb, Robert Gower, James Henry, Robert Alexander, and James McDonald, in the summer of 1776, the party being guided by Thomas Wilson, who had previously explored the country as a hunter. This company, who were from Topsham, in this state, ascended the Kennebec, as far as Hallowell, in canoes, and from thence travelled by land, over a bad road, until they reached their destination. When they arrived at Farmington Falls, they found two Indian camps, and discovered that a considerable tract of land, extending from the upper part of the present site of the village down the river to the edge of New Sharon, had been cleared. They proceeded up the river about a mile from the falls, where they concluded to locate; and, having fixed upon the spot, made a chain from basswood bark, with which they measured off the land into farms;

having defined the boundaries of which, they returned to Topsham, to obtain their tools, and a stock of provisions. In two weeks they were again at the scene of the proposed new settlement, and commenced assiduously their labors in the clearing of their respective lots. From this period till 1781, this company, with others, continued to make improvements in different parts of the town. About this time the first families moved in, some coming from Massachusetts and others from New Hampshire; all of whom were compelled to endure those inconveniences incidental to the majority of the settlements in New England.

Farmington was incorporated February 1, 1794, and is drained by Sandy river and its tributaries. Small streams and springs everywhere abound, affording water to every farm and family in town. The soil is generally good and fertile, especially in the intervals and uplands adjacent to them; though some of the high lands, particularly those in the northwest section, are somewhat rocky, and a little difficult to cultivate. The superior quality of these lands for grazing, however, well recompenses the labors of the husbandman. Apple and other fruit-trees are cultivated with success, and many orchards are springing up. Limestone has been discovered in many places; but it is of a poor quality, and unfit for mechanical purposes.

Farmington, from Hunter's Hill.

Farmington has three villages, — the Centre, the Falls, and the Upper Village, — the former of which is the principal one, containing nearly one

11 *

hundred dwelling-houses, twenty stores, and several manufacturing establishments. In this village are located an academy, a bank (with a capital of $75,000), a court-house, jail, and a fire-proof building for the county offices. There are six church edifices — Congregational, Methodist, Baptist, Free-will Baptist, and two Union houses; twenty-seven school districts, with twenty-six public schools; several private schools; and two post-offices — Farmington and Farmington Falls. Population, 2,725; valuation for 1858, $684,957.

FAYETTE, situated in the western part of Kennebec county, was originally called Sterling plantation. A part of the town was granted to Robert Page and associates, by Massachusetts, and it was settled soon after the Revolutionary war. Fayette was incorporated February 28, 1794. The surface is somewhat hilly, — the principal elevations being Oak and Berry hills, which lie in the southern part. There are several ponds and streams, skirted with some fine meadow land. The inhabitants are engaged to a considerable extent in raising stock. The manufacturing interests consist of one wood turning shop, establishments for making scythe-snaths, rakes, oars, leather, pails, edge-tools, and carriages; three saw-mills, two shingle machines, and one grist-mill. Fayette has two church edifices (Baptist and Union), eleven school districts and parts of three others, with ten schools; two villages, and two post-offices, called Fayette and North Fayette. Population, 1,085; valuation, $194,777.

FOXCROFT, Piscataquis county, situated on the north side of Piscataquis river, opposite the town of Dover, was one of the five townships conveyed by Massachusetts, in 1796, to Bowdoin College. The first efforts at settlement were made by Nathaniel and Samuel Chamberlain in 1805, and the town was incorporated February 29, 1812, taking its corporate name from Joseph E. Foxcroft, who was one of the principal proprietors under the auspices of the college. It is watered on the north by Sebec lake, and on the south by Piscataquis river. The soil is well adapted to agricultural purposes. There is a village, situated on the river, where there is an academy, and a post-office. There are four religious societies — Congregational, Baptist, Free-will Baptist, and Universalist, the two former of which have church edifices; and eleven school districts, with six schools. Manufacturing is carried on by two saw-mills, one shingle mill, one carding machine, one carriage builder, one chair manufacturer, one tannery, one fork maker, two pail-makers, one machinist, and one sash, door, and blind maker. Population, 1,945; valuation, $142,707.

FRANKFORT, the northern frontier town of Waldo county, is situated on the west side of Penobscot river, at the head of winter navigation. As early as 1760, there were settlers about Fort point and Sandy point, some of whom had been soldiers, and had assisted in building the fort now in the town of Prospect. They named their plantation Frankfort. The north line of what was then called Frankfort is the south line of the present town, at that time called Marsh Bay. In 1789, a town was incorporated, embracing what was then Frankfort, with some additions, which was, in 1793, divided into three towns, — Prospect, the longest settled, retaining the old records, but not the name.

A petition from the settlers on the Waldo Patent having been presented to the legislature in the year 1800, commissioners were appointed by that body to decide upon the terms by which the settlers should hold titles to their lands. The Frankfort settlers were ruled out, because, in the resolve, the lands to which they laid claim were represented as belonging to General Knox, though, in reality, of the land known as the "Ten Proprietors' Tract," which included Frankfort, he owned only a part. This loss of the titles to their lands proved a great misfortune to the settlers of Frankfort; because, by the resolve above alluded to, the land was disposed of at one dollar an acre; while in 1806, when Knox sold out to Thorndike and Company, two dollars per acre were demanded. Even this would not have been so much felt had not embargo, non-intercourse, and war soon followed; which, with interest accumulating, made the circumstances of the case doubly trying.

The war of 1812 proved disastrous to Frankfort. Through mere distress, many enlisted in the army and never returned. One of her citizens was killed at the battle of Hampden, and two were wounded. Privateering nearly destroyed the coasting trade, and rendered lumber, and even vessels, almost valueless. A brig, laden with lumber, belonging to James Little, was taken from his wharf and made a prize of, during the war.

On the return of the British fleet from Bangor in 1814, they anchored off Frankfort, where they remained some days. Under a threat of bombardment, they demanded provisions. The selectmen of the town agreed with George Halliburton to supply a yoke of oxen, which he did, on the supposition that the town would pay him therefor. When, however, Halliburton called for his money, payment was refused. He sued the corporation, and the supreme court ruled that selectmen could not force a town to pay for provisions thus furnished.

Before the British ascended the river for the purpose of capturing the *Adams* at Hampden, there had been stored on the McGlathry wharf, a prize cargo of cocoa, which it was thought prudent to haul into the country for safety. While this was being done, however, a tender, with a lieutenant and fourteen men, came from one of the British men-of-war, and commenced taking the cocoa on board. Lieutenant Morse, having escaped with a small American force from Machias, and hearing of this circumstance, came suddenly upon the British and took them prisoners. Discharging the cocoa that had been taken on board, he fired the tender and set her adrift.

The surface of this town is broken and rough. There are several fine quarries of granite, immense quantities of which are annually wrought and shipped to the various ports of the United States. Ship-building is one of the prominent branches of industry. John Kempton, of Oak point, built the first vessel in Frankfort; and during the past ten years there has been an average of six vessels per annum, varying from ten to 1,600 tons burden. A short distance from the river, there are some well-cultivated and productive farms; potatoes, English grain, and hay, being the staple commodities. The town is drained by Marsh river, which enters on the west, and falls into the Penobscot. On the southeast of this stream several saw-mills, grist-mills, and shingle, lath, and clapboard machines are in active operation. Joshua Treat, the ancestor of the present generation of Treats, erected the first mill.

Mount Waldo and Mosquito mountain are situated in the south part of the town, three quarters of a mile apart. The former was for a long time known as Mount Misery, so named on account of two lads, who were overtaken by a violent snow-storm, perishing near it. In 1815, a party of excursionists ascended the mountain, and the question arising as to its name, it was decided to call it Waldo, which was given in due form. Mosquito mountain is an immense pile of granite, having between it and the river a large marsh, containing several pools of stagnant water, where mosquitos are bred in myriads: hence the name of the mountain. Those who have never visited this spot can scarcely form a conception of the immense swarms of mosquitos that are here encountered.

Frankfort has three villages, of which Frankfort, at the head of winter navigation, is the principal. The others are known as Ellingwood Corner, and Frankfort Mills; the latter being a thriving little place, set like a gem among the mountains. It has also two hundred miles of roads, a high school, and six churches, two of which are Methodist, two Congregational, one Baptist, and one Catholic. Post-offices have been established at Frankfort, Frankfort Mills, Ellingwood Corner, and North Frankfort. Manufacturing operations are carried on by seven saw-mills, four shingle mills, three grist-mills, one tannery, one carding machine, five ship-builders, three pail-makers, one carriage builder, and two brickmakers. There are twenty-four school districts, with twenty-six schools. Population, 4,233; valuation, $608,242.

FRANKLIN is situated in the middle division of Hancock county, at the head of Taunton bay, and was incorporated in 1825. It is well watered by ponds, on the streams leading from which are some good mill-sites. The soil is good, but little is done in an agricultural point of view, — the principal kinds of business being lumbering and ship-building. The town contains eleven school districts, with fourteen schools; a few mills, a machinist, one tannery, three ship-builders, one brickmaker, and one post-office. Population, 736; valuation, $78,461.

FRANKLIN COUNTY has Somerset on the east, Oxford on the west, and extends from Androscoggin and Kennebec upon the south to Canada East upon the north. The act establishing this county was passed March 20, 1838, by which it was made to embrace seventeen towns and twenty-nine townships and parts of townships, enumerated in the following order: — "New Sharon, Chesterville, Wilton, Temple, and Farmington, in the county of Kennebec; and Jay, Carthage, Weld, Berlin, Madrid, townships numbered six, letter E., and D. in the county of Oxford; thence extending northerly from the northwest corner of letter D. on the line betwixt townships numbered three and four, through the several range of townships to Canada line, so as to include three tiers of townships west of the west line of the Bingham Purchase in said county of Oxford; and Industry, New Vineyard, Strong, Avon, Phillips, Freeman, Salem, Kingfield, townships numbered four in the first range west of Kingfield, three and four in the second range, and the south half of township numbered four in the third range of the Bingham Purchase in the county of Somerset." The county comprises an area of sixteen hundred square miles, and is not yet more than half settled, the northern and northeastern part being principally a dense wilderness. The surface, as a whole, is mountainous, although there are no continuous ranges. Mount Blue, in the southern part, has an elevation of 2,804 feet, the eastern peak of Mount Abraham, in the eastern part, 3,387 feet, and Saddleback, in the centre of the county, about four thousand feet, above the level of the sea. The towns in the southern part are generally fertile, particularly those situated upon Sandy river.

Farmington is the capital. The county is embraced in the western judicial district of Maine, the law terms of which are held at Portland. The jury terms of this court, for both civil and criminal business, are held at Farmington, on the third Tuesdays of April and October. Population in 1850, 20,027, showing a loss of 774 since the census of 1840,

Franklin county being the only one that has suffered a decrease since the last decennial period; valuation, $2,700,662.

FREEDOM is situated in the western part of Waldo county, and belonged to the Plymouth patent. The first opening was made here in 1794, by Stephen Smith, of the town of Nobleborough, a soldier of the Revolution, who arrived on the 20th of November of that year, and, with the assistance of his brothers Joshua and John, and one James Naddocks, erected a small log-house a short distance south of the burying-ground in South Freedom. After completing this rude habitation, and clearing a small portion of land in the immediate vicinity, they departed for the winter. But in the May following, Mr. Smith with his family, consisting of a wife and seven children, returned and took up their abode in the log-house. The next June, John Smith, known afterwards as Father Nehemiah, arrived in Freedom; and he was followed at subsequent periods by Rev. Aaron Gould, Isaac Worthing, and James and Joshua Smith. Jason Wood, Frost Gerry, Gideon Robinson, Colonel Brown, Benjamin Comings, Bradstreet Wiggins, William Sibley, and Rev. Reuben Keen are among a few of the prominent names, in addition to those already mentioned, associated with the early history of the town. Many of the settlers came from New Hampshire.

The plantation name of Freedom was first Smithstown; afterwards Beaver Hill. In 1813 it was incorporated under its present name. The southern portion of the town was the first settled, though not naturally more favored in soil and mill privileges than other sections; and here was erected the first school-house, the teacher being Benjamin White, subsequently member of congress. Freedom ranks, in an agricultural point, as an average town. Sheepscot river serves as a partial boundary on its southerly side, and Sandy stream passes through the village on its way to the waters of the Kennebec — furnishing within one mile some of the best sites for mills and tanneries in the country, which have been improved in several places. Besides this stream, there are two ponds, known as Duck and Sandy ponds.

The only business locality here has recently sprung up, from a comparatively thick and gloomy forest, to one of the most thriving inland villages in the country. For much of its growth and prosperity it is indebted to the efforts of William Buxton, an accomplished Englishman, who was the first settler in this quarter of the town. There is but one church edifice, which is owned and occupied by the Congregationalists and Baptists. There are ten school districts, with nine schools, and an academy, which was incorporated February 18, 1836. The manufactures consist of leather, lumber, and flour. Two post-offices have been established, one at Freedom, and the other at South Freedom. Freedom contains one saw-mill, two grist-mills, one shingle mill, one tannery, two pail-makers, and three carriage builders. Population, 948; valuation, $146,537.

FREEMAN, Franklin county, joins Strong on the north, and is the westerly of the two townships granted by the state of Massachusetts to the sufferers of Falmouth (now Portland), in the burning of the town by the British, during the Revolutionary war. It was surveyed and settled. under the agency of Reuben Hill, about 1797. William Brackly, David Hooper, Alexander Fasset, Samuel Weymouth, and Messrs. Burbank, Morton, and Borton were some of the first settlers.

The town was incorporated March 4, 1803, and takes its name from Samuel Freeman, late of Portland, who was one of the principal owners at the time of the settlement. Freeman derives little advantage from water-power, but has a productive soil, though rather hard to cultivate. The northerly part, or what is called Freeman Ridge, is said to be the best for tillage.

Freeman has nine school districts, with nine schools, but no church edifice. It has one post-office. It has also three saw-mills, one machine shop, two shingle mills, one carriage builder, one chair manufacturer, one door, sash, and blind maker, one edge-tool maker, one pail-maker, one ship-builder, and one tannery. Population, 762; valuation, $76,677.

FREEPORT is situated in the eastern part of Cumberland county, on the sea-shore, and originally belonged to North Yarmouth. It lies between Cousins river on the southwest, and Prout's Gore on the northeast, and was called Harrasacket settlement, from the name of the river that runs through it. There were settlers on this grant as early as 1750, but their names we have been unable to ascertain. It was incorporated as a town February 14, 1789, (receiving its present name probably from the openness of its harbor,) and at this time included within its limits the present town of Pownal. The principal occupations of the people are ship-building and farming.

Freeport has four villages, five church edifices (Congregationalist, Baptist, Free-will Baptist, Universalist, and a Union house), seventeen school districts, with thirty-four schools; and two post-offices, called Freeport and Oak Hill. Manufacturing operations are carried on by two saw-mills, one shingle mill, nine ship-builders, one grist-mill, three pail-makers, one carriage builder, and two brickmakers. The Kennebec and Portland Railroad passes through the central part. Population, 2,629; valuation, $563,146.

Friendship is a frontier town, situated toward the southeast part of Lincoln county, between Waldoboro' and Medunoook rivers. It was originally included in the Waldo Patent, and contains about eight thousand acres of main land, besides two islands lying in close proximity to it, one of which is nearly three miles long, and bears the name of Friendship Long island; the other being less than half as large, and called Moses island. The inhabitants hold the titles to their lands by deeds from General Waldo. The Indian name of the town was "Meduncook," and signifies "Sandy harbor," but why it should have been so called is beyond conjecture, for the shore of the town is rockbound; and, in some places, there are high, bold bluffs, where ships may safely lie at anchor in twenty feet of water.

Settlements were commenced in the year 1750. In the southern part, a garrison was erected on an island, called from this circumstance Garrison island, which at low water is connected with the main land. James Bradford was one of the first persons here. He and his comrades settled on this island and its immediate vicinity, in order to be able to find protection in the fort on the approach of the Indians. The outbreak of the French and Indian war in 1755 so imperilled the existence of this peaceful settlement, that it was deemed politic, not only to strengthen the garrison, but to recommend all the families in the settlement to take up their residence therein. They all complied with the suggestion except Bradford, who was repeatedly urged to move his family in with the rest; but he steadily refused, saying, that "he did not think it necessary, as his house was in full view of the garrison, which he could easily reach on the approach of the Indians."

One morning, however, while Mr. Bradford was engaged in pounding corn, a party of Indians were seen, from the garrison, approaching the house. The alarm-gun was fired; but the concussion of pestle and mortar was so loud that the gun was not heard by Mr. Bradford nor by any of his family; neither were the savages perceived by any of them until the moment they entered the house. The savages instantly dispatched Mr. and Mrs. Bradford with their tomahawks. A daughter, of some twelve or fourteen years of age, who had sought a momentary concealment under the bed, sprang from her hiding-place, and caught the infant as it fell unharmed from her mother's arms, with which she fled through the open door to the garrison. The Indians pursued, and, not being able to overtake her, one of them threw a tomahawk, which inflicted a deep and fearful wound in her side; but the heroic girl, clasping the babe still more firmly with one hand, and with the other holding her side, succeeded in reaching the garrison. She recovered from the wound, and subsequently removed to Vermont, where she became the mother of a large family. Her two young brothers were taken by the savages to Canada, where they remained, the one seven and the other fourteen years, after which they made their escape.[1]

Friendship was incorporated in 1807. The surface is very rough and ledgy; covering which is but a thin layer of sand and alluvium. Ship-building is prosecuted to some extent, — averaging about one vessel of one hundred tons per year. The town has one church — Methodist; two ship-builders, two grist-mills, one shingle mill, three saw-mills; six school districts, with the same number of schools; and one post-office. Population, 691; valuation, $70,107.

FRYEBURG, in the southern part of Oxford county, on the line separating Maine from New Hampshire, was granted in 1762, to General Joseph Frye, an officer in the king's army, in consideration of his gallant deeds on the frontier.[2] Nathaniel Smith made the first settlement in that year, on the west line of the town, — the same site on which the Indians built their village. Among other early settlers were Moses Ames, John Evans, David Evans, Samuel Osgood, David Page, Nathaniel Merrill, Caleb Swan, Joseph, Simon, Richard, and Nathaniel Frye, and Joseph Frye, Jr., who came principally from Concord, N. H., and Andover, Mass. To reach here, they had to penetrate an unbroken wilderness for sixty or seventy miles. Their nearest white neighbors for a long time were at Saco; and Sandford, some sixty miles distant, was their place of resort for articles of necessity. The only mode of conveyance was on horses, and their guides were the marked trees of the forest. The settlers obtained the titles to their lands from General Joseph Frye, the original grantee.

Fryeburg is celebrated for a memorable battle, fought between Captain John Lovewell and his followers and the Pequawket Indians. Captain Lovewell and his men, having made several successful expeditions prior to this last, which we are about to notice, left Dunstable April 16, 1725. The expedition consisted of forty-six men, who, from the adjoining towns, had volunteered for the arduous and perilous undertaking. After a long and tedious march, in which they were deprived of the services of three men by sickness, and others who were

[1] This family were descendants of Governor Bradford, of Massachusetts.

[2] General Frye had been at Fort William Henry, and escaped, with the gallant Monro, the fearful carnage which cast such a stain upon the honor of Montcalm. He was an officer in command of a company, and, it has been faintly hinted, opposed the surrender of the fort. On his return, he was presented with an elegant silver-mounted sword and tankard.

left to care for them, their number being thus reduced to thirty-four, they reached Saco pond on Thursday, May 6, 1725, and, having encamped on the westerly side, prepared themselves for an encounter. Hesitating what course to pursue, but conscious of the proximity of the Indians, they remained here till Saturday morning. Having breakfasted, they assembled for their accustomed morning devotion, which had scarcely been commenced by the chaplain, when a gun was fired, and they espied an Indian on a point of land projecting into the pond on the opposite side. A hurried consultation was held, and they concluded that the design of the Indian's firing, and of discovering himself, was to draw them that way; but that the main body of the enemy was at the north of the pond. They soon took up their march, which lay along the margin of the pond, and near the northwestern shore they crossed the Indians' "carrying place," a path which led from the pond to their settlement. At the northeast end of the pond, on a slightly elevated plain, they divested themselves of their packs, and commenced a more cautious march. They had gone but a short distance, when they discovered an Indian, who had been out hunting; and all immediately "squatted." He came unsuspectingly toward them, and, when near enough, several guns were fired at him; but they all missed their mark. Seeing certain death, the Indian resolved to defend himself manfully; and the action was as speedy as the thought. He fired at the English, and Lovewell and another were wounded, — the captain mortally. Another gun was fired, and the Indian fell dead. From this point, Lovewell's party returned to their packs.

Paugus, the captain of the Indians, had arrived with his warriors that morning, at their landing-place on the shores of the pond; and scarcely had Lovewell crossed the "carrying place," in search of his foe, when the wily sachem, pursuing the well-beaten path to his village, discovered and counted the packs, and thus ascertained the number of white men. They instantly sprang into ambush, and were scarcely concealed in the brakes, when Lovewell[1] and his men came up and commenced searching for their packs. Springing from the thicket with a horrid yell, the savages fired their guns directly over the heads of the whites, and ran towards them with ropes, demanding if they would have quarter. "Only at the muzzle of your guns," replied the intrepid Lovewell and his men, and the fight commenced. Seizing the advantage, the little party of whites rushed towards the Indians, firing, as they pressed on, and, killing many, drove them several rods. The Indians soon rallied, however, and, maddened by the unexpected resistance,

[1] Lovewell, though mortally wounded, still led his men, but fell before the retreat.

rushed furiously on, killing Lovewell and eight others, and wounding three by their first fire. The English, thus in number reduced, and seeing the Indians about to surround them, commenced a retreat, which was made in good order, bravely contesting each inch of ground as they went. They were soon brought to a stand by a large brook on their right, a ridge of rocks on their left, and a pond in the rear.

Here the fight continued furious and obstinate till the going down of the sun, and till but nine of the English remained uninjured. Wawa, out of about eighty Indians, could lead but twenty uninjured from the field; and, though they had the advantage at sunset, they fled, leaving the dead unburied. Paugus,[1] the brave chief, had been slain, and thirty-nine of his bold followers had been killed and wounded. About midnight, it being certain the Indians would not renew the contest, the shattered remnant of the little party assembled themselves together to examine into their situation. To remain in the very centre of an enemy's country, maddened by the loss of their brave chief, and destitute of all food, was impossible; but to return they must leave not only their dead unburied, but their wounded companions unprotected, to die by the torture of the savages. Farrar, one of the wounded, expired during their consultation; and two of the number wounded — Lieutenant Robbins and private Usher — urged and commanded their companions to return, and leave them to their fate. As the moon was rising, they bade adieu to their companions, and, taking a last look at the scene of their dreadful encounter, commenced their memorable return. They had gone but a mile and a half when four of the men — Farwell, Davis, Frye, and Jones — declared themselves unable to go on; and, like the brave fellows they had already left, they were unwilling to detain the company, and desired them to proceed. Their number being now reduced to sixteen, they divided into three parties, fearing to make too large a track, by which the Indians might pursue them. One of these parties reached the fort at Ossipee, but found it deserted. "The only

[1] Paugus was killed in single combat by one Chamberlain, of Groton. Wearied by the protracted contest, both had come to opposite sides of the brook to quench their thirst and wash their guns, which had become foul by frequent firing. Their guns could almost touch, so narrow was the space between them. As they washed their guns, conversing familiarly with each other, Chamberlain assured Paugus that he should kill him, and Paugus returned the threat, bidding him defiance. Carefully drying their guns, they commenced loading at the same time. Their movements exactly corresponded, and the balls of both were heard as they were sent home by the rods at the same instant. The gun of Chamberlain primed itself, and that of Paugus did not. Striking the breach upon the ground it primed, and raising it with deliberate aim he fired, and Paugus fell dead upon the bank. As he fell, the well-aimed ball from his rifle passed through the thick locks on the top of Chamberlain's head, but left him unwounded.

coward among their number fled in the beginning of the battle, and ran directly to the fort, where he gave the men such a frightful account of what had happened, that they all fled, and made the best of their way home." The main party of eleven, leaving the Ossipee fort, continued on, and reached Dunstable May 13th, in the night. Those who were left behind during the march, with the exception of two, — Lieutenant Farwell and Mr. Frye, — after enduring the greatest privations which the imagination can conceive, succeeded in reaching places of safety, and recovered from their wounds. Thus mournfully terminated this expedition. Trees, perforated by the balls, may be seen on the shore of the pond to this day; and the older citizens of Fryeburg relate to the visitor the bloody engagement of early Pequawket with all the ardor of youth.

Fryeburg was a favorite resort of the Indians; and, for many years after the dispersion of the Pequawket tribe, solitary members continued to linger around their old home. Old Philip, Tom Hegon, and Swarson are familiar names with the old people yet. Many of them entered into the service of the Americans in the war of the Revolution, and rendered good service, for which they received suitable testimonials from the government.

Fryeburg was incorporated in 1776, and was in early times the principal, and, in fact, the only village, of the White mountains. It was, for long years, the centre of attraction and trade. Its favorable situation in respect to the seaboard towns, and the rapidity with which the village grew, gave it great prominence in its early days. Every neighborhood and settlement sent its representatives weekly to the village to trade, and its one long street was then a scene of bustle and activity. Unlike most of our villages, it sprung up, in a comparatively few years, to its full size. It stands on a broad, level plain, slightly elevated above the intervals of the Saco, which encloses it in one of its huge folds. The only elevations of note are Mount Tom and Stark's hill, the former near the centre of the town, and the latter at the head of the village.

There are six ponds, namely, Bog pond, Kezar pond, Charles pond, Kimball pond, Pleasant pond, and the far-famed Lovewell's pond. The Saco is the only stream. Fryeburg is a good farming town, and contains two villages, one at the south part, the other at the north; three church edifices — Congregational, Methodist, and Universalist; three post-offices — Fryeburg, North Fryeburg, and East Fryeburg; four tanneries, three saw-mills, one grist-mill, one foundery with steam-power, one pail factory, one wheel factory, a tin-shop, two brickmakers, two carriage builders, and two blacksmith's shops. In the south village, there is a fine and commodious brick building, in which the Fryeburg academy is in successful operation;[1] besides sixteen school districts, and the same number of schools. Population, 1,523; valuation for 1858, $506,883.

GARDINER, Kennebec county, was originally a part of Pittston, from which it was separated in 1803. The original name was Cobbossee Contee, which was changed to the one it now bears out of respect to the Gardiner family, who were the owners of the soil, at the time of incorporation, when there were 104 tax-paying residents, and four non-resident tax-payers. The town meetings were held in the old Episcopal meeting-house, or "church house," as it was then called. The only buildings then in existence, and which are still standing, were the old post-office, the Plaisted house, the Jewett house, and the cottage now or lately occupied by S. L. Plummer. The first settlers were from Falmouth, (now Portland), whence they sailed in the fall of 1760. Their names were Mr. Thomes, Benjamin Fitch, Jacob Loud, Ezra Davis, James and Henry McCausland, and William Philbrook. They ran their vessels into a creek, formed by the mouth of the river, which was then navigable some distance up, where their craft lay all winter. Fishing and trading seem to have been the chief occupations until 1794. About 1751, settlers began to flock in to what was then called the Kennebec Purchase. As late as 1775, the only mill on the purchase was in this settlement; and the settlers of old Norridgewock and Canaan were obliged to bring their corn here in their canoes. In the year 1787, there were about twenty houses, a grist-mill, a double saw-mill, and one or two stores in the vicinity of Cobbossee pond, and on both sides of the stream leading therefrom. The roads to the principal towns were not as commodious as they are now; but they were as good as could be expected in such times.

In 1786, Major Seth Gay built the first wharf, and General Dearborn established the ferry. At that time, shad, herring, salmon, and sturgeon were taken in abundance in Cobbossee pond. The first farm was cleared by Ebenezer Byram and Seth Gay, on the road at the east side of the river, near Warromontogus stream, soon after which others, on Beech hill, were cleared. There were then large quantities of white and red oak on both sides of the river, much of which was cut and sent to England; also fine spruce, pine, and ash, from which oars were made, and sent to Boston. The shores of all the ponds and streams were well wooded, and lumber was constantly being sent to the new mill (as it was called) to be manufactured for the Boston market.

[1] One of the early preceptors of this academy was the late Hon. Daniel Webster.

In 1799, the population of Gardiner was eight hundred, 150 of whom were at Bowman's point, then a part of Hallowell; and there were not over twenty houses from Gardiner to Stage island, at the mouth of the river. The first steamer on the Kennebec river was the "Waterville," which commenced running in 1826. It was not till 1834 that even stage travelling was a permanent thing. In 1827, the attempt to establish an hourly was made, but proved a failure. In 1829, the steam-ferry was chartered. In 1851, the first train of cars entered Gardiner. In 1820, the old church was purchased for a town-house, and permission given for all denominations of Christians to use it for worship whenever they wished. It was burned on the night of July 4, 1833, and is supposed to have been a sacrifice to rum. In 1822, the lyceum was established by R. H. Gardiner, and Professor Hale installed as principal. The institution continued to languish till 1848, when it was organized as an academy. In 1851, a public high school was opened in the building.

Gardiner city was chartered in 1849. It is situated at the head of summer navigation on the Kennebec. The common is situated in the pleasantest part of the city, about 125 feet above the river. It contains about five acres, on the summit of Church hill, from which the view stretches over a wide and pleasant country. The land was given by R. H. Gardiner. The physiognomy of the city is certainly striking. It has a rough, day-laboring look, which inspires the stranger at once with a feeling of security and attachment. The soil is mostly a clayey loam; the rocks are granite. The surface is undulating, and the water soft. It contains 10,448 acres.

There are ten places of public worship — two Baptist, one each Congregational, Episcopal, Free-will Baptist, Universalist, Roman Catholic, Swedenborgian, Methodist, and Christian; eight school districts, with fifteen schools; two post-offices, Gardiner and West Gardiner; three banks with an aggregate capital of $250,000; two bookstores, a printing-office, a paper-mill, a woollen factory, six saw-mills, two grist-mills, three tanneries, two hotels, and all the manufactures and accommodations usually found in such a place. During the season of navigation, Gardiner is the busiest place on the Kennebec. Population, 6,486; valuation, $2,098,000.

Garland is situated among the northern tier of towns in Penobscot county. Its exterior lines were run in 1792, by Ephraim Ballard and Samuel Weston. In 1796, the legislature of Massachusetts passed a resolve, granting to the trustees of Williams College two townships of land, to be assigned from any unappropriated lands belonging to that commonwealth in the district of Maine. Garland was one of the townships selected under the provisions of this resolve; and in 1798, the trustees of Williams College conveyed it to Levi Lincoln, Seth Hastings, Samuel Sanger, Samuel Sanger, Jr., Calvin Sanger, and Elias Grout. The township took the name of Lincoln, from one of the proprietors.

In the year 1800, Moses Hodsdon, assisted by Daniel Wilkins, David A. Gove, and a Mr. Shores, ran the lines between the lots. The first two lots selected in the township with reference to settlement were those of Mr. Gove and Mr. Wheeler. In 1802, openings were made by sixteen or eighteen individuals, from the western part of Maine and from New Hampshire, nearly all of whom afterwards became settlers. On the 22d of June, 1802, Joseph Garland, of Salisbury, N. H., arrived with his wife and three children, being the first family here. This circumstance afterwards gave the name to the township. In 1805, twelve families had taken up a permanent residence. In the autumn of 1802, a saw-mill was built by the proprietors; and, in 1803, several frame buildings were erected. The first school was opened by William Mitchell, in 1806, in the house of Joseph Garland. In 1811, the township was incorporated, there being at that time about fifty legal voters within its limits.

Garland is six miles square, the southern part, embracing more than one half of the whole area, being quite level, not very stony, and a good farming section. The northern part is traversed from east to west by a very high range of hills, which is intersected near the east line of the town by a deep ravine, known as the "Notch," apparently designed by nature as the point of egress for the people of Piscataquis county. A county road has been located, to run through the Notch; and the practicability of building a railroad through it from Bangor to the flourishing villages of Foxcroft and Dover, with a branch to the iron and slate localities of the Piscataquis region, has been discussed by the citizens. Numerous small streams originate at the summit of the range of hills, some running towards the Penobscot, and others finding their way into the Kennebec. The Kenduskeag runs from a small pond, lying partly in Dexter and partly in Garland. It takes a southeasterly course through the latter town, and makes itself useful on its way by driving one grist-mill, four shingle mills, five saw-mills, and other machinery.

The people are, for the most part, engaged in farming. The several mills cut out considerable quantities of the coarser kinds of lumber, and the manufacture of boots and shoes is prosecuted to some extent. There are two churches — Congregational and Baptist; nine school districts, with eleven schools; a high school, established in 1818, and well sustained; and two post-offices, one at Garland and the other at West Garland, which are the only villages in town. Population, 1,247; valuation, $132,004.

GEORGETOWN, Sagadahoc county, originally embraced several islands at the mouth of the Kennebec river, and included the present towns of Phipsburg, Bath, and Woolwich; but it has been shorn of its territory from time to time, until it has become reduced to a single island, formerly known as Parker's island, which was purchased of the natives, in 1650, by one John Parker, who was the first occupant after 1668. Yet it is thought by some, a small detachment of Popham's colony commenced a settlement on it. The occupancy of this island has continued under Parker's title from the time of his purchase to the present day, (excepting during the intervals occasioned by the Indian wars), and some of Parker's posterity are now proprietors of a part of the land, on which they live. The act of incorporation was obtained in 1716, while it embraced its greatest extent of territory.

About one half of the town is tolerable farming land, well adapted to grazing. The inhabitants are principally employed in coasting and fishing, though raising stock, and the manufacture of butter and cheese, receive attention. The town has three villages, Robin Hood's Cove, the principal one, Riggs's Cove, and Harmon's Harbor; two church edifices — Methodist and Free-will Baptist; nine school districts, and two post-offices. Some business is done by two saw-mills, two shingle mills, one grist-mill, one pail-maker, and one ship-builder. Population, 1,121; valuation, $155,390.

GILEAD is situated in the western part of Oxford county, on the boundary line between Maine and New Hampshire. Its settlement was commenced about the year 1780. In 1781, Williamson says there were but two families here; and on the 4th of August of that year, both of the men were killed by the Indians. A few years afterwards, several families moved in from Massachusetts and New Hampshire. Accessions were made from year to year, and on the 23d of June, 1805, it was incorporated, taking its name from a large Balm of Gilead tree, still standing near the centre of the town.

During the terrible storm of 1826, — memorable on account of the destruction of the Willey family, — slides took place on many of the mountains around this town. From Picked hill, thousands of tons of earth and rocks, with trees, came rushing down, destroying every thing that lay in their course. The darkness was intense, and the vivid lightnings and long streams of fire (caused by the concussion of the rocks which covered the sides of the mountains,) only served to increase the wildness and sublimity of the scene. The deluge of rain, the peals of thunder, and, above all, the deafening roar of the descending slides, were truly terrific, and the valley rocked as though shaken by an earthquake. No lives were lost; but the frightful scene, though brief, had more terror crowded into it than occurs in an ordinary lifetime.

The surface of Gilead is mountainous, and considerable portions are covered with forests, which, till very recently, were much infested with bears, especially during the summer months.[1] The earlier annals of the town are full of the thrilling adventures which the inhabitants encountered in hunting these animals.

Gilead is drained by the Androscoggin, which runs through its entire length from east to west, on the borders of which is some of the best land in this region. Wild river, an impetuous mountain stream, here falls into the Androscoggin. Gilead is so situated as to escape almost entirely the frosts of autumn. The valley is walled in on two sides by high ranges of mountains, shaggy and rude, between which there is a continual current of air, which preserves from the frosts the crops in the valley and on the slopes. The Grand Trunk Railway passes through this town into New Hampshire. There are two churches here (Congregational and Methodist), six school districts, with eleven schools, and one post-office. Three grist-mills, one shingle mill, and one brick-yard, are among the mechanical establishments. Population, 359; valuation, $47,622.

Glenburn, Penobscot county, about ten miles north of Bangor, was called Dutton until 1837, when it became an incorporated town, and received its present name. The surface is generally level, and the town is watered by Kenduskeag river and Pushaw pond, the latter forming its eastern boundary. Glenburn is more than an average farming town for this section of country, and the people seem to be proud of their occupation — agriculture. There is no water-power in town, and this may account in a measure for the number of fine farms and prosperous farmers. There are two saw-mills and two shingle mills on the banks of the Pushaw pond; but they do little more than supply the necessary building material required by the inhabitants. The town has one church edifice — Congregational; two post-offices — Glenburn and West Glenburn; and seven school districts, with the same number of schools. Population, 905; valuation, $86,821.

Gorham, in the southern part of Cumberland county, adjoining Portland, was No. 7 of the seven townships granted by the state of

[1] In the fall of 1804, it required all the vigilance and courage of the inhabitants to preserve their cattle and hogs from these ferocious denizens of the forest. The infuriated beasts would rush almost into the houses of the settlers, and young hogs were caught up and carried off before the very eyes of their owners.

Massachusetts to eight hundred and forty men, who were engaged in the Narraganset war. The settlement was commenced, soon after the grant was made, by John Phinney and Messrs. Bryant, Cloutman, Read, McClellan and others. They early took the precaution to defend themselves from the attacks of the Indians by the erection of block-houses; but these did not fully secure the inhabitants. An attack was made by a party of Indians on the 19th of April, 1746, when Bryant was killed in his field, his house assailed, five of his children killed and scalped, and the mother taken captive, carried to Canada, and sold. Other incursions were made from time to time, sufficient to keep up a constant state of apprehension and alarm, and at one time there were two men, by the name of Peale, killed.

In 1762 the town was surveyed, and, two years after, it was incorporated. From that time its growth has not been retarded by the reverses which many of the other towns of New England have suffered, and it now maintains a position of substantial independence. The town is pleasantly located, and has a soil of a superior quality. There are four villages, most of which are places of considerable business. Gorham is watered by Presumpscot river, and is traversed by the York and Cumberland Railroad. There are six churches — three Free-will Baptist, two Methodist, and one Congregational; eighteen school districts, an academy, a female seminary, a carpet factory, a tannery, a gunpowder mill, several saw and grist-mills, and two post-offices — Gorham and West Gorham. Population, 3,088; valuation, $684,732.

Gouldsborough, the most easterly town of Hancock county, lies between Frenchman's bay and Gouldsborough harbor. It covers a large, broken surface of some thirty thousand acres, and has an extensive sea-coast, with numerous islands and harbors. At least one third of the town is unfit for cultivation. It was originally granted by the legislature of Massachusetts to Nathan Jones, Francis Shaw, and Robert Gould of Boston, who settled it with lumbermen from Portland, Saco, and other places in that vicinity. It was incorporated February 16, 1789, receiving its corporate name in honor of Robert Gould, one of the original proprietors. General David Cobb, of Revolutionary fame, was for many years a resident of this town. There is one Baptist church here; there are also three saw-mills, three grist-mills, two tanneries, sixteen school districts, with the same number of schools; and two post-offices — Gouldsborough and West Gouldsborough. Population, 1,400; valuation, $125,931.

Grafton, in the northwest part of Oxford county, was first settled in

1830 by William Reed, Jesse Smith, Abraham R. York, Stephen Emery, and James Brown, the four latter having obtained their titles from the first-named settler. The northerly portion of the town is abundantly timbered with pine and spruce, while the southerly portion is very mountainous and broken, — there being only one pass, or notch, through which a road could be opened. The soil, however, is fertile. A plantation was organized in 1840, which was called Holmes until 1852, when it was incorporated as a town by its present name. The most noticeable streams are Cambridge, flowing north into the Umbagog lake, and Bear river, flowing south to the Androscoggin, on each of which is a saw-mill. Lumbering and farming constitute the occupations of the inhabitants. There are two small ponds, which are abundantly supplied with trout; and Speckled and Saddleback mountains are the principal eminences. Grafton has three school districts, and one post-office. Population, 200; valuation, $25,000.

GRAY is situated in the central part of Cumberland county, and was originally owned by inhabitants of Boston, to whom it was granted December 3, 1735, upon petition to the general court of Massachusetts, representing that they had large families, and were in straitened circumstances. Several years intervened before a settlement of the township could be effected; but in the mean time there were frequent meetings of the proprietors in Boston, generally held at the Sun Tavern, and sometimes at the British Coffee-house. One of the first settlers — probably the first — was Moses Twitchell, who came from Westboro', Mass. Jabez Matthews and William Webster followed soon after; and in the course of fifteen or twenty years, several other families moved in. In 1756, the proprietors made a report of the progress of the settlement to the legislature, in which they state that they had laid out sixty-three lots of sixty acres each for settling lots, had built a meeting-house, erected thirty-six dwelling-houses, and cleared a part of the lands, as required by the conditions of the grant; but that they had been put to great expense and suffering.

The settlers were in constant fear of hostile Indians, who at one time came upon the settlement in great numbers, destroyed the cattle, burnt the meeting-house and all the dwelling-houses, and obliged the settlers to flee to places of safety. After peace was concluded with the Indians, some of the inhabitants returned, and erected a new meeting-house, as well as a block-house, fifty feet long and twenty-five feet wide, around which they erected a garrison, one hundred feet long and seventy-five feet wide, which was supplied with military stores. Soon after, a rumor of war with France terrified the settlers, and they fled the second time; but the fort was not altogether forsaken, and, gradually, families obtained sufficient confidence to venture to take up a permanent abode here. At first the township was without a name, being known only as a proprietory lying on the back of North Yarmouth, in the county of York. About the year 1756, it began to be called New Boston. In 1778, by act of legislature, it was incorporated and called Gray, as it is supposed, in honor of Thomas Gray, one of the proprietors. The town furnished men and supplies for the Revolutionary war, and Moses Twitchell, the first settler, died in the public service in Canada. The last war with England called many from this town to the defence of their country.

The principal business is farming, although lumbering was formerly carried on to a large extent. The land is good for tillage, much of it being a clayey or sandy loam. The village called Gray Corner is situated near the centre of the town, upon an elevated plain, surrounded by hills. There are five religious societies — Congregational, Free-will Baptist, Protestant Methodist, Episcopal Methodist, and Universalist; as well as six stores, one public-house, two factories, two saw-mills, a new steam mill; a bank, capital, $50,000; an academy, chartered but not in operation; a railroad, chartered but not built; eleven school districts, with 718 scholars; and two post-offices, Gray and North Gray. Population, 1,788; valuation for 1856, $240,000.

GREENBUSH, Penobscot county, on the east side of the Penobscot, opposite Argyle, is twenty-three miles from Bangor. It was incorporated in 1834. The surface is somewhat varied, though the soil is on the average of a fertile character. It is drained by Olamon and other affluents of the Penobscot river. The village is a pleasant and thriving place. The town contains seven school districts and one post-office. Population, 457; valuation, $22,096.

GREENE, Androscoggin county, lies on the east side of the Androscoggin river, five miles above the falls at Lewiston, and six miles northeast of Auburn. It extends on the river six miles to Leeds line, is connected with Turner by a bridge, and is bisected by the Androscoggin and Kennebec Railroad. The settlement was commenced about the year 1775, when it was called Littlesborough. The settlers obtained their titles from the Pejepscot proprietors. Among the first inhabitants were Benjamin Merrill, Joseph Herrick, and Luther Robbins, the latter of whom was the first representative to the Massachusetts legislature after the incorporation of the town in 1788, in which office he continued, with one or two intervals, until the separation of Maine from Massachusetts in 1820.

Greene has but little water-power, and only three small ponds, the principal of which is the Sabattis pond, three miles long and one wide, on the southeast side of the town. The land is somewhat uneven, but the soil is quite productive. There are two villages, Greene and Greene Corner, with a post-office at each; two church edifices, one occupied by the Baptists, the other by the Universalists and Free-will Baptists alternately. Greene has two shingle mills, two saw-mills, one grist-mill, one tannery, three carriage builders, and three pail-makers; and thirteen school districts, with twenty-three schools. Population, 1,348; valuation in 1858, $259,553.

GREENFIELD, in the eastern part of Penobscot county, about twenty miles northeast from Bangor, was first settled in 1812 by Jeremiah Lord, Samuel Wheeler, and William Costagin from Salem, Mass., Peter Witham from Thomaston, and Miles Stone from Easton, Me. They obtained their titles from William Bingham or his heirs, through John Black, the agent. The town was incorporated in 1831; its surface is uneven, and it is watered by the Olamon and Sunkhaze streams, — the former running through nearly its entire length. Agriculture receives but little attention beyond the common wants of the inhabitants; the lumbering business, however, is carried on to some extent in the manufacture of shingles and clapboards. There are one saw-mill, two shingle mills, and one clapboard mill here; as also one post-office at Winslow Mills; and five school districts, with seven schools. Population, 305; valuation, $45,000.

GREENVILLE, Piscataquis county, is situated on the southern shore of Moosehead lake, thirty miles from Dover. It was incorporated in 1836, and, from its recent origin, has but little of note to commend it to the researches of the historian. The surface is hilly; but the soil is of the most fertile character, and with the aid of a thrifty and industrious population, Greenville will eventually take its rank among the best sections of country in the state. From the variety of its scenery and its location on the margin of the beautiful Moosehead, it has become, within the past few years, a place of summer resort. A view of the lake is here given, with the little steamer, which plies regularly between Greenville and Mount Kineo, in the foreground. Wilson pond lies within the limits of the town, by which with a few streams it is drained. The industry of the inhabitants is chiefly devoted to agriculture. There is a small village or settlement on the lake, which is rapidly increasing.

There are several mills in Greenville, three school districts, and one post-office. Population, 326; valuation, $36,150.

View at Greenville, on Moosehead Lake.

Greenwood is situated nearly in the centre of Oxford county. The settlement was commenced in 1802, by William Yates from Minot, who was followed the next year by Thomas Furlong from Danville, and Timothy Patch from Westbrook. Several others came in 1804; and in 1805 there were thirteen families. The town was incorporated in 1816.

The surface is very broken. It is watered by nine ponds, three of which fall into the Great Androscoggin river at Bethel; the other six form the head waters of the Little Androscoggin. Agriculture is the leading pursuit. Considerable attention is paid to fruit-growing, with good returns, some of the orchards producing two hundred barrels of apples in a year. One good mill privilege is already occupied. There are two villages — Greenwood, and Locke's Mills, with a post-office at each; and twelve school districts, with the same number of schools. There is but one church edifice, which is occupied by the Methodists. There are four saw-mills, two shingle mills, one grist-mill, and one pail-factory. Population, 1,118; valuation, $59,861.

Guilford in the southern part of Piscataquis county, was settled in 1806, by Robert Low, Jr., Robert Herring, Jr., and John and Nathaniel Bennett, — all from New Gloucester. The township was conveyed by Massachusetts to Bowdoin College in 1794; and by that college to

Robert Low. It was called Lowtown until 1816, when it was incorporated under its present name. The northern part is uneven and broken, but the south part has some very productive farms. The town is watered by Brainerd and Salmon stream ponds, and by Salmon stream and Piscataquis river, which flow southerly through it. Agriculture is the leading pursuit. There is only one village, in which are two church edifices, one occupied by Baptists, and the other by Methodists and Universalists. There are two post-offices, Guilford and Centre Guilford; and nine school districts, with fifteen schools; also two saw-mills, four shingle mills, one tannery, one grist-mill, one chair factory, one carriage builder, one brickmaker, and two pail-makers. Population, 834; valuation, $94,714.

HALLOWELL, Kennebec county, is situated on the west bank of the Kennebec river, and was a part of the Plymouth Kennebec Patent. The first permanent settlement after the devastating Indian wars that swept the region of which this was a part, was made within a few years after the erection of Fort Western in 1754, at a place called "the Hook," where the village now is. Inhabitants or resident traders were here at least a century earlier. The original lots, a part of which are in the present Hallowell, on the west side of the Kennebec, were four, each a mile wide, extending from the river to Winthrop pond. Two were granted in 1760 to Dr. Gardner, one to Mr. Pitts, and one to Mr. Hallowell, two of them Plymouth proprietors. The town was incorporated April 26, 1771, having a territory of nearly sixty thousand acres, extending upon both sides of the river, and embracing, besides its own present limited territory, what is now comprised in Augusta, Chelsea, Farmingdale, and a part of Manchester. On the 20th of February, 1797, the northerly part of it was cut off and incorporated by the name of Harrington, which, however, at the next session of the legislature, on the 9th of June following, was changed to Augusta.

About the year 1793, Charles Vaughan, a wealthy merchant of Boston, whose family were among the proprietors of the Kennebec Purchase, and who with them owned all the lands comprising the present village of Hallowell, — so called after his maternal grandfather, — took a strong interest in promoting the settlement of this section, and spared no expense to develop its resources. He designed Hallowell to be the great town at the head of navigation on the Kennebec, and built a distillery and a large brewery, capable of making more malt liquor than was then consumed in the whole of New England. He also erected a very large and expensive flour mill, furnished with the best machinery then in use; and built wharves, stores, and houses necessary for these branches of business. But as these establishments were all greatly in advance of the times, and consequently unprofitable, they gradually went to decay, and were abandoned.

In 1850, Hallowell lost all of its territory on the east side of the river, by the incorporation of Chelsea; and so much upon the west side as was taken to form Manchester: and again, in 1852, Farmingdale was taken from it, leaving it the smallest municipality in the county. Hallowell received a city charter August 29, 1850, and was divided into four wards.

The surface is somewhat uneven, but the soil suitable for agriculture, which engages considerable attention. The city contains five church edifices — Congregational, Methodist, Baptist, Unitarian, and Universalist; three school districts, with ten schools; one academy, supported by private individuals, and one post-office. It has also three ship yards, one steam saw-mill, two tanneries, two machine shops, a linseed oil factory, three carriage shops, four pail-making establishments, and two brick-yards. There are three banks, with an aggregate capital of $275,000. The population in 1850 was 4,769, since which the incorporation of Chelsea, Manchester, and Farmingdale, has probably reduced it to about 2,400; it has not suffered a proportionate reduction in valuation, which, in 1858, was $1,225,510.

HAMPDEN is the southeastern frontier town of Penobscot county, situated on the west side of Penobscot river, between Frankfort and Bangor, and contains an area of 23,040 acres. Benjamin Wheeler, the first settler, came from Durham, New Hampshire, about the year 1767, and "pitched his tent" at what was known as the "Basin," at the mouth of the Soadabscook stream. Wheeler, being a carpenter by trade, soon erected mills, and from him the place took the name of Wheelersborough. For the first ten or fifteen years after the arrival of Wheeler, the progress of the settlement was very slow; and, being disturbed by the English after their occupation of Bigaduce (now Castine), in 1779, the settlers retired through the woods to Kennebec, and from thence to Woolwich and Falmouth (now Portland). Returning in 1783, they resumed the settlement; and, in 1796, the township was surveyed and lotted by Ephraim Ballard, every inhabitant receiving a lot of one hundred acres. If he were a settler before January, 1784, he paid six dollars; but if afterwards, and before January, 1794, he paid fifty dollars. The residue of the town was assigned by the government to General Knox, to make up for a deficiency in the Waldo Patent. After the conclusion of peace, large accessions arrived from Cape Cod, and the town was incorporated January, 1794, though it appears from the records that it acted in a municipal capacity as early as 1784. Its corporate name was adopted in memory of the famous Englishman, John Hampden.

General John Crosby was one of the early settlers. He came from Woolwich about 1775, and commenced as a farmer on the estate now occupied by Ivory Frost. He afterwards entered largely into commercial business, and carried on an extensive trade both with Europe and the East Indies. He died May 25, 1843, at the advanced age of eighty-six. Another prominent man among the early settlers was General Gabriel Johonot, a Frenchman by birth, a brave and distinguished officer in the American army during the Revolution. He was a friend and correspondent of General Washington; and, during a long and active life, exerted a great influence in the affairs of the town. Hon. Martin Kinsley, General Jedediah Herrick, Enoch Brown, and John Godfrey were early and prominent citizens of the town. Hon. Hannibal Hamlin, now a senator in congress from this state, settled here as a lawyer about 1832.

During the last war with England, Hampden suffered probably the most of any town in the state. The United States corvette, the *Adams*, of twenty-four guns, Captain Charles Morris, homeward bound from a cruise, arrived off Penobscot bay in the latter part of August, 1814, at which time there was a large British fleet in the vicinity, under command of Rear Admiral Griffith. On entering the bay, the *Adams* struck a sunken rock, causing her to leak badly. Captain Morris proceeded up the river to repair, and arrived at Hampden during the last week of the month, and commenced dismantling his ship. The British admiral, learning the situation of the *Adams*, determined to take her; and immediately despatched two sloops of war, one brig, and several transports, with seven hundred regulars, under command of Colonel Henry John, of the 60th regiment. Captain Morris made every preparation for defending his ship; landed her guns, and erected two batteries, one on the wharf, and another on a hill two hundred yards below the wharf. The militia had collected to the number of six hundred, under command of General Blake, of Brewer, who took up a position on the ridge, where the house of James A. Swett now stands, for the purpose of opposing the advance of the enemy on the main road, they having landed at Bald Hill cove. General Blake had taken no precaution to have breastworks thrown up for the protection of his troops, and had failed to make any arrangements by which a successful resistance might have been made; nor did he even do so much as post sergeants in the rear of his line to prevent the troops from retreating. At daylight, on the morning of September 3, the British forces were in motion on the road from Frankfort; and when within three hundred yards of General Blake's position opened their fire, and advanced with fixed bayonets in "double quick time." His force, being outflanked, immediately gave way, and made a precipitate retreat. The British troops pressed on to Captain Morris's batteries; and as the men had no protection in the rear, they were driven from their guns at the point of the bayonet.

Captain Morris blew up his ship, and with his men retreated to Bangor, thence to Portland. The English commander was greatly provoked at losing his prize; and, for three days, he permitted the sailors, marines, and land-force, full liberty on shore. They committed the most wanton excesses in the plunder of the citizens and the destruction of property. The furniture in nearly all of the houses in the village was entirely destroyed, and the cattle and hogs belonging to the farmers were killed. Even the sanctuary of the Most High did not escape their sacrilegious hands. They entered the meeting-house, tore the Bible and psalm-book in pieces, and cut down the altar and pews with their cutlasses.

This proved a heavy blow to the inhabitants of Hampden. Many who had been independent were rendered almost destitute by this calamity. But this was not all. When the English force left, they took about eighty of the citizens to Castine, as prisoners of war. They were released in a short time, on the promise of the selectmen of the town to pay one thousand dollars as a ransom. Peace being concluded soon after, the ransom was never paid. The inhabitants, by their industrious habits, in a few years recovered from the losses they thus sustained, and have since continued prosperous and thriving.

The surface of the town is somewhat rolling, but well adapted for agricultural purposes. The principal stream, and the only one of any note, is the Soadabscook, running through the town from west to east, and affording water-power for fifteen saw-mills, three paper-mills, and two grist-mills. Hampden has one cloth-dressing mill, three shingle mills, two ship-builders, three brickmakers, and two carriage builders. There are three natural ponds, situated in the northwest part of the town, named Great, Little, and George; two villages, both situated on the river road, about one mile apart, known as the Upper and Lower Corners; four post-offices, one of which is at Hampden, one at Hampden Corner, one at West Hampden, and one at East Hampden. The first meeting-house was built by the town in 1796, and for thirty years was the only place of worship. It is now standing, and in good repair, and for the last twenty years has been used as a town-house. There are now six church organizations and six church edifices, namely, two Methodist, two Baptist, one Congregational, and one Universalist; also, fifteen stores, eighteen school districts, with twenty schools, and an academy, which was incorporated in 1803, and has ever since been in successful operation. Population, 3,195; valuation, $423,441.

HANCOCK, in the southern part of Hancock county, having Taunton bay on the east, and Skilling bay on the west, is about thirty miles southeast from Bangor. The first settlers were Philip and S. Hodgkins, who came from Georgetown, in this state, in 1766. A. G. Crabtree, Oliver Wooster, Thomas Googing, Thomas and James McFarland, and Reuben and Moses Abbott soon followed. These settlers belonged to Maine and Massachusetts, and were accompanied by their families. Thomas Moon, Francis Grant, William Gatcomb, James Smith, John Cook, and Richard Clark, with their families, were also among the early settlers. The inhabitants obtained the titles to their lands from Massachusetts.

Hancock was incorporated in 1828, the greater part of it having been set off from the town of Sullivan. Tracts were also annexed to it from No. 3 township, and from Trenton. The surface is generally even; but the agricultural advantages which it possesses are not improved to any great extent. There are two streams having sufficient water-power for mills, one of which is known by the name of Kilkenny, and the other by that of Egypt, on which are one grist-mill, four shingle mills, and four lath-mills. Besides the mills already noticed, there is one propelled by steam, manufacturing all the varieties of lumber, and having a grist-mill connected with it. Near the centre of the town is a small village, in which there are two meeting-houses — Baptist and Free-will Baptist. The principal occupation of the inhabitants is seafaring. There is a considerable number of vessels owned here. Hancock contains a boot and shoe manufactory, two stores, eight school districts, and two post-offices — Hancock and North Hancock. Population, 960; valuation, $128,822.

HANCOCK COUNTY is one of the seaboard counties of eastern Maine, and lies mainly between 44° 10′ and 45° 20′ north latitude, having Washington county upon the east, and Penobscot bay and county upon the west. No county has undergone more changes in territorial limits; notwithstanding which, by reference to the map, it will be seen that neither this nor Penobscot county has yet attained a natural shape. Hancock and Washington were the fourth and fifth counties in the then province of Maine, the act establishing them being passed June 25, 1789. The easterly line of this county, separating it from Washington, from the ocean as far up as townships Thirty-three and Thirty-four, was then the same as at present; but the westerly line ran on the westerly side of Penobscot bay through a part of what is now Waldo county, northeasterly to the north line of the Waldo Patent, thence northerly to the highlands.[1] A portion of it was taken, in 1816, to form Penobscot county, and, in 1827, to form Waldo county. The west and north lines of Hancock are still as awkward as possible, having no regard to the Penobscot river, (which is the natural division of the counties,) further up than the north line of Bucksport, then turning east as far as Mariaville, then north as far as Lowell in Penobscot, and again east to Washington county, yielding to Penobscot quite a number of towns on the east side of the river. The territory of Hancock is, however, sufficiently large, being about one hundred miles long from north to south, including bays and islands, and forty in width. It has twenty-eight incorporated towns, nineteen inland plantations, and nineteen island plantations. The Union river and bay divide it into nearly equal parts, called Eastern and Western Hancock. It is distinguished for the number and magnitude of its islands, its capacious bays, roadsteads, and harbors, its rivers, lakes, and ponds, and its bold and magnificent scenery. Its commercial interests and relations abroad are extensive and important. Agriculture is the leading pursuit in the interior, but along the rivers and upon the coast the principal business is lumbering, fishing, ship-building, and coasting.

Penobscot became the shire town in 1789, but this distinction enured to Castine upon its incorporation from a part of Penobscot in 1796. On the 17th of February, 1837, Ellsworth became the shire town.

This county belongs to the eastern judicial district, the law terms of which are held at Bangor. The jury terms of the supreme judicial court, for both civil and criminal business, are held at Ellsworth, on the fourth Tuesdays of April and October. Population, 34,372; valuation, $4,621,567.

Hanover, in the western part of Oxford county, was incorporated in the year 1843, being taken from that part of Bethel lying upon the northerly side of the Androscoggin river. It is a small town, beautifully situated, and is about eight miles from the Grand Trunk Railway. It comprises some of the best interval farms in the county. Hanover was called by the Indians, Sudbury-Canada, and was first settled by Nathaniel Segar from Newton, Mass., in the spring of 1774. He returned

[1] "The proclamation of 1763, and commissions to governors," — the "Quebec bill," passed in 1774, — the "definitive treaty of peace," of September 3, 1783, — and the act of 1791, dividing Canada into the Upper and Lower provinces, all speak of "the highlands, which divide the rivers emptying themselves into the St. Lawrence, from those which fall into the Atlantic ocean." The term is, therefore, here applied to the northern limits of Maine.

in the autumn to Newton, and remained in the United States service most of the time until 1780, when he again came to Bethel, and commenced clearing a farm, on which he worked until the 3d of August, 1781, when he was taken and held captive by the Indians for sixteen months. After his captivity he returned to Bethel, where he spent the remainder of his days. Jonathan Bean, from Standish, settled here in 1780, on the farm now owned and occupied by Abner Brown; and Jesse Duston from Haverhill, Mass., settled here soon after, on the farm now owned by Adam Willis; Moses and Stephen Bartlett from Newton, Mass., were also among the first settlers. Phineas Howard, from Temple, N. H., purchased the land comprised in this town from Massachusetts, about the year 1792, and from him it was called Howard's Gore, until the time of its incorporation.

The surface is broken and uneven, and is watered by Howard's pond, lying about a mile from Androscoggin river. This pond is noted for its abundance of speckled trout. The stream that flows from it into the Androscoggin river furnishes water-power for two wheelwright shops, one furniture shop, one grist-mill, one saw-mill, one threshing machine, one shingle machine, and one woollen factory. The majority of the people are devoted to agriculture. A village is situated near the Androscoggin river, in which is a Methodist meeting-house and a post-office. There are four school districts, with seven schools. Population, 266; valuation, $38,212.

HARMONY, Somerset county, is a six mile square township, and was originally granted by the state of Massachusetts to the trustees of Hallowell academy, of whom it was purchased by Charles Vaughan. It was settled in 1796, and was then known as Vaughanstown, which name was changed to the one it now bears June 15, 1804, the time of its incorporation.

Harmony has a tolerably productive soil, in the cultivation of which the inhabitants are principally engaged; and has one village, situated in the central part; a saw-mill, a grist-mill, two shingle mills, a carding machine, and a carriage builder; ten school districts, with sixteen schools; one Methodist and one Baptist church; and one post-office. Population, 1,107; valuation, $130,286.

HARPSWELL, Cumberland county, directly south of Brunswick, formerly called Merryconeag peninsula, comprises within its limits Erascohegan, Bailey's, Haskell's, Orr's, and House islands, beside several smaller ones. The first permanent settlement was commenced in 1720, and the town was incorporated in January, 1758.

The soil is tolerably good, consisting in part of gravel, clay, and brown mould, which, by a proper mixture, produces good crops. Something is done annually in ship-building; and the fisheries are a source of considerable profit. The inhabitants are all in comfortable circumstances, the town being without a pauper. There are five church edifices on the Neck, one on Erascohegan island, and one on Bailey's island; and fifteen school districts, with twenty-four schools. Population, 1,534; valuation, $314,941.

HARRINGTON, Washington county, at the head of Narraguagus bay, was No. 5 of the six second-class townships east of Union river, granted by the General Court of Massachusetts, in 1762, to an association of petitioners. The settlement was commenced a few years after the grant was made, and it was incorporated as a town, June 17, 1796, when it contained a population of 177. There are several mill privileges here, some excellent harbors, and one small village. The surface is level, but the land is good for nothing in an agricultural point of view. Harrington has considerable navigation and trade for a town of its size, and much business is done in lumber. There are two religious societies — Baptist and Episcopal Methodist, both of which have church edifices; ten school districts, with nine schools; and two post-offices. Also, two saw-mills, three shingle mills, a tannery, a grist-mill, two lath manufactories, two brickmakers, and eighteen ship-builders. Population, 963; valuation, 109,318.

HARRISON is situated in the northwest of Cumberland county, and was formed from parts of the towns of Otisfield and Bridgton. It was incorporated March 8, 1805, and derived its name from Harrison Gray Otis, of Boston, who owned a large quantity of land in it. Harrison is small as to territory, but it compares well with other towns as regards its agricultural products. It has two villages — Harrison and Bolster's Mills; its mechanical establishments consist of one saw-mill, two grist-mills, one tannery, one foundery, two machine shops, one carriage factory, and one wire factory, the latter employing about fifteen hands. The trade comprises produce, lumber, and stock. The Cumberland and Oxford canal affords excellent facilities during the summer season, for transportation to Portland. There are five church edifices — Congregational, Baptist, Free-will Baptist, and two Methodist; thirteen school districts, with twenty-four schools; and one post-office. Population, 1,416: valuation, $253,625.

HARTFORD, in the eastern part of Oxford county, was settled soon after the close of the Revolutionary war, and incorporated in 1798. It is watered by numerous ponds and small streams, and has some very good farming land. Hartford has one village, called Hartford Centre; one church edifice, occupied by all denominations; sixteen school districts, with twenty-six schools; and one post-office; also one saw-mill, one grist-mill, two shingle mills, and a tannery. Population, 1,293; valuation, $175,000.

HARTLAND, in the southeast part of Somerset county, was formerly called Warren's Town, No. 3. It was first settled about the year 1800, by William Moor, a native of Goffstown, N. H., who came to what is now Hartland village, and built mills. About the same time, James Fuller, Simeon Starbird, Daniel Ham, Eben Ordlin, Joseph Bowley, Uzziah Withee, and Benjamin Church, with a few others, came from different towns in New Hampshire, and made a permanent settlement. Their descendants are now among the most wealthy and influential citizens. Dr. John Warren, of Boston, was the original proprietor of the township; and from him the settlers derived their titles. Hartland was organized as a plantation in 1811, and incorporated as a town in 1820.

The surface is generally uneven, with a soil of more than common fertility, considering its rocky nature. Agriculture receives fair attention, encouraged by the East Somerset Agricultural Society, which holds its annual exhibitions at Hartland. Moose pond, partly in this town, is about seven miles in length and six in breadth, furnishing a constant supply of water for the mills and mechanical establishments situated at its outlet. Here is located the neat and flourishing village of Hartland, the only one in town. The Baptist meeting-house is the only church edifice. The St. Albans Academy is a flourishing institution; besides which there are ten school districts, with eleven schools. The only post-office is known by the name of Hartland.

An extensive tannery, in full operation, adds much to the thrift and prosperity of the village. The nearest railroad station is at Pittsfield, on the Penobscot and Kennebec Railroad, seven miles distant. Manufactures are receiving greater attention than formerly, although the very excellent water-power still invites a much further investment of capital. The village was formerly and extensively known as St. Albans till 1846, when it was set off from the latter town by an act of the legislature. Population, 960; valuation, $83,166.

HEBRON, in the southeast corner of Oxford county, about thirty-five miles southwest of Augusta, was granted by Massachusetts, on the 8th day of March, 1777, to Alexander Shepard, Jr., of Newton, Mass. This grant was three, or, perhaps, four miles square, and comprehended that portion of territory adjacent to Buckfield. It was distinguished by the name of Bog Brook by the early settlers; and by them it has been represented to have been made in consideration of the chart of a coast survey of Maine, which, they say, was the work of an Englishman, who employed Shepard to assist him in the undertaking. The survey having been completed at the time when the people of the colony began to look fiercely toward the mother country and to pay all her demands in a currency that was not quite so acceptable as cash, the Englishman abruptly quitted America, and his chart, or a copy of it, was left with Shepard. This chart was purchased of Shepard by the state government, and the grant made in payment therefor. Subsequently, Shepard extended his claim over all the isolated tract, of which the above grant was only a part, and which covered more than thirty-six thousand acres. No information is given as to the authority on which he founded his extended claim; but it seems that government recognized it, except as to some small portions.

In the year 1778, Captain Daniel Buckman, with his family, moved here: they were probably the first family on the grant. John Greenwood, Asa Bearce, and Abner Curtis came in soon after: they remained but a few years, and returned to Massachusetts. In 1780 and 1781, a large number of persons arrived from that state, and commenced permanent settlements. Among the names of these were Barrows, Bumpas, Benson, Cushman, Weston, Keen, Richmond, and Thayer, some of whom had large families. The settlement now assumed an animated appearance, — dense columns of smoke curling upward from clearings in all directions. Many of the settlers were fresh from the battle fields of the Revolution; and it was well that they had thus become inured to hardships, and were ready to compete with difficulties, for ere comfort could be secured, stern obstacles stared them in the face.

The original name was Shepardsfield, which was retained until the 6th of March, 1792, when the town was incorporated under its present name. From its shape, — extending something like fifteen miles, from Norway to Turner, — the voters experienced some inconvenience in assembling at a given spot; and, to remedy the difficulty, the town was divided, about January, 1829, — the southwesterly part being called Oxford; the northeasterly part retaining the name of Hebron. The surface of Hebron is generally hilly. In the north part is Streaked mountain, extending partly into Paris and partly into Buckfield. It is a large and rather smooth elevation, rising to the height of about sixteen hundred feet above the field below, which is rather high land. It is composed principally of solid rock, which, with the little shrubbery growing on its surface, gives it the appearance from which it derives its name. This mountain is surrounded by a number of others, which, though not so high, yet make a prominent feature in the adjacent landscape. Some of them are immediately connected with Streaked mountain, and, in some places, are rough, rocky, and precipitous; but on their declivities are some good farms.

Hebron is well watered by ponds and small streams, the three principal of which are Bog brook, the Middle branch, and Matthew's pond, on which there is considerable interval. Some of the land is hard and rocky, while other portions are free from stones and easy to cultivate. Every article common to this latitude can be grown here; and there are advantages for orcharding possessed by few other towns. The people generally obtain their livelihood by agriculture, and the most of them are industrious and prosperous.

Among the early settlers who have acted an important part in the affairs of Hebron may be mentioned Deacon William Barrows; who, besides being forward in every other effort that would promote the public good, was mainly instrumental in the founding of Hebron academy, which was incorporated February 10, 1804, and is a flourishing and useful institution. Hebron is noted for being the birthplace of the late Governor, Albion K. Parris.

There are two meeting-houses in Hebron — Baptist and Free-will Baptist; eight school districts, with nine schools; one saw-mill, a shingle mill, a pail factory, a blacksmith's shop, a shoemaker's shop, and two post-offices — Hebron and East Hebron. Population, 839; valuation, $113,854.

HERMON, Penobscot county, joins Bangor on the west, and is one of the four towns assigned to General Knox by the state to make up the deficiency of eighty-three thousand acres in the Waldo Patent. The settlement was commenced about 1790, by Julius Hewes, William Patten, Collins Howes, Jotham Mason, and a few others, nearly all of whom came from New Hampshire. Immigration at first was very small; and when the town was incorporated, in 1814, there were not over twenty families in it. Hermon is now nearly all cleared up, and has a productive soil. The surface is rolling, but not hilly or broken. The fields are well fenced, and yield luxuriant crops. There are a few families in the northern part of idle, dissolute habits, who have given to strangers a false impression of the character of the people. Hermon is watered by the Kenduskeag and the Soadabscook rivers, neither of which has any mill privileges. It has one small village; three post-offices — Hermon, North Hermon, and Hermon Pond; one church edifice — Universalist; and fourteen school districts, with twelve schools. Population, 1,374; assessors' valuation for 1858, about $183,000.

Hiram, in the extreme southern part of Oxford county, lies on both sides of the Saco river. Benjamin Ingalls, John Watson, Thomas Veazie, John Bucknell, Benjamin Burbank, and one Foster, were among the earliest settlers, having arrived here about the year 1788. They were followed the next year by many others; and from this time the town was rapidly settled by emigrants, principally from this state, New Hampshire, and Massachusetts. Among the distinguished men who have been residents in this town, was General Peleg Wadsworth, an officer in the Revolutionary war, who was born in Duxbury, Mass., in 1748. He purchased a tract of land in Hiram in 1790, from a committee appointed by the general court of Massachusetts, and commenced clearing a farm on the land for his oldest son, Charles L. Wadsworth, in 1792 or 1794.

Hiram was incorporated in 1807. It is rather uneven at the centre, but on the Saco and Ossipee rivers (the latter of which divides the town from Cornish) are some fine tracts of interval; and, on the north side of the Ossipee, are some tracts of pitch-pine plain. The most noted mountains are called Bill Morrill (named from an old hunter) and Mount Misery. Saco river runs through a part of the town, and turning divides it from Baldwin. Ten Mile brook, Cleman's, Spectacle, Image, Hancock, and Bryant's ponds, furnish excellent water-power for mills and other machinery.

There are two small villages, one on the west side of Saco river, at the bridge, where are a few dwelling-houses, a store, a tavern, harness-maker's shop, blacksmith's shop, town-house, and school-house. Upon a small stream, not far from the bridge, is a grist-mill, with two runs of stones; and, underneath, machinery for sawing shingles, clapboards, staves, and heading; also, a cooper shop. The other village is half a mile easterly from the bridge. The town contains one meeting-house, owned by the Methodists and Free-will Baptists, but occasionally occupied by other denominations; five saw-mills, two grist-mills, two stores, one carding and fulling-mill, several shingle machines, and two blacksmith's shops. A number of cooper shops are in operation, and several shoemakers' shops, in which shoes are manufactured for Lynn, Mass., and other places. A large amount of sale-work, so called, is made by the women of this town for the clothing merchants of Boston. There are fifteen school districts, with twenty-five schools, and one post-office. Population, 1,210; valuation, $143,761.

HODGDON, Aroostook county, is distant from Augusta 178 miles, and from Houlton five miles. John Dural, James Daggett, James U. Parker, Joseph Kendall, Jabez Bradbury, Thomas Lander, Charles Tryon, Rufus Wiggin, James Ham, Joseph Gerow, Joseph E. Jackins, and Daniel Smith were among the first settlers. They obtained the titles to their lands from John Hodgdon, the proprietor.

Hodgdon was incorporated in 1833. The surface is smooth, there being but one hill, which is called Westford Hill. It is watered by a stream called Meduxnekeag. Hodgdon is formed of two half townships — the north half being the Groton Academy grant, and the south half, the Westfield Academy grant. It has three saw-mills, one grist-mill, two clapboard machines, and several shingle and lath machines. The first saw-mill and the first grist-mill were built in 1828–9, by Jabez Bradbury.

There are four churches — one Baptist, one Methodist, and two Free-will Baptist; also, one post-office, and eight school districts, with fourteen schools, having an aggregate attendance of 480 scholars. Population, 862; assessors' valuation for 1857, $65,659.

HOLDEN, Penobscot county, is situated on the east side of Penobscot river, opposite Bangor, the town of Brewer intervening. It was incorporated from Brewer in 1850. The surface is somewhat uneven; but there are some fine and productive farms. The town contains one Congregational church; eight school districts, with eight schools; four saw-mills, two of which are run the whole year, and two but two months of that period; and two post-offices — Holden and East Holden. Population, about 600; valuation, $119,943.

HOLLIS, York county, was a part of the tract of land purchased by Small and Shapleigh of the Indian sagamore, Captain Sunday.[1] A truck-house was erected here at an early date, and stood about ten miles above Saco Lower Falls. The plantation name of the town was Little Falls, which was changed on its incorporation, February 27, 1798, to Phillipsburg, and subsequently to the one it now bears. The surface is moderately uneven. Water is supplied by Kelliok pond and Saco river, the latter of which forms the eastern boundary. The inhabitants are engaged for the most part in agricultural pursuits. The villages are three in number — Hollis Centre, Moderation Bar Mills, and Salmon Falls. The two latter are on the Saco river, or rather are divided by it, being partly in Buxton. They are both manufacturing

[1] See Parsonsfield.

villages of some note, and send much lumber to market. The church edifices are Methodist and Free-will Baptist. There are fifteen school districts, with twenty-three schools; two post-offices — Hollis and Hollis Centre; seven saw-mills, three grist-mills, nine shingle mills, two carriage builders, two pail-makers, and one brickmaker. Population, 2,683; valuation, $247,894.

HOPE, Waldo county, on St. George's river, twenty miles southerly from Belfast, began to be settled about 1782. It was a tract of land bought by Charles Barrett, of New Ipswich, N. H., who sold to the settlers; and was called Barrettstown. Some of the early inhabitants were Reuben and Simon Barrett, Reuben Safford, Enoch and Walter Philbrick, Samuel and Daniel Bartlett, William Howett, Sampson and Stephen Sweetland, Micah Hobb, and Fergus McLain, who came from different towns in New Hampshire and Massachusetts.

The town was incorporated under its present name, in 1804. In 1843, two and a half miles of its territory, on the north side, was annexed to Appleton, divesting Hope of St. George's river, and two villages of some importance. The surface is uneven, but the soil, a rich loam, is of an excellent quality, and the agricultural facilities are of the best character. There are three mountains — Mount Hatchet in the centre, and two others in the northern part, of the town. Hope is watered by a lake lying in the western section, two and a half miles long by one and a half wide, at the outlet of which are several mills; and by two ponds. There are three meeting-houses — Baptist, Methodist, and Universalist; seven school districts, with fourteen schools; and two post-offices — Hope and South Hope; also, two saw-mills, one grist-mill, one shingle mill, one edge-tool factory, and one pail factory. Population, 1,108; valuation for 1858, $219,943.

HOULTON, the shire town of Aroostook county, was settled by two families, named Houlton and Putnam, from Massachusetts, about the year 1807. The nearest settlements to them at this date were Bangor and Calais, the former distant one hundred and twenty, and the latter ninety, miles. Houlton was incorporated in 1831, taking its name from one of the two first settlers. The surface is composed of large swells, which yield wheat, hay, and potatoes in abundance. A branch of the St. John river furnishes ample supplies of water. In the year 1830, a military station was established here by the United States government; but, war breaking out with Mexico, the troops were removed in 1847, since which the barracks and buildings erected for their accommodation have remained unoccupied, and are fast going to decay. The village is a flourishing one, and contains the county buildings. Houlton has two church edifices — Methodist and Congregational; and two religious societies without edifices — Baptist and Roman Catholic; nine school districts, with eight schools; an academy, and one post-office; also three saw-mills, two grist-mills, two tanneries, a carding machine, a chair factory, a machine shop, two carriage builders, and one brickmaker. Population, 1,453; valuation, $141,599.

HOWLAND, Penobscot county, is situated on the west bank of the Penobscot river, forty miles above Bangor. It was incorporated in 1826; and is drained by the Piscataquis river and its tributaries, the Penobscot forming its eastern boundary. The surface is varied with rich intervals on the margins of the rivers, the banks of which are low and very beautiful. The town has one village, several saw-mills, one church edifice (Methodist), five school districts, and two post-offices — Howland and North Howland. Population, 214; valuation, $24,114.

HUDSON, Penobscot county, was originally purchased of the Commonwealth of Massachusetts, by William Sullivan, of Boston. Its settlement was commenced in 1800 by Luke Wilder, David Pierce, Wareham Briggs, Tristram Warner, and was gradually continued by others. In 1824, it was organized into a plantation under the name of Jackson; and in 1825, it became an incorporated town, with the name of Kirkland, which it retained until changed in 1854. The land is stony and hard, notwithstanding which there is grass enough for raising neat stock. The inhabitants, for the most part, are engaged in the lumber business. There is one village, near the centre of the town, on the Little Pushaw stream, containing two saw-mills, two shingle and clapboard mills, one furniture manufactory, two cooper shops; and a post-office; a Free-will Baptist church, and seven school districts, with seven schools. Population, 717; valuation, $41,296.

INDUSTRY, Franklin county, formed from the northwest corner of the Plymouth Patent or Kennebec Purchase, is bounded on the west by Farmington and New Sharon, and north by New Vineyard, a part of which has been set off to Industry. The first settlements were made by James and John Thompson, Zoe Withe, Thomas Johnson, and William Allen, about 1793 or 1794. Benjamin Cottle, Daniel Luce, Peter Daggett, Jabez Norton, Peter West, James Winslow, John Gowner, and Lemuel Howes were also early settlers. The lands were first taken up as each individual chose to select, and held by possession,

14*

being afterwards purchased of those claiming proprietorship under the original grant.

Industry was incorporated June 20, 1803. The soil is very productive. The Bull-Horse or Clear-Water pond, situated in the northwest corner, affords an excellent stream of water, on which are a first-rate grist-mill, saw-mill, tannery, and starch factory, which, with a store and a number of mechanics' shops, form a place of considerable business, near the outlet of the pond. In the northeast part is a village known as West's Mills, having a fulling-mill, carding-machine, and a number of stores and shops. There are six church edifices — two Methodist, Baptist, Congregational, Free-will Baptist, and a Union house; fourteen school districts, with thirteen schools; and two post-offices — Industry and West's Mills. Population, 1,041; valuation, $147,545.

ISLANDPORT, belonging to Hancock county, is pretty well out to sea, and is defined by the act incorporating it, February 11, 1857, as "the plantation of Long Island, lying south from Mount Desert some eight miles, and east from Isle Haut some twelve miles." It is a little spot of five hundred acres, not more than half of which is cleared of wood. The first settler was one Barks, who came some time previous to the year 1820. Others settled before 1823, among whom were William Rich, Thomas Rice, William Pomeroy, Joseph Remick, Franklin Spofford, John Perkins, Amos, Jacob, and Ezra B. Lunt. The settlers hold their titles by occupancy, no claimant by purchase having found the place sufficiently valuable to attempt to oust them. The principal occupations of the inhabitants are fishing, and coasting in a small way, — shipping paving-stones to Boston, and kiln-wood to Rockland, coming under the latter head. A school-house, which has also been used a part of the time as a chapel, was erected four or five years since, by contributions of people in Massachusetts, at a cost of about three hundred dollars. A Baptist church was formed some years since, but its organization has not been kept up. There are some twenty-five families on the island, making a population of 152.

ISLESBORO', Waldo county, lying near the centre of Penobscot bay, consists of several small islands, the principal of which is Long Island. It is twelve miles in length, and three miles in its greatest width, — a singular feature being, that in the middle it does not exceed three rods.

One of the first settlers on Long Island was a man by the name of Gilkey. He had scarcely made any efforts at improvement, when the Revolutionary war broke out, and he was impressed into the British service; his wife and two young children being left destitute on the island, to gain a subsistence as best they could. After the close of the war, other families moved in, and in 1789 it became an incorporated town, and is now quite thickly settled.

Sea-going is the principal pursuit of the inhabitants; and as a specimen of what is done in this line, it may be mentioned, that one hundred and fifty-three vessels sailed from Islesboro' in 1855, many of which were owned in town, while all the masters were residents there. Islesboro' has eight school districts, with the same number of schools; four meeting-houses, one of which is used principally for a town-house; and two post-offices, one at Islesboro' and the other at North Islesboro'. Population, 984; valuation, $95,104.

ISLES OF SHOALS is a name applied to a cluster of eight islands, situated nine miles from Portsmouth (N. H.) light-house, a part of which belong to York county, Me., and a part to New Hampshire. The largest contains three hundred and fifty acres, and the smallest but one acre. They were discovered by the celebrated John Smith in 1614, and named by him Smith's Isles. They are little else than a bed of rocks raising their unsightly heads above the water, covered for the most part with a thin soil; and but for their advantageous situation for carrying on the fisheries, would probably never have been inhabited. For more than a century previous to the Revolution they were very populous, containing at times six hundred inhabitants, having a court-house upon one island, and a meeting-house upon another. From three to four thousand quintals of fish were annually caught and cured here, and seven or eight schooners, besides numerous boats, were employed in the fisheries. Only faint traces, however, of its ancient business and population now exist. William Pepperrell and a Mr. Gibbons from Topsham, England, were among the first settlers. The former was an ancestor of the celebrated Sir William Pepperrell, of Kittery. Population, 29.

JACKSON, in the northern part of Waldo county, about fourteen miles from the city of Belfast, is five and a half miles in length from north to south, and five miles wide from east to west. The first settlement was made in 1798, by Benjamin Cates, of Gorham, from whom Cates hill takes its name. Joel Rich arrived the next year, and settled on what is known as the Rich Hill, where two of his sons now live. Nicholas Hamlin, Benjamin Skillings, John Cates, George, Elisha, and Ebenezer Morton, and Nathaniel Knight, most of them from Gorham, were among the earliest settlers.

Jackson was organized into a plantation in 1812, and incorporated as a town in 1818. General Henry Knox was the original proprietor under the Waldo Patent. He sold a few lots to settlers, and afterwards disposed of the whole tract to Israel Thorndike, David Sears, and William Prescott. Thorndike, although residing in Boston, had a taste for agricultural pursuits, and cleared up and cultivated a large farm, which he stocked with numbers of cattle, horses, sheep, and poultry. He set out an orchard with five hundred apple trees, and planted a large garden. This place, still known as the Great Farm, has passed into the hands of persons who have not felt disposed to cultivate it so extensively as formerly, and, as a consequence, it has fallen into decay.

The surface is very much broken. There is but one stream, called the Great Farm brook, formed by other brooks, which take their rise in the northwesterly part, and unite near the Great Farm. The Congregationalists own and occupy the only church edifice. There are eight school districts, with eight schools, and one post-office; also, four saw-mills, two shingle mills, one carding machine, a pail factory, one machine shop, and one carriage builder. Population, 833; valuation, $176,379.

JAY, in the southern part of Franklin county, on both sides of the Androscoggin river, was formerly known as Phips's Canada, and was granted to Captain Josiah Phips and sixty-three others, for services in the French war of 1755. It was incorporated in 1795, and named for Hon. John Jay, the eminent patriot and statesman. It was a large township, embracing twenty-seven thousand two hundred acres, about one third of which, lying on the west side of the river, was incorporated as Canton, in 1821.

The conditions of the original grant were, that it was to be divided into rights of four hundred acres each; one to be reserved for Harvard College, one for the first settled minister, one for the use of the ministry, and one for the use of schools. It was early surveyed, and divided into lots of one hundred acres each. A settling committee was appointed by the associates, who subsequently purchased the whole, and so managed the business that the original owners received little or no benefit from the grant. Actual settlements were not commenced till after the Revolutionary war. Simon Coolidge, Oliver Fuller, Samuel Eustis, Scarborough Parker, Moses Crafts, Isaac West, Thomas Fuller, Joseph Hyde, Nathaniel Jackson, Samuel Jackson, William Godding, and William Atkinson were some of the first settlers.

In the village, on what is called Jay hill, where James Starr settled as early as 1802, are two stores, a tavern, and a meeting-house. Near Jay hill is a toll-bridge across the Androscoggin, a first-rate grist-mill, and a saw-mill. A small village, known as Bean's Corner, has sprung up in the northeast section, where a number of the sons of the late Mr. Bean, of Readfield, settled at an early day. Jay has derived little benefit from water-power or floating capital, but was settled by, and possesses, a population of industrious, independent yeomanry. There are three meeting-houses in all. At first the people had only occasional preaching; but a Baptist church was formed in 1799, which became large and flourishing. A considerable Methodist society is in existence, who have stated preaching. There are also two small Free-will Baptist churches; nineteen school districts, with twenty-two schools; and two post-offices — Jay and North Jay. Population, 1,733; valuation, $220,551.

JEFFERSON, Lincoln county, at the head of Damariscotta river, distant from Augusta twenty-four miles, numbers among its first settlers John Weeks, Ezra Parker, Jonathan Fish, Jonathan Eames, Jonathan Linscott, Joseph Jones, and Thomas Kennedy, most of whom brought their families with them. Jefferson, as also Whitefield, was formerly included in the territory originally known as Ballstown, so named in honor of its first settler, John Ball. That portion now included in Jefferson was settled a few years before the Revolutionary war.[1] Many of the first settlers came from Woolwich and Boothbay; they obtained the titles to their lands from Massachusetts.

Jefferson was incorporated in 1807. The surface is uneven and hilly. Besides the Damariscotta, there are two other ponds, known as Dyer and Pleasant, the streams emptying into and draining which furnish some very good mill privileges. About half a dozen saw-mills are in operation, as well as machinery for the manufacture of shingles, staves, and other articles. About the head of the Damariscotta pond, there are several considerable clusters of houses, and some very pleasant scenery. Farming is the principal occupation of the inhabitants. There are two Baptist churches; fifteen school districts, with twenty-seven schools; and two post-offices — Jefferson and West Jefferson. Population, 2,225; valuation for 1858, $275,262.

JONESBOROUGH, Washington county, lies at the head of Englishman's bay, and joins Machias on the west. It contained under the grant to John C. Jones and others, January 1, 1789, an area of 48,160 acres,

[1] John, son of Thomas Kennedy, who was born in 1774, and came here with his parents from Newcastle, in 1778, is still living. Weeks, Parker, Eames, and Jones were then here. John Jones and a Mr. Richardson, who had been here earlier, returned and took up a permanent abode soon after Kennedy.

which included "Buck's Harbor," and "Little Kennebec," the former now belonging to Machiasport, and the latter to Machias; also the whole of what now constitutes the town of Jonesport. Judah Chandler, who arrived here about 1763–4, is supposed to have been the first settler. Chandler was accompanied by two men named Bucknam, but it is not known whether they ever took up a permanent residence. He built his house and mill in 1764, on the side of the hill between the house of Joshua Whitney and the present mills. This mill was subsequently rebuilt by Captain Ephraim Whitney; and more lately, the present substantial mill was erected nearly on the site of the old one by his son, Porter Whitney, — a grandson of one of the first settlers, Joel Whitney, who came from Falmouth (now Portland) about 1767. Captain Whitney was a member of the Massachusetts legislature two years, of the convention to form a constitution for Maine, in 1820, represented his district in the new state, and filled several offices of honor and trust for his town. Captain Samuel Watts, from Falmouth, settled in 1769, and Josiah Weston in 1772. The latter married Hannah, the daughter of Captain Watts, in 1774. The history of this noble woman, who was conspicuously connected with the capture of the British schooner *Margaretta* at Machias, in the month of May, 1775, is intimately connected with that of Jonesborough. She lived to her ninety-seventh year, having died in 1855.

Previous to its incorporation, this town was called Chandler's River, and was one of the best timbered sections in the state; but that policy which too often has made a disposition of the forests afterwards to be regretted, prevailed here, and thus cut off, in a great measure, one of the sources of wealth. In 1785, the first ship was sailed up the river by Captain Locke, for purposes of trade. Corporate privileges were conferred on Jonesborough, March 4, 1809; the name was given in honor of the proprietor. The first town meeting was held on the 27th of March, in that year.

There have been built at different periods a grist-mill and lath mills. On the east side of the river, some three miles below the settlement, the "tide mills" were erected; a mill at Englishman's river; and one at Beaver brook, in the Farnsworth district. The first meeting-house was built in 1841. There are two religious societies, one Baptist, one Congregationalist; six school districts, with the same number of schools; and one post-office. Population, 466; valuation, $45,754.

KENDUSKEAG, Penobscot county, is situated on Kenduskeag river, eleven and a half miles northwest from Bangor. Its history is contained in the articles on Levant and Glenburn, from each of which a portion was taken, and incorporated under its present name, February 20, 1852. Five of its original settlers are now residents of Kenduskeag, namely, three sons of Major Hodson, a son of Pecallis Clark, and Lemuel H. Hasey. All the others are deceased or have removed.

The surface is very even, and easily cultivated. Agriculture is regarded with increasing interest, and yields an ample return for the labor bestowed. There is a good water-power on the Kenduskeag, which is chiefly employed in manufacturing large quantities of lumber, while in other sections considerable is done in the manufacture of shoes, iron castings, and other articles. There are five school districts, with six schools; two church edifices, one owned by the Congregationalists and Baptists (occupied alternately by each), and the other by the Universalists; one village, formerly known as Levant; and one post-office. Population in 1850, 839; valuation, from the assessors' books for 1858, $137,565.

KENNEBEC COUNTY, situated quite centrally in the state, almost equally divided by the river from which it was named, was the sixth county organized, the act establishing it having been passed February 20, 1799. Its present limits are very small as compared with its original territory, which embraced the whole northern (much the larger) portion of Lincoln county, to Canada. The southerly line ran nearly the same as at present, on the south sides of Harlem (now China), and Pittston, thence to Purgatory stream, at its junction with Cobbossee Contee stream, along the south side of Monmouth and of Greene, now in Androscoggin county, to the Androscoggin river. Cumberland county then ran to the northern line of the state upon the west, and Hancock upon the east. Somerset county, erected in 1809, cut off more than four fifths of this original territory; Waldo county, established in 1827, took four towns upon its east; Franklin county, in 1838, took five towns upon the northwest; and Androscoggin, in 1854, four towns upon the west, — so that the county is now in extent but a shadow of its former self. It comprises within its limits nearly all that tract of land granted to the Plymouth colony, January 16, 1629; and has twenty-seven towns and two plantations. Its agricultural capabilities are second to those of no county in the state, it being well watered by the Kennebec and its tributaries, as well as by numerous large ponds, possessing also a fine rolling surface and a rich soil; and the many well-cultivated and beautiful farms in the county prove that these natural advantages have not been undervalued. The facilities for communication, by steamboat and railroad, are unsurpassed in the state. It is traversed by the Kennebec and Portland, the Androscoggin and Kennebec, and the Penobscot and Kennebec Railroads.

Augusta has been the shire town from the beginning, and is the seat of the middle district of the supreme judicial court, which holds a law term here, commencing on the third Tuesday of June. This district embraces the counties of Lincoln, Kennebec, Somerset, and Sagadahoc. The jury terms of this court for civil and criminal business commence on the first Tuesday of March, third Tuesday of August, and fourth Tuesday of November. Population, 58,018; valuation, $12,145,888.

KENNEBEC PURCHASE. Some notice of this valuable territory, and of the company that managed it, seems important here, for the reason, that to the earnest efforts made by that company for a long series of years to procure the settlement of this region may be attributed, in a great measure, the superior development of wealth, population, and general resources, in the numerous towns on either side of the river.

This tract was granted in 1629, by the council established at Devon, in England, to Governor Bradford and his associates, of the Plymouth colony, and was described as "lying in and between and extending itself from the utmost limits of the Cobbossee Contee, which adjoineth to the river Kennebec, towards the Western ocean, and a place called the falls of Nequamkike,[1] and a space of fifteen miles on each side of the Kennebec."

Under this grant, the Plymouth company claimed the mouth of the Kennebec, it being valuable for trade and its fisheries, the revenue to be derived from which seems to have been the sole object of the company's desire. In 1640, Bradford and his associates surrendered this grant to all the freemen of the colony of New Plymouth. In 1648, and again in 1653, the colony obtained Indian deeds of the land extending from Cushnoc, now Augusta, to the Wessernnset (a stream falling into the Kennebec a little below Norridgewock), where the northern limits of the patent were finally fixed. They built three forts, and sent magistrates; but, being an infant colony themselves and at so great a distance, they were unable to protect the colony here, and to continue the trade, which was regarded as a monopoly, and consequently became unpopular. For a number of years, from 1640 to 1661, they resorted to leases, which also became troublesome; and, at the last-named date, they sold out their entire interest for £400 to Antipas Boies, Edward Tyng, Thomas Brattle, and John Winslow, together with all additions that had been made to it by Indian grants. These persons and their heirs held the patent for nearly a century, without any efficient attempt at settlement, regarding it, like their predecessors, as valuable only for fishing, and

[1] The exact location of these falls is somewhat uncertain; on an old map of the Kennebec in possession of the Maine Historical Society, they are stated to be about sixteen miles above Cobbossee Contee stream, which would be near North Sidney.

trading with the natives. In September, 1749, a meeting of the proprietors was called, and new proprietors were admitted; and in 1753, the legislature of Massachusetts having passed a general act permitting proprietors of common and undivided lands to assume a corporate character, a corporation was formed by the name of "the Proprietors of the Kennebec Purchase from the late colony of New Plymouth," which continued to be their legal title, though commonly called the Plymouth company. At this time, their claims were quite extensive under the purchase, reaching from Casco bay to Pemaquid, and from the ocean to Carritunk falls. Four other claims gave them much trouble — those of Clark and Lake, the Wiscasset company, the Pejepscot company, and the Pemaquid proprietors. After sundry lawsuits and references, running over a period of ten years to 1763, these claims were compromised, releases were given, and the boundaries of the patent were included within lines which ran on the east side of the river, from the north line of the present town of Woolwich (the southern boundary), northerly, half-way between the Kennebec and Sheepscot rivers; and on the west side of the river, within a line fifteen miles distant from every part of the river. The patent, as thus established, extended from Merry-Meeting bay to Norridgewock, and about thirty-one miles in width, with the Kennebec in the centre, including also Bath and Phipsburg below the line. The meetings of the Plymouth company continued regularly from 1749 to 1816, — a period of sixty-seven years, — when affairs were wound up, during the first twenty-five of which strenuous efforts were made to induce settlements within their grant. Very liberal terms were proposed in the form of free grants of considerable tracts to each family, besides provisions for a certain time, with the condition only that five acres should be cleared and a small house built within three years. Some settlements were made upon these terms. Still larger tracts of whole townships were granted, on condition that one hundred persons should settle within three years. The proprietors had, for many years, as their chief manager of affairs, a man of great energy and liberality — Doctor Sylvester Gardiner. Within eleven years after he assumed the control of the company's concerns, £5,000 had been assessed on the shares to promote the prosperity of the patent, besides which, Doctor Gardiner expended large sums from his private fortune. He built a large sloop, which was kept constantly running from Boston to the Kennebec in summer, and in winter to the Sheepscot; he erected houses and mills at Eastern river, (now Dresden village); and two saw-mills, a grist-mill, fulling-mill, a wharf, stores, and many houses at Gardinerston (now Gardiner); cleared farms and built houses at the Chops, Lynde's Island, Swan Island, Pittston, and Winslow, and was at great expense in bringing settlers and furnishing them supplies. His exertions gave great stimulus to the settlements, and for many years his grist-mill (the only one in that region) was patronized by settlers coming thirty miles with their meal bags upon their backs, or in canoes by the river. A court-house was erected by the company at Pownalborough; and forts were built for the protection of the settlers. In fact, almost every facility was extended to settlers, short of a complete surrender of all right and title in the lands covered by the patent.

But in spite of unremitting efforts, claims were entered upon slowly, nearly every one who received a large grant as an inducement to bring in settlers failing to comply with the conditions. In the earlier history of the company, the obstacles which stared them more fully in the face, was the unwillingness of settlers to subject themselves to the dangers apprehended from savages, who had been rendered fiercer by the ill-treatment received from early settlers and mere adventurers;[1] and a further reluctance on their part to enter and clear dense forests. After the Revolution, the Indians were no longer a bugbear, but as many members of the company had been loyalists, who had forever quit the new republic, without any assignment of their interests, suspicions were, to a considerable extent, excited as to the validity of any title deed from the company. Still further difficulties were encountered from mere squatters, who acknowledged no allegiance to the company, and refused to pay any thing for their lands. As early as 1796, these settlers in Ballstown (now Jefferson) had become sufficiently numerous to act in a body, and prevent individuals from agreeing to any measure not approved by the majority. They at first advanced the doctrine (which was subsequently decided untenable by the highest tribunal), that this corporation, under the general law establishing landed corporations, could only sell land when necessary to raise money to pay debts. As the company temporized with them, they became more resolute, and refused to allow any survey unless they could previously know what was to be the price of their lands; and when the company began to enforce their rights, still more serious consequences ensued. In 1809, Paul Chadwick, while engaged in a survey, was waylaid and murdered by an armed party, who shot at him from the woods. The party, with a single exception, were taken and lodged in jail; an armed force was raised to rescue them; the militia were ordered out to preserve order and defend the prison. At the trial, against the strongest evidence, the prisoners were acquitted. The result, however, — as the squatters perceived they had only heaped expense upon themselves, and the com-

[1] The conduct of Popham and his colony may be particularly cited. See ante, p. 12.

pany were alarmed at the slender prospect of enforcing their rights, — tended to promote a compromise. Previously to this, in 1802, steps had been taken in this direction, by the appointment, upon petition to the general court, of commissioners for the mutual adjustment of differences; and, as a basis of action for the commissioners, the settlers were to be divided into three classes; — those who had gone on to their land previously to the Revolution, when the company offered lots to all who would enter and improve them; those who went on during the war; and those who had taken up lots subsequently. The price was to be lowest to those in the first class, and highest to those in the last. The state agreed to pay half the expenses. The terms were satisfactory to all but the Jefferson settlers. They, however, submitted, upon a further modification of terms by the legislature, by which they were to relinquish all claim, and receive deeds of their lots, upon payment of five dollars in each case, as a fee; and the original claimants were to receive an equivalent in the unlocated lands of the state. Three disinterested persons, not inhabitants of Massachusetts nor Maine, were to be commissioners, and execute the will of the state. Jeremiah Smith, who had been chief justice and governor of New Hampshire, William H. Woodward of the same state, and Judge Howell of Rhode Island, were appointed to this office. This commission settled the last great controversy in Maine respecting land titles.

Such were the hindrances to rapid settlement, growing partly out of extraneous circumstances, but chiefly, it must be admitted, through an inherent prejudice against an attempt on the part of great landed corporations, — hence, supposed to be made up of the opulent, — to apportion out "God's heritage" to those who claim partnership alone with nature, in giving to the soil whatever it has of wealth or utility. The Plymouth Company, having done all that seemed honorably to be required of them, in 1816, divided among the proprietors those lands that were susceptible of convenient division, and disposed of the remainder at auction, in Boston.

KENNEBUNK, York county, is a seaboard town and port of entry, situated twenty-five miles south of Portland. Sir Ferdinando Gorges was the original proprietor, and in 1643 granted it to Lieutenant John Sanders. Goodman Sanders, son of John, took possession of the grant, and is supposed to have built the first house. Previous to the year 1653, when the town was incorporated, Goodman Burke had a house upon the sea-shore, a few rods from the mouth of Kennebunk river. This house and those of Sanders and one Stover Batsom were probably built for the accommodation of travellers passing from the settlements of Piscataqua and York to those begun at the eastward. After 1653 there seems to have been little addition made to the settlement for many years.

In 1679, the falls and water privilege on Mousam river were granted to Jonathan Corwin and Eleazer Hawthorne, from Scotland, who brought with them several mechanics. They erected a saw-mill, grist-mill, blacksmith shop, and dwelling-house, and soon opened a fine business with Boston, by the shipment of lumber to that city. In this, however, they were, in 1688, disturbed by the Indians, who burned the mills — when these men moved to the west. The house seems afterward to have been occupied only by the mechanics employed by them. The grants of land previously made, were, in consequence of the implacable enmity of the Indians, not regarded as of any value. In 1703, the war again broke out; its devastation extended to all the settlements from Casco to the Piscataqua. This war lasted till 1713.

The first house erected after the close of the war was that of William Larrabee. In 1714, John Look built a house just below Larrabee, on a point of land since known as "Butland's ship-yard;" and in 1715 one was built by Thomas Wormwood, a few rods from Look's, and in front of the one which is or was occupied by Joseph Gooch, both which were used as garrisons. Though it was now a time of peace, yet such was the distrust felt towards the Indians, that those who were disposed to settle in the province chose rather to locate near the garrison towns. Hence these four houses were the only ones built up to 1720. In 1721, John Webber, Richard Boothbay, and Samuel Sawyer built houses, and these were the only additions made until after the Lovewell war in 1722. This war lasted three years, and was conducted with great asperity on the part of the Indians. Sawyer was killed in this outbreak, as were also William Wormwood, Ebenezer Lewis, and John Felt. The three last were surprised by a party under Wawa while rafting timber on the Gooch creek. The account of this was given by Wawa himself, after the close of the war.[1] About 1735, a large fortification was erected on Mousam river, called Fort Larrabee, in honor of Stephen Larrabee, son of William, before spoken of. This garrison

[1] Hutchinson relates this as occurring "at a saw-mill on Kennebec river." The same perverted account has been copied into other histories of the Indian wars. Hutchinson was simply misinformed. Tom Wawa, referred to here, was the king of one of the tribes of Indians who frequented this neighborhood, and lived on Great hill. He was a distinguished warrior, and a leader in most of the depredations committed on the inhabitants of this part of the then county of York. Though in most cases driven by a savage spirit to acts of the most relentless cruelty, yet occasionally he was known to manifest more of the feelings of civilized man than any of his companions.

remained until 1762, when it was torn down. Within its walls the whole of the people were collected in time of danger, thinking themselves secure from any attack the savages might make. The fort occupied more than an acre of ground.[1]

In 1745, the war with the Indians was again renewed, and continued for years. The settlements at this period were so extensive that the Indians became more cautious. Attempts were made once or twice to surprise the settlers at the village of Sergeant Larrabee. On one of these occasions they would probably all have been murdered but for the fidelity and vigilance of a dog belonging to Larrabee, which, by repeatedly barking, gave warning of the approaching danger, and thus afforded them opportunity for escape. After the close of this war, fears having subsided, the settlement made steady progress. Lands were cleared, buildings erected, and improvements made, in almost every direction. What is now the principal village was then one unbroken wilderness, with the exception of two or three houses; while the western side of the river was destitute of any habitation, save a camp, which was erected for the accommodation of the hands employed at the saw-mill, which was subsequently destroyed by a freshet, said to have been the most destructive ever known here.

The inhabitants took quite an active part in the Louisburg expedition. Some of them also served in the army in the vicinity of Lake George in the year 1756–7, and also with General Abercrombie in the rash attack on Ticonderoga. About the year 1759, the French war closed, and the joy of the people was unbounded.

In 1760, the settlement was extended considerably. To give the reader some idea of the value of real estate about this time, a two story tenement was rented for *one* dollar a year, the parties having the privilege of taking as much wood from the land adjoining as was necessary for their consumption during that time; and land on the western side of the river was sold at the rate of an acre of ground for a yard of calico. In the year 1760, the village, which had been built on the banks of the

[1] Sergeant Larrabee, who defended this fort with great bravery, is said to have been ever on the watch for his foes. The Indians thought to take the fort by stealth on a certain dark night, and accordingly Wawa secreted himself and a few chosen men under a cart which had been left a few rods from the wall, intending to scale the walls when the garrison were asleep; but Larrabee, in his watchful care, noticed something rather strange in the look of the cart, and tried the effect of a heavy charge of buckshot, aimed just below the body of the cart, when the scene changed suddenly, and retreating footsteps were heard. In the morning, blood was found there; and Wawa, after the war, confessed to have been wounded by the shot of Larrabee at that time. He also said that it was owing to Larrabee's strict watch that the garrison was saved.

15*

river, ceased to exist. Most of the houses were torn down; the inhabitants deeming the present site of the town the more desirable location.

In the year 1774, a factory for iron-works was erected on what is now the island, a short distance below the lower dam. The iron ore was brought, some from Saco, some from Maryland ridge, and some from the land on the western side of the main road leading from Wells. A similar factory was built about the same time at the western end of the present lower dam. A grist-mill was also erected the same year, near the middle of the dam at the lower iron-works. Three salt factories were also erected, which were worked five or six years, yielding a handsome profit in consequence of the scarcity of the commodity. Stores and dwellings continued to be erected with a persevering spirit, so that in 1784 the settlement presented quite a flourishing and business-like appearance.

The travelling, in the early times, was entirely on the seaboard. But the water, in consequence of the rising of the tide at the mouth of Kennebunk river, was of so great a depth that travellers were unable to pass it. As the communication between the different parts of the province began to increase, it became necessary that this evil should be remedied. Accordingly, after the close of the war, in 1714, a ferry was here established by order of court. John Reynolds was appointed the first ferryman. The tolls which he was authorized to receive were: "For a man and horse, sixpence; for a single man, two pence."[1]

As early as 1755, ship-building was a prominent branch of industry; in fact, to this Kennebunk owes her population and wealth. The first vessel was built in 1755, by John Bourne, of Wells; and from this time forward, the business progressed rapidly. Most of the vessels were then built on the Mousam river, a fact which, to some, may seem rather inexplicable, on account of the present shallowness of that stream. This, however, will be explained by subsequent facts. A few years after the close of the Revolutionary war, it was deemed highly probable that the quantity of shipping would increase, and, accordingly, it was considered important that the facilities for the passage of vessels up and down the

[1] It will be noticed that there was no toll fixed for the transportation of carriages. This may be explained by the fact that, at this time, and till many years afterwards, no carriages of any description were used. The first chaise seen here was that of Judge Paine, in 1755. Everybody in the neighborhood went to see the great curiosity. It is a little remarkable that previous to the year 1770 no sleigh had ever been used or seen, in Kennebunk. Mr. Little, the minister of the parish, contrived something which was intended to answer the purpose; but no adequate description can be furnished of its appearance.

river should be augmented. It was supposed that the long arm of the river, next to its mouth, might be advantageously cut off, and an outlet made to the sea, which would considerably shorten the distance from the bend, and possibly at the same time give them a greater depth. A corporation was formed, and many gentlemen from the neighboring towns embarked in the enterprise; but, after considerable labor and expense, the plan failed, and the river was left in a far worse condition than before. These difficulties soon put an end to ship-building in the Mousam river. Fishing was also carried on to some extent, and till as late as the year 1760, salmon, bass, and shad were very abundant in the Mousam river. Even at the present day, shad may be caught in the stream. Until about the commencement of the Revolutionary war, herds of deer were found in the neighborhood, and moose also were seen in considerable numbers.

Among the men who used their utmost endeavors for the permanent settlement of Kennebunk were Joseph Storer, Stephen Larrabee, John Mitchell, Nathaniel Kimball, Richard Kimball, William Rutland, — who was a second Larrabee in fearlessness, — Ichabod Cousins, Rev. Daniel Little, and many others. Much might be written about the usefulness of these pioneers, but space will not permit. Kennebunk took quite a prominent part in the Revolutionary struggle for liberty. In fact, says a reliable writer, "There was not an able-bodied man in town who did not have something to do in the struggle." Many of them were employed in the Penobscot expedition.

The surface of Kennebunk is generally level, and is suitable for the purposes of agriculture. There are two rivers — one called the Kennebunk, in the eastern part, on which most of the ship-building is done. A lock, costing about $6,000, has been constructed on this river, whereby vessels of any burden can be built and safely carried down from the Landing village. The other river is the Mousam, a new outlet to which was made a few years ago at the sea, whereby vessels drawing eight or nine feet of water can now enter with safety. Ship-building and a seafaring life are the main occupations of the inhabitants. A merchant marine of over fifty ships is owned in Kennebunk, and there are many vessels built annually. There is a large number of fine residences and stores; and, in proportion to population, Kennebunk is second to none in the state for wealth. The principal places of business are called the Village, the Landing, and the Port. The Unitarians, Congregationalists, Methodists, and Christians have each a house of public worship, and the Baptists have two. Twelve school districts, with fourteen public schools, afford ample facilities for the education of youth; and the

Ocean bank (with a capital of $100,000), the Atlas Marine Insurance Company, and the Kennebunk Mutual Fire Insurance Company, are institutions which are held in estimation. There are four or five saw-mills and a yarn factory, doing some business. The only post-office is at Kennebunk village. Population in 1857, about 3,300; valuation for 1858, $1,155,296.

KENNEBUNKPORT, York county, is bounded on the east by Little river, which separates it from Biddeford, and was formerly known by the name of Cape Porpoise. It must have been settled about the summer of 1619. If not then, the exact date is not known. After its discovery by Gosnold, in 1602, it was probably visited every summer by fishermen and traders, who built small huts for their summer residence, usually returning to Europe in the winter. Folsom says, "the settlement on Cape Porpoise was probably made about the same time as that at Winter Harbor. It presented many advantages for fishermen, many of whom made it a place of resort, and perhaps of abode, as early, probably, as any other point of the coast."

The Plymouth Company, February 12, 1629, granted a patent to John Oldham and Richard Vines, of a tract of land four miles in breadth, on the sea-shore, extending eight miles into the country, on the west side of Saco river. Vines took legal possession on the 25th of June, and several families that came over with him settled near Little river, within the limits of this town. This, probably, was the first permanent settlement, it being a matter of uncertainty whether persons ever spent the winter here previous to that time. This grant of land to Vines was entirely independent of the settlement known as the "Cape Porpoise Plantation," and had no connection with that at Little river. That this was the spot where the first settlement was made is rendered more certain from the fact that the inhabitants could here defend themselves from the attacks of the Indians, or more readily escape, than they could on the main land. There was no part of America to which there were so many conflicting claims, grounded on different grants from European powers, as to that portion in which Cape Porpoise is included. No less than six grants were made to different parties by various crowned heads of Europe.

In 1653, Cape Porpoise was brought under the control of Massachusetts, and was incorporated; yet, on account of its limited wealth and population, it was deemed little more than an adjunct of Saco. By an agreement made with the inhabitants, President Danforth — whose government of Maine concluded June 18, 1684 — was to give them a deed of the town, which deed was executed on the 26th day of June of that year.[1]

During the government of Andros, and when on his visit to Maine, he ordered the inhabitants of Cape Porpoise to put their roads in a better state of repair, which, as usual, were neglected. Although the Province, up to 1685, had generally increased in population and wealth, Cape Porpoise remained in a poor condition. Four mills constituted the whole of its business; and although it had sustained the appearance of being a separate municipality, by choosing officers and keeping a record, it was now only spoken of as a parish. In May, 1688, Andros destroyed even the appearance of its independent existence, by placing it under the jurisdiction of Saco, which guardianship, at most, lasted but a few months.

During the war entered into by Governor Andros against the eastern Indians, Cape Porpoise suffered much from their attacks; and, for more security, a company under the command of Lieutenant Puddington was stationed at the fort on Stage island. After Governor Andros's return to Massachusetts in 1690, his troops all deserted, and the Indians began to appear in greater numbers. The inhabitants of the Cape withdrew to the fort for protection, while those who resided between the Cape and Kennebunk river went to Wells. The fort was soon besieged by the Indians; and as the point of the island, on which it was built, was surrounded by deep water at all times, and the Indians were stationed at the narrow neck of land which leads to the main part, the whites were therefore completely prevented from escape, having only a poor boat wherewith to make their retreat. After sustaining the attacks of the Indians for some time, they became fearful of being surrounded, and withdrew to the southern part of the island, which, being narrow, left them exposed only on one side.

They remained for some time thus at the mercy of their savage enemies, almost destitute of provisions, and with no expectation of aid or relief from their critical situation, when Nicholas Morey, who was lame, offered to take the old boat and seek assistance. Accordingly, as soon as it was dark, he embarked; and, by sitting at the whole end of the frail bark, was enabled to keep the defective part out of water. Although the weather was pleasant, there was but little chance of his reaching Portsmouth in safety; but, buoyed up by the hope of assistance, the little band continued to defend themselves during all the next day, without provisions and only with a very limited supply of ammunition. Night coming on, and being closely besieged by a cruel, blood-

[1] This deed is still in existence.

thirsty foe, their situation was indescribably trying. Slight as the prospect of relief was, long, lingering looks were cast towards Portsmouth, when, late in the afternoon, they descried a small sloop standing directly towards the cape. Mr. Morey had arrived in safety at Portsmouth, and returned with this providential succor. When the sloop came into the harbor, a small swivel was discharged from her at the Indians, who immediately fled. The inhabitants were taken on board, and did not return till 1699. Scarcely had they experienced the pleasures of peace and safety, when the French again endeavored to excite the Indians to acts of hostility against them. War was declared between England and France, May 4, 1702, and the year following, hostilities recommenced. Five hundred Indians attacked the principal settlements in Maine, and "Cape Porpoise, being inhabited only by a few unsettled fishermen, was wholly desolated." How many of the inhabitants were killed or taken prisoners is not known. It is probable, that, having anticipated an attack, most of them made their escape. In 1713, a treaty of peace was made with all the eastern tribes; and many of the inhabitants returned to their homes and recommenced business.

In 1717, a petition was presented by the inhabitants of Cape Porpoise to be reincorporated, which petition was granted by the General Assembly of Massachusetts, and the name changed to that of Arundel. The assembly directed that a garrison should be erected on Montague Neck; but it does not appear that the order was executed, as no remains of a garrison are distinguishable on that spot. It does not appear that the inhabitants attempted to renew the settlement at Stage Harbor; but erected their buildings at what was called Folly Harbor, where the village at Cape Porpoise now stands. Inducements to obtain grants of lands were held out to settlers, who began to flock in from various parts of New England; and the town was more flourishing and populous than at any former period. Among the first settlers were William Scadlock and his sons William and John, Morgan Howell, Joseph Bowles, William Frost, Christopher Spurrell, Stephen Batson, Gregory Jeffery, Charles Potum, Thomas Warner, Griffin Montague, John Baker, William Reynolds, Roger Willine, Peter Turbat, Richard Hix, William Thomas, Thomas Merrill, John Barrett, and John Purrington, or Puddington.

This prosperous condition of affairs, however, was destined to be of short duration. The Indians began to assume a threatening attitude about 1721, and in 1722 Lovewell's war commenced. Several garrisons were erected; but, despite these arrangements for their protection, many of the inhabitants sought safety in places less liable to attack. In August, 1723, a man was either killed or carried off by the Indians;

and this was only the precursor of other deeds of heartlessness and diabolism. The settlers, however, supported their trials with heroic fortitude; and their deeds exhibit not only great presence of mind, but almost inimitable daring. In December, 1725, a treaty of peace was signed with the Indians, and in 1726, the inhabitants ventured from their garrisons, and looked forward to more prosperous times.

This treaty was ratified at Falmouth in August, 1726, and the Indians appeared to be satisfied with it. The French, however, induced them to violate the treaty, and several parties were sent out, one of which attacked the house of Philip Durrill, who lived where Durrill's bridge now is. The whole family was carried off, and all, with the exception of a boy, brutally murdered. In 1727, peace was permanently secured, and its good effects were soon evident in Arundel. The population increased greatly up to 1730, and land, as a natural consequence, became more valuable.

War again troubled the inhabitants in 1755, the period of the expedition to Louisburg. A company from this town were engaged in the enterprise, which was commanded by Captain Thomas Perkins, and many lost their lives. The Indians committed no depredations during this war, though the inhabitants were kept in a constant state of alarm. In October, 1748, the treaty of peace was signed at Aix-la-Chapelle, and prosperity again began to smile upon the inhabitants. Cape Porpoise was then, as it always has continued to be, much frequented as a harbor. Several vessels were owned by the inhabitants; and, altogether, affairs began to wear a business-like aspect.[1]

Nothing of further importance occurred till the war of the Revolution, in which the town of Arundel was not behindhand. She raised money to defray the expenses of ammunition, etc.; and, in 1775, many of the inhabitants repaired to Cambridge to join the army, several of whom were engaged in the memorable battle of Bunker Hill. Arundel then, it would seem, exhibited more energy than at any preceding period in her history.

The only incident of local importance that occurred during the war was the following: On the 8th of August, 1781, an English brig, of eighteen guns, came into Cape Porpoise harbor, and took a schooner and a sloop belonging to Newbury. They carried off the schooner; but the sloop, having got ashore, was destroyed by fire. While the English had possession of these vessels, Samuel Wildes, who was partially

[1] In 1764, there were in Arundel 127 houses, 138 families, 833 white inhabitants, and five negroes. Those who had owned slaves within the twenty years preceding were Mr. Prentice, Mr. Hovey the minister, Robert Cleeves, Thomas Wiswall, Samuel Hutchins, John Fairfield, Gideon Walker, Andrew Brown, and Jonathan Stone.

insane, paddled into the harbor in a small canoe, and ordered them to give up the vessels and leave the place. After joking with him for a short time, they asked him aboard the brig. This he refused to do, and turned to pull ashore, when they wantonly fired seven muskets at him, wounding him in several places. When he got ashore, he was unable to stand from loss of blood, and remained in a critical situation for some time. The inhabitants were aroused at this outrage, and soon collected on Trott's island, with the intention of crossing over to Goat island, near which the brig was anchored. To prevent this, the brig sent a crew of men to the latter island; while a schooner of ten guns, which was in company with the brig, kept up a continual discharge of grape-shot. The infuriated citizens at length succeeded in crossing, when the English, finding they were likely to be outnumbered, retreated to their boats, closely followed by the inhabitants, who opened a deadly fire. So destructive was this attack, that the English turned to come on shore, for the purpose, as was afterwards supposed, of giving themselves up as prisoners. But the Americans, being under no regular command, and suspecting the British were returning to the attack, redoubled their fire, and compelled them to go back. Only one, it is said, of their number, was able to climb up the vessel's side, and it was thought sixteen or seventeen were killed. Captain James Burnham was the only one killed on the American side. Two pieces of cannon were afterwards carried on Trott's island, which so annoyed the British that they were compelled to take their vessel out of the harbor, which was accomplished only after the ammunition of the Americans was expended. February 19, 1821, the name was changed from Arundel to Kennebunkport.

The face of the country is moderately uneven, with little swampy or waste land. The soil is clayey, and produces grass in abundance. In the southeast part it is rocky, and affords large quantities of valuable building stone. The salt marshes are also very valuable. Within the limits of Kennebunkport there are no less than sixteen islands. Kennebunk river is navigable about half a mile from its mouth, and has two falls, about two miles from the bar, over which the tide flows at half flood. Goffe's Mill creek empties into Kennebunk river, between the upper and lower falls. Cape Porpoise, at the extremity of the cape, is a small but convenient harbor, and is the only safe one for coasting vessels between Portsmouth and Portland. The main entrance is between Folly island, on the west, and Goat island — where there is a lighthouse — on the east. There are from twenty-five to thirty feet of water in the harbor at low water, and it is sufficiently capacious for the largest class of merchant vessels. At high water, several hundred coasting vessels can harbor with perfect safety. Batson's river is a little to the eastward of the cape. It is never used for a harbor, but is sufficiently deep for small fishing craft. Little river, which was called Eastern or Northern river on the early town records, is a small stream: vessels of two hundred tons burden have been built there. Brimstone and Great are the only two ponds. The highest hill is Mount Seargery, or Seargo, which is seen some distance at sea.

There are many substantial wharves and several piers built by government. There are about eighty miles of public road; also fifteen or twenty bridges and a large number of expensive causeways, besides eight bridges over Kennebunk and Little rivers, two of which have draws.

The principal pursuits are farming, fishing, ship-building, quarrying, and the lumber business. From the close of the Revolutionary war to 1790, the wealth of Kennebunkport, by lumbering and ship-building, increased amazingly. In 1812, in consequence of the embargo laid on shipping, the owners, who were never engaged more profitably, suffered severely in their pecuniary affairs. Kennebunk river was crowded with dismantled vessels, and, in order to protect them, a small fort was built on Kennebunk point, and a battery near Butler's rocks, on the eastern side of the river. Several privateers were fitted out; but all of them except one were captured by the English. In 1815, business again revived, and was carried on with great activity. In 1820, the amount of tonnage owned in this port was 7,509 tons; and its valuation in 1821 was $324,122.

Trade declined considerably in 1826, and it has never fully recovered from this shock. There is, however, at the present writing, an increasing spirit of enterprise, which will, undoubtedly, eventually overcome this lethargy. Ship-building is carried on with something of the old spirit, and the fishing interests are gradually increasing. Agriculture, too, has also wrought itself into favor; but lumbering has in a great measure ceased, in consequence of the scarcity of timber. The custom-house was removed to Kennebunkport in 1815: the building is of brick, and was, till recently, the only one of that material in town.

There are three business places, known as Kennebunkport, Cape Porpoise, and North Kennebunkport; seven church edifices — three Methodist, two Congregational, one Baptist, and one Union; thirteen school districts, with sixteen schools; and two post-offices — Kennebunkport and North Kennebunkport; also two steam and several hydraulic saw-mills, two tanneries, several grist-mills, a brass foundery, and two ship-yards. Population, 2,706; valuation, $1,400,000.

KINGFIELD, Franklin county, twenty miles from Farmington, in a direction nearly north, was formerly plantation No. 3, range one, Bingham's Purchase, and was surveyed by Solomon Adams in 1808. Settlements were commenced here about 1806, by a Mr. Blanchard from Weymouth, Rev. Nathaniel Gilbert of Kingston, Mass., Eben Pillsbury, Solomon Stanley, Joseph Longley, Benjamin Foster, William Trask, Charles Pike, and others.

It was incorporated January 24, 1816, and received its name in honor of William King, the first governor of Maine, a principal proprietor. It is watered by the Seven Mile brook, two branches of which meet near the southeast corner, where mills were early put in operation, and where there is a considerable village. There are some fine interval lands along the streams, and the town is noted for its surrounding mountain scenery. Meetings are sustained a part of the time by most of the religious societies, and several churches have been organized; but houses of public worship have not yet been built. There are five school districts, with the same number of schools; one grist-mill, two saw-mills, one shingle mill, one carriage builder, and one post-office. Population, 662; valuation, $73,273.

KINGSBURY is a new town in the southeast part of Piscataquis county, embracing an area of 23,040 acres of average farming land. It is watered by two of the head branches of Piscataquis river; was incorporated in 1836; has three school districts, with a like number of schools; and one post-office. It has also one grist-mill, one saw-mill, and one shingle machine. Population, 181; valuation, $22,639.

KITTERY lies on the sea-coast, in the southwestern part of York county, and originally comprised, besides its present territory, that of Eliot, Berwick, South Berwick, and North Berwick, all of which was known as the Plantation of Piscataqua. It formed a portion of the estate of Sir Ferdinando Gorges. Settlements were commenced as early as 1623, under the patronage of Gorges and Mason, who appointed Walter Neal agent for the disposal of the lands. Neal entered upon the business of settlement with commendable activity; and, before the expiration of the year 1634, had conveyed by grant or sale all the lands comprised in this tract. He then returned to England, and was succeeded by Francis Williams. The titles to the land derived through Neal have ever remained valid.

In 1647, the territory was endowed with town privileges by the court of elections, and its records begin March 19, 1648. Twenty-seven years after, the Indian wars commenced, and, during their continuance, the history was but a constant alternation of war and peace. The inhabitants, while the foe were prowling about their dwellings, and ever and anon alighting upon their unsuspecting victims, became, as it were, familiarized to the scenes of this barbaric strife. The stirring events of those days were not in more striking contrast with the present quietude than were the social manners of the people. Ardent spirits, in the days of yore, were almost indispensable in all social gatherings, whether for pleasure or mutual aid. Even at ordinations, the reverend divines must needs have a glass of brandy to quicken the fervor of their devotions. In a bill of expenses incurred on such an occasion in the vicinity of Kittery Point, there are charges for eight quarts of rum, and two of brandy, for the clergy and council. At funerals the practice was still worse, and can only be surpassed by an Irish wake, where fighting and other indecencies are indulged in. The intoxicating cup was freely circulated, and the sighs and tears of sympathizing friends were awakened by potations of spiced rum; but they prayed as heartily as they drank, which was strong evidence of their sincerity, and may, in a measure, be a redeeming point for the unholy indulgence.

Although civil dissensions and political changes occurred to impede the general prosperity, yet the population and wealth gradually increased until the disastrous war of King Philip. The following are among the names of some of the early settlers: John Andrews, Philip Babb, Mary Baylie, John Bursley, Humphrey Chadbourne, William Chadbourne, Nicholas Frost, Charles Frost, William Everett, Nicholas Shapleigh, and Thomas Withers. The people of Kittery joined the inhabitants of York, Saco, Wells, and Cape Porpoise in the petition of August 12, 1656, to Oliver Cromwell, to be continued under the Province of Massachusetts, under whose jurisdiction they placed themselves November 20, 1652.

Until 1636, the fur trade, fishing, and lumbering were the chief employments of the first settlers. About this time a large number of families — some of them farmers — were sent here by Mason and Gorges, and with them ample supplies of stock, provisions, and agricultural implements. The number of mills increased on the small rivers, and lumber and ship-timber soon floated down in gondolas to Kittery Point and New Castle, whence they were shipped to various ports, European and American. But the most lucrative, extensive, and durable business was the fisheries. It required but a small outfit, rarely failed of a good return, and always met with ready sale or a profitable exchange in American or foreign ports. Ship-building was an early and very extensive branch of industry on the Piscataqua and its tributary streams; and, from the fact that foreign merchants could supply themselves at a lower price here than elsewhere, many vessels were built.

A garrison house was erected on the point previous to the commencement of King Philip's war, and as early as 1700 a fort was erected. The celebrated Colonel Church, a desperate enemy of the Indians, in his eastern expedition in 1704, had orders to send his sick and wounded to what is now Portland, or to Pepperrell's fort at Kittery Point. This fort was probably a private concern, or built at the expense of the inhabitants. In 1714, the province of Massachusetts, in order to prevent the levying of improper duties by New Hampshire, made Kittery Point a port of entry, and adopted measures to retain it as such.

One of New England's distinguished heroes — Sir William Pepperrell, Bart. — was born in Kittery, in 1696. His father was a hard-working Welshman, who emigrated to the Isle of Shoals, and there, amid storms and struggles, from the humble calling of a fisherman, rose to the condition of a wealthy merchant, and bequeathed to his son the fortune and position of a gentleman. Young Pepperrell had as much taste for warlike pursuits as for the counting-house, and prospered by following both. The breaking out of the French war in 1745 afforded him the opportunity to be a hero, and he was not slow to avail himself of it. He was among the first to discover, that, if the French were to be subjugated in America, the preliminary step was the reduction of their Sebastopolian stronghold — Louisburg — on the island of Cape Breton. The enterprise was ultimately resolved upon, and Pepperrell placed at the head of the expedition. The fortress was taken, and the title of baronet was conferred upon the intrepid leader. Sir William died on the 6th of July, 1759, leaving a princely fortune, which, in a brief hour, was scattered broadcast by the confiscation act of 1778. His funeral obsequies were attended by a large concourse of people, and every mark of respect exhibited. The drooping flags at half mast on both shores of the Piscataqua, the solemn knell from neighboring churches, the responsive minute-guns from all the batteries, and the mournful rumbling of the muffled drums, announced that a great man had fallen, and was descending to the tomb. The old mansion of Sir William, now standing upon the point, is plain in its architecture; and, before being curtailed ten feet from each end, contained a great number of rooms. The lawn in front extends to the sea; and the restless waves, over which Sir William successively sought fortune and fame, still glitter in the sunbeams, and dash around the desolate mansion. The fires of hospitality are extinguished; and its present occupants are the families of poor fishermen. But little of its former elegance and ornamental work now remain.

The surface of Kittery is generally of an even character. It is compactly built, and there are many good stores and private residences.

Near the centre is a large body of water, called Spruce creek, which empties into the Piscataqua. There are two villages — Fore Side and Kittery Point, both places of considerable importance. Coasting and fishing are the principal pursuits from which the trade springs, and almost every branch of mechanical industry is prosecuted. The religious denominations have here five church edifices — Congregational, Free-will Baptist, Episcopal, Methodist, and Christian. The town is divided into thirteen school districts, and has two post-offices — Kittery and Kittery Point. Population, 2,706; valuation, $290,492.

KNOX, Waldo county, lies equally distant from the Kennebec and Penobscot rivers, and is distant northwest from Belfast twelve miles. The settlement was first commenced in the year 1800; and the territory comprising it formerly belonged to the Waldo Patent. It was incorporated February 12, 1819, and received its name in honor of General Henry Knox, of Revolutionary fame. Knox contains an area of 17,000 acres, the principal portion of which has been bereft of its native growth of timber, and is now yielding ample crops to the husbandman: two villages — Knox and East Knox, with a post-office at each; three church edifices — Methodist, Baptist, and a union house; nine school districts; four saw-mills, one shingle mill, two carriage builders, and one pail-maker. Population, 1,102; valuation, $133,194.

LAGRANGE, Penobscot county, on the west side of Penobscot river, thirty-one miles north from Bangor, was incorporated in 1832, and is watered by Birch stream and its branches, and by the east branch of Dead stream. The soil is good, and well timbered. It produces large quantities of wheat, and the usual varieties of grain common to the state. Lumbering is as yet the chief pursuit of the inhabitants. It has one church edifice (Free-will Baptist), four school districts, with seven schools; one grist-mill, one saw-mill, two shingle mills, one carriage factory, and one post-office. Population, 482; valuation, $38,300.

LEBANON, on Salmon Falls river, in the western part of York county, was granted by the General Court of Massachusetts, in 1733, to settlers, by whom it was inhabited a few years afterwards. Its Indian name was Towwoh, and it was incorporated under its present name, June 25, 1767. Lebanon has an extensive territory, and agriculture forms a large share of the attention of the people. It has two villages; four church edifices — Congregational, Baptist, and two Free-will Baptist; one seminary, chartered and endowed by the State, and now in a flour-

16*

ishing condition; twenty school districts, with nine schools; four saw-mills, three grist-mills, one shingle mill, one tannery, and four post-offices — Lebanon, Centre Lebanon, West Lebanon, and North Lebanon. Population, 2,208; valuation, $354,809.

LEE, Penobscot county, is situated twelve miles east of Lincoln, on what is called the upper route from Bangor to Calais, equally distant, or sixty miles from each city. It was originally granted by the state of Massachusetts to Williams College, and was sold by the trustees of that institution to parties living in Cumberland county. An unfortunate lawsuit, relative to the title of the land, retarded for many years the settlement, as well as its prosperity. After a long period of litigation, which ended only in the Supreme Court of the United States, the case was decided in favor of the settlers. The first inhabitants took up their residence in 1824; and at that time there was no road nearer than Passadumkeag, twenty-eight miles below. Jeremiah Fifield and his wife, who are still living, were the first who moved in. In 1832, the town was incorporated, having at that time about four hundred inhabitants.

The land is generally good, and was originally covered with a dense forest of hard wood, — hemlock, spruce, and pine. There are large quantities of first-rate land here, both wild and partially cleared, which only requires skilful cultivation to make it productive. The facilities for lumbering have been such, and the apparent inducements so tempting, that too many have sought for an annual harvest in the forest, rather than in the field. The consequence is that the pine forests have melted away without yielding adequate returns for the labor bestowed; and those who have been engaged in the business denounce Maine as unfit to live in, and have gone or are going to "the Far West" to find happier homes in the prairie wastes of other states.

In 1845, the legislature incorporated the trustees of the Lee Normal Academy, and endowed it with half a township of land, which the trustees subsequently sold for about $4,000. This sum now constitutes a permanent fund for the support of the school. Many of the first settlers understood the value, and prized the institutions of learning, and religion. Public worship has been maintained from the first settlement, — the Baptists, Congregationalists, Free-will Baptists, and Universalists having each performed their part in sustaining worship, and in giving a moral and religious tone to the character of the people. The first mill erected was in 1827, and was built on the Mattabunk stream, at the place where the village is now located. There are two Free-will Baptist churches in Lee; eight school districts, with nine schools; and one post-office. Population, 917; valuation, $68,151.

LEEDS, Androscoggin county, is situated about twenty miles west from Augusta, and adjoins Wayne and Monmouth on the east. The first settlement was made during the Revolutionary war by Thomas and Roger Stinchfield, Josiah Fish, and Daniel Lane (the two former coming from New Gloucester, Me., and the two latter from Sandwich, Mass.), who located themselves near Leeds Centre. They were followed soon after by the Gilberts, the Jenningses, and Messrs. Cushman, Freeman, and William Fish. The settlement was called Littlesboro', from the fact of its being claimed by the Pejepscot proprietors, of whom Josiah Little was a principal one, and agent for the company. Their title came by deed from Warumbee and other Indian chiefs to Richard Wharton and others, July 7, 1684. Richard Wharton and Thomas Purchas, two of the proprietors, then resided at Twenty Mile Falls, on the Androscoggin river. Under this title, Little laid claim to the whole township, and the settlers purchased their lands of him; but the Plymouth company opposed Little's claim, and held, by decision of the courts, the eastern part. The consequence was, that the settlers in that section had to repurchase their lands of that company.

From its first settlement it bore the name of Littlesboro', but in 1801 it was incorporated as Leeds. Leeds is an agricultural town, and contains many excellent farms. The surface is moderately uneven, and the soil generally good. The Androscoggin pond lies on the east, between Leeds and Wayne, and has its outlet in Dead river, which runs through here and empties into the Androscoggin river. The water-power is inconsiderable, there being but two saw-mills and one grist-mill in operation. The principal business is carried on at North Leeds and Curtis's Corner. The inhabitants are generally moral and industrious, and there are quite a number of active and enterprising men. The Androscoggin Railroad, from its junction with the Kennebec and Androscoggin Railroad, passes directly through to Farmington. There are four churches — two Baptist, one Methodist, and one belonging to the Friends; thirteen school districts; and four post-offices — Leeds, Leeds Station, North Leeds, and South Leeds. Population, 1,652; valuation, $225,330.

LEVANT, Penobscot county, is situated about ten miles northwest of Bangor. The first settlement was made by William and George Tebbets, and Messrs. Boobar and Knowland, some time prior to the year 1800. In 1801, Major Moses Hodsdon, from South Berwick, settled on the land now occupied by the village in Kenduskeag, which was recently taken from Levant and added to the former town. In 1802, Major Hodsdon erected a saw and grist mill, three dwelling-houses, a store, and blacksmith's shop, which were the first framed buildings erected in these parts, and in fact the only ones, save three or four others, which were standing at that time between here and the Kennebec river. Major Hodsdon was largely engaged in surveying, and in the purchase and sale of lands. Shortly after his arrival, his brother and others followed, who gave a rapid impetus to the settlement.

The inhabitants held the titles to their lands from William Wetmore, who purchased of the state in 1792. Kenduskeag plantation was the original name, which was retained until the period of incorporation, 1813, when the present name was given. The surface is uneven, though the soil is fertile. It is drained by Kenduskeag river and its branches. The village is situated on the river, where are several mills. There are three stores, one fulling-mill, one tannery, one grist-mill, and six saw-mills; two churches — Universalist and Methodist Episcopal; nine school districts, with ten schools; and two post-offices — Levant and West Levant. The population, in 1850, was 1,841; but the incorporation of Kenduskeag has probably reduced it to 1,200; valuation, $169,397, which has also been correspondingly reduced.

Lewiston, situated in the central part of Androscoggin county, making a nearly oblong square upon the easterly side of the Androscoggin, running upon the river about twelve miles, was a part of the Pejepscot claim. It was first entered for settlement in the spring of 1771 by Paul Hildreth and David Pettingill, with their families, who came from New Gloucester, and located about half a mile below the falls. In the spring of 1772, Lawrence J. Harris, of Dracut, Mass., immigrated hither with his large family, and brought men and materials for the erection of mills. Under an arrangement with Captain Moses Little, of Newbury, and Colonel Bagley, then the Pejepscot claimants, Mr. Harris was to receive two large lots of land around the falls, and one hundred acres for each of his five sons, the title of which land remained in his family until 1810, and is now included in the very valuable tract owned by the Franklin Company. Until that time, the nearest saw-mill was at North Yarmouth, twenty-five miles distant.

The next settler was a Mr. Varnum, also from Dracut. In 1773, a part of the territory was surveyed and lotted for the Pejepscot claimants by Amos Davis, D. Purinton, and Nathaniel Ingorsal. Davis moved with his family, January 25, 1774, from New Gloucester, and Israel Herrick became a settler at the same time. A memorandum, made at that date by Davis, states that Thomas and Jonas Coborn were also residents. The Revolutionary war brought in other settlers, who sought refuge further from the coast; among whom, in 1776, were

James Garcelon (the progenitor of all the Garcelons in this country), with his five sons (one of whom was Colonel William Garcelon of Lewiston), and two daughters; Josiah Mitchell, Joel Thomson, Stephen Coffin, Mark Pettingill, Joel and Jesse Wright, and Solomon Cummings. Many others settled previous to 1780. In 1788, there were seventy-five families. Daniel Davis kept the first school, in a log house near the falls. Lewiston was incorporated February 18, 1795. The Friends organized the first religious society. Amos Davis built them a house upon his own premises. They erected another house in 1811. The Baptists organized a society, and built a house in 1818; and the

Lewiston, Me.

Free-will Baptists in 1820. Lewiston is somewhat broken in surface, but well cultivated, and contains many good farms. It has excellent clay for making bricks; also several valuable ledges, furnishing the best of building materials, which is shown in the beauty of the dwelling-houses, and the substantial character of its stores and manufacturing establishments. This town is connected with the most flourishing and populous portions of the state by railroad. But its distinguishing features are its almost unrivalled water-power, and the extensive application of it to the propulsion of a great variety of machinery. A correct view of Lewiston Falls, from a beautiful photograph by Messrs. Locke, taken at a point near the toll-bridge, is given in connection with the article upon Androscoggin county. The river breaks over a ledge of rocks which crosses it diagonally, creating a natural fall of forty feet in a distance of two hundred feet, which, by the aid of dams, has been increased to fifty feet. This water-power is now owned by the Franklin Company. Its use may be best shown by a brief synopsis of the several manufacturing interests.

The Franklin Company, the successor of the Lewiston Water-Power Company, has a capital of $400,000; runs one mill with five thousand spindles, and employs about 125 operatives; the manufactures are white cottons. Another mill is being fitted to accommodate fifteen thousand spindles. — The Bates Manufacturing Company, which went into operation in April, 1852, has a capital of $800,000; two mills, with thirty-six thousand spindles, 812 looms, and one thousand operatives; manufactures fine white cotton sheetings and shirtings, fancy cotton stuffs, and cotton flannel; average annual product, three million yards; monthly pay roll, from $15,000 to $20,000. — The Hill Manufacturing Company has a chartered capital of $1,000,000, with $385,000 invested; one mill, with 414 looms and 22,400 spindles; manufactures fine cotton goods for bleaching; consumes annually 1,750 bales of cotton; employs four hundred operatives, with a monthly pay roll of $7,800. The gross sales for year ending June, 1855, amounted to $310,000. Since then 2,368 spindles have been added, and the sales have proportionally increased. — The Lewiston Bagging Company has a capital of $150,000, of which $75,000 is invested; one mill, which was built in 1854, and went into operation in 1856; seventy-four looms and 4,500 spindles; manufactures grain sacks, with an average of 2,500 sacks daily, which are sold at $23 per hundred; employs 120 operatives, with a monthly pay roll of about $3,000. — The Lewiston Falls Manufacturing Company has a capital paid in of $59,000, and is wholly devoted to woollen goods, chiefly cassimeres, tweeds, and flannels. It runs five sets of machinery, employs about thirty males and thirty females, and uses annually 160,000 pounds of wool. — The Sabattis Manufacturing Company is situated at the outlet of Sabattis pond, in Lewiston, Webster, and Greene; has a capital of $30,000; runs three sets of machinery; manufactures flannels, and uses about 80,000 pounds wool annually.

The Lewiston Furnace Company manufacture steam-engines, boilers, and machinery of all kinds, including Reynold's patent variable cut-off for steam-engines; it has a capital of $35,000, employs forty hands, and has a monthly pay roll of about $1,200. It is owned by Reynolds, Steinmetz and Company. — John Ferguson has a large machine shop in one of the buildings of the Franklin Company, which is employed upon mill shafting and gearing. It has eight engine lathes. Another machine shop is carried on in one of this company's buildings, by Mr. Whipple, for the manufacture of wooden machinery. — There are also a corn and flour mill, having four runs of stones, capable of making 150 barrels of flour per day; a saw-mill having one gang and one single saw capable of cutting five million feet of lumber annually, with all the appliances for the manufacture of shingles, laths, sashes, blinds, doors, and bobbins; also a large card factory.

Lewiston has increased surprisingly within a few years, through its manufacturing interests. The Maine State Seminary, incorporated in 1855, and endowed by the state, is located here. There are also fourteen school districts; nine religious societies — Congregational, Methodist, Baptist, Episcopal, Roman Catholic, Friends, two Free-will Baptist, and a Universalist, all except the last having meeting-houses; and one post office. Population, about 7,000; valuation for 1859, $2.427.615.

LEXINGTON, Somerset county, is situated on the western side of the Kennebec river, twenty miles from Norridgewock. It was incorporated in 1833, and has several ponds flowing into Seven Mile branch of Kennebec river, which afford fine mill seats. The surface is moderately uneven, but the soil is good, offering profitable investments for the farmer. Lexington has a thriving population, and lumber forms the principal source of wealth. It contains one church edifice (Free-will Baptist), one saw-mill, nine school districts, with ten schools; and one post-office. Population, 538; valuation, $43,288.

LIBERTY, in the western part of Waldo county, eighteen miles from Belfast, was formerly comprised in the Waldo Patent. It was incorporated in 1827, and is diversified with rocky eminences and fertile valleys, well adapted to the pursuit of agriculture. It is watered by George's pond, and by several smaller streams. Liberty contains one church edifice (Free-will Baptist), nine school districts, with the same number of schools; two extensive tanneries, an iron foundery, a machine shop, a planing machine, saw-mills, stave mills, shingle mills, carding-machines; and two post-offices — Liberty and South Liberty. Population, 1,116; valuation, $99,715.

LIMERICK, in the northern part of York county, bounded south by Little Ossipee river, has an area of about 14,000 acres. The settlement was commenced, about the year 1775, by persons from Biddeford, Saco, York, Kittery, and Newbury, Mass.; and among the early immigrants were some from Limerick, Ireland. James Sullivan, afterwards governor of Massachusetts, was an early resident, but soon abandoned the farm, and entered his brother John's law-office, in Durham, N. H. The town was incorporated March 6, 1787. Among the petitioners for incorporation were Jacob and John Bradbury, Abijah Felch, Joseph and Thomas Gilpatrick, William Durgin, David Clark, Thomas Lord, John Hodgdon, Jr., John Mills, and John Wingate. Thomas Paul, afterwards "the black preacher" in Boston, was an apprentice at the tannery of Dea. Mills. The Baptists organized a branch church here in 1793 — an independent one in 1796, when they ordained Ebenezer Kingman as pastor. The Congregational church dates from 1795, over which Ed mund Eastman was ordained the same year. Alpheus Felch, United States senator from Michigan, John Fairfield and J. W. Bradbury, senators from this State, when boys, attended the Limerick Academy together, the first being a native of the town. The Freewill Baptist church was organized in 1822, and the Freewill Baptist newspaper, "The Morning Star," was started here. There are ten school districts, an academy, and a post-office, three saw-mills, three shingle-mills, a grist-mill, and two tanneries. Population, 1,473; valuation, $235,780.

LIMINGTON, York county, formerly called Ossipee Plantation, containing about 27,000 acres, is bounded north and east by the Saco river, and was a part of Francis Small's Indian purchase. Its settlement was begun about 1773. At the time of incorporation, February 9, 1792, upwards of one hundred families were here, Small's heirs being largely represented. Among the petitioners for a town were Joshua, Daniel, Isaac, William, and Benjamin Small, Dominicus McKenney, Jonathan Boothby, Jesse, John and Philemon Libby, Amos Chase, and Ephraim Clark. No less than seventy inhabitants remonstrated, on account of the uncertainty of their land titles by reason of lawsuits then pending, and also on account of poverty. The Congregational church was organized in 1789. The Baptist church dates from 1802. Besides these, are two Freewill Baptist churches, and a Society of Friends, all having meeting-houses. There are three post-offices — Limington, East Limington, and North Limington; seventeen school districts, an academy and seminary; also five saw-mills, three grist-mills, three shingle machines, and a carriage manufactory. Population, 2,116; valuation, $346,786.

LINCOLN, Penobscot county, is situated on the east side of Penobscot river, fifty miles north from Bangor, and covers an area of 57,600 acres. Israel Heald, John Carpenter, Alfred Gates, Benjamin Hammond, Stephen Chase, Humphrey Merrill, Ira Fisk, and others first settled, about the year 1825: possibly there may have been some previous to this. A part of Lincoln was purchased from the state by Governor

Lincoln and others; the remainder being sold to settlers. Those who located on the Lincoln purchase came mostly from Oxford county; those settling in other parts were from New Hampshire. Improvements were rapidly made; and mills were erected at an early day on the Mattanawcook stream, where the lower village now stands. The building of the military road from here to Houlton gave encouragement to the settlement, while its central location, which made it a rendezvous for lumbermen, gave it an additional impetus.

The surface is broken. Back from the river the land is rocky, and hard to cultivate; while near the river, it is free from stone and less stubborn. Nearly half the territory is under cultivation. This town has produced a large growth of valuable pine timber, which has mostly been cleared. That which remains is spruce and hemlock. Water is supplied by a great number of ponds, — Mattanawcook being the principal, — nearly all of which have their outlets in the Penobscot river. There are two villages, two miles apart; one, called the Lower village, situated one mile from the Penobscot river, on the Mattanawcook stream; and the other, called the Upper village, situated on the Penobscot, at the mouth of the Cumberlassis stream. At the upper village are a carding mill, saw-mill, grist-mill, a shingle machine, and a clapboard machine; at the lower village, a double saw-mill, a grist-mill, a tannery, a shingle machine, and a clapboard machine. Considerable business is done in axe making, and in wagon and sled making. A steamboat ascends the Penobscot from Oldtown to Mattawamkeag, landing at the upper village. The Oldtown and Lincoln Railroad is surveyed to Lincoln Centre, which, when built, will prove highly advantageous. At the outlet of Long pond, about three miles from the upper village, are a saw-mill and a shingle and clapboard machine. A Baptist church was organized here soon after the settlement of the town; but no edifice was erected until 1840. There are four post-offices — South Lincoln, Lincoln, Lincoln Centre, and North Lincoln; an academy with a fund of about $3,000; and twelve school districts, with the same number of schools. Population, 1,356; valuation. $127,663.

Lincoln County, situated a little west of the centre of the sea-coast of Maine, is a twin sister of Cumberland, both of which were established on the 19th of June, 1760, as the second and third counties in the province. The easterly line of Cumberland was then the westerly line of Lincoln, and for a long time this line in part remained unbroken; but other counties have interloped, and this ancient sisterly connection of counties has ceased. From the time of its formation, until the erection of Hancock and Washington counties in 1789, Lincoln extended over quite three fifths of the territory of the province. Its westerly line was "from Small point northwesterly upon Casco bay to New Meadows river, and up said river to Stevens's carrying place at the head of said river; thence across said carrying place to Merry Meeting bay and Androscoggin river, and up said river thirty miles; thence north two degrees west on a true course to the utmost limits of the province." Its north was Canada, its east, Nova Scotia, and its south, the ocean. Hancock county came across Penobscot bay and river, and took in nearly the whole of the Waldo Patent. In 1799, the organization of Kennebec took four fifths of what remained after the formation of Hancock. Lincoln then continued undisturbed until 1827, when it parted with six towns to form Waldo; and it had an equal run of time again, down to the organization of Androscoggin and Sagadahoc, in 1854, when the former received three towns from it, and the latter was made entirely from it; all these creations and enlargements of other jurisdictions apparently pushing little Lincoln out to sea, or restricting it certainly within bounds which inlets of the sea make far into, and broad rivers almost traverse.

This county now contains twenty-five towns and three plantations; nineteen of these towns are situated either on navigable rivers or on the seaboard. The three plantations are Matinicus Isle, Monhegan Isle, and Muscle Ridge, all sparsely peopled. At the west is Sheepscot river, for the accommodation of Southport, Boothbay, Westport, Wiscasset, and Alna. More centrally located is the Damariscotta river, affording like facilities to Bristol, Newcastle, Damariscotta, and Nobleborough. The Muscongus river opens water communication to Bremen, Friendship, and Waldoborough, and the St. George river does a like service for Cushing, Warren, St. George, and Thomaston, while the broad Penobscot supplies South Thomaston and Rockland. The people of the county are very generally devoted to fishing and maritime interests. Pownalborough was made the shire town at the outset, and has ever continued so, although under another name; that part of it which remained after the incorporation of Dresden having, on the 10th of June, 1802, received from the legislature the name of Wiscasset, as being more generally known in the commercial world by that cognomen.

The district court of the United States holds one term at Wiscasset, commencing on the first Tuesday of September. The county belongs to the middle district for the state courts, the law term of which is held at Augusta. The jury terms of the supreme judicial court for civil and criminal business commence on the fourth Tuesday of January, and the first Tuesday of October; and for civil and criminal business on the first Tuesday of May. Population, 47,048; valuation, $8,191,197.

LINCOLNVILLE, Waldo county, is situated on the western shore of Penobscot bay, and is some seven miles in length, and about four miles in width. John Studley, and a man by the name of Wilson, were the first settlers, having arrived in the year 1774. The surface is broken, rocky, boggy, and mountainous. It is watered by several ponds, known as Canaan, Fletcher, Molyneaux, Andrews, Pitcher, and Knights; and is drained by the Megunticook and Duck-trap streams. Peaked mountain, situated in the northwest part, is the highest elevation, having an altitude of about eight hundred feet.

There are three small villages — Duck-trap, French's Beach, and Lincolnville Centre; three church edifices — Methodist, Baptist, and Freewill Baptist; seventeen school districts, with thirty-three schools; two post-offices — Lincolnville and Centre Lincolnville; also, four saw-mills, three shingle mills, two grist-mills, one tannery, one carriage builder, and two ship-builders. Population, 2,174; valuation, $248,890.

LINNEUS, in the southeastern part of Aroostook county, at the head waters of the Mattawamkeag and Meduxnekeag rivers, was first settled by Daniel Neal, from New Brunswick, in 1826. It was surveyed into lots in 1827. Colonel Moses Burleigh, from Palermo, who settled in 1830, is now living, at the age of seventy-seven. He was a captain in the militia of Maine, in the war with Great Britain, in 1812; and was, with his company, called into service, and stationed at Belfast when the British came up the Penobscot river to capture the corvette *Adams*, lying at Hampden. He represented his district in the Massachusetts legislature several years; and after the separation of Maine, was for several years in the legislature of that state.

Linneus was incorporated in 1836. It was originally granted by Massachusetts to endow a professorship of botany. Much of the surface of the land is gently undulating; though a small portion at the northwesterly part is rather hilly and stony. The soil generally is of an excellent quality, and well adapted to grazing, and the usual productions. From eighty to ninety-two bushels of Indian corn to the acre have been produced. Limestone of an excellent quality is found in abundance in the northwest part, and is pronounced by Dr. Jackson, state geologist, to be equal in quality to the Thomaston limestone. Many beautiful specimens of magnetic iron ore have been found in different parts. There are several small ponds, — one at the northwest corner of the town; another near the northeast corner, in both which salmon trout of a large size are found. Besides these, there are several smaller ponds. Linneus has eight school districts; two post-offices — Linneus and North Linneus; one saw-mill, two stores, and two black-smith's shops. Population, 561; valuation, $25,199.

LISBON, Androscoggin county, originally belonged to the Pejepscot Purchase, and formed a part of Bowdoin until June 22, 1799, when it was incorporated under the name of Thompsonborough, which, not being satisfactory to the inhabitants, was changed February 20, 1802, to the one by which it is now designated. In an agricultural point of view, Lisbon holds an important position; and, from its location, it is inferred that it will, at no distant day, attain a reputation second to none of the towns in the interior of the state. It lies on the east side of the Androscoggin river, on which there are falls known as the Ten-mile Falls. There are two villages — Lisbon and Little River, with a post-office at each; four church edifices — Congregational, Baptist, Free-will Baptist, and Methodist; eleven school districts, an academy, a public library; five saw-mills, and three grist-mills. Population, 1,495; valuation, 263,167.

LITCHFIELD is the most southerly town in Kennebec county, and is separated from the Kennebec by Gardiner on the east. Prior to its settlement, it was frequently visited by two hunters from Topsham — Andrew Jack, and one Graves, who came in pursuit of beavers, otters, bears, and other game. The former moved here about the year 1790. The settlement was commenced about 1775 or 1776, — the settlers erroneously presuming that the land was owned by the state. The principal proprietors were Charles W. Apthorp, of New York, Nathan and James Bridge, Dr. J. P. Sheafe, Messrs. Wood and Boardman, John Pitts and Lady Temple, who derived their titles from the Plymouth company. The settlers paid from $1.75 to $4.00 per acre for their land. Among the early inhabitants were Benjamin Hinckley, Eliphalet Smith, a family named Tibbets, William Potter, Barnabas Baker, Thomas Smith, Benjamin Smith, Andrew and David Springer, John Dennis, James Lord, and Joseph Sawyer.

Litchfield was incorporated in 1795. It has never been the theatre of any Indian attacks, or other important events. The surface is moderately uneven, though not broken. The land is well suited to agriculture, producing fine crops of corn, grain, and hay. It is well watered, — the eastern, northern, and part of the western boundaries being ponds and streams of water, which are skirted with intervals, yielding a large quantity of hay. Purgatory ponds form a continued chain, extending through nearly the whole western part; and derive their name, so tradition says, from the abundance of flies and mosquitos, which harassed some hunters, who at one time encamped on the banks of one of them. Loon pond is a beautiful sheet of water. Litchfield is intersected by streams, affording excellent mill sites. Oak hill, a considerable elevation, extending from north to south through the western portion of the town, is rather rocky, but notwithstanding has some good farms upon it. The principal pursuits of the inhabitants, exclusive of farming, may be conjectured from the following summary: — five saw-mills, four grist-mills, one carding machine, three shingle machines, and one match factory; also one hoe and fork factory, where one thousand dozen of these tools are made annually. There are two villages — North Litchfield and Litchfield Corner, both prosperous; three post-offices — Litchfield, South Litchfield, and Litchfield Corner; three church edifices, occupied by Baptists, Free-will Baptists, and Congregationalists; and fourteen school districts, with sixteen schools. The Litchfield academy was incorporated in 1845, and endowed by act of legislature in 1849. It has a good library, apparatus, maps, charts, globes, and an extensive cabinet of minerals and curiosities. Many excellent teachers have received their education at this school. The Litchfield Liberal Institute was incorporated in 1846, and has received from the state three hundred dollars. Population, 2,100; valuation for 1858, from assessors' books, $436,612.

LITTLETON, Aroostook county, is an eastern frontier town, and joins Houlton on the north. The northern half was granted to Framingham academy in 1801, and was surveyed in 1802. The southern half is the northern part of a township granted to Williams College, the southern half of which grant now constitutes the northern half of Houlton. The area of the town is 22,040 acres. That part of Littleton which was formerly granted to Williams College was made over to that institution by the commonwealth of Massachusetts in 1800, and was located the next year by Park Holland. The progress of this settlement has been very slow, which is evidenced by the fact, that, until 1856, it did not possess a sufficient number of inhabitants to entitle it to incorporation. The southern half of the town is now quite thickly settled. A large proportion of the land is good, and is being profitably cultivated. Population, 255.

LIVERMORE, Androscoggin county, is the westerly portion of a township six and three quarters miles square (exclusive of 1,000 acres allowance for sway of chain, and 3,042 acres for ponds and rivers), which was granted, in 1771, to Samuel Livermore and others, to make up the loss sustained on account of the grant, in 1736, of a township between Merrimack and Connecticut rivers, in consideration of military services in 1710, at the reduction of Port Royal, in which township the proprietors had laid out roads and erected a saw-mill and other buildings, but which, upon the settlement of the State line, fell within New Hampshire. In 1774, the proprietors voted £4. each to the first ten settlers, provided they should build houses before 1776. A meeting of the proprietors was notified at Waltham, Mass., in May, 1775; but the war prevented attendance, and no meetings were held till March, 1779. In this year, Dea. Elijah Livermore, the chief proprietor, came here from Waltham, but is said to have withdrawn for a period, on account of danger from the Indians. He was residing here permanently in 1782, and contracted with the proprietors to build a mill. His brother Samuel, the first-named proprietor, — who served as attorney-general in New Hampshire under Governor Wentworth, in the same capacity under the State government, as delegate to the Continental Congress, as chief justice, and United States senator, — never took up his abode here. The second settler was Samuel Benjamin, a lieutenant in the Revolutionary army, who came from Watertown, Mass., in 1782. In June, 1783, Samuel Sawin, and in 1784, Abijah Sawin and Thomas Coolidge, came also from Watertown. The town was incorporated February 28, 1795, when there were upwards of sixty families, among whom were Hon. Reuel Washburn, Israel Washburn, Samuel Hillman, Sylvanus Boardman, David Learned, John Walker, William Hurd, and Ransom Norton. "The three Washburns" in congress — Israel Washburn, Jr., of Orono, Elihu B. Washburn, of Illinois, and C. C. Washburn, of Wisconsin, are sons of Israel Washburn; and Hon. Hannibal Hamlin, United States senator, and Elijah L. Hamlin, of Bangor, are grandsons of Dea. Livermore. Bishop Soule, of the Methodist Episcopal Church South, was born in Livermore. That part of the town upon the east side of the Androscoggin river was incorporated in 1843, by the name of East Livermore. The land rises in gentle elevations from the river, there being little interval upon its banks.

There are two villages — Bretton's Mills and North Livermore; three church edifices — Methodist, Baptist, and Universalist; eighteen school districts, with thirty-six schools; four saw-mills, three shingle mills, two grist-mills; one hay-rake factory, one pill-box factory, and one match factory; also three post-offices — Livermore, Livermore Centre, and Livermore Falls. Population, 1,764; valuation, $271,633.

LOVELL, in the westerly part of Oxford county, is a part of what is called the Pequawket country, so named from the tribe of Indians, who had their head-quarters at Fryeburg, where the gallant and unfortunate Captain Lovewell and his little band of thirty-four followers had their desperate fight. Some years after, the legislature of Massachusetts granted a tract of land to the suffering heirs of Captain Lovewell and his company; but when the line was run between Maine and New Hampshire, it was found that this township (now called Pembroke), was in New Hampshire; and the legislature of Massachusetts, to make up for the loss thus sustained, granted to them another lying on the easterly side of Saco river, which was to be called New Suncook, and was to be six miles square, or equal to that amount of land. The usual conditions of a grant were fulfilled in this case. The southeasterly part of the township, as originally granted, is now incorporated as Sweden.

The settlement was commenced about the year 1779, in the southwesterly part, near Saco river, by Noah Eastman, Stephen Dresser, John Stearns, Captain John Wood, Oliver Whiting, Joseph McAllaster, Annias McAllaster, Benjamin Stearns, Josiah Heald, Levi Dresser, John Whiting, Abel Butters, James Kilgore, and others.

Lovell was incorporated on the 15th of November, 1800. The surface, as a general thing, is uneven; but the soil is good. There are five ponds, the principal of which, called Kezer pond, from an old hunter, is a magnificent sheet of water, having three bays, about one mile wide and eight miles long; also, two small rivers — one, the outlet of Kezer pond, emptying into the Saco; the other taking its rise from five small ponds, mostly in the town of Waterford, known by the name of Kezer. At a short distance from these ponds, the stream becomes narrowed by a ledge, and, falling over the precipice, winds its way along the easterly part of the town, and passes through a very pleasant village, supplying excellent water-power. This village is doing considerable business for a place of its size. The houses are well built and pleasantly situated.

There are three churches in Lovell — one Methodist and two Congregational; three post-offices — Lovell, Centre Lovell, and North Lovell; and fifteen school districts, with twenty-five schools. Population, 1,193; valuation for 1858, $222,000.

LOWELL, Penobscot county, distant forty miles northerly from Bangor, was first settled by Alpheus Hayden and Levi Done, of Canaan, Somerset county, who removed here March, 1819. These settlers, and others who soon followed, purchased their lands of the state. The son of Alpheus Hayden, the first person born here, was called Lowell, for whom the town was named. In 1841, the legislature annexed to Lowell what was called the Strip, north of township No. 1, Bingham's Penobscot purchase. The settlers of this plantation purchased their lands of the Bingham heirs. Mary C. Dean (afterwards the wife of Stephen Kimball, of Bangor) was the first school teacher, and the Rev. Pindar Field the first minister of this plantation. Both these individuals were held in very high estimation by the people, and the plantation, which had been previously called Page's Mills settlement, was named *Deanfield*, in honor of them. In 1842, the legislature annexed what was called the Cold Stream settlement to Lowell.

Lowell was incorporated February, 1837, under the name of Huntersville, which was changed by the legislature the next year. The surface is uneven, and in some places broken. The land is somewhat stony but fertile, and will well reward the labor of the husbandman. There are large tracts of meadow land upon the rivers and streams, and large quantities of lumber for building purposes. The pastures on the hills are excellent for grazing. Several high elevations of land lie in the north part. The Passadumkeag river passes from east to west, some six or eight miles, through the town; and the stream Escutussis, from the lake of the same name, empties its waters into the Passadumkeag river.

The inhabitants of Lowell are engaged somewhat in manufactures. At Page's Mills, on the Passadumkeag river, there is a large tannery; also a mill for the manufacture of lumber, consisting of one single and one gang saw-mill, and a clapboard, lath, and shingle mill. One mile above, at the mouth of the Escutussis stream, there is another establishment for the manufacture of lumber, consisting of one saw-mill and one shingle and clapboard mill. All the above are new establishments, having been erected within a year. Ascending the Escutussis one mile, another saw-mill is reached; and, one hundred rods above, are a corn-mill, a flour mill, a clapboard mill, and a shingle mill, which are known by the name of Porter's mills. Two miles above this, at the outlet of the Escutussis lake, are the Verney mills, comprising a saw-mill and a shingle mill. In addition to the above, the inhabitants are quite extensively engaged in lumbering on the upper waters of the Passadumkeag, furnishing thereby large quantities of lumber to be manufactured on the main Penobscot river below.

The principal villages are at Page's Mills, formerly so called, and Porter's Mills. Some of the inhabitants of these villages have united with Burlington and built a meeting-house, not far from the town line, which is usually occupied by the Congregationalists. A portion of the inhabitants of Cold Stream settlement are connected with the Baptist church in Enfield. The people on Long Bridge are connected with a Free-will Baptist church. There are six school districts, and two post offices —

the Lowell post-office, at Page's Mills, and the East Lowell post-office, at Porter's Mills. Population, 378; assessors' valuation for 1858, $36,000.

Lubec, Washington county, is situated on the peninsula opposite Campo Bello island, and was settled about 1780. It formed a part of Eastport until June 21, 1811, when it was incorporated under its present name, from Lubec in Germany. This town is possessed of an admirable harbor, which is of sufficient capacity for vessels of the largest draught — is never obstructed by ice — is easy of access, and well protected by Grand Menan and Campo Bello islands. The principal place of business is built on a point of land jutting out into the harbor, — a beautiful location, — and presenting a fine appearance. Lubec, from its situation, enjoys a very extensive trade with the Bay of Fundy and the great waters of Passamaquoddy bay, coasting and the cod and mackerel fisheries being the principal branches of business. West Quoddy Head light-house is situated at the western entrance into Passamaquoddy bay. Lubec contains two church edifices (Congregational and Methodist), fourteen school districts, one tannery, three grist-mills, nine saw-mills, and three post-offices — Lubec, Lubec Mills, and West Lubec. Population, 2,814; valuation, $240,153.

Lyman, in the central part of York county, was purchased in 1660, of an Indian sagamore named Fluellen, by John Saunders, John Bush, and Peter Tarbitt, who sold their deed in 1668, to Harlackindine Symonds. Symonds afterwards disposed of his title to Roger Haskins and thirty-five others, and, under their proprietorship, the town was settled in 1767. It was called Loxhall when incorporated, March 11, 1778, which name was changed to the present one, February 26, 1803, as a token of respect, it is believed, to Theodore Lyman, of Boston, originally of York, Me. When first organized, the people in their parochial affairs were connected with Alfred and Sandford, from which they separated in 1787 or 1788. John Low first represented Lyman in the general court in 1786.

Like most of the towns in the immediate neighborhood, the surface is generally smooth, and the land well adapted to the necessities of an agricultural community, Lyman being essentially of that class. In shape it is oblong, and is generally thickly settled. There are four ponds, called respectively Kennebunk, Swan, Bunganaul, and Barker's, which afford sufficient water for all purposes. The Baptists have two church edifices, and the Congregationalists and Methodists one each. Lyman Centre and Goodwin's Mills are the only two villages.

There are two saw-mills, one carding-machine, one grist-mill, one carriage factory, and one brick-yard. Education receives proper attention, there being twelve school districts, with twenty-two schools. Lyman, Lyman Centre, and Goodwin's Mills are the names of the post-offices. Population, 1,376; valuation, $202,753.

MACHIAS is the capital of Washington county, and a port of entry. The first knowledge the English obtained of this place was in 1633, while the fierce contest was going on between France and Great Britain for supremacy on this continent. They erected a trading house here during the spring of that year, put in a stock of goods, and commenced a traffic with the natives. This trading house the English intrusted to the keeping of five or six armed men, who they thought might be able to defend it from pillage by the Indians; and, if menaced by the French, give such timely warning to the proper authorities as would enable them to make arrangements for its defence before the enemy could arrive. In this they were deceived, for when La Tour, the French commander, in the spring of 1634, learned of this establishment, he immediately started from Port Royal, and made a descent upon it, capturing it after a slight resistance on the part of the armed force, two of whom were killed. The survivors he took prisoners, and, with the goods they had in charge, returned to Port Royal, from whence the prisoners were liberated shortly afterwards, — the goods apparently being retained as lawful prize. From this time, for upwards of one hundred and twenty years, no attempt was made by either nation to settle the wilderness of Machias.

In 1761–62, a great drought prevailed in the eastern part of Maine; and the people living on the seaboard, in order to procure hay for their cattle, pushed further into the wilderness east of the Penobscot, and became acquainted with this place, and the advantages it offered for settlement. They thereupon petitioned the general court of Massachusetts for a grant of the territory, which petition was allowed in 1770. Of the eighty petitioners for this grant, no less than fifty-four were from Scarborough.[1] Among the settlers in 1763, were persons named Scott, Libby, Stone, Larrabee, Hill, D. Fogg, and J. Foster, most of whom were at West Falls. The Messrs. Foster, Munson, Sevey, and Scott,

[1] In regard to the settlement of Machias, a statement has gained currency, that the settlers fled here to escape punishment for participation in the King riot, which occurred at Scarborough, on the 19th of March, 1776. This can scarcely be true; for the riot did not take place till six years after the grant had been made to the signers of the petition. It is not, however, improbable that some of the culprits might have fled here for concealment for a time among their former townsmen.

settled at East Falls. In 1765, Morris O'Brien and his sons built a double saw-mill at the former place. Other persons came in, and before 1770 several mills were erected on both East and West rivers, and one on Middle river.

In 1775, an affair occurred which acquired for the inhabitants much credit. Captain Ichabod Jones, of Boston, having obtained from Admiral Graves permission to freight his (Jones's) vessel with provisions, and carry them to this settlement, upon condition of returning with a cargo of wood and lumber for the British troops, arrived here early in June, accompanied by the *Margaretta*, an English schooner, well armed, under the command of Midshipman Moor. Jones had a meeting of the settlers, who consented to allow the vessel to load. But Benjamin Foster and a party from East river conceived the bold design of making the British schooner their prize, and her officers prisoners. The first attempt proved unsuccessful; but afterwards, aided by Jeremiah O'Brien and his sons, they succeeded in capturing the schooner without much loss of life on either side, — two of the Machias men having been killed and several wounded, while the commander of the British schooner fell in the encounter, with several of his men. Nor did the exploits of these brave men end here. They succeeded subsequently, by a bold stratagem, in capturing a British schooner of seventy or eighty tons with her tender, and making their commanders prisoners. For their heroism, they afterwards received the thanks of the provincial congress.

In 1777, in consequence of the expedition planned against Fort Cumberland, St. John's, and other places on the Bay of Fundy, Machias became a general rendezvous for the American forces, and the British admiral at New York sent the *Rainbow*, two frigates, and an armed brig to frustrate the expedition. They arrived in August, and came to anchor in Machias bay; and, after committing several depredations in the immediate neighborhood, proceeded to the foot of the falls in Middle river, where they were received by Major Stillman and party on the one side, and by Joseph Neptune, chief of the Passamaquoddy tribe, on the other, and were effectually repulsed. Every man in the place able to bear arms was upon the shore, as well as between forty and fifty Indians, who raised and kept up a hideous yell, which so reverberated as to induce the supposition that the forests were full of wild savages. Discouraged by these appearances, and by the vigor and spirit with which they were resisted, the British squadron in a day or two left the place, and the town was not molested again during the war.

Machias was incorporated June 23, 1784, and formerly embraced within its limits East Machias, Whitneyville, Machiasport, and Marshfield. In 1781, the first church was organized, and in 1794, the first meeting-house erected. A convention being held at Portland in 1786 to consider the expediency of the separation of Maine from Massachusetts, the people of Machias resolved that it was not expedient to urge such separation. This action was repeated in 1791.

Its excellent location, the fertility of its soil, and its navigable privileges, which are equal to any on the coast, render Machias one of the most flourishing towns in the state. It is watered by Machias river, which flows across the northeast corner. Machias does a business annually in ship-building, lumbering, and manufacturing, of upwards of $2,000,000. There are two meeting-houses — Congregational and Methodist; one school district, with eleven schools; a post-office, a printing-office, two founderies, sixteen saw-mills, lath and shingle mills, a carriage manufactory, grist-mill, a telegraph station, a court-house, a jail, two hotels, and other buildings and conveniences. Population, 1,590; valuation, $600,000.

Machiasport, Washington county, is an Atlantic frontier town, situated on the western shore of Machias bay. It originally belonged to Machias, and was separated and incorporated in 1826. It has a great number of mills; and the inhabitants are very extensively engaged in the lumber trade, as also in fishing and coasting. It is a port of entry, and has an excellent harbor. The railroad to Whitneyville, a distance of eight miles, conveys the lumber from that place to this town for shipment. It was in this part of old Machias that the Plymouth colony established their trading house in 1633. It was subsequently occupied by the French several years. The details of other portions of the history are involved in the article on Machias. There are five churches — one Baptist, one Congregational, two Free-will Baptist, and one Second Advent; nine school districts, several saw-mills, one grist-mill, and one post-office. Population, 1,266; valuation, $106,405.

Madison, Somerset county, is situated on the east side of Kennebec river, and was incorporated in 1804. It is watered by a pond, the outlet of which is at Skowhegan; and the soil is of the greatest fertility. The inhabitants are, for the most part, engaged in agricultural pursuits, for which there is a wide field. Madison has three villages, pleasantly situated; three church edifices — Congregational, Free-will Baptist, and Universalist; nineteen school districts, with thirty-two schools; three saw-mills, two grist-mills, two shingle mills, and two post-offices — Madison, and East Madison. Population, 1,769; valuation, $281,045.

MADRID, Franklin county, is something more than twenty miles northwest from Farmington. The first settlements were commenced about 1807 or 1808 by Abel Cook, David Ross, John Sargent, Lemuel Plummer, Miller Hinkley, Joseph Dunham, Ebenezer Cawkins, and Nathaniel Wells. It was formerly owned by Mr. Phillips, and subsequently passed into the hands of Jacob Abbot, whose heirs still own the unsettled land, amounting to nearly half the township.

Madrid was incorporated in 1836. Some of the land is good, while other portions are unfit for cultivation. It has three saw-mills, a grist-mill, two clapboard machines, and two shingle machines. As yet there is no house of public worship. Meetings are held in school-houses; and though the town is but partially settled, the inhabitants have sustained stated meetings on the Sabbath most of the time from the earliest date of their arrival. There are seven school districts, with twelve schools; and one post-office. Population, 404; valuation, $23,964.

MANCHESTER, Kennebec county, is situated about four and a half miles west of the Kennebec river, extending from east to west about three miles, and from north to south about eight miles. The first settlement was commenced in 1775. Nathaniel Floyd, a native of Plymouth, Mass., took up a "settler's lot" in the south part; and the same year, Thomas Allen, a native of Braintree, Mass., obtained of the government a lot in the north part, which remains in the family until the present day, and is now owned by a grandson of said Thomas Allen (William H. Allen, president of Girard college). In 1776, Captain John Evans and Francis Fuller of Cape Cod, and Reuben Brainard of Haddam, Conn., took up lots; Samuel Cummings, of Stoughton, Mass., took up one in 1778; and several other persons soon after. From this time to 1790, settlers came in from Massachusetts in such numbers that most of this part of the country was taken up in farms.

Manchester was incorporated August 12, 1850, by the name of Kennebec, and is composed of parts of Hallowell, Litchfield, Winthrop, and Readfield. A strip upon the northeast side of Manchester was annexed to Augusta in 1856. The name was changed, April 18, 1854, to Manchester. The surface is somewhat uneven. A large portion of the Cobbossee Contee pond, a beautiful sheet of water, about nine miles long by one mile wide, interspersed with numerous islands, lies in the southwestern part. The principal occupation of the inhabitants is agriculture, which at the present time is carried on by many on scientific principles with good success. There are two manufacturing establishments, — one of painted carpetings, and one of hay forks and manure forks. In the eastern part is a fine quarry of excellent granite, from which large numbers of blocks are excavated annually and shipped to other states. There are three church edifices in Manchester, one occupied by the Baptists, one by the Society of Friends, and one as a Union meeting-house; seven school districts, with the same number of schools; one village, and one post-office. Population, 1,000; valuation, 277,448.

MARIAVILLE, Hancock county, is situated on the west bank of Union river. The first settler was a Mr. Fabrick, who arrived here about 1802. Captain Benjamin Epps, Daniel Epps, Emerson Alcott, Seth Alcott, James Fletcher, James Hapworth, and Elisha Goodwin settled here soon after. The principal inducement which brought these pioneers to this region was the timber, from which they expected to reap a profitable harvest, but were disappointed.

Mariaville was incorporated into a plantation in 1820; and, in 1822, it was reduced to its present limits, by taking from its territory the present towns of Aurora, Amherst, and Waltham. It was incorporated in 1836. The surface is broken, and in some parts rocky to a considerable extent. Union river furnishes supplies of water. Situated on West brook is a tannery, which is doing a very good business. There are also two grist-mills and one saw-mill, besides two clapboard and two shingle machines. There is one church edifice, owned and occupied by the Baptists; five school districts, with eight schools; and one post-office — North Mariaville. Population, 374; valuation, $36,847.

MARION, situated in the eastern part of Washington county, was incorporated in 1834. It is watered by a large pond on the west, which separates it from East Machias. The surface is hilly, and the soil of a variable description; but chiefly of a moderately productive character. The village is situated in the northeast part, on the post-road leading to Dennysville. The town contains several saw-mills; three school districts, and one post-office. Population, 207; valuation, $21,369.

MARSHFIELD, Washington county, was formerly the northern part of Machias, and received its act of incorporation, June 30, 1846. The people are, for the main part, engaged in farming operations; but ship-building and lumbering are carried on to a moderate extent. The town is pleasantly situated, and is increasing in importance and population. It has two school districts, with the same number of schools; three saw-mills, four shingle mills, two grist-mills, and one carding-machine. Population, 294; valuation, 41,354.

MASARDIS, Aroostook county, is situated upon both sides of the Aroostook, opposite the mouth of the St. Croix river. Colonel Thomas Goss was the first settler, who, previous to the Aroostook war, in 1839, ran away from his family in Levant, and eloped with a widow Nelson. During his flight, he went to New Brunswick, and made his way round by the St. John and the Aroostook to this town, and commenced its settlement. He remained here in solitude until the breaking out of the Aroostook war, when a son of his, from Levant, who had been drafted into the service, discovered his residence, and was greatly surprised to identify his father. This son soon after moved here with his family, and was followed by John Nolan, who married a daughter of widow Nelson. The widow died in 1840; and after her death Goss united his fortunes with an Irishwoman, and pushed on up the river road, and commenced a settlement in No. 12, range 6, between the Aroostook river and Portage lake.

In the spring of 1839, at the time of the war, Leonard Reed moved here with his family, and was followed by Abiel McAllishe, Joseph Pollard, Cyrus McKinney, Alexander Woodward, William Fitzgerald, and a man by the name of Fogg. The first settlers were mostly men of intemperate habits; and their influence has been seriously felt upon the present inhabitants. While a great improvement has been going on in the way of temperance in other parts of the state, Masardis has been backward in the march; and is as far behind to-day as she was twenty years since. Masardis was incorporated in 1839.

The surface is level, and along the river the soil is a rich alluvium; but, back from the river, it is not so good. As yet no church edifice has been erected, and most of the few houses are near the mouth of the St. Croix, which is crossed by a bridge. A post-office is established here; and there are three school districts. The first store, of which there are but few, was opened by one Woodward, who made a fortune in the rum traffic. Population, 122; valuation, $10,209.

MASON is situated in the western part of Oxford county, and was a grant of land to Fryeburg academy. It was incorporated in 1843. We are unable to give any account of its early settlement, or of the manufacturing or agricultural interests of this town. It has one school district, with two schools; one grist-mill, two saw-mills, and one shingle mill. Population, 93; valuation, $12,022.

MATTAMISCONTIS is a very poor township, situated in Penobscot county, on the west bank of the Penobscot river, near Lincoln. It was incorporated in 1839, but the population has been and still is so small that they have not been able to support their town organization. There were fifty-four inhabitants here in 1850, but there are not half that number now. Valuation, $6,000.

Mayfield, Somerset county, is situated on the east side of Kennebec river, twenty-nine miles from Norridgewock. It was incorporated in 1836, and originally formed a part of Bingham's Kennebec Purchase. It is drained by the south branch of Piscataquis river, and by a tributary of the Kennebec. The town is up to the present time but sparsely settled, and hence its resources, if it has any, are as yet undeveloped. It contains two school districts, and one church edifice (Free-will Baptist). Population, 133; valuation, $3,435.

Maxfield, Penobscot county, is situated on the west side of Penobscot river, forty-five miles north from Bangor, and was incorporated in 1824. It is watered by Piscataquis river and Sebois stream, furnishing good water-power, which is used in propelling several saw-mills. The surface is undulating, with a varied soil, particularly adapted to the production of grain. It has one church edifice (Free-will Baptist), two school districts, with two schools, and one post-office. Population, 186; valuation, $8,784.

Medford, in the southeast part of Piscataquis county, twenty miles from Dover, was incorporated in 1824, by the name of Kilmarnock, which was changed to its present name in 1856. It is watered by the Piscataquis river, and by the outlet of Scootum lake. The well timbered soil is adapted to the growth of grass. It contains one church (Free-will Baptist), three school districts, and several mills. Population, 322; valuation, $30,378.

Medybemps, in the eastern part of Washington county, became a corporate town in the year 1841. It has a pond on the north, by the outlet of which it is drained. As yet it is of moderate capacity, but from the character of the soil, the plentifulness of its woodlands, and its favorable location, it will eventually prove a good place for settlement. It has three school districts, and one post-office. Population, 287; valuation, $19,739.

Mercer, Somerset county, lies on the east bank of the Sandy river, about seven miles from its intersection with the Kennebec at Indian Old Point,—formerly the site of the village of the Norridgewock Indians, and celebrated as the place where that tribe and their priest

Father Râsle, were destroyed in 1724. The settlement was commenced soon after the close of the Revolutionary war, — about 1784. Tradition says, Nathaniel Emery, many years a pensioner, was the first settler. He was emphatically the pioneer of the town, — his custom being to fell a few acres of trees, build a log house, then sell his improvements and commence again. Prominent among the first settlers were Nahum Baldwin, from New Hampshire, Samuel Hinckley, from Georgetown, Me., Nathaniel Davis, of Cape Ann, Mass.,[1] Joshua Greenleaf,[2] Ambrose Arnold, and eight or ten others. The first settlements were commenced on the river lots, and the intervals there, prior to settlement, were covered with a stately growth of maple, elm, butternut, and other kinds of hard wood, indicative of a strong and productive soil.

With the exception of the river lots, Mercer was mostly an unbroken wilderness until 1801, after which it was rapidly settled; and, in a few years, there was not an unoccupied lot. The titles to all the land, except that in the easterly part, were obtained from the Plymouth company. It was incorporated in 1804. In 1835, twenty families, with their farms, were annexed from Starks. In 1840, a portion of Mercer, containing twenty-five families, was set off to form Smithfield; and in 1841, another portion, containing twelve families, was given to New Sharon.

The surface is gently undulating, with one large swell, called Beech hill, nearly in the centre, which contains over twenty beautiful farms. The landscape, as seen from Beech hill, is surpassed at but few locations in the country. North pond, in the southeast corner, is three miles long by two wide, and lies partly in Mercer, partly in Smithfield, and partly in Rome. It is well stocked with fish of various kinds. The only village lies on the Big stream, which passes through the town from north to south, and falls into the Sandy river, two miles below. There are four stores, a tin and sheet-iron manufactory, a carriage and sleigh factory, a starch factory, a shovel-handle factory, a tannery, two saw-mills, a grist-mill, four shingle machines, three blacksmiths' shops, and other operations. Besides these, there are four churches — Congregational, Universalist, Methodist, and Free-will Baptist; eight school districts, with eighteen schools; and one post-office. Population, 1,186; valuation, $146,504.

Mexico, Oxford county, is situated on the north side of Androscoggin river, twenty-five miles from Paris, and was incorporated in 1818.

[1] Mr. Davis was in early life a soldier, and was at Fort William Henry, having narrowly escaped the massacre that followed the taking of that fort.

[2] This gentleman settled here in 1785, and died in 1856, at the advanced age of ninety-three years.

18*

When a plantation it was called Holmanstown. It is watered by two of the tributaries of the Androscoggin river, and is possessed of a good soil, and has average water-power. It has one church (Universalist), six school districts, with the same number of schools; a tannery, two saw-mills, two shingle mills, and a post-office. Population, 482; valuation, $57,480.

Millbridge, Washington county, was set off from Harrington, Steuben, and Cherryfield, in 1848. It is watered by the Narraguagus river, at the mouth of which there is a thrifty little village, and tide-mills for sawing lumber and grinding grain, which cost in their erection upwards of $100,000. Considerable ship-building has been done here. The principal business of the inhabitants is fishing and coasting. Some few vessels are employed in the foreign trade. Millbridge has one village; two church edifices — Union and Methodist; eleven school districts, with eleven schools; and one post-office. Population, 1,170; valuation for 1858, $250,000.

Milford, Penobscot county, is situated on the east side of Penobscot river, opposite Oldtown and Orono. It was incorporated in 1833, and is at present the terminus of the Bangor and Oldtown Railroad. The surface is level, but the soil is generally poor and swampy. The principal business in which the inhabitants are engaged is lumbering. There is one village here, and there are four school districts, with five schools, one saw-mill, one shingle mill, and one post-office. Population, 687; valuation, $128,876.

Milo is situated in the southeast part of Piscataquis county, eighteen miles from Dover, and was incorporated in 1823. It is a beautiful township, situated on the fertile banks of Sebec and Pleasant rivers, at their union with the Piscataquis, by which it is watered. The surface is pleasantly diversified, and well adapted to the production of grain. The village contains a number of dwellings, stores, and workshops, and there are a few mills and manufactories. It has two churches (Congregational and Free-will Baptist), seven school districts, and one post-office. Population, 932; valuation, $89,416.

Minot, Androscoggin county, originally comprised in the town of Poland, was granted to a man by the name of Baker, by Massachusetts, to make up for the loss of a similar tract granted to him, which was found to be in New Hampshire. Moses Emery was the first settler, having arrived in 1772. Messrs. Bray, Wellcome, Safford, Hawke, Buckman, Dwinal, Shaw, and Vareal were among those who followed shortly afterwards. Minot was incorporated February 7, 1802. On the arrival of the first settlers, there were several Indians belonging to the Anasagunticook tribe in the immediate vicinity. The first meeting-house was built May 29, 1805, and the second July 3, the same year. Auburn was incorporated from the eastern part of Minot in 1842.

The surface is hilly, but not mountainous, and is well adapted to agriculture, which is the principal pursuit. The Little Androscoggin river furnishes water-power of a serviceable and profitable description. Lumber is an article of manufacture, comprising pine boards and plank, clapboards and shingles, (split and sawed,) oak and other hard wood plank, sugar-boxes for the Havana market, and shooks and staves. Some business is also carried on in the manufacture of leather — boots, shoes, saddles, and harness. There are four religious societies — Congregational, Universalist, Methodist, and Free-will Baptist; eight school districts, with eleven schools; and three post-offices — Minot, West Minot, and Mechanic Falls. Population, 1,734; valuation, $297,184.

Monhegan Island belongs to Lincoln county — is situated just outside of the entrance to Muscongus bay, and is only a plantation. The name is of Indian origin, and signifies "Grand Island." It was discovered by Captain George Weymouth in 1605, who gave it the name of St. George's island, dividing the honor of the name between his patron saint and himself. This name, however, it did not long retain, its former one being considered more appropriate. Monhegan Island has always been a place of resort for European fishermen and traders; and the winter of 1618–19 was spent here by a part of the crew sent over by Sir Ferdinando Gorges. In 1623–4, Prince mentions it as "a settlement of some beginnings," and as a "plantation of Sir F. Gorges." In 1626, Abraham Shurt was sent over by Elbridge and Aldsworth, the owners of the Pemaquid Patent, to purchase the island from Abraham Jennings of Plymouth, the owner, for which he gave £50. It was depopulated in King Philip's war; but was soon after resettled, and has ever since continued in a thriving condition.

The island comprises upwards of a thousand acres of good land, has a bold shore on all sides, a large projection of rocks at its northeastward part, and has one good harbor. There are 103 inhabitants, about fourteen dwelling-houses, and a school-house, where the children are educated and religious meetings held. The people are industrious, prosperous, and well informed; and are engaged in fishing — both at home and on the Grand Banks — and in agriculture. Several vessels are owned on the island. There are no officers of any kind — the people's affairs being governed and guided to suit themselves, conformably to certain rules and usages which they have laid down. There is a light-house on the island, which was erected in 1824. Valuation, $3,506.

On the island of Mananas, which is merely an adjunct of Monhegan, is a rock bearing inscriptions, which have caused a good deal of research and inquiry among antiquaries, though the result has not been very satisfactory. The characters are about eight inches in length, and penetrate quite deeply into the rock. They appear upon what seems to be a stratum softer than the main ledge, which is hornblende, and they all stand in proper parallels with each other, and obliquely to the course of the stratum. Every effort hitherto made to prove these characters of Indian or Scandinavian origin has failed. Dr. Hamlin has taken a cast of the inscription in relievo, and sent it to the American Antiquarian Society at Copenhagen for examination; but no report has yet been received. He did not pretend to recognize the simple Runic characters in these inscriptions; and, although at first inclined to regard them as the attempts of some illiterate Scandinavian, he, as well as others who have investigated the matter, have concluded that they are mere fissures in the rock.

MONMOUTH, Kennebec county, is about fifteen miles west from Augusta, midway between the Kennebec and Androscoggin rivers. The first settlers were Thomas Gray, Joseph Allen, Philip Jenkins, Reuben Ham, and Jonathan Thompson, who came from Brunswick in 1776; and in the winter of 1777 moved in with their families. After two years, Ichabod Baker, John Welch, Alexander Thompson, Hugh Mulloy, and John and Benoni Austin arrived. About 1781 came Peter Hopkins and James Blossom, and not long after about thirty others, among whom were General Henry Dearborn, Simon Dearborn, Benjamin Dearborn, and John Chandler. The first settlers found here quite a tribe of Indians, who gradually disappeared.

The settlement was first called Freetown, under the belief that the land was free to every settler. Shortly after it was called Bloomingboro'. The first plantation meeting was held the 24th day of August, 1781. The following is a copy of the notification: — "By the desire of a number of inhabitants of Bloomingboro', the whole are hereby notified to meet at the house of Mr. Ichabod Baker's, on friday ye 24th day of August, 1781, at 12 of the clock, in order to act on the following articles: First, to chuse a Morderator; 2dly, to chuse a Clark; 3dly, to see if the inhabitants will think proper to chuse one man to act as Capt. for the preasant year; 4thly, to see if the inhabitants will except of the proposals made to them by the Committee of the general court; 5tly,

Monhegan Isle

to act on any other thing, that shall be thought proper by said inhabitants.

"PETER HOPKINS,
"HUGH MULLOY,
"CHRISTOPHER STEPHENS.

"*Bloomingboro', August y^e 20th*, 1781."

"At the Meeting, — Chose Peter Hopkins, Morderator; 2dly, chose Hugh Mulloy, Clark; 3dly, chose Peter Hopkins to act as Captain the preasant year; 4thly, voted that the Destrict wherein we now reside shall be known by the name of Wales, beginning at the South line of Winthrop, and running Southward eight miles, or thereabouts; 5thly, voted, that whatever tax, or taxes, the Hon. Gen. Court shall think proper to lay on said Destrict, we levi and raise within ourselves.

"HUGH MULLOY, *Clark.*

"*Wales, Aug. ye 24th*, 1781."

At the next plantation meeting, April 22, 1782, they chose assessors, and voted to raise £8 to defray plantation charges. Many of the settlers never dreamed of paying for the soil, but erroneously believed they could hold their claims by possession. The township was a part of the Plymouth right, and had been sold to different individuals, among whom were the Hon. James Bowdoin, General Henry Dearborn, and Samuel Sawyer; and a portion remained, taxed, in the first land-tax bill, to William Vassal, one of the Plymouth Company. The settlers obtained their titles from the owners above named, or their representatives; the land costing them from one to three dollars an acre.

The plantation was incorporated under the name of Monmouth, January 20, 1792, — so named by General Henry Dearborn from Monmouth, New Jersey, in the battle of which, June 28, 1778, he was engaged. At this time the place contained about fifty-five families. At the first town meeting, April 2, 1792, it was voted to raise £30 for the support of schools; £100 to make and repair highways; £15 for preaching, and £6 to defray town charges, all to be paid in corn and grain, excepting the highway appropriation. In 1794, a contract was made for carrying the mail through Monmouth, — this being the first mail route that was established to Hallowell and Augusta east of Portland. Up to 1794, the settlers were chiefly without public religious instruction. In 1793, however, the Rev. Jesse Lee formed a Methodist circuit in the province, and the first Methodist society in Maine was formed here during the next year, for which a meeting-house was finished in 1796. This society now numbers nearly two hundred members.

In the same year, a meeting-house was constructed, to be used for religious worship and town meetings, on land given for the purpose by Lady Temple, a non-resident proprietor. The house was partly finished, so that the meetings were held in it in 1799, and it was completed in 1800. It stood some forty years, when, becoming dilapidated, it was taken down, and the Monmouth town-house built in its place.

Among the distinguished individuals who have been residents of Monmouth may be mentioned Generals Henry Dearborn and John Chandler. At the close of the Revolutionary war in 1783, General (then Colonel) Dearborn came into the settlement, and became proprietor of 5,225 acres of land, made a farm, built mills, and made Monmouth his home for a number of years. He spent a portion of the time here for the remainder of his life. He was greatly respected among the settlers. General Chandler was the poorest man in the settlement; and was an itinerant blacksmith. His talents were of a high order; and, by perseverance and industry, he became wealthy. From poverty he rose to be a major-general in the militia, a brigadier-general in the war of 1812, a representative in congress, United States senator, collector of the port of Portland, and filled several other important offices. Among others who have been residents may be mentioned General James McLellan, a distinguished merchant of Bath; Colonel Greenleaf Dearborn, of the United States army; General Ira Blossom, of Buffalo, N. Y.; and the Hon. Anson G. Chandler.

There are three villages, all important places of business: North Monmouth, East Monmouth, and Monmouth Centre. North Monmouth village is at the outlet of Wilson pond, so named from one Wilson, who was drowned in it by the Indians. This village has two manufactories for making boot-webbing and binding, a shovel and hoe factory, a tannery, machine shops, turning shops, a sleigh and carriage manufactory, boot and shoe shops, mechanic shops, stores, and mills. The water-power is excellent, and the place is rapidly growing. At East Monmouth village, situated at the outlet of the South pond, are mills, a carpet factory, and a store. At the Centre village, situated at the outlet of Cochnawagan pond, are mills, a sash, door, and blind manufactory, stores, and the Monmouth Mutual Fire Insurance office. The Androscoggin and Kennebec Railroad passes through Monmouth.

Monmouth is one of the best agricultural towns in the state, with not a lot of waste land in it. There are five houses for religious worship — the Methodist chapel; the Union house at North Monmouth, occupied by Methodists, Christians, Congregationalists, and Universalists; the Union house at East Monmouth, occupied by Methodists and Baptists; the Baptist house on Monmouth Ridge; and the Congregational house at Monmouth Centre. Monmouth academy is one of the oldest and most efficient institutions of the kind in this state. There are three post-offices — Monmouth, North Monmouth, and East Monmouth; and fourteen school districts. Population, 1,925; valuation of taxable property for 1858, $516,700.

MONROE, Waldo county, joins Frankfort on the west. The first settlement was commenced soon after that of Frankfort. It was at first called Lee plantation; and in 1822, when it became an incorporated town, it received its present name, James Monroe being then president of the United States. The surface is broken. It is watered by the north and south branches of Marsh stream. The inhabitants are principally engaged in agriculture; and of late considerable interest has been taken in the cultivation of the various kinds of fruit-trees adapted to the climate. There are two small villages; twelve school districts, with twenty-three schools; three post-offices, called Monroe, Monroe Centre, and North Monroe; and one church edifice, owned and occupied by the Free-will Baptists, Universalists, and Methodists. There are also three shingle mills, one carding-machine, one tannery, one grist-mill, one pail factory, and one carriage factory. Population, 1,606; valuation, $184,206.

MONSON, Piscataquis county, is situated eighteen miles northwest from Dover, and was incorporated in 1822. It is watered by Piscataquis river and Wilson's stream, which furnish good water-power for mills. The surface is of a varied cast; a large portion of which is wild land. It is settled by an industrious class of people, who have furnished themselves, as far as practicable, with the various essentials necessary to comfort, and the prosecution of their limited business. There are two church edifices — Congregational and Baptist; eight school districts, with eleven schools; an academy, generally well attended; some mills and other machinery, and one post-office. Population, 654; valuation, $66,733.

MONTICELLO, Aroostook county, bounded south by Framingham academy grant, (now part of Littleton,) was incorporated July 29, 1846. The river Meduxnekeag passes through it from west to east, and furnishes good water-power. Monticello is situated in a very fertile section of country, and holds out, from the productiveness of its soil, the best inducements for the settlement of industrious and energetic farmers. The surface is densely covered with timber, the preparation of which for market at present forms the principal pursuit of its inhabitants. There are seven school districts, and one post-office. Population, 227; valuation, $16,518.

MONTVILLE, Waldo county, is distant from Augusta twenty-six miles, and from Belfast fourteen miles. The first settlement, according to Williamson, was made as early as 1780; though circumstances lead us to suppose that it was not commenced till 1783. A Mr. Stannard had a temporary abode here about 1778–79, but moved away about the time of the arrival of the first settler, James Davis, a Presbyterian minister, originally from Massachusetts. Two years after, Mr. Davis's two sons, William and Joshua, arrived; also another Davis, a distant relative of James, all of whom settled in the neighborhood of what is now known as Liberty. These families intermarried, and soon became so numerous that the place was called Davistown, which name it retained till the date of its incorporation. William Clark and Archibald McAlister, from Jefferson, then Ballstown, settled here soon after; and, about 1793, Timothy Barret, a native of Concord, Mass., came to Montville, and lived as a hermit till within about three or four years of his death, in 1847, at the supposed age of eighty-five. Montville was the second grand division of the grant, known as the "Twenty Associates' Proprietary," the most of which was subsequently owned by Joseph Pierce, of Boston, from whom the settlers obtained the titles to their lands.

Montville was incorporated February 18, 1807. The surface is quite uneven, being broken into hills and mountains. Near the centre there is a considerable mountain, called the Hogback, on the west side of which the water flows into the Sheepscot river, on the east side into the George's river, and on the north side into the Sebasticook. The inhabitants are mostly engaged in agriculture, notwithstanding the broken condition of the country. The slopes of the hills furnish good pasturage, and in many places excellent tillage. Lumber is here manufactured, but of late only to a limited extent, as the forests are nearly exhausted.

The Rev. Moses McFarland, born in 1781, came here in 1799, commenced preaching in 1805, and still frequently occupies the pulpit. Hon. Ebenezer Knowlton, a representative from this district in the congress of 1855–7, is also a preacher, and was, in 1845, speaker of the house of representatives of Maine. There are four church edifices — three of which are occupied by the Free-will Baptists; four post-offices — Montville, Centre Montville, South Montville, and East Montville; and sixteen school districts. Population, 1,881; assessors' valuation for 1858, $347,000.

MORRILL, Waldo county, historically included in Belmont, from which it was taken, was incorporated March 3, 1855, named in honor of Anson P. Morrill, late governor of the state. The first settlements were commenced in 1801–2 by James Weymouth, Benjamin Smith, Joseph Coming, and Nathaniel Cushman. All these settlers purchased their lands from General Knox, the original proprietor under the Waldo Patent.

The town is moderately uneven, but with very little waste land. Agriculture is the leading occupation. Morrill is watered by Cross's pond and Passagassawaukeag stream. The manufactures consist principally of lumber. There are four saw-mills, one grist-mill, four shingle mills, and five stave mills. About twenty thousand lime-casks are annually manufactured, besides large quantities of staves, shingles, and boards. It has one village; also one church, owned and occupied by the Baptists, Free-will Baptists, Methodists, and Christians; six school districts, with the same number of schools; and one post-office. Population, 750; valuation of real and personal property, $80,512.

MOSCOW, Somerset county, formerly township No. 1, in the second range on the east side of Kennebec river, belonged to Bingham's Purchase, and was incorporated January 30, 1816. It is twenty-eight miles from Norridgewock, and is said by Williamson to have been settled in 1773, which is certainly somewhat earlier than several settlements below this on the Kennebec. The land was surveyed and lotted in 1812, at which time a petition to the legislature was started for incorporation. It was signed by the greater part of the adult male residents, as it represented "that there were between thirty and forty heads of families in said township." The petition further set forth the usual occasion for corporate rights — "that the roads were bad and out of repair," and that they had no legal means of enforcing a contribution towards their support from the unwilling. This place sometimes, naturally enough, went by the name of Bakerstown — Nathan Baker and no less than six other Bakers being among the petitioners; but it should not be confounded with Bakerstown, which was the original name of Poland, Minot, and Auburn. The petitioners asked for incorporation by the name of Northfield; but after the action of the several legislatures from 1813 to 1816, the town emerged by the name of Moscow.

The soil is good, and there are many well-tended farms, which yield to their owners good supplies of grain and the other staple products of this part of the country. Water is supplied by a pond, and by a branch of the Kennebec river. There are two religious denominations — Baptist and Free-will Baptist; eleven school districts; one post-office — West

Moscow; and a saw-mill and shingle mill are among the mechanical operations. Population, 577; valuation, $48,616.

MOUNT DESERT is an island at the southern extremity of Hancock county, and is the most extraordinary one on the coast of Maine, perhaps on the whole coast of America. It is remarkable for its size, its singular topography, its bold and wild scenery, and, still more, for its wilder and stranger history. Mount Desert is especially a mythical region. Whoever visits it, if he is familiar with its earliest records and legends, will, as he sits upon some bold pinnacle of its mountains, and glances over its sea-cradled islands, its sun-burnished creeks, its mountain lakes, and its alp-like ravines, almost expect to see the savage emerge from some glen, or to see lying at anchor the rude shallop of two hundred years ago; or, stranger still, to behold some wanderer from England, France, or Spain, in the habiliments of his time, with steeple hat, peaked beard, slashed doublet, and sword by his side, climbing the sea-wall thrown up by the ocean, to seek his rude cabin upon the shore.

Mount Desert, from its imposing appearance, was a natural attraction to the earliest voyagers. From the early part of the sixteenth century, this region was visited, and its waters made to contribute largely to the luxuries of the tables of the European nobility. Later, or in the early part of the seventeenth century, it was a familiar locality to the voyagers De Monts, Gosnold, Pring, Weymouth, and Smith. It is also distinguished as the place where the first Jesuit mission in America was planted—soon to, however, be uprooted.[1] Port Royal (now Annapolis, Nova Scotia) had just been founded, when Father Coton, the provincial of the Jesuits, at the suggestion of Henry IV., undertook a mission, to be established at that place, for the conversion of the natives, and selected Peter Biard and Enemond Masse to be the apostles to New France. These men went to Bordeaux to embark in 1608, but were unable to obtain passage until 1611, when, through the favor of the Marchioness de Guercheville, who bought the shares of two Huguenot merchants in a vessel, and made them over to the missionaries, they sailed with Biencourt, a son of Potrincourt, the patentee of Port Royal, and arrived at that place June 12, of that year. Through some misunderstanding with Biencourt, their plans were suddenly frustrated by his absolute refusal to allow them either to establish a mission or to return to France. Madame de Guercheville, learning of their condition, resolved upon another mission for them, and, by securing aid from the queen and ladies of the French

[1] Biard, Relation, etc., p. 235; L'Escarbot's Histoire, etc.; Champlain's Voyages; Charlevoix's Histoire, etc., vol. I. 122-140.

court, soon equipped a vessel under command of La Saussaye. In the mean time Biard had visited the Kennebec. La Saussaye, with Du Thet, and Fathers Quentin and Lalemam, arrived at Port Royal in March, 1613,—took on board Biard and Masse,—set sail again, and landed on the east side of Mount Desert Island. Here they set up a cross, founded a mission settlement under the name of St. Saviour, and proceeded to erect a small fort and houses. Biard and Masse are said to have visited an Indian village on the other side of the island, and to have wrought a miracle to save the life of a child. The fort was soon finished, and the vessel about to leave, when it was delayed by a storm. Samuel Argal, from Virginia, being upon the coast with an armed vessel and some fishing vessels, and being obliged to make a harbor, heard of the young settlement, and at once resolved to surprise it. The French, being a part on board their vessel, and a part in the fort, with no cannon, were easily overpowered. Du Thet was mortally wounded, and was buried the next day beneath the broken mission-cross. Some were permitted to escape to Port Royal, and the remainder were carried prisoners to Virginia, but, by means of disasters to Argal's fleet, finally escaped to France. No further attempt at settlement was made until 1761, when Abraham Somes came here and built a house at the head of the sound, ever since known as Somes's Sound.

The inhabitants suffered much during the Revolutionary war, both from the attacks of the enemy and for the want of necessaries; but their patriotism is abundantly shown by the records of the town from 1776 to the close of the war. The British never had a permanent occupation of the island during the war; consequently, what the inhabitants suffered was from their predatory excursions, pillage, stealing of stock, and those embarrassments incident to a constant state of alarm from attacks which might be expected at any moment. The period of the last war with England presents but little of interest in this town. The same patriotism, however, that was manifested during the Revolution, was exhibited during this war. Two hundred dollars per annum was appropriated for powder and ammunition; and the place was kept in a state of defence.

The act of incorporation of Mount Desert bears date February 17, 1787. From this time the inhabitants set to work with commendable spirit to populate their beautiful town. This island is now divided into three distinct municipalities,—Eden, Tremont, and Mount Desert,—containing an area, in the aggregate, of 60,000 acres. Its topography is a natural curiosity. Contrary to the ordinary level formation of islands, it exhibits evidences of convulsions of nature, which have thrown up huge granite mountains to the number of thirteen, and given to the scenery of the island striking and picturesque features. These thirteen mountains are situated to the west and north. Their crests meet the sky; and from the receding ship the mariner may be gazing at them as the last that is visible of his native land, while, to the homewardbound sailor, a view of their hazy tops sends gladness to his heart, assuring him as it does of proximity to family and friends. The altitude of the highest peak is stated by Williamson to be 2,300 feet; by Dr. Jackson, in his Geological Survey, 1,900 feet; and by C. O. Boutelle, of the United States Coast Survey, 1,556 feet. On the summit of one of these mountains there is a pond of some acres, without any visible inlet or outlet. The whole island abounds in ponds and streams, which are filled with fine fish.

Mount Desert has become noted, during the last few years, as a place of summer resort, and Nahant may yet look to her laurels. A steamer plies regularly between this place and Rockland, connecting with steamers to Belfast, Bangor, Portland, and Boston. There are eleven school districts, with seventeen schools; two post-offices — Mount Desert, and Winter Harbor; three religious societies — Baptist, Congregational, and Methodist; one carding-machine, four ship-builders, one tannery, and one carriage builder. Population, 782; valuation, $79,181.

MOUNT VERNON is situated in the northwest part of Kennebec county, and was included in the Kennebec Patent. Settlements were made as early as 1774, and the town was incorporated June 28, 1792, receiving its name from the plantation of General Washington. Mount Vernon is a very pleasant spot, having a fine soil; while its productions are numerous and profitable to those who make agriculture a business. It is watered by several ponds, which afford good water-power. Mount Vernon has three villages; three churches — a Baptist, a Free-will Baptist, and a Union house; thirteen school districts, with nineteen schools; one grist-mill, two saw-mills, one shingle machine, one turning machine, one planing mill, one clothing mill, and one post-office. Population, 1,479; valuation, $239,056.

NAPLES, Cumberland county, distant from Portland thirty miles and from Augusta sixty-three, was formed from Otisfield, Harrison, Raymond, Bridgeton, and Sebago, and a tract of about seven thousand acres, called Songo river, not previously within the limits of any incorporated town. In 1849, additions were made from Otisfield; and, in 1851–2, from Sebago, making the present area of land 16,500 acres. Lying within its limits is the south end of Long pond, consisting of fifteen hundred acres; also Brandy pond, eleven hundred acres; Cold

Rain pond, fifty acres; and Trickey pond, six hundred acres, — making in all some 3,300 acres of water. The whole area falls but little short of twenty thousand acres. Sebago pond makes the southern boundary for two or three miles.

Songo river, leading from Brandy to Sebago pond, is six miles in length. This river, being navigable by the aid of one lock, forms a connecting link between the ponds for the Cumberland and Oxford canal. A small steamer, for carrying passengers and towing boats and rafts of logs, plies upon the river. Crooked (sometimes called Pequawket) river, a tributary of Songo, is, as its name indicates, very tortuous, and forms most of the eastern boundary. It flows through here, being some fifteen or twenty miles in length. Muddy river, entering near the northwesterly corner, flows southeasterly to Sebago pond. Both the latter streams furnish mill-sites.

The formation of Naples is granitic, in which are injected many veins and dikes of quartz and trap. The granite contains a large proportion of mica and felspar, rendering it coarse and of little value as a building material. There are some localities, however, where the rock assumes the character of gneiss, and quarries well. Many granite and gneiss boulders, some of large size and worn as from the action of currents, are scattered here and there, evidently brought from the hills at the north-northwest. These are easily worked, and supply the demand for home use. Specimens of flesh-colored felspar are found, which are very beautiful.

Naples was endowed with corporate privileges in 1834. The general surface is pleasantly diversified with hill, valley, and plain; pond, river, and brook. There is a great variety of soil, from the arid, sandy plain to the moderately tough clay; though the major part, being the detritus of a granite formation, is a gravelly loam, with many pebbles and boulders of all sizes interspersed. The hills are not precipitous, but afford good grazing for the flocks and herds.

Agriculture is the chief occupation of the inhabitants in summer. Probably nine tenths of the taxable property consists of farms, farm stock, and implements. Farming is pursued with little system or science; each one seemingly endeavoring to produce a variety, instead of relying upon a leading crop. Hay is the most valuable crop, and is consumed at home. Lumbering, in winter, affords employment for many, though the stately old forests of pine, oak, and hemlock, for the last fifty years, have sadly dwindled away before the woodman's axe.

Naples has three saw-mills, two grist-mills, and one establishment for the manufacture of mackerel-kits, half and quarter barrels. Shoe-making and bootbinding furnish occupation for many fingers in times when

19*

the trade is good. Naples and Ede's falls are the only two villages, at each of which there is a post-office. A town-house, used also as a church for all denominations, is the only public edifice in town. There are twelve school districts, with an average winter attendance of 264 scholars. Population, 1,025; assessors' valuation for 1858, $246,441.

NEWBURGH lies on the south line of Penobscot county, in the second range of towns west of Penobscot river. It was originally a part of the tract granted to General Henry Knox for his military services in the Revolutionary war, and was sold by him to Benjamin Bussey, who continued to own all the unoccupied land till his death. The settlement of Newburgh was very much retarded by the exorbitant price demanded for land by the proprietor; but after his death, the lands being offered at a more reasonable rate, purchasers were readily found, and the settlement increased rapidly. Among the original inhabitants were Freeman Luce, Edward Snow, Levi Mudgett, James Morrison, Abel Hardy, Thomas Morrill, Ezekiel Smith, George Bickford, and Daniel Piper, who arrived here about the year 1794.

Newburgh was incorporated in 1819. The surface is varied, — the north and westerly part being somewhat hilly and rocky, while the southeasterly part contains extensive tracts of interval, situated along the banks of the Soadabscook, by which the town is watered. The soil is well adapted to the cultivation of Indian corn, potatoes, English grain, and hay; and a very laudable enterprise is manifested in raising the various kinds of fruit-trees common to this latitude. Formerly, large quantities of hemlock bark and cord wood were hauled to the markets on the Penobscot river; but that business is now nearly abandoned for the more profitable employment of agriculture. Newburgh has one church edifice — Free-will Baptist; nine school districts, with the same number of schools; four saw-mills, five shingle machines, one wool-carding and cloth-dressing establishment; and three post-offices — Newburgh, Newburgh Centre, and South Newburgh. Population, 1,399; valuation, $115,354.

NEWCASTLE, Lincoln county, lies on a tongue of land formed by the Sheepscot and Damariscotta rivers, at the head of tide-water, about fifteen miles from the ocean, and twenty-four southeasterly from Augusta. It is more than six miles in length and four in breadth. The earliest settlement, supposed to have been about the time Pemaquid and Arrowsic were settled, was made upon the Sheepscot side of the peninsula, and covered an area of about four hundred rods in length, and ninety-two in width. All that is definitely known of this early settlement is contained in the traces of habitations found, the next century after, by the inhabitants, who, with their descendants, have since held undisturbed possession. A street ran the whole length of the neck, upon both sides of which, at uniform distances, were laid out the two-acre lots into which the homesteads were usually divided; and on these, cellars and other traces of this ancient settlement have been discovered. Easterly from these were the farms of one hundred acres, reached by a road called the "king's highway," which also led to the woods and the mill, which latter was situated on a stream about a mile from the settlement, now called Mill Brook. On the highest point, opposite the falls and overlooking the town, was a small fort. No means are presented of ascertaining correctly the population of this place at that early time; but Sullivan, in his history of Maine, quoting from the account of Sylvanus Davis, says: "There were in the year 1630, eighty-four families, besides fishermen, about Pemaquid, St. George's, and Sheepscot."

In 1665, Robert Carr, George Cartwright, and Samuel Maverick, commissioners appointed by the Duke of York, arrived at Sheepscot, this being a part of the territory claimed by him as within his patent from the crown.[1] They met at the house of John Mason, appointed Walter Phillips clerk, erected the whole territory into a county, by the name of Cornwall, called the plantation at Sheepscot New Dartmouth, established the line between this place and Pemaquid, and summoned the inhabitants to appear and take the oath of allegiance to the Duke, twenty-nine only of whom complied with the order. They vested the civil power in a chief constable, three magistrates or justices of the peace, and a recorder. The justices were Nicholas Raynal, Thomas Gardiner, and William Dyer. This government lasted till 1675, when the desolations of King Philip's war reached this coast. The people of Arrowsic fell before the tomahawk, and their habitations were laid in ashes. A little girl only escaped. She fled through the woods fifteen miles to Dartmouth, and sounded the alarm; and the terrified inhabitants escaped in a ship just built by Sir William Phips, which was then lying in their harbor nearly ready for sea. But their settlement shared the fate of Arrowsic.

Upon the close of the war, about three years subsequently, the settlers began to return and rebuild. Commissioners John Palmer and John West, appointed by the Duke's governor at New York, and Colonel Dungan, arrived at Sheepscot in 1686, and began to lay out the town in lots as before; but were regarded with hatred for their avarice, favoritism, and extortionate practice in their apportionment of land.

[1] See ante, article on Bristol, p. 67.

Their rule, however, was abruptly terminated by the second Indian or French war, upon the accession of William of Orange to the throne, in 1688; and these precincts were again laid in ruins, and continued so for nearly thirty years; the native forests, in the mean time, reclaiming heritage where cultivated gardens and the abodes of living men so lately had existed.

In 1718, Rev. Christopher Tappan, of Newbury, sent two men to inclose a portion of this territory, which he had bought of the claimants as early as 1702, a part of which then belonged to the settlers driven away by the Indians, and the other part to Walter Phillips, of Salem, whose title was derived from Indian sagamores by three several purchases, in 1661, 1662, and 1674. Tappan himself arrived in 1733, began to survey his lands on the Sheepscot side of the town, and laid out forty-five one hundred acre lots, two of which were allotted to the first settled minister and the first parish. The latter remains in the same hands at the present time. Tappan's title to the east of Mill river, however, was disputed by William Vaughan and James Noble, who held under the Pemaquid Patent. After a sharp litigation, Vaughan's title prevailed, and the settlers there hold under him to this day, while those on the west side of the river derive title from Tappan.

Newcastle was incorporated June 19, 1753, being the twelfth incorporated town in Maine. Being between two rivers, it has become naturally divided into two villages, one on the Sheepscot and the other on the Damariscotta side. The latter is the largest, and contains several stores, ship yards, an academy, bank, printing-office, and public-house. A free bridge connects it with Damariscotta. A toll-bridge connects Sheepscot with Alna. Newcastle formerly furnished large quantities of lumber and ship-timber for the market, but since the scarcity of these materials, attention has been turned more to farming and ship-building, the latter of which has, however, become temporarily quiet through some heavy failures. A considerable business has also been done in brick making. There is a variety of soil, which is well adapted to the usual agricultural productions, of which hay is the chief, a considerable quantity being shipped for sale, after supplying the ordinary wants of the place.

There are three church edifices — the Union at Sheepscot, Congregational at Damariscotta Bridge, and Roman Catholic at Damariscotta Mills; five religious societies — two Congregational, a Baptist, Methodist, and Roman Catholic. The academy was incorporated in 1801, with a grant of land for its endowment, — has a good fund, and has maintained a school the greater part of the time since its commencement. There are fourteen school districts, with twenty-six schools, the amount of money raised for the support of which, including the bank tax, is about $1,800. A newspaper (the Lincoln Democrat) is also published. There are two post-offices — Newcastle and Sheepscot Bridge; and one bank, with a capital of $50,000. Population, 2,012; valuation, $392,503.

NEWFIELD (previously the plantation of Washington), in the northwest part of York county, contains 14,543 acres of good land, and was embraced within Small's Purchase in 1661. It was surveyed in 1778 — settled the same year — and incorporated in 1794. Rev. John Adams was settled in 1781, when there were but five families. Josiah Towle was the first representative to the legislature, in 1806. The Little Ossipee and its tributaries furnish ample supplies of water. The principal buildings and business operations are situated upon Mount Eagle, a beautiful swell of land in the southern part. A mineral polish, much in use, is found here. Newfield has two villages, four church edifices (two Free-will Baptist, one Congregational, and one Methodist), ten school districts, three saw-mills, three grist-mills, three shingle machines, an iron foundery, a carriage factory, and two post-offices — Newfield and West Newfield. Population, 1,418; valuation, 212,832.

NEW GLOUCESTER, in the northerly part of Cumberland county, is situated partly between Poland and Danville in Androscoggin county. It was granted by act of the general court, May 27, 1735, to the inhabitants of Gloucester, Mass., who were instructed to lay out a township of six miles square in the vicinity of North Yarmouth, if the land could there be obtained; and if not, in some other place convenient, in the eastern parts. It was ordered, that it should be laid out into sixty-three equal shares; one of which was to be reserved for the first settled minister, one for the support of the ministry, and one for the support of schools. The further conditions of the grant were: first, that on each of the other lots, the proprietors should, within five years, have a good family settled; second, that they should have a meeting-house built; third, that they should have a good orthodox minister permanently stationed; and for the due performance of this contract, each settler was bound in the sum of forty pounds, — failing to do which, the defaulter's share should revert to the province. It was at once settled by inhabitants from the parent town, who built a dozen log houses on Harris hill, and a mill on Royall's river. In 1743, they had erected nineteen framed houses — and two bridges across the river, at a cost of £400 — had made twelve miles of road, and cleared considerable land.

The survey was made by Edward King, and the plan dated June 20,

1737. The grantees failing to fulfil the conditions, by reason of the Indian troubles, many of those who had already settled were ordered off by the governor. In April, 1753, a petition having been presented by the grantees, asking for longer time to fulfil the conditions, eighteen months were allowed them. The first attempt at resettlement was made in March, 1754, when it appears a block-house was erected, which was subsequently a provincial garrison, a storehouse and asylum for settlers, and, for sixteen years, a place of public worship. It was sold at auction, in 1772, for seven bushels of corn, and stood until 1788. Through pecuniary and other inducements, in 1756, twenty men undertook the settlement of the place, agreeing to dwell here a year. Isaac Parsons removed here in 1762 — was the first magistrate in the plantation — was a representative to the legislature in 1783, and during other years — and held several other honorable offices. James Stinchfield was among the earliest settlers, having removed hither with his father's family in 1753. He was engaged in the erection of the first fort — was distinguished in the hunt, and in Indian warfare, and was, for some time, a leading man in town. The first proprietors' meeting in the plantation was held in November, 1763. Rev. Samuel Foxcroft was ordained minister of the first church in 1765.

New Gloucester was incorporated in 1774, and has been one of the most distinguished towns in the state. Being a half shire with Portland, the courts sat here from 1791 until the organization of Oxford county in 1805, when they returned to Portland. The first post-office was established in 1793. The surface is beautifully diversified, and presents, in some parts, a delightful rural prospect. Its husbandry, and its public and private buildings, are evidences of independence, industry, taste, and skill. The highest land is under cultivation; and there are good roads and comfortable dwellings on every eminence. There are six saw-mills, two grist-mills, two tanneries, four churches — Congregational, Baptist, Universalist, and Shakers'; fourteen school districts, with twenty-two schools; and three post-offices, called New Gloucester, Upper Gloucester, and West Gloucester. Population, 1,848; valuation, $327,670.

New Limerick, Aroostook county, is six miles long, east and west, and three miles wide. True Bradbury, Eben Bradbury, Jonathan Hayes, John Felch, and Samuel Morrison were among the first settlers, — the most of whom emigrated from Limerick, York county. The town was surveyed in 1809, by Benjamin Marshall, and was incorporated in 1839. Not more than a quarter of it is cleared, though more than half is occupied by settlers. There are three schools, with an average of forty scholars. Population, 160; valuation, 13,383.

NEWPORT is situated in the western part of Penobscot county, and is distant twenty-five miles from Bangor. The settlement was commenced about the year 1808, — the earlier inhabitants being William Martin, Isaac Lawrence, Nathaniel Burrill, John Whiting, Daniel Bicknell, John Ireland, and Elam Pratt, most of whom came from Bloomfield, Somerset county, and purchased their land of Benjamin Shepard, who lived in Bloomfield at that time.

The township was called East Pond plantation until its incorporation, June 14, 1814. The surface is generally level; and a large pond of about fifteen miles circumference lies nearly in the centre, in which the east branch of the Sebasticook river takes its rise. The principal village, situated at the outlet of the pond, covers about one square mile. and is divided by the Sebasticook river. The water-power offers superior inducements to capitalists; and this, in connection with the opening of the railroad from Bangor to Waterville, will, without doubt, soon make Newport one of the most flourishing villages between the Kennebec and Penobscot rivers.

The chief employment of the inhabitants is agriculture; but in different parts of the town are a number of saw-mills, for the manufacture of boards and shingles. Besides these mills, there are a grist-mill, foundery, cabinet shop, eight stores, a number of harness and blacksmith's shops, and a carriage manufactory, where are manufactured annually carriages to the amount of $10,000, which, for durability and finish, are not excelled by any in the state. There is one church edifice, in which the several denominations worship; there are also eight school districts, and three post-offices — Newport, East Newport, and North Newport. Population, 1,210; valuation, $195,203.

NEW PORTLAND, situated in the western part of Somerset county, is six miles west from the Kennebec river, and forty-five miles west-northwest from Augusta. This township, with that of Freeman on the west. was granted by Massachusetts to the sufferers of Falmouth (now the city of Portland), which was burnt by Captain Mowett in 1775. It was organized into a plantation in 1808. The first settlement was commenced by David Hutchins of Chelmsford, Mass., who moved, with his family, from thence to what was then called Sheepscot (now Newcastle), in 1784; and next into the wilderness on Seven-Mile brook, where he made the first opening in the at that time dense forests of New Portland. His son, James, was two years old when he moved here, and is still living on the identical farm cleared by his father. Josiah Parker arrived in 1786 from Groton, Mass., where he was born. He served in the fourth regiment Massachusetts militia, in the war of the

Revolution, was honorably discharged at West Point, and was still living (May, 1856), in the ninety-second year of his age. He has borne an honorable and arduous part in the affairs of New Portland, as he previously did, in his younger days, in the service of his country. Ebenezer Richardson from Sedgwick came in the same year, and John and William Churchill from Bingham, in 1788; Eben Casley from Gorham, Samuel and Benjamin Gould, Solomon Walker, Charles Warden, from Woolwich, and John Dennis from Groton, N. H., arrived and settled here subsequently. Dennis was a blacksmith, and was the first man who could repair the axe, the harrow-tooth, or the ploughshare for the pioneer settler. Four of the early settlers are now living, at the advanced ages of ninety-two and ninety-six. All of them are pensioners.

In 1809, in accordance with a vote of the town, Beniah Pratt was invited to become the town minister, which he accepted; but, for some cause, was not settled. In 1815, Samuel Hutchins, son of the first settler, was called and settled, and had part of the ministerial lands. The Free-will Baptists were the first principal sect, to which the divines above named belonged. In 1810–11, a Baptist church was collected and organized, over which Oliver Peabody was ordained pastor.

New Portland was incorporated in 1808. The surface is uneven, lying in large swells; though the land will admit of high cultivation. Seven-Mile brook, rising near the base of Mount Abraham and Mount Bigelow, flows through from northwest to southeast, dividing the town into two nearly equal parts. Besides Seven-Mile brook, there are two small streams, respectively named Lemon and Gilman. These three streams furnish an abundant water-power, which is made useful in driving three or four saw-mills and several grist and flour mills. The agricultural interests will compare favorably with those of any other town of its age in the state. Dr. Charles T. Jackson, in his Geological Report, published in 1838, says: "New Portland is large and flourishing, having a pretty good soil, bearing crops from twelve to forty bushels to the acre, according to the dressing. From the specimens of the wheat seen at the flour mill, I should not consider it generally of the first quality, it not being full and heavy; but there were some samples that were excellent. From the nature of the soil, I should have anticipated such a result; for it is of granitic origin, and is poor in lime, a deficiency easily remedied, as limestone occurs in the vicinity in loose masses, but by searching may be found in place."

There are three small villages — New Portland, East New Portland, and North New Portland, at each of which there is a post-office; three houses of public worship — one occupied by the Universalists and Congregationalists, one by the Free-will Baptists, and one by various denominations; and eighteen school districts, with twenty-five schools. Population, 1,460; valuation, $230,631.

NEWRY is situated in the west part of Oxford county. The first settlement was made in 1781, by Benjamin Barker and his two brothers, from Methuen, Mass., and Ithiel Smith of Cape Elizabeth, Me. The titles to the land were derived from Massachusetts. The plantation name was Sudbury-Canada. It was incorporated with its present name, June 15, 1805. The surface, in its general aspect, is wild and mountainous. Bear and Sunday rivers — fine streams — flow through nearly parallel, in a southerly direction, falling into the Androscoggin. Newry has one village, two public-houses, a store; three post-offices — Newry, North Newry, and South Newry; two religious societies — Methodist and Free-will Baptist; and six school districts, with six schools. Population, 459; assessors' valuation $43,000.

NEW SHARON is situated in the extreme southeasterly part of Franklin county, bordering upon the counties of Somerset and Kennebec. Prince Baker, a native of Pembroke, Mass., arriving in 1782, was the earliest settler. He was soon followed by Nathaniel Tibbits, Benjamin Chambers, Benjamin Rollins, James Howes, and Samuel Prescott. The township was purchased from the state of Massachusetts by Prince Baker and others, February 14, 1791. It was incorporated June 20, 1794, and contains 28,600 acres, most of which is excellent soil. New Sharon has an advantage in location over most of the towns in the county, as to access to market and water communication.

The mills at the Falls were first built by Abel Baker, in 1801. They afterwards passed into the hands of Abel Mayhew, and were rebuilt by him and much improved. The bridge was built about 1809 or 1810, and has since been rebuilt with permanent stone abutments. The water privilege at the village is superior, and the location possesses many advantages for a business place. It has, in addition to the grist-mill, a saw-mill, shingle machine, starch factory, one or more tanneries, fulling-mill, carding machine, a number of blacksmith shops, and several stores. At Weeks's mills, in the northwest part, there is a set of mills, a starch factory, and a considerable village. New Sharon has six churches — Baptist, Methodist, Congregationalist, Universalist, Free-will Baptist, and a free meeting-house; two post-offices — New Sharon and East New Sharon; and nineteen school districts, with the same number of schools. Population, 1,732; valuation, $293,526.

NEW VINEYARD, Franklin county, is situated east of Strong and north of Industry, and is distant from Augusta forty miles, and from Farmington eight miles. It was purchased from the state by an association of individuals belonging to Martha's Vineyard, Mass., together with Jonathan Knowlton, of Farmington, who acted as their agent. After the survey, it was divided by lot among them. Nearly all the first settlers came from Martha's Vineyard; hence it took the name of New Vineyard from the commencement of its settlement. Daniel Collins and Abner Norton commenced improvements and removed their families here in the fall of 1791. They were the only families who remained in the place the following winter. They were soon after followed by Samuel Daggett, Jonathan Merry, James Manter, Ephraim Butler, John Spencer, Cornelius Norton, David Davis, John Daggett, Benjamin Benson, Joseph Smith, Henry Butler, Herbert Boardman, Charles Luce, Henry Norton, William Farrand, Seth Hillman, Ezra Winslow, and Calvin Burden. Settlements north of the mountains were commenced soon after by people mostly from Middleboro', Mass., among whom were George Pratt, Eleazer Pratt, Paul Pratt, Elias Bryant, Simeon Hackett, Jabez Vaughan, Zephaniah Morton, and Beniah Pratt.

New Vineyard was incorporated February 22, 1802. The soil is generally good, especially in the northerly and easterly sections. There is quite a range of mountains extending nearly across the centre, from east to west, dividing the waters of the Sandy river from those of the Seven-Mile brook. The principal stream is the outlet of Porter's pond in Strong, which discharges into the Seven-Mile brook, and on which are a number of valuable mill-sites. A first-rate grist-mill, two saw-mills, a clover mill, a shingle machine, and various other kinds of machinery; one store, a number of mechanics' shops and dwelling-houses, form a considerable village, which has been known as Vaughan's Mills.

There are two churches — one Congregational and one Free-will Baptist; ten school districts, with twelve schools; and two post-offices — New Vineyard and East New Vineyard. Population, 635: valuation, $65,538.

Nobleborough is situated in the central part of Lincoln county, on the east bank of Damariscotta river, and contains an area of about ten thousand acres. It originally formed a part of the possessions of Elbridge and Aldsworth, known as the Pemaquid Patent,[1] and was settled about the same time as Newcastle, which is situated on the opposite side of the river. It was a favorite resort of the natives for hunting and fishing; and they resisted, with the bravery of desperation, the erection of the

[1] See Bristol.

white man's cabin on their fair plantation. Nobleborough was involved in the bloody issue that depopulated more flourishing but less beautiful towns along the coast; and, during the whole period of the Indian wars, the blood of the white man and the savage was mingled together in saturating the soil. After the barbarous contest was decided, the inhabitants were involved for many years in a harassing controversy about the title to their lands, which was not settled until 1814. The territory was claimed under the Brown right, and the title was pursued till 1765, by James Noble, who had married the widow of William Vaughan. Vaughan either commenced or revived the settlement under Colonel Dunbar about 1730; but it had a slow growth, as there were only thirty men here able to bear arms at the commencement of the Revolution. Noble and his coadjutors were dispossessed in 1765, though they did not abandon their claim.

The town was incorporated November 20, 1788, and named by Arthur Noble, one of the heirs of the proprietor; but the name was not popular with the people, principally because of their antipathy to all who were proprietary claimants. It is connected with Newcastle by two bridges across the Damariscotta, which are about two miles apart. Nobleborough has done considerable heretofore in lumbering and ship-building, but the people are now generally engaged in agricultural pursuits.

Rev. Adoniram Judson, father of the world-renowned missionary to Burmah, was settled over the second Baptist church here in 1819. There is a great curiosity in Damariscotta, opposite the upper falls, being a bank from twelve to fifteen feet in depth, composed of oyster shells, deposited here, in all probability, by the natives, years before the discovery of the continent. This large oyster bank has led some to think, that here was situated the far-famed mythical city of Norumbega. In 1849, the town was divided, and the southern part incorporated by the name of Damariscotta. There are four church edifices — three Baptist and one Methodist; twelve school districts, with twelve schools; two saw-mills, one lath machine, one shingle machine, seven stores; and two post-offices — Nobleborough and Damariscotta Mills. Population, 1,408; valuation, $234,312.

Norridgewock, situated in the southern part of Somerset county, is the shire town. It is built on both sides of the Kennebec river, — is thirty miles north from Augusta, and fifty-five west from Bangor. Its name is of Indian origin, and signifies "smooth water." It is noted for having been the head-quarters of a powerful tribe of Indians, sometimes called the "Canibas," and sometimes the "Norridgewogs," belonging to the Abnaki nation. Norridgewock was taken possession of by the French as early as 1610. Rasles spent thirty-seven years of his life here, as a missionary to the Indians, and acquired such an influence over them that he controlled all their affairs. The village even now is a beautiful place; but when inhabited by the Indians, it was almost a second paradise. It stands in a lovely and sequestered spot, a point around which the waters of the Kennebec, not far from their confluence with those of the Sandy river, sweep past merrily, as if to the music of the rapids above.

Destruction of Norridgewock, and death of Rasles.

All the forays of the Norridgewock Indians upon the unprotected English settlements along the coast were, it is believed, instigated by Rasles, the Jesuit priest.[1] Conference after conference was held, and

[1] "Father Rasles was distinguished for his literary attainments. He was thoroughly educated, and wrote the Latin with classical purity. He made himself fully acquainted with all the Indian dialects, and prepared a dictionary of the Abnaquies' language, which is preserved in the library of Harvard College. He taught many of the Norridgewocks to write, and held a correspondence with some of them in their own language. He was a zealous Catholic, and devoted himself to the service of the church. He was mild in his

treaty after treaty made, between the English and the Indians, in almost every one of which the English thought themselves overreached; but, whenever they attempted to put a different construction upon them, for the purpose of securing more important advantages, the sagacious priest would inform the Indians of their designs, and thus frustrate them. Nor was this all. Whenever they suffered in any respect at the hands of the English, a terrible retribution invariably ensued, either in the burning of hamlets or the murder and pillage of the settlers; and when the English were at war with the French, the Indians were always found on the side of the latter.[1] In all the ulterior designs of the English upon the Indians, whether in wresting their territory from them or in cheating them in trade, they were held in check by their dread of this tribe. Under these circumstances, only one remedy remained, which was the destruction of the village, and the murder of Rasles and his Indians. Accordingly, on the 12th August (old style), 1724, a detachment of two hundred and eight men from Fort Richmond stole up the Kennebec, and reached the fated village. The Indians remained ignorant of the contemplated attack till the shots of their enemies had penetrated their wigwams, causing death and destruction. Rasles, the object of the savage vengeance of the English, was killed; but, not satisfied with this, they scalped him, and carried the scalp to Boston. The Indians, when they beheld the bleeding corpse of their idolized priest and counsellor riddled with bullets, immediately, in the greatest consternation, took to flight, and attempted to cross the river; but their pursuers, following close behind, shot them in the water; and those few even who succeeded in reaching the opposite bank were killed before they could gain a place of safety. The English then returned to the village; and, having secured Rasles' papers and other effects, burnt down the church and the wigwams, and then withdrew, with such precipitation that it seemed rather a flight than a victory.[2]

manners and convincing in his speech; his conversation had a charm that would compel the savages to listen to him." — Allen's *History of Norridgewock*, pp. 42, 43.

[1] It may seem strange to some that the Indians were always found on amicable terms with the French, while they were ever making inroads upon the settlements of the English. But the means used by the two nations were entirely opposite. While the French, with their social fascination and flexibility of character, used every method of conciliation towards them, — giving them warlike implements, accompanying them on their hunting excursions, and becoming intimately identified with them by marriage, — the English looked upon them with detestation and horror, taking every opportunity for their extermination, and using every means to annoy and exasperate them. The gorgeous display and the imposing ceremonials of the Romish church also exerted an irresistible influence upon the mind of the rude savage.

[2] Mass. Hist. Coll. vol. xviii. p. 254.—Upon this memorable event in our annals, Father

20*

Writers have disagreed in opinion as to the justness of the retribution thus meted out to Rasles and his proselytes.[1] But it would seem that the dispassionate verdict of men at this day, — remote from the fierce jealousies of two great nations contending for territory, from the wounded pride and disappointment embittered by the duration of the contest, — should be rendered against such a wholesale massacre, and that milder, more reasonable, and Christian means might have been resorted to in pacifying the savages, who, it must be admitted, had grave charges to prefer against the English, of treachery, chicanery, and double-dealing practised by them from the time they first placed foot on American soil. Vestiges of the ancient settlement are in existence even now. Broken utensils, glass beads, and hatchets, have been turned up by the plough of the husbandman, and are preserved as valuable relics by the people in the neighborhood.

No attempts at settlement were made till after the Revolution. Some persons, however, emigrated here in 1772 and 1780, from Massachusetts and New Hampshire; but, not being imbued with the spirit of enterprise, or failing to see the advantages which the place possessed for ultimately becoming a thriving settlement, some of them pushed further up the river, while others returned again to Massachusetts. When peace was proclaimed, the town received as settlers a large number of young men, who, inured to active labor from their infancy, had their robust constitutions more perfectly developed by hard service in

Charlevoix should be heard. "There were not," says he, "at the time the attack was made, above fifty warriors at Norridgewock; these seized their arms, and ran in disorder, not to defend the place against an enemy who was in it, but to favor the flight of the women, the old men, and the children, and to give them time to gain the side of the river, which was not yet in possession of the English. Father Rasles, warned by the clamors and tumult, and the danger in which he found his proselytes, ran to present himself to the assailants, hoping to draw all their fury upon him, that thereby he might prove the salvation of his flock. His hope was vain; for hardly had he discovered himself when the English raised a great shout, which was followed by a shower of shot, by which he fell dead near to the cross which he had erected near the centre of the village. Seven Indians who attended him, and who endeavored to shield him with their own bodies, fell dead at his side. Thus died this charitable pastor, giving his life for his sheep, after thirty-seven years of painful labors." — *Historie Generale de Nouvelle France*, II. 382–4.

[1] One writer says, "The inhumanity of the English on this occasion, especially to the women and children, cannot be excused, and greatly eclipses the lustre of the victory." — *History and Biography of the Indians of North America*. By S. G. Drake, p. 312. Whittier, in his graphic and picturesque style, has commemorated the murder of the aged pastor and his flock in verse. A granite obelisk, three feet square at the base, and eleven feet high, with an inscription recording the massacre, marks the spot where the Indian church once stood. It was erected by Bishop Fenwick, of Boston.

the American army. To their efforts alone must be attributed the permanent settlement of Norridgewock. The celebrated Benedict Arnold passed through here in October, 1775, on his perilous expedition to Quebec.

Norridgewock was incorporated in June, 1778; and in the summer of 1794 the first meeting-house was erected, at the public expense. In relation to this circumstance, the records state that it was "voted to get one barrel of good West India rum, and two hundred pounds maple sugar, to be used at the raising of the meeting-house." The court-house was built in 1820, and remodelled in 1847, at a cost of about $7,000; and the present bridge across the Kennebec river was built in 1849, at a cost of $11,000.

Norridgewock contains about twenty-six thousand acres, the surface of more than one third of which is level, and free from stone. The soil is generally better adapted for tillage than for grazing, and is mostly of good quality and easily cultivated. Limestone is found here in abundance; but, being mixed with slate, is unfit for building purposes. A granite quarry is situated on Dodlin hill, on the south line of the town, from which large quantities of good stone are annually excavated. Agriculture is the principal pursuit of the inhabitants, who are an industrious people, the greater part of whom have enough and to spare of this world's goods. Their perseverance and energy have enabled them to recover from the pecuniary shocks experienced by the land and timber speculations of 1837.

There are two villages, called the South and the North, in the latter of which the county buildings are located. Each of these villages is in a thriving condition, there being quite a number of dwelling-houses in each, besides stores and offices. In the way of manufactories, the south village surpasses the north, — having a good flour-mill, a saw-mill, a carding-machine, and other operations. Roads have been constructed to almost every place of note, and so great has been the progress in this line, that but little expense would be necessary to connect every farm by a good road. There are six religious societies in Norridgewock — Methodist, Congregationalist, Baptist, Free-will Baptist, Christian, and Universalist, with three meeting-houses; two post-offices — Norridgewock and South Norridgewock; a female academy, erected in 1837, by voluntary subscriptions; and sixteen school districts, with fifteen schools. Population, 1,848; valuation, $344,406.

North Berwick, situated in the southwest part of York county, formed a part of Berwick, in which its history is included. It was set off and incorporated in 1831. The surface is uneven, and the soil is for the most part sandy and not very productive. There is one village, called Doughty's Falls; two church edifices, belonging to the Baptists; nineteen school districts, and twenty-six schools; one factory, having an invested capital of $50,000; two saw-mills and two grist-mills; two other mechanical establishments; and one post-office. Population, 1,593; valuation, $331,148.

NORTHFIELD is situated in the central part of Washington county, and is watered by the west branch of Machias river. It was incorporated March 21, 1838, having been previously township No. 24 in the east division of the county. It has three school districts, with a maximum attendance of eighty-three scholars. Population, 246; valuation, $24,950.

NORTH HAVEN, Waldo county, is situated at the entrance of Penobscot bay, and originally formed a part of Vinalhaven, from which it is separated by a strait, or thoroughfare, about a mile in width. It was for some time known as North Fox Island. It has suffered considerably in consequence of the advantages taken of an act, passed by the legislature of 1850, giving the majority of the inhabitants the right to have such roads as they deemed fit. The majority decided upon having no roads at all; or, what is worse, to have roads fenced up with gates and bars, wherever the owners of land might wish to locate them, which have proved of no public convenience or utility whatever. The minority made a violent opposition, and have brought the matter before every legislature since the passage of the obnoxious act. At the session of 1857, the controversy was referred to the county commissioners for settlement.

North Haven was incorporated by the name of Fox Isle, June 30, 1846, which was changed July 13, 1847. The surface is generally even. Hay is the staple production. The inhabitants are engaged principally in fishing and farming. There are four small villages, one post-office, six school districts, with eleven schools; one church edifice, owned and occupied by the Baptists; four dry and West India goods stores, and one public-house. Population, 806; valuation, $82,550.

NORTHPORT, Waldo county, is situated on the west side of Penobscot bay, and joins Belfast on the south. The prime movers in the settlement were Thomas Burkmar, Samuel Bird, David Miller, Colonel Thomas, Stephen and John Knoulton, H. Flanders, Adam Patterson, Mark and John Welch, Zachariah Lawrence, Captain Ebenezer Frye, Major Benjamin Shaw, David Alden, Henry Pendleton, and Micajah Drinkwater. These men arrived but a short period prior to the Revolutionary war; and hence had scarcely more than discussed their plans of settlement, ere they were called off to the more stirring and dangerous life of the army. No further efforts at settlement were made till the conclusion of peace, when there were accessions of emigrants from different parts of the state.

During the time the English occupied Castine, a descent was made by them on this town, when several of the citizens were plundered. Shots were exchanged from the shore; but no damage was done on either side. One shot, however, from the English struck the house of Jones Shaw, and is still to be seen imbedded in one of the corner boards, where it will remain, doubtless, as long as the house stands.

Northport extends nine miles on Penobscot bay, and is about four miles wide, its surface being considerably broken, particularly along the shore. It is drained by Saturday cove and Little Harbor streams. In the southwest part is situated Knight's pond, a considerable body of water, having its outlet in Duck-trap stream, and falling into the bay in Lincolnville. The principal avocations of the inhabitants are farming and fishing. The town was incorporated February 13, 1796.

There is one church edifice, which was erected about the year 1835, and is occupied by all denominations. There are two small villages, Brown's Corner and Saturday Cove — which takes its name from the circumstance of the Rev. John Murray having arrived in this cove on a Saturday, and remaining over Sunday, on which day he preached to his crew, and those few hearers who could be gathered from along the shore. There are two post-offices, called Northport and East Northport; and ten school districts, with the same number of schools. Population, 1,260; valuation, $146,735.

North Yarmouth, Cumberland county, is situated a short distance from Casco bay, and originally embraced Yarmouth, Cumberland, Pownal, and Freeport. Some attempts at settlement were made as early as 1640, as a fortification was found here on the arrival of the settlers at that time, which had been occupied by George Felt, who purchased it of John Phillips, a Welshman. In 1646, William Royall purchased the farm, which, with the river, yet bears his name. In 1645, John Cousins lived on the neck of land which divides the branches of Cousins river, and owned all the island which still bears his name. Richard Bray, James Lane, John Maine, John Holman, Messrs. Shepard, Gendall, and Seward, Thomas Blashfield, Benjamin Larrabee, Amos Stevens, Thomas Reading, and William Haines were among the early settlers. During the first Indian war, in 1675, the settlement was destroyed, and the inhabitants abandoned the place, to which they did not return till the conclusion of peace, in 1678.

North Yarmouth was incorporated on the 22d of September, 1680, and was laid out on the land commonly called Maine's point, in a very compact manner, with the view of defending it from the attacks that might be made by the Indians.[1] In 1688, another assault was made upon the settlement by the savages, and the thirty-six families comprising its population abandoned their stock and improvements, and sought a refuge from the fury of the natives. Captain Gendall, the most wealthy and enterprising of all the settlers, a Mr. Scales, and several others, fell victims to the Indians' revengeful cruelty. Nineteen years of Indian warfare intervened; and when the settlers ventured again (about 1713) within the precincts of their former home, they found the sites of their habitations covered by a young growth of trees. Nothing daunted, however, they went to work with vigor, and the settlement again presented tokens of civilization and improvement. New proprietors were admitted, among whom were Gilbert and Barnabas Winslow, Jacob Mitchell, Seabury Southworth, and Cornelius Soule, descendants of the first settlers at Plymouth.

Till after the year 1756, the Indians were exceedingly troublesome. In 1725, William and Matthew Scales were killed, as was also Joseph Felt, whose wife and children were carried into captivity, from which they were afterwards released. Joseph Weare, grandson of Felt, pursued the Indians on every opportunity with unrelenting hate. His deeds of daring, and the number of natives put to death by him, would form a thrilling narrative. Joseph Sweat was killed June 16, 1746, and Philip Greely on the 9th of August of the same year, at the Lower Falls, where a party of thirty-two Indians had secreted themselves for the purpose of surprising Weare's garrison. These events continued till May 4, 1756, when the Indians attacked the house of Thomas Maines, killing him and an infant in the arms of Mrs. Maines, and taking a girl, named Skinner, captive. Beside those mentioned above, there were four persons killed and some eight or ten carried into captivity. No further depredations were committed after the date last named.

The comparative quiet which the cessation of Indian hostilities had given to the inhabitants was interrupted by the war of the Revolution, and the town, on the 20th of May previous to the Declaration of Independence, "voted unanimously to engage with their lives and fortunes to support congress in the measure." No place in New England can boast of a more steadfast and consistent career in the crisis than North Yarmouth. One among the distinguished individuals who have resided

[1] North Yarmouth was called *Wescustogo* by the Indians, and it is more than probable that they had a settlement on Lane's island, as several evidences have come to light, in the shape of skeletons of the aborigines, which would give reason for the supposition.

here was Rev. Ammi R. Cutter, who officiated as a clergyman for some years, and afterwards studied medicine. He commanded a company under General Pepperrell in the memorable expedition to Louisburg, and remained there as surgeon to the garrison the winter following the surrender of that place.

The surface is generally even, and the land of a good quality. North Yarmouth is watered by Royall's river, which runs directly through it. It contains two church edifices — Congregationalist and Methodist; nine school districts, and nine schools; two saw-mills, one grist-mill, and two post-offices — Centre and East North Yarmouth. Population, 1,121; valuation, $395,501.

NORWAY, in the southerly part of Oxford county, is estimated to contain about twenty-five thousand acres, consisting of a tract, estimated at six thousand acres, purchased of Massachusetts in 1787; a six thousand acre tract granted to Mr. Lee, and called the Lee Grant; and two other tracts, known as the Cummings Gore, and the Kent Gore. The township was brought to the notice of the first settlers by the reports of hunters, who travelled through its territory in pursuit of deer and other game, with which the forests abounded. James Stinchfield, Jonas Stevens, and some others, came into the township on a hunting excursion around the great Pennessewasse pond and other streams, and, seeing the beautiful growth of wood and other indications of fertile soil, determined to settle here.

In 1786, Joseph and Jonas Stevens, Jeremiah and Amos Hobbs, and George Lessley, came and commenced vigorous efforts in clearing lands and erecting dwellings. Shortly, three of them brought their families. Many others soon followed; and the place began to wear a populous aspect. Captain Rust, a large proprietor of land, performed many acts of kindness to the settlers, for which he was very much beloved and esteemed; and, in honor of him, the township received its name, which it retained until its incorporation, March 9, 1797. At this date, the inhabitants were thinly scattered about in small clearings, dotted here and there with log houses, many of them with large families of young children, often poorly clad and fed; notwithstanding which, they were not without their comforts and consolations. Many of the earlier settlers were soldiers in the Revolution; one of whom, Phineas Whitney, served throughout the war, and was at the battle of Bunker Hill, being one of the last to leave the field. In 1843, the records of the town from the beginning were destroyed by fire.

Norway has a fertile soil, and is watered by the great Pennessewasse pond, which furnishes good water-power for mills and other machinery.

By industry and economy, rapid advances have been made in agricultural improvements — in buildings, and in mechanical and mercantile business. Norway has five meeting-houses — two Congregational, and a Universalist, Free-will Baptist, and Methodist; thirteen school districts, with fifteen schools; a prosperous academy, a weekly newspaper, twelve or fifteen stores, ten blacksmith shops, two iron founderies, seven saw-mills, two grist-mills, clapboard, shingle and lath machines, a plough factory, one large carriage factory, a large paper-mill with the latest improvements, carding and clothier's mills, and a variety of boot and shoe establishments; as also two post-offices — Norway and North Norway. Population, 1,963; valuation, $326,473.

Oldtown, Penobscot county, is situated on the west side of the Penobscot river, about twelve miles above Bangor. Its history will be found in that of Orono, of which it formed a part until March, 1840, when it was incorporated as a separate town. The inhabitants, mostly from the western part of the state, were enticed here by the hope of making a fortune in the lumber business; and are an enterprising, active, and intelligent population. They seem to be a homogeneous compound of people from various nations, particularly Irish, Germans, Canadians, and Scotch.

The surface is generally pretty even. A "horseback," so called, runs the entire length, from north to south, which, according to the testimony of geologists, has been formed by the action of water. The town is drained by Penobscot river, and Pushaw and Birch streams. Agriculture is but little attended to, the inhabitants being principally engrossed in the lumber business, which is very extensively carried on. There are twelve gangs and fifty-nine single saws employed in sawing boards and timber, and some fifty machines used in the manufacture of clapboards, shingles, laths, and other small lumber. The Bangor, Oldtown, and Milford Railroad, the second completed in the United States, passes through here. The Penobscot Railroad, now building, will also pass through. A noticeable feature in Oldtown is the boom in Penobscot river, erected some years since at a cost of $100,000. Its object is to stop all the lumber coming down the river, and prevent its going out to sea. During the rafting season, there are three hundred men or more employed in rafting out the lumber which is driven into it. The largest quantity ever rafted in one year was in 1855, — 181,000,000 feet. There was estimated, at one time, to be six hundred acres of logs in the boom, from which some idea can be formed of the magnitude and importance of the lumber business.

There are four villages — Upper Stillwater, Greatworks, Pushaw, and

Oldtown village, which latter contains a majority of the inhabitants. In this village is located the Lumberman's Bank, with a capital of $75,000. There are also five dry goods and four variety stores, four groceries, two millinery shops, three clothing stores, one tin manufactory, and one saddlery. It has eight school districts, with sixteen schools; seven churches — Congregationalist, Baptist, Episcopalian, Universalist, Methodist, Union, and Roman Catholic; three post-offices — Oldtown, Upper Stillwater, and West Greatworks. Population, 3,087; valuation for 1858, $496,094.

ORIENT, in the southern part of Aroostook county, was surveyed in 1831 by General John Webber, and the settlement was soon after commenced by Abraham Longley and others. It became an incorporated town in 1856, and was made up of Orient gore, and the east half of township No. 9, lying west of the gore, and south of the town of Amity, near the monument, in the county of Aroostook. The westerly part is broken; but the easterly part, bordering on the Cheputnetecook lake, is quite level, has a tolerably good soil, and is partly cleared. It has one post-office, and three school districts. Population, 205.

ORLAND, Hancock county, situated on the east bank of the Penobscot river, was one of the six first-class townships granted by Massachusetts, in 1762, to David Marsh and 559 others. It became an incorporated town, February 11, 1800, and its surface is rough and broken. It is watered by a chain of ponds extending nearly its whole length, called Toddy ponds, having their outlet in the Penobscot river. Besides these there are Cragie's and Long ponds, lying mostly in Bucksport, as also Great pond. Orland is not very valuable for agricultural purposes, and as a consequence the inhabitants are principally engaged in other pursuits, mainly lumbering, ship-building, and fishing. There is one village in Orland, three church edifices — Methodist, Congregational, and Universalist; eighteen school districts, and twenty-two schools; six saw-mills, two grist-mills; and one post-office. Population, 1,579; valuation, $277,433.

ORNEVILLE, in the southeast part of Piscataquis county, was incorporated in 1832, under the name of Milton, afterwards changed to Almond, and then to Orneville. It is watered by several ponds and by the Pushaw river, a tributary of the Penobscot. The surface is rolling and the soil good. It contains eight school districts, with the same number of schools; one post-office; two grist-mills, three saw-mills, and two shingle mills. The Bangor post-road passes through the village. Population, 424; valuation, $28,926.

ORONO, Penobscot county, is situated on the west bank of the Penobscot river, and joins Bangor on the north. It was originally the property of Massachusetts, and was settled, in 1774, by Jeremiah Colburn and Joshua Ayres. It embraced an island in the Penobscot river, which was settled soon after by John Marsh, and consequently called Marsh Island. The McPheters, the Whites, and the Spencers were early settlers. John Bennoch, a native of Scotland, came here from Boston about 1808, and Andrew Webster, father of the late Col. E. Webster, settled about the same time. They were the most active and enterprising among the lumbermen on the river, and contributed largely in laying the foundation of the present prosperity of Orono. The plantation name was Stillwater. It included Oldtown as a part of its territory until 1840, the period of its incorporation. The present name was derived from a distinguished chief of the Tarratine tribe of Indians, who had his residence here, and whose devotion to American liberty was regarded as a strong reason for thus perpetuating his memory.

The surface is generally even. Immediately on the banks of the Penobscot there is some fine tillage land; but back from the river it is poor and unproductive. Marsh island is connected with the main land by a covered toll-bridge. The Bangor and Oldtown Railroad passes through the western part, and the Orono and Milford follows up the west bank of the Penobscot, both crossing the Stillwater branch, as well as the main river, to Milford, which at present is the terminus of both. Lumbering and fishing were the principal occupations of the inhabitants for many years; but, of late, they have turned their attention more to agriculture. There are two sets of saw-mills on the first dam, having three gangs and twenty single saws, together with shingle, lath, and clapboard machines; and on the second dam, three gangs and twenty-seven single saws, a portion of which are in operation. There is also at this place another block of mills, called the Basin mills, drawing the water by which they are propelled from the main river. They contain two gangs and about twenty single saws, besides several shingle, lath, and clapboard machines. This block has superior advantages over the others in not being affected by drought, and by having facilities for securing and containing a large number of logs. The town has one village, part of which is situated on the main land, and a part on Marsh Island; three church edifices — Congregational, Methodist, and Universalist; the Orono Bank, with a capital of $50,000; two post-offices — Orono and Upper Stillwater; and one school district, with twelve schools. Population, 2,785; valuation, $259,930.

ORRINGTON, Penobscot county, is situated on the east bank of Penobscot river, and formerly comprised within its territory Brewer and Holden. It was settled by mariners from Massachusetts, who had been compelled, in the Revolutionary war, to leave their legitimate business and seek other employments. As soon as hostilities ceased, many of these settlers, with their sons, sought again a life on the ocean. Captain Brewer and Simeon Fowler were among the early settlers, and purchased from the government a tract of land on Penobscot river, containing 10,864 acres, for which they paid £3,000 in consolidated notes. The remainder was granted to Moses Knapp and others. The survey was made in 1784, and the town was incorporated in 1788.

The surface is a medium between that of Bucksport and Brewer — not so hilly and rocky as the former, and not so level, sandy, or loamy as the latter. It is drained by Brewer and Wentworth streams, which flow diagonally through the town, and fall into the Penobscot. Orrington has three small villages; four church edifices — three Methodist and one Congregational; twelve school districts, with thirteen schools; seven saw-mills, two grist-mills, two shingle mills, one wood-turning establishment, one tannery, and four post-offices — Orrington, South Orrington, East Orrington, and Goodale's Corner. Population, 1,852; valuation, $256,605.

OTIS, Hancock county, is bounded on the north by Ellsworth. The first settlements were commenced about fifty years ago. Among those who were prominent pioneers in the work of improvement were Isaac Frazer, W. M. Jellison, Nathan Young, Allan Milliken, James Gilpatrick, Benjamin Davis, and others. The first farms were cleared in 1823, the titles to them having been obtained from Leonard Jarvis. Otis was incorporated in 1835. Its surface is quite uneven. Some of the rivers which flow into Frenchman's bay have their source here, and Union river passes the northwest corner. On Flood's pond several mills are built, and Springy pond is the site of a clapboard mill. On Beech Hill pond there are other mills, owned by residents of Ellsworth. The principal portion of the inhabitants are Free-will Baptists; as yet, however, they own no church edifice, and from necessity hold their meetings in the school-houses. There are three school districts, with the same number of schools; and one post-office. Population, 124; valuation, $19,341.

OTISFIELD, in the northern part of Cumberland county, thirty miles from Portland, was formerly a plantation under the same name. It was incorporated in February, 1798. The soil is very good, and as an evidence of its productiveness, it may be stated, that, in 1837, it yielded four thousand four hundred and twenty-five bushels of wheat. It is watered by Pequawket river, which empties into Sebago lake, and by Thompson's pond. There is a pond known as Long pond, lying partly in this town and partly in Casco, having its outlet in Pequawket river. Otisfield contains two church edifices, one Congregational, the other owned by Methodists and Free-will Baptists; twelve school districts, with twenty-four schools; three saw-mills; four shingle machines; a capital invested in trade of about $6,000; and three post-offices — Bolster Mills, Otisfield, and East Otisfield. Population, 1,171; valuation, $211,185.

Oxford, in the southerly part of Oxford county, originally formed a part of Hebron, from which it was incorporated in 1829. It was settled during the closing years of the Revolutionary war by Captain Isaac Bolster from Worcester, John Caldwell from Ipswich, Job and Joseph Cushman and Peter Thayer from Plympton, Daniel Whitney, Daniel Bullen, Zadoc and Abraham Dean, Elliot Richmond, Daniel and Asa Bartlett, Nathaniel Fuller, Holmes Thomas, Zebulon Chadbourne, James Soule, and James Perry from different places, — all from Massachusetts. These settlers came within a few years of each other. The progress of the settlement was slow, — more so from the various obstacles that deterred settlers from pushing out into the wilderness, than from any difficulties presented by the soil or position of the place. William C. Whitney settled here in 1796, and remained until about 1840, having held several important offices. J. S. Keith and J. J. Perry are distinguished residents, both having been members of the state senate. Mr. Perry recently represented this district in the Congress of the United States, and has been chosen to the thirty-sixth Congress.

The surface is somewhat hilly, but nearly all of it capable of cultivation. Water is supplied by the Little Androscoggin river and the outlet of Thompson's pond, on which there are some good mill-sites. There are in Oxford three saw-mills, a grist-mill, two woollen factories, a tannery; two villages — Welchville and Cragie's Mills; three religious societies — Congregational, Methodist, and Baptist, — the two former of which have houses of public worship; ten school districts, and ten schools; and two post-offices — Oxford and Welchville. Population, 1,233; valuation, $183,800.

Oxford County extends about one hundred miles in length upon the western boundary of the state, and made originally the northern parts of York and Cumberland. The act establishing it was passed March 4, 1805. Its southerly line then began upon the Androscoggin, at the southeasterly corner of the town of Turner, and ran west to the present easterly line of the county; thence southerly and westerly as the line now runs, taking in Hebron, Norway, Waterford, and the towns of Sweden, Denmark, and Hiram, since incorporated. Great Ossipee river was made its southern limit, Canada its northern, and its western the state of New Hampshire. In 1838, the county of Franklin received five towns and a large number of plantations from Oxford, making more than half its territory. In 1854, it gave two towns to form Androscoggin county. It has now thirty-four towns and eighteen plantations and parts of plantations, covering an area of about seventeen hundred square miles, the northern portion of which is mostly unsettled. Some parts are rough and mountainous; but the greater portion is fertile, and well adapted to cultivation, especially that along the rivers and lakes. The county is well watered by the Androscoggin, Saco, and their tributaries, and in the northern part are the large lakes Umbagog and Mooselockmeguntic. It is traversed by the Grand Trunk Railway.

Paris has always been the shire town. The county belongs to the western judicial district, the law terms of which are held at Portland. The jury terms of the supreme judicial court for civil and criminal business commence at Paris on the second Tuesdays of March, August, and November. Population, 35,463; valuation, $5,349,340.

PALERMO is situated in the west part of Waldo county, twenty-four miles from Belfast. It was formerly called Sheepscot Great Pond, and the petition for incorporation was presented in 1801, which set forth, among other things, that they had "a great proportion of roads to make and maintain within their bounds, and ten miles of road at least out of their limits, which road led to the head of navigation on Sheepscot river, their nighest market." The petitioners were fifty-five in number, among whom were Gabriel Hamilton, Jacob Greeley, Jabez Lewis, James Dennis, William C. Hay, Joseph Whittier, Charles Lewis, Samuel and Stephen Longfellow, John Glidden, and Joseph Bowler. The township was surveyed in August, 1800, by William Davis, and contained 27,100 acres. It was incorporared by its present name (Lisbon was the one mentioned in the petition), June 23, 1804.

The surface is varied with hill and dale, but not mountainous; and the soil is good, consisting mainly of a gravelly loam. Palermo has one village, called Branch Mills; two Baptist church edifices; fifteen school districts, with thirteen schools; three post-offices — Palermo, Palermo Centre, and East Palermo; three saw-mills, two grist-mills, three shingle machines, and one starch factory. Population, 1,659; valuation, $177,886.

PALMYRA, in the southeast part of Somerset county, twenty-five miles from Norridgewock, was purchased of Massachusetts by a Mr. Barnard of New Hampshire, for twelve and a half cents per acre, and was afterwards sold by him to Dr. John Warren of Boston. It was surveyed, in 1798, by Samuel Weston. The first settler was Daniel Gale, who removed his family here in 1800. It was incorporated in 1807, and a post-office was established in 1824. The surface is rolling, and the soil very productive of grass and grain, to the cultivation of which, attention is mostly directed. Palmyra is drained by the outlet of Moose pond, — the west branch of Sebasticook river, — which affords water-power. The town contains one church edifice (Union), fifteen school districts, with the same number of schools, and the various elements necessary to the comfort and convenience of a country town. Population, 1,625; valuation, $162,897.

PARIS, the shire town of Oxford county, is situated forty-seven miles northwest from Portland, and about forty-two miles west from Augusta. It extends from northeast to southwest about twelve miles, and from southeast to northwest about six miles, and contains about seventy square miles. It was originally granted to Captain Joshua Fuller and his sixty-four privates, by Massachusetts, in 1771. The first settlement was commenced in 1779, near the centre of the town, by John Daniels, John Willis, Benjamin Hammond, Lemuel Jackson, and Uriah Ripley. Joseph Daniels, born in February, 1784, who is still living, and has always been a resident, was the first native citizen. The first settled minister was James Hooper, Baptist, who was ordained in Lemuel Jackson's barn, June 25, 1795. Mr. Hooper remained in charge of his church forty years. In 1803, the Baptists erected a house for public worship at Paris Hill. Paris was incorporated June 20, 1793, and became the shire town upon the incorporation of the county in 1805. It has furnished six members of congress, namely, Levi Hubbard, Albion K. Parris, Enoch Lincoln, Timothy J. Carter, Rufus K. Goodenow, and Charles Andrews, of whom the last only was a native.

The surface is uneven, Streaked mountain, on its eastern line, being its highest elevation. It presents every variety of soil except clay, very little of which is found. It is superior for pasturage and hay crops, and is one of the best stock and dairy towns in the state. The orchards are large and productive, and a source of great income. The first apple-tree and pear-tree were brought by Lemuel Jackson from Massachusetts in 1780, and both are still in good condition. Moose pond, in the north part, is the only sheet of water of any magnitude. The Little Androscoggin runs its entire length from northwest to southeast, and furnishes several fine water privileges, which are occupied by saw and grist-mills, a woollen factory, manufactories for cane-seat chairs, cast-iron ploughs, and portable galvanized iron ovens. Boots and shoes are manufactured to some extent. In the north part is a beautiful spring, whose waters are strongly impregnated with sulphur and nitre. Snow's falls, on the Little Androscoggin, is one of the wildest and most picturesque waterfalls. Mount Mica, in the eastern part, is much resorted to by the scientific to obtain specimens of mica, green and red tourmalines; other minerals being also found here in abundance. The Grand

County Buildings upon Paris Hill.[1]

Trunk Railway runs the entire length of the town. It crosses the Little Androscoggin upon a granite bridge, erected at a cost of $60,000.

There are three villages — Paris Hill, South Paris, and North Paris, the first of which contains fifty-five dwelling-houses and the county buildings, and, from its high elevation, enjoys a fine air and delightful prospect. The Oxford Normal Institute, at South Paris, has for years been a flourishing literary institution. The Paris Hill academy, erected and sustained solely by individual effort, is well patronized, and has a very desirable location. There are eighteen school districts; four church edifices — one Congregational, two Methodist, and one Baptist; five post-offices — Paris, South Paris, West Paris, North Paris, and Snow's Falls. Population, 2,882; valuation for 1858, $340,800.

[1] The above view was taken in January, 1858, and has as much scope as could well be obtained by the camera, on account of the sharp elevation of the hill above all neighboring points. The foreground of the picture indicates the mode of the artist's arrival.

PARKMAN, in the southern part of Piscataquis county, fifteen miles from Dover, was incorporated in 1822, and received its name from Dr. George Parkman, who was murdered by Dr. Webster. It is watered by a branch of Piscataquis river; and the surface is generally even, with a soil excellently adapted to agricultural development. The manufacture of butter and cheese receives considerable attention. A thriving little village, called Parkman Corner, has sprung up near the centre of the town. The people have intelligence, thrift, and industry, and are reaping the benefits arising from these characteristics. There are three church edifices (Methodist, Free-will Baptist, and Congregational); fourteen school districts, with twenty-four schools; two post-offices — Parkman and Parkman Centre; one grist-mill, two saw-mills, and two shingle mills. Population, 1,243; valuation, $117,194.

PARSONSFIELD is the northwestern corner town of York county, on the boundary line between Maine and New Hampshire, and contains an area of twenty-two thousand acres. It is a part of the tract sold by the Indian sagamore, Captain Sunday, to Francis Small and Nicholas Shapleigh, in 1661. Small removed to Cape Cod, where he died soon after, and, on the division of the property in 1771, this portion of the purchase fell to the claimants under Shapleigh, — Alexander Scammel, Joseph Moulton, and Philip Hubbard, — who conveyed it to Thomas Parsons and thirty-nine associates. The tract was shortly afterwards surveyed into one hundred acre lots, two of which were reserved for each proprietor, nine for the use of schools and the support of the ministry, and one for a mill privilege. The next year (1772), twelve families settled, which were increased during the four years following to forty families. Among the names of the early inhabitants were John and Gideon Doe, of Newmarket, N. H., who settled in 1775. Parsonsfield was incorporated March 9, 1785; and the first warrant for a town-meeting was issued by Simon Frye, of Fryeburg, justice of the peace.

The surface is rough and hilly, and the soil requires a considerable dressing to make it productive. Cedar, Wiggin's, and Randall mountains are the three principal elevations. Water is supplied by Great brook, which flows into the Ossipee river, and by Spruce, Long, and Mudgett ponds. There are four villages — Kezar Falls, Middle Road, Weeks Corner, and North Road, all of them small; eight church edifices — four Free-will Baptist, one Congregational, one Baptist, one Friends' and one Union; a seminary, under the direction of the Free-will Baptists; seventeen school districts, with thirty-four schools; and six post-offices — Parsonsfield, North Parsonsfield, South Parsonsfield, East Parsonsfield, West Parsonsfield, and Kezar Falls. There is a set of saw, shingle, and grain mills at Kezar Falls; and one in the west part of the town, known by the name of the Lord mills; besides some six other mills of less note. Population, 2,322; valuation for 1857, $490,000.

PASSADUMKEAG, Penobscot county, on the east bank of Penobscot river, thirty-two miles from Bangor, was incorporated in 1833. It is drained by Passadumkeag river, and the surface is varied, with a fertile soil, promising bountiful harvests to the industrious farmer. The admirable location of the village of Passadumkeag will eventually secure for it the trade of a large section of country. The lumber business engrosses the principal attention of the inhabitants. The town contains some excellent mill privileges; has four school districts, with the same number of schools; and one post-office. Population, 295; valuation, $20,066.

PATTEN, Penobscot county, eighty miles north from Bangor, was first settled in 1834, by Henry Blake. It was lotted at different times by Caleb Leavitt, John Webber, Zebulon Bradley, and David Haynes, and is well timbered. About half of the 155 lots have settlers. The town was incorporated in 1841, taking its name from Amos Patten, the first proprietor. Crystal and fish streams flow through it. It has four saw-mills, two grist-mills, a hotel, academy, meeting-house, five school districts, and a post-office. Population, about 550; valuation, $46,177.

PEJEPSCOT PURCHASE. The Pejepscot settlements originated in the enterprise of Thomas Purchas and George Way, in 1624–5.[1] They claimed on both sides of the Androscoggin to the falls at Lewiston, southwardly to Maquoit, also the Merryconeag peninsula, Sebascodegan and other islands. Upon the breaking out of the Pequot war, Purchas, wishing to strengthen the position of the settlements, which were very much exposed to the ravages of Indians, by a conjunction with Massachusetts, assigned this territory to Governor Winthrop by deed, executed August 22, 1639, with a provision that Purchas himself, his heirs and associates, should for ever have the protection of government, and that they should be allowed always to occupy the lands that they might clear within seven years ensuing.[2] Purchas continued unmolested in the enjoyment of his lands for thirty or forty years, and grew wealthy from trading with the natives. But his neighbors, the Anasagunticooks, had become very much excited during King Philip's war, and feeling a strong

[1] Williamson (vol. I., p. 266,) says, they settled at the head of Stevens river, which is in Bath; but some claim the honor for Brunswick.

[2] 1 Haz. Coll. 457.

aversion to him, a party of them, on the 5th of September, 1675, plundered his house during his absence, and left without offering any personal violence to the inmates, but with the threat that "others would soon come, and treat them worse." This promise was soon fulfilled, and the settlements were desolated. The colonial charter of Massachusetts being vacated in 1684, the inhabitants of Maine felt less interest in a government regulated solely by appointment from the crown, and began to resume purchases of the Indians. A very important deed of conveyance was executed July 7th of that year, by Warumbee and five other sagamores of the Anasagunticooks, to Richard Wharton. It was at first supposed the conveyance included the lands between Cape Small point and Maquoit, thence extending northward, on the western side of the Androscoggin river, four miles in width, to the Upper (Lewiston) falls; and from there, five miles in width, on the other side of the river, down to Merry-Meeting bay, including the islands upon the coast. The deed premised that Thomas Purchas, the first possessor of the tract, settled near the centre of it sixty years before, and obtained, according to report, a patent from England; that Nicholas Shapleigh had, at some time, purchased of the sagamores Merryconeag peninsula, Sebascodegan island, and the other islands between Cape Small point and Maquoit, and had died, seized of them; that the widows and heirs of Purchas and Shapleigh, after a few reservations, had joined in a quitclaim of the whole to Wharton; and that the six sagamore grantors, wishing to encourage him in settling an English town there, and in promoting the salmon and sturgeon fishery, as well as in consideration of the money they had received, did grant and confirm unto him the afore-described tract. They reserved to themselves, however, the use of all their ancient planting grounds, and the usual privileges of hunting and fishing. From the indefinite description of the boundaries in the deed, and from the doubt as to what "falls" were intended, a great controversy arose. Some of the subsequent proprietors have claimed as high up the river as the great falls in Rumford.

The Indian ravages in 1690, which again laid waste the Pejepscot and surrounding country, quieted controversy for several years. Some attempts at resettlement were made in 1699; but Wharton dying insolvent, the tract was sold, in 1714, to Messrs. Winthrop, T. Hutchinson, Ruck, Noyes, Watts, Minot, Mountford, and two others, for only £100, who at once applied to the general court for confirmation of the purchase as they bounded it,[1] and encouragement in settling and defending

[1] They supposed it ran "from five miles above the uppermost falls of Androscoggin river, on a northeast line, over to Kennebec river, including what land lies to the south-

the three proposed new towns of Brunswick, Topsham, and Harpswell. Their prayer was granted, and Fort George was built and garrisoned for their defence. The legislature gave further confirmation in 1726, but with this clause — "saving all other interests that may be found therein." The history of this purchase had now reached a point where controversy could not be allayed without the arbitrament of law; or, this failing, till the parties, — worn out with tedious litigation, — should be more disposed to a compromise.[1] The case occupied much time at a term of the court in 1754, being conducted by two of the ablest advocates in the country — the attorney-general, Jeremiah Gridley, for the Plymouth company, and the renowned James Otis, for the Pejepscot proprietors. A compromise was arranged, after much difficulty, in 1758, but was not finally carried out till 1766, when the Pejepscot proprietors released to the Plymouth company the lands between New Meadows and Kennebec rivers, — comprising the present towns of Phipsburg and Bath, — and determined the line between them, on the south of the latter company, to run from the mouth of the Cathance river, W. N. W., and the west line to be fifteen miles from Kennebec river.[2] But, in regard to the true running of the compromise line, disputes afterwards arose, which were not decided until the present century. Massachusetts had, in 1787, defined the Twenty-mile falls to be Lewiston falls, which gave the proprietors all below that point on the west, and below a line near the north line of Leeds on the east. Dissatisfied with this, they procured a reference in 1798, composed of Levi Lincoln, Samuel Dexter, and Thomas Dwight, and refused to abide by the award made in 1800; but were compelled to do so by actions brought on the award, decided against them in 1814, by which the tract was limited as fixed by the legislature, embracing, on the west side of the Androscoggin, Brunswick, the greater part of Durham and Danville, a corner of Poland, and the present town of Auburn; and, on the easterly side, Topsham, a part of Lisbon, all of Lewiston and Greene, and three fourths of Leeds.

PERU, Oxford county, bounded north by the Androscoggin river, is twenty-eight miles from Augusta. The original grant of two miles square was made by Massachusetts to Merrill Knight, Daniel Lunt, Wil-

ward of that line, down to Merry-Meeting bay" — which confirmation only increased the difficulty, by coming into collision with the Kennebec proprietors, or the Plymouth company.

[1] "These proprietors had waged a paper war some time before they carried their controversy into court. Pamphlets were published on both sides, in which personal abuse was not spared." — Smith and Deane's *Journal*, p. 157, note 1, by William Willis.

[2] See Kennebec Purchase, ante, p. 169.

liam Brackett, and a Mr. Bradish of Falmouth. The settlement was commenced by Knight, who came with a large family about the year 1793. He was soon followed by Lunt and Brackett, and by William Walker, Osborn Trask, and Brady Bailey, also from Falmouth. Many others soon settled upon the same tract, the descendants of whom form a considerable portion of the population of Peru. The remainder of the township was afterwards purchased of the state, in tracts or grants, by E. Fox, Lunt, Thompson, and Peck, and separated into as many grants, designated as Peck's, Fox's and Thompson's grants, and Lunt's upper and lower tracts, the upper tract including the original grant of two miles square. From these proprietors the settlers obtained their titles.

The township was organized as a plantation in 1812, and incorporated as a town in 1821. The surface is uneven and broken. On the Androscoggin, which forms its northeasterly boundary, there is generally a narrow interval, between the river and highland, very smooth and fertile. Bordering upon Spear's stream are also several farms of like smoothness and fertility. Wheat and other grain were formerly among the staple productions; but of late these have been superseded by corn, oats, hay, and grass. The soil of Peru continues good and equally free from stone to the very summit of the hills, on which may be seen some of the best plough fields.

The only mountains of note are Black Mountain and Tumble-down Dick, more commonly called Dick. Black Mountain received its name from its black appearance when first discovered, being at that time covered with a dense growth of pine, spruce, and hemlock, to its very summit. Dick is a small mountain, which, when viewed from a distance, resembles Mount Washington. On the north it rises gradually to its summit, and on the south it breaks off in an abrupt and frightful precipice, never scaled by man or beast. At the foot of this mountain is a small pond, known as the Cranberry pond. Further to the east, in the southerly and easterly part of the town, is Worthy pond, which is some two miles in length. The small Cranberry pond is the source of the east branch of Twenty Mile river. Spear's stream crosses the town, draining much of its waters and those of Franklin plantation into the Androscoggin.

Hon. Samuel R. Thurston, first delegate to Congress from Oregon Territory, was a native of Peru. He died on his passage between San Francisco and Oregon, *en route* home. James H. Withington, formerly the able and successful principal of Hallowell academy, was also a native.

There is a small place of business on Spear's stream, formerly known as Putnam's Mills, having a grist-mill, saw-mill, shingle and lath mill;

Pembroke Iron Works.

a cabinet-maker, blacksmith, and two stores. Peru has two post-offices — Peru and West Peru; one church edifice, owned and occupied by the Episcopal Methodists; and eleven school districts, with twenty-two schools. Population, 1,109; valuation in 1858, $133,804.

PEMBROKE, Washington county, is situated on an arm of Passamaquoddy bay, and adjoins Perry on the east. The first settlers were Hateville Leighton, Edmund Mahar, and William Clark, who arrived here about 1774. They were soon followed by Robert Ash, M. Denho, Joseph Bridges, Zadock Hersey, Caleb Hersey, Samuel Sprague, Theophilus Wilder, Bela Wilder, Moses Gardiner, Stephen Gardiner, and M. Dunbar, most of whom came from Maine and Massachusetts. It is said, but without proof, that Theophilus Wilder settled here as early as 1740. These settlers brought with them the industrial and frugal habits, respect for law, love of order, and the stern virtues, of an illustrious ancestry. They obtained the titles to their lands from General Benjamin Lincoln, of Revolutionary memory, and other proprietors. The Indian name was Pennamaquon.

Pembroke was originally incorporated as a part of Dennysville; but was set off and incorporated as a separate town in 1832. The surface is uneven, but there are no mountains of note. A considerable portion of the land is suitable for agricultural purposes, but the citizens have not as yet turned their attention that way. There are, however, a few good farms, sufficient to settle the question that farming can be made profitable. Among the natural curiosities of this section of country are the far-famed Cobscook falls, caused by the tumultuous rushing of a vast column of water through a narrow passage, over rugged rocks, into and out of an immense basin or reservoir. It bears some resemblance to Hurl-gate, New York; the scene here, if possible, being more terrific and wild than there.

Prior to the year 1844, some three or four small vessels were built here; and, in that year, Hon. S. C. Foster permanently established the ship-building business, and pursued it for a number of years, during which he built a large fleet of vessels. There are now seven ship-yards. Pembroke has one of the best harbors on the coast of Maine. The town has been settled for nearly a century, and though about one hundred sail of vessels visit the harbor annually, not one was ever lost within its precincts. A large factory for the manufacture of iron has been erected, the main building of which is 171 feet wide and 160 feet in length, a view of which is here given. It was erected under the auspices of General Ezekiel Foster, an enterprising merchant of Eastport, and is situated on the Pennamaquon stream, near the head of tide-water, which furnishes it with unsurpassed water-power, rarely interrupted by drought. The dams are built of stone, at a trifling expense, and are entirely free from any hazard by flooding. This factory is supplied with all the essentials necessary to the prosecution of an extensive business, and the grounds and general arrangements are made with special reference to convenience, utility, and economy. The proprietorship has changed hands two or three times, and the establishment is now owned by Messrs. William E. Coffin and Company, of Boston. The quantity of iron spikes, rivets, and nails produced at this factory in 1856 did not fall short of five thousand tons. The iron produced here is said to be equal to any manufactured on the globe.

The southern shores of Pembroke are washed by the sea; the harbor is easy of access, and its proximity to the fishing grounds renders it one of the best locations for carrying on that important branch of business in this region, the resources of which are inexhaustible; it has a water-power unemployed, except for unimportant purposes, sufficient to carry several large factories. Its advantages for farming, lumbering, fishing, manufacturing, ship-building, and carrying on the freighting business, warrant the belief, that, eventually, Pembroke will raise its head among the important towns of the state. Pembroke contains two church edifices, one a Union church, and the other a Baptist; eleven school districts, with the same number of schools; one post-office, one stone factory, three saw-mills, one grist-mill, four shingle machines, four lath machines, and one rolling-mill, connected with which is a spike, nail, and rivet factory. Population, 1,712; valuation, $158,994.

PENOBSCOT, Hancock county, is situated east of Penobscot bay, opposite Belfast. It formerly embraced within its limits Castine and a great part of Brooksville, extending from Orland, by the shores of Penobscot river and bay, around by Cape Rozier to Buck's harbor. What year the settlement was commenced is uncertain. The birth of the first child, Mary Grindle, which took place in 1765, leads us to suppose, however, that it occurred about that period. Some of the early settlers were Charles Hutching, Giles Johnson, Elijah Winslow, Jonathan Wardwell, Pelatiah Leach, Andrew Herrick, David Dunbar, Elijah Littlefield, and Eliphalet Lowell, nearly all of whom came from towns in Maine. The settlers obtained the titles to their lands from the proprietors.

Penobscot was incorporated in 1787. The surface is generally smooth and even, there being no eminences of any note. There are two ponds, each being about three miles in circumference, on the outlets of which there are good mill-sites. There is a small village at the head of the Northern bay, having three stores, and other places of business.

The manufactures consist of two or three coopering establishments, four or five shoe factories, three saw-mills, and three grist-mills. Agriculture is the principal occupation of the inhabitants; though even that is not prosecuted very extensively. There are three meeting-houses — two Methodist, and one Union meeting-house; fourteen school districts, with the same number of schools; and two post-offices — Penobscot, and North Penobscot. Population, 1,556; valuation, $160,286.

Penobscot County, situated towards the easterly part of the state, is of a long, irregular shape, presenting three dissimilar rectangles, and has an area of two thousand seven hundred and sixty square miles. The act establishing it was passed February 15, 1816, under which it was made to include "all that territory in the county of Hancock which lies north of the Waldo Patent, on the west side of Penobscot river, and north and west of the following lines on the east side of said river; beginning at said river at the south line of Orrington, Brewer, and the gore east of Brewer, to the west line of the Bingham Purchase; thence northerly by said Bingham Purchase, to the northwest corner thereof; thence easterly on the north line of said Bingham Purchase to the county of Washington." The county then embraced two or three times its present area. The organization of Piscataquis county, in 1838, deprived Penobscot of the five ranges of townships north of Dexter, Garland, Charleston, Bradford, and Lagrange; and the next year, Aroostook received from Penobscot the ranges of townships numbered three, four, and five north of Mattawamkeag. In 1843, Penobscot was again cut down by annexing to Aroostook ranges of townships six, seven, and eight north of township numbered eight. Its territory remains as it was left at that time, and but little more than half of it has yet been settled. There are forty-seven towns and forty-one plantations. The surface is diversified with hill and dale; but there are no elevations of note. The soil is generally fertile, and produces good crops of hay, wheat, corn, and potatoes. The manufacture and shipping of lumber have for many years monopolized the capital and energies of the people; but as these employments are becoming less lucrative by reason of the large influx of timber from the region of the great lakes of our country, attention is more and more turned to that sure basis of the wealth and prosperity of a state, — agriculture. The Penobscot — that crowning glory of God's handiwork among the rivers of Maine — traverses the entire length of the county, and receives in its course the waters of the Mattawamkeag, Piscataquis, Passadumkeag, Greatworks, Pushaw, and Kenduskeag rivers, and many others of less magnitude. About one half the length of the excellent military road from Bangor into Aroostook lies within this county. It is also traversed by the Penobscot and Kennebec, and the Bangor, Oldtown, and Milford Railroads, and will be the route of the projected European and North American Railroad, if that great connecting link shall ever be completed.

Bangor has always been the capital. The supreme judicial court holds a law term here for the eastern district (which embraces the counties of Waldo, Piscataquis, Penobscot, Hancock, Washington, and Aroostook), on the fourth Tuesday of May. The jury terms of this court for civil business commence on the first Tuesdays of January, April, and October; for criminal business, on the first Tuesdays of February and August. Population, 63,089; valuation, 89,094,465.

PERKINS, Sagadahoc county, is an island in Kennebec river, formerly called Swan island, a part of Dresden, from which it was incorporated June 24, 1847; and is four miles long by two hundred rods wide. It is noted for being at one time the residence of the bashaba of the Abnaki nation. It is well situated both for agricultural and mercantile business. It has one school district, with a maximum winter attendance of fourteen scholars. Population, 84; valuation, $26,721.

PERRY, Washington county, is washed on its eastern shore by the waters of the Passamaquoddy, and on the south by those of Cobscook bay, giving, by their numerous indentations, an extent of about forty miles of sea-coast. This township was sold by the state of Massachusetts, in 1783 or '84, to General Benjamin Lincoln and others, on condition that the proprietors should place here twenty settlers within a given time, and give to each one hundred acres of land. This was very soon accomplished, for Perry was a fine timbered township, and the lumber was easily got to market, which was a very prominent object with new settlers. For many years, the forest furnished the principal means of subsistence. The trade of the settlers was mainly with St. Andrew and Robbinston, carrying thither timber, spars, shingles, and other articles, and bringing back provisions and rum. In process of time, however, there were a few trading houses built on Moose island (now Eastport), which diverted a part of the trade of the town in that direction. It seems surprising, that men could sustain life as the people here did; and the wonder increases, when we consider that they had under their feet a soil, and around them a climate, capable of furnishing all of the necessaries, and many of the luxuries, of life.

This state of things continued till 1808, when even the settlers in this remote part of an almost unknown region felt the effects of the political tornado that was desolating Europe. Bonaparte had stopped the

English in their shipment of timber from the Baltic, which as a consequence diverted their trade to her colonies on this side of the Atlantic. St. Andrew grew up very rapidly; and the timber trade became the business of the whole surrounding region. This was then the California of the country. One man alone got out timber in ten days which he sold for $300; and it was no uncommon thing for men to bring home $500, and even $1000, at a time, as the proceeds of their lumber. But where is it all now? It is not in Perry. It seems to be a law of nature, that a curse must always attend the lumber business, and that poverty must be its constant attendant. Money could be obtained so much more easily by lumbering than by the slow returns of agricultural pursuits, that the inhabitants neglected to avail themselves of this sure source of independence, if not of wealth; and, in process of time, they found themselves, with their improvident and wasteful habits, living from hand to mouth, their market destroyed, their resources cut off, and their families destitute.

The climate is salubrious, not subject to the extremes of heat and cold, — the thermometer seldom rising above 75° or falling below 10°. The shores are bold, allowing vessels of one hundred tons, in most places, to lie so near as to be laden from the bank by wheeling from fifty to eighty feet. The tide rises thirty feet. The surface is free from mountains or large hills. The southern part of the town is very rocky and uneven; the northern part, more level. There is a lake ("Boyden's") in the northwest part, emptying into Passamaquoddy bay by Little river, affording by its falls numerous mill-sites. Farming is the most common employment of the inhabitants, who live pretty equally distributed along the coasts of the two bays, forming nowhere a settlement which can properly be called a village. At Little river, however, there is a meeting-house, (Congregational,) a school-house, post-office, store, blacksmith shop, three saw-mills, and a grist-mill. The only other church edifice is a Roman Catholic chapel at Pleasant Point. There is a Unitarian society. The post-office is furnished with a mail *occasionally*, — when the postmaster can find some market-man willing to convey it from Eastport, — as a regular conveyance would not pay the expense, and the government is too poor. Beside the mills before mentioned, there are several shingle and lath mills, one fulling-mill, and a carding-machine. There are thirteen school districts, with twelve schools. Population, 1,324; valuation, $115,374.

PHILLIPS, Franklin county, lies about seventeen miles northwesterly from Farmington. It was formerly called Curvo, a name it received from Captain Perkins Allen, on account of its resemblance to a port he

22*

had visited in a foreign voyage. Improvements were commenced as early as 1790 or 1791, — Perkins Allen, Seth Greeley and son, Jonathan Pratt, Uriah and Joseph Howard, and Isaac Davenport, being among the first settlers. The town was endowed with corporate privileges, February 5, 1812, and received its name in honor of Mr. Phillips, the former proprietor. The soil is productive, the water-power superior, and the situation such as to command most of the trade and other business of the interior of the county; while the inhabitants find a ready cash market for all their surplus wool, seed, and most other articles.

Phillips formerly embraced a territory of about nine miles in length, and five in width; but, in 1823, a section from the northeast corner was set off to form a part of Salem. There are two important villages on the Sandy river, near the southern extremity of the town. The lower village has a noble waterfall, a superior grist-mill, a tannery, a fulling-mill, a carding-machine, and other operations. The Upper Village, a thriving little place, half a mile above, has several stores, a tannery, a bridge, a saw-mill, a starch factory, with other manufactories; and, still higher up, there are a grist-mill and saw-mill.

An object of striking interest in Phillips is a deep ravine, connecting with a large basin, from forty to sixty feet deep, in loose sand, which is the site of a pond of about eighty acres, that had probably stood for ages, till within ten years. In 1847, the Messrs. Noyes, two brothers from Weld, erected a grist-mill upon a small stream that discharges its waters into the Sandy river at Bragg's Corner. After constructing their dam about one hundred rods above, on the stream, they found the water-power insufficient, and conceived the further design of tapping this pond on top of the hill, about half a mile up the brook, and at a height of seventy feet above it, which they did by constructing a plank flume, bulkhead, and gate, so as to regulate the flow from the pond. After the completion of the work, and while they had retired temporarily to their farms to increase their means for future operations, a leakage was discovered in the flume, which threatened to undermine the pond. The house of a Mr. Shepard was above the mill, near the pond. Alarm was felt and given; the neighbors assembled; some were engaged in sounding the pond, and others in examining the works, when one of the number seized and shook one of the flume-posts to test its strength, and the water gushed through. The stream quickly wore through the indurated clay, a thin layer of which made the bottom of the pond, then increased with immense velocity, widening and deepening the chasm, until the impetuous torrent swept all before it, scattering the buildings of Mr. Shepard and the mill into a thousand fragments, and even hurling the rocks from their foundation beds. Mrs. Shepard and her children barely escaped by flight to an adjoining hill. No vestige of the former appearance of the surroundings below now remains.

The religious societies are the Methodist, the Free-will Baptist, and the Congregational. In the Upper Village there is a Methodist meeting-house, and in the Lower Village a Union meeting-house. Phillips has seventeen school districts, with twenty-seven schools; and one post-office. Population, 1,673; valuation, $208,745.

PHIPSBURG, Sagadahoc county, is a peninsula, bounded on the north by Bath, east by the Kennebec river, south by the ocean, and west by Quohog bay. It originally belonged to the Pejepscot Purchase, and included the ancient Cape Small point and Cape Small point harbor. It is noted as the place where the Popham, or Sagadahoc colony, passed the tedious winter of 1607–8. In 1716, the Pejepscot proprietors conceived the project of making this a fishing settlement, and prosecuted the enterprise very successfully in making surveys, cutting out roads, and erecting houses. Dr. Oliver Noyes, one of the proprietors, was the principal director and patron. He named the settlement Augusta;[1] and, at a meeting of the inhabitants, held November 6, 1717, it would seem that the settlement was thriving, and had a goodly number of inhabitants. From the record it appears, that Captain John Penhallow, of Portsmouth, N. H., author of the "Indian Wars," had taken up his residence here, and was a prominent and useful inhabitant.

In 1716, Dr. Noyes erected a stone fort one hundred feet square, for the purpose of protecting the settlers, who were now coming in very fast. A sloop, named the *Pejepscot*, was obtained, and employed between Augusta and Boston, carrying out lumber and fish, and bringing back merchandise and settlers. The settlement continued to flourish until the time of Lovewell's war, when it was depopulated, the houses burnt, and the fort destroyed by the Indians. In 1737, the proprietors made another effort to rebuild Phipsburg, and sundry persons from Falmouth, encouraged by them, removed to the town. The names of those upon the record are Eben Hall, Eben Hall, Jr., Cornelius Hall, James

[1] Williamson labors under a mistake in confounding the history of this town with Old Cushnoc, or what is now Augusta, the state capital; for, in the Pejepscot records, now with the Maine Historical Society, we find the following: "Whereas, at a meeting of the proprietors of Pejepscot, on the 23d of April, 1718, it was voted that there be allowed and granted to our partner, Oliver Noyes, Esq., his heirs and assigns, three hundred acres of land in Agusta township, which is comprehended within the limits of Georgetown," [that town then included the peninsula of Phipsburg,] "in consideration of the expense and loss he has been at in settling said town." .... — *Pejepscot Records*, p. 7.

Doughty, David Gustin, Jeremiah Springer, Nicholas Rideout, John Owens, and others. The names of some of these are familiar at the present day as old settlers. It is probable, however, that there is no authentic knowledge of any of the first settlers. Phipsburg was incorporated with its present limits in 1814, receiving its name in honor of Sir William Phips.

The surface is rough and ledgy. Ship-building is prosecuted to some extent, but the occupation of the inhabitants is divided between fishing and farming. Phipsburg has two small villages, one called Parker's Head, and the other Cobb's Mills; three church edifices — Congregational, Methodist, and Free-will Baptist; twelve school districts, with fourteen schools; and two post-offices. Population, 1,805; valuation, $365,622.

Piscataquis County is one of the large northern counties, with uncleared regions yet to be opened wider to the sunshine of life. It was established March 23, 1838, partly from Somerset, but more largely from Penobscot. It then embraced "all the territory north of the south lines of Parkman and Wellington in the county of Somerset, and the north lines of Dexter, Garland, Charleston, Bradford, and south line of Kilmarnock, now Medford, in the county of Penobscot." The east line ran northward between the eighth and ninth ranges of townships, and the west line was continued from the west lines of Wellington, Kingsberry, and Shirley northward to the Kennebec river, and by the west shore of Moosehead lake to Canada. By act of March 12, 1844, Piscataquis gave to Aroostook all the territory north of townships numbered ten, and it remains, in form and size, as it was left at that time. It contains 110 townships, twenty-three of which are settled and incorporated. The remainder of these townships consists principally of wild land, most of which has been lotted to settlers. Like Aroostook county, it is well watered. The chief rivers are the Piscataquis, the east and west branches of the Penobscot, Sebec river, Pleasant river, besides a great number of tributaries of these rivers. The principal lakes are the Pemadumcook, Chesuncook, Sebec, Scootum, and Moosehead; the latter of which is the largest in the state, and forms part of the boundary line between Piscataquis and Somerset counties, containing within its limits several large islands. The greatest length of this lake is thirty-five miles, varying in width from four to twelve miles. The county contains 3,780 square miles, the surface of which is diversified with hills and valleys. Katahdin is the only mountain of note in the county.

Dover has been the county seat from the organization. It belongs to the eastern judicial district, the law terms of which are held at Bangor.

View on the Upper Penobscot,—Mount Katahdin in the distance

The terms of the supreme judicial court, for both civil and criminal business, commence on the last Tuesday of February and second Tuesday of September. Population, 14,735; valuation, $1,905,883.

Pittsfield, in the southeast corner of Somerset county, is about nine miles in length from north to south, and from seven to eight miles in width from east to west, being narrower across the north and south ends than in the other parts. It was formerly known as the Plymouth Gore, and was included in a grant to the Plymouth company, its eastern line being on the eastern line of that grant. The first settlement was made in 1794, by Moses Martin, of Norridgewock, at a bend of the Sebasticook about two miles below the village. His farm is still occupied by his son David, a gentleman some sixty years old, who has held several honorable offices. George Brown of Norridgewock, William Bradford, and one Wyman of Vassalboro' came in 1800. Brown and Wyman built the first mills; John Sibley and John Spearing came from Fairfield in 1804, and settled on the westerly side, east of Sibley's pond. John Merrick, from Hallowell, settled in 1806. Dominicus Getchel came from West Anson, in 1811; Joseph McCauslin from Hallowell, in 1813, and John Webb from Waterville, in 1815. Timothy McIntire and Stephen Kendal settled about the same time, and were prominent in the early affairs of the town.

In 1815, Pittsfield was organized into a plantation by the name of Sebasticook; but, after ineffectual attempts to enforce the collection of taxes, it was abandoned. It was incorporated by the name of Warsaw, June 19, 1819. The first town-meeting after its incorporation was held at John Webb's dwelling-house, July 19, 1819. Stephen Kendal was elected delegate to a convention to frame a state constitution, September 20, 1819; and, on December 6 of the same year, the town cast nineteen votes — the whole number — for the new constitution. In the winter of 1824, the name was changed from Warsaw to Pittsfield, in honor of William Pitts, who was then a proprietor of land here; and, in 1828, a portion of the Ell of Palmyra, so called, containing 4,200 acres, Joseph Warren of Boston being the proprietor, was annexed to Pittsfield. The first settlers obtained the titles to their lands from the Plymouth company.

From the singular shape of Pittsfield, the impression is that it must have been a piece of land which had been left from the laying out of other towns around it. It is situated on a large swell, inclining to the south, between the Kennebec and Sebasticook rivers, the waters on the western side running into the Kennebec, and those on the eastern side into the Sebasticook. The western branch of the Sebasticook runs through the eastern part. On this river is an excellent water privilege, where there are mills and other machinery. At this place there is a thriving village, which is the only one in Pittsfield. The railroad from Waterville to Bangor here crosses the Sebasticook.

The surface is remarkably level, there being no eminence or hill of any note. The original forest was composed of yellow birch, rock maple, beech, hemlock, white ash, and cedar. The soil on the Sebasticook is a sandy loam, entirely free from stone; and back from the river it is deep, rather moist, and, in some places, rather stony. This is an excellent farming town, — corn, wheat, oats, rye, barley, and potatoes being cultivated extensively; and recently the farmers have been turning their attention to fruit-growing, in which they have met with tolerable success. The inhabitants are principally engaged in farming, though there are a few mechanics. The Sebasticook river, mentioned above, is the only river of note; and the Sibley pond, which lies in the northwest corner, the only pond of note. There are two post-offices — Pittsfield and East Pittsfield; ten school districts; and one church edifice — Free-will Baptist. Population, 1,166; assessors' valuation for 1857, $222,520.

PITTSTON, Kennebec county, lies on the eastern side of the Kennebec river, seventy-eight miles from Bangor, fifty-three from Portland, and six from Augusta. Among the Massachusetts archives is a bill filed with the act of incorporation, which styles ancient Pittston, "Randolph." It passed through all necessary stages to become a law except the signature of the governor. It passed its readings, and was delivered into the hands of John Pitt, January 15, 1779. When, a fortnight later, it was brought forward, it was named Pittston, after his Honor, and so incorporated.[1] It is not known that more than one white person penetrated as far as Pittston and established a residence prior to Philip's war. This is supposed to have been one Alexander Brown, who located a house on an interval known by the name of "Kerdoormeorp," and afterwards as "Brown's farm," in 1670. He remained there, engaged in sturgeon-fishing, until Philip's war broke out; soon after which, in 1676, he was murdered by the Indians, and his house burned. In 1716, Noyes built a fort near Nahumkeag Island, which was also destroyed by the Indians. In 1751, Captain North laid out lots one mile wide on the river, and extending five miles west, from Nahumkeag Island to old Richmond fort.

From old maps and records, it appears that the government of Massa-

[1] Hanson's History of Gardiner and Pittston.

chusetts built Fort Halifax, in 1754, on the Kennebec. About this time, Dr. Gardiner began his plans, from which first sprang the settlement of ancient Pittston. This region filled up rapidly from 1759; and Dr. Gardiner, from various donations, became almost sole owner of Gardiner and Pittston, and of much of the territory in other parts of the old Kennebec province. In 1764, James Winslow received a deed of ninety acres of land in what is now Pittston, on which he settled the year previous. The names of Berry, McCausland, Philbrook, Tibbetts, Smith, Colburn, and Bailey, are found among the records of settlers from 1761 to 1765. From the settlement of the plantation down as late as 1790 the civil affairs seem to have been in a very loose state, — no governing power exercised; and to collect debts or obtain justice was next to impossible. Things assumed a different face on the appointment of General Dearborn as marshal, 1790. General Dearborn's house then stood near where now stands the Gardiner Bank. "Near the spot occupied by the town-house stood a whipping-post, where many an unruly varlet received the barbarous reward of those times for his offence, as meted to him by General Dearborn. Benjamin Shaw was usually the constable, and laid on the lashes. So great was the fear felt by culprits of his strength, that when he wished to make an arrest he had only to send his jackknife to the victim, and they were few who failed to return the knife to its owner." Much of the early history of Pittston is identified with that of Gardiner, and the first settlers were more or less connected with each.

The town of Pittston contains an area of 21,300 acres. It is about seven miles long from north to south, and five miles wide from east to west. The soil is very excellent, and diversified with hills and valleys, ponds and streams. At the time of its settlement, much of the timber was white oak. The "Pebble hills" are situated in the southwestern part, on the "Haley farm." They consist entirely of small pebbles drifted into eminences, and, although excavations to the depth of some eighty feet have been made, nothing else is found. The village of Pittston is beautifully located on the bank of the Kennebec, has good water-power, and is celebrated for the thrift and energy of its people. The principal occupations of the inhabitants are ship-building and agriculture. Pittston has nineteen school districts, with thirty-six schools; an academy in a very flourishing condition; two Methodist, two Congregational, a Baptist, and one or two other churches; and three post-offices — Pittston, East Pittston, and North Pittston. Population, 2,823; valuation, $593,319.

PLOUGH PATENT was a tract of land extending from Casco bay to Cape Porpoise on the seaboard, and about forty miles into the country. It was a grant issued in 1629 to John Dy and other citizens of London by the Plymouth Council, and included lands which had been granted to Mason and Gorges in 1622. It also covered the lands which had been granted earlier in the year 1629 to the patentees of Saco and Biddeford. The cause of this singular proceeding on the part of the council, of making a grant of lands previously held under former grants, has never been discovered. It is, however, generally attributed to their ignorance of the situation of this part of the country. The name of the patent is supposed to have been derived from the name of the ship, "the Plough," in which the grantees, or persons sent by them, came over from England. There is, however, no satisfactory evidence that any of the original owners of the Plough Patent ever visited their new province.

Gorges remained undisturbed in that part of his possessions covered by this patent until 1646, when it was sold to Alexander Rigby, a member of the Long Parliament. Gorges resisted the claim of Rigby; but, as Gorges was a royalist and Rigby a republican, and as the republicans were in power, it was, to say the least, a most unfavorable occasion for Gorges to urge his claim, however just and honorable it might have been. In 1647, Gorges died, leaving the matter unsettled, and Rigby master of the field. Rigby died in 1650, and, for a brief season, the distracted province enjoyed repose; but before the noise of the previous contention had died away, the colonists of Massachusetts Bay, by a wonderful stretch of the limits of their charter, declared themselves the rightful proprietors of the province of Maine. The matter did not subside here; but again and again became a bone of contention, and remained unsettled until the Massachusetts Colony, by the positive command of King Charles II., yielded up the province to a son of Sir John Gorges, an heir of Sir Ferdinando. In the year 1677, Massachusetts purchased the province for £1,250 sterling; and thus ended the long contest for a jurisdiction, which, after all, was deemed of no more value than a few hundred pounds.

PLYMOUTH, in the westerly part of Penobscot county, twenty-two miles from Bangor, was incorporated in 1826. Martin stream runs through it into Newport pond, affording water-power which is made serviceable in propelling mills. The soil is productive, and well timbered with the usual varieties. The Penobscot and Kennebec Railroad passes the northwest corner of the town. There are six school districts, with seven schools; one post-office, and one church — Baptist; also one grist-mill, two saw-mills, and one carriage factory. Population, 925; valuation, $80,272.

POLAND, Androscoggin county, eight miles above Lewiston, adjoins Cumberland county, and is thirty-six miles southwest of Augusta. It was originally called Bakerstown, and embraced Minot and Auburn within its limits. Nathaniel Bailey and Daniel Lane were the first settlers; and John Newman followed in 1769. Chandler Freeman with his family, and Joseph Freeman and his wife, moved here in 1784; and, in 1786, Samuel Pool came in. The first religious meeting was held in 1784, in the house of Chandler Freeman; his father, Joseph Freeman, officiating. The first church (Congregational) was formed September 8, 1791; and, two years afterward, Rev. Jonathan Scott was called to preach. The town was incorporated February 17, 1798. When the place was first settled, game abounded, and there are many anecdotes related of the narrow escapes which the inhabitants had in hunting.

Poland is almost exclusively an agricultural community, though the land is only of an average quality. Water is supplied by several ponds, and by the Little Androscoggin river, on which the town is situated. A very pleasant and thriving little village has been built up by the industry and perseverance of the inhabitants. A family, of the denomination called "Shakers," have located here, and have supplied themselves with six hundred acres of the best land within the precincts of the town. They are in no way different from others of this sect, and pursue all those habits of thrift and economy for which they are peculiar. The Grand Trunk Railway passes through Poland. There are three religious denominations — Congregational, Methodist, and Freewill Baptist; twenty-three school districts, with twenty-five schools; three post-offices — Poland, East Poland, and West Poland; four saw-mills, one grist-mill, one tannery, and one carriage factory. Population, 2,660; valuation, $333,168.

PORTER, Oxford county, lies one hundred miles southwest from Augusta, and forty miles west-northwest from Portland. The Great Ossipee river separates it from Parsonsfield, in the county of York, and the New Hampshire line makes its western boundary. This township, containing 18,500 acres (including Timothy Cutler's upper grant of 3,500 acres), was purchased of Massachusetts on the 24th of September, 1795, by Dr. Aaron Porter of Biddeford, Caleb Emery of Sanford, Thomas Cutts of Pepperrellborough, and their associates, for the sum of £564 lawful money. By the provisions of their grant, they were required to appropriate 320 acres for schools, a like number of acres for the first settled minister, and a like number for the support of the ministry. They were also required to appropriate one hundred acres of land for each of the following settlers, who settled in the township before the 1st day of January, 1784, namely: Mesheeh Libby,[1] Stephen Libby,[1] John Libby, and James Rankins. These four were the only settlers until 1787, when Benjamin Bickford, Benjamin Bickford, Jr., Samuel Bickford (from Rochester, N. H.), and Benjamin Ellenwood from Groton, became settlers. About 1791, David Allord, Joseph Clark, and Moses Drown from Rochester, N. H., arrived, and became permanent residents. Most of the original settlers were soldiers of the Revolution; and in their newly selected home, encountered, for fifteen or twenty years, all those hardships and privations incident to a pioneer life.

Porter was incorporated February 20, 1807. It is six miles in length by four and a half in width, and contains about twenty-three square miles. The territory, it is said, was a portion of the Pequawket territory; and, at the time of its purchase, adjoined Fryeburg. At the time of its incorporation, however, about two fifths of its northerly portion was annexed to Brownfield. The surface is generally uneven, containing many hills of considerable height, on which is excellent pasturage. A large number of cattle are annually raised for market. The soil is well adapted to the raising of Indian corn, potatoes, wheat, rye, and oats, which are cultivated to a considerable extent. There are many good orchards of natural and grafted fruit, of nearly every description.

Mine mountain, though not large, is celebrated on account of its having been operated upon for mining purposes about the year 1802, by William Towle. He discovered what he supposed to be gold and silver near the top of its southern slope, and perforated it at right angles with the slope nearly one hundred feet, by burning and blasting; but, finding nothing save small portions of lead, iron, and a very small portion of silver ore, he finally abandoned the enterprise as useless. Rattlesnake mountain, so called from the large number of rattlesnakes found here, was visited by the first settlers, who annually captured a large number of these reptiles for the purposes of procuring their skins and oil; at the present day there are none of them to be found in the vicinity. Quite a number of good water privileges exist, the most of which are occupied. There are also a number of ponds, the two largest of which are the Colcord and Bickford ponds, the former covering about 150 acres, and the latter about one hundred. At the outlet of each are a saw-mill, a grist-mill, a shingle machine, and a clapboard machine. Spectacle ponds, which take their name from their form, situated in the southeast portion, though not of any great size, are beautiful sheets of water.

Porter was originally well timbered with white pine and white and

[1] These two settlers were the first in town, having arrived here about the year 1781. They came from Rye, N. H.

red oak; but it has nearly all disappeared, and a young growth is now rapidly appearing. There are three meeting-houses, all of which are free; one village, situated on the Great Ossipee river, about four miles from the New Hampshire line, in which there are three stores, one meeting-house, one saw-mill, one shingle machine, one wheelwright's shop, three blacksmith's shops, and a post-office. There are also thirteen school districts, with the same number of schools. Population, 1,208; valuation, $165,198.

PORTLAND, Cumberland county, situated on Casco bay, was originally embraced within the town of Falmouth, as were also Westbrook and Cape Elizabeth, together with a number of large and valuable islands in Casco bay, lying at the mouth of the harbor. The first settlement was made in what is now Portland, by George Cleeves and Richard Tucker, who established themselves near the mouth of the Spurwink river, in 1630. This tract, however, being claimed by Robert Trelawny and Moses Goodyear, merchants of Plymouth, England, by virtue of a grant made to them by the council of Plymouth, a contest was commenced between John Winter, the agent of Trelawny, on the one part, and Cleeves and Tucker on the other. Winter succeeded, in the Provincial court, in sustaining the title of Trelawny; and the ejected parties sought refuge, in 1632, on the Neck, now Portland.

This Neck, Cleeves declared, was known first by the name of Machigonne: being a neck of land which was in no man's possession or occupation, he seized upon it as his own inheritance, by virtue of a royal proclamation of King James of England, by which proclamation the king freely "gave unto every subject of his who should transport himself over into this country upon his own charge, for himself and for every person that he should so transport, 150 acres of land." Cleeves further declared, that he "continued the occupation from year to year under this possession, without interruption or demand of any; at the end of which time, being desirous to enlarge his limits in a lawful way, he addressed himself to Sir Ferdinando Gorges, the proprietor of the Province of Maine, and obtained, for a sum of money and other considerations, a warrantable lease of enlargement, bounded as by relation thereunto had doth and may appear."[1] This was the origin of Portland, which was first called Cleeves's Neck, then Munjoy Neck, and sometimes Casco and Old Casco, from its position on Casco river and bay.

[1] This statement is made in an action, which Winter brought against Cleeves in 1640, to recover possession of this tract also, claiming the whole under the grant made to Trelawny; but in this he failed, and Cleeves was left in full possession.

Portland is probably as rich in historical associations as any locality in Maine; and to trace them through their various phases would require a greater space than the limits of this work will permit. In July, 1658, the settlement received the name of Falmouth, from Massachusetts, and its limits are thus stated: "Those places formerly called Spurwink and Casco bay, from the east side of Spurwink river to the Clapboard islands in Casco bay, shall run back eight miles into the country." Previous to 1675, the period of the first Indian war, the settlements embraced in this territory had advanced rapidly. The part now occupied by Portland had, however, fewer inhabitants than were at other points, — Cleeves occupying the eastern extremity of the Neck,[1] the family of Michael Mitton (Cleeves's son-in-law) the western, and Tucker the central part. When that war commenced, there were five or six persons with their families on the Neck, namely: Thomas Brackett, George Munjoy, John Munjoy, his son, George Burroughs, the minister, and Elizabeth Harvey, the daughter of Cleeves.[2] Every thing was very prosperous at this time; but the Indians left not a vestige to tell the tale that here had been a habitation, or any marks of improvement. Thirty-four persons were killed in the whole town; among them Thomas Brackett, John Munjoy, and Isaac Wakely upon the Neck. The family of the first were taken into captivity.

During the continuance of the war, no white person ventured within the desolated locality; but after the conclusion of peace, in November, 1678, George Bramhall purchased the hill which yet bears his name, and prosecuted the tannery business. Anthony Brackett, one of the old settlers, with others, in 1679, resumed their former sites, or procured grants of new lots. In 1680, Fort Loyal was erected at the foot of the present India street, in which, in September of that year, Governor Danforth held a court for the purpose of organizing a new settlement, arranging the inhabitants in a more compact manner, in order that they might better withstand future attacks from the savages. Evidences of renewed activity were manifest, and houses and buildings were erected in different directions. The character of the inhabitants here at that time was superior. Among them were Peter Bowdoin, or, more properly, Pierre Baudouin, and his son-in-law Stephen Boutineau,[3] Philip Barger, Philip Le Bretton, Augustin Jean (the ancestor of the Gustins now liv-

[1] Cleeves's house fronted on the bay, just east of India street, and his corn-field stretched westerly to near Clay cove.

[2] Mitton, her former husband, was at this time dead.

[3] These were French Huguenots, who fled from France on the repeal of the edict of Nantes. Mr. Bowdoin was a physician of Rochelle, who subsequently established himself in Boston, and was the ancestor of the distinguished family there of that name.

ing here), George Burroughs,[1] the minister, Thaddeus Clark, the Bracketts, Sylvanus Davis, John Graves, Henry Harwood, the Ingersolls, Robert Lawrence, and Edward Tyng. In ten years, the inhabitants in Falmouth had increased to seven hundred. Twenty-five families resided on the Neck; and every effort was being made in the way of progress, and peace and plenty were rewarding their labors, when the blast of war warned them that prosperity could not be enjoyed without interruption.

In the autumn of 1689, Major Benjamin Church, of Plymouth Colony, a terrible enemy of the Indians, who had been commissioned as commander of an expedition to the eastward, arrived here most opportunely to thwart the designs of a body of French and Indians, some seven hundred strong, who came in at the same time, and landed on Peak's island. Measures were immediately taken for defence; the troops landed with as little noise as possible, and the next morning, an hour before daybreak, marched, accompanied by many of the townsmen, "to a thick place of brush, about half a mile from the town." The enemy, too, had not been idle; for, during the night, they had shifted their quarters to the upper portion of the Neck, and at day-dawn, September 21, approached the farm of Anthony Brackett, whose house stood where the one now or lately occupied by Mr. Deering stands, at the junction of the roads. Brackett's sons gave the alarm, and Captain Hall's company, being in advance, hastened to meet the enemy, which they did in Brackett's orchard, where the action was principally fought. Church, on hearing the alarm, soon came to the rescue with a reinforcement, and a supply of ammunition, which was transported across Back Cove Creek by one of the friendly Indians. The reserve force of the English took up a position on this side of the creek, prepared to support Captain Hall. After contending hotly for some time, Major Church informed Captain Hall that he designed assaulting the enemy in the rear, and immediately advanced up the creek to execute his purpose; but the enemy, perceiving it, made a precipitate retreat, hotly pursued, to the forests. Finding that they were met with a number equal, if not superior, to their own, they gave up the idea of further depredations that season. Eleven were killed on the English side, and ten wounded, of whom Mr. Freeze, Mr. Bramhall, and one friendly Indian, died of their wounds. Captain Brackett was also killed, as well as a negro belonging to Colonel Tyng. Had it not been for the timely intervention of

[1] Mr. Burroughs fell a victim to fanaticism, having been tried for witchcraft at Salem, May 8, 1692, and executed on the 19th of August following.

Church, the whole people must have been utterly cut off. As it was, the enemy saw their plans frustrated by the unexpected movements of the Major; and that they would soon be completely in his power: they therefore, after an action which had lasted six hours, made a hasty retreat; but, as the sequel shows, with a determination to renew the attack, whenever a favorable opportunity should occur. Many of the inhabitants, fearing this, sought places of greater security; but a large proportion, through the assurance of Church that he would endeavor to return the next spring with a protecting force, remained. A garrison of fifteen soldiers, with a commander and gunner, was left by Church in the fort, and sixty soldiers in the town, when he departed, with the sincere thanks, but deep regret, of the settlers. A quiet but anxious winter was passed, during which garrisons were sustained in Fort Loyal, at Lawrence's stone house on the hill, at George Ingersoll's, foot of Exchange street, and in another part of the Neck not known. The enemy did not remain long inactive. Captain Willard, of Salem, who was in command at this point, was taken off with the regular troops for other operations, leaving the defence of the place entirely to the inhabitants, which the enemy were not slow to discover. In May, 1690, the force which, in February, destroyed Schenectady, N. Y., joined the eastern Indians, and soon after appeared in Casco bay, where they took Robert Greason, belonging to this place, prisoner. Captain Sylvanus Davis commanded Fort Loyal, and ordered that the people should not leave their garrisons, but keep constant watch to prevent surprise. Lieutenant Clark and thirty men, however, with more zeal than precaution, neglected this advice, and precipitated the destruction of the settlement. Being desirous to gain some information with regard to the enemy, they proceeded to the summit of the hill (probably Munjoy's), which was covered with woods, having a lane with a fence on each side, and a block-house (probably Lawrence's) at the end. When they came up, they found the cattle looking alarmed towards the fence, afraid to pass into the wood; and the party immediately suspected that the enemy were in covert there. Lieutenant Clark and his men concluded that the best way to get rid of the difficulty was to boldly face it, and, in the hope of intimidating the enemy, advanced quickly to the fence with a loud shout. But the enemy were fully prepared for them, and poured upon the little party a deadly fire, which killed the lieutenant and thirteen men, when the remainder ran hastily to the block-house. This was attacked; but was defended with great bravery all night, when the inmates abandoned the garrison, and sought security in Fort Loyal. On the morning of May 16, the enemy burnt the house, and forthwith turned their attention to the fort, which they besieged with their full force, consisting of about four or five hundred French and Indians, under command of Mons. Burniffe. The fort stood on a rocky bluff (now occupied by the station of the Atlantic and St. Lawrence Railroad), under which the enemy worked with perfect security, being out of reach of the guns, and in no danger, by their superior number, from a sortie from the small force within the fort. The siege was prosecuted actively five days and four nights, in which they "killed the greater part of the English, and burned all the houses." Being ultimately worn out by the continued watching and defence, the besieged capitulated on the 20th of May. The articles of capitulation, which were solemnly sworn to by the French, were disregarded, and the commander "suffered," says Captain Davis, "our women and children and our men to be made captives in the hands of the heathen, to be cruelly murdered and destroyed, many of them, and especially our wounded men; only the French kept myself and three or four more, and carried us overland to Canada." The captives arrived at Quebec, June 14, after twenty-four days' march through the wilderness. Captain Davis, after four months' captivity, was exchanged.

Thus sank this rising settlement a second time. Among those killed were Lieutenant Clark, Thomas Cloice, Seth Brackett, Thomas Alsop, Edward Crocker, George Bogwell, and a soldier from Lynn, named James Ramsdell. Captain Robert Lawrence and Anthony Brackett, Jr., were mortally wounded; and James Ross and Peter Morrill were among the prisoners. Ross was likewise wounded, having had his collar-bone split and cut off, and suffered considerably from the Indians while in Canada; for which he received, in 1726, a pension of five pounds per annum. John Parker[1] and his son, James, who sought refuge in Fort Loyal from the Indians on the Kennebec, were also among the killed.

In August, 1703, the settlements at Falmouth called Spurwink and Purpooduck were entirely destroyed, — no less than twenty-two being killed and taken captive in the former place. Purpooduck, having a population of nine families, was visited by the Indians, when all the men were from home, and twenty-five of the inhabitants butchered in the most barbarous manner, while eight were taken prisoners. Some of their atrocities are too horrible to describe.

Some of the inhabitants began to return to Falmouth about 1708; but the settlement on the Neck was not permanently resumed until after the peace of Utrecht, in 1713. Elisha Ingersoll, Major Samuel Moody, Benjamin Larrabee, Benjamin Skillings, Zachariah Brackett,

[1] This gentleman was the great-great-grandfather of the late Isaac Parker, chief justice of Massachusetts, and son of John Parker, who came from Biddeford, England, to Saco, Maine.

Richard Collier, Samuel Proctor, James Doughty, Mark Rounds, James Mills, Ebenezer Hall, Thomas Thomes, John Wass, John Barbour, and John Gustin settled principally on the Neck, between 1716 and 1718.[1] In 1722, further troubles with the Indians retarded the growth of the settlement. In 1725, after the close of hostilities, there were about forty-five families in the place, twenty-seven of whom were upon the Neck. A meeting-house, which was in course of construction five years previous, was completed in 1728, and stood on the junction of the present King and Middle streets. A church had been formed the previous year, over which Rev. Thomas Smith was ordained pastor, being the only minister in the settlement for many years. A saw-mill and grist-mill were in operation; and at this time, the settlement at Falmouth was considered, with one exception, — that of York, — the chief one in the state. In September, 1733, Robert Bayley was employed as schoolmaster.

A gradual and steady progress was made from this time, with some slight interruptions from the Indians; and, in 1749, there was a population of some 2,346, of which 720 were on the Neck, with 120 dwelling-houses (all of wood, many of them but one story high, and generally unpainted), most of which were below the present site of Centre street. That part above Centre street was covered with wood and swamp; and was, in the strictest sense of the term, an "eminent wilderness." The business was transacted at the lower end, around the foot of India street, where was the landing. The principal business occupations were in lumber and wood, and in fish. Ship-building was also a prominent branch of business. In 1752 there were seven schooners and fifteen sloops owned on the Neck; now the shipping exceeds over 79,000 tons. The people were hardy and industrious, and all the rich men, and those who have been rich, in Portland, were either mariners or mechanics, or descendants of persons in those occupations. Among the most prominent men here at this time were the Moodys, Freeman, Longfellow, Fox, Waldo, Westbrook, Cushing, Noyes, John Wiswell, and the two ministers, Smith and Allen. In 1735, the settlement was made the half-shire town with York, and the Court of Common Pleas and Sessions of the Peace were appointed to be held alternately, in January and October, here and at York. There was no regular mail east of Portsmouth till 1760, and then but once a week. Previous to that time, letters were reserved till a sufficient number accumulated to

[1] Many of these, and others who came in, were new settlers, and located on the land without any shadow of title, which, as a consequence, led to endless disputes between the old proprietors and the new, which were ultimately settled in the supreme court in May, 1731.

pay for the expense, when they were despatched either on the back of a man or a horse. Several important conferences were held here with the Indians, which gave the place considerable distinction.

Many of the inhabitants took part in the various expeditions carried on by the English against the French in the subjugation of Canada, and a number lost their lives in the service. The difficulties which hastened the Revolution brought on the destruction of Falmouth or Portland the third time. Several circumstances raised the ire of the British against the town, one of which, in March, 1775, was the trouble with Thomas Coulson, a tory, for whom a vessel, arriving about this time, brought rigging and stores for a new ship he had built, and also a considerable cargo of goods and merchandise. These the Committee of Safety and Inspection determined ought not to be used, according to the agreement of the "American Association," and ordered that they should be returned to England in the vessel that brought them. Several attempts were made by Coulson to carry out his designs, in opposition to the command of the committee; but he was held in check by threats from the populace. Finally, through his instrumentality, the *Canseau* sloop-of-war, Captain Mowett, arrived in the harbor, and through her protection Coulson accomplished what otherwise he had failed to do, — rig his vessel, and put on board the goods and merchandise. Considerable opposition was met from the populace, and none of them could be hired to assist Coulson, but were pressed into the obnoxious service by the petty tyranny of Mowett. This conduct on his part, as might be imagined, made him very unpopular with the citizens; and on May 9, the captain, with his surgeon, and Rev. Mr. Wiswell, Episcopal minister, were, while on shore, made prisoners by a party of volunteers under the direction of Colonel Samuel Thompson of Brunswick. This was followed by a threat from the sailing-master of the *Canseau*, that if Captain Mowett was not released he would lay the town in ashes, which caused great consternation, and a general stampede amongst some of the inhabitants. Thompson, notwithstanding this threat, and the expostulations of some of the first citizens, refused to set the prisoners at large till night; when, through excessive importunity, they were released on parole, — General Preble and Colonel Freeman being pledges for their appearance at nine the following morning. Mowett, however, failed to appear, which so exasperated the volunteers, who had in the mean time collected in considerable numbers from the towns in the vicinity, that they threatened to attack the vessel, provided Mowett continued in the harbor; and exhibited other marks of displeasure and discontent. Coulson's dwelling-house was rifled, his boats drawn through the streets, and several persons, who were thought to be tories, were dealt with in a manner which soon proved to have been very ill-advised. The crowd at last dispersed, and Mowett, accompanied by Coulson in his own ship, left the harbor for Portsmouth.

On Monday, the 16th of October following, a squadron of four armed vessels, consisting of the *Canseau*, the *Cat*, a ship of war, a large cutter schooner, and a small bomb ship, arrived in the harbor, and anchored about a league from the town. They were commanded by Captain Mowett; but the people were at a loss to divine the object of the visit, unless it were to obtain without charge a supply of provisions from the islands, which the inhabitants took measures to prevent. The next day, however, the mystery was cleared up. The vessels were towed up towards the wharves, and, about four o'clock in the afternoon, were moored in line near the compact part of the town. A messenger with a flag was sent on shore by Mowett, who brought a letter from the captain, filled with regrets which he did not feel, and making assertions which were wholly untrue. The substance was, that, in consequence of the bad behavior of the inhabitants towards the mother country, he had orders "to execute a just punishment on the town of Falmouth," and gave them two hours to remove themselves and what was valuable from its precincts. Not having given any just cause for such a proceeding, the people were greatly surprised; and a meeting was held, at which a committee was appointed to confer with the captain, and learn, if possible, the reasons for this summary vengeance, which was about to be taken on them. The reply of Captain Mowett was, "my orders I have received from Admiral Graves, and they direct me to repair to the place with all expedition, take my position near the town, and burn, sink, and destroy; and this without giving the people warning! The note you have received is of special grace, at the risk of my commission." They used every argument with him against the execution of such a cruel mandate, till time was allowed to consult the admiral; but he only replied that his orders applied alike to every seaport on the continent, and concluded by offering some very humiliating conditions, which were the delivery over to him of various munitions of war, — by the fulfilment of which they might save the town from destruction till communication was had with the admiral. These terms the people, in order to gain time, complied with in part; but decided, at a meeting in the morning, not to fulfil *in toto*. In the last conference held with Mowett, the committee conjured him, by every claim of justice and humanity, to spare the work of destruction for a short period; but his only answer was, that he would give them *thirty minutes, and no more*.

About nine the same morning, the firing was opened from the vessels on the ill-fated town, and was urged with considerable briskness, — balls weighing from three to nine pounds being poured like showers of hail upon the most thickly built part. What was not accomplished by the guns was done by armed parties from the vessels; and though the watchful citizens succeeded in protecting some buildings from destruction, many parts of the village were soon in a blaze. The cannonading lasted some nine hours; and, with the exception of the Congregational meeting-house, about one hundred of the poorer dwelling-houses, and a few wharves, every thing[1] in the once thriving town was one mass of blackened ruins. One hundred and sixty families, which the day previous were in comfortable circumstances, were thrown upon the world, almost without food, or covering to protect them from the inclemency of the winter, fast approaching. After the accomplishment of his work of devastation, Mowett with his fleet departed. "Yet his name lives to be execrated, and his dark deeds are portrayed, to teach base men what indelible infamy shall cleave to their memories long after their relics have mouldered to their original element."[2] The last visit which was made by the British to the town was by Captain Symonds, in a large war ship, shortly after this destruction, and when the inhabitants were engaged in erecting forts for defence. He commanded them to desist from the work; but finding the inhabitants paid no regard to him, and that his ship was exposed to an attack, he made a precipitate retreat. Cape Elizabeth was incorporated from Falmouth, November 1, 1765; Portland, July 4, 1786; and Westbrook, February 14, 1814.

Portland is the capital of Cumberland county. It was incorporated as a city in 1832. The peninsula projects eastwardly into the bay, is about three miles in length, and has an average width of three fourths of a mile. Its surface rises from each shore, forming throughout an elevated ridge, which, at its extremities, rises again into considerable hills, presenting a marked outline and very beautiful appearance. The city is regularly laid out and handsomely built, particularly its more modern portions, which are noted for their elegant buildings. The streets, and many of the houses, are lighted with gas. The main street occupies the ridge of the peninsula, extending from hill to hill. Many of the streets are lined with elm and other shade trees, presenting a truly delightful appearance. The natural advantages of the city for trade and commerce have been well improved by its enterprising citizens. The harbor is capacious and safe, and is considered among the best in the United States. It is protected by islands from the violence of storms.

[1] St. Paul's church, the new court-house, the town-house, the public library, the fire-engine, about 130 dwelling-houses, 230 stores and warehouses, a great number of stables and outhouses, and about one half the merchandise, furniture, and goods were destroyed.

[2] Williamson, vol. ii., p. 437.

has a good entrance, and is defended by Forts Preble and Scammel. the former of which is garrisoned by United States artillery. The foreign commerce of the city is chiefly with the West Indies and Europe, the chief exports being lumber, ice, fish, and provisions. The coasting trade is principally with Boston, and, during the summer, steamboats run daily to that city. On the 30th June, 1857, the total tonnage of the district was 145,242 tons, of which 109,926 tons were registered, and 35,316 tons enrolled and licensed. The registered tonnage consisted of 85,696 tons permanent, and 24,229 tons temporary. The enrolled and licensed tonnage consisted of 34,437 tons "permanent," which were employed as follows: In coasting trade, 29,722 tons; in cod fishery, 2,704 tons; in mackerel fishery, 2,011 tons; and 878 tons. "licensed under twenty tons," which were in the cod fishery. The number of vessels built in 1857 was twenty, namely, eighteen ships and barques, and two schooners, with an aggregate tonnage of 12,925.

Portland has several public buildings, the principal of which are the City Hall, the Court-house, Grand Trunk Railway Depot, an Athenæum, incorporated in 1827, and containing a library of upwards of six thousand volumes; and several spacious hotels, among which may be mentioned the Machigonne House, now in process of erection by the Hon. John M. Wood, said to be the largest building in the state. The new custom-house and post-office building, recently erected on Exchange street, is a stately granite structure, and is a credit to the United States government, and an ornament to the city. At the eastern extremity of the city is a tower, seventy feet high, and 220 feet above tide water, which was erected for the purpose of observing vessels at sea. and is furnished with signals. The harbor is connected by the Cumberland and Oxford canal, twenty and a half miles long, with Sebago pond, and thence with Long pond.

Four important railroads now centre at Portland, and contribute greatly to its prosperity. The Portland, Saco, and Portsmouth Railroad. fifty-one miles long, was opened in 1842, completing the line of railroad from Boston to this city, one hundred and five miles. The extension of this route, called the Kennebec and Portland Railroad, is completed to Augusta, sixty miles. The York and Cumberland Railroad, now open to Buxton, eighteen miles, when completed will connect, at Great Falls, with the Boston and Maine Railroad. The construction of the Atlantic and St. Lawrence Railroad, or the Grand Trunk Railway, as it is now more usually called, commenced in 1846, from each terminus — Portland and Montreal — and was completed in 1853. Over this important thoroughfare passes a large portion of the products of the North and West for shipment to Europe.

DANIEL WEBSTER

There are twenty-two churches in the city, and seven banks, with an aggregate capital of $2,075,000. The capital of the city is chiefly employed in commerce, coasting and inland trade, and the fisheries; hence its manufactures are, for the most part, those incident to a mercantile city. The Portland Company, with a capital of $250,000, have a large establishment for the manufacture of locomotives and railroad cars. Much attention is given to education in the public schools, which consist of a classical school for boys, a high school for girls, four grammar-schools, (two for boys and two for girls,) and the primary schools. There are also numerous private schools, and an academy; and three daily newspapers — *The Advertiser* (Republican); *State of Maine* (Republican), and *Eastern Argus* (Democrat), which also issue tri-weekly and weekly editions. Besides these, there are seven weeklies, namely: *The Transcript* (Literary); *Christian Mirror* (Orthodox Congregational); *Zion's Advocate* (Baptist); *Journal and Inquirer* (Maine Law); *Pleasure Boat* (Miscellaneous); *Cold Water Fountain* (Temperance); and *The Scholar's Leaf* (Educational), issued semi-monthly. There is one post-office. Population estimated at 30,000; valuation for 1858, $22,260,290.

POWNAL is situated in the eastern part of Cumberland county, and contains an area of about 18,000 acres. Its early history is merged in that of Freeport, of which it formed the northwest part until March 3, 1808, when it was incorporated by its present name. In May, 1807, the inhabitants, at a town-meeting, chose a committee, consisting of Barstow Sylvester, Josiah Reed, and Thomas Means, in behalf of the lower part of the town, which is now Freeport, and Edward Thompson, Lebbeus Tuttle, and Jabez True, for the upper part (or the proposed new town), to agree to a line of separation. The committee reported that they had agreed upon a line, which report was accepted on the 18th of May, as certified by John Cushing and Cornelius Dillingham, selectmen. The petition to the legislature had forty-one signatures, among which appear those of Edmund Cleaves, Jacob Davis, Joseph Hutchins, Nathaniel Noyes, Benjamin A. Richardson, Edward Thompson, William Sawyer, Benjamin Humphrey, and Jabez True. An order of notice on the petition was made returnable to the next general court, when the act was passed. The surface is undulating, and the soil generally of a productive character. The inhabitants are devoted principally to agricultural pursuits. Pownal is watered by the eastern branches of Royall's river, none of which have sufficient power for propelling machinery. There are three religious societies — two Methodist and one Congregational; twelve school districts, and three post-offices — Pownal, North Pownal, and West Pownal; also one grist-mill, and one carriage factory. Population, 1,074; valuation, $241,550.

PRINCETON is situated in the eastern part of Washington county, on the Baring and Houlton road, at the outlet of the chain of lakes which extend some thirty miles westwardly toward the Penobscot river. The head of these lakes is near the source of the Passadumkeag, a tributary of the Penobscot river. When clear of ice, these lakes and their tributaries are navigable to the remotest point, at all seasons of the year. A heavy and valuable growth of hard and soft timber borders their shores, from which immense quantities are cut annually for the mills at Baring and Calais, and yet the supply is not sensibly diminished. But few settlements have as yet been made upon the banks of these streams, which are said, in many places, to contain excellent land. A railroad has just been completed from tide-water at Calais to Princeton, a distance of twenty miles, called the Lewey's Island Railroad, which has its terminus at a wharf on the lower lake. By this road immense quantities of lumber will be taken annually to market.

There is an excellent water-power at this place, having all these lakes as a reservoir, which is now only partially occupied, but which erelong will be one of the lumber marts of Maine. The Lewey's Island Railroad will be one of the links in the projected European and North American Railroad, and this town will be one of the depots through which will flow the productions of two continents. This will not happen in a day; but time will consummate the enterprise. The town was incorporated in 1832, and has four school districts and two post-offices — Princeton and South Princeton. Population, 280; valuation, $24,314.

PROSPECT, Waldo county, is situated on the west side of Penobscot river, and has about eight miles of shore, extending from the northerly line of Stockton to Marsh bay. The first historical event of note was the erection of a small fort by Governor Pownall,[1] on the spot now known as Fort Point, in Stockton, — vestiges of which are still standing, — commenced in the year 1758, and completed July 28, 1759, at a cost of £4,969 17*s*. 6*d*., the expenses being reimbursed by parliament. The ditch by which it is surrounded was originally about twelve feet deep, but rubbish has accumulated in it to such an extent that it is now not over six feet in depth. The old well which supplied the garrison with water is still in existence, though partially filled up. This fort was

[1] See *Gov. Pownall's Journal*, in Maine Hist. Coll. V. art. 6.

erected, as stated by the governor, in his speech to the General Court, June 1, 1759, "that the last door which the enemy had to the Atlantic (by the Penobscot) might be shut forever." That body approved the measure, and called the fortification *Fort Pownall.* A garrison was kept here until the Revolutionary war. Gen. Jedediah Preble had command of it until 1763; Col. Thomas Goldthwaite until 1770, when he was superseded by John Preble, son of the general, but was reinstated by Gov. Hutchinson the next year. Being a tory, he permitted Capt. Mowett, with a man-of-war, to take possession of it, in 1775, and the latter dismantled it. In the year 1779, Col. Cargill, of Newcastle, fearing its occupation by the enemy, burned all the erections to the ground.

The first inhabitants, some of whom had been soldiers in the French and Indian wars, settled near the above fort. John Odom, who settled at Sandy Point, about three miles above the fort, and who built the first mill on the Penobscot river, a Mr. Clifford, a Mr. Treat, Charles Curtis, from whom Curtis Point takes its name, and two or three men by the name of Colson, were among the first settlers. Phœbe, a daughter of Mr. Curtis, born February 15, 1770, was the first child claiming nativity in the town. Captain John Odom, the grandson of the Odom alluded to above, is a resident here. He was born March, 1787, and is the oldest sea-captain in Prospect, having followed the sea for forty-five years. He was impressed into the British service, and was at the battle of Corunna, at which Sir John More was killed, where he acted an important part in carrying off the wounded and providing for their wants. He obtained his release from the British service soon after that battle and returned home in 1811, since which he has been engaged in maritime pursuits.

Prospect was incorporated February 29, 1794, at which time it was seventeen miles in length from north to south. Searsport was taken from it in 1845, and Stockton (much the larger part) in 1857, leaving but thirteen square miles to Prospect. About one fourth of the land is fertile, the remainder rocky and mountainous. The south branch of Marsh river runs through the town, and is crossed by three bridges. Ellis, Seavey, and Half-moon ponds are considerable bodies of water, and are each crossed by a strong bridge. Heagan mountain, in the northeast, and Mack mountain, in the west, are the two principal elevations. Sammy's Eddy affords shelter and anchorage for vessels. To the north there is a large marsh, covering an area of two or three hundred acres, which may yet become a source of wealth as a fertilizer. In the vicinity of Fort Knox, a short distance above the ferry to Bucksport, lead ore has been exhumed; but whether it will prove an article of commerce, further developments must determine. The principal business was ship-building, which, since the division, has been mainly transferred to Stockton. In 1854, there were five vessels built, one of which was a ship of 1,200 tons; and in 1855, there were as many more. A superstition was quite rife here, some years ago, respecting some treasures, which were supposed to have been buried by pirates, at a place called the "Cod Lead," a gravel mound, near the north line of the town, directly east of Mosquito Mountain. An immense amount of digging has been performed; but, as yet, money has failed to make its appearance to reward the toilers.

The United States government is erecting a stupendous fortification at East Prospect, which, when finished, will command the entire river above and below. It is called Fort Knox, in honor of General Knox, of Revolutionary fame. Prospect has one village, called North Prospect; but no church edifice. Seven school-houses are distributed through the town, and there are two post-offices — North Prospect and Prospect Ferry. Some manufacturing is done by three saw-mills, one shingle machine, and one grist-mill. Population in 1858, about 900; valuation $101,000.

RANGELY, situated in the western part of Franklin county, comprises an area of 25,792 acres, most of which is wild land. Settlers have been moving into this township for a few years past, and taking up lots, encouraged principally by the lumbermen of Portland and Bangor, who have been doing considerable business about Mooselockmeguntic lake, a part of which lies here. Rangely had for a short time a plantation organization, which was terminated March 8, 1855, by its becoming an incorporated municipality. There are four school districts, with four schools, a Free-will Baptist society, one post-office, one shingle mill, one grist-mill, and one saw-mill. Population, 200; valuation, $21,000.

RAYMOND, Cumberland county, was granted by Massachusetts to William Raymond and company, in 1767, in consideration of their services in the expedition to Canada, and formerly comprised within its limits the town of Casco. The settlement was commenced by Captain Joseph Dingley, in 1771; but there were few families until after the Revolution, when such additions were made to the population from year to year, that, on the 21st June, 1803, it was incorporated, taking its name from Captain Raymond, one of the proprietors.

The soil is hard, gravelly, and, in many places, very stony. A large proportion of the timber growth is white oak, an article of considerable trade. The inhabitants are temperate, economical, and industrious; uniting with these qualities hospitality and liberality in their donations towards benevolent objects. Raymond has been heavily burdened with taxation for public and private purposes. There are three small villages — Raymond, East Raymond, and North Raymond, with a post-office at each; three religious societies — Free-will Baptist, Methodist, and Union; ten school districts, with eighteen schools; also two saw-mills and two grist-mills. Population, 1,142; valuation, $126,901.

READFIELD, Kennebec county, originally constituted the northern part of Winthrop, and was incorporated from it under its present name, March 11, 1791. Its settlement was begun about the year 1760, the same time as that of Winthrop, and the first clearings were made on the south of Chandler's pond. The surface is gently undulating, and the soil strong and productive. It is well watered by ponds and small streams, one of which is Carlton pond, and the other a branch of North pond. The town contains three villages — Kent's Hill, Readfield Corner, and East Readfield; four church edifices — two Methodist, one Free-will Baptist, and one Union; twelve school districts, and twenty-three schools; the Maine Wesleyan Seminary, at Kent's Hill, a flourishing school for young ladies and gentlemen; three post-offices — Readfield, Kent's Hill, and Readfield Depot; the Readfield Woollen Manufacturing Company, employing about twenty-five hands, and having a capital of $20,000; one grist-mill, two saw-mills, one tannery, and one oil-cloth carpet factory. The Androscoggin and Kennebec Railroad passes through the centre of Readfield. Population, 1,985; valuation, $439,723.

RICHMOND, on the west bank of Kennebec river, in Sagadahoc county, was incorporated from the northern part of Bowdoinham in 1823. All that tract of land extending from the mouth of the stream that falls into the Kennebec, at the northerly extremity of Swan Island, up the Kennebec to the mouth of the Cobbossee Contee, and extending back from the Kennebec ten miles, was purchased of the Indians by Christopher Lawson, on the 10th of October, 1649, and was sold by Lawson, July 2, 1650, to Messrs. Clark and Lake. Richmond comprises nearly or quite one half of this tract, and the other half is now Gardiner. In 1719 and 1720 a fortress, called Fort Richmond, was erected here, for the purpose of facilitating the peltry trade with the natives, and for the better security of the settlers against Indian depredations. This fortress was maintained until 1754, when it was dismantled. On the incorporation of Bowdoinham, Richmond was included within its limits, and for many years was involved in a violent controversy between its rightful owners and the proprietors of the Plymouth Patent on the north, who claimed it as a part of their possessions. The advantages that were afforded

24 *

for ship-building and navigation were not lost sight of by the early settlers. The best of ship timber (oak) was easily procurable. There were also as good facilities for launching vessels and sending them to sea as could be desired; and, as a consequence, the inhabitants have always been more or less interested in navigation. The town possesses, for the most part, an even surface, and a tolerably productive soil. Communication is had daily by steamboat between Augusta, Boston, Portland, and Bath. The Kennebec and Portland Railroad renders communication with many of the principal cities and towns easy and expeditious. There are six church edifices — one Congregational, two Free-will Baptist, one Methodist, one Union house, and one Baptist; eleven school districts, with thirty-four schools; two post-offices — Richmond and Richmond Corner; one large steam mill, one door and sash factory, one brass foundery, one large furniture factory, and twenty-two stores. Population in 1850, 2,056, which had increased, in 1857, to about 3,000; valuation at the former date, $405,475, which had increased at the latter date to near $1,000,000.

RIPLEY, Somerset county, was the southern half of Cambridge, and was originally granted by the state of Massachusetts, September 27, 1803, to John S. Frazy, who conveyed it to Charles Vaughan and John Merrick. The survey of the town was commenced in 1809, and completed in 1813. It was settled in 1804 — incorporated December 11, 1816, and named in honor of General Ripley, an officer who distinguished himself in the last war with England. The surface is somewhat uneven, but the soil generally good. It is watered by Maine stream, which forms the northern boundary, and by Indian stream, which has its head waters here. Ripley has one church edifice (Free-will Baptist); five school districts, with ten schools; a few mills, one tannery, and two post-offices — Ripley and West Ripley. Population, 641; valuation, $57,648.

ROBBINSTON, Washington county, situated on the west side of the Saint Croix, opposite Saint Andrew, New Brunswick, was granted by the state of Massachusetts, October 21, 1786, to Edward H. and Nathaniel J. Robbins, in honor of whom the town was named. There were two families here at the time the grant was made, and several others moved in shortly afterwards. Williamson says a post-office was established here as early as 1796. The proprietors entered into the business of clearing a settlement with commendable zeal, and erected a storehouse and other buildings. On the 15th of January, 1810, a committee was chosen by the inhabitants, consisting of John Brewer, Thomas Vose, John Balkham, Obadiah Allen, Abel Brooks, Job Johnson, and Thaddeus Sibley, to present their petition to the legislature for incorporation; and after the usual order of notice made returnable to the next legislature, (from which it appears John Balkham was plantation clerk,) the town was incorporated February 18, 1811. For many years Robbinston was the centre of trade for the neighboring towns. Ship-building and commerce were carried on to such an extent that the harbors of this town and Saint Andrew, as well as Passamaquoddy bay, were white with shipping. The ports of Europe furnished ready markets for the class of ships built here, but, with the changes of fashion in ship-building, the trade has declined, and left to the place but a fraction of its pristine glory in this business.

More nearly allied with Robbinston than any other place, from its close proximity, is Neutral island, (so called from its position in the middle of the river, which divides the two countries). It is quite small, its area probably not much exceeding six acres; and is noted only for having furnished, as is supposed, the winter-quarters of the explorer, Pierre De Monts, in 1604–5.[1] Apprehending danger from the savages, he erected a fortification upon the north part, which entirely commanded the river. Traces of this, still in existence, were found in 1798, by the commissioners appointed by England and the United States, sent to determine the boundary in this vicinity, some dispute about the same having grown out of the indefiniteness of the treaty of 1783.[2] Great mortality prevailed among De Monts's men in that dreadful winter, generally supposed to have been from scurvy; but, in the opinion of some, from drinking water from the wells (several of which were dug by De Monts), poisoned by the Indians, in retaliation for injuries received. There is but one house on the island — the residence of the keeper of the light-house. This light-house was erected in 1856. The British government relinquished all claim to the island upon the final settlement

Site of the old fortification at Neutral Island.

[1] L'Escarbot's Hist. De Monts's Voyages; abridged in 5 Purchas's Pilgrims, p. 1619. — *Harv. Coll. Library.* "The colony of De Monts was made up of Romanists and Protestants. Among the latter was L'Escarbot, who was a Huguenot minister." — *Bartlet's Frontier Missionary*, p. 240, note. Consequently, Neutral Island was the first Protestant preaching-ground upon this continent.

[2] Holmes's Am. Annals, p. 149, note 3; Williamson's Maine, vol. I. p. 190, note.

of the northeastern boundary: one half of it belongs to the heirs of Stephen Brewer, and the other half to the United States.

But to return, after this digression, to Robbinston. The attention of the people is now devoted chiefly to agriculture. From the shortness of the season of vegetation in this latitude, and the consequent rapid growth, productions escape in a great measure the fluctuations of climate, and the many diseases incident to more southern latitudes. Accordingly the best potatoes, and other garden vegetables, are raised here, which are much sought for abroad. The surface is nearly level, but gradually rises in a gentle slope away from the river. Boyden lake is a fine sheet of water, about five miles in diameter, furnishing excellent trout fishing. There are also three or four smaller ponds, the streams issuing from which, and terminating in the Saint Croix, supply water-power for three saw-mills, a grist-mill, lath machine, and a sugar-box machine. There is also a tannery. Robbinston has two church edifices — Congregational and Methodist; eight school districts, and one post-office. Population, 1,028; valuation, $152,767.

Rockland, Lincoln county, is situated on the west side of Penobscot bay. It was first visited in 1767, by John Lermond and his two brothers, from the Upper St. George, now the town of Warren, who erected a camp and got out a cargo of oak staves and pine lumber, but did nothing in the way of settlement. From this circumstance, the place was for a long time known as Lermond's Cove. Its Indian name was Catawamteak, signifying "Great Landing-place;" so named, doubtless, on account of its having been a sort of stopping-place for parties in their passage around Owl's Head in their course along the shore, or when proceeding to St. George for the purpose of trading and fishing. The place was permanently settled about 1769, by Josiah Tolman, Jonathan Spear, David Watson, James Fales, John Lindsay, Constant Rankin, Jonathan Smith, and John Godding, who erected log huts, and commenced clearing up and cultivating their lots. John Ulmer, of Waldoboro', moved here in 1795, entering into the business of lime-burning, of which he was the pioneer.

For the want of mill privileges and other business advantages, the growth of the place was at first somewhat slow. Habitations were scattered; and at Lermond's Cove, where the city now stands, there was, in 1795, but one house, that of John Lindsay. After Thomaston, to which this place belonged, was incorporated, it was known as the Shore village; but, on the establishment of a post-office here, about the year 1820, it took the name of East Thomaston, and was finally incorporated by that name, on the division of the parent town in 1848. In

1850, the name was changed to that of Rockland, and in 1853 it received a city charter.

The surface of the city is rough and broken. Along the shore it is somewhat low; but, a short distance in the rear, there is a beautiful series of mountains, known as the Camden range, extending from Thomaston to Camden, where they terminate. At the extreme northwest there is a large meadow, a portion of which lies in Thomaston. There are few places in New England whose growth has been as rapid and substantial as this. At present the inhabitants are furnished with almost every convenience which modern ingenuity has invented. The city is lighted with gas; and an aqueduct, having its source at Chickawaukie pond, brings to the inhabitants an abundant supply of pure soft water, the pond being entirely fed by springs from the adjacent mountains. This aqueduct is constructed of sheet iron, cased inside and out with hydraulic cement, — the improvement of J. Ball and Company, of New York.

The principal business is ship-building and lime-burning. In 1854, eleven ships, three barks, six brigs, and four schooners, the total tonnage of which was 17,365 tons, were built at this port, most of which were owned by the citizens. This, however, exceeds the average annual tonnage. The *Red Jacket*, of 2,500 tons register, one of the largest and finest ships that ever sailed from an American port, was built here in 1853. She made the quickest passage across the Atlantic ever made by a sailing vessel, and the quickest from Australia to Liverpool and back. There are in this town twelve lime quarries, owned and worked by companies, and 125 lime-kilns, which annually turn out about nine hundred thousand casks, employing upwards of three hundred vessels in their transportation to the various ports of the United States.

There are seven churches in Rockland — two Baptist one Free-will Baptist, one Congregational, one Methodist, one Universalist, and one Episcopalian; one public library, the Athenæum, containing 1,800 volumes; eight school districts, with twenty-three schools; two newspaper establishments, both weekly — the Rockland Gazette, and the United States Democrat; two marine railway corporations; several wharf companies; one steam navigation company, owning one steamer, called the *Rockland*, which plies semi-weekly between Rockland and Machias, touching at intermediate landings; three banks — the Rockland, the Lime Rock, and the North, with a combined capital of $300,000; two fire and marine insurance companies; and one post-office. The population, in 1850, was 5,052; valuation for the same year, $1,039,599. The present population is estimated to be about 8,500, and the valuation for the year 1858 is $3,148,499.

ROME, Kennebec county, is distant from Augusta nineteen miles, and from Farmington sixteen miles. The first settlement was commenced about 1780. Among the early inhabitants were Benjamin Furbush of Lebanon, Trip Mosher of Dartmouth, Mass., Stephen Philbrick of New Hampshire, Stabard Turner, and Joseph Halho, who obtained their titles to their lands from Charles Vaughan, R. G. Shaw, and Reuel Williams, the proprietors.

Rome was incorporated in 1803. The surface is broken and uneven, with some high elevations of land. There are two large ponds partly located here, one of which is called Long pond, the other Great pond. Their waters abound in trout, perch, and pickerel. At the outlet of Great pond, which is the line between Rome and Belgrade, there is a factory, which annually manufactures from 100,000 to 150,000 gross of spools for thread. Agriculture is the chief employment of the inhabitants. One half of the town is good tillage land, the other half is rather rocky and unproductive. The farmers, however, as a general thing, succeed in making a good living. There are two religious societies — Free-will Baptist and Christian; eight school districts, with the same number of schools; one post-office; two stores, one grist-mill, one saw-mill, and one shingle mill. Population, 830; valuation, $79,097.

ROXBURY, Oxford county, adjoins Rumford on the south, and is thirty miles north from Paris. It was incorporated in 1838, and is watered by Swift brook, a branch of the Androscoggin river, which flows through its centre. The surface is elevated, and there is some good soil. Timber is plentifully distributed over its lands. There are five school districts, with five schools; one post-office, one grist-mill, one saw-mill, and one shingle mill. Population, 246; valuation, $15,929.

RUMFORD, Oxford county, is situated on both sides of the Androscoggin river, fifty-one miles from Augusta and twenty from Paris. It was granted by Massachusetts to Timothy Walker, Jr. and his associates, of Concord, N. H., to make up losses which they and their ancestors sustained in maintaining the controversy with the town of Bow, growing out of the purchase of Concord. This town was first called New Penacook to distinguish it from Penacook,[1] N. H. Jonathan Keyes, and his son Francis, came here from Massachusetts, in June, 1782; and, a few years later, Philip and David Abbott, Jacob, Benjamin, and David Farnum,[2] Benjamin Elliott and wife, Benjamin Lufkin

[1] Baxter's History of Concord.

[2] Mrs. Jacob Farnum, who has attained the age of ninety-four, and Mrs. David Farnum, eighty-eight years old, are both still living here: also Samuel Akley, a Revolutionary pensioner, and a soldier in General Knox's regiment of artillery, now ninety-six years old.

and wife, Stephen Putnam and wife, John Martin, Daniel Martin, and Kimball Martin, became permanent residents. The above principally came from Concord, N. H. The settlers obtained the titles to their lands from Timothy Walker and associates, or their descendants.

Rumford was incorporated in February, 1800. The surface is very level; and on the rivers are some fine intervals. Some portions lie in large swells, rising almost to mountains. The only elevations worthy of notice are the White Cap and Glass-face mountains, the former of which rises six hundred feet, and the latter four hundred feet, above the surrounding country, both noted for their large growth of blueberries. The former annually yields some thousand bushels of the finest berries produced in the State, and is the resort of from fifty to a hundred persons per day, during the blueberry season. The soil is very fertile, owing doubtless to the disintegration of the neighboring limestone.

There are four rivers passing through or near Rumford, the Androscoggin, Ellis, Concord, and Swift, the latter of which divides the town from Mexico. Besides these, there are various other streams, on which are erected mills for the manufacture of lumber. The Rumford falls are the grandest of any in New England. They are produced by the bounding waters of the great Androscoggin, as they sportively leap over abrupt and craggy ledges of granite, and dash their spray high in air. There are at present three or four waterfalls at this place, while, anciently, there must have been others of greater magnitude, for large holes are seen worn high upon the rocky banks, where the waters have not run in modern times. The whole pitch is now from 160 to 170 feet. The third fall, having a nearly perpendicular descent of eighty-four feet, immediately arrests the attention of the traveller. In 1833, Rufus Wiggin and Nathan Knapp built a stone flume around the head of this fall, to divert the water to their mills. After its completion, Mr. Knapp stepped on to the wall, to see if it was tight, when thirty feet of it were forced over by the water, and he, being precipitated in an unbroken descent to the bottom, was drowned. His body was found the next spring at Livermore, some twenty miles down the river. There are now located on these falls an excellent flour mill, with two sets of burr-stones; a saw-mill, a shingle machine, and an axe factory, employing some ten hands, and producing very fine axes. About three miles north of Rumford Point village, on the farm formerly owned by Samuel Lufkin, there is a paint mine, where a mineral spring has deposited the ochreous red oxide of iron. The paint is capable of being wrought advantageously for the manufacture of red ochre, since the quantity is large, and is constantly forming by gradual deposition from the water of the spring. Near this mine is a good supply of bog iron ore. On the farm of Alonzo Holt, black lead, or plumbago, has been found in considerable quantities. Limestone abounds in several places, but more particularly at Rumford falls. It is of very good quality, and would yield a profitable return, if worked.

There are seven stores, one tannery, two superior grist-mills, each having two or three sets of burr-stones; six saw-mills, six blacksmith's shops, three shops for the manufacture of cabinet work; and three wheelwright shops, in which are manufactured wagons, sleighs, and other articles. A year or two since, a steamboat was built just below Rumford falls, which was to run from the foot of the falls to Canton, to connect with a railroad at that place. There are four small villages — Rumford Corner, Rumford Point, Rumford Centre, and East Rumford; three churches — owned by the Congregationalists and Methodists, but occupied by other denominations; four post-offices — Rumford, Rumford Point, Rumford Centre, and East Rumford; and thirteen school districts, with twenty-six schools. Population, 1,375; valuation, in 1856, $165,150.

Saco, York county, is a seaboard town, situated on the eastern bank of the Saco river. It was originally granted, by the Plymouth Company, to Thomas Lewis and Captain Richard Bonython, by patent, bearing date February 12, 1629, (old style,) and is described as "that tract of land lying on the north side of the Swanckadocke (Saco) river, containing, in breadth, from northeast to southwest, along by the sea, four miles in a straight line, and extending eight miles up into the main land." The patentees took passage for the New World the following year, and on the 28th of June, 1631, took legal possession of their grant; but as to the number of colonists who accompanied them, or the precise date when the settlement was commenced, information is not given, — there being no records of the town affairs kept until 1653, when the inhabitants passed under the jurisdiction of Massachusetts.

About this date, commissioners were sent here from Massachusetts, with full powers to arrange all matters, local as well as general, in this province, as they thought proper. It was, among other things, "ordered that Saco shall be a township by itself, and always shall be a part of Yorkshire, and shall enjoy the privileges of a town, as others have and do enjoy." It seems, however, that Saco was not represented in the general court until 1659, and not again until 1675, the year in which it was totally destroyed by the Indians, which was the last time during that century.

Some time during the seventeenth century, the grant of Richard Vines, now Biddeford, was added to the territory of Saco,[1] and was retained until 1718, when the last meeting of the inhabitants of both sides of the river was held, under the old name of Saco. A petition was gotten up at this meeting for the division of the town, when that part of Saco on the west side of Saco river was set off, and incorporated under the title of Biddeford,[2] so named from a town in England, from whence some of the settlers came. That part, however, on the east side of the river, being but sparsely populated, was only a sort of plantation, having no corporate authority, except that given by the order of the Massachusetts commission in 1653. It remained thus until 1762, upwards of a century, when, there being a sufficient number of inhabitants, the general court was petitioned by them for an act of incorporation, which was granted in the month of June of that year, by which the name was changed to Pepperrellborough, in memory of General Pepperrell. This name never seemed to be fully satisfactory to the people, though they retained it till 1805, when it was abolished, and the ancient name of Saco reëstablished. Since that period, no event has occurred of sufficient importance to be added to the history.

Saco has been generally prosperous, and is now a thriving place. The surface, taken as a whole, is generally even, and most of the land is capable of being cultivated. There is one village, situated on the banks of the Saco river, of sufficient importance to be created into a city, and much larger even now than some that already possess a city government. The river between Saco and Biddeford is spanned by four bridges, one of which is the railroad bridge of the Portsmouth, Saco, and Portland Railroad, which crosses north of the village. The principal business is manufacturing. The York corporation have erected five mills for the manufacture of colored cotton goods, running thirty-five thousand spindles and eight hundred looms, employing two hundred and fifty males and nine hundred females, and turning out six million yards annually. The pay-roll of this large establishment averages $20,000 monthly. Very little is done here in the lumber business, — there being but two saw-mills, which manufacture principally lumber for boxes. Ship-building is not very extensive. There are, however, a number of small vessels owned here, which are mostly employed in the coasting trade.

[1] Josselyn, in his voyages, published in 1672, says: "Saco adjoins Winter harbor, [Biddeford,] and both make one scattering town of large extent, well stored with cattle, arable land and marshes, and a saw-mill."

[2] "November 14, 1718. — On petition of H. Scammon, *et als.*, that part of Saco on the west side of Saco river was set off, and incorporated by the name of Biddeford." — *Records of the General Court.*

There are two banks in Saco — the York and the Manufacturer's — with a capital of $100,000 each; one public library, the Athenæum; one academy; nine churches — one Congregational, one Baptist, one Unitarian, one Episcopal, one Methodist, two Free-will Baptist, one Universalist, and one Roman Catholic; nine school districts, with twenty-three schools; and one post-office. Population, 5,798; valuation, $2,239,831.

SAGADAHOC COUNTY is bounded by Cumberland, Lincoln, Kennebec, and Androscoggin counties, and by the ocean. Being comparatively of diminutive size, — scarcely three hundred square miles, including its waters, — wonder is naturally excited, upon inspecting the map, as to the necessity for such a county. As its territory was wholly within Lincoln county, the seat of which was Wiscasset, a good deal of inconvenience was experienced, by people belonging to towns upon the west side, in crossing the river for county business, there being no bridge below Gardiner. To remedy this difficulty as far as possible, eleven towns, — namely, Arrowsic, Bowdoin, Bowdoinham, Georgetown, Woolwich, Perkins, Phipsburg, Richmond, Topsham, West Bath, and the city of Bath, — were set off, by an act passed April 4, 1854, from the parent county to form Sagadahoc; and to the inhabitants was referred the selection of a county seat, upon which they chose Bath. The name of the county is of Indian origin, and was formerly applied to the mouth of the Kennebec river, being thought to signify "flowing out of the waters." With a single exception — Bowdoin — the above towns are all upon either the ocean, bay, or river.

The county belongs to the middle judicial district, the law term of which is held at Augusta. The jury terms of the supreme judicial court, for civil and criminal business, commence on the first Tuesday of April and 3d Tuesday of August; and for civil business exclusively on the 3d Tuesday of December. Population, 21,669; valuation, $5,597,710.

SALEM, Franklin county, situated fifteen miles to the north of Farmington, was formed of parts of Freeman, Phillips, and No. 4, in the first range, Bingham's or the "Million Acres" Purchase, and is very conveniently situated. Benjamin Heath 2d, from Farmington, made the first "chopping," about 1815, to which he and John Church 1st and Samuel Church removed in 1817, and they, with Messrs. Double and Hayford, were the first settlers in the place. It was incorporated in 1823 by the name of North Salem, which was afterwards changed by leaving off the "North." It is drained by the westerly branch of the Seven Mile brook, which empties into the Kennebec at Anson. The soil is free and productive. Here is a valuable mill privilege, at which is situated a village, containing two stores, a saw-mill, grist-mill, starch factory, and several other operations.

The inhabitants have no meeting-house; but meetings on the Sabbath are sustained a part of the time, principally by the Methodists and Free-will Baptists. There are nine school districts, with five schools; and one post-office. Population, 454; valuation, $60,029.

SANFORD, York county, comprised a part of the tract of land along the Saco river, purchased in 1661, by Major William Phillips, of the Indian sagamores Fluellen, Captain Sunday, and Hobinowell. This purchase was confirmed by Gorges, in 1670, to the major, or his son, Nathan; and September 29, 1696, Mrs. Phillips devised the township to Peleg Sanford, a son of her former husband, and from him it derived its name. The first permanent settlement was made about the year 1740; and February 23, 1768, the town was incorporated. In 1794, Sanford lost a part of its territory by the incorporation of Alfred. Sanford is generally even, and is watered by Mousam river, which has its source in a pond in Shapleigh, and flows through the entire town. There are two villages; five church edifices — two Congregational, two Baptist, and one Free-will Baptist; sixteen school districts, with seventeen schools; three factories, seven saw-mills, three grist-mills, three shingle machines, three clapboard machines; one bank, the Mousam River, with a capital of $50,000; and three post-offices, — Sanford, South Sanford, and Springvale. The York and Cumberland Railroad, now in process of construction, will pass through the town. Population, 2,330; valuation, $334,654.

SANGERVILLE, Piscataquis county, lies west of Penobscot river, and was formerly known as No. 4, in the sixth range of townships north of the Waldo Patent. It was settled in 1806, by Phineas Ames; and was, for some time after, called Amestown. It was incorporated June 13, 1814, taking its name from Calvin Sanger, an early and large proprietor; and at that time contained forty families, among whom were Samuel M. Clanathan, Walter Leland, Ebenezer, Nathaniel, John, and William Stevens, John and Ebenezer Causley, Ellis Robinson, Edward Magoon, Phineas, Daniel, and Samuel Ames, Nathaniel Stevens, Jr., Thomas Riley, Aaron Woodbury, and Samuel and James Waymouth.

Sangerville is a beautiful township, and is in a thriving condition. Its surface cannot be called mountainous; yet it is so elevated between the Penobscot and Kennebec rivers, that the waters of its three ponds meet the ocean by both of these streams. There are four church edifices — two Free-will Baptist, one Congregational, and one Methodist; thirteen school districts, with the same number of schools; three post-offices — Sangerville, South Sangerville, and East Sangerville; four tanneries, four shingle mills, three saw-mills, and two grist-mills. Population, 1,267; valuation, $192,300.

SCARBOROUGH is in the extreme southern part of Cumberland county, — having Portland upon the northeast, and Saco upon the northwest. The first settler was one Stratton, who located on a couple of islands, both called, until recently, Stratton's islands. In 1631, the tract of land now forming Scarborough was granted to Captain Thomas Cammock, a nephew of the Earl of Warwick, to whose influence, in all probability, he was indebted for obtaining the patent to so valuable a territory. Captain Cammock was the first legal proprietor in Scarborough, having received his grant of 1,500 acres, situated between Black Point and Spurwink rivers, from the Plymouth Council. He soon after, however, disposed of his grant, and went to the West Indies, where he died, in September, 1643. For three years after Cammock's settlement at Black Point, there was no other part of the grant occupied, except by Indians. The majority of those who settled were men of small means, were unable to purchase land, and hence were compelled to become the tenants of Cammock.

The next principal settlement was at Blue Point, now a part of Saco; Richard Foxwell, Henry Watts, George Deering, Nicholas Edgecomb, Hilkiah Bailey, Edward Shaw, and Tristram Alger being the earliest settlers. The third principal settlement was that made at a place called Dunstan, which was settled by two brothers, named Andrew and Arthur Alger, who purchased a large tract of land of the Indians residing at this place, and retained their possession of it by virtue of their Indian title. The settlement at Black Point seemed to increase more rapidly than the other two, and soon became one of the most flourishing and important places on the coast. Its excellent situation, both for farming and fishing, induced many to settle here, in preference to any other part.[1] Its growth was very rapid for those days, and has rarely been equalled in the same section of country since that time. Thirty-eight years prior to 1671, Captain Cammock's house was the only one at Black Point; and in 1791, about a century afterwards, there were 2,235 inhabitants in

[1] Josselyn says, in 1671, "Six miles to the eastward of Saco, and forty miles from Gorgeana (York), is seated the town of Black Point, consisting of about fifty dwelling-houses, and a magazine or doganne, scatteringly built. They have a store of neat cattle, and horses near upon seven or eight hundred, much arable and marsh land, salt and fresh, and a corn mill." — *Josselyn's Voyages*, p. 200.

the settlement.[1] Henry Josselyn, brother of the distinguished voyager, arrived in 1634. He acted as chief agent for Mason at Piscataqua, in which capacity he officiated till Mason's death in 1635, when he removed, and settled at Black Point the same year. He became largely interested in lands in the settlement, and became somewhat distinguished as a politician.[2] John Josselyn, the voyager, resided here a few years with his brother, Henry.

Scarborough received its name and bounds by an order from the commissioners of Massachusetts, who were appointed in May, 1658, to take the inhabitants of the province of Maine under their jurisdiction, and receive from said inhabitants a pledge that they would recognize the authority of Massachusetts. The "articles of submission" were eleven. Number seven reads thus: "That those places which were formerly called Black Point, Blue Point, and Stratton's Island, thereunto adjacent, shall henceforth be called by the name of Scarborough; the bound of which town, on the western side, beginneth where the town of Saco endeth, and so runs along on the western side of the river Spurwink, eight miles back into the country." The name was given in remembrance of old Scarborough, England. The Indian name was "Owascoag," and signifies a place of much grass. In 1659 or 1660, John Libby settled here. He was the first of the name in Scarborough, and probably the first in New England. He came from Broadstairs, Kent county, England, remained here for many years, and was one of the most prominent men in the settlement. He is the common ancestor of the large number of individuals who bear the name and reside in this vicinity. He died in 1682.

In 1675, this town, and the settlements for some distance around, were attacked simultaneously by the Indians. Fortunately, apprehending a collision with the natives, Massachusetts had, a short time previous, sent down a small detachment for the protection of the Scarborough settlements. This detachment was placed under the command of Captain Scottow, and stationed at his garrison on the Neck; and before the close of King Philip's war, was increased by an additional force of 130 English, and forty friendly Indians, which force scoured the coast as far eastward as Casco. The Indians, however, had scattered themselves in such a manner that the English were unable to bring them to an

[1] As late as 1791, the census returns show a very slight difference in population between Portland and Scarborough. The returns for the two towns stood thus: Portland, 2,240; Scarborough, 2,235. Compare these figures with those of 1850, and note the difference.

[2] He resided here until 1668, when, according to Williamson, he removed to Pemaquid, where he remained until 1675, when he removed to the Plymouth Colony.

engagement; and, after remaining at the garrison house of Henry Josselyn at Black Point for a short time, the detachment returned again to Massachusetts. This was a very unfortunate proceeding; for no sooner had the Indians heard of the departure of the Massachusetts force than they made a descent upon the garrison at Scarborough, and captured it. The inhabitants, fortunately, having previously abandoned the town, the Indians remained in the neighborhood but a short time. The Indian troubles becoming more and more complicated, the Massachusetts government sent down in June, 1677, two hundred friendly Indians and about forty English soldiers to protect the settlements. They were under the command of Captain Benjamin Swett and Lieutenant Richardson, and came to an anchor off Black Point. Captain Swett, being informed of the presence of Indians in the vicinity, landed a detachment of his men, which, being joined by some of the inhabitants, consisted of ninety in all. They started the next day, June 29, in pursuit of the marauders; but had not proceeded far before they were ambushed, and a bloody hand-to-hand fight ensued. Captain Swett displayed great presence of mind and great personal courage; and his efforts to bring off the dead and wounded from the field and convey them to the rear—upon which the savages hung with desperate fury—were truly commendable. He was several times severely wounded; and, being exhausted by fatigue and the loss of blood, he was grappled by the savages, thrown to the ground, and barbarously cut in pieces. Sixty out of the ninety men who departed on this expedition were left dead or wounded on the field, and the remaining thirty succeeded in making good their retreat to the fort.

In 1681, the work of erecting the great fortification at Black Point was commenced,—a work rendered necessary for the greater security of the inhabitants from the attacks of Indians, to which they were more or less daily exposed. It was the largest and strongest fortification ever built here; and the remains of it are still to be seen. During the several Indian wars, the inhabitants were so harassed by the attacks of the Indians, that the settlements at Scarborough and its vicinity were broken up, the settlers driven from their comfortable homes, and compelled to seek new dwelling-places less exposed to the incursions of the savages. The precise date of the second settlement, after the evacuation of 1690, is not known, but is supposed to have been about 1702 or 1703. The new settlers were a little band of seven persons, who came from Lynn in a sloop, and who, for at least a year, were the only inhabitants. A peace had been concluded with the French and Indians; and these settlers came here, in all probability, under the expectation that this peace would be permanent; but they, in common with other pioneers in the newly revived settlements around them, were sadly disappointed. In August, 1703, a band of five hundred French and Indians, under the command of Beaubarin, a Frenchman, made a sudden descent upon the settlements along the coast from Casco to Wells. They attacked the fortification at this place, which was garrisoned by only the little band from Lynn. The assaulters sent a flag of truce, and demanded a surrender of the fort; but the garrison, though small in numbers, were not deficient in courage, and refused to surrender, or treat with the enemy on any terms. The whole force of five hundred French and Indians then surrounded the fort, and commenced the work of undermining. The prospects of the gallant band within the fort were now gloomy indeed, and the courage of some began to fail. They then thought that it would be advisable to abandon the defence; but Captain John Larrabee, whose courage and presence of mind did not forsake him in this hour of danger, immediately assumed the command, solemnly declaring he would shoot down the first man who mentioned the word "surrender." He then made every preparation to give the enemy a warm reception, as soon as they should reach the cellar of the fort, and calmly awaited the result. Before, however, the Indians had completed half the distance they had to dig, a heavy rain storm came on, which continued two days.[1] The soil gave way under the influence of the excessive rains, and filled up a large portion of the excavation, so that the assailing party were now exposed to the fire of the garrison, which harassed them so much that they became disheartened, and departed in search of easier prey, leaving the brave commander of the fort and his companions as undaunted as they were unharmed. Soon after this event, settlers again began to come in, but so slowly that no town government was organized until 1720. For many years the settlers paid little or no attention to agriculture, — depending on the salt marshes for hay for their cattle during the winter; and, for their own support, looked as much to the sea as to the land.

During the eleven years of Queen Anne's war, Scarborough was the scene of many tragic acts. No pitched battles were fought by large forces of Indians or English; but a continued guerilla warfare was sustained between small squads of Indians and some of the more daring of the settlers. There were two men living here who particularly distinguished themselves in this kind of warfare. Their names were Charles Pine and Richard Hunniwell, both of whom were bitter enemies of the Indians, who often had occasion to experience their vengeance

[1] An accident like this occurred at Thomaston, when the Indians made an attack on the garrison at that place. (See Thomaston.)

with terrible effect. One or two well authenticated traditions have come down to us, and the narration of them here, as illustrating the unhappy state of things existing in this neighborhood, may not be out of place. On a time, when the Indians were holding their nightly pow-wows in an old shell of a house, standing on Plummer's Neck, Pine, always ready to improve every occasion for a trial of his skill as a marksman, took his two guns with him, well loaded, and made his way to the old house. Climbing up among the beams, he secreted himself, and silently awaited the result of his adventure. Soon after dark, he heard the expected Indians whistling in the woods around him; and, on peeping out through the crannies of his hiding-place, saw about twenty of them coming up to the old house. He was now three miles from the garrison, and as that was the nearest aid he could hope to obtain, he ran great risk. He was not a man, however, who was easily frightened, so he remained perfectly quiet till the two foremost of the Indians had entered the door-way, when he fired and killed them both. On seeing two of their number killed, the rest of the Indians took to flight, not even waiting to examine the bodies of their fallen comrades. Pine, satisfied that he would not be molested, came down from his hiding-place, and, taking the guns of the murdered Indians with him, proceeded to the garrison with as much expedition as possible.

Hunniwell was a more ferocious and irreconcilable foe of the Indians, and was known as the "Indian killer." Pine's cruelty resulted more from a love of adventure than from any decided hatred he bore to his savage enemies. Hunniwell's detestation was such, that he would murder them, whenever and wherever he could get the opportunity. This is doubtless to be attributed to a desire to revenge the death of his wife and child, whom the Indians are said to have murdered. There are many traditions respecting him; but one will suffice. At one time, while mowing, he observed some Indians on the opposite side of the river, who soon recognized him as the "dreaded Hunniwell." The Indians, seeing his gun standing by a stack of hay some distance from him, determined to entrap him; and one of them volunteered to perform the hazardous duty. Crawling up under cover of the bank of the river, the savage eluded discovery, and succeeded in reaching the spot where the gun was placed, unperceived by Hunniwell, who continued at work, apparently unconscious of his approach. When the Indian had got up within a few yards of Hunniwell, he pointed the gun towards him, and called out, saying, "Now me kill you, Hunniwell!" Scarcely had these words been uttered before Hunniwell sprang towards him, shouting at the top of his voice, "You infernal dog! if you fire at me, I will cut you in two with this scythe!" He did fire, however, as Hunniwell approached, but the latter escaped unharmed, the charge passing over his head; and, as the gun was heavily loaded, it kicked terribly, throwing the Indian on his back, from which posture he never rose again, Hunniwell having carried out his threat to the letter. After finishing his bloody work, he took the head of the murdered savage, and, putting it on a pole, exhibited it to the astonished gaze of the Indians on the opposite side of the river, calling loudly to them to come over and share the same fate. This inveterate Indian destroyer was finally murdered by the savages, in the autumn of 1710.

Another story is told of one James Libby, a descendant of the first settler of that name, which, having more of the comic than the tragic about it, will perhaps be a fitting close to these exciting traditions: "Mr. Libby had a mare, to which he was much attached, and of whose speed he was continually boasting. Riding out a few miles one day, and finding himself in the neighborhood of Indians, he turned towards the garrison. An Indian immediately sprang from the thicket as he passed, and gave him chase. Libby, not being a courageous man save when out of danger, urged his mare to her utmost speed. The path was clear, and the ground even; and, for a while the contest seemed to be doubtful. At length the Indian had gained so far upon the horse as actually to put his hand upon the rump of the animal; and in a moment more Mr. Libby and his favorite mare would have been captured. At this juncture, a brother of his who commanded the garrison, and one of his comrades, appeared, at sight of whom the intrepid Indian let his prey escape. The sight of Libby, with his eyes almost starting from their sockets, his body thrust forward on the horse's neck, and his legs far in advance of the mare, to keep them from the reach of his pursuer, so convulsed his brother and comrade with laughter, that neither of them could steady their muskets to fire at the Indian. The savage took advantage of this opportune circumstance, and escaped to the woods. From that day forth, Libby was never heard to boast of the speed of his favorite mare."

Libby pursued by the Indian.

In 1719, the number of settlers had so increased that it was thought expedient to organize a town government; and, in March, 1720, the proprietors met together for that purpose. The records, which had been taken to Boston for safety during the Indian troubles of 1690, were again delivered to the town agent. Few places in New England suffered so much, in proportion to the population, as Scarborough, during the first and second Indian wars. About one hundred deaths are recorded as having occurred here during those contests, by savage hands; and many others must have taken place, of which no account can be obtained.

After the peace of 1749, the inhabitants severally returned to their wonted occupations, and were soon established again, in the enjoyment of that undisturbed quiet and prosperity with which they had been favored prior to the wars. For many years, the lumbering business engaged the whole attention of the inhabitants. Saw-mills were erected on every available spot, until ten or twelve were in successful operation. From this time there seems to have been no event, worthy of historical note, till the breaking out of the war of the Revolution. The people of Scarborough were not found wanting, either in expressions of opinion, votes of supplies, or in prompt action. A company of fifty men was raised, and marched to Massachusetts, where it joined the continental army then stationed at Cambridge, soon after the battle of Lexington. Most of the able-bodied men in town served some portion of the time during the war. In addition to this service, a large number of the inhabitants were engaged in the disastrous expedition to Bigaduce (Castine), in 1779. From the close of the Revolution up to the present time, the condition of the town has been one of almost uninterrupted prosperity. Its history for this period is but the simple record of the blessings attendant upon honest labor, and the quiet pleasures incidental to life at a country fireside.

Scarborough is an agricultural town of large extent, with broad salt marshes; and has three villages — Dunstan's Corner, Scarborough Corner, and Blue Point, which is partly in Saco. It has some mechanical operations in an ordinary way, — among them an edge-tool manufactory, a carding-machine, a saw-mill, grist-mill, and shingle mill. It has four religious societies — two Free-will Baptist, a Methodist, and Congregationalist; eleven school districts, with twenty-one schools; and one post-office. Communication is had with most of the large cities by means of the Portland, Saco, and Portsmouth Railroad, which has a station at West Scarborough, and one at a place called Oak Hill. Scarborough is the native place of Rufus King, New York; William King, first governor of Maine; and Cyrus King, member of Congress — all brothers.

Scottow's hill, in this town, is rendered famous as the place where the signal-fires of old were lighted, and where the beacon telegraphed to the surrounding country the approach of danger. Population, 1,837; valuation, $386,549.

SEARSMONT, Waldo county, originally formed a part of the Waldo Patent, and afterwards fell into the hands of Sears, Thorndike, and Prescott, the large land proprietors. The first efforts at settlement were made in 1804, and the town was surveyed in 1809. It was incorporated February 5, 1814, taking its name from the first named of its three proprietors. The soil is productive, and there are several beautiful ponds. Searsmont has two villages — Searsmont and North Searsmont, having each a post-office; two church edifices — Baptist and Methodist; fifteen saw-mills, two grist-mills; and twelve school districts, with the same number of schools. Population, 1,693; valuation, $201,760.

SEARSPORT, Waldo county, was formerly comprised in the town of Prospect, from which it was set off and incorporated in 1845. David Sears, with Thorndike and Prescott, was the principal proprietor under the Waldo Patent, and, on his death, it descended to his son, David Sears, of Boston. All that now remains in the possession of the family is Brigadier's island, which is owned by David Sears, Jr., a resident of Boston. This island comprises about one thousand acres, seven hundred of which are covered with wood. It is two miles long by one broad, and makes a delightful summer residence for the proprietor. About the year 1830, a company of fishermen wished to purchase the island, for the purpose of establishing a fishing depot, and offered $25,000 therefor.

The surface of Searsport is uneven; but back from the river there is quite a large quantity of farming land. There is a village located on the Penobscot, which is a landing-place for steamers plying on the river. Some very fine thorough-bred stock, cattle, and sheep are now being raised. The inhabitants are largely interested in ship-building and navigation. David Sears, Sr., recently presented the town with the sum of $1,000, which was appropriated to the erection of a town-hall. There are four church edifices, Methodist, Baptist, and two Congregational; eleven school districts, with fourteen schools; and two post-offices — Searsport and North Searsport. Population, 2,208; valuation, $502,819.

SEAVILLE, Hancock county, is composed of five small islands, situated in Ellsworth bay, at the mouth of Union river. It was formerly a part of the town of Mount Desert, from which it was set off and incorporated in 1838. The first settler in this vicinity was one Christopher Bartlett, from Rhode Island, who came here about ninety years since, the descendants of whom in the fifth generation are still residing in this town. The names of the principal islands of which Seaville is composed are Bartlett's, Hardwood, and Robinson's. Bartlett's island contains about six hundred acres, half of which is suitable for farming, while the other part is rocky; and has on the east side a good harbor. Hardwood island has two hundred acres, most of which was, till recently, covered with wood, though the soil is excellent. Robinson's island has about three hundred and fifty acres. The people are engaged in cultivating the soil, and in sea-going. There are four school districts, with the same number of schools. Population in 1857, 160: valuation for the same year, $29,780.

SEBAGO, Cumberland county, is distant from Augusta eighty, and from Portland thirty, miles. The early history of Sebago is blended with that of Baldwin, it having been the northerly part of the grant made in 1774, by the colonial legislature of Massachusetts, to Whittemore, Lawrence, and their associates, the survivors of John Fitch and Company. In 1826, twenty-four years from the incorporation of Baldwin, the act was passed for dividing it into two townships. The first town-meeting after the incorporation was held on the 13th day of March of that year. In 1830, by act of the legislature, a part of Denmark was added to Sebago. Those of the early settlers who devoted their energies to the permanent improvements needful in so rough a country, have left enduring monuments to their memory.

The prosperity of Sebago, in its general interests, has been as great as could be expected under the circumstances. The addition made to its territory falls far short of what it has lost. In forming Naples, some four thousand seven hundred acres have been taken from the northeastern portion of Sebago. Nearly one thousand acres were added in the portion transferred from Denmark; and four lots of one hundred acres each have been added to the southeast corner, from Baldwin, since the first division of the town. It has always been a severe tax upon the people to make and maintain the roads over its hilly surface, and among its granite rocks, as well as to build the bridges over its rapid streams. Intemperance in this, as well as in other new towns in Maine, was once very prevalent, and did much to retard its prosperity. The divided and unsettled state of its religious affairs for a number of years has operated against its prosperous development; but with all these disadvantages there has been substantial progress.

The surface of Sebago is very uneven, and generally rocky; but the soil is strong, and there are many good farms within its limits. Pine to some extent, and large quantities of the other kinds of timber usually found in the forests of Maine, are still standing. The rivers and streams furnish abundant water-power; and the location of Sebago, on the west shore of Sebago lake, affords convenient facilities for sending produce to the seaboard by the Oxford and Cumberland canal. A light draft steamer daily passes across the lake in summer, conveying passengers from Portland through this and its connecting rivers to Bridgton, *en route* for the White Mountains. The improvement of late years in education, morals, temperance, and in productive industry, inspires the hope of still better things in the future. The town raised in the year 1856 for repair of roads and bridges, $1,500; for support of schools, $600; for the support of the poor, and town charges, $200. It is free from debt, with a small surplus of funds in the treasury. There are three churches — one Congregational, one Methodist, one Free-will Baptist; ten school districts, with eighteen schools; a town-house; and two post-offices — Sebago and Sandy Beach. Population, 850; valuation, $70,162.

Sebec, Piscataquis county, is situated at the end of Sebec pond, and is distant eighty-seven miles from Augusta, and ten from Dover. The original settlers were Ezekiel Chase, Biley, James, and Jonathan Lyford, Jeremiah Moulton, and others. Mr. Chase came from what is now called Bingham, in this state; the Lyfords from Canterbury, N. H., and Mr. Moulton also from New Hampshire. The first settlement was made in September, 1803, when Chase moved his family into town. The Messrs. Lyford followed the next spring, and Mr. Moulton and others soon after. Sebec was owned by Richard Pike, Philip Coombs, and the Messrs. Coffin, of Newburyport, from whom the settlers obtained the titles to their lands. The Indian name of the lake was Sebecco, from which the town derived its name.

Sebec was incorporated in 1812. The surface is mainly uneven. There are a few intervals on the Piscataquis river, which make very good farms. Sebec lake is twelve miles long, and from one to three miles wide. Sebec river empties the water of said lake into the Piscataquis river, some five miles from the outlet of the lake, in Milo. Piscataquis river, the centre of which is the southern boundary of the town, divides Sebec from Atkinson. There are three small ponds near the centre, lying north and south, which empty into the Piscataquis by three distinct streams; also a number of smaller streams, which empty into the Sebec river and lake, one of which is of sufficient volume to propel machinery.

At the outlet of the Sebec lake there is a small village, having a woollen factory, saw-mill, tannery, and a number of machine shops. This village has suffered very much by fire, a saw-mill, grist-mill, and woollen factory having been burnt within a few years. There is another small place of business, in which are two stores and some machine shops. Agriculture is the principal pursuit of the inhabitants. There is but one church edifice, which is occupied by the Congregationalists, Baptists, and Methodists alternately; two post-offices — Sebec and South Sebec; and ten school districts, with sixteen schools. Population, 1,223; valuation for 1856, $115,000.

SEDGWICK, situated in the southwestern part of Hancock county, was one of six townships granted by Massachusetts, in 1761, to David Marsh and three hundred and fifty-nine others. It was provided that these townships, which were to be each six miles square, should be located in a regular contiguous manner between the Penobscot and Union rivers. The grantees individually bound themselves in the penal sum of £50 to fulfil the conditions of the grant, which were, to settle each township with sixty Protestant families within six years after obtaining the king's approbation, to fit for tillage three hundred acres of land, to erect a meeting-house, and to settle a minister. If the grantees failed to execute their portion of the contract, Sedgwick and the other townships were again to become the property of Massachusetts.

In 1763, some settlements having been made by Captains Goodwin and Reed, and John and Daniel Black, at what was known as Naskeag point, and, a few years later, by other persons in other parts of the town, the general court, in 1789, quieted their fears of ejectment by granting each settler a lot of one hundred acres. The settlement of Sedgwick progressed slowly; and January 12, 1789, it was incorporated, and named in honor of Major Robert Sedgwick. In 1817, five thousand acres were taken off to form Brooksville; and again, in 1849, about two fifths of the remaining twenty-two thousand acres were taken off to form the town of Brooklin.

Sedgwick is quite broken, and in some parts ledgy. It is drained by Benjamin river, which forms the dividing line between Sedgwick and Brooklin; and in the western part there is a pond. Sedgwick can boast of two excellent harbors, to which vessels of one thousand tons may have ingress and egress without difficulty. There are five ship-yards, owned by different individuals, in which are built about three vessels per annum, which are employed in the coasting, fishing, and West India trades. The inhabitants are principally engaged in agriculture and sea-going. The clam and other fisheries yield an annual revenue of upwards of $15,000, which is increasing every year. There are two small villages in Sedgwick; three post-offices — Sedgwick, North Sedgwick, and West Sedgwick; ten schools and ten districts, and two church edifices, both occupied by the Baptists. The Congregationalists have a society, but no meeting-house; at present they worship at a place called Dodge's Hall. Population, 1,235; valuation, $119,748.

SHAPLEIGH, York county, adjoins Alfred on the west, and was formerly called Hubbardston. Its territory was a part of the original purchase obtained of the Indian chief, Captain Sunday, by Francis Small, of Scarborough, who conveyed an undivided portion of the tract to Major Shapleigh.[1] The original deed of Small was found in 1770, and the descendants of the two tenants in common made partition, August 5, 1771, when the territory comprised in this township fell to the claimants of Shapleigh. Doubts afterwards arising whether it might not be without the limits of the original purchase from the sagamore, and in order that the title might not be disputed, the inhabitants obtained a confirmation of the grant from the state, October 30, 1782. The first efforts at settlement were made in the year 1772, when a saw and grist mill were erected by Simeon Emery. In 1773, Joseph Jellison and his son moved in, and were soon after followed by James Davis, William Stanley, George Ham, and others. Settlements were prosecuted with much vigor, so that in 1778 there were over forty families here.

Shapleigh was incorporated March 5, 1785, taking its name from its original owner. Nearly one fourth of its surface are plains, lying in the north and northeast part; the remainder is divided into precipitous hills, pleasant swells, meadows, and extensive ponds of water. Little Ossipee river, having its source in Balch pond in this town, forms the northern boundary, and Salmon Falls river the western boundary. Ponds and streams of water are abundant, the principal of which are Square pond and Long pond. The land, generally speaking, is suitable for cultivation, requiring, however, attention and care. There are many beautiful landscapes, equal to any in the state. In 1830, Acton was set off from Shapleigh, and in 1844 a portion of the northeast corner was annexed to Newfield. The town contains three villages — North Shapleigh, Emery's Mills, and Ross's Corner; seven religious societies — a Congregational, two Baptist, two Free-will Baptist, and two Methodist, one each of the two last having no house, fifteen school districts, with twenty-

[1] This tract was supposed to embrace Parsonsfield, Shapleigh, a part of Limerick, Newfield, Limington, and Cornish The first three were assigned to the Shapleigh claimants; the three latter to the Small claimants. Some disputes were afterwards raised as to the justness of this decision, the Shapleigh proprietors claiming one half of Newfield and Cornish.

three schools; five saw-mills; two grist-mills; several other mechanical works; and three post-offices — Shapleigh, North Shapleigh, and Ross's Corner. Population, 1,848; valuation, $201,771.

SHIRLEY, in the western part of Piscataquis county, was incorporated in 1834. It formerly contained much timber, which, having been mostly cleared off, leaves the inhabitants to turn their attention to agriculture, for which the town is well adapted. It is watered by the higher branches of the Piscataquis river, on which are erected mills for the manufacture of lumber. Stages pass daily between Bangor and that favorite summer resort, Moosehead Lake. There are three school districts, with three schools; a post-office, a grist-mill, a saw-mill, and a shingle-mill. Population, 250; valuation, $38,012.

SIDNEY, in the county of Kennebec, situated on the western side of Kennebec river, is the next town north of Augusta. It originally constituted a part of Vassalborough, from which it was set off and incorporated January 30, 1792, being named in honor of the renowned English republican, Algernon Sidney. The earliest settlements were made along the river, and upon the borders of Snow's pond, in 1774. Sidney contains twenty thousand acres, of which one thousand is bog, but the rest excellent soil for grain and grass. This is one of the best agricultural towns in Maine, and the inhabitants are nearly all independent farmers. There is a considerable portion of the primeval forest of beech, birch, and maple yet standing in the central part.

There are three stores and two blacksmith shops; two churches of the Baptist denomination, a Free-will Baptist, a Universalist, and a Methodist, one of the Friends, and one Union house, occupied by the Congregationalists and Free-will Baptists. The streams here are small, with no good mill privileges; yet there are some half dozen small saw-mills located upon them, which are operated during the spring freshets, and a grist-mill, that runs a short time in the spring and fall. There is a mutual fire insurance company, which was chartered in 1856; but no other corporation, and no large manufactories. The only literary institutions are the public schools, of which there are twenty, with a large attendance of pupils in proportion to the number of people. There are three post-offices — Sidney, North Sidney, and East Sidney. Population, 1,955; valuation, $458,556.

SKOWHEGAN, Somerset county, lies on the north bend of the Kennebec river. The territory comprising this town was originally a part of Canaan, from which it was separated February 5, 1823, and incorporated under the name of Millburn. This name it bore until the year 1836, when, through the efforts of many of its citizens, the one it now bears was substituted in its place. Skowhegan is an Indian word, and signifies "a place to watch." In ancient days, it was noted as a "place to watch" and catch salmon, and other varieties of fish. Skowhegan has an area of 19,071 acres, forty-eight of which are covered with water, and 324 devoted to roads. There are five churches — a Baptist, a Congregationalist, a Methodist, a Christian, and a Universalist; eleven school districts, one post-office; a tannery, one grist-mill, two shingle mills, one marble-worker, and four carriage builders. Population, 1,756; valuation, $331,370.

SMITHFIELD, in the southern part of Somerset county, was incorporated February 20, 1840. It was formed from parts of Mercer and Dearborn, and the whole of the territory called East Pond Plantation. It is watered by a handsome sheet of water, called Milk pond. The soil is good, its inhabitants industrious; and, from its location, the town obtains a good market for its surplus productions. It has a few saw-mills, and manufacturing establishments; two church edifices (Free-will Baptist), eleven school districts, with twenty-one schools; and one post-office. Population, 873; valuation, $77,058.

SMYRNA, Aroostook county, fifteen miles west from Houlton, embraces an area of 23,040 acres, and is yet but sparsely settled. It was incorporated in 1839. It has six school districts, with seventy-two scholars. Population in 1850, 172; valuation, $8,121.

SOLON, Somerset county, lies on the east side of the Kennebec river, due north from Norridgewock, from which it is separated by the intervening town of Madison. The first settler was William Hilton, of Wiscasset, who moved here during the fall of 1782, and purchased five hundred acres of land on the river, in the southwest part. Mr. Hilton lived on this farm for sixty-four years, raised a family of thirteen children, and died, at the advanced age of eighty-seven years, respected as a man of integrity and worth. The next year, 1783, William Hunnewell, from Wiscasset, moved to a farm adjoining Hilton's; and in 1787–8, Calvin and Luther Pierce, from Westmoreland, N. H., Moses Chamberlain and Jonathan Bosworth, from Easton, Mass., Eleazer Whipple, and Joseph Maynard, settled on the river, in the northwest part. In 1798–9, the south part was settled by James, Jonas, and Nathan Jewett, from Groton, Mass., and Jonas Heald and Caleb Hobart, from Pepperell.

Solon was incorporated February 23, 1809, and organized on the

26*

27th of March following. The surface is undulating, with rich, alluvial land along the banks of the river. Near the centre is a high elevation of land, called Parkman's hill. The only pond worthy of notice is the Wesserunset, situated in the northeastern part, covering an area of about five hundred acres. This pond is the head of the east branch of a stream bearing the same name, which falls into the Kennebec, and forms the western boundary. Carritunk falls, on the Kennebec, are situated about a mile from the north line of the town, and have a descent of twenty feet. The scenery in the vicinity of the falls is picturesque and romantic. Fall brook enters the Kennebec two miles south of the north line, and flows through Solon village, affording valuable mill sites. There are already situated on this stream two saw-mills, one flour-mill, one shovel-handle manufactory, two fulling and carding machines, and two blacksmith's shops. The principal pursuit of the inhabitants is agriculture, in which the majority of the population are engaged, and from which they reap a profitable return. Grain and hay are the staple productions. There are four churches — Congregationalist, Baptist, Methodist, and Universalist, two of which have church edifices. The one situated at the village is occupied by the above-mentioned denominations in rotation; the one at South Solon by the Congregationalists. The town has one hundred dwelling-houses and shops, six stores, one hotel, one tannery, two lawyer's offices, two post-offices — one at Solon, and one at South Solon; seven school districts, with thirteen schools, and a high school, which is in a prosperous condition. Population, 1,419; valuation, $179,706.

Somerset County is one of the enormous counties of the state, embracing an area of three thousand eight hundred square miles. It was the northerly portion of Kennebec county, and was established March 1, 1809, its southern boundary then running, as now, south of Detroit, Pittsfield, Canaan, Fairfield, Smithfield, Mercer, and as far west as the west line of Phillips in Franklin county. Hancock was then upon its east, and Oxford — four years its senior — upon the west. It gave to Franklin the towns of Industry, New Vineyard, Strong, Avon, Phillips, Freeman, Salem, Kingfield, and three and a half townships north of these towns; to Piscataquis two ranges of townships, and to Aroostook six townships. It now has one hundred and eleven townships, twenty-nine of which are settled and incorporated. Norridgewock has always been the shire town. The upper portion of the county is drained by the head waters of the St. John river and the west branch of the Penobscot. The Kennebec, the principal river, has its rise in Moosehead lake. It flows centrally through the county, and receives several small streams in its course. The surface is varied, and there are several small ponds, such as Brassua, Wood, Attean, Long, Allen, etc., interspersed over its territory, all of which are fine sheets of pure, clear water, well filled with the various species of fresh water fish. Agriculture is the leading pursuit. The productions are principally wheat, corn, and potatoes. The county belongs to the middle judicial district, the law terms of which are held at Augusta. The jury terms of the supreme judicial court, for both civil and criminal business, commence on the third Tuesdays of March, September, and December. Population, 35,581; valuation, $4,935,697.

South Berwick, York county, adjoins Quampheagen falls, extending as far as Salmon falls. It was originally a part of Kittery, and was settled simultaneously with Strawberry bank, now Portsmouth. It was called "the Parish of Unity." Berwick was separated from Kittery in 1700, and South Berwick, taken from Berwick, was incorporated in 1814. It includes all the lands within the first territorial parish, and a small part of York, lying north of Agamenticus, since annexed. Among the first settlers were Humphrey Chadbourne, Shapleigh, Heard, Frost, and Emery, — all ambitious and enterprising, — the first of whom purchased a tract of land of the Indians to commence a permanent settlement.[1]

In 1675, the dwelling-house of John Tozier, at this settlement, was attacked by a party of Indians, led on by Andrew of Saco and Hopehood of Kennebunk, two daring warriors. Tozier was absent on an expedition to Saco with Captain Wincoll, and his family was left without any male protector. Circumstances often make heroines as well as heroes; and in this case the courage and coolness of a girl, eighteen years of age, were most singularly exemplified. She saw the approach of the Indians, and, shutting the door of the house, kept it closed till it was cut in pieces by the tomahawks of the savages, and the family had escaped from the dwelling. Foiled in their intentions, the Indians wreaked their vengeance on the heroic girl, and, leaving her for dead, started with all haste after the family. Two of the children they overtook, and one of them, being too young to travel, was immediately killed; the other they kept with them six months. The girl, who was left for dead, revived after the departure of the Indians, and, going to the garrison at Salmon falls, was healed of her wounds, and lived for many years.

The day following, (September 25,) a large party of Indians set fire to the buildings of Captain Wincoll, near Salmon falls, and were pur-

[1] Upon part of this land the academy is located.

sued by the men belonging to the garrison; but darkness put an end to the pursuit. October 7, of the same year, the place was again attacked, and a man and two youths were shot. Nor was this all; on the 16th of the same month, about one hundred Indians assailed the house of Richard Tozier, killing him and taking his son captive. Nine men, sent by the commander of the garrison, Lieutenant Roger Plaisted, to watch the movements of the enemy, were surprised, and three of them killed. Plaisted and twenty of his men, while bringing in the bodies for interment, were attacked by a party of one hundred and fifty of the enemy, who had been concealed behind some logs, and a fierce conflict ensued. The contest was unequal, and all the men except Plaisted, his eldest son, and one of the garrison, made their escape. Plaisted would not surrender, although frequently urged to do so, and fought with almost unexampled courage, till he was all but cut to pieces with the hatchets of his enemies. His son and his fellow-soldier also fell nobly supporting the heroic man. Another son, engaged in the contest, died a few weeks after, of his wounds.

During the Revolutionary war (1775), two full companies marched from Berwick to the scene of action, one being commanded by Captain Philip Hubbard, and the other by Captain Daniel Wood. The latter was promoted to the rank of major; and Captain Ebenezer Sullivan, brother of General John and Governor James Sullivan, succeeded to the command. Berwick has the honor of having furnished as many men, in proportion to the population, to fight the battles of independence, as any other town in the state.

The principal river, a branch of the Piscataqua, was called Newichawannock. Quampheagen landing is at the head of tide navigation upon this river, and here is the factory of the Portsmouth Company. The Great Works river rises in Berwick, and flows circuitously into the above-named branch at Yeaton's mills, below Quampheagen. It received its name, because two Englishmen, named Leders, purchased of the town of Kittery five hundred acres of land on both sides of the river, including the Falls and the "Great hole," where they erected a mill of eighteen saws. The first settlers were attracted to this heritage, because it was one dense forest of pine, hemlock, and oak, and because of the facilities afforded for lumbering. They had no taste for agriculture or the fisheries; but, in process of time, lumbering failing, their successors took to the cultivation of the land, and they soon found that the soil was strong and retentive. They inclosed gardens, planted orchards, and cultivated fruit, vegetables, corn, and the grains; but hay is the staple. The lands of the late Judge Hayes, (who was a skilful farmer,) furnish a small part of the view given in this article, and exhibit some of the results of scientific agriculture. The trade of South Berwick was early quickened by the wood and lumber business, which was pushed into the interior towns. Ship-building was carried on advantageously. Merchants built their own vessels and employed them, and a profitable interchange of commodities with the West Indies gave employment to many of the inhabitants.

The manufacturing interests of South Berwick are considerable. The company at Great Works manufactures woollen goods; the Portsmouth company at Quampheagen has 250 hands, and manufactures cotton goods; and the company at Salmon Falls, on the opposite side of the river, has two large mills employed in the manufacture of cotton cloth. The magnificent establishments at Dover and Great Falls are within four miles of this place. Three of the principal railroads pass through the limits of the town. The Portsmouth, Saco, and Portland Railroad and the Boston and Maine Railroad meet at the junction in South Berwick, on the margin of Great Works river, twelve miles from Portsmouth, and six miles from Dover. A cross railroad is now completed, diverging at Brock's crossing on the Eastern road, ten miles from Portsmouth, and extending near the factories of Great Works, Quampheagen, and Salmon Falls,to Great Falls, a distance of six miles, where it connects with railroads leading to Rochester, Alton, and Wakefield.

South Berwick has five churches: one Congregational, — which has been in existence more than a century and a half, over which John Wade was settled in 1702, and Jeremiah Wise, his successor, in 1707, who continued as pastor till his death, in 1756, — two Baptist, one Methodist, and one Free-will Baptist. Some of the most prominent men who have lived and died in this town during the present century, were Colonel Jonathan Hamilton, Hon. John Lord, John Cushing, Esq., General Ichabod Goodwin, Timothy Ferguson, Esq., Hon. William A. Hayes, and Hon. C. N. Cogswell.

Berwick Academy (a view of which is given on the next page), located near the centre of the town, upon commanding ground, which was the gift of the late Benjamin Chadbourne, was incorporated in 1791, and endowed with a township of land. Samuel Moody was the first preceptor. The grounds, which are adorned with hedges and shrubbery, are inclosed with a substantial wall. A building of chaste architectural appearance, designed by Richard Upjohn, of New York, has recently been erected. There is also a large and commodious boarding-house. The institution is under the supervision of a board of fourteen trustees, at the head of which is Francis B. Hayes, of Boston. There are three scholarships in the institution, each of which provides one hundred dollars per annum for a meritorious graduate of the academy while in college. The school is under the charge of

Berwick Academy.

one of the most skilful teachers and its prospects are at present more auspicious than at any former period.

There are in town sixteen school districts, with an attendance of 750 scholars; two banking institutions — the South Berwick Bank, with a capital of $100,000, and the South Berwick Savings Institution; a mutual fire insurance company, and one post-office. Population, 2,592; valuation, $619,409.

SOUTHPORT is an island at the mouth of Sheepscot river, and belongs to Lincoln county. It formerly belonged to Boothbay, from which it was set off and incorporated by the name of Townsend, February 12, 1842. This name was changed to the present one, June 12, 1850. The inhabitants are mostly fishermen; and have thirty-five vessels, averaging eighty tons each, employed in this branch of business. Southport has one church edifice, which belongs to the Methodists; five school districts, with five schools; and one post-office. Population, 543; valuation, $37,126.

SOUTH THOMASTON is situated in the extreme easterly part of Lincoln county, and extends into the Atlantic on the south in the form of a peninsula, and into Penobscot bay on the east in the form of a high bluff or promontory. The first permanent settler was Elisha Snow, who came from Brunswick in 1767. He built a saw-mill on the Wessaweskeag stream, at the site of which has sprung up the largest village in South Thomaston. Snow was soon followed by Lieutenant Matthews, Richard Keating, John Bridges, and James and Jonathan Oberton. In 1773, Joseph Coombs, a young man who had but recently attained his majority, came here, and erected another saw-mill in close proximity to the one Snow had built; and soon after, in company with Snow, erected a grist-mill. The Indian name of this place was Wessaweskeag, which signifies "river of many points." The name was contracted by the settlers at first to "Weskeag," afterwards to "Keag," and finally it has degenerated to "Gig," which is a familiar appellation at the present time. The settlements at Wessaweskeag, — which included South Thomaston, Thomaston, Rockland, St. George, Warren, Cushing, Friendship, and other places, — were known in earlier times as Upper and Lower St. George. South Thomaston was incorporated from Thomaston in 1848.

The Baptist church of South Thomaston, with one exception, is the oldest one of that denomination which was established between the Kennebec and Penobscot bay, having been constituted June 27, 1784, under the pastoral charge of Rev. Isaac Case. A meeting-house was erected by this society in 1796, which was enlarged and improved in 1847. It is the only church edifice in South Thomaston. In April, 1784, Elisha Snow, the first settler, was baptized, and, September 27, 1794, was settled as sub-pastor of this church. In 1808, he became senior minister, and continued thus till removed by death, January 30, 1832, at the age of ninety-two years.

The surface is rough and rocky along the coast, but back some distance there is some good land, which has been laid out in farms. It is watered by the Wessaweskeag stream, which supplies many good mill-sites. Owl's Head, a view of which is here given, is a high, rocky bluff, projecting into Penobscot bay, and has a light-house on its summit, as seen in the engraving, making it a noted landmark for seamen approaching this coast. There are three villages — Keag, Owl's Head, and Ingraham's Hill; the two latter having chiefly sprung up since 1850. Ship-building is the leading occupation; but, owing to

Owl's Head.

a general depression in this business, it fell off in 1857. In 1854, there were built five ships, three barques, and three schooners. There are twelve school districts, and eighteen schools; two post-offices — South Thomaston and Owl's Head; one set of mills, consisting of a grist-mill, two planing machines, one up and down saw, one circular saw, and one shingle machine; five stores, a sail-loft, a cigar manufactory, two shoemaker's shops, and one carpenter's shop. Population in 1850, 1,120, which has probably increased about 200; valuation for 1857, $406,401.

SPRINGFIELD, Penobscot county, lies east of Lee, on the road from that place to Calais. It was first settled in 1830. The first trader was James Butterfield, who is still living, and doing an extensive and profitable business. Springfield was incorporated in 1834, at which time it contained about three hundred inhabitants. From various causes, the population since that time has increased but slowly. One of the main drawbacks was, that the town, soon after its incorporation, became involved in debt to the amount of $6,000, or about one fourth of the whole taxable property. This burden was imposed upon the people by the location of two county roads, when but one was necessary, which has ever since retarded the prosperity of the town. By the excellent management of the officers, however, this debt is now nearly extinguished.

The north half of the township was granted by the legislature to Foxcroft academy, and was sold by the trustees to parties in Bangor for thirty-one cents per acre. It was heavily timbered with pine and spruce, immense quantities of which have been taken from it, and much still remains. The south half was sold by the state to settlers and others, and contains some of the best land in Maine. In 1837, the state offered a bounty on wheat, and Springfield took the prize — Samuel C. Clark having produced that year 1,340 bushels of wheat, besides 435 bushels of other grain, making 1,775 bushels in the whole. Agriculture is the principal pursuit. Notwithstanding the financial embarrassments, a large number of the inhabitants are in independent and easy circumstances, not one of whom brought his wealth with him. The good buildings and well-cultivated farms prove that the people have not labored in vain.

Public worship has generally been sustained on the Sabbath. A large and elegant meeting-house, which will cost some $2,500, is nearly completed, and will be dedicated shortly. It will be an ornament to the place. The common schools are well cared for, and for several years a high school was sustained. There are eight school districts; two Free-will Baptist churches; one grist-mill; two saw-mills; and one post-office. Population, 583; valuation, $29,422.

STANDISH, Cumberland county, on the line of York, is equal to eight miles square, including a large portion of Sebago lake, and an island of five hundred acres. The territory composing it was granted April 30, 1750, in one township, not in two, as has been erroneously stated,[1] to Captain Humphrey Hobbs and Moses Pearson and their respective companies for military services in the siege of Louisburg, and was laid off next to Gorham, one of the Narraganset townships; and it was provided that they should "take associates of the Cape Breton soldiers, so called, and not exclude the representatives of those who were dead, so as to make the whole number of grantees 120; sixty of whom were to settle in distinct families within three years, and sixty more within seven years;" and they were to give bonds to the treasurer of the province that each man should build a house sixteen feet by eighteen, and seven feet shed, and clear up five acres of land. Jabez Fox, Ezekiel Cushing, and Enoch Freeman were a committee to receive and transmit the bonds to the treasurer.

The settlement was commenced in 1760. Rev. John Thompson, the first minister, was ordained in October, 1768, and remained until 1783. At the time of his ordination, the number of families in the plantation did not exceed thirty. During the Revolutionary war, however, there were considerable accessions of persons who removed hither to escape the ravages of the enemy.

Among the noticeable incidents in the history of this town is the effect caused by the following missive to the almost petrified inhabitants, which appears upon the journal of the house of representatives, dated February 19, 1783: "On representation that the plantation, called Pearsontown, neglected to apply to be incorporated only to avoid paying taxes, they being qualified therefor, — Resolved, that Mr. Stephen Longfellow, Jr., notify the inhabitants of said plantation to show cause, etc., on the first Wednesday of next June, why they should not be incorporated into a town." They did "show cause," — not against incorporation, but, in the language of injured innocence, why they should not be subjected to the provisions of an *ex post facto* law. The general court had, November 1, 1782, passed a general act providing a more effectual method for collecting taxes in unincorporated plantations, and had also, it seems, following up the spirit of the resolution just quoted, in 1784, ordered an assessment of taxes upon this plantation from the year 1764,

[1] Williamson, vol. II., p. 281.

a period of twenty years. This act brought out an appeal from the inhabitants, not surpassed in earnestness by the remonstrances of the colonies against the exactions of the mother country.[1] They further asked for incorporation. This solemn appeal caused the hearts of the lawmakers to relent; and an act was immediately passed to abate £571 18s. from the sum previously ordered, being the amount of taxes up to 1780, and to stay execution on the remainder for six months. The town was incorporated November 30, 1785, and is said to have been named from respect to the courage and character of Miles Standish. Edmund Mussey was the first representative to the legislature, in 1806. Much of the land consists of pine plains; but there is good farming land, which is well watered by Sebago lake and little streams connecting with it. There are four villages, known as Standish Corner, Steep Falls, Bonnie Eagle, and East Standish, each of which has a post-office; eight saw-mills, and two grist-mills; six church edifices — two Methodist, two Free-will Baptist, a Unitarian, and a Congregational; sixteen school districts, and an academy. Population, 2,290; valuation, $329,206.

STARKS, Somerset county, lies on the west side of the Kennebec river, at its junction with the Sandy river. James Waugh, of Townsend, Mass., was the first settler, who, prior to his removal, had resided for

[1] A petition dated September 27, 1784, signed by John Sanborn, George Freeman, Jonathan Philbrick, Daniel Lowell, and Daniel Hasty, "in the name of the plantation," was presented to the legislature. They say: "Your petitioners are ready to declare that they have not even a wish to be excused from their full and just proportion of public burdens, according to their utmost abilities, and that they had no such object in view in their late application. It was their humble opinion, and they beg leave to say it is their serious opinion still, that the hardships they have suffered in bringing forward a settlement in the midst of a howling wilderness, exposed to the incursions of the native savages, Indians, and wild beasts, — twenty miles to the nearest market, — to which they make their way through roads almost impassable at first, and which required vast labor to render them comfortably passable, — your petitioners say it is their serious and unshaken opinion that the inhabitants of this plantation, induced by poverty to settle in a desert, and subdue overgrown forests, — destitute to this time of the conveniences, and frequently of the necessaries, of life, have borne a burden full equal to the rest of the inhabitants of the commonwealth, taking into the account the small assistance they have afforded in men and supplies in the late war. Few, if any, persons in the plantation could have had any knowledge of such taxes, as most of them were residents of other and distant places, where they paid taxes for a number of years after the levy of a part of these taxes. Your petitioners confess themselves perfectly confounded at the prospect of a burden sufficient to crush them and their unhappy families to ruin. They are still resolved, however, to confide in the wisdom and justice of representatives of the body of the people."

some years in Clinton. The history of the arrival of this settler is briefly this: Hearing that the New Plymouth Company were making liberal offers for the encouragement of settlers, he thought he would avail himself of this favorable opportunity to secure a home; and, in 1772, with his knapsack, dog, and gun, started up the Kennebec in pursuit of a farm. He ascended as far as the mouth of the Sandy river, and, near it, selected a lot. In 1774, he returned, accompanied by three of his neighbors, who brought with them their families, all of whom forthwith turned their attention to clearing the lands and building suitable habitations. In 1790, only sixteen years subsequent to the arrival of Waugh and his three comrades, there were three hundred and twenty-seven persons within the limits of the town.

Starks was incorporated February 28, 1795, and received its name from Major-General John Stark, the hero of Bennington. It contains an area of seventeen thousand one hundred and fifty-four acres; of which three hundred and sixty-three acres are in roads, and two thousand two hundred and twenty-four in waste lands. It is drained by Sandy river. The level appearance and general fertility of the soil lying upon this river are subjects of frequent remark and commendation. Agriculture is the leading pursuit of the inhabitants. Starks is advancing in its industrial enterprises, and in all that adds to the prosperity and dignity of a town. There are two church edifices, both occupied by the various religious denominations alternately; thirteen school districts, with twenty-four schools; several saw-mills and grist-mills; one tannery; and one post-office. Population, 1,446; valuation, $211,276.

ST. ALBANS, situated in the eastern part of Somerset county, contains an area of 23,040 acres. It was sold by the state of Massachusetts, in 1799, to John Warren of Boston, and was very soon after settled. The act of incorporation was passed June 14, 1813. The surface is undulating. Water is supplied by Indian pond, and by a stream, that forms its outlet, falling into the Sebasticook. The town has one village, centrally situated, two religious societies — Congregational and Free-will Baptist; fifteen school districts, and sixteen public schools; two saw-mills, two shingle mills, and one post-office. The occupation of the inhabitants is principally agriculture, the products of which form the main portion of the trade of the town. Population, 1,792; valuation for 1857, $200,000.

ST. GEORGE, a peninsula in the eastern part of Lincoln county, is bounded on the southeast by the ocean, and on the west by St. George's river. It originally comprised a part of Cushing. It is stated that a settlement was commenced here by two families, as early as 1635; but, for want of encouragement, little further progress was made, and it was known for a long time merely as an English frontier. When this section of country was first settled, this peninsula was noted for the immense flocks of wild ducks, geese, and other waterfowl, that had their haunts on it, and on the adjacent islands in the bay; in killing which the natives, as well as the English, had rare sport.

During Lovewell's war, in the spring of 1724, St. George was the scene of a most tragic encounter between the whites and natives. Captain Winslow, a descendant of the governor of that name, having been left in charge of the fort at Thomaston, time hanging heavily on his hands, proposed taking a pleasure excursion down the river to the islands. Accordingly, on the morning of May 11, the weather being fine, he selected a party of sixteen from the garrison to accompany him, and proceeded in a couple of staunch whale-boats to the scene of the intended rendezvous. It was said by those Indians who saw them, that they had a fine time in shooting fowl on the islands; and the sport must have been enticing, as they did not set out on their return till the evening of the next day. While on their homeward voyage, they were attacked by a large party of Indians in ambush on the banks of the river, and every one of them murdered; leaving only their savage enemies to relate the story of their melancholy fate. Cotton Mather preached a funeral sermon on the death of young Winslow and his companions, in which he commemorated the event in fitting terms.

St. George was incorporated in 1803. It has superior facilities for navigation, and a large number of vessels are employed in the lumber and coasting trade, and in the prosecution of that lucrative branch of business — the fisheries. Ship-building is carried on to some extent, averaging three or four vessels annually. The town has three Baptist societies; eighteen school districts, with thirty-four schools; a number of stores, a grist-mill, five ship-builders, and two post-offices — St. George and Tenant's Harbor. Population, 2,217; valuation, $233,820.

STETSON, situated in the western part of Penobscot county, contains an area of 23,040 acres. It is a town of recent settlement, and was incorporated in 1831. The surface is quite level, and the soil good for agricultural purposes. It is watered by two ponds, one lying near the centre, having its outlet in Newport pond, and the other in the southern part. The Penobscot and Kennebec Railroad passes across the southwest corner. Stetson has one village; an academy; one church edifice — Union; eight school districts, and seven schools; a tannery, doing a large business; one saw-mill, one grist-mill, and two post-offices — Stetson and East Stetson. Population, 885; valuation, $78,987.

STEUBEN is situated on the sea-coast, in the southwesterly part of Washington county, and was Number 4 of the six second class townships granted in 1762 by Massachusetts to an association of petitioners; but, the grantees failing to comply with the terms upon which the grant had been made, it reverted to the state, and a new grant was made August 26, 1794, to Thomas Ruston. On the 27th of February, 1795, Steuben was incorporated, receiving its name in honor of the celebrated Baron Steuben. The progress of the settlement, notwithstanding its advantageous location for commerce, was slow. The surface is uneven, and the soil hard and rocky. The leading pursuit of the inhabitants is seafaring. A number of vessels are owned here, varying from six hundred tons downwards. Steuben has one village, two church edifices — Methodist and Universalist; four saw-mills; two grist-mills; a few shingle, lath, and clapboard machines; eleven school districts, with eighteen schools; and one post-office. Population, 1,122; valuation, $119,136.

STOCKTON, Waldo county, fifty-two miles from Augusta, extends about ten miles upon Penobscot bay and river, having an area of eighteen square miles. It was incorporated from Prospect, March 13, 1857. Here, out upon a bluff promontory rising abruptly, on the south and east, sixty or seventy feet, known as Fort Point, is the site of Fort Pownall, described more particularly in the article on Prospect. There are no streams in Stockton, and but one pond, called Tide-Mill. Sandy Point Fort Point cove, and Cape Jellison are good harbors, affording sufficient depth of water for the largest merchant vessels that sail on the Penobscot, with excellent anchorage accommodations. A light-house, erected in the year 1837, stands on Fort Point, which has an elevation of 123 feet above the level of the sea. It has a fixed light, the lamps being about eighty-seven feet from the ground.

There are three villages, two of which — Hichborn's Corner and Sandy Point — are of considerable size; the other is but a small settlement of four or five families, near Tide Mill pond. The Universalists and Congregationalists are the principal religious denominations, the former having two church edifices, and the latter one. There are twelve schools, each of which has a good school-house; two post-offices — Stockton and Sandy Point; twelve stores, with a capital of $16,000; four saw-mills, three shingle mills, two lath mills, one carding-machine,

27 *

one cloth-dressing mill, one tannery, four ship yards, six blacksmith's shops, and several other small mechanic shops. Population, by estimate, about 1,800; valuation, at the time of the separation from Prospect, $232,000.

STONEHAM is a small town in Oxford county, occupying the place of a wedge between Lovell and Albany. It was incorporated in 1834, and has some trade in manufactured lumber, such as boards, shingles, shooks, and hoops. There are two saw-mills, and two stave mills — the latter of which are used in manufacturing red oak staves for cigar boxes; one village — East Stoneham; six school districts, with the same number of schools; and one post-office, situated at the village. Population, 484; valuation, $25,390.

STOW, Oxford county, is seventy-five miles from Augusta, and thirty from Paris. The original settlers were Isaac James, Micah and Simeon Abbott, from Andover, Mass., William Howard of Keene, N. H., and Samuel Farrington of Fryeburg, Me. The first settlement was commenced in 1770. The Abbotts obtained the titles to their lands in part from the proprietors of Fryeburg, in part from William Steele of Concord, N. H., and in part from Judge Phillips of Andover, Mass.; and Mr. Howard obtained his from Jonathan Robinson of Fryeburg. Stow was a part of the Pequawket tract, so called from a tribe of Indians who resided within its limits.

Corporate privileges were conferred on Stow in 1834. The surface is rather uneven, but not broken. Speckled mountain is situated in the northern part, and Great and Little Cold rivers supply abundance of water. Agriculture is the principal pursuit of the inhabitants. There are one village, one post-office; one church, owned by the Methodist denomination; and eight school districts, with thirteen schools. Population, 471; valuation, in 1856, $65,525.

STRONG, Franklin county, lies directly north of Farmington, on the Sandy river, and was formerly known as Middletown. The first settlement was made as early as 1784, by William Read, from Nobleborough, in this state, who was followed by Edward Flint, John Day, David and Joseph Humphrey, Jacob Sawyer, William Hiscock, Benjamin Dodge, Timothy Merry, Eliab Eaton, Peter Patterson, Robert McLeary, and one Ellsworth, all from the same place or vicinity. Richard Clark and Joseph Kersey settled about 1792. The township was purchased of the state by an association of individuals, of whom William Read was one, and who acted as their agent in the purchase and survey of the town.

The state reserved one lot for a Mr. Pierpole, on which he had settled, after leaving Farmington falls. He put up the second framed house, where he remained till 1801, when he left, and went to Canada with his family. The inhabitants of this town, as well as those located higher up the river, frequently had to go to Winthrop to mill, and, for some years, were compelled to use mortars.

Strong was incorporated January 31, 1801, taking its name from the circumstance of the act of incorporation being the first act of the kind which bore the signature of Caleb Strong, governor of Massachusetts. It embraces a territory of seven miles from north to south, and five from east to west. The soil is strong and fertile, though the surface is somewhat uneven. It has a considerably large pond in the eastern extremity, at the outlet of which stand a saw-mill and a clover-mill. There is a grist-mill on the Sandy river; and on the northeast branch of the Sandy river are a grist-mill, saw-mill, fulling-mill, carding-machine, starch factory, tannery, and various kinds of mechanic shops, and a very pretty village. Just below this village, a bridge crosses the Sandy river. A meeting-house is situated at the northeast branch of the Sandy river, one at the lower part of the town, and one in the easterly section, all of which are chiefly occupied by the Episcopal Methodists. There is another meeting-house in the northeast part, owned and occupied by the Congregationalists. There are eleven school districts, with fourteen schools; and two post-offices — Strong and East Strong. Population, 1,008; valuation, $169,091.

SULLIVAN, Hancock county, which previous to its incorporation was called New Bristol, is pleasantly situated on the northern side of Frenchman's bay. The township was granted to David Bean and associates, in 1761, by the colonial government of Massachusetts, on condition that the grant should be ratified by the king within eighteen months. It was sent out accordingly, but the king refused to comply with the request. The first settlers came from York, and arrived here in 1762, among whom we find the names of Simson, Bragdon, Sullivan, Bean, Preble, Gordon, Blaisdell, Johnson, Card, and Hammond. At the commencement of the Revolution, nearly two thirds of these settlers moved back to York, from which county they never returned. The principal object which had attracted them hither was the lumber trade. In 1798, the settlers made application to the legislature of Massachusetts to secure their lands. In 1800, the legislature passed resolutions granting to each of the settlers one hundred acres by each man's paying into the public treasury the sum of five dollars. Those who moved back to York put in a claim for damages sustained, and the legislature granted them fifty acres each. After these lots were appropriated to the settlers, there remained about nine thousand acres, which the resolve gave to Bowdoin and Williams Colleges. The Indian name of the town was Wakeag, signifying "a seal." It was incorporated February 16, 1789, taking its name from one of the original settlers. The surface is very uneven, but the soil is generally good. In 1841, an earthen pot containing French coins, of about the date of 1725, was dug up here, the value of which was somewhat more than four hundred dollars. Some little attention is devoted to manufactures, as well as to shipbuilding. In the eastern part are two streams, which furnish water-power for several mills, at which a considerable amount of lumber is manufactured. Sullivan has one church edifice, occupied by the Baptists, Methodists, and Universalists; seven school districts, with seven schools; and two post-offices, Sullivan and East Sullivan. Population, 810; valuation, $107,255.

SUMNER, Oxford county, is situated in the very heart of the Oxford hills, having Peru on the north, Hartford on the east, Buckfield on the south, and Paris and Woodstock on the west. Sumner was originally united with Hartford, under the respective names of East and West Butterfield; but, in 1798, it was separately incorporated, and the name of Sumner given to it, from Governor Increase Sumner. The first settlement was made in 1783, in the southeast part, by Increase Robinson and Noah Bosworth. Most of the first settlers came from Plymouth county, Mass., and were Revolutionary soldiers. Among the earliest settlers were Increase and Joseph Robinson, Simeon Barrett, Noah Bosworth, Hezekiah Stetson, John Briggs, John Crockett, Benjamin Heald, Meseeh Keen, Barney Jackson, and Oliver Cummings. They obtained the titles to their lands from the state of Massachusetts.

The first blow struck by the axe, in what is now the centre of the town, was by Oliver Cummings, from Dunstable. The first settlers, among other privations, were compelled to go to Turner, a distance of ten miles by "a spotted line," to mill, carrying their grain on their backs. Increase Robinson afterwards erected a saw-mill and a grist-mill, the first of which has been rebuilt, and the last replaced by a shingle machine and starch factory, besides which there are two saw-mills, two grist-mills, one shingle machine, one clover-mill, and one powder-mill. The surface is somewhat broken and uneven. A portion of Black mountain, noted for its large growth of blueberries, is located in Sumner; as also three ponds, known by the names of Pleasant, Labrador, and North ponds. Twenty Mile river, which has its rise in Franklin plantation, passes through to Buckfield; and the east branch of this river, having its rise in Peru and emptying its waters into Twenty Mile river in Buckfield, divides this town from Hartford. There is one village, called Jackson. The inhabitants are engaged, for the most part, in agricultural pursuits.

There are five religious societies in Sumner, namely, Congregational, Baptist, Free-will Baptist, Methodist, and Universalist; only the two former of which have meeting-houses. There are fourteen school districts, with twenty-six schools; and three post-offices — Sumner, West Sumner, and East Sumner. Population, 1,151; valuation, $168,070.

SURRY is situated in the southerly part of Hancock county, on Patten bay. The earliest settlers were John Patten, Hopkinson Flood, Andrew Flood, Leonard Jarvis, Wilbraham Swett, Matthew Ray, James Ray, Samuel Joy, Isaac Lord, James McFarland, and Hezekiah Coggins, who came mainly from the western part of the state. They settled here about the year 1785. The town was incorporated March 21, 1803. Stephen Conary, a soldier of the war of 1812, is a resident of this town. He was wounded in the hand by the accidental explosion of a musket, while opposing the landing of a party of British soldiers on the shores of Wiscasset.

Surry has an area of about 21,025 acres, the surface of which is considerably broken. It is well watered by two ponds, lying between Surry and Ellsworth, called Patten's ponds — Patten's stream being the outlet; also one near the line between Surry and Penobscot, called Toddy pond. The productive industry of the town is about equally divided between agriculture, ship-building, and the lumber business. During the past ten years, thirty vessels, of different sizes and models, have been built, averaging two hundred tons each. There are two societies — Methodist and Baptist, each having a house of public worship; also one small village, situated at the head of Patten's bay, at which there is a post-office; eight school districts, with seventeen schools; one grist-mill, two saw-mills, one shingle mill, and three ship-builders. Population in 1850, 1,189; valuation for 1856, from the assessors' books, $132,588.

SWANVILLE is situated in the eastern part of Waldo county, and formed a part of the Waldo Patent. It was formerly known as the plantation of Swan. The petition for incorporation was presented by James Leach and thirty-seven others, in November, 1816, and set forth that they had one hundred ratable polls, fifty-six legal voters, and fifty-eight soldiers enrolled in the militia; that Mr. Sullivan, the present proprietor, had appointed an agent to make conveyance to settlers, who had recently made many purchases, and the settlement, in consequence, was rapidly increasing. The petition was allowed February 19, 1819. The face of the country in Swanville is not very level; but the soil is tolerably productive. There is one village, known by the name of the Mills. There are six school districts, with nine schools; one post-office, three saw-mills, and two blacksmith's shops. No church edifice has yet been erected; but religious meetings are sometimes held. Population, 944; valuation, $102,999.

SWEDEN, situated in the western part of Oxford county, forty-five miles northwest from Portland, and sixty-seven southwest from Augusta, formed a part of the grant made to Captain Lovewell's little company, by the commonwealth of Massachusetts, for services in the Indian wars, and was called the Pequawket country, from the Pequawket Indians, (a branch of the Sokokis tribe,) who lived here. The first settlement was made by Samuel Nevers, from Burlington, Mass., in 1794. He was followed, in 1795–6, by Benjamin Webber from Bedford, Jacob Stevens from Rowley, Andrew Woodbury and Micah Trull from Tewksbury, and Peter Holden from Malden, Mass. Nevers and Trull, Mrs. Holden and Mrs. Woodbury, were still living in January, 1857, at a good old age, and on the farms they originally occupied, whilst their companions in the privations, dangers, and hardships of a pioneer life, have within the last few years been gathered to their fathers. Nevers is now in his ninety-first year. At the age of seventeen he embarked on board the *Hyder-Ally*, Captain Baldwin, a vessel fitted out in Boston as a privateer during the Revolutionary struggle, and which was captured by the British brig *Chatham*. He was impressed into the British service, where he remained about one year, when the vessel put in to New York, and he effected his escape.

Sweden was incorporated in the year 1813. The soil is good for farming purposes, and is particularly adapted to the growth of grains. Kezar river crosses the west part, and on the northeast are two ponds, by which the town is drained. There are eight school districts, with eight schools, three church-edifices — Congregational, Methodist and Free-will Baptist; and one post-office. Population, 696; valuation, 124,268.

TEMPLE, in the south part of Franklin county, lies west of Farmington and north of Wilton, and takes its name from a town in New Hampshire, from which many of the early settlers emigrated. Temple was formerly known as No. 1 of Abbot's purchase; and the first settlements were commenced about 1796. Joseph Holland and Samuel Briggs were the first two who moved into the place. They were soon followed by James Tuttle, Moses Adams, John Kenney, Jonathan Ballard, William Drury, Asa Mitchell, Samuel Lawrence, Gideon and George Staples, and others. Mr. Tuttle, who settled at the centre of the town, was soon succeeded by Benjamin Abbot, who was one of the most useful and respected citizens in the place. He died in 1823, aged fifty-three.

Temple, at the commencement of the settlement, was owned by Benjamin Phillips of Boston, but was surveyed and settled under the agency of Jacob Abbot, late of Brunswick, in this state, who subsequently purchased the residue of Mr. Phillips's eastern lands. Temple was incorporated June 20, 1803. It is somewhat mountainous, embracing quite a portion of the Blue ridge; but the land is good for grazing. The best of sheep are raised here. It is watered principally by the Starling or Davis Mill stream, on which there are a grist-mill and some two or three saw-mills, a starch factory and machine shop.

There are two meeting-houses — Congregational and Methodist. Stated meetings have been continued from the period of the first settlement by these societies, and also by the Free-will Baptists. Temple has nine school districts, and one post-office — Temple Mills. Population, 785; valuation, $72,550.

THOMASTON, situated in the eastern part of Lincoln county, on St. George's river, is bounded on the north and east by the city of Rockland, on the south by St. George and Cushing, and on the west by Warren, and originally belonged to the Muscongus, afterwards known as the Waldo Patent. The first information of this place dates as far back as 1630, at which time a trading-house was erected by the proprietors on the eastern bank of the river, for the purpose of traffic with the natives. No attempt, however, was made to settle it for nearly a century subsequent to that period. In 1719–20, two strong block-houses were erected; and the old trading-house, which was situated directly in front of the spot where the residence of the late General Knox now stands, was remodelled, being made into a sort of fort, the large area between this and the block-house being inclosed with palisades. These improvements were made for the purpose of encouraging the immigration of settlers, assuring them, as it would, of security in case of attack from the Indians. As a still further inducement, the proprietors built a double saw-mill on a stream ever since known as Mill Creek; erected thirty frames for dwellings, and maintained a garrison of twenty men, under command of Captain Thomas Westbrook.[1]

[1] Report of Committee of General Court, 1731. Waldo's petition to Gov. Belcher. Mass. MS. Papers, vol. CXIV., pp. 116–152.

The Indians regarded this preparation for a settlement by the English as an unwarrantable encroachment upon their rights, and as an attempt to wrest from them the fairest portion of their eastern possessions. They earnestly protested against these proceedings; in reply to which, the English asserted that they (the Indians) had sold the land to Governor Phips, the deed having been signed by one of their chiefs, Madockawando. In reply to this, the Indians maintained that the Madockawando, and Sheepscot John, who signed the deed, were not Penobscot Indians, one belonging to Machias, and the other in the vicinity of Boston; consequently, these chiefs had disposed of what did not rightfully belong to them, and the deed was therefore null and void. These representations, however, failed to convince the English, and they refused to give the Indians any further compensation than that which had been paid them by Governor Phips through Madockawando.

The Indians, failing to persuade or frighten the English to abandon their designs, determined on attacking the infant settlement. The government, anticipating the attack, accepted the proposition of the proprietors to make this a public fortress, and sent down a force of forty-five men with cannon, and all the necessary munitions of war.[1] On the 15th of June of that year (1722), the Indians made a descent upon the place, burning the saw-mill, setting fire to a sloop in the harbor, and destroying all the houses and frames, that had been erected but a short time before. They then made a vigorous assault upon the fort and block-houses, and it was with the greatest difficulty and hazard that the garrison saved them from destruction.[2] The Indians retired for a short time only to rally again in greater force. In July, only a few weeks later, they renewed the attack, and prosecuted the siege with unremitting perseverance for twelve days;[3] but they were unable to alarm the garrison until they had made considerable progress in undermining one side of the fort, when, fortunately, heavy rains came on, causing the banks of the trenches to cave in upon the besiegers, and forcing them to abandon the enterprise. During this siege the Indians lost twenty of their number, while the garrison lost but five.

This failure, instead of dispiriting the savages, seemed to spur them on to renewed exertions; and, on the 28th December, 1723, they made another onslaught upon the fortress, continuing the siege for thirty days, at the end of which Captain Westbrook, who had previously been succeeded in the command of the place by Captain Kennedy, came to the

[1] Mass. Rec. x., p. 380. Com. Rep. 1812, p. 60.

[2] Report of Committee of General Court, 1731.

[3] Williamson's Hist. Maine, vol. II., p. 115. — Eaton, in Annals of Warren, says the attack was made August 14.

rescue, and put the Indians to flight.[1] Even this did not damp their ardor, and still another effort was made the following year to seize the fortress; but this also proving unsuccessful, all further attempts were abandoned.

In 1729, Waldo had engaged a clergyman and 120 families to come here and settle; but, owing to the proceedings of Colonel David Dunbar, who enjoyed a brief authority in this province, they did not arrive as soon as they intended, and the settlement of the place was again deferred. In 1732, it was visited by Governor Belcher, for the purpose of learning from the Indians their wants and their grievances, and of making such provision for them as might be necessary. He listened to their several complaints, assuring them of redress; and, after distributing presents among them and drinking the king's health, he departed. In a subsequent message to the legislature, he pronounced a high eulogium upon the soil, rivers, and natural advantages of the country; and, among other things, recommended the rebuilding of the fort, it being then in a state of decay, and there being an abundance of good stone and lime to aid in its erection.[2]

Not at all discouraged by the past frustration of his plans, Waldo succeeded, in 1735, in entering into an engagement with twenty-seven persons to settle on his lands on the St. George; but they, having but recently arrived from Europe and not being acquainted with the management of new lands, accomplished but little in the way of husbandry. Waldo, however, continued with renewed activity to make improvements on his settlements. He erected a grist-mill on the river in 1740, — a strong proof that the settlers had made some progress in agriculture, and were beginning to raise a sufficiency of grain to supply themselves with bread. Harassing conflicts with the Indians made frequent inroads upon the settlement for some time after. Nothing of a permanent character seemed to exist here until the arrival of Mason Wheaton, who settled on Mill river in 1763.

There are various opinions concerning the derivation of the name the town bears. Williamson, the historian of Maine, says, it was named in honor of Major-General John Thomas of Massachusetts, an officer in the American army, who died at Chamblee in the early part of the Revolutionary war. Others say it was named from Thomaston, in Ireland, from whence some of the original settlers came. The town was incorporated in 1777. General Peleg Wadsworth and Major-General Henry Knox were residents of this town.

[1] Hutchinson's History, vol. II., p. 276.

[2] Indian Conference of 1732; and Waldo's petition.

The surface is gently undulating, and drained by Oyster and Mill rivers and Weskeag stream, the latter of which forms a part of the eastern boundary. There are some fine farms in Thomaston; and, were it not that the inhabitants are extensively engaged in quarrying, lime-burning, and ship-building, there might be many more. There are several valuable quarries of limestone; but they are not worked as extensively as formerly, Rockland having taken the lead in this branch of business. The inhabitants, therefore, are turning their attention more exclusively to ship-building. The state prison is located here. The following statistics will doubtless prove interesting: Whole number received since July 2, 1824, 1,186; discharged on expiration of sentence, 845; on writ of error, one; pardoned, 205; died, 29; escaped and not retaken, 9; removed to insane hospital, 4; number remaining, December 31, 1856, 93. There are only one village, extending over a large part of the town; one post-office; five societies — two Baptist, one Congregational, one Methodist, and one Unitarian, each of which, except the Methodist, has a house of public worship. There are a few Catholics in town; but they have no resident priest, though they have services occasionally. There are two banks, doing business on a capital of $50,000 each; one steam mill; an iron foundery; one newspaper establishment; two public libraries; and one post-office. Population, 2,723; valuation, in 1858, $2,124,023.

THORNDIKE, situated in the northwest of Waldo county, is bounded west by Unity, north by Troy, east by Jackson, and south by Knox, and formed a part of the Waldo Patent. It was originally called Lincoln plantation, and the petition for incorporation was dated May 4, 1818, and signed by Joseph Shaw, Joseph Higgins, and Stephen Jones. It was requested in the petition, that the name should be called New Gorham, but it came from the legislators' hands, February 15, 1819, with the name of Thorndike, given to it in honor of the principal proprietor.

The face of the country in Thorndike is quite broken, and the soil requires more than ordinary attention to make it productive. It is watered by a tributary of the Sebasticook, which flows through in a northwest direction, and by the head waters of Marsh river, which rises in this town, and flows easterly, falling into the Penobscot. There are two church edifices — Free-will Baptist and Quaker; ten school districts, with ten schools; two post-offices — Thorndike and East Thorndike; five country retail stores; and three saw-mills. Population, 1,029; valuation, $141,604.

TOPSFIELD, situated in the north part of Washington county, on the second range north of Bingham's Penobscot purchase, was incorporated in 1838. It is a fine location for new settlers and others, who wish to retire from the world and live in seclusion. A small Baptist church was organized here in 1840. Topsfield has one post-office; four school districts, and four schools, with an aggregate of ninety scholars. Population, 268; valuation, $26,642.

TOPSHAM, Sagadahoc county, is about ten miles long and four miles wide, and contains 25,000 acres. It is very pleasantly located on the easterly side of the Andrescoggin river, and the first attempt at settlement was made about the beginning of the eighteenth century. Three men, accompanied by their families, arrived here about that time; the names of whom, save one (who was called Gyles), are now unknown. Stimulated by the prospect of gain, their designs appear to have been to traffic with the natives, rather than make this their permanent abode. One of them built a house and resided at Fulton's point, another at the head of Muddy river, and the third — Gyles — on Pleasant point, at each of which places, not many years since, the cellars and the rude chimneys of their dwellings were clearly traceable.

It is more than probable that the settler at Fulton's point arrived several years prior to the others; for it is stated, that, in 1750, there was a tree upward of one foot in diameter growing in the cellar. There is also a tradition asserting that this settler lived for some time on apparently friendly terms with the natives; but having, on one occasion, been absent in quest of provisions, the Indians massacred his family and burnt his house. He returned; but, fearing he might share the same fate as he supposed had befallen his family, he went to Europe. Both the other families were murdered by the natives. Gyles and his wife were shot while gathering their crops; and the children were taken into captivity, all of whom, except a son, were ransomed by the officers at the garrison of Fort George. The son alluded to was detained in captivity for three years, when he made his escape, and for some years afterward was commander of the garrison at Brunswick, where he composed an account of his captivity, published a few years since by S. G. Drake of Boston, entitled "Tragedies of the Wilderness." The terrible fate which befell these pioneers deterred others from venturing within the precincts of Topsham for many years subsequent to their death. About the year 1730, a few families took up their residence here; and from this period a settlement has been maintained, though for several years many perils and dangers fell to the lot of those who moved into the town. The inhabitants did not feel wholly secure from the attacks of the savages till after the peace of Versailles in 1763, when they began to look forward to brighter days. From the discouraging aspects thus presented, the population increased but slowly, and in 1750 there were but eighteen families in Topsham, most of whom were Scotch-Irish. From this time the population gradually increased, and in 1764 the town was incorporated.

The surface is made up of hills and ravines, but there is a good proportion of arable land. Some of it is sandy, and not very productive. The water-power of the Androscoggin river is sufficient for several factories, — there being three falls within the space of half a mile, — most of which is wholly unemployed. Topsham was celebrated formerly for its business in ship-building; but at the present time it has been entirely discontinued. Lumbering was also prosecuted to a considerable extent; but it likewise has greatly diminished. The Sagadahoc Agricultural and Horticultural Society, which erected its building here in 1856, promises to be very serviceable to the community and the farming interest generally. The structure is commodious and the grounds well laid out, with accommodations for the exhibition of stock. It is situated in the vicinity of the railroad station. The town is easy of access by the Kennebec and Portland Railroad, which passes through, half a mile below the village, at the falls of the Androscoggin. Topsham contains one village; three church edifices — Baptist, Congregational, and Free-will Baptist; ten school districts, and thirteen schools, consisting of primary, grammar, and high schools; one planing and five saw mills; one blind factory; one grist-mill; and one post-office. Population, 2,010; valuation for 1857, $822,611.

TREMONT, Hancock county, situated in the southwest part of Mount Desert island, was formerly a portion of that town, from which it was detached and incorporated June 3, 1848, by the name of Mansel, which was changed to the present one August 8, same year. It contains within its limits the islands called Moose, Gott's, and Langley's. The general characteristics of the soil are similar to those of the parent town. Its trade is principally in fish and lumber. The town has one Union meeting-house, thirteen school districts, with the same number of schools; two saw-mills, two shingle mills, four blacksmith's shops, and three post offices — Tremont, Southwest Harbor, and Seal Cove. Population, 1,600; valuation, $150,000.

TRENTON, Hancock county, on the sea-coast between Union river and Frenchman's bay, was formerly known as No. 1 of the six second-class townships granted by Massachusetts in 1762.[1] It was confirmed to Paul Thorndike and others, June 21, 1785; and the first settlement, of which we can find any account, was made in 1763. At Trenton point, however, there are appearances of a settlement commenced some time anterior to this, probably by the French. Trenton was incorporated February 16, 1789. Its surface is undulating, but the soil is not under cultivation to any great extent, the people being principally engaged in lumbering and fishing. It is watered by Jordan's river, which divides it into Eastern and Western Trenton. There are twelve school districts; three post-offices — East Trenton, Trenton Point, and West Trenton; and two church edifices, both Baptist. There have been four Baptist churches formed in Trenton — the First Trenton, in 1809; the West Trenton and Third Trenton, in 1839; and the East Trenton, in 1844. Population, 1,205; valuation, $148,720.

TRESCOTT, in the southeast part of Washington county, formerly called No. 9, is bounded northeasterly by Lubec, southeasterly by the Atlantic ocean, and southwesterly by Whiting. It was incorporated February 7, 1827. It comprises the harbors of Moose Cove, Bailey's Mistake, and Haycock; is flourishing in trade and navigation; contains eight school districts, with ten schools; and five saw-mills and one grist-mill. Population, 782; valuation, $62,349.

TROY, Waldo county, is thirty-nine miles northeast from Augusta, and twenty from Belfast. The original settlers were Henry Warren, Charles Gerrish, Charles Gerrish, Jr., Enoch Bagly, Enoch Bagly, Jr., Jonathan Bagly, Christopher Varney, John Smart, Andrew Bennett, John Rogers, James Work, Nehemiah Fletcher, Hanson Whitehouse, Francis, Charles, and Thomas Hollman, and Joseph Green, most of whom came from different parts of this state, and settled here from 1801 to 1813. The first clearing was made about the year 1801 by John Rogers, who acted as agent for the proprietor. After this date the plantation was rapidly filled up by an industrious and thrifty population. The first settlers obtained the titles to their lands from General Bridge of Chelmsford, Mass., and from Benjamin Joy of Boston, Mass., who owned about seven eighths of the land. Bridge's claim was a transient one, and subsequently fell into the hands of Benjamin Joy and Jonathan C. Hastings of Boston. When the settlement was organized into a plantation, it received the name of Bridgestown, in honor of General Bridge, who erected the first mill.

[1] Williamson says that the original grant was dated January 27, 1764.

28*

Troy was incorporated, in 1812, by the name of Kingville, since which time, by legislative enactments, it has borne the names of Joy, Montgomery, and latterly, Troy. The surface is generally uneven, rising into large swells, with table-lands and valleys, all of which are very fertile. There is a large, dry bog in the northwest part, which may at some future day be made useful as a fertilizer. There are a number of small streams, which are materially affected by drought. Several mills are erected on these streams; but their business is necessarily small, on account of being compelled to cease operations during the dry season. In the western part, however, there is water-power for mills and machinery, furnished by the Carlton stream, which is formed by a union of small streams, — being the inlet of the Twenty-five-mile pond. The town is drained by branches of the Sebasticook river. Agriculture is the chief employment of the inhabitants. There is but one meeting-house in town, which is open to all denominations. The only regularly organized religious society is that of the Methodist denomination. Other denominations hold meetings at the free meeting-house, town-house, and school-houses. There are twelve schools, having an average attendance of about six hundred and nine scholars; and one post-office. Population, 1,484; valuation for 1856, $172,212.

TURNER, Androscoggin county, lies on the west bank of the Androscoggin river, ten miles above Lewiston Falls village. It is ten miles long from north to south, is about four miles wide on the north, and six miles on the south. The original grant was made by the general court of Massachusetts, in 1735, to Major James Warren and others, survivors of Captain Joseph Sylvester's company, for their services in the expedition against Canada in 1690; but, upon running the boundary line between the provinces of Maine and New Hampshire, their township was found to be within the limits of the latter state, and their claim consequently void. On the representation of these facts by Charles Turner and others, agents for the claimants under the original grantees, the general court, on the 25th of June, 1765, made up for the loss by a grant of the present territory, under the name of Sylvester township, on the usual conditions for making a settlement; but, through the remissness of the proprietors, no attempt was made to improve their grant until 1773, when, upon their offer of a lot of land and ten dollars to every one who should become a settler, five young men, — Elisha and Thomas Records, Daniel Staples, Abner Phillips, and Joseph Leavitt, came from Plymouth county, Mass., and began to clear land. They returned to their families in winter, and came again in the following summer with several others; but the first who made a permanent settlement with his family was Israel Haskell, who came from New-

Gloucester in the spring of 1775. Two other families followed him during the summer. Among the early settlers were William and Chandler Bradford, Dea. Daniel Merrill from New Gloucester, and a Mr. Copeland. In 1785, according to the statement of the petition for incorporation, the settlement numbered forty-five families. The act to incorporate was passed July 7, 1786. Rev. Charles Turner had occasionally visited the plantation, and preached: but no church was gathered until the Presbyterian, which was organized in 1784, and of which Rev. John Strickland, a native of Hadley, Mass., and graduate of Yale College (1761), became pastor, and continued such until 1792. He was followed by Rev. Amasa Smith, of Belchertown, Mass., in 1804, and by Rev. Allen Greely in 1810. This church gradually lost its Presbyterian character, and in 1803 became Congregational. The Baptists organized a church in 1824, and there are two Universalist societies; all of them having meeting-houses. There is a ministerial fund, yielding an annual income of $360, which is divided among the churches having settled pastors, in proportion to their respective numbers. Turner is a good farming town—has a large water-power, as yet but little occupied. There are several mills, among which are three grist-mills, and five saw-mills. There are nineteen school districts, with forty schools; and four post-offices, called Turner, East Turner, North Turner, and North Turner Bridge. Population, 2,537; valuation, $418,832.

Union, in the northeast part of Lincoln county, originally embraced an area of 34,560 acres. It was included in the Waldo Patent, and was purchased of the Waldo heirs by Dr. John Taylor of Lunenburg, Massachusetts, in 1774, "for the consideration of £1,000, lawful money." Taylor commenced the settlement the same year he made the purchase, offering such inducements to settlers, that, in a few years, the whole tract was lotted and taken up; and on the 20th of October, 1786, it was incorporated. It then contained nineteen families, nearly all of whom had emigrated from Massachusetts. There are many pleasant reminiscences connected with the history of the early settlers, which, were this the proper place, might be profitably related. They were devout Christians, and, being isolated, made every effort to cultivate those feelings of friendly intercourse which make life blessed.

Union and Dresden are the best agricultural towns in the county. The picturesque varieties of hill and dale, water and woodland, render the scenery, in the summer season, truly beautiful. There are five ponds, three of which lie partly in other towns; and some two or three streams, besides the St. George's river, by which the town is drained; also, four villages, known as Union Common, East Union,

North Union, and South Union; three post-offices — Union, North Union, and East Union; four churches — Baptist, Methodist, Congregationalist, and Universalist, the latter of which own a part of the Baptist meeting-house; two carriage factories, one edge-tool, one shovel-handle, and one woollen factory; and fourteen school districts, with the same number of schools. Population, 1,974; valuation, $341,621.

UNITY is situated in the northwest part of Waldo county, thirty-five miles from Augusta. It formerly belonged to the Plymouth Patent, and its settlement was commenced about the year 1782. It was incorporated June 22, 1804; the harmony of feeling on political questions at the time finding expression in its name. The soil, in some parts, is tolerably productive; but, as a whole, farming is not a very profitable business. Unity is watered by Twenty-five-mile pond, which lies between it and Burnham. The town has one village; four church edifices — Congregational, Quaker, Methodist, and Union; thirteen school districts, with the same number of schools; four saw-mills, four grist-mills, four shingle machines, two or three tanneries; and one post-office. Population, 1,557; valuation, $236,031.

VASSALBOROUGH, Kennebec county, lies on the east side of Kennebec river, and joins Augusta on the northeast, extending along the river ten miles. It was settled, about 1760, by emigrants chiefly from Cape Cod. Williamson says that, in 1768, Vassalborough contained but ten families; and, in 1771, the year it was incorporated, the inhabitants voted "to raise £30 lawful money, for the support of a minister and other necessary charges." At that time the area of the town was much larger than now, Sidney, on the west side of the river, being included within its boundaries. It continued thus until January 30, 1792, when Sidney was set off.

The surface is beautifully diversified, and the soil excellent. Taber hill and Cross hill are the only two eminences. Webber pond is a large body of water, lying a short distance from the centre. Part of China lake lies on the eastern side of the town. The water-power is excellent. The principal business is the manufacture of woollen goods, and tanning. At East Vassalborough village are two grist-mills, a saw-mill, a woollen factory, and a large amount of machinery otherwise employed. At North Vassalborough is a woollen manufactory, which produces about $300,000 worth of goods annually, employing about two hundred operatives. For many years the tanning business was carried on very considerably, and is still prosecuted to some extent. There are eight church edifices, two occupied by the Friends, the most numerous denomination, one Baptist, one Congregational, two Methodist, and two Union; also, twenty-three school districts, one academy, and the Oak Grove Seminary, owned and directed by the Friends; three thriving villages; and six post-offices — Vassalborough, Brown's Corner, East Vassalborough, North Vassalborough, Seward's Mills, and South Vassalborough. Population, 3,099; valuation, $648,288.

VEAZIE, Penobscot county, is a small town on the west side of Penobscot river, taken from Bangor and incorporated March 26, 1853. It was named in honor of General Samuel Veazie, and is about two miles square. It has a very pretty village. The principal business is the manufacture of lumber. It has one public-house; two church edifices, owned by the Congregationalists and Baptists; one school district, with four schools; and one post-office. Population, 800; valuation, $255,231.

VIENNA is situated in the northwest part of Kennebec county, twenty-two miles from Augusta. It was surveyed, in 1792, by Jedediah Prescott, and, September 25, 1800, thirty-five of the inhabitants of the place — then called Wyman's Plantation — petitioned for incorporation, representing the plantation to contain sixty ratable polls. Among the signers were Noah Prescott, Joseph Chapman, Timothy White, Abel Whittier, and John Carr. A remonstrance was made by several other of the inhabitants, on the ground that "the petitioners were inhabitants of a place known to them by the name of Goshen, a tract of land wide from them by nature's laws," and that Chester was conveniently accessible for religious and town purposes. This remonstrance, however, was ineffectual, and the town was incorporated February 20, 1802, Jedediah Prescott being authorized to call the first meeting. The face of Vienna is uneven, there being several hills interspersed through it, while on the eastern side lies Thomas's or Gilman mountain, which extends into Rome. The soil is generally fertile. Kimball, Kidder's, Graves's, Egypt, and McGurdy ponds lie in different parts of the town; and Flying pond, a considerable body of water, is situated on the southerly line. There are two villages — Vienna and North Vienna; two churches — Free-will Baptist and Methodist; nineteen school districts, and one post-office; also a peg factory, propelled by steam, one grist-mill, two saw-mills, three shingle machines, and three blacksmith's shops. Population, 851; valuation, $126,125.

VINAL HAVEN, Waldo county, is what was known in the early history of New England as the South Fox Island, taking that name from the number of silver-gray foxes found here. It was a favorite place of resort for the early voyagers, on account of its "safe and convenient harbors." A permanent settlement was not established until 1765, and even then the inhabitants did not enjoy an undisturbed quiet. During the progress of the Revolution, the English at Castine impressed many of the islanders into their service in erecting fortifications there, while others escaped, leaving their houses and effects to be reduced to ashes by the plundering soldiery. On the conclusion of peace, the inhabitants returned to the island, and obtained from Massachusetts valid titles to their lots. Seventy-two of the number purchased the entire island, north and south, from the commonwealth, for £246.

This town, including North Haven, contains an area of 16,527 acres. It has a bold shore, with good harbors on every side, running in between projecting bluffs. It was incorporated June 25, 1789. The surface of the island is very broken; not more than one third of it being suitable for cultivation. Some fishing and coasting vessels have been built here, but on account of the scarcity of timber, the business was long since given up. The leading pursuit of the inhabitants is fishing. There are two light-houses on the island, both of which are single lights; also a small village called Carver's Harbor, having a post-office. Population, 1,252; valuation, $103,921.

WALDO, Waldo county, lies north of Belfast, the northwest corner of Belfast touching the southwest corner of Waldo. It contains about eleven thousand six hundred acres. When Waldo plantation was organized, July 6, 1821, it consisted of the so-called "Three Mile Square," or "Six Thousand Acre Tract," only, which was, in September, 1800, set off on execution from the goods and estate of Brigadier-General Waldo of Boston, deceased, to Sarah Waldo, administratrix of the estate of Samuel Waldo, of Falmouth, Maine, deceased; and, according to the transcript, was nine hundred and eighty rods square, and was appraised at $8,000 by Robert Houston, James Nesmith, and Daniel Clary, of Belfast. The first clearing on this tract was made in 1798, near the southeast corner, one hundred rods from the Belfast line, by William Taggart, and a Mr. Smith from New Hampshire. This "possession," as it was called, subsequently had several owners; but no family resided on it until November, 1811, when Henry Davidson moved in, and continued thirty-six years. About the year 1800, Jonathan Thurston, of Belfast, made an opening where Hall Clements (who came here in 1822 or 1823) now resides, and his family was the first on the tract. A third opening was made where Comfort Whitcomb now resides, in 1805, by Josiah Sanborn, from Exeter, N. H. In 1809, the tract was surveyed by Malcolm and Gleason into sixty lots, in six ranges of ten lots each. In 1810, when the third United States census was taken, there were not probably more than four or five families on the tract, and there was no return made of these. In 1824, Waldo plantation was enlarged, by the annexation of about five thousand three hundred and eighteen acres from Swanville, which that town made no effort to retain; and, in 1836, a gore of about one hundred and fifty acres, lying between Knox and the "Three Mile Square," was annexed. The plantation, thus enlarged, constitutes the present town.

Waldo was incorporated in 1845. A large portion of the land is rocky, uneven, or broken, and unfit for cultivation, and will probably, for many generations, be reserved for the growth of forest trees. There are, however, some excellent farms and prosperous farmers. At the annual cattle-shows of the county, a fair proportion of premiums is awarded to Waldo. It is watered by the Passagassawaukeag, or Belfast river, and by Wescott's stream, on which are seven saw-mills, one grist-mill, and some shingle machines.

There is no place in Waldo that can with propriety be called a village; nor is there any extensive manufactory of merchandise. The Baptist church, which existed here twenty-five years ago, has become extinct. Ten years ago, the Free-will Baptists were in a prosperous state, and built a meeting-house. Recently, in consequence of the death of one prominent member, and the removal of some others, the church seems to be in a languishing state, and their meeting-house has now become free to all denominations. There is a small society of Methodists, who are visited by a circuit preacher once in two weeks. In December, 1847, the post-office was removed one mile, to the head of tide-water in the city of Belfast, three miles northwest from the court house. It still retains the name of Waldo post-office. In this little village is a meeting-house; and the Rev. Joseph R. Munsell is pastor of a Congregational church, a few of whose members reside in Waldo. There are three stores, one tannery, and one saw-mill, stave and shingle machines, and sundry mechanical operations. One mile east of this, at a place called The Point, at the head of sloop navigation, are four stores, which do extensive business. There are seven school districts, with fourteen schools. Population, 812; valuation, $81,597.

WALDOBOROUGH, Lincoln county, on an arm of the sea, for many years called Broad Bay, was included within the Muscongus or Waldo Patent. It was settled, through the persevering efforts of Waldo and the other patentees and claimants, by Scotch-Irish and German emigrants, between 1733 and 1740. Shortly afterwards, the town was attacked by the Indians, and burned to ashes; and those not tomahawked were carried away captives. Immediately after the ratification of the treaty of Aix-la-Chapelle, in 1748, the settlement was revived; and, in 1752–3, Samuel Waldo, son of the General, visited Germany, and issued his proclamation, promising every emigrant, settling upon his father's possessions, one hundred acres of land; and it is fair to presume, that, as an additional incentive to emigration, he promised them exemption from the grasping hand of capricious landlords, and a toleration of their religious and political opinions, untrammelled by priestly surveillance.

Influenced by such encouraging prospects, about 1,500 people removed from Germany, and here lived in contiguous neighborhoods till 1763–4, when the lands on the west side of Muscongus river were claimed by Drowne, as being without Waldo's Patent. They submitted to pay for their lands the next year, but very soon after the Brown claim was extended over the same lands. Upon the settlement of the Waldo heirs with the commonwealth of Massachusetts, they (the Waldo heirs) released all the lands on the west side of the river, and thus the German settlers planted there by Waldo were left without any indemnity or remuneration. Displeased with such treatment, and disappointed in their expectations, three hundred families sold their estates for the most they could obtain, and removed to the southwestern part of Carolina, where some of their German brethren had settled. There was, however, a large and flourishing community left on the spot, which was, in 1773, incorporated into a town, and named in honor of General Waldo. A Lutheran church was organized on the arrival of the German settlers, and a minister settled in 1762. In 1786, Waldoborough was made a shire town, and remained such till 1800, when the courts were removed to Wiscasset. Conrad Heyer, the first male citizen of Waldoborough, was born April 10, 1749, and died February 19, 1856, at the advanced age of 106 years, ten months, and nine days. He served in the Revolutionary war, and was wont to relate his adventures in that struggle with peculiar zest. His father was one of the emigrants brought over from Germany by General Waldo. He was buried on the 17th of June, 1856, with military honors. The funeral obsequies were largely attended, not only by the citizens of Waldoborough, but by those of adjoining towns, thus exhibiting the respect in which this venerable man was held.

The surface is agreeably diversified. There are some good farms; but generally the soil is not very productive. Within the limits of

Waldoborough are several islands, the names of which are Upper Narrows, Hog, Poland's, Hadlock, Hungry, Otter, Jones's, Garden, and several smaller ones. Farming, seafaring, and some little ship-building, engage the industrial energies of the people. The village was greatly injured by fire a few years since, but has been rebuilt. The new buildings evince much improvement upon the former ones. The town is drained by Muscongus river, which has a sufficient fall to be made available in propelling machinery. Waldoborough has a bank with a capital of $50,000; two post-offices — Waldoborough and North Waldoborough; six church edifices, — two Congregational, one Methodist, two Baptist, and one Lutheran; twenty-nine school districts, with thirty-two schools; fourteen ship-builders, two carriage builders, six saw-mills, three grist-mills, two carding-machines, one tannery, and two brickmakers. Population, 4,199; valuation, $941,088.

WALDO COUNTY has the Penobscot bay and river upon the east, Penobscot county upon the north, and Kennebec and Lincoln counties upon the west; and extends somewhat beyond the original limits of the Waldo Patent. The act establishing it was passed February 7, 1827, giving it jurisdiction over "all that portion of the territory of the county of Hancock lying westward of the Penobscot bay and river, with the town of Islesborough in said county, and the towns of Camden, Hope, Montville, and Palermo, and the plantations of Appleton and Montville (now the towns of Appleton and Liberty), in the county of Lincoln, and the towns of Freedom, Unity, Montgomery, and Burnham in the county of Kennebec." By act of January 22, 1828, the limits of this county were enlarged eastward, by making the line dividing it from Hancock "the middle of the channel of the Penobscot river and bay, commencing in the middle of said river, at the northerly line of the county of Waldo, and descending the same, leaving Orphan island on the east, and Islesborough on the west, till it intersects a line drawn due east from the southern corner of this county of Waldo." It has thirty-one towns, of which Belfast is the shire.

The surface is uneven, and, in some parts, mountainous. The chief eminences are Mounts Waldo, Knox, and Meganticook. The maritime interests of the county surpass its agricultural, having its largest side and seven of its leading towns upon the bay and river, which have attained an eminence in ship-building, in commerce, and in the fisheries, enjoyed by few towns on the coast of Maine. The principal rivers are the Sebasticook, Duck-trap, Passagassawaukeag, Marsh, and Meganticook. There are also some ponds.

This county belongs to the eastern judicial district of the state, the law terms of which are held at Bangor. The jury terms of the supreme judicial court for civil and criminal business commence on the first Tuesdays of May and October; for civil business only, on the first Tuesday of January. Population, 47,230; valuation, $6,800,981.

WALDO, LINCOLNSHIRE, or MUSCONGUS PATENT, was a tract of land granted by the council of Plymouth, March 13, $16\frac{29}{30}$ o. s., to John Beauchamp of London, and Thomas Leverett of Boston, England. This grant was more generally supposed to cover the territory between the Penobscot and Muscongus rivers, from the sea-coast so far northward, to an unsurveyed line running east and west, as would embrace a territory, without interfering with any other patent, equal to thirty miles square. But the vague description of its boundaries gave rise to another construction; for it is quite evident, from later transactions, that claims were made under it of territory east of the Penobscot.[1] The patentees are supposed to have come to this country,[2] but to have made no attempt at settlement. Beauchamp died, and the lands descended from the survivor, who was the father of John Leverett, Governor of the Province, to his great-grandson, John Leverett, President of Harvard College, who divided the patent, August 14, 1719, into ten shares. The "ten proprietors" assigned two thirds of their lands to the "twenty associates," and held the remainder. "At this period," says Williamson (Vol. II. 97), "there was not a house between Georgetown and Anapolis, except a fish-house on Damariscove Island, nor until the time St. George's fort was built by the proprietors, in 1719–20." This fort, in 1722, was made a public garrison. It resisted successfully repeated attacks from Indians and French, the last attack being in 1758, by a body of 400. The site of it was in front of the mansion of Gen. Knox, in Thomaston. Attempts of the proprietors to promote the settlement were for a few years frustrated, on account of the claim to territory and jurisdiction by David Dunbar, surveyor of the King's woods; but Samuel Waldo, a merchant of Boston, who had a large interest, was chosen agent for the proprietors, and after two years' attendance, and solicitation at the Court of London, at his own expense, August 11, 1731, obtained an order ousting Dunbar. At this time there were probably 150 families between the Muscongus and Kennebec. Mr. Waldo was now un-

[1] The patent is found entire in 1 Haz. State Papers, 304–5, but is too long for insertion here. The clause of it, which was particularly ambiguous, reads — "and the utmost limits of the space of ten leagues, on the north and north-east of a river in New England aforesaid, commonly called Penobscot, towards the north and north-east." See Report of Com. of Legislature, July 4, 1785.

[2] Eaton's Annals of Warren, p. 19.

sparing in his efforts and outlays to obtain settlers, — with what success is more particularly set forth in the various towns embraced under the patent. He was patriotic, and, in 1745, was appointed by Gov. Shirley a brigadier-general in the expedition against Louisburg. In 1753, his son visited Germany, and issued a circular promising to every one, who should emigrate and settle on the patent, one hundred acres of land, and such aid as he might need before harvest. A large number of honest and industrious people came and settled about Broad bay and Broad cove; but many of them, disheartened by the hardships incidental to a new country and by adverse claims, returned, or emigrated to other parts — some 300 families, in 1773, to the southwest part of Carolina. In the last French and Indian war, it was deemed necessary further to guard the mouth of the Penobscot, and Governor Pownall, with 333 men, made an expedition from Boston to this river, to erect a suitable fort, which was completed in July, 1759, at Fort Point, in the present town of Stockton, and called Fort Pownall. He was accompanied by General Waldo, who fell dead of apoplexy on the east side of the river, just above the first falls (near Eddington bend), May 23, 1759. His remains were taken back to the fort, and interred the next day with the honors of war. In the revolution, most of the Waldo heirs were "absentees." In September, 1778, an act was passed confiscating the estates of 310 persons, among whom was Thomas Fluker, a son-in-law of General Waldo; Gen. Henry Knox, Fluker's son-in-law and administrator, at a low figure, bought up the rights of the heirs. Complaints about title being still made by the settlers, the legislature, by act of July 4, 1785, determined the bounds of the patent, extending the same six miles north of the old line, on condition that all claim east of the Penobscot should be released; and by act of March 9, 1797, appointed Nathan Dane, John Sprague, and Enoch Titcomb, commissioners to quiet the settlers, dividing them into three classes — settlers *before*, *during*, and *after* the war, then in possession, or who had transferred to others then in possession. The six mile extension of the patent struck into the Plymouth patent, on the north-west, for which interference a new survey, ordered February 23, 1798, gave four townships (Bangor, Hampden, Newburg, and Hermon) to the patent.

WALES, Androscoggin county, is bounded north by Monmouth, east by Litchfield, south by Webster, and west by Greene; being only four and a half miles long and four wide. It was settled in 1773. Among the first inhabitants were Samuel Waymouth, from Berwick; Jonathan and Reuben Ham; James Wetherell, John Andrews, and John Ham, from Brunswick; and Joseph Small, from Limington, — at whose house the first plantation meeting was held. The settlers purchased their lands of proprietors under the old Plymouth Company. In April, 1803, the settlers met, organized as a plantation, and chose Joseph Small clerk, which office he filled thirty years. At this meeting it was voted to raise $50 for plantation expenses, $150 for schools, and $150 for roads. For the first twelve or fifteen years, there were no saw-mills or grist-mills within twenty miles; and the settlers were compelled to carry their bags of corn on their shoulders this distance, with no path except marked trees to guide them. The only meats they had were such as they could procure with the rifle — moose, deer, bear, and other game.

The surface is uneven, but not broken. There are two elevations of land, one in the southeast part, called Hodgkins hill, which rises to the height of six hundred feet; the other in the southwest, called Sabattis mountain, on the southeast side of which is a cave, called the "Devil's den." In this cave are found some of the finest specimens of red ochre. How far the cave extends is not known. Sabattis pond lies partly in this town; but there is no stream of water of sufficient capacity for mills. The soil is good, and adapted to any crop; and agriculture is becoming the chief occupation of the settlers. There are seven school districts, with the same number of schools, and two church edifices — one occupied by the Baptists, the other by Baptists, Free-will Baptists, Methodists, and Universalists; one post-office, one carriage manufactory, and one marble shop. Population, 612; valuation, $111,632.

Waltham, Hancock county, is situated on the east bank of Union river, opposite Mariaville. The settlement was commenced about the year 1805 or 1806, by Samuel Ingalls, Lebbeus and Eben Kingman, Ebenezer Jordan, and others. The progress of it has been very slow. It was incorporated in 1831. The town has two saw-mills, one church edifice (Baptist), two schools, with an average attendance of eighty-two scholars, and one post-office. Population, 304; valuation, $41,881.

Warren, Lincoln county, on both sides of St. George's river, at the head of navigation, was originally known as the "Upper town of St. George," and belonged to the Muscongus, afterwards the Waldo Patent. The first settlement was begun under the auspices of Waldo, the proprietor, in 1736, at which time, says Eaton, "with the exception of a trading house, mill, and fort, which had been erected on the banks of the St. George, one hundred and five years previous, no marks of civilization existed, and no inroads were made upon that unbroken forest, which over the whole country sheltered the moose and the Indian alike from the scorching suns of summer and the howling storms of winter."

Waldo made a similar contract with the settlers here to that made by him for the settlement of Thomaston; and, in the summer of 1736, forty-seven persons, having cast lots for their possessions, located themselves. Waldo furnished the inhabitants with provisions, and they occupied themselves principally in getting out cord-wood and staves, and sometimes in hunting and fishing. Agriculture was not much prosecuted, the people understanding but little about the management of new lands. A spirit of harmony prevailed among them, which some of our modern settlements would do well to emulate. In 1752, the town received an accession to its numbers by the arrival of some German emigrants; and from year to year the numbers were augmented — English, Scotch, Irish, and Germans being among the settlers.

Warren was incorporated in November, 1776, taking its name from General Joseph Warren, who fell so gloriously at the battle of Bunker Hill. The surface is broken, having some considerable eminences, the most notable of which are Mount Pleasant and Crawford mountain, the former commanding an extensive view of the neighboring towns, the Atlantic ocean, Penobscot bay, and its islands. The soil is variable in character, but amply rewards the labors of the husbandman. Limestone and granite are found in abundance, and are extensively quarried. The town is drained by Back river, and by Little, Southwest, and Crawford's ponds. The coasting trade was formerly a branch of business much followed; but latterly it has almost entirely ceased. Ship-building, however, has steadily advanced, as well in the number, as in the size and quality, of the vessels. Between the years 1770 and 1850, there were built 224 vessels, varying from fifty-three to 1,127 tons burden. Agriculture and ship-building are now the principal pursuits, and the facilities for their prosecution are of the best kind. There are four religious societies, Congregational, Baptist, Methodist, and Free-will Baptist; twenty school districts, with nineteen schools; an academy, endowed by a grant of half a township of land; a post-office; also a woollen factory, and other mechanical works. Population, 2,428; valuation, $707,730.

Washington is situated in the northerly part of Lincoln county, thirty-five miles easterly from Augusta, a part of it formerly being included within the limits of the Plymouth Patent, and a part under the Waldo Patent. It was made up of the "westerly part of Union, and several gores and strips of land adjacent thereto," and was incorporated by the name of Putnam, upon the petition of thirty-eight of the inhabitants, February 27, 1811. Among the petitioners were Mark Hatch, James Laughton, John Bowmin, David Colamy, John Laughton, Benjamin Speed, William Starrett, Thomas Nelson, James Daggett, Samuel Stickney, and Sanford Rhoades, most of whom were probably early settlers. The name was changed to Washington, January 31, 1823.

The surface is uneven, and in some parts rocky. It is watered by a large pond, and a branch of the Muscongus river, which takes its rise in this pond. The town is purely agricultural, having no more trade or mechanical business than is requisite for the ordinary wants of the place. It has one village, three church edifices — Methodist, Congregational, and Union; twelve school districts; and three post-offices — Washington, South Washington, and North Washington. Population, 1,756; valuation, $143,560.

Washington County originally made the whole eastern frontier of Maine, having been established by the same act that spoke Hancock county into existence, June 25, 1789. Its western boundary was the eastern line of Hancock.[1] It was bounded "south and southeast by the sea or western ocean, on the north by the utmost northern limits of this commonwealth, and easterly by the river Saint Croix; comprehending all the lands within this commonwealth to the eastward of the line of the county of Hancock aforesaid, including all the islands on the sea-coast of said easternmost county." In 1839, it surrendered to Aroostook all the territory "north of the north line of the fourth range of townships, north of the lottery townships."[2] The area of the county is about twenty-seven hundred square miles. It had, by the census of 1790, a population of 2,758. Its sea-coast extends for about fifty miles, and abounds in bays and inlets, which afford excellent harbors. It is drained by the Schoodic, the St. Croix, and the east and west Machias rivers, and contains numerous lakes, the most important of which are the Schoodic and the Baskahegan. The surface is undulating, and the soil back from the seashore is fertile. The people are beginning to show an active interest in railroad enterprise, which has materially aided the growth of some of the older counties. Machias was made the shire town at a time when it was the only corporate town in the county, and has continued to be the county seat. At the time of organization, the terms set for the common pleas and court of sessions were in June and September for both this and Hancock counties; but all matters happening in either, whereof the supreme judicial court had cognizance, were to be heard and tried at their annual term at Pownalborough.

The county now belongs to the eastern judicial district, the law terms for which are held at Bangor. The jury terms of the supreme judicial

[1] See Hancock county, ante, pp. 151-2.

[2] See Aroostook county, ante, p. 33.

court commence at Machias on the first Tuesdays in January and October, and the fourth Tuesday in April. Population, 38,811; valuation, $5,244,431.

WATERBOROUGH, York county, is a part of a tract of land purchased by William Phillips in 1661–4, of the Indian sagamores Fluellen, Hobinowell, and Captain Sunday. John Smith made a settlement in 1768, the first of which any thing definite is known. In 1770 there were eight families here, those of John Smith, John Scribner, Robert Harvey, Alexander Jellison, William Deering, Scammon Hodsdon, William Philpot, and William Nason, who came from Scarborough and Berwick, and from New Hampshire, all of whom lived in log huts. Colonel Josiah Waters of Boston, and others, claimed this town under an old Indian deed, and in 1771–2 sent Moses Banks to lot and survey the same; but the Revolution commencing shortly after, and part of the original proprietors turning tories, nothing further was done till 1784, when Colonel Waters had the plantation surveyed, and sold the lots to 118 actual settlers for twenty-five cents to one dollar per acre. Waterborough was originally known as Massabesick plantation, which name it retained till its incorporation, March 6, 1787. It was made a shire town of York county in 1790, and the courts of common pleas and sessions were holden here till their removal to Alfred in 1807. The first church was organized in 1780.

Waterborough contains 26,491 acres. The land lies mostly in swells or ridges running from north to south, which were covered with white, red, and yellow oak, beach, maple, and birch. There are large tracts of pine plain, on which was formerly a heavy growth of timber, now cleared. This land is quite barren, and of little value, while that on the swells is equal to any in the county. Ossipee mountain, lying in the centre of the town, is, with one exception, the highest in the county, and is a station for the United States coast survey. There are several ponds, covering about one thousand acres, there being considerable meadow land, originally flowed by beaver dams upon the streams which flow into them. The people are engaged in farming.

There are two villages — Waterborough and Waterborough Centre; two church edifices — Baptist and Free-will Baptist; fifteen school districts, with fourteen schools; and two post-offices — Waterborough and Waterborough Centre. Population, 1,989; valuation, $200,332.

WATERFORD, Oxford county, is distant from Augusta fifty-seven miles, and from Paris fourteen miles. David McWaine, who arrived in 1775, from Bolton, Mass., was the first settler, and for five or six years was the only person in town. Among those who settled subsequently were four brothers by the name of Hamlin, five or six brothers named Brown, and four families named Jewett, Saunders, Chaplin, and Greene, who came from Rowley, Mass. The other settlers came principally from Bolton, Harvard, and Stow. The titles to the lands were obtained from the proprietors, Jonathan Houghton, Henry Gardiner, David Sampson, Jonathan Whitcomb, and others.

Waterford was incorporated in January, 1797. The surface is rather uneven and somewhat mountainous, but the land is good for agriculture, which engrosses most of the attention of the inhabitants. There are twelve ponds — Thomas's pond, in the centre of the town, containing 484 acres; Long pond, Bear pond, Island pond, Bog pond, Moose pond, containing 182 acres; Duck pond, Pappoose pond, and four ponds known as the Kezar ponds, the largest of which contains 124 acres. The only river of any size is Crooked river; and the only hills of any note are the Tyrum, Bear, and Hawk, each of which is some five hundred feet in height. There are three villages; three church edifices — Congregational, Methodist, and Universalist; three post-offices — Waterford, North Waterford, and South Waterford; and fifteen school districts, with twenty-four schools. Population, 1,448; valuation, $263,096.

WATERVILLE, Kennebec county, — the early history of which is embodied in that of Winslow, from which it was taken and incorporated in 1802, — lies on the west side of the Kennebec river, and is six miles long by a little more than six wide, having quite an irregular western boundary. It has two villages, called respectively Waterville and West Waterville. The former contains about twenty-five hundred inhabitants, is situated on a fine alluvial plain at the head of boat navigation, and is one of the most attractive villages in the state. The west village lies on the outlet of Snow's pond, which is partly in Belgrade. The surface generally is rolling, and the soil good. Agriculture is the leading pursuit, though considerable lumber is manufactured at the east village, besides some manufacturing in axes, hoes, and scythes at the west village. A paper-mill and foundery on Emerson's stream (which runs from Snow's pond), are doing a moderate business. There is a fine fall of water of about twenty feet on the Kennebec, situated at the east village, called Ticonic falls; but this privilege is as yet but partially improved. Richmond lake and McGrath's pond lie on the west. There are two post-offices, one at each village; six church edifices — two Baptist, two Universalist, one Congregational, and one Free-will Baptist; fourteen school districts, with twenty-two schools; an academy and college, both in the east village. Waterville College was chartered in 1820, and, though the state has done but little for its endowment, private individuals have contributed largely to its funds, and furnished it the means for conducting with success a liberal system of education. It has educated many of our public men; and, from its central position, seems destined to exert an important influence upon the educational

Waterville College.

interests of the state. There are three banks — the Ticonic Bank, Waterville Bank, and People's Bank, having an aggregate capital stock of $350,000. In the summer season, a small steamboat plies between Waterville, Augusta, and Gardiner; while three railroads, the Androscoggin and Kennebec, Penobscot and Kennebec, and Somerset and Kennebec, concentrate here. The village is well supplied with public-houses, has many fine residences, and several blocks of buildings for business purposes. A weekly paper is published, called the Eastern Mail. Population, 3,964; valuation, $1,018,362.

WAYNE, Kennebec county, is situated about sixteen miles northwest of Augusta, and was first settled by Reuben Wing, Reuben Besse, Job Fuller, Samuel Norris, Isaac Dexter, and others, who came from Sandwich, Mass., about the close of the Revolutionary war. These settlers, as was then the custom, located themselves in close proximity to the meadows, so that they might easily procure grass for their cattle. They purchased their land from the Plymouth Company. The township was called New Sandwich until its incorporation in 1798, when it received its present name, in honor of Anthony Wayne, a general in the Revolution. When it was first settled, — although adjoining the thriving town of Winthrop, — it was considered as beyond the pale of civilization, and the Botany Bay of the state. Rev. David Thurston gives an anecdote, in his history of Winthrop, of an itinerant fiddler, who came into that town to pursue his profession; which being particularly obnoxious to the inhabitants, he was warned by the sheriff to leave instanter. But the poor vagabond, at his wits' end, inquired whither he should go. The sheriff replied — "Get out of the world! go to Wayne!" However truly this may have applied to Wayne then, at the present day it is one of the most enterprising and flourishing towns in the county.

The surface is uneven and broken, particularly in the southern part, which is also very rocky; notwithstanding which, the soil is good for farming, and the inhabitants are active in developing its agricultural resources. The water-power is excellent, there being a chain of four ponds, commencing with Flying pond in the south part of Vienna, all flowing into Wing's pond (which has its outlet in Androscoggin pond) in Wayne village. There are two important places of business — Wayne village, at the outlet of Wing's pond, and North Wayne village, at the outlet of Lovejoy's pond. At the former there are mills and manufactories of various descriptions; three churches — one Methodist, one Baptist, and one Free-will Baptist; five stores, and several mechanic shops. The village is very pleasantly situated, and in a flourishing condition. At North Wayne village is situated the North Wayne scythe manufactory, which annually turns out a large quantity of scythes, and gives employment to a considerable number of workmen. Here also is a Methodist church. This village is situated about three miles northeast from Wayne village, and is a thriving place. There are fourteen school districts, and two post-offices — Wayne and North Wayne. Population, 1,367; valuation, $233,339.

WEBSTER, Androscoggin county, is distant from Augusta twenty-seven miles, and was first settled, about 1774, by Robert Ross, from Brunswick, who located on the shores of the stream which bears his name. The next settlement was made a short time after, in the south part of the town, by one Mora, said to have been a deserter from the American army. The place is still known as Mora's meadow, and is upon land owned by Eliphalet S. Bryant. About the same time, Timothy Weymouth, from Berwick, settled, and built a mill for Jesse Davies.

Edmund, Nahum, and Jonathan Weymouth, John Henry, Timothy Tibbetts, Foster Wentworth, Abner and Ephraim Jordan, Levi Temple, James Maxwell, William True, Phineas Spofford, Elias Moody, and Edmund Weymouth, Jr., made settlements about 1780. The lands first settled, as well as all within the territorial limits of Webster, were finally decided to be within the grant made to the Plymouth Colony in 1629. Webster was originally within the territorial limits of Bowdoin, which was divided, and the western part incorporated, with the name of Thompsonborough, June 22, 1798. This name was changed to Lisbon, by act of legislature, February 20, 1802; and, March 7, 1840, Lisbon was divided, and the northern part incorporated, with the name of Webster.

Captain Jeremiah Nowell, a native of Webster, was the captain of the vessel which carried Jerome Bonaparte and his wife — Miss Patterson, of Baltimore — to France, and brought the latter and her child back to America.

The surface and soil are various. Along the Sabattis river are very considerable elevations and depressions. The rock formation is chiefly gneiss, impregnated with iron, which crops out upon its greatest elevations. For the most part, the intermediate elevations consist of drift, varying in depth from twenty to one hundred feet. In the southern part, on the eastern margin of the Sabattis river, lies a level tract of considerable extent, consisting of clay, portions of which are formed of alluvial deposits. Mount Sabattis lies in the northwestern part, on the line of division of Webster and Wales, and was occupied, during 1853 and 1854, as a station of the Coast Survey. The completion of the railway from Portland to Lewiston gives the industrial resources of Webster means for development, and will make its fine farming lands and extensive water-power substantial elements of wealth. Sabattisville is the principal and only village. There are three church edifices — Baptist. Free-will Baptist, and Union; eleven school districts, with twenty schools; and two post-offices — Webster and Sabattisville. Population, 1,110; valuation for 1856, $257,289.

WELD, Franklin county, formerly known as No. 5, or Webb's Pond Plantation, is a large town, containing about forty-eight square miles, and is about ten miles from the court-house in Farmington. It was settled about 1800. Nathaniel Kittredge, Caleb Holt, James Houghton, Abel Holt, and Joseph and Abel Russel, were among the first settlers.

Weld was surveyed by Samuel Titcomb, surveyor to the state. It was lotted by Philip Bullen, in 1797, and originally purchased of the state by Jonathan Phillips, of Boston. Sales to settlers were commenced by Jacob Abbot, of Wilton, N. H., who, in 1815, purchased, in company with Benjamin Weld, of Boston, Mr. Phillips's unsold lands in Maine. Mr. Abbot proceeded to the settlement of this and other towns, and procured the location of the Coos road, by the state, from Chesterville, through Wilton, Carthage, and Weld, passing the notch by Mount Metallic, thence through Byron and East Andover to New Hampshire. Mr. Abbot died at Brunswick, in 1820, aged seventy-four. He was succeeded by his son, the late Jacob Abbot, who died in Farmington, January 21, 1847, at the age of seventy.

The town was incorporated February 2, 1816, and derived its name from Mr. Weld, then one of the owners. Webb's pond is a considerable body of water. Webb's river rises from this pond, and, running southerly through Carthage, falls into the Androscoggin at Dixfield village. The land around the pond is level, but ranges of mountains hem it in, and impart a picturesque and romantic aspect to the landscape scene. On the south is seen Bear mountain, in Carthage; on the east, Mount Blue, the summit of which is 2,360 feet above Webb's pond, and nearly 4,000 feet above the sea; on the north is Mount Metallic, and on the west is Ben Nevis. There is a considerable village on the eastern side of Webb's pond, on the Coos road, known as Holt's village, where there are two or three traders, a good grist-mill, a blacksmith's shop, tannery, carding-machine, and several good dwelling-houses. About two miles above, on the same road, there is another village, containing a town-house, starch factory, saw-mill, store, and blacksmith's shop. A Congregational church was early organized in the town, of which David Sterret was the first pastor. They have a convenient meeting-house in the eastern part of the town. Rev. Lemuel Jackson, from Greene, opened a religious meeting in 1804, and a Baptist church was constituted in 1809. Various preachers have since labored in the place. Two hundred members have been received since its formation, and about one fourth of that number remain. A small Free-will Baptist church has recently been organized. There are eleven schools, having an attendance of about 425 scholars; and one post-office. Population, 995; valuation, $92,232.

Wellington, Piscataquis county, is distant from Augusta sixty miles, and from Dover twenty. The first settlement was made about 1814, by James Knowles, who came from New Hampshire, and located in the south part of the town, on the farm where he now resides. The same spring, David Staples, from Newfield, settled on the west side of the town; and the ensuing summer James B. Potter and John Ward, from Bowdoin, located in the northwest part of the town. In 1818,

James Davis and Elisha Boston, from Shapleigh, also settled in the southwest part. These were soon followed by others, and the settlement progressed rapidly. The town being a part of what was called the Bingham Purchase, the settlers obtained the titles to their lands of Black, an agent of Bingham's heirs. This purchase subsequently fell into the hands of a Mr. Bridge, and the town was called Bridge's town, until its incorporation, in 1828, under its present name. The surface is uneven, being diversified by hills and valleys. In the northern part there is a hill of greater size than the rest, called by the inhabitants Ball mountain. Higgins's stream, the only one of any size, — having a saw-mill erected on it, — runs through the town. The inhabitants are chiefly employed in agriculture. The only other manufactory in town is a sash, blind, door, and furniture factory, which has a steam-engine. Wellington possesses one church edifice, owned and occupied by the Free-will Baptists; one post-office; and eleven schools. Population, 600; valuation, $45,000.

WELLS, situated on the sea-coast, in York county, was first settled by persons from Exeter, N. H., it is believed about the year 1640, and, according to the statement of Folsom, the title was derived from the Indians.[1] One Wawa, a noted Indian chief, resided here about 1750, and pretended to claim the territory in Wells, and that of adjoining towns. It formerly comprised within its limits the territory of Kennebunk, and contained forty thousand acres, one thousand of which is salt marsh. It was formerly a portion of the possessions of Sir Ferdinando Gorges, who, in 1641, presented five thousand acres of it to Thomas Gorges, deputy governor of Maine and mayor of Gorgeana. He was permitted to select whatever portion he pleased, and made choice of the tract near the small river Ogunquit, in the southwesterly part of Wells. A portion of this tract — about four or five hundred acres — was conveyed by Gorges, on the 17th of April, 1643, to Rev. John Wheelwright (brother-in-law of the celebrated Anne Hutchinson), who had been banished from Massachusetts for his *antinomian* principles; and another grant was made by Gorges, July 14, 1643, to Wheelwright, Henry Boad, and others. The former tract lay along the shore eastward of Ogunquit

[1] John Wadlow, or Wadleigh, removed from Saco to Wells before 1649, to whom an Indian, named Thomas Chabinoke, devised "all his title and interest to Namps-cas-coke, being the greatest part of Wells, upon condition that he should allow one bushel of Indian corn annually to 'Old Webb,'" (his mother). This tract extended from the sea as far up as the Great falls on Cape Porpoise [Mousam] river, and from Negunket to Kennebunk river. This title proved valid. — *Folsom*, p. 120.

river, and the latter between that river and the Kennebunk. The land was parcelled into lots by Boad and Edward Rishworth.

Wheelwright settled here about 1643, as did also Mr. Storer and Francis Littlefield, who immediately began a regular plantation. In July, 1653, Wells submitted to the jurisdiction of Massachusetts, and twenty of her citizens took the freeman's oath of allegiance. Among the names were Samuel Austin, John J. Barrett, John Barrett, Henry Boad, Joseph Bowles, John Buck, Nicholas and William Cole, Joseph Emerson, John Gooch, William Homans, Ezekiel Knight, Arthur, Francis,[1] Thomas, and Edmund Littlefield, Francis Littlefield, Jr., Thomas Millot, and John Smith. The plantation, called by the Indians Webhannet, was created into a town at the same time, and had a population of about one hundred and fifty-six. Wells was visited by the Indians under command of Mogg, October 18, 1676, who ordered the garrison to capitulate; which was imperatively refused by the commander. No attempt was made to attack the fort, but two persons were killed and one wounded, while thirteen of the cattle were destroyed.

On the 10th of June, 1692, the place was again attacked. The inhabitants at the time were dispersed among the fortified houses, and Storer's fort had only fifteen men, under command of Captain Converse, for its defence. The day previous (the 9th of June), however, ammunition, provisions, and fourteen men, fortunately arrived in two sloops. The alarm of approaching danger was given the same day by the cattle, which ran precipitately from the woods, in a bleeding condition; and Captain Converse immediately gave orders for all to prepare for defence, — the whole night being passed under the greatest anxiety. On the morning of the 10th, John Diamond, a passenger in one of the sloops, was captured by Indian spies; and shortly afterwards about five hundred French and Indians appeared, under the command of M. Burniffe, General Labrocree, and a few other Frenchmen, attended by Madockawando, Egeremet, Moxus, Warumbee, and several other sagamores. Having learnt the strength of the garrison from Mr. Diamond, they were certain of victory, and went so far as to portion out the

[1] Francis Littlefield came from England, and his parents, supposing him dead, named another son Francis, who, in process of time, also sought his fortune in the New World, and came to Wells, when he was agreeably surprised to find that the brother, thought to be dead, was still hale and hearty. He took up a farm near the one occupied by Francis the elder; and a short time after, two other brothers settled. From them, all of those who bear the name are supposed to have descended — no less than sixty-eight of whom are legal voters of Wells.

spoils. They immediately attacked the fort, and sustained the assault during the day; while another party, having in the mean time constructed a breastwork, endeavored to destroy the sloops, which were set on fire several times by means of fire-arrows. The crews, however, succeeded not only in extinguishing the flames, but in keeping up such a steady fire that the enemy were compelled to abandon the breastwork. Many other attempts were made to destroy the sloops, but they were all equally unavailing; while a continual fire from the small arms was sustained, with cries of "Surrender! surrender!" which were received by the crews with derision. At night the enemy asked, "Who's your commander?" to which was replied, "We have a great many commanders." "You lie!" cried an Indian; "you have none but Converse, and we'll have him before morning!"

The next morning, July 11, which was Sunday, a party of six men, who had been sent to Newichawannock by Captain Converse a few hours before the enemy appeared, arrived in the vicinity of the fort, and were, as a consequence, very much exposed to capture; but the corporal having by stratagem impressed the Indians with the belief that Converse was near them, they fled, and he and his men succeeded in entering the fort unharmed. The French and Indians this day concentrated their whole force, and began to move with great precision towards the fort, when one of Captain Converse's soldiers sighed a surrender. "Utter that word again," said the captain, "and you are a dead man! — All lie close, — fire not a gun till it will do execution!" The enemy came forward with a steady step, and gave three shouts, when the entire force opened into three ranks, and fired all at once. The cannon (some of which were twelve-pounders), and the small firearms from the fort, returned a perfect blaze of fire; and the repulse was so complete that the attack was not renewed. Many of the women in the garrison handed ammunition, and several of them fired the cannon at the enemy. The enemy, thwarted in their designs upon the fort, made a vigorous effort by means of a fire-float eighteen or twenty feet long, filled with combustibles, to destroy the sloops, which had wellnigh succeeded, when a counter breeze sprang up, and they were thus saved from destruction.

The enemy were completely disappointed in every effort made, and they could hope for no success in attempting to undermine the garrison, in consequence of the level nature of the ground. Not one in the fort was killed, and only one of the mariners. A flag of truce was sent by the leaders, who offered Captain Converse the most seducing terms, all which he refused. A short conversation then ensued,[1] after which

[1] 2 Mather's Magnalia, pp. 532–536; 2 Hutchinson's Hist., p. 67.

the Indian holding the flag of truce fled. A few shots were indulged in till dusk, and, about ten o'clock, the enemy evacuated the town. Probably this was one of the most extraordinary sieges during the war, and has scarcely a parallel. Several of the enemy fell, among whom was Labrocree; and the Indians, to avenge his death, put John Diamond to torture. "They stripped, scalped, and maimed him; slit his hands and feet between the fingers and toes; cut deep gashes in the fleshy parts of his body, and then stuck the wounds full of lighted torches, leaving him to die by piecemeal in the agonies of consuming fire." In August, 1703, Wells, which had been thus bravely defended, was again attacked, and with such desperation that, in a short time, it sustained a loss of thirty-nine in killed and prisoners, besides many wounded. In 1712, Wells probably would have met with further injury, had it not been for the strong arm of Massachusetts, which was then most opportunely extended for her relief.

A church was early gathered, under the auspices of Mr. Wheelwright, who was much beloved by his flock. The first Congregational church was organized in 1701, being the second in the state; and, about the year 1780, a society of Baptists was organized. Since 1812, two societies of Free-will Baptists have been formed. Courts were holden at Wells from time to time for nearly half a century; and it was represented in the general court of Massachusetts for three years, from 1653 to 1676. At the session of Congress in January, 1824, a grant of $5,000 was made to Wells, for the purpose of improving the main harbor; and, the year following, the money was expended in erecting a pier eight hundred feet in length.

Wells has a variety of soil, though its general character is sandy. Almost one fifth of the whole town may be considered waste land, being barren heaths, ledges, and pitch-pine plains. The salt marsh, too, is generally considered poor, the average crop of hay not exceeding half a ton per acre; though experiments have been made upon it sufficient to demonstrate that, when subdued, it will prove valuable. Though a number of the inhabitants are engaged in the cultivation of the soil, it is doubtful if a sufficient supply of corn and grain can be raised to supply home consumption. The principal article of export is wood, which is for the most part sent to Boston, Salem, and Newburyport. Considerable ship-timber has been cut, and vessels of various sizes have been constructed in years past. Water is abundant, there being nine small rivers or brooks coursing through the town in various directions, which afford water-power a part of the year for thirteen saw-mills, five grist-mills, four shingle machines, and one fulling-mill. There are eight churches — two Congregational, two Baptist, one Methodist, and three

Free-will Baptist; sixteen school districts, with sixteen schools; one steam saw-mill, and three post-offices — Wells, Wells Depot, and Ogunquit. The Portland, Saco, and Portsmouth Railroad has a station in Wells; and many persons, during the summer months, take advantage of the accommodation thus afforded to visit Wells beach, a delightful resort. Population, 2,945; valuation, $428,628.

WESLEY, twenty-five miles from Machias, is situated in the central part of Washington county, among the forests, and can scarcely be said to be within the pale of civilization. It was incorporated in 1833, and has one church (Methodist), four school districts, with four schools; and one post-office. Population, 329; valuation, $29,743.

WEST BATH, Sagadahoc county, is a small town detached from Bath, and incorporated February 14, 1844. It has neither village nor post-office; but contains one church (Methodist), five school districts, one saw-mill, one grist-mill, one clapboard machine, one shingle machine, and one lath machine. Population, 603; valuation, $88,645.

WESTBROOK, Cumberland county, was a part of Falmouth, to which it belonged until 1814, when it was set off and incorporated. It contains about 15,000 acres, and is a very beautiful town, the surface being moderately diversified with swells. It is watered by Presumpscot river. Westbrook has three villages — Saccarappa, Stroudwater, and Woodford's Corner, all of which are places of considerable business; but the first named is the principal. The Westbrook Seminary, situated on Stevens's Plains, is well patronized, and a highly successful institution. The Presumpscot canal passes through the western part of Westbrook, and affords excellent facilities for the transportation of merchandise, as does also the York and Cumberland Railroad. The Portland Manufacturing Company have a mill at Saccarappa for making sheetings, stripes, and ducks, which runs six thousand spindles. The Cumberland Paper-Mills, running fourteen engines, employ 120 hands, manufacturing one thousand tons of paper annually: value, $250,000. There are five church edifices — two Congregational, one Free-will Baptist, and two Universalist; seventeen school districts; and two post-offices — Stevens's Plains, and Saccarappa. Population, 4,852; valuation, $1,201,922.

WEST GARDINER, Kennebec county, lies west of Gardiner city, from which it was set off and incorporated August 8, 1850. The inhabitants were moved to petition for a separate organization from the fact that they would be more conveniently situated for town business and other

30 *

matters. The first town meeting was held August 21, 1850. Its history, up to that period, is so interwoven with that of Gardiner as to leave no room for comment; and, during the subsequent seven years, nothing of importance has occurred. The people are industrious, thrifty, and contented. The territory contained in West Gardiner amounts to about ten thousand acres, and its general appearance is of a rural character. Cobbossee Contee stream flows in on the northern limits, and Cold stream from the north, while Cobbossee Contee river forms most of the eastern boundary. There are three church edifices — two Free-will Baptist, and one Baptist; eight school districts, with sixteen schools; and one post-office. Population, 1,260; valuation of real and personal property for 1858, $710,459.

WESTON, lying in the extreme southeastern portion of Aroostook county, one hundred and thirty-five miles northeast of Augusta and about ninety miles northeast from Bangor, was formerly known as the Hampden Academy grant, having been incorporated March 17, 1835. It was settled soon after 1820, by William Butterfield and Dr. Otis Smith. The soil of Weston is of a good quality, but as yet has been neglected, and much of it remains to be improved. Baskahegan river passes through its southwestern corner, and Grand lake, an extensive body of water, forms its eastern boundary. Roads pass through it, leading to the principal points of trade. Manufacturing is not a very prominent branch of business — there being but three carpenters, one lumber dealer, and one carriage manufacturer in the town. Agriculture, for the most part, seems to occupy the attention of the people. Weston has a Methodist society, six school districts, with six schools; and one post-office. Population, 293; valuation, $28,140.

WESTPORT, Lincoln county, is an island situated in Sheepscot river, between Woolwich and Boothbay, and was formerly known as Jeremisquam. It is eleven miles long and about a mile wide, and originally formed a part of Edgecomb, from which it was set off and incorporated in the year 1828. The surface is uneven. The principal pursuit of the inhabitants is sea-going. The town has one church edifice, occupied by the Methodists and Free-will Baptists; six school districts, with the same number of schools; three saw-mills, four grist-mills, and one post-office. Population, 761; valuation, $101,511.

WHITEFIELD, in the western part of Lincoln county, contains an area of 29,000 acres. It was claimed by the Plymouth proprietors; but they failed to establish a right thereto. It was settled, about 1770, by Irish

Roman Catholics, and was then the western part of Ballstown, now Jefferson, to which it remained attached till June 19, 1809, when it was incorporated, receiving its name in memory of the celebrated Rev. George Whitefield. Soon after the close of the Revolutionary war, many of the veterans of the struggle for the independence of the colonies settled in Whitefield, and cleared away its immense forests of pine and oak timber, the latter of which was used for ship-building. The lumbering business was successfully prosecuted for a time; but it has somewhat diminished at the present writing, and the inhabitants are engaged in agricultural pursuits.

Whitefield is watered by Sheepscot river, and the head waters of East River. On the Sheepscot are some excellent mill privileges; but they are not improved to such an extent as they might be, for the want of capital and enterprise. There are three small villages — Whitefield, North Whitefield, and Cooper's Mills, — each of which has a post-office; four church edifices — two Union, one Baptist, and one Roman Catholic; eighteen school districts, and thirty-five schools; four single saw-mills, and one gang saw-mill; four grist-mills; and about six shingle machines. Population, 2,160; valuation, $278,160.

Whiting, Washington county, is situated at the head of Machias bay, eleven miles from Machias, and was incorporated in 1825. Lumbering has been an important employment, but it has latterly declined. The town has one village, one grist-mill, five saw-mills, one church (Congregational), six school districts, with six schools; and one post-office. Population, 470; valuation, $61,260.

Whitneyville, Washington county, lies four miles above Machias, on Machias river, and was originally contained in Machias, from which it was incorporated February 10, 1845. It is small in territorial extent, and has one school district and one post-office. Population, 519; valuation, $86,052.

Williamsburg, Piscataquis county, is an uneven, rough township, and is particularly noted for its excellent roofing slate. It was incorporated in 1820, and has been on the retrograde ever since. It has a post-office, and three school districts. Population, 134; valuation, $22,018.

Wilton is the largest town, excepting Farmington, in Franklin county, and joins Farmington on the east. It is eight miles from the court house in that town, and thirty-two miles northwest from Augusta. The first settlement was made at the place now called East Wilton, in

1789, by Samuel Butterfield, accompanied by his brother, Henry Butterfield, then sixteen years of age, who came through the woods from Farmington in search of a location on which to build a mill. After exploring the stream for some distance, Samuel fixed upon the spot where the dam of the Wilton factory now is, and directed Henry to commence chopping the trees, and clearing a spot on which to haul the timber. These were the first trees cut. The township had been previously granted by the state of Massachusetts to Captain Tyng and his company, of Concord, Massachusetts, for destroying an Indian by the name of Harry. It was explored in 1785, by Solomon Adams and others, located by Samuel Titcomb, surveyor for the state, and lotted by Solomon Adams in 1787. The explorers called it Harrytown, in memory of the ill-fated Indian; but the first settlers called it Tyngtown, in memory of the grantee. Samuel Butterfield erected a saw and grist mill at East Wilton, and settled in Wilton in 1790. With him Isaac Brown was contemporaneous; and William Walker, Ammial Clough, Joseph Webster, Silas Gould, Ebenezer Eaton, Josiah Perham, Ebenezer Brown, Joshua Perley, and Josiah Blake soon followed. Henry Butterfield, who in 1789 cut the first trees within the limits of this town, is still living at East Wilton, having attained a good old age. In his long and eventful life he has seen a territory, which he entered through a pathless forest, converted into fertile and fruitful fields, dotted over with beautiful habitations. Captain Hammon Brown, the first male child born here, is still living.

Wilton was incorporated in 1803. In the southerly part is Wilson pond, a fine sheet of water, two miles in length, and some half-mile in width. From this pond issues a stream, which runs north and northeast through the town until it enters Farmington, and thence empties into the Sandy river. On this stream are two villages, Wilton Upper Village and East Wilton. The Upper Village is situated upon the high land surrounding the outlet of the pond, whilst the stream goes pitching and foaming upon either side of the street for about 150 rods, affording water-power for almost any amount of machinery. It has ten stores, two taverns, and a large number of shops where the various mechanical occupations are carried on. East Wilton is a beautiful village, having two or three stores, several mechanic shops, and other business interests. Wilton Factory, which has done a large business, and the Farmers' and Mechanics' Tool Factory, are located in this village. At the outlet to Varnum's pond in the north part are a grist-mill and a saw-mill. There are five religious societies — Congregational, Methodist, Universalist, and two Free-will Baptist, each of which has a church edifice; twenty school districts, with thirty-nine schools; four post-offices — Wilton, East Wilton, North Wilton, and East Dixfield. Capital invested in trade, $100,000; in manufactures, $50,000; annual proceeds, $75,000. Wilton is in a flourishing condition. The railroad from Portland to Farmington, recently completed, runs directly through the town. Population, 1,909; valuation, $320,566.

WINDHAM, Cumberland county, extends down the Presumpscot river to Saccarappa Falls, and was granted by Massachusetts, December, 1734, to Abraham Howard, Joseph Blaney, and fifty-eight others, belonging to Marblehead. In June, 1735, the town was located, and the lots laid out and disposed of to the proprietors, — those designated as "the home lots" being so laid out as to protect them from the ravages of the Indians. Some disputes arose between Windham and Gray and Falmouth regarding the boundary lines; but they were finally amicably settled, after much embarrassment and expense to all parties. After this, the grantees made many improvements, such as building bridges, locating roads, and erecting a meeting-house. It was first called New Marblehead, which it retained until its incorporation in 1762, when it received its present name, from a town in the county of Norfolk, England. Captain Thomas Chute was the first settler, having arrived July 30, 1737. He was shortly after followed by William Mayberry, John Farrar, Stephen Manchester, and Abraham Anderson: all of these, and many of those that subsequently settled, came from Marblehead, Mass. Settlements were commenced under the most discouraging aspects; but the settlers had dared the dangers, and they were not the men to flinch when obstacles presented themselves.

In the spring of 1744, a substantial fort was erected in the centre of the settlement, by order of the general court of Massachusetts, to protect the settlers from the threatened attacks of the Indians. This fort was furnished, at the expense of the town, with two swivel guns and the necessary ammunition. The inhabitants remained within its walls from 1745 to 1751, which was a period of great suffering and danger. During this time none of the inhabitants lost their lives by the hands of the Indians, though one (William Maxfield) was wounded, and four (William and Joseph Knight, William Bolton, and Seth Webb) were taken prisoners, who, after a short time, were released. From 1751 to 1754, the inhabitants enjoyed a short respite from the harassing warfare of the Indians, and came forth from the garrison, erected new buildings, and made many improvements, while there was a visible increase in the population. These "good times" were of short duration, however. Peace had scarce found a comfortable abiding place, ere, frightened by the voice of war, she again (1754) unfolded her wings and took her flight. The inhabitants put their settlement in a good state of defence — converting three dwelling-houses into garrisons, which, with the fort already mentioned, were sufficient for the protection of the settlers. In February, 1756, the Indians surprised and made prisoner of Joseph Knights, who escaped from them, and rendered efficient service, by giving warning to several of the settlements of the approach of the Indians. The last and principal attack of the savages on Windham was made May 14, 1756, by Poland, king of the Rockomeca tribe, and about twenty of his followers. On the morning of that day, Ezra Brown and Ephraim Winship left the fort, accompanied by four men and four boys as a guard, for the purpose of working on Brown's lot. To reach the lot, they had to travel through a wood; and Brown and Winship, being some distance in advance, were fired upon by the Indians, when Brown was shot dead and Winship severely wounded, — the Indians taking their scalps. Four of the party (two men and two boys) in the rear, hearing the report, hastened back to the fort, while the others — Abraham Anderson, Stephen Manchester, Timothy Cloudman, and Gershom Winship, the two latter lads — determined to pursue the Indians and avenge their companions, or perish in the attempt. The little party soon came upon the savages, who, seeing them, sought concealment behind the trees. The result of the contest was, that Poland the king, and two of his followers, were killed by the little band of Spartans, when the Indians retreated, leaving behind them several trophies. Subsequently, several men from the fort fell in with another Indian laden with booty in the shape of a quarter of beef, at whom they fired some shots for the purpose of making him surrender the beef and himself; but not taking the hint, he fell a victim to his cupidity, or stupidity; for he was brought to the ground by another shot, from the effects of which he afterwards died. The danger of Indian depredations having abated, the people indulged again in those pursuits which go to make up the sum of happiness in this world, in which they remained undisturbed till the breaking out of the Revolution, when the councils of war were substituted for those of peace. The people of Windham brought with them into the contest that zeal which alone can spring from the consciousness of being engaged in a just cause. Officers were chosen to impart military instruction, ammunition and military accoutrements purchased, the ordnance belonging to the town put in proper condition, and every thing done, with their moderate means, to advance the cause locally and generally. Many men from this town, under command of Captain Richard Mayberry, served through the campaign of 1777 till the surrender of Burgoyne in

October of that year. No less than seventy-one men performed service, and $2,280 in silver money were given by the town for the prosecution of the war.

Windham has agricultural advantages of a good order, — the soil being loamy and easily worked. There are inexhaustible quarries of granite in the south part. The inhabitants are mainly engaged in cultivating the soil. The principal stream is the Presumpscot, which has ten falls lying partly in Windham, affording excellent water power for mills and manufactories, seldom affected by freshets or drought. Black, Calley Wright's, and Inkhorn brooks, are in the south part. Pleasant river has many advantageous mill seats; and in the north part of the town there are several ponds. Duck pond, in the east, is partly in Windham and partly in Westbrook. Little Sebago pond, part of which lies here and part in Gray, is of considerable magnitude, a portion of which was drained of its waters by the making of an artificial outlet at the south end. In June, 1814, this outlet increased to such size that the waters did much damage, carrying away a number of mills and bridges on Pleasant and Presumpscot rivers, and doing other damage. Windham contains six villages — Little Falls, Oak Hill, Great Falls, Windham Centre, Windham Hill, and the Upper Corner; six churches — two Congregational, one Friends', two Baptist, and one Universalist; eighteen school districts, with thirty-four schools; two social libraries; eight saw-mills, one corn and flour mill, two shingle mills, one fulling-mill, two carding-machines, one woollen factory, one keg factory, one chair-stuff manufactory, two tanneries, and a powder factory having eight or ten mills. There are three post-offices — Windham Centre, South Windham, and North Windham. Population, 2,380: valuation for 1850, $407,708; valuation for 1857, $1,021,698.

WINDSOR, Kennebec county, lies on the east side of Kennebec river, and joins Augusta. It belonged to the Plymouth Patent, and Reuel Williams was the principal agent. Its first settlement was commenced in 1790 by Walter Dockindoff, Thomas Labalister, Prince Keen, Samuel Pierce, John Linn, Dr. Stephen Barton, Benjamin and Joseph Hilton, Joseph Linscott, and Joseph Trask. The act of incorporation was passed March 3, 1809, when the town received the name of Malta, which was changed to Gerry in 1820, and to the present one in 1822. Joseph Trask, Jr., was born October 30, 1790, and was the first native citizen of Windsor. Quite an excitement was created here in 1809, by the murder, on the 8th of September, of Paul Chadwick, employed by the proprietors of the Plymouth Patent to survey Windsor, which they claimed as part of their territory, and whose authority the settlers generally were determined not to recognize.[1]

Windsor is laid out perfectly square, and its surface is hilly, but not mountainous. From some of its highest elevations very pretty views are obtained of the surrounding scenery. The principal stream is the western branch of the Sheepscot, which passes through from north to south, affording excellent water privileges for mills and factories. The Barton brook is the next in size, besides which there are the Harriman, Colburn, Dearborn, and Cotton brooks, and several other smaller streams: there are also seven ponds. The southerly end of Three Mile pond lies in Windsor. When the first settlement was commenced, the town was remarkable for the quantity and quality of its pine and oak timber, and its hemlock and hard wood. As a consequence, lumbering formed the main occupation of the inhabitants for a number of years. Saw-mills were erected in different parts of the town, many of which have discontinued their operations in consequence of the scarcity of timber. At the present time, agriculture takes the lead over other pursuits; and since it has gained favor, Windsor has steadily increased in wealth and importance, — showing that the soil is susceptible of a high state of cultivation, which is well improved.

The most thickly settled points are South Windsor, Pope's Mills, and Taylor's Corner. There are three churches — Baptist, Methodist, and Union; thirteen school districts, with the same number of schools; two post-offices — Windsor and South Windsor; three saw-mills, four shingle mills, two grist-mills, one clothing mill and carding-machine, and three public-houses. Population, 1,793; valuation, $260,427.

WINN, Penobscot county, lies on the east bank of the Penobscot river, north of Lincoln, at the junction of the Mattawamkeag river. It is a new town at the head of steamboat navigation on the Upper Penobscot, and has borne the name of Five Islands. Winn was incorporated March 21, 1857, and named from John Winn of Bangor, a principal proprietor. It contains 22,040 acres. It has two schools, with sixty-five scholars; and one post-office. Population, 111; valuation, $12,000.

WINSLOW, Kennebec county, on the east side of the Kennebec river, eighteen miles above Augusta, formerly embraced the territory of Waterville, — having been laid out on both sides of the Kennebec river, and then containing seventy-two square miles. The beautiful and grand

[1] See Kennebec Purchase, ante, p. 170.

Falls of Ticonic (anciently Teconnet, signifying the junction of the two rivers, [Kennebec and Sebasticook]) — the flats favorable to the planting of Indian corn — the fish and game with which the waters and woods abounded — all these presented features which made the site of this town a favorite abiding-place for the aborigines. The same natural advantages readily attracted the attention of the white settler. The first farming ever attempted here was made upon the flat below Fort hill, by Morris Fling, about the year 1764, and was, for a long time after the settlement, known as Fling's field. The whole region, at the time of Fling's arrival, was a dense pine forest. In those days there was no bridge over the Kennebec, no dam on the Ticonic falls, no bridge across the Weskerangan; the only habitations or signs of improvement being a large block-house on the heights, and two on Fort hill proper.

In 1676, under the direction of a council of war then sitting in Massachusetts, Abraham Shurt, of Pemaquid, met the Indians here for a parley, and exerted his powerful influence, as he did at Pemaquid, to prevent the ravages of King Philip's war, then extending over all the eastern settlements. He was received by the Indians in the "great wigwam," or fort; but he was unsuccessful in his efforts to ward off the terrible blow; hence nearly a century elapsed before any considerable settlement was made here. Winslow was incorporated in 1771, and received its name in honor of General John Winslow, who had command of the expedition employed in the erection of Fort Halifax. The inhabitants first met in a municipal capacity, May 23, 1771, in the fort, where most public meetings were held for many years afterwards.

Among the ancient public buildings in this town was Fort Halifax, a portion of which is now standing, but is fast going to decay. It was erected on the point of land between the rivers Kennebec and Sebasticook, in 1754, by Governor Shirley, of Massachusetts, and was the last of the line of forts on the Kennebec river, built as defences during the French and Indian war. There were no settlers here at the time of its erection; and though it was of no real benefit to the section of country in which it was situated, it served, in a measure, as a protection and safeguard to the settlements in the vicinity of Massachusetts, and those further down the river, from the depredations of the Indians, who entertained a wholesome dread of a company of soldiers coming out upon them from the fort. There is no evidence that this fort was ever attacked by the Indians; in fact, they did not dare to make a direct assault, but occasionally attempted to cut off supplies. The balls which were found in it were fired by friendly guns, which is evident from the fact, that most of them were in the first story and a few in the yard side, — at which place there were no port-holes, — whereas, in the second story, where the majority of the soldiers were most likely to be, and where they surely would have been in case of an attack, there were no bullet-holes whatever. The fort was never attacked by the French, — the only enemy who could have captured it, — for the reason that they were called to more important fields of action. Two years previous to the close of the war, the fort was garrisoned by 130 men under Captain William Lithgow, and, after him, Captain Ezekiel Pattee, commanded. At the peace of Paris, 1763, it was abandoned.[1]

Fort Halifax.

There is but one village in Winslow, and that is of very limited size. It is situated at the junction of the Sebasticook with the Kennebec river, half a mile below Ticonic falls; and, being well shaded, possesses rare natural beauty. At the falls there is a natural dam, which, at a trifling expense, might be raised so as to give a water-power of almost unlimited extent; and, on the east side of the river, a canal might easily be excavated even as far as the Sebasticook, with waste ways at suitable distances to return the waters again to the Kennebec; thus furnishing sites for a large manufacturing business, perfectly safe from floods, and as enduring as the rocks on which they would rest. The Somerset and Kennebec Railroad, from Augusta to Winslow, built on the east side of the Kennebec, crosses the river at the falls. In the vicinity are considerable tracts of land, which are yet uncleared. The Mile brook, a stream valuable for manufacturing purposes, is the outlet of China pond, and falls into the Sebasticook a mile above its mouth. There is some waste land in town; but much of the soil is perhaps not exceeded by any in New England. The original settlers came from Massachusetts. The Puritanic descent of the inhabitants is abundantly apparent from the intelligence, taste, and industry to be found on every hand. There are four houses for public worship — one Congregational, two Methodist, and one Baptist. The town has a post-office, and sixteen school

[1] The corner-stone of this fort was recently exhumed, and deposited in the state-house at Augusta. It bears the following inscription: — "THIS CORNER | STONE LAID | BY DIRECTION | OF GOVERNOR | SHIRLEY. 1754."

districts, with twenty-nine schools. Population, 1,796; valuation, $400,000.

WINTHROP, Kennebec county, originally called Pondtown, lies on the west side of Kennebec river, and was formerly included in the Kennebec Purchase. The south line of the town was five miles long, the west line nine miles, and the north, seven miles. What the eastern boundary was, is unknown. The first settler is supposed to have been Timothy Foster, in 1765, who located his tent by the great pond, on the lot now owned by Jacob Robbins. The next was Squier Bishop, in 1767. Soon after, the families of Foster, Fairbanks, Stanley, and Pullen were settled near Bishop. For a long time these people, having been used to cultivated farms only, suffered intensely, and must have perished but for the abundance of game and wild fruit. They soon received a lesson in backwoods life, however, in witnessing the management of three brothers, — Nathaniel, William, and Thomas Whittier, — who felled some twenty acres of timber, burned it off, and planted their corn without ploughing, to the no small curiosity of the other settlers. After 1769, settlers poured in rapidly, and the township began to show the progress of civilization.

The first saw-mill was built in 1768, on the stream where now stands the cotton factory, by John Chandler, who, soon after its completion, erected a grist-mill. To get the mill-stones from the river is said to have taken "the whole strength of the settlement nearly a week." For building these mills, he received a grant of four hundred acres, in two lots of two hundred acres each, one near the pond, and the other where he should choose in the province. The first road was cut through and cleared out to the "Hook," now Hallowell. Previous to this, the settlers travelled by a guide of spotted trees. These guide-paths afterwards became roads. The first tax levied in town was paid by a bounty on a wolf's head, by Benjamin Fairbanks, in 1784.

Winthrop was incorporated in April, 1771; and the first town meeting was held on the 20th May in that year, at the inn of Squier Bishop. Soon after this, Nathaniel Fairbanks built a tannery near Deacon Metcalf's, and afterwards carried on business at the village. In 1791, Cyrus Baldwin built a fulling-mill where the woollen factory now stands, which passed through the hands of Benjamin Allen, Liberty Stanley, and John Cole; the latter also had a blacksmith's shop, with a trip-hammer in operation. In 1806, Nathaniel Perley opened a canal from North pond and erected a grist-mill. This he afterwards sold to the Cotton Manufacturing Company. The Winthrop Woollen and Cotton Manufactory was incorporated in 1809, and went into operation in 1814.

The first man who made cider in this town was Ichabod How, who, in the absence of a mill or press, pounded a quantity of apples in a sap-trough, and extracted the juice by means of a cheese-press, thus obtaining a few gallons, with which he, and his neighbors for a long distance round, made merry in a great gathering. The first movement towards schools was in 1774. Little was done, however, until 1782, on account of the breaking out of the Revolutionary war, which seemed to swallow up every other care, when £20 were appropriated for this purpose, and the town was divided into six school districts. The first school was taught by Benjamin Brainard, in the house of Benjamin Fairbanks.

Winthrop contains 25,540 acres, the surface of which is rather uneven; the land is of a good quality, and well wooded. It is adapted to the growth of the different grasses and grains, and to fruit raising. Some of the scenery is beautiful. From the town-house, when the air is favorable, the hills in Dixmont, seventeen miles west of the Penobscot, and a section of the White Mountains, are plainly visible. In the western part lies Mount Pisgah, which extends nearly across that portion of the town. South pond, a large body of water, is partly here; as is also North pond. Berry and Narrows pond, two smaller bodies of water, lie within the limits of Winthrop, and Cobbossee Contee Great pond covers a large surface in the eastern section. There are two oil-cloth factories, a factory for making window blinds and sashes, a woollen factory, a bank, incorporated in 1853, with a capital of $75,000; a celebrated water-cure establishment, and an agricultural society, incorporated in 1818. The first church in town was built in 1774, and the first preacher was Thurston Whiting. There are now a Congregational, Baptist, Methodist, and Universalist church, and a meeting-house belonging to the Society of Friends; ten school districts, and two post-offices — Winthrop and East Winthrop. Population, 2,154; valuation, $500,757.

WISCASSET, Lincoln county, is situated on the west side of Sheepscot river, twelve miles from its mouth, and is the shire town of the county. The settlement was commenced in 1663, by George Davie, who, according to Mr. Bradford, lived about half a mile north of the point where the jail now stands. He purchased of the Indians a tract of several hundred acres, embracing within its limits the present village of Wiscasset; and during the summer of that year, he, assisted by his brother and two other persons, erected several buildings, and made improvements of various kinds, as well as encouraged the location of other settlers. On the breaking out of King Philip's war, in 1675, the people were obliged to leave their homes, and flee to a place of greater security; and, for nearly sixty years afterwards, the town was entirely depopulated.

Robert Hooper came here with his family, consisting of four persons, in 1730, and may be considered the first settler. He was a man of energy and determination, and soon erected a small but comfortable dwelling, by the side of a large rock, on the eastern side of where Water street now runs. At that time, with the exception of a few acres of land, which the Davies had cleared more than half a century before, the whole country was a wilderness. Hooper brought with him a few articles of furniture, a small stock of cattle, and a number of fruit-trees, which went far towards comfort in such an inhospitable neighborhood. For nearly four years this hardy pioneer toiled on, unaided and alone, in his wilderness home. In 1734, Michael Seavey, Robert Groves, Sheribiah Lambert, and a man by the name of Foye, immigrated from Rye, N. H. Josiah Bradbury, Nathaniel Rundlett, Richard Holbrook, Colonel Kingsbury, and Benjamin Holbrook arrived about the same time; and, a few years later, John Young, and three others, by the name of Taylor, Boynton, and Chapman, settled on the Cross river, about two miles south of Wiscasset point. Being men of energy, they soon went to work in good earnest in clearing away the lands. From this time forward, the settlement progressed steadily, additions being made to its numbers every year; and, in 1740, it had become a plantation of thirty families, numbering one hundred and fifty persons.

About the year 1743, a fortification — some relics of which are yet to be seen — was erected on the hill near the residence of Captain William H. Clark. It is related of this fort, that in the latter part of September, 1744, a party of twenty Indians arrived before it, in a dense fog, for the purpose of attacking it. The only inhabitants in it at the time were two women and a girl, the men being at work in the fields, some distance off. Discovering, as the mist cleared away, their savage enemies, they barricaded the doors, and, disguising their voices, called to a number of imaginary persons to put the place in a state of defence. The Indians, believing that there was a large force within the fort, became alarmed, and abandoned their design. The fort was thus saved by stratagem, adding another to the numerous instances already on record, of the presence of mind and heroism of the women of those early days. In the summer of 1745, a man, who had been at work on the Seavey farm, while returning to the garrison, and being about sixty rods distant, was shot dead by an Indian concealed in the forest. Soon after this, in order to secure better accommodation to all the inhabitants, two block-houses were built, — one on what is now called Brim-

31 *

stone hill, and the other on Seavey's hill, — about three quarters of a mile distant from each other. No remains of either of these block-houses are now to be seen.

The attention of the settlers was very early directed to ship-building and maritime pursuits. Timber for masts and spars was very plenty; and, being in good demand, it became a very important branch of business, the land being cleared up for the sake of its valuable timber, rather than for agricultural purposes. The settlement was incorporated in 1760, by the name of Pownalborough, in honor of Governor Pownal of Massachusetts, and embraced within its limits Alna and Dresden. It was incorporated under its present name in 1802. During the Revolutionary war, the town having no defences, the British sloop-of-war *Rainbow* came up the river, anchored in the harbor, and laid the town under contribution to furnish supplies for the ship; threatening the place with destruction, and the inhabitants with the halter, if they refused. There was no alternative but a compliance with their demands; for, being entirely destitute of any armament, they were wholly at the mercy of the invaders.

On the conclusion of peace, the business of Wiscasset with foreign ports became very extensive; and at home the place was the chief mart of trade for the entire country around. She then saw her palmiest days. Most of her inhabitants were more or less interested in navigation, and her marine floated on every sea; but the embargo of 1807 on shipping, being laid at an unfortunate time, dealt a stunning blow to her business and prosperity, the destruction of which was completed by the war of 1812; and, to this day, the town has never succeeded in retrieving its fallen fortunes.

Wiscasset has a most excellent harbor. A United States surveying commission, in 1813, strongly recommended to the navy department the propriety of establishing a navy yard here. The river spreads out into a broad bay, and becomes admirably fitted for such a purpose. One hundred of the largest sized vessels can anchor here in from twelve to twenty fathoms of water. Vessels rarely find difficulty in entering this port; and, when Boston harbor is frozen over as far as the Castle, the harbor at Wiscasset is perfectly free from ice. A high bridge has been thrown across the river, directly above the harbor, which has a draw of thirty-four feet, through which vessels of 1,000 tons pass without difficulty. The surface of the town is hilly, making a view of it very interesting and romantic. It is drained by Sheepscot river, Monsweag stream, and Ward's brook, the two latter falling into Monsweag bay. Gardner's pond lies partly here and partly in Dresden. Judge Bailey, Abiel Wood, son of General Wood, Judge Orchard Cook, and John D.

McCrate, citizens of this town, have each represented the people of this district in Congress. There are three churches — Episcopalian, Methodist, and Congregationalist; one bank, the Mariner's, with a capital of $75,000; one village, one post-office, six school districts, with eight schools; an academy, a select school, a court-house, and a jail. Population, 2,332; valuation, $605,096.

WOODSTOCK, Oxford county, comprises two half townships, one of which was granted by the state of Massachusetts, June 14, 1800, to Dummer Academy, and the other, February 7, 1807, to Gorham Academy. It was incorporated February 7, 1815, and its surface is mountainous. There are several beautiful ponds, which form mill-streams, and fall into the Little Androscoggin river. The alluvial lands that skirt the ponds and streams are very productive. Hon. Sidney Perham is a resident of this town. Woodstock contains two villages — North Woodstock and Bryant's Pond; three church edifices — Universalist, Baptist, and Methodist; eleven school districts, and twenty schools; five saw-mills, three clapboard machines, three shingle machines, one carriage manufactory, one sash and door manufactory, and two post-offices — Woodstock and North Woodstock. Population, 1,012; valuation for 1857, $165,000.

WOOLWICH, Sagadahoc county, lies on the eastern shore of Kennebec river, twelve miles above its mouth, and was first settled by Edward Bateman and John Brown in 1638, who, the next year, purchased from Robin Hood, an Indian chief, most of the territory of which the present town is composed. Subsequently, a large portion of the tract was claimed by Thomas Clark and Sir Biby Lake, and by the settlers under them, by whom mills were erected as early as 1660. In the second Indian war, the settlers were murdered, or compelled to resign their homes. The cellars and wells then constructed are still pointed out as vestiges of this ancient settlement. Persons moved in again about 1726, after Dummer's treaty with the Indians, soon after which it became a precinct of Georgetown, and remained such till its incorporation on the 20th of October, 1759. Its plantation name was Nequassei, and its present name was conferred upon it after Woolwich, England, — the turns and courses of the water on the Thames and Kennebec, near a place called "Fiddler's Reach," situated in proximity to each of the towns, being almost the same. The titles to the land were obtained either by actual settlement under the grantees of Robin Hood, or else from Thomas Clark and Sir Biby Lake. Sir William Phips, the first royal governor of the province of Massachusetts, and the commander of the first expedition against Canada, about 1690, was a native of Woolwich, having been born on a peninsular projection into Mousweag bay, in the southeast part, February 2, 1650.

The general appearance of Woolwich is rough and broken, though there are neither very large hills nor very ample lowlands. A portion of the land is very heavily wooded, the timber being extensively used in ship-building. The soil is well adapted to the growth of every kind of produce, for which the state is noted. Woolwich contains twenty thousand acres. Nequasset pond is a beautiful sheet of water, lying near the centre, two miles in length, and alternating from a half to three quarters of a mile in width, having an outlet into Nequasset bay, at the southwest part of the town, where is a fall sufficient for mills. There are four small villages — Day's Ferry and Sagadahoc Ferry, near the Kennebec; Nequasset, at the foot of the pond of that name, and Monsweag in the eastern part.

The inhabitants are principally devoted to farming, though all trades and professions are represented. Ship-building is carried on to a limited extent — there being one ship yard affording business the greater part of the time; two saw-mills and two grist-mills are in operation the most of the year. There are six church edifices — two occupied by the Congregationalists, two by the Methodists, one by the Baptists, and one by the Free-will Baptists; eight school districts, with the same number of schools, and one post-office. Population, 1,420; valuation, $346,365.

Yarmouth is a small town on Casco bay, in Cumberland county. It is an old settlement with a new name, having formed a part of North Yarmouth until 1849, when it was set off from the parent town and incorporated by its present name.[1] There are two large villages, called the Corner and the Falls. The trade or business is principally of a commercial character — ship-building and navigation. Hay, potatoes, and brick are the principal articles of exportation. Yarmouth is watered by Royall's river, which runs through it lengthwise, and affords an abundant water-power, upon which are located several saw-mills and grist-mills, one cotton factory, and five tanneries. The other manufacturing establishments are — two brick-yards, which manufactured, in 1856, three million bricks; two potteries, two cabinet factories, two wheelwright shops, four establishments for building boats, and one for making blocks for vessels, one wood-turning establishment, one sash and blind factory, and one plaster mill. Yarmouth has been divided into

[1] For the account of its settlement, see North Yarmouth.

nine school districts, having sixteen public schools, two seminaries, and an institute. There are four church edifices — Congregational, Baptist, Methodist, and Universalist; and one post-office. Population, 2,144; valuation for 1857, $955,319.

YORK is a seaboard town, situated in the southwest part of York county. It comprised a part of the patent granted to Sir Ferdinando Gorges, and was selected by him as the seat of government for his Province of Maine. On the 10th of April, 1641, while then a wilderness, it was chartered by Gorges as a borough, the boundaries of which were "to extend three miles east and west, north and south, from the church, chappell, or place ordained for a chappell or oratory, belonging to the plantation of Agamenticus." Over this borough, Thomas Gorges, a cousin of Sir Ferdinando, was appointed mayor; with Edward Godfrey, Roger Garde, George Puddington, Bartholomew Barned, Edward Johnson, Arthur Bradington, Henry Simpson, and John Rogers, as aldermen. Edward Godfrey was appointed a justice of the peace, and Roger Garde, recorder, town clerk, etc.[1] This charter was in existence but one year; for, on the 1st of March following, Gorges issued a new one, erecting his seat of government into a city, and considerably extending its boundaries, which are thus described: "From the beginning of the entrance of the river, commonly called and known by the name of *Agamenticus*, and so up the said river seven English miles, and all along the east and northeast side of the sea-shore three English miles in breadth from the entrance of the said river, up into the main land, seven miles, butting with the seven miles from the sea-side up the said river, the breadth of the said three miles opposite thereunto."

Its name was changed to Gorgeana, and it was appointed to have a corporation, consisting of a mayor, twelve aldermen, and twenty-four common councilmen. The corporation retained the name of Gorgeana, and sometimes Agamenticus, until about the year 1652, when the Massachusetts government, supposing that the charter made to Sir Henry Rossewell and others, by Charles the First, included New Hampshire and a large part of the province of Maine, sent down commissioners from Boston, for the purpose of establishing a government at Agamenticus, naming the town York, and the territory lying east of Piscataqua river, Yorkshire, or York county, the boundaries thereof being three miles to the northward of Merrimac river. York enjoyed its city privi-

[1] The following is a copy of the oath drawn up by Gorges, to be administered to all freemen: "You shall true liege men be, and true faith and troth bear unto our Sovereign lord the king, his heirs and successors, and unto the lord proprietor of the Province of Maine, his heirs and assigns. So help you God."

leges, conferred upon it under the name of Gorgeana, until 1662, when it was made a *town*, — an apparent falling off from its previous dignity. In 1716 it was made the shire town of York county, then called Yorkshire.

The settlements in the plantation of Agamenticus were made principally on the sea-shore, near the mouth of York river; and before 1641, the commissioners of Sir Ferdinando Gorges held courts of justice at a place called Mount Saco. The settlements on the south side of the river increased to a considerable extent; so much so, in fact, that, before the year 1740, occasional preaching was had there on the Sabbath.

In each of the first three wars with the Indians, the tribes made great efforts to destroy the place entirely, though without success. Early in the morning of Monday, February 5, 1692, at the signal of a gun fired, the town was furiously assaulted at different places by a body of two or three hundred Indians, led on and emboldened by several Canadian Frenchmen, all of the marauders having marched thither upon snow-shoes. The surprise was altogether unexpected and amazing; and consequently the more fatal. A scene of the most horrid carnage and capture instantly ensued; and, in one half hour, more than 150 of the inhabitants were expiring victims or trembling suppliants at the feet of their enraged enemies. The rest had the good fortune to escape into Preble's, Harman's, Alcock's, and Norton's garrisoned houses, the best fortifications in town. Though well secured within the walls, and bravely defending themselves against their assailants, they were several times summoned to surrender. "Never!" said they. "Never! till we have shed the last drop of blood." About seventy-five of the people were killed; yet, despairing of conquest or capitulation, the vindictive destroyers set fire to nearly all the unfortified houses on the northeast side of the river, which, with a large amount of property left, were laid in ashes. Apprehensive of being overtaken by avenging pursuers, the Indians hastened their retreat into the woods, taking with them as much booty as they could carry away.[1] Nearly a hundred of these unhappy people were taken prisoners and carried a long journey,[2] aggravated by a thousand hardships and sufferings, — severe weather, snow, famine, abuse, and every species of wretchedness.[3] So late as the year 1744, there was considerable anxiety felt as to the attacks of the Indians; and it was customary for the men to take their muskets with them on the Sabbath, to be stacked, during the time of service, in the meeting-house.

[1] Williamson, vol. I., p. 629.

[2] It is supposed they were taken to Sagadahoc. — *Williamson.*

[3] Mather's Magnalia, vol. II., p. 530.

In June, 1744, during the morning service, there was an earthquake; and the men in the gallery, supposing, from the rumbling noise and the outcry of the women, that the Indians had made an attack upon the church, seized upon their guns, hastened down stairs, and prepared to discharge them upon their imaginary foes as they were passing the meeting-house door.

Prior to the destruction of the town by the Indians in 1692, the principal road passed near the mouth of the river, over the Long Sands and the Short Sands, to a point of land which retains the name of Betty Allen's Point, where one Elisha Allen conveyed people across the river. In process of time a ferry was established, where the toll-bridge is now built, called Trafton, from the first ferryman. Another was established where the Great Lower Bridge, erected in 1761 by Major Samuel Sewall, architect, now stands. After the erection of this, the ferries over the river were discontinued. The meeting-house used for public worship in 1692 stood on the northeast side of Meeting-house Creek, within gunshot of Harman's garrison. This building was replaced in 1719 by a new one, more commodious, which was removed in 1746, and the present one, which was finished in 1748, erected on the same ground.

It is related of the Rev. Samuel Moodey, a Calvinistic minister, who settled here in 1700, that, in the expedition to Louisburg in 1745, he volunteered as chaplain to General Pepperrell. Induced in some measure by the example of this divine, three full companies were formed in the town, and embarked in the campaign, leaving scarcely a sufficient number to cultivate the soil. Many of these patriots never returned, or when they did, died of a fever, called the Cape Breton fever. Mr. Moodey, it is supposed, received the seeds of this disease, of which he died in November, 1747. It is said of this minister, that, in his natural disposition, "he was dogmatical and absolute, and very irritable; greatly feared and beloved by the people of his charge, over whom he had an uncommon power."

The surface is broken, and, in some parts, rocky; while, along the seashore, it is marshy to a considerable extent. To the northwest there are some very fine farms, which are worked with energy, and yield a profitable return; though, on the whole, but a small portion of the land is fit for cultivation. The town is regularly laid out, with streets intersecting each other at right angles; the buildings on which are comfortable and neatly constructed. The principal harbor is at the mouth of York river, having water sufficient for vessels of three hundred tons burden. It is distant about six miles from Portsmouth, N. H. The entrance to this harbor is difficult, being narrow and crooked. Cape Neddock cove, four miles northeast of York river, is navigable about a mile from the sea, at full tide only, — the sand-bar at its mouth preventing vessels of any considerable burden passing at low water. Cape Neddock and Bald Head are the headlands. The former is a little to the south of Cape Neddock river, and the latter forms the southeast part of Wells bay. At the end of this cape, a small hillock, called "the Nubble," is situated; and nine miles southward of this lies Boone island. Agamenticus mountain, from which the town originally took its name, situated in the north part, is a considerable elevation, and a noted landmark. The United States Coast Survey have erected an observatory on its summit, the prospect being, it is said, one of the grandest in the country.

The principal business of the inhabitants is agriculture. Some employ themselves in navigation, — in fishing, coasting, and voyaging to different parts of the world. The trade and commerce of the inhabitants, for a considerable period after the destruction of the place in 1692, were small and inconsiderable, — two small coasting sloops being the only vessels owned in town up to 1740. At length, great exertions were made to purchase a vessel for the purpose of sending her to the West Indies; which having been accomplished and the voyage proving successful in a pecuniary way, encouragement was given to further essays in this line; and, in 1756, soon after the commencement of the French war, there were several sloops and schooners employed in the coasting trade to Halifax, and carrying lumber from the eastward to Boston. Some of these vessels were also employed as transports to Louisburg and Quebec until the peace of 1763. Ship-building was carried on to a considerable extent at the commencement of the Revolution; but, before its close, by captures and disasters, the merchant marine of the town was reduced to two old sloops. On the acknowledgment of the independence of the United States, ship-building again revived, and many engaged in it beyond their ability. The embargo laws, however, put a stop to the enterprising spirit which had been infused into the inhabitants, and reduced many of them to penury. At present, the ship-building interests are in a good condition, the shipping in 1854 amounting to 1,825 tons, enrolled and licensed. There are six churches — Baptist, a Christian, two Congregational, and two Methodist; three post-offices — York, Cape Neddock, and Scotland; five villages, of which York village, in the centre of the town, is the principal, and has considerable trade; and fourteen school districts, with thirty schools. Population, 2,980; valuation, $516,609.

York County, at the extreme southwest of the state, is renowned for its antiquity, being coeval with the province of Maine, chartered to Sir Ferdinando Gorges, April 3, 1639,[1] — thus running back to the essayed establishment over the territory of a feudal government but little short of absolute royalty in all its appointments. Then, the people had hardly a shadow of the right of self-government, and this old domain saw the judges and other officers appointed by the lord proprietor, and removable at his will, the regulation of the courts being entirely within his pleasure. But, to the honor of the people, no such system was accepted by them. Sir Ferdinando proposed to divide the province into four counties or bailiwicks, — east, west, north, and south, — these into eight hundreds, and the latter into parishes and tythings, as the people should increase or convenience require; but the division was in fact made by the river Kennebunk into two districts or counties, "east and west." Without any formal designation on the part of the court, these counties gradually acquired the names of York and New Somerset, for the former of which the inferior courts were to sit at Agamenticus, and for the latter at Saco; but a general court for the whole province was to be held annually (June 25), at Saco. This court was composed of seven persons, who were styled "Councillors of Sir Ferdinando Gorges, for the preservation of justice through his province." The inferior courts had no jurisdiction in capital felonies, or in civil actions involving titles to land. Among the prerogatives claimed by the court was the compulsion of all parents in the western division to bring their *unbaptized* children to the ordinance; and whoever should refuse, after the settlement of a minister in his plantation, and after "the worshipful Thomas Gorges" and Edward Godfrey (the deputy governor and senior councillor of the province) "should enjoin upon him the duty," was to become answerable, at the next court, for contempt.

In 1646, Alexander Rigby, who had become the purchaser of Lygonia, or the Plough Patent,[2] and thereby involved in a sharp contest with the government of Gorges on the question of jurisdiction, received in his favor the judgment of the governor-general and commissioners of the American plantations, to whom the subject had been referred, by which the jurisdiction of Gorges was narrowed down to Wells, Gorgeana (York), and Piscataqua (Kittery), and the northern Isles of Shoals, or the territory between the Piscataqua and Kennebunk rivers. Cleeves, the deputy-president of Rigby, at once opened a court at Saco,

[1] The first volume of York county records begins in 1640; and the volumes are numbered regularly down to the present time. — *Williamson*, vol. i., p. 283, note.

[2] See Plough Patent, ante, p. 261.

at which place and at Casco, the courts were held until their virtual dissolution by the death of Rigby in 1650. The death of both Gorges and Rigby, the fall of the English monarch, the succession of the republic, and the consequent dissensions and alternation of strength in the provinces, rendered the territory of Maine easy of acquisition by Massachusetts, which regarded it with a wishful eye. Accordingly, the purchase of Lygonia was completed in 1652, the Gorges patent having previously been purchased of Sir Ferdinando's heir. This territory, extending just north of the river Presumpscot, was erected into a county by the name of Yorkshire, and a court established, to be holden alternately in Kittery and Agamenticus (York), at appointed times, twice a year, by such magistrate or assistant as the general court might from time to time designate, aided by three or five resident associates elected for the purpose within the county. The jurisdiction and authority were to be coequal with similar courts in Massachusetts.

After the restoration of monarchy, the state encountered some troubles by the revival of claims under the former patents, but they were again quieted by the purchase, in 1677, of a release from the Gorges heirs for £1,250.

A county by the name of Devonshire was formed in 1674, by Massachusetts commissioners, out of the territory between the Sagadahoc and George's rivers, being a part of the dominions claimed by the Duke of York under his patent; but neither the name nor jurisdiction seems to have been long retained. The French and Indian wars rendered the province desolate until early in the next century.

In 1716, the general court, "in order to render justice commensurate with its jurisdiction," ordered "that all the lands, families, and settlements eastward of Sagadahock," within the limits of the provincial charter, be annexed to Yorkshire; and that York be the shire town for holding all the courts and keeping the registry of deeds. In 1735, the legislature ordered that the inferior courts should be holden alternately in January and October at York and Falmouth, the latter thereby becoming the half shire town, at which time the county appears to have acquired the name of York. In 1760, the two new counties of Cumberland and Lincoln being established, the bounds between the former and York were made to run, as at present, northerly of Saco, Buxton, and Limington to the point where the northwest line of "Pearsontown" (Standish) intersects the river Saco, "and from thence north two degrees west on a true course as far as the utmost northern limits of this province." This northern section above the Great Ossipee was cut off to make up a portion of Oxford county, in 1805; since which the bounds of this once great jurisdiction have remained undisturbed. In

1802, the supreme court, which had for the two previous years been held at Kennebunk, was, after a severe contest, removed to Alfred, and, at the first session, the bench was occupied by Judges Dana, Cushing, and Thacher; but the courts of sessions continued to be held at several places for some years longer. In 1807 they ceased at Biddeford, in 1814 at Waterborough, and in 1833 at York, thus making Alfred the exclusive shire town.

York belongs to the western judicial district, the law terms for which are held at Portland. The jury terms of the supreme judicial court commence on the first Tuesdays of January and April, and the third Tuesday of September.

The county contains an area of about eight hundred square miles. It is separated from New Hampshire chiefly by the Piscataqua and Salmon Falls rivers, and is bounded on the southeast by the ocean, which gives it the advantage of several good harbors. An accurate survey of York harbor has been completed under the superintendence of Professor Bache, of the Coast Survey. Ship-building and maritime pursuits are on the decline, the attention of the people being more generally given to agriculture. The surface is somewhat rough and uneven, and, along the coast, rocky. The county is watered by the Saco and its tributaries, by the Kennebunk, Mousam, Wells, York, and Little Ossipee rivers, besides those before mentioned, and some ponds of greater or less size. It can boast also of Mount Agamenticus, some 680 feet above the level of the sea. It is traversed for about thirty miles by the Portland, Saco, and Portsmouth Railroad, and by the York and Cumberland Railroad, projected from Portland to Great Falls, N. H., but which has been completed only eighteen miles, to Hollis. Population, 60,098; valuation, $12,390,335.

ADDITIONS AND CORRECTIONS.

JONESPORT, situated on the sea-coast in Washington County, Me., eighteen miles southwest from Machias, formed a part of the town of Jonesborough until 1832. The settlement of the town was commenced some years previous to the Revolution, by the Kellys, the Sawyers, and some others. John Shorey was an early settler, and took up a residence on Rogue's Island, at the mouth of Chandler's river. The inhabitants suffered much during the Revolutionary war, on account of the scarcity of provisions; deriving for weeks together their only sustenance from the clam beds. But little attention has ever been devoted to the cultivation of the soil. Fishing, coasting, and getting out cord wood for the Rockland and Boston markets, are the principal occupations of the people. Some business is done in boat-building. Moose à Bec Reach, situated opposite, is quite a noted thoroughfare, and affords a convenient harbor, as well as a safe passage for vessels in a stress of weather; still, many, particularly large English vessels, bound up the Bay of Fundy, or up the River St. John, by endeavoring to make the land here, are driven ashore, and the scattered remnants of their cargoes are promptly picked up and accepted as a precious boon by the poorer inhabitants. The islands at the mouth of Indian river are encircled by navigable waters. Head Harbor Island, having an area of about three hundred acres, is situated below the east entrance of "the Reach," and has a very barren soil. Beals's Island, cut off from the main land by "the Reach," contains about one thousand acres, and is inhabited by several families. The town has eleven school-districts; one religious society — Baptist, and one meeting-house — Union. Population, 826; valuation, $54,602.

ELLIOTSVILLE, Piscataquis county, Me. The act of March 19, 1835, incorporating this town, was repealed March 26, 1858.

ISLANDPORT, Hancock county, Me. The act of February 11, 1857, incorporating this town, was repealed March 27, 1858.

GREENFIELD, Hancock county, Me., and townships numbers One and Two were set off from Hancock county, and annexed to Penobscot county, by act of March 13, 1858.

JEFFERSON, Lincoln county, Me. A small part of this town was set off and annexed to Newcastle, March 11, 1858.

DANVILLE, Androscoggin county, Me. All that part of this town embraced within Auburn village, was annexed to Auburn, February 19, 1859.

SEAVILLE, Hancock county, Me. Bartlett's Island was annexed to Mount Desert, and the remainder of Seaville to Tremont, February 24, 1859.

PRESQUE ISLE, Aroostook county, Me., or Letter F., R. 2, (see ante, 971,) was incorporated as a town, April 4, 1859.

MAYSVILLE, Aroostook county, Me., or Letter G., R. 2, was incorporated as a town, April 4, 1859.

LYNDON, Aroostook county, Me., was incorporated out of the parts of half-township H., and the township of Eaton which lie west of the Aroostook river, April 5, 1859.

WINTERPORT, Waldo county (northerly half of Frankfort), incorp. March 12, 1860.

UPTON, Oxford county, incorporated from Letter B., February 9, 1860.

MATTAWAMKEAG, Penobscot county, incorporated from township No. 1, Indian Purchase, E. Penobscot river, February 14, 1860.

DANFORTH, Washington county, incorporated from half township R. 4, north of Bing. Penob. Purchase, and township No. 8, R. 4, March, 17, 1860.

SUPPLEMENT.

TOWNS AND PLANTATIONS IN MAINE.[1]

AROOSTOOK COUNTY. THE spirit of immigration to this county having recently been stimulated to an unwonted degree, some information respecting the various settlements will be in place. There are three or four principal centres of population, nearly all, however, lying in the first and second ranges, along the Military road, and within ten or fifteen miles of the river St. John. These are Houlton, Bridgewater, Presque Isle, and Fort Fairfield. There are two or three other less important districts, chiefly in the fifth and sixth ranges, such as Patten, Masardis, Ashland, and Portage Lake. The latter are situated along the Aroostook river and the easterly branches of the Penobscot. Indeed, such is the supply of timber along these streams, and so great are the facilities for getting it to marketable ports, that these localities will unquestionably become populous, before new-comers will find an inducement to penetrate further into the wilderness. It is estimated that no less than five hundred *bonâ fide* settlers have taken up lots during the year 1858.

Of the two million acres held by the state, nearly one half, or 964,000 acres, lie in this county, and these are all that are yet offered for purchase. By the laws of the state, lots in the lands designated by the state for settlement, not exceeding two hundred acres to each person, may be sold at fifty cents per acre, for which he gives his notes, payable in one, two, and three years in labor upon the roads. In order to receive a deed, he must establish his residence on the lot within two years, and, within four, build a comfortable dwelling-house, and clear not less than fifteen acres, ten of which must be laid down to grass. When all conditions shall have been fulfilled, he may hold his land, to the extent of 160 acres, free from attachment and execution for debt, as long as the value of the land does not exceed one thousand dollars. Other safeguards against transfer, solely for speculation, are provided.

There are two principal causes of attraction to the lands in Aroostook county, which are nearly as extensive as the whole state of Massachusetts, and capable of sustaining a vast population. These are the richness of the soil and the excellent roads. The Aroostook soils are mostly of limestone alluvion, with a depth varying from two to six feet, of great fertility, and as well adapted to the production of large crops of wheat, rye, barley, oats, buckwheat, and potatoes, as any land at the East or the West. The uplands are

[1] Such towns as have been incorporated since the body of the work was in type, together with some of the more important plantations, are given here. In the greater number of cases, the figures given for population are estimates based upon the last census reports, upon the votes given for the last two or three years in the several towns and plantations, and upon the number of scholars returned in the latest school reports, and are supposed to be a near approximation to the actual numbers.

crowded with all varieties of hard wood which are indigenous to rich soils. Along the rivers is a luxuriant growth of blue-joint and other grasses, which attain a height of four or five feet. In the first range, some townships are so free from stones that even a sufficiency for wells and cellars is not readily obtained. That part of this territory which is believed to present the greatest inducements to immigrants is what is known as the Valley of the Aroostook, and the tract south of this, extending fifty miles more or less, embracing the five easternmost ranges of townships, drained in part by tributaries of the St. John, but principally by those of the Penobscot. In some of these townships scarce a lot of 160 acres can be found, which is not capable of being made a good farm. Wheat is grown less than formerly, the fly, rust, and mildew having been found serious obstacles to its profitable culture, although in several sections this evil is yet unknown. Twenty to twenty-five bushels to the acre are set down as a good crop, while, in several instances, no less than fifty have been raised. The average production of oats, barley, and rye, under good treatment, may be set down as fifty bushels of oats, thirty of barley, and from thirty to thirty-five of rye. Buckwheat yields from forty to fifty bushels; Indian corn (not yet extensively produced), nearly forty bushels; and potatoes, from two to three hundred bushels. It is asserted, that, for ten years past, not more than one fourth of this crop has ever been lost by disease in any part of this region. The yield of turnips, with very little care, is about five hundred bushels; of carrots, from six hundred to twelve hundred bushels; and of clover and herd's-grass seeds, from six to ten bushels to the acre. The pasturage is abundant, the autumnal feed lasting until covered with snow, while the cattle find a plenty of fresh and nutritious grass as soon as snow disappears in the spring. Another fact which greatly enhances the value of lands here is, that droughts, which are so often destructive in the Middle States and the West, very rarely, if ever, occur in Aroostook. The cost of clearing land averages about ten dollars per acre.

Excellent roads were mentioned as a second inducement to settlers. In this respect the county is provided with what is never found in new sections, unless, as here, the strong arm and deep purse of the general government come to aid. Two principal thoroughfares — the Military and the Aroostook roads — run northerly through to the St. John. Besides these are several roads connecting the eastern and western settlements, and the eastern with towns along that noble river. A summary of the distances of a few of the principal points from Bangor is given below.[1] The present rates of transportation over these roads are so high that resort is had by the eastern settlements to the St. John, during the summer months, for bringing up nearly all the supplies and articles of domestic trade. The question of a railroad from Bangor, through this county, is now warmly urged upon the people of Maine; the more so for the reason, that the St. Andrew and Quebec Railroad, now nearly completed to Woodstock, a few miles from Houlton, threatens to give our Provincial neighbors a monopoly of the trade, if not to encourage a feeling of common interest between the people of this region and the Provinces.

[1] From Bangor to head of steam navigation at Mattawamkeag Point
" " by railroad to Milford, 12 miles, thence by travelled road to Mattaw. Point } 61 miles.
" " to the "Forks" at Molunkus, 10 miles from " " 71 "
" " " Houlton, by military road, 47 " " Molunkus, 115 "
" " " Presque Isle, 40 " " Houlton, 160 "
" " " Fort Fairfield, 11 " " Presque Isle, 169 "
" " " St. John River, at Mouth of Violette brook, 30 miles from " " 191 "
" " " Ashland, by Aroostook road, 75 " Molunkus, 146 "
" " " Presque Isle, " " 24 " Ashland, 170 "
" " " Fort Kent, by Fish river, 48 " " 194 "

Another inducement to settle in Aroostook, which should be first, but which, in the haste to be rich, is generally last considered, is the remarkably healthy character of the climate. The cold is less intense than in many places in New England farther south, while the clearness of the atmosphere has no tendency to induce disease, either contagious or organic.

The legislature of 1858 incorporated two new towns in this county, which, with those given in the body of the work, make thirteen. A brief historical and statistical notice of these, together with such townships as have been opened by the state to settlers, and make a respectable show of inhabitants, is here given.

B. PLANTATION is a half township in range 1, next north of Bridgewater, containing 11,520 acres. It was designated for settlement in 1855. The Presque Isle of the St. John runs through it, and furnishes very excellent water-power. From this fact, and from its location on the Aroostook road, near Presque Isle, a populous settlement, at an early day, must be the result. Mars Hill post-office is in this township. Population, about 150.

BANCROFT PLANTATION, about seventy-five miles from Bangor, is situated in the southeastern part of the county, on the Mattawamkeag river, and is commonly known as Baskahegan Gore. It has a post-office, and three school districts. Population, upwards of 200.

BARKER PLANTATION is made up of a part of Number 1, range 3, and that part of Bancroft township lying west of Mattawamkeag river. It has one school district. Population, about 30.

BELFAST ACADEMY GRANT is a half township, and joins the west line of Houlton. It was located in 1809. It has four school districts, and 136 scholars. Population, about 300.

BENEDICTA PLANTATION, about eighty miles from Bangor, includes township Number 2, range 5. The west half of this township was purchased of the state of Massachusetts by Bishop Benedict J. Fenwick, and was settled about the year 1837, by Irish Catholics. A chapel and college building have been erected, but the college is not yet patronized. The east half of the township belongs to the state, and was lotted for settlement, in 1858, by Daniel Barker. Considerable progress has already been made in the settlement. Both halves are watered by the Molunkus stream. The plantation has one school district, with 162 scholars; and the Conway post-office. Population, about 350.

BRIDGEWATER, about twenty-one miles from Houlton (the shire town), lies in the first range of townships, and is made up of two half townships, Bridgewater Academy Grant and Portland Academy Grant. The first-named grant was settled in 1827, by Nathaniel Bradstreet, who built mills on the Presque Isle of the St. John, or Bridgewater river, about ten miles above its confluence with the St. John. The next settlers were Joseph Ketchum, James Thorn, John Young, Joseph Bradstreet, and Samuel Harvey. The lands were held, until 1852, by the Trustees of Bridgewater Academy, when John D. Baird purchased them, and built a store and extensive lumber mills upon the site of the old mills, as well as a potash manufactory and a grist-mill. The first settlers on the Portland Academy Grant were Orrin Whitney, Dennis Nelson, David Foster, Jason Russell, William Harvey, George Oliver, and others, who came here about the time of the Aroostook war, during which a company of riflemen was stationed here. The town was incorporated, March 2, 1858, and, upon organization, Elbridge Webber was chosen town clerk.

The town is in a good farming region, but as yet its agricultural resources have not been fully developed, on account of the superior facilities for lumbering. There are two small villages, Bridgewater Corner and Baird's Mills, and one post-office. At the Ketchum place is the "Half-way House," where passengers from Houlton to Presque Isle stop for refreshment. About two million shingles annually made in these parts are brought here for sale. There are four school districts; also four blacksmith's and one carriage-maker's shop. Population, about 700.

CRYSTAL PLANTATION, which is township Number 4, range 5, was first settled by William Young, who came here in 1838. It is well watered by westerly branches of the Mattawamkeag river, and has one saw-mill. Large clearings have been made, and there remained unsold, May 1, 1858, only 6,404 acres. There are about thirty settlers; three school districts, and two school-houses. Population, about 200.

DAYTON PLANTATION is township Number 5, range 5. Like Crystal Plantation, it is watered by the head branches of the Mattawamkeag. It has not kept pace with some of the neighboring townships. The first settlers were Nicholas Cooper and Samuel Houston, who came here together in 1839. There is one school district. Population, about 60.

EATON PLANTATION, about forty-seven miles north from Houlton, embraces the western half of the grant to the town of Plymouth, and the original grant to William Eaton, which was made in consideration of services rendered by him in the Revolutionary war. On the Aroostook river here are some well-cleared farms, in a high state of cultivation; and a carriage road has been opened from the mouth of the Carribou stream, in letter H. Plantation, to Fort Fairfield, passing through a portion of the Plymouth grant and entirely through Eaton. A negotiation has been opened between the proprietors of these two grants and the governor and council of Maine for an exchange of these for other tracts, which, when carried through, will bring into the market some very choice lands. There are here four school districts and a post-office. Population, about 400.

FORT FAIRFIELD, about forty-five miles from Houlton, was "so much of township letter D., first range west from the east line of the state, as lay south of the Aroostook river, together with so much of the township granted to the town of Plymouth, as lay south-easterly of the same river." It was first settled as early as 1816, by people from the British Provinces, who came up the river in canoes. They located themselves on front lots near the river, and lived many years without roads, having no communication with other parts of Maine, and confessing allegiance to the British crown. Upon the breaking out of the northeastern boundary troubles in 1839, the state authorities sent a military force here. Fort Fairfield (from which the town has been named) was built the same year, consisting of two block-houses and the officers' head-quarters; and roads were opened from the Penobscot. The main fort has been demolished; the other, erected for the protection of the boom, and the officers' head-quarters, are still standing, the latter being occupied as a dwelling-house. The township was lotted in 1840, by Thomas Sawyer, Jr., surveyor-general of the State, from which time there has been a steady increase in population. The town was incorporated March 11, 1858.

The surface is generally smooth, with some swells, and is well watered by the Aroostook river and its tributaries. The soil is very fertile, and easily cultivated. Lumber is the chief article of manufacture and trade: and the facilities for getting it to the ocean are very good. Tow-boats pass up and down the Aroostook, and the St. John is navigable for steamboats to Grand Falls, eighteen miles above the mouth of the Aroostook, and for tow-boats 120 miles further, to the Big Rapids above the mouth of the Great Black river.

The town has one village, three religious societies — Methodist, Congregational, and Baptist, — nine school districts, and three post-offices, — Fort Fairfield, Maple Grove, and Fremont: also three saw-mills, a clapboard-mill, a grist-mill, and a plaster-mill. Population, about 700.

FREMONT PLANTATION is letter C., range 1, and is bounded north by Fort Fairfield. It was lotted by Noah Barker in 1856. Every settling lot is now taken up by immigrants, and a considerable portion has been improved. The first settler was a man by the name of Bartlett, who was soon followed by Henry Wilson, the latter of whom travelled by a spotted line from Presque Isle, and settled near the middle of the township in 1853. The township offers superior inducements to settlers, and those already here are a persevering and industrious class of people. Much interest is manifested in the organization of district and Sabbath schools. Isaac Wortman, a gentleman of wealth from Brooklyn, N. Y., has taken up lands here, and laid the foundation of a princely estate. He felled forty acres of forest in 1856. The legislature of 1857 granted him 640 acres of land as an inducement to erect mills, and such mechanical establishments upon the river De Chute as will materially aid in the progress of the settlement. Fremont has one school district. Population, about 150.

G. PLANTATION is bounded north by H. Plantation and the Eaton Grant, and south by Presque Isle, and contains 19,665 acres, a part of which has been lotted. The road from Presque Isle northward to the St. John passes through it, and the Aroostook river makes such a detour southwards, then taking its course directly north, that it twice nearly traverses the township. On this are some mills. The land is very productive, and Indian corn has been grown here with good success, the yield having been found equal to fifty-one bushels to the acre, although the average crop does not probably exceed forty bushels. There are eight school districts, and 174 scholars. Population, 500.

GOLDEN RIDGE PLANTATION is Number 3, range 5, mostly east of the Aroostook road, and was set apart for settlement in 1855. It contains 22,111 acres, and is watered by the Molunkus stream. It has a fertile soil, and is being rapidly settled. Alfred Cushman, who came here about the year 1833, was the first settler. Mr. Cushman, in one instance, from two bushels and a half of seed, reaped 175 bushels of wheat on four acres, one acre of which proved too wet, and yielded only about half as much as the rest, thus indicating fifty bushels to the acre on three acres. The corn crop here has proved excellent, yielding 210 bushels of sound ears to the acre. There are probably one hundred settlers, some forty of whom came here in the summer of 1858. The other settlers have generally made large clearings. There are two saw-mills, two school-houses, six school districts, and one post-office, called Number Three. Population, about 300.

H. PLANTATION, in range 2, about fifty miles north from Houlton and eight from Presque Isle, embraces the westerly half of the township of which Eaton is the east half, and township I. directly north of these two half townships. Half township H. was lotted in 1839, by H. W. Cunningham, and is a tract possessing many advantages for the settler. The inhabitants were mostly from Kennebec and Oxford counties. Among those who first arrived were Winslow Hall from Hartford, and I. Hardison from China. Nearly all of the lots are already taken up, and but 3,157 acres were remaining in May, 1858.

A post-office, called Lyndon, is located here. There are two clapboard-mills, a saw-mill, and two grist-mills in this township. Township I. was lotted in 1856, by Noah Barker, and but little of it has yet been taken up. Alexander Cochrane and brother were the first settlers here, having taken up a residence since 1840. There are several French settlers here from Madawaska, one of whom keeps a public-house. There is a shingle-mill in this part of the township. The plantation contains seven school districts, with 162 scholars. Population, about 325.

HANCOCK PLANTATION, in the extreme north part of Aroostook county, joins the western boundary of Madawaska Plantation, but has no definite limits. Fish river runs through its territory and falls into the St. John. At the junction of these two rivers, the United States government, in 1839, built Fort Kent, designed for the defence of the frontier. The fort consisted of a common block-house, connected with which were two houses for the accommodation of the officers, barracks for the soldiers, and buildings for the use of the commissary department. The land upon which they were erected was leased by the state to the United States, and was to continue in the possession of the latter as long as it should be occupied for a military post. The troops were withdrawn late in the autumn of 1843, since which time the fort has been under the charge of an agent of the federal government. Noah Barker, the land-agent of this state, in March, 1857, requested of the war department a surrender of the lease, on the ground that the lands are no longer occupied as a military post; and the surrender was ordered in October of the same year.

The region adjacent to Fort Kent is probably one of the healthiest within the limits of the United States, and the climate, though rigorous, seems to be promotive of the most robust health. Fevers and other diseases of a malarious origin are unknown; and in many instances, pulmonary symptoms, quite strongly marked in persons arriving here, have disappeared after a brief residence. The inhabitants are largely made up from the French "side of the house." There is one post-office — Fort Kent; and there are nine school districts. Population, about 1,000.

HAYNESVILLE PLANTATION, in the southeast part of Aroostook county, about eighty miles from Bangor, joins Orient, and embraces the west half of township Number 9, Greenwood's survey, and that part of Pickering and Morrill's gore lying south of the west branch of Mattawamkeag river, as well as township Number 2, range 3. A small village has grown up on the southwest side of the river, on the military road, containing a post-office, two stores, and two public-houses. This place is better known as the "Forks of the Mattawamkeag." There are three school districts. Population, about 100.

ISLAND FALLS PLANTATION is Number 4, range 4, and was organized as a plantation in the autumn of 1858. It was lotted in 1855–6, and contains an area of 23,040 acres, a small portion of which has been disposed of to settlers. The first settler was Levi Sewall, who came here in 1842. Thirty-two new settlers took up their residence here in the year 1858. It is an excellent farming township, and is traversed by the head-waters of the Mattawamkeag river, which have their course through a large pond situated upon the east line of the township. The road from Patten to Smyrna passes through the northerly part. Population, about 100.

LEAVITT PLANTATION, ninety-five miles from Bangor, embraces Number 3, range 2, as also that part of Pickering and Morrill's gore lying northeast of the west branch of Mattawamkeag river. There are two school districts, with forty scholars. Population, about 75.

LIMESTONE RIVER PLANTATION, about fifty-four miles from Houlton, is E., range 1. and was lotted in 1847, by Charles K. Eddy. In May, 1858, 1,280 acres had been disposed of to settlers. On the Limestone river, a saw-mill and clapboard machine have been erected. This river derives its name from the abundance of limestone found in the region. A post-office has been established here. Population, about 100.

MACWAHOC PLANTATION is Number 1, range 4, being the next township northeast of Molunkus. The Military road runs through the southeast part of it, and the Macwahoc stream passes through its entire length from north to south, emptying into the Molunkus stream not far below Molunkus pond. There are two school districts. Population, about 130.

MADAWASKA PLANTATION, in the extreme north part of Aroostook county, about 195 miles from Bangor, embraces Numbers 18 and 19, ranges 4 and 5. The settlement derived its name from the river Madawaska, which falls into the St. John about thirty-six miles above the Grand Falls, and 160 miles above Fredericton. The original settlers arrived soon after the treaty of 1783, and the first grant of land was made to Joseph Muzzerol and fifty-one other French settlers, in the month of October, 1790, by Thomas Carlton, then lieutenant-governor of the province of New Brunswick. The land thus granted lay at intervals between the Verde (Green) and Madawaska rivers (which are about nine miles apart) and on both sides of the St. John river. The grant comprised fifty-one several lots or plats of land, sufficiently large for a homestead for each settler. The second grant was to Joseph Soucer and others, in August, 1794, by lieutenant-governor Carlton, and contained 5,253 acres lying below Green river. These, and one made to Limo Hibert, in May, 1825, of 250 acres opposite to and along the Madawaska river,[1] were the only grants, on this side of the St. John.

The inhabitants are exclusively French, or of French descent, and came here from Acadia upon the breaking up of that settlement by the English. They are principally Roman Catholics. The plantation is divided into four parishes—Grand River, Madawaska, Chatauquay (Cat-corner), and St. Francis, at each of which is a church edifice. There are thirteen school districts, and one post-office. Population, about 1,400.

MARS HILL PLANTATION, in range 1, about thirty miles north from Houlton, was granted by the state of Massachusetts to Revolutionary soldiers. It was lotted in 1801; and when the boundary line was run between Maine and New Brunswick, it was found that a half-mile strip, thus lotted, was within the territory of the latter province. The proprietors of the township are Messrs. Madigan and Trueworthy. The surface is rough and broken. Mars hill, from which the plantation was named, about three miles long, and estimated to be 1,700 feet high, is situated in the eastern part. The post-office called Mars Hill is in the half township B., range 1, which bounds this on the south. Population, about 50.

MOLUNKUS PLANTATION, Aroostook county, seventy-one miles northeasterly from Bangor, is township A., range 5, and includes the tracts marked, on the state plan, Fiske and Bridge, and Chamberlain. It has one school district, and a post-office called South Molunkus. Population, about 100.

NUMBER ELEVEN, range one, lies between Amity and Hodgdon, on the Houlton and

[1] Madawaska river is wholly in the province of New Brunswick; consequently the grant in 1825 must have been mostly, if not wholly, in that province.

Baring road, ten miles south of Houlton, and was designated for settlement in 1855. It embraces 11,520 acres, 6,747 of which remained unsold May 1, 1858. It was lotted in 1856, by Daniel Cummings, and there are already a few settlers here. There are five school districts. Population, about 100.

NUMBER TWELVE, range three, is next west of Presque Isle and G. Plantation, situated upon the road from Ashland to Presque Isle. It was lotted in 1843, and the settlement is making rapid progress. A branch of Presque Isle stream runs through its southern part. Population, about 100.

NUMBER FOUR, range four, was lotted in 1855 and 1856. It contains an area of 23,040 acres, a small portion of which has been disposed of to settlers. The road from Patten to Smyrna passes through the northerly part, and it is traversed by the head waters of the Mattawamkeag river, which have their course through a large pond situated upon the east line of the township.

NUMBER NINE, range four, is next southeast of Masardis, and was lotted in 1839. It is watered by the Masardis stream, on which are some old mills.

NUMBER TWELVE, range four, was partly lotted in 1855, by Noah Barker, and the survey was completed in 1858, by Daniel Barker. Rapid progress is making in the settlement. Here are the Castle Hill post-office, and a public-house, at the half-way point between Presque Isle and Ashland, on the road leading from Fort Fairfield *via.* Presque Isle to Ashland. The township is not yet organized into a plantation, but its citizens vote at Salmon Brook. The Aroostook river passes through the northwest corner of the township. Population, about 150.

NUMBER ONE, range five, is a half township, situated between Molunkus and Benedicta plantations, but has not, as yet, an organization. The Aroostook road runs through it, as also the Molunkus stream. The Rawson post-office is located here, although the township is as yet sparsely settled.

NUMBER FIVE is the name of a plantation embracing township Number 5, range 6. Thomas Myrick was the first settler. The township lies next north of Patten, and the Aroostook road passes through it. Population, about 150.

NUMBER ELEVEN, range six, is the next township west of Ashland, and has a good location. The Aroostook road and river, as well as the village of Ashland, are within a mile of the east line, and the Machias river runs through the centre from west to east, discharging its waters into the Aroostook. The township was lotted in 1839. It has mills.

PLYMOUTH PLANTATION, Aroostook county, is all that part of the Plymouth Academy Grant in range 1, which lies northeasterly of the Aroostook river, and which is not included in Fort Fairfield and Eaton Plantation. The river passes southeasterly and northeasterly through the township. The road to Limestone River Plantation, thence easterly to the St. John, also passes through the township. The proximity of Plymouth to Fort Fairfield gives it superior advantages as a place for settlement. There are thirty-two scholars in the public school. Population, about 100.

PORTAGE LAKE PLANTATION, about ten miles north from Ashland and 160 from

Bangor, is Number 13, range 6, and is bisected by the Aroostook road. The beautiful lake, the name of which is borne by the township, is at the head of the chain of lakes having their outlet northward into Fish river. But a small portion of the lots here remain unsold. It is an excellent farming township, and possesses an advantage over some of the neighboring places in the length of summer, frosts not generally making their appearance until about two weeks later than in Number 11, which is twelve miles further south. The wheat-fly has never troubled the grain here. Hon. Nathaniel Blake, who has done much to promote the settlement of the plantation, has usually had a wheat crop of twenty-five bushels to the acre. There are three school districts with 134 scholars, and a post-office. Population, about 300.

PRESQUE ISLE is F., range 2, situated forty miles north from Houlton, and 160 from Bangor. The first improvement here was made in 1828, by Dennis Fairbanks, who soon afterwards erected a mill. The township was partly surveyed in 1839, by Thomas Sawyer, Jr., and the survey was completed in 1856, by Noah Barker. Presque Isle is situated in the midst of a large tract of the finest settling land in New England, and is surrounded on all sides by townships, which are fast filling up with an intelligent and industrious people. Its position, therefore, must soon place it among the first towns in northern Maine. The soil is rich, and its agricultural resources are extensive, which fact, coupled with the capacity of the stream for mills, has brought in a considerable population. Immigration hither, for the last two or three years, has been rapid, and the township is mostly settled. Some attention has been given, through the exertions of members of the North Aroostook Agricultural Society, to the introduction of choice breeds of cattle. The grass crops in this region are very heavy, and a large quantity of grass-seed is put up for market. The village of Presque Isle is situated partly in letter F. and partly in letter G. The people of these two townships have petitioned the legislature of 1859 for incorporation into one town, by the name of Presque Isle. Several roads connect here,—a branch of the Aroostook from Ashland, the Military road northward and southward, and two roads from the St. John through Fremont Plantation and Fort Fairfield. Presque Isle stream flows northward into the Aroostook, and the Presque Isle of the St. John passes southward into the St. John. There are here one post-office, one newspaper—the Aroostook Pioneer—the only one in the county, seven school districts, with 189 scholars, a high school, and a public-house: also, a saw-mill and grist-mill, a clapboard and shingle machine, a carding, spinning, and weaving machine, five stores, and establishments for the manufacture of furniture, harnesses, carriages, &c. The place is fast increasing in numbers and importance. Religious services are held regularly on Sundays in the high-school building. Population, about 600; valuation, about $70,000.

REED PLANTATION, about nine miles northeast from Molunkus, is Number 1, range 3. The Military road passes through it, and it is watered by the Wytopitlock stream, running south into the Mattawamkeag.

ROCKABEMA PLANTATION, which is Number 6, range 5, is about forty-four miles from Molunkus, and is traversed by the Aroostook road. Limestone abounds in this region. There are two school districts, with thirty-seven scholars; and two post-offices—Moro and Rockabema. Population, about 75.

SALMON BROOK PLANTATION embraces township Number 13, range 3, and is situated next westerly of letter G. and H. plantations, ten miles from Presque Isle, and fifty from Houlton. On the south side of the township is a strip of land two miles wide, along

33

the Aroostook river, which was lotted in 1842, by William P. Parrott, and is now nearly all settled. The remaining part of the township was lotted, in 1855, by Rev. E. Knight, but as yet has very few settlers. Mr. Knight also laid out a road from the junction of Salmon brook with the Aroostook river to Lyndon post-office in H., range 2. The principal portion of the lands on this road are now being taken up with a view to settlement. Iron ore abounds in this region. A post-office, called Salmon Brook, is established here, and on the stream of the same name are a saw-mill, grist-mill, and a carding machine. There are two school districts, with ninety-six scholars. Population, about 300.

UMCOLCUS PLANTATION is Number 9, range 6, and adjoins the southwest corner of Masardis. It was lotted for settlement, in 1839 and 1840, by H. W. Cunningham and Noah Barker, and is perhaps better known as the "Ox-bow," named from a singular bend which the Aroostook river makes in passing through the township. The Umcolcus stream comes from the south, and falls into the Aroostook near the Ox-bow. Here are a good saw-mill and a grist-mill, which have been in operation since about the year 1842. The post-office is on the Aroostook road, in Number 8, range 5, which township was also lotted, in 1839, by Noah Barker, and in which is a limestone quarry. There is one school district, with forty-one scholars. Population, about 80.

VAN BUREN PLANTATION is in the extreme northeast part of the county, 190 miles from Bangor, being bounded north by the river St. John, east by New Brunswick, south by Limestone Plantation (E., range 1) and H. Plantation, and west by Madawaska Plantation, and embraces, as will be perceived, nine townships. At the mouth of Violette brook, in M., range 2, there is a settlement containing a post-office, a public-house, a saw-mill, a clapboard-mill, and a store. A large proportion of the population here consists of French, who retain their own language. At this point the inhabitants of the plantation assemble to vote. L., range 2, included in this plantation, was set apart by the legislature for settlement, and was partly lotted, in 1858, by Lore Alford. Several Yankee settlers are about entering here to make farms. G., range 1, and M., range 2, were also located and designated for settlement in 1858. Numerous streams run through the several townships, such as the Violette, Toussaint, Little Madawaska, and Limestone; and the soil of the whole region is of a character to invite immigration. The Grand Falls, on the St. John, are within three miles of the eastern limits of the plantation. There is also another post-office, by the name of West Van Buren. There are said to be 585 scholars. Population, about 1,200.

FRANKLIN COUNTY: —

DALLAS PLANTATION is township Number 2, range 2, west of Bingham's Kennebec Purchase. The Acquessuck or Rangely lake is near the township upon the west; but the waters of Dallas chiefly fall into the Saddleback stream, which flows in a northeasterly direction into Dead river. Population, 123.[1]

E. PLANTATION is a gore of land situated between Phillips and Number 6 upon the south, and Rangely Plantation upon the north. Here is the water-shed between the Androscoggin and Sandy rivers. There are two school districts. Population, 86.

EUSTIS PLANTATION contains township Number 1, range 4, west of Bingham's Pur-

[1] An enumeration of the inhabitants of all the plantations in Franklin county was made November 9, 1858, from which these figures are derived.

chase, which adjoins Somerset county. The Saddleback stream here unites with Dead river. The soil is mostly good, and there are many excellent farms. Population, 315.

JACKSON PLANTATION (known as Copeland Town) embraces township Number 1, range 3. It adjoins Somerset county, and is a part of what is called "Dead River Settlement," lying westerly and southwesterly of Flag Staff Plantation and Dead river. It is a good farming region, but, as yet, lumbering forms the chief business. A new county road is about to be laid out by the county commissioners through this region, passing west of Mount Abraham, and connecting the Sandy river valley with the Dead river country. The Saddleback stream passes through the township. Population, 63.

NUMBER THREE is township Number 3, range 2, of Bingham's Purchase. It is next north of Kingfield, and is watered by the north branch of Seven-Mile brook, which empties into the Kennebec at North Anson. There is some settling land, but the township is mostly valuable for its timber. Population, 39.

NUMBER SIX is the westerly portion of what was once incorporated as the town of Berlin, but which, as no organization was effected under the charter, again relapsed into the plantation state. The easterly half was afterwards annexed to the town of Phillips. Population, 59.

PERKINS PLANTATION, a small, irregular tract of land, was formerly known as Number Four, and was set off from Carthage, which bounds it upon the west. Weld is upon the north, Dixfield upon the south, and Temple and Wilton are upon the east. It lies in a narrow gorge between rugged mountains. There are three school districts, and seventy-two scholars. Population, 177.

RANGELY PLANTATION embraces townships Number 2 and 3, range 1, next west of Madrid. Its waters run westerly into Rangely and Mooselockmeguntic lakes. Population, 183.

HANCOCK COUNTY:—

SWAN ISLAND PLANTATION includes Swan and Burnt Coat islands, situated about ten miles from the mainland, and easterly of Deer Isle. There are four school districts, with 187 scholars. It has a post-office. Population, 423.

WETMORE ISLE, formerly a part of Prospect, is situated in Penobscot river, opposite Bucksport, and contains an area of about five thousand acres. It originally belonged to the Waldo patent, and fell into the possession of an orphan girl, an heir of General Waldo: hence it bore, for many years, the name of Orphan Island. It was finally purchased by a man named Wetmore. The island was settled in 1763 by three families, who took up their residence on its southern margin. At that time there was not another settler above them on the river. The chief means of subsistence to the inhabitants is fishing and hunting, the land being too poor to yield any thing in the shape of grain or vegetables. There are four school districts and seven schools here. Population, 405; valuation, $56,595.

KENNEBEC COUNTY:—

UNITY PLANTATION is in the extreme northeast part of Kennebec county, having Unity in Waldo county on the east. It is the only territory in the county not under municipal government. It has one school district, with thirty-three scholars. Population, 110.

LINCOLN COUNTY:—

MATINICUS ISLE, a plantation belonging to Lincoln county, is opposite to St. George, and several miles from the mainland. It has one school district, and a post-office. Population, 120.

MUSCLE RIDGE is also a plantation easterly from St. George, but nearer the coast than Matinicus. It consists of several small islands, and has three school districts. Population, 56.

SOMERVILLE, the most northerly town in Lincoln county, about fifteen miles easterly from Augusta, was, until its incorporation, March 25th, 1858, called Patricktown Plantation. The settlement was commenced in 1784, John Evans, William and David Gilpatrick, Ichabod Marr, Joseph Tobey, Porter Dodge, Enoch Gove, and Daniel Brown being the first men on the ground. The land belonged to the government, and was purchased more than twenty years since by Hon. Reuel Williams, and Messrs. Dorr and Russell, from whom the settlers have derived title. The principal occupations of the inhabitants are lumbering and farming. The town has two villages — Sand Hill and Sheepscot; two church-edifices — Baptist and Second Advent; seven school districts, and one post-office; also, five saw-mills, two grist-mills, eight shingle-machines, eight stave-machines, and one clapboard-machine. Population, 552.

OXFORD COUNTY:—

B. PLANTATION adjoins the New Hampshire line, and has Umbagog lake partly upon the north and west border, and is well watered by streams contributing to this lake and to the Androscoggin river. It has four school districts, and a post-office. Population, 174.

FRANKLIN PLANTATION is a tract of land west of, and about half as large as, the town of Peru. It has four school districts. Population, 188.

HAMLIN'S PLANTATION is a small quadrangular tract of land southeast of Bethel. It has one school district. Population, 108.

MILTON PLANTATION is a tract of land on the south side of Rumford, and about two thirds its length. It has two school districts. Population, 166

NUMBER FIVE, in ranges 1 and 2, is the name of a plantation. The Margalloway river passes southwards through a large portion of it, and the Umbagog chain of lakes is upon the east side. It has two school districts. Population, 105.

RILEY PLANTATION is west of Newry and east of Gorham, N. H. It has not, thus far, made a very rapid advance towards a prosperous settlement. Population, 60.

PENOBSCOT COUNTY:—

MATTAWAMKEAG PLANTATION is Indian township Number One, being that part of the Indian Purchase which lies east of Penobscot river. The river Mattawamkeag runs westerly through its southern part. Mattawamkeag Point, the half-way place from Bangor to Houlton, at the junction of these two rivers, and at the head of steamboat navigation upon the Upper Penobscot, is a village of some importance, containing an excellent hotel, several stores, and a post-office. Population, about 300.

NIKERTOU PLANTATION embraces a tract containing upwards of 100,000 acres, and is made up of two townships, that were formerly granted by the state to the Penobscot Indians, the Hopkins Academy Grant, township A., and Emerson and Fish township. It is well watered by the west branch of the Penobscot, by the Twin lakes, and the Millinoket stream. It has four school districts, with 105 scholars, and a post-office. Population, about 250.

NUMBER ONE, north division, was set off, together with Greenfield and Number Two, in 1857, from Hancock county, and annexed to this county. It adjoins Greenbush, which borders upon Penobscot river, and has the Passadumkeag river upon the north, a branch of which passes nearly through this township. Population, 142.

NUMBER FOUR, range one, is bounded north by Springfield and south by Number Four, north division, in Hancock county. Sysladobsis lake lies partly within the township. There are three school districts. Population, 161.

NUMBER FIVE, range six, is next north of Patton, on the Aroostook road. Nearly half of the land has been sold, and habitations are springing up. A road has also been laid out to some ponds and mill privileges in the northwest part. Fifty-seven scholars were reported in the last school returns. Population, about 150.

PRENTISS, Penobscot county, about sixty miles from Bangor, having Carroll upon the south, is what was township Number 7 in the third range of townships north of Bingham's Penobscot Purchase. The original proprietors were Seth Paine and members of his family, Hon. Israel Washburn, Jr., and Hon. Henry E. Prentiss, in honor of whom the town was named. Major John Judkins, who came here with his family, consisting of five sons and two daughters, June 25, 1838, was the first settler. His original habitation was a rude hut covered with elm bark, which he put up in less than two days. The next year E. and I. Averil, J. T. Baldwin, and others, came into the settlement. A post-office by the name of Deerfield was established in 1855, and on the 27th of February, 1858, the town was incorporated. Water is supplied from one of the branches of the Penobscot. Prentiss has six school districts; also, a saw-mill and grist-mill. This is said to be one of the best settling towns in the State. There are fifty-two legal voters, and a population of about 300.

WOODVILLE, a plantation lying on the west bank of Penobscot river, opposite the mouth of the Mattawamkeag river, is township Number 2, Indian Purchase, which was lotted by Noah Barker in 1835, under a resolve of the legislature granting said township, in lots of 200 acres each, to the Maine or Massachusetts soldiers in the Revolution. Many of the lots have been bought up by speculators: hence the tardiness of its settlement. There is a carriage road through it, leading from Chester to Nikertou, or Forks of the Penobscot river. A post-office, by the name of North Woodville, has been established here. Ninety-six scholars are reported. Population, about 225.

SOMERSET COUNTY:—

DEAD RIVER PLANTATION embraces township Number 3, range 3, of Bingham's Kennebec Purchase. It is situated upon the south bend of the Dead river, and has some very good farms. Mt. Bigelow lies upon the south. There is one post-office. Population, about 100.

33 *

FLAG STAFF PLANTATION is Number 4, range 4, of Bingham's Kennebec Purchase, and is said to have derived its name from the circumstance of Arnold's erecting a flag here, when on his expedition to Canada. It is watered by the Dead river and its tributaries, on which are some mills. There is some excellent farming land, and good progress has been made in the settlement. A public-house occupies the site of the flag. It has a post-office. Population, about 75.

FORKS is the name of a small settlement in Number 1, range 4, west of Kennebec river, and at the junction of the same with Dead river, about fifty-five miles north from Augusta. It is also called Salmon Stream Town. It has three school districts, and a post-office. Population, about 150.

MOOSE RIVER PLANTATION, sometimes known as Jackman's, is Number 4, range 1, north of Bingham's Kennebec Purchase. It is watered by Moose river, which runs easterly into Moosehead lake; and the main road up the Kennebec river and thence to Canada passes through the township. Population about 125.

NUMBER ONE, range two, west of Kennebec river, is what is called Pleasant Ridge. It has three school districts, with sixty-two scholars. Population, 143.

NUMBER TWO, range two, is next west of Number 1, and has three school districts, and fifty-one scholars. Population, 144.

NUMBER ONE, range three, east of the Kennebec river, is what is called Carritunk, and has five school districts, with ninety scholars, and one post-office — Carritunk. Population, about 200.

WASHINGTON COUNTY:—

BIG LAKE PLANTATION lies on the north side of Big Lake. It is visited during the summer months by hunting and fishing parties, but as yet is sparsely settled. It has one school district. Population, 126.

DANFORTH PLANTATION is in the extreme north part of the county, south and west of the Schoodic lakes. It has one school district. Population, 168.

NUMBER SEVEN, range two, is Kossuth. It has two school districts. Population, 61.

NUMBER NINE, range four, is a township formerly belonging to Waterston and others, and contains the Baskahegan lake, fully one third of its territory being thus covered with water. It has two school districts. Population, about 75.

NUMBER FOURTEEN is in the southeasterly part of the county, west of Dennysville. It has three school districts, with sixty-three scholars, and a post-office. Population, about 125.

TALMADGE PLANTATION is in the northerly part of the county, in the second range. It has a considerable lake in the west part, and is also watered by streams emptying into Big lake. There are two school districts. Population, about 70.

WAIT PLANTATION lies next east of Talmadge, and is watered by Schoodic river and its branches. It has one school district, and a post-office. Population, 81.

APPENDIX A.

POST-OFFICES.

The following list contains some names of post-offices newly established, some of which have been casually omitted in the body of the work, and some in towns where the number of offices is stated, but where the names, although differing from those of such towns, are not given.

MAINE.

Albany, North
Amity,
Anson, West
Ashland — Aroostook,
Atkinson,
Atkinson, South
Baldwin, West
Bangor,
Bangor, North
Bangor — Six Mile Falls,
Bangor, West
Bath,
Beddington,
Beddington, South
Bethel, East
Bethel, West
Boothbay — Hodgdon's Mills,
Boothbay, North
Bowdoin Centre,
Bowdoin, West
Bowerbank,
Bridgton, North
Bridgton, South
Bridgton, West
Brooksville, South
Brooksville, West
Brownville, North
Buckfield, North
Bucksport — Buck's Mills,
Burnham,
Casco, New,
Dexter,
Dexter, South
Dixmont, North-east
Forks — Parlin Pond,
Freedom, West
Freeport, South
Fryeburg Centre,
Fuller, Washington Co.
Gouldsborough — Prospect Harbor,
Great Pond, Hancock Co.
Greenbush—Olamon,
Hartford, South
Highland, Somerset Co.
Hollis — Bar Mills,
Hollis, North
Jackson, Washington Co.
Jacksonville, Franklin Co.
Jefferson, South
Kennebunk Depot,
Leeds — Curtis's Corner,
Levant, South
Lincoln Plant'n, Oxford Co. — Wilson's Mills,
Linneus,
Livermore, North
Livermore, South
Mariaville — Tilden,
Milford — Greatworks,
Monmouth, South
Newburgh, North
Newcastle, North
New Limerick,
Northfield,
Palermo, North
Palmyra,
Parkman, South
Penobscot, South
Phipsburg — Cape Small Point,
Seaport, Hancock Co.
Shapleigh — Emery's Mills,
Shirley — Shirley Mills,
Sidney, West
Smyrna,
Smyrna Mills,
St. George, South
Troy Centre,
Vienna, North
Wales, East
Warren, North
West Bath — Winnegance,
Windham, East.

(391)

APPENDIX D.

SENATORS AND REPRESENTATIVES IN CONGRESS.

A blank indicates that the incumbent has been elected for a full term yet unexpired.

MAINE.

Senators.

Bradbury, J. W.	1847—1853
Chandler, John,	1820—1829
Evans, George,	1841—1847
Fairfield, John,	1843—1847
Fessenden, Wm. Pitt,	1854—1859 1859—
Hamlin, Hannibal,	1849—1851 1851—1857 1857—
Holmes, John,	1820—1827 1828—1833
Moor, Wyman B. S.	1848—1849
Parris, Albion K.,	1827—1828
Ruggles, John,	1835—1841
Shepley, Ether,	1833—1837
Sprague, Peleg,	1829—1835
Williams, Ruel,	1837—1843

Representatives.

Abbott, Nehemiah,	1857—1859
Allen, Elisha H.,	1841—1843
Anderson, Hugh J.,	1837—1841
Anderson, John,	1825—1833
Andrews, Charles,	1851—1852
Appleton, John,	1851—1853
Bailey, Jeremiah,	1835—1837
Bates, James,	1831—1833
Belcher, Hiram,	1847—1849
Benson, Samuel P.	1853—1857
Bronson, David,	1841—1843
Burleigh, William,	1823—1827
Butman, Samuel,	1827—1831
Carey, Shepard,	1843—1845
Carter, Timothy J.,	1837—1838
Cilley, Jonathan,	1837—1838
Clapp, W. H.,	1847—1849
Clark, Franklin,	1847—1849
Clifford, Nathan,	1839—1843
Cushman, Joshua P.	1821—1825
Dane, Joseph,	1821—1823
Davee, Thomas,	1837—1841
Dunlap, Robert P.,	1843—1847
Evans, George,	1829—1841
Fairfield, John,	1835—1839
Farley, E. Wilder,	1853—1855
Fessenden, Wm. Pitt,	1841—1843
Foster, Stephen C.,	1857—
Fuller, Thomas J. D.	1849—1857
French, Ezra B.,	1859—
Goodenow, Robert,	1851—1853
Goodenow, Rufus K.	1849—1851
Gerry, Elbridge,	1842—1851
Gilman, Charles J.,	1857—1859
Hall, Joseph,	1833—1837
Hamlin, Hannibal,	1843—1847
Hammons, David,	1847—1849
Harris, Mark,	1822—1823
Herrick, Ebenezer,	1843—1845
Herrick, Joshua,	1821—1827
Hill, Mark L.,	1821—1823
Holland, Cornelius,	1831—1833
Jarvis, Leonard,	1831—1837
Kavanagh, Edward,	1831—1835
Kidder, David,	1823—1827
Knowlton, Ebenezer,	1855—1857
Lincoln, Enoch,	1821—1826
Littlefield, Nathaniel S.,	1841—1843 1849—1851
Longfellow, Stephen,	1823—1825
Lowell, Joshua A.,	1839—1843
Marshall, Alfred,	1841—1843
Mason, Moses,	1834—1837
Mayall, Samuel,	1853—1855
McCrate, J. D.,	1845—1847
McDonald, Moses,	1851—1855
McIntire, Rufus,	1826—1835
Morse, F. H.	1843—1845 1857—1859 1859—
Noyes, Joseph C.,	1837—1839
O'Brien, Jeremiah,	1823—1829
Otis, John,	1849—1851
Perry, John J.,	1855—1857 1859—
Parks, Gorham	1833—1837
Parris, Virgil D.,	1838—1841
Randall, Benjamin,	1839—1843
Reed, Isaac,	1852—1853
Ripley, James W.,	1827—1831
Robinson, Edward,	1838—1839
Sawtelle, Cullen,	1845—1847 1849—1851
Scammon, J. F.,	1845—1847
Severance, L.,	1843—1847
Smart, Ephraim K.	1847—1849 1851—1853
Smith, Albert,	1839—1841
Smith, F. O. J.	1833—1839
Sprague, Peleg,	1825—1829
Stetson, Charles,	1849—1851
Somes, D. E.	1859—
Washburn, Israel, Jr.	1851—1859 1859—
Whitman, E.	1821—1822
Wiley, James S.,	1847—1849
Williams, Hezekiah,	1845—1849
Williamson, Wm. D.	1821—1823
Wood, John M.	1855—1859
Wingate, J. F.	1827—1831

APPENDIX E. Popular and Electoral Vote for President, with Names of Electors.

MAINE, 1820–1856.

1820–1.

Candidate	Popular Vote	Elect. Vote
James Monroe	4,946	8
Scattering	548	

Electors.
Joshua Wingate, Jr.,
William Moody,
Elisha Allen,
William Chadwick,
Samuel Tucker,
Lemuel Trescott,
Joshua Gage,
Josiah Prescott,
Levi Hubbard.

1824–5.

Candidate	Popular Vote	Elect. Vote
J. Q. Adams	10,289	9
Andrew Jackson	3,088	
In House of Rep's Adams had	7	

Electors.
James Campbell,
Thomas Fillebrown,
Nathaniel Hobbs,
Joshua Taylor,
Benjamin Chandler,
Stephen Parsons,
James Parker,
Benjamin Nourse,
Asa Clapp.

1828–9.

Candidate	Popular Vote	Elect. Vote
J. Q. Adams	20,766	8
Andrew Jackson	13,927	1
Scattering	94	

Electors.
Thomas Fillebrown,
Simon Nowell,
Joseph Prince,
James C. Churchill,
Joseph Southwick,
Levi Hubbard,
Ebenezer Farley,
John Moor,
John S. Kimball.

1832–3.

Candidate	Popular Vote	Elect. Vote
Andrew Jackson	33,985	10
Henry Clay	27,332	
Scattering	844	

Electors.
Isaac Lane,
James C. Churchill,
Joseph Sewall,
Nathan Cutler,
Silas Barnard,
Ellis Burgess,
Rowland H. Bridgham,
Ephraim Fletcher,
Samuel Moore,
Joseph Kelsey.

1836–7.

Candidate	Popular Vote	Elect. Vote
Martin Van Buren	22,890	10
Wm. H. Harrison	15,200	
Scattering	1,114	

Electors.
Sheldon Hobbs,
Jonathan Smith,
Benjamin Burgess,
John H. Jarvis,
Shepard Cary,
Reuel Williams,
Joseph Tobin,
John Hamblet,
William Thompson,
Sam'l S. Heagan.

1840–1.

Candidate	Popular Vote	Elect. Vote
Wm. H. Harrison	46,612	10
Martin Van Buren	46,190	
James G. Birney	195	

Electors.
Charles Trafton,
Isaac Illsley,
Edward Robinson,
Isaac Hodson,
Samuel Small,
R. K. Goodenow,
Thomas Fillebrown,
B. P. Gilman,
Joseph Huse,
Thomas Robinson.

1844–5.

Candidate	Popular Vote	Elect. Vote
James K. Polk	45,721	9
Henry Clay	34,382	
James G. Birney	4,976	

Electors.
James W. Bradbury,
John Stickney,
Ichabod Jordan,
Levi Morrill,
John Foster,
Alfred Pierce,
Thomas Bartlett,
Nathaniel Robinson,
Joshua A. Lowell.

1848–9.

Candidate	Popular Vote	Elect. Vote
Lewis Cass	39,927	9
Zachary Taylor	35,149	
Martin Van Buren	12,173	

Electors.
Rufus McIntire,
Hugh J. Anderson,
Oliver L. Sanborn,
Thomas D. Robinson,
A. Wiswell,
Edward L. Osgood,
Asa Clark,
Andrew Masters,
David R. Straw.

1852–3.

Candidate	Popular Vote	Elect. Vote
Franklin Pierce	41,411	8
Winfield Scott	32,208	
John P. Hale	7,925	

Electors.
Rufus McIntire,
John C. Talbot,
George T. Shepley,
Reuben Lowell,
Jonathan G. Fuller,
Oliver Moses,
David Richardson,
Isaac W. Tabor.

1856–7.

Candidate	Popular Vote	Elect. Vote
John C. Fremont	65,514	8
James Buchanan	38,036	
Millard Fillmore	3,235	

Electors.
Noah Smith, Jr.,
Sidney Perham,
Edward Swan,
Knott Crockett,
Isaac Gross,
Moses H. Pike,
Aaron P. Emerson,
James Morton.

APPENDIX F.

GUBERNATORIAL VOTE IN MAINE, TOGETHER WITH THE GOVERNORS AND ACTING GOVERNORS.

1820 TO 1858.

Year	Candidate	Votes
1820.	WILLIAM KING,	21,083
	Scattering,	1, 31
1821.	ALBION K. PARRIS,	12,887
	Joshua Wingate, jr.	3,879
	Ezekiel Whitman,	6,811
	Scattering,	811
1822.	ALBION K. PARRIS,	15,476
	Ezekiel Whitman,	5,795
	Joshua Wingate, jr.,	755
	Scattering,	154
1823.	ALBION K. PARRIS,	18,550
	Scattering,	850
1824.	ALBION K. PARRIS,	19,779
	Scattering,	660
1825.	ALBION K. PARRIS,	14,206
	Scattering,	1,046
1826.	ENOCH LINCOLN,	20,689
	Scattering,	874
1827.	ENOCH LINCOLN,	19,969
	Scattering,	489
1828.	ENOCH LINCOLN,	25,745
	Scattering,	2,364
1829.	JONA. G. HUNTON,	23,315
	Samuel E. Smith,	22,991
	Scattering,	245
1830.	SAMUEL E. SMITH,	30,215
	Jona. G. Hunton,	28,639
	Scattering,	238
1831.	SAMUEL E. SMITH,	28,292
	Daniel Goodenow,	21,821
	Scattering,	106
1832.	SAMUEL E. SMITH,	31,987
	Daniel Goodenow,	27,651
	Moses Carlton,	869
	Scattering,	90
1833.	ROB'T P. DUNLAP,	25,731
	Daniel Goodenow,	18,112
	Thomas A. Hill,	2,384
	Samuel E. Smith,	3,024
	Scattering,	101
1834.	ROB'T P. DUNLAP,	38,133
	Peleg Sprague,	33,732
	Thomas A. Hill,	1,076
	Scattering,[1]	90
1835.	ROB'T P. DUNLAP,	45,208
	William King,	16,860
	Scattering,	615
1836.	ROB'T P. DUNLAP,	31,837
	Edward Kent,	22,703
	Scattering,	148
1837.	EDWARD KENT,	34,358
	Gorham Parks	33,879
	Scattering,	286
1838.	JOHN FAIRFIELD,	46,216
	Edward Kent,	42,897
	Scattering,	486
1839.	JOHN FAIRFIELD,	41,038
	Edward Kent,	34,749
	Scattering,	208
1840.	EDWARD KENT,[2]	45,574
	John Fairfield,	45,507
	Scattering,	98
1841.	JOHN FAIRFIELD,	47,354
	Edward Kent,	36,790
	Jeremiah Curtis,	1,662
	Scattering,	347
1842.	JOHN FAIRFIELD,	40,855
	Edward Robinson,	26,745
	James Appleton,	4,080
	Scattering,	100
1843.	H. J. ANDERSON,	32,029
	Edward Robinson,	20,973
	James Appleton,	6,746
	Edward Kavanagh,	3,221
	Scattering,	170
1844.	H. J. ANDERSON,	48,942
	Edward Robinson,	38,501
	James Appleton,	6,245
	Scattering,	105
1845.	H. J. ANDERSON,	34,711
	Freeman H. Morse,	26,341
	Samuel Fessenden,	5,867
	Scattering,	486
1846.	JOHN W. DANA,[2]	36,031
	David Bronson,	29,557
	Samuel Fessenden,	9,398
	Scattering,	678
1847.	JOHN W. DANA,	33,420
	David Bronson,	24,246
	Samuel Fessenden,	7,352
	Scattering,	275
1848.	JOHN W. DANA,[2]	39,760
	Elijah L. Hamlin,	29,929
	Samuel Fessenden,	12,037
	Scattering,	553
1849.	JOHN HUBBARD,	37,636
	Elijah L. Hamlin,	28,056
	George F. Talbot,	7,987
	Scattering,	102
1850.	JOHN HUBBARD,	41,203
	William G. Crosby,	32,120
	George F. Talbot,	7,267
	Scattering,	75
1851.	By a change in the constitution of the State, providing for the session of the Legislature in the winter instead of summer, all State officers elected in 1850 held office until 1852—no election being held in 1851.	
1852.	John Hubbard,	41,999
	WM. G. CROSBY,[2]	29,127
	Anson G. Chandler,	21,774
	Ezekiel Holmes,	1,617
	Scattering,	190
1853.	A. Pillsbury,	36,386
	WM. G. CROSBY,[2]	27,061
	Anson P. Morrill,	11,027
	Ezekiel Holmes,	8,996
	Scattering,	157

[1] 1429 votes, distributed among the several candidates and included in the above returns, were rejected.
[2] Chosen in convention of the Senate and House of Representatives.

1854.	A. P. MORRILL,	44,565
	Albion K. Parris,	28,462
	Isaac Reed,	14,001
	Shepard Cary,	3,478
	Scattering,	127
1855.	A. P. Morrill,	51,441
	SAMUEL WELLS,[1]	48,345
	Isaac Reed,	10,610
	Scattering,	81
1856.	HANN'L HAMLIN,	69,574
	Samuel Wells,	43,628
	George F. Patten,	6,554
	Scattering,	58
1857.	LOT M. MORRILL,	54,655
	Manasseh H. Smith,	42,968
	Scattering,	255
1858.	LOT M. MORRILL,	60,380
	Manasseh H. Smith,	52,440
	Scattering,	78

GOVERNORS AND ACTING GOVERNORS OF MAINE FROM 1820 TO 1860.

Names.	When Inaugurated.	Termination of Office.	Remarks.
William King,	June 1, 1820,	May 28, 1821.	Resigned.
William D. Williamson,	Acting, May 28,, 1821,	Dec. 5, 1821.	Resigned, (Pres't of Senate).
Benjamin Ames,	" Dec. 5, 1821,	Jan. 2, 1822.	———, (Speaker of House).
Daniel Rose,	" Jan. 2, 1822,	Jan. 4, 1822.	———, (Pres't of Senate).
Albion K. Parris,	Jan. 4, 1822,	Jan. 4, 1827.	
Enoch Lincoln,	Jan. 4, 1827,	Oct. 8, 1829.	Deceased.
Nathan Cutler,	Acting, Oct. 12, 1829,	Feb. 10, 1830.	———, (Pres't of Senate).
Jonathan G. Hunton,	Feb. 10, 1830,	Jan. 8, 1831.	
Samuel E. Smith,	Jan. 8, 1831,	Jan. 2, 1834.	
Robert P. Dunlap,	Jan. 2, 1834,	Jan. 19, 1838.	
Edward Kent,	Jan. 19, 1838,	Jan. 4, 1839.	
John Fairfield,	Jan. 4, 1839,	Jan. 12, 1841.	Office declared vacant by legislature.
Richard H. Vose,	Acting, Jan. 12, 1841,	Jan. 13, 1841.	———, (Pres't of Senate).
Edward Kent,	Jan. 13, 1841,	Jan. 6, 1842.	
John Fairfield,	Jan. 6, 1842,	March 7, 1843.	Resigned.
Edward Kavanagh,	Acting, March 7, 1843,	Jan. 5, 1844.	———, (Pres't of Senate).
Hugh J. Anderson,	Jan. 5, 1844,	May 18, 1847.	
John W. Dana,	May 18, 1847,	May 13, 1850.	
John Hubbard,	May 13, 1850,	Jan. 18, 1853.	
William G. Crosby,	Jan. 18, 1853,	Jan. 6, 1855.	
Anson P. Morrill,	Jan. 6, 1855,	Jan. 4, 1856.	
Samuel Wells,	Jan. 4, 1856,	Jan. 8, 1857.	
Hannibal Hamlin,	Jan. 8, 1857,	Feb. 26, 1857.	Resigned.
Joseph H. Williams,	Acting, Feb. 26, 1857,	Jan. 8, 1858.	———, (Pres't of Senate).
Lot M. Morrill,	Jan. 8, 1858.		

[1] Chosen in convention of the Senate and House of Representatives.

GENERAL INDEX.

N. B. Where the former names of towns are given, the present name also occurs in ( ); v. indicates a village: p. o. a post-office.

O.

P.

Q.

R.

S.

T.

ERRATA AND ADDENDA.

P. 13, l. 3. Read (*La Saussaye*), instead of (*Suassaye*).

P. 23, l. 33. For *eighteenth*, read *seventeenth*.

P. 123, l. 26. For *Marston*, read *Martin's*.

P. 193. LINCOLN, Me. Besides the Baptist Church mentioned here there are two Churches — Congregational and Methodist.

P. 305, l. 15. For *Milk pond*, read *East* and *North ponds*.

P. 305, l. 18. For *church edifices*, read *religious societies*.

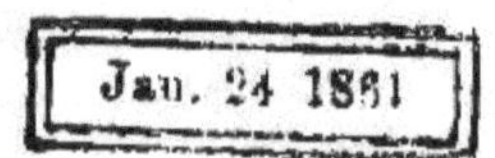

Hon. J. W. Hathaway graduated at Bowdoin College in 1820; studied law with Hon. John Holmes of Alfred; settled in Bluehill in 1823; was elected to the legislature in 1824; moved to Ellsworth in 1825, and during the two following years was elected to the State senate. In 1837, he moved to Bangor, and devoted himself to the practice of his profession until February, 1848, when he was appointed judge of the District Court of the State; which office he held until May, 1852, when that court was abolished. He was then appointed a judge of the Supreme Court for the term of seven years, on the expiration of which, May, 1859, he returned again to practice at the bar.

Natives of Concord, N. H., and sons of the late Hon. William A. Kent. Edward was a graduate of Harvard University, studied law with Hon. Benjamin Orr of Topsham, Me., and commenced practice in Bangor in 1825; he represented this town in the State legislature of 1829 and 1830; was governor of the State in 1838 and 1841; and U. S. consul at Rio de Janeiro from 1849 to 1853; in 1854, he returned to Bangor, and resumed the practice of law, in connection with his brother as above, until appointed judge of the Supreme Judicial Court, in May, 1859. George was a graduate of Dartmouth College; studied law with Judge Green of Concord, N. H., and Hon. William Sullivan of Boston, Mass., where he was admitted to practice, and settled soon after in his native town; he represented Concord in the legislatures of 1828 and 1838; was for several years cashier of one of the banks in that place; editor and joint proprietor of the New Hampshire Statesman and Concord Register; and subsequently an editor in Indianapolis, and in Boston — coming to Bangor, as a lawyer, 1854.

MILLETT & BANGS,

No. 19, West Market Square, - - - - - - - - BANGOR,

MANUFACTURERS AND DEALERS IN

BOOTS AND SHOES

Of all Fashionable, Desirable, and Staple Kinds.

IMPORTERS OF GENTS' FRENCH BOOTS.

MANUFACTURERS AND WHOLESALE DEALERS IN

BOOT AND SHOE MOCCASINS.

A SUPERIOR QUALITY OF

MEN'S AND BOYS' THICK BOOTS.

AS ALSO,

Fine French, and American Single Sole, Half Welt, and Double Sole

CALF BOOTS.

LADIES' BOOTS, SHOES, AND SLIPPERS

Manufactured to order, of any desirable material, and in the most modern styles.

LADIES' BALMORAL BOOTS, SNOW BOOTS, ETC.

COPPER TIPPED BOOTS AND SHOES,

For Sale in Bangor *only* by

MILLETT & BANGS,

And by their Agents in the towns of Penobscot and Aroostook counties. Millett & Bangs are exclusive proprietors of the right to manufacture and sell the COPPER TIPPED SHOES in and for the counties of Penobscot and Aroostook, excepting the towns of Newport, Levant, and Dexter, under letters patent granted to George A. Mitchell of Turner, Me., January 5, 1858, for *Metal Tips for Boots and Shoes.* All infringements of their Right will be prosecuted according to law.

SOLE LEATHER, WAX LEATHER, KIP and CORDOVA UPPER LEATHER;

FRENCH, GERMAN, AND AMERICAN CALF SKINS;

Harness Leather; Collar and Seat Leather; Split, Buff, and Grain Leather; Picker and Lace Leather, Kid and Goat Skins, Linings, Bindings, and Colored Roans; English Lastings, Serge de Berris, Satin Français and Eugenie Cloths, Lasts, Pegs, Shoe Findings, and Shoemakers' Tools.

GENTS' DRESS HATS,

And every thing new and desirable in the way of Fur, Wool, and Cloth Hats and Caps; Fur Collars and Gloves; Buck Gloves and Mittens; Dress and Street Gloves for Gents and Boys.

This firm entered into copartnership and commenced the Shoe, Leather, Hat, and Cap business in their present location, in May, 1858, and by close application to business, strict integrity, and careful attention to the wants of their patrons, have met with unprecedented success, and may now be ranked as the leading establishment of the kind in Bangor.

They have the largest stock of Leather and Manufacturers' Goods in Eastern Maine, and sell as much stock as all the other dealers in the city. Those who would receive respectful attention personally, or have orders faithfully executed, will be sure to notice their advertisement, or visit them when in the city.

NOROMBEGA AIR-TIGHT COOKING STOVE.

This New Stove was made in 1859, to fill a large and increasing demand for a more convenient Cooking Apparatus. It is plain and substantial, extra heavy, and in good taste; it takes in wood 24 inches long. The whole top is made to take out, and a large 20 gallon Iron Boiler or Brass Kettle can be placed directly over the fire. The Oven is large and capacious, which, united with its large and long fire-room, makes it the most desirable Stove in the market. We manufacture this Stove ourselves and spare no pains to make it a first-rate Cooking Stove.

We shall keep supplied with pieces to REPAIR at all times. We warrant them to give satisfaction after a fair trial, or take them back and refund the money.

We make the same Stove with EXTENSION TOP, with Copper Reservoir Boiler for hot water, and Iron Warming Closet, or Sheet Iron Drum in place of Reservoir Boiler, to increase the heat in cold weather. We shall sell the *Norombega Air-Tight Cooking Stove* at the very lowest prices, wholesale or retail, relying on large sales to repay us for the heavy expenses of getting up this beautiful Stove. We have a large Stock of Goods in our line which will be sold cheap and on liberal terms, at wholesale and retail.

All kinds of TIN AND SHEET IRON WORK done to order. MARBLE MANTEL PIECES AND GRATES, HOT AIR FURNACES for WOOD OR COAL. TIN WARE

Sold to Peddlers and Traders at Reduced Prices.

WOOD & BISHOP.

Nos. 1, 2, & 3, Broad Street, Bangor, Me.

FRANKLIN HOUSE,

HARLOW STREET, BANGOR, ME.

This well and favorably known Hotel, having the past season been enlarged, remodelled and refurnished, has now all the appointments of a first class Hotel.

The subscribers having leased the above House for a term of years, and having had several years' experience in the business, flatter themselves by strict and personal attention to merit a liberal share of public patronage.

In location, this House has no superior, being in a central position, and on one of the pleasantest streets in the city.

In connection is a large and commodious Stable in the care of attentive ostlers. Also, a Livery Stable, which will always be supplied with first class teams.

Stages leave this House daily for all parts of the country.

O. M. SHAW,
HENRY McLAUGHLIN, } SHAW & McLAUGHLIN.

WARREN'S COUGH BALSAM!

Has been found, by experience, to be the BEST REMEDY *for the various Diseases of the Lungs and Throat, such as* ASTHMA, BRONCHITIS, CONSUMPTION, CROUP, INFLUENZA, PLEURISY, PNEUMONIA, *or* INFLAMMATION OF THE LUNGS, *and* WHOOPING COUGH.

In these complaints this medicine *has no superior;* and while thus efficacious, it is perfectly safe to administer to persons of all ages. With the return of cold weather invariably appear Coughs and Colds, which, if neglected, may lead to slow disease or swift decline. As a fire, which at its first beginning might have been quenched by a single pailful of water, if unchecked becomes in a short time a conflagration which, in spite of all after effort shall consume a city; so a cold or cough at its first appearance, may be cured by a few doses of WARREN'S COUGH BALSAM, which, if allowed to run on even for a few days, may eventually prove fatal. This Cough Balsam possesses the two-fold advantage of being at once *valuable as a curative* and *invaluable as a preventive* of all the Diseases of the Throat, Lungs, and Bronchia.

In ASTHMA, however violent and distressing, this Balsam gives prompt relief.

In BRONCHITIS and PNEUMONIA it relieves the irritation, loosens the cough, and promotes a favorable expectoration.

In CROUP its powers are almost magical. This insidious disease, coming literally "like a thief in the night," may be speedily and effectually arrested by a few timely doses of this Balsam. Every family should keep it in the house, and thus avoid the dangerous delay occasioned by sending out for the medicine when needed for immediate use.

☞Prepared and sold by AMBROSE WARREN, *Botanic Druggist*, No. 1 Granite Block, East Market Square, Bangor, Maine.

NEW ENGLAND BUSINESS DIRECTORY.

800 PAGES, OCTAVO, PRICE, $3.00.

CONTAINING THE NAMES OF MORE THAN

100,000 Business Men,

WITH MUCH OTHER VALUABLE INFORMATION.

Just published and for sale by ADAMS, SAMPSON & CO.,

No. 91 WASHINGTON STREET, Boston, Mass.

WING & INGALLS,

DEALERS IN

Corn, Flour, Pork, Fish, W. I. Goods, Groceries, and Grass Seeds of all Kinds.

No. 54, WEST MARKET SQUARE, BANGOR, MAINE.

A. A. WING, O. H. INGALLS.

THE

HISTORY AND DESCRIPTION

OF

NEW ENGLAND,

GENERAL AND LOCAL.

BY A. J. COOLIDGE AND J. B. MANSFIELD.

BEAUTIFULLY ILLUSTRATED

With Views of most of the CITIES and many IMPORTANT PLACES, drawn and engraved by some of the best Artists in the country, from the most recent Ambrotype and Photographic Pictures, together with some views of interesting Historical Events;

And accompanied with a Township Map of each of the New England States.

The design of it is to furnish, in a brief, but complete, elegant, and attractive form, the history and topography of New England. The work opens with the discoveries by Cabot and his successors; presents a view of the aboriginal inhabitants, their character and condition; records the extinguishment of their race, as decreed by the hand of progress; and traces the important events of every locality from its settlement to the living present. It embraces the topographical features of the country, the boundaries of the States, counties, and towns, the hydrographical description of the coast, according to the United States Survey, the principal travelled roads, all the railroads, public institutions, custom-houses, and light-houses, the location of villages and post-offices; together with statistics of the population, productive industry, and of the educational, religious, and other material interests of every town and city. It also contains a complete list of the Senators and Representatives in Congress from the organization of each State to the present time; also of the Presidential Electors and of the Governors and the Gubernatorial Candidates, with the Electoral and Popular Vote; and a carefully prepared Index.

As the Publisher has been at great expense in the preparation and bringing out of the work, and expects to be remunerated only by a large sale, the price has been fixed so low at the outset, as to invite the attention and bring it within the means of every one, to whose love of literature is added the merit of earning his own bread by his daily toil.

VOLUME FIRST — MAINE, NEW HAMPSHIRE, AND VERMONT, 1050 pp.

The same also in SEPARATE STATES:

MAINE,	1 vol.	425 pages.
NEW HAMPSHIRE,	1 vol.	350 "
VERMONT,	1 vol.	300 "

To the numerous testimonials of the highest character, the

LEGISLATURE OF MASSACHUSETTS

has added its recommendation of this work. The following is from the Report of the Committee on Education, submitted by Hon. Charles W. Upham: —

"That they have examined the volume of the aforesaid work relating to the States of Maine, New Hampshire, and Vermont, and have no hesitation in expressing in the strongest terms their conviction that, if the remaining volume, embracing the States of Massachusetts, Connecticut, and Rhode Island, is executed in the same style as the present, the work will be eminently worthy of being placed in our schools, as a book of reference.

"It presents the history of New England colonization, and of the States included in the volume already printed, in the most compact, lucid, and attractive form. The history, topography, and institutions of the several cities and towns, bear the impress of accuracy, fulness, and faithful research. It is a work, in its design, and, so far as executed, in its character and merit, which ought to be in every school-room in New England.

"By the fourth section of the thirty-sixth chapter of the General Statutes, it is provided that the school committees of the cities and towns of the Commonwealth 'may, if they see fit, appropriate' twenty-five per cent. of the amount received by them, annually, from the School Fund, 'to the purchase of books of reference' for the use of the schools.

"The Committee have no doubt that the work referred to their consideration will be found to possess the properties that will commend it to school committees, as particularly desirable as a book of reference in all schools."

SOLD ONLY BY SUBSCRIPTION.

A. J. COOLIDGE, 39 COURT STREET, BOSTON.

Zeitfracht Medien GmbH
Ferdinand-Jühlke-Straße 7
99095 Erfurt, Deutschland
produktsicherheit@kolibri360.de